POLICE SCIENCE SERIES

LEONARD'S POLICE OF THE
20th CENTURY

LEONARD AND MORE'S POLICE ORGANIZATION
AND MANAGEMENT, 3rd Ed.

LEONARD AND MORE'S THE GENERAL ADMINISTRATION
OF CRIMINAL JUSTICE

PERKINS' THE ELEMENTS OF POLICE SCIENCE

PERKINS' POLICE EXAMINATIONS

THE IANNARELLI SYSTEM OF
EAR IDENTIFICATION

VOLLMER'S THE CRIMINAL

POLICE ORGANIZATION

AND

MANAGEMENT

THIRD EDITION

By

V. A. LEONARD, B.S., M.A., Ph.D.
Professor Emeritus Department of
Police Science and Administration
Washington State University
Pullman, Washington

and

HARRY W. MORE, B.A., Ph.D.
Professor and Chairman Department of
Administration of Justice
San Jose State College
San Jose, California

Police Science Series

Mineola, New York
THE FOUNDATION PRESS, INC.
1971

Leonard Police Org. & Man. 3rd Ed. **F.P.**

Dedicated to the individual police officer, ambitious
for study and advancement, who is looking
forward to a professional career in the
American police services

*

PREFACE

Police service stands at the threshold of a new era in standards of performance. *POLICE ORGANIZATION AND MANAGEMENT* offers a comprehensive inventory of tested principles and procedures in the organization and administration of the police enterprise—geared to the requirements of a modern social order. The basic manuscript was originally written as a dissertation for the Ph.D. degree at Ohio State University, under the title, *A Theory of Police Organization and Administration.* Today, it is more than a theorem; it is a part of the facts of life.

The first edition in book form was published in 1951. The second edition appeared in 1964. The professional reception accorded this work prompted the preparation of the third edition in order to put into the record pace-making developments that have occurred in recent years.

Police service has mounted important gains in the march toward professionalization. It has been necessary to revise much of the material in the second edition in order to accommodate the changes and developments that have appeared on the American police scene. Five new chapters have been added, including:

CHAPTER 5. ADMINISTRATIVE ALTERNATIVES, presenting alternatives to the conventional police department, including *The Metropolitan Police Authority, The Federated Police System, Integrated Police-Fire Services, Contract Law Enforcement, City-County Consolidation,* and *The In-resident State Police System.*

CHAPTER 7. THE POLICE TRAINING FUNCTION—providing a more extended treatment of the important advances that have been made in this area of the police operation.

CHAPTER 11. IMPROVEMENT OF APPREHENSION CAPABILITY—stressing the yield for the administration of criminal justice flowing from prompt arrest. Here, the key role of the police communications system in the apprehension process receives appropriate attention, together with a view of electronic data processing and the fantastic performance of the computerized National Crime Information Center at the Headquarters of the Federal Bureau of Investigation in Washington, D. C.

CHAPTER 14. THE TIDE OF VIOLENCE—concerned with the anatomy of violence and violent crime, and an approach to solutions in connection with this current social phenomenon.

CHAPTER 15. CHALLENGE AND ASSESSMENT—an analytical review of the several reports presented by the President's Commission on Law Enforcement and the Administration of Justice, including: *The Challenge of Crime in a Free Society, Task Force Report: The Police, Task Force Report: Science and Technology, Task Force Report: Juvenile Delinquency and Youth Crime, Task Force Report: Organized Crime,* Task Force Report: *Crime and Its Impact—an Assessment.*

Additional new material appearing in the Third Edition include:
Minority groups and militant activists.
Dominance of an idea in organization.
Intelligence and internal investigation.
Civilian Review Boards.
Coordinated state-wide recruiting of police personnel.
Police-Community relations.
The police salary structure.
Roll Call Training.
Teaching methods.
The police library.
Recent developments in police training at the university and college level.
Lateral mobility of police personnel.
The State Board Qualifying Examination concept.
Conditions of service.
Report writing.
Need for a nation-wide police retirement and pension system, similar to that of the Teachers Insurance and Annuity Association in the academic field.
The criminal identification system.
The Fluid Patrol System.
Legal aspects of patrol service.
An analysis in depth of the investigative process.
The police laboratory.
The interrogation of a criminal suspect.
Police surveillance.
The point system of traffic violator control.
An extended treatment of traffic engineering.

Criminal justice administration in general and the law enforcement field in particular will note the appearance of Dr. Harry W. More,

Jr., as co-author of the third edition. A former member of the White House Detail in the United States Secret Service and former Chairman of the Department of Criminology at Indiana University of Pennsylvania, he is now Chairman of the Department of Administration of Justice, at San Jose State College (California). He presides over a faculty of nine full-time members, two part-time, one full-time instructor in charge of an $85,000 community relations program, and an impressive segment of the total enrollment of 23,500 students at that institution.

He is the author of *THE NEW ERA IN PUBLIC SAFETY*, *CRITICAL ISSUES IN LAW ENFORCEMENT*, and co-author with the writer of *THE GENERAL ADMINISTRATION OF CRIMINAL JUSTICE*; in addition, he is a consistent contributor to the professional journals in the field. Dr. More brings to his assignment as co-author of the third edition a wide and varied experience.

The third edition of *POLICE ORGANIZATION AND MANAGEMENT* offers a broad application to the fundamental problems of police organization and administration, including the municipal police, state police and sheriff's departments, together with commercial and industrial security, since it shares with the police field proper, many problems in common. In addition, it is designed and written as a textbook for introductory courses in police science and administration at the university and college level.

V. A. L.
H. W. M.

February, 1971

SUMMARY OF CONTENTS

TABLE OF CONTENTS

TABLE OF CONTENTS

CHAPTER 3.   THE POLICE EXECUTIVE—Continued

CHAPTER 4. INTERNAL ORGANIZATION—Continued

CHAPTER 5. ADMINISTRATIVE ALTERNATIVES ____ 101

CHAPTER 6. POLICE PERSONNEL SELECTION _____ 117

TABLE OF CONTENTS

XIV

CHAPTER 8. POLICE RECORDS ADMINISTRATION—

Continued   **Page**

CHAPTER 9. PATROL—MAJOR COMPONENT OF

TABLE OF CONTENTS

TABLE OF CONTENTS

CHAPTER 15. CHALLENGE AND ASSESSMENT—
Continued

APPENDICES

TABLE OF CONTENTS

TABLES

†

POLICE ORGANIZATION
AND
MANAGEMENT

Chapter I

INTRODUCTION

SOCIETY has organized itself on many fronts for self-protection and the promotion of human welfare. The evidence may be seen by looking in any direction. Organization is a strong characteristic of business and industry which serve to meet the various needs and requirements of the people of this country. The educational system in the United States reflects the presence of organization on an impressive scale. In terms of national security, the military services and the total defense establishment fulfil an important purpose in this respect.

It was an organization of portentous magnitude that put men on the moon and that even today, contemplates projected excursions into planetary space. Organizations without number serve the security, business, social and spiritual needs of man. The list is endless.

Government itself, represents the greatest single organization within the geographical limits of the country. How well it is organized and the extent to which performance meets the needs of the society it serves, are matters of overwhelming importance. This is especially true of the American police system.

On the law enforcement front, organization finds expression at the national, state, local and even international levels.

Internationally, nations have combined their police strength. Governments have joined forces in the creation of a major police agency, the International Criminal Police Organization, known as INTERPOL, with general headquarters in Paris, France. Its purpose is to promote mutual cooperation among the different countries in the investigation and apprehension of criminal offenders who operate across international boundary lines. Some sixty-three countries, including the United States, are now members of this important organization.

Included among federal law enforcement agencies are:

The U. S. Department of Justice.
The Federal Bureau of Investigation.
Department of the Treasury.
     Bureau of Customs.
     Internal Revenue Service.
     Bureau of Narcotics.
     United States Secret Service.
     United States Coast Guard.
Bureau of Postal Inspectors.

At the state level of government are to be found:

The State Police.
The State Attorney General.
State Crime Laboratories.
State Bureaus of Criminal Records and Identification.
State liquor control units.
State Police Training Commissions.
State Crime Commissions.
The New England Inter-State Police Compact.

In addition to police agencies located within the framework of government, business and industry have in an increasing number of instances, developed their own private police or security forces. The railroad police are well known. In recent years, plant protection and security has become a major operation on the American scene.

But it is at the local level of government—the county and primarily the municipality, that the major advance against the problems of crime and the criminal goes on day after day, month after month and year after year. In this respect, it is to the examination and appraisal of the nation's police forces that this book is dedicated.

Perhaps no arm of government is more vulnerable to observation in this respect than is police service. The press, literature, pulpit, radio, television, motion picture, pressure groups and the public generally, have not been lax in focusing attention on the police uniform, what it stands for, the nature of the man inside and the nature of his performance. That this close surveillance of the police by the people they serve has in general been good for the service, is unquestioned, although in too many instances, opinions and criticisms have been uninformed and unjustified.

In the march toward professionalization, most observers, including the police themselves on occasion, have overlooked *line performance* as the basic point of departure and this oversight has resulted in a loss of perspective and a general failure to recognize the relationship between organization and the attainment of police objectives. An accelerated professional tempo in the American police services requires the application of patterns of organization and administration based upon the dynamics of performance in field operations. Operating strength in the line merits acceptance as a controlling factor of high validity in the organization and administration of a police department. Referred to variously in the text as "line power," "combat strength" or "striking power," it concerns the quality and quantity of performance at the point in police organization where the delivery of police service is actually made—*the line*.

The line operations of a police department are directed toward the execution of plans in the field where contact is made with police objectives. These objectives include the protection of life and property, maintenance of the peace and public order, control and prevention of crime and vice, traffic control, and a large number of regulatory responsibilities. Line performance is, therefore, the point at which the investment in organization and administration comes to a focus and it is at this point that the return on the expenditure of public funds for police service may be measured.

Line performance is a product of the kind and amount of work performed in the effort to realize police objectives. Maximum work standards are determined by the quality and quantity of power available in the line. Thus, line power is an expression of the competence exercised in the field operations of a department; it is contingent upon the resources that are available to the enterprise in terms of personnel and equipment, and the manner in which they are articulated through organization and administration into a program.

Up to and including the first quarter century of the 1900's, the police system, in common with many other social institutions, trailed behind developments in science and industry in the process of adapting itself to the needs of modern society. For many years, the average American police department, because of the lagging development of professional standards, was by far the weakest member of the official family. Health, public works, park, recreational and school departments moved forward rapidly but the police, although registering slight gains, remained far behind the rest of the public services in the march toward better government. The result in terms of unused resources, wasted public funds, failure to achieve objectives in the critical areas of crime control and prevention, and traffic administration was a matter for serious concern.

Criminal case loads of American police departments and admissions to penal institutions revealed little if any gain in the solution of these problems.[1] The social and economic losses resulting from retarded traffic flow, traffic congestion and traffic accidents, continued to follow a menacing upward trend.[2] Vice, little understood by either the police or the people, gained strength as a corrupter of men and government.

The reasons for this condition have escaped the attention of most observers. While it is clear that police administration trails other public services in standards of efficiency and performance, organized police service is little more than a hundred years of age, and most of the gains to be credited to this branch of the public service have been achieved almost within the life span of some now living. An inventory of the comparatively youthful career of this new enterprise reveals creditable evidence of progress toward professionalization even within this short time. But the advance is slow and is opposed by almost insuperable odds.

Despite this weight of millstones about its neck, American police service began to thrust forward after the turn of the century in a series of brilliant advances. A number of changes were moving across the field as police organization and administration gradually began to seek membership in the hierarchy of the professions.

The fingerprint identification system with its contributions of speed and accuracy in the identification of known offenders, was followed in quick succession by motorization of the police force and the adoption of radio communication. These new developments taken together, have almost served to synchronize the arrest with the depredation. Other technological improvements, whose utility had already been demonstrated in other fields of endeavor, were appropriated in turn by the police. Verdicts began coming from test tubes in scientific crime laboratories as the disciplines of chemistry, physics, the microscope, photography, spectrography and other instruments of scientific crime detection were brought into play. Where formerly guilt was determined by the night stick confessional and other "third degree" methods, it came to be a matter of inductive proof painlessly established by an ensemble of scientific facts. Circumstantial evidence had come into its own.

More was involved in these developments than the promise of immediate gains in police efficiency. Certainly, motorization and radio communication marked a strategic increase in the mobility of the force

[1] Annual Reports of American Police Departments; Uniform Crime Reports.

[2] Reports of the National Safety Council.

and amplified the striking power of a crime fighting organization. Similarly, the facilities of the crime detection laboratory shortened the investigative process and materially increased the percentage of case clearances and convictions. The way of the transgressor became doubly hard with the rapidly mounting risk of apprehension and the threat of a verdict of guilty.

The real significance of these new developments, however, was that for the first time scientific disciplines came to be associated with police service. From that point on, the invasion of the field of police organization and administration by scientific method has gone forward, gaining steadily in momentum. Organizational patterns, personnel, record systems, communications, criminal investigation and identification, crime prevention, traffic control and other phases of police administration have come under the influence of these new forces. It may be said that the people of the United States are now at the threshold of a new concept of police service geared to the requirements of a modern social order.

Police service is moving through a significant period of transition. Concepts and procedures that find general application today would have seemed strange indeed not too many years ago. In the early twenties the mere mention of the potential value of radio in patrol operations was enough to provoke ridicule. A contemporary issue of a police journal, The Michigan State Trooper, (March 1927) carried an editorial with the heading, "Radio Not For the Police." Scientific crime detection was comparatively unknown. The mass production line of Henry Ford, the pyramiding registration of automobiles, and the problems of traffic accidents, parking and congestion were yet to come. The record system as an administrative tool of control had not received police recognition.

The distribution of the force was regarded as a very simple matter. The complexities of patrol operational planning and execution had not yet captured the attention of police executives. The nearest approach to the basic administrative problem of scientific beat construction was to divide a map of the city into equal parts, or to set up patrol area boundary lines on the basis of population density. The necessity and possibilities of a beat formula were matters yet to be placed on the agenda of police management.

The technological advances of the past three decades and their application to the police enterprise—including motorization of the force, radio communication and scientific crime detection—have multiplied enormously the service potential of this branch of government; at the same time, they have lulled police administrators and the communities they serve into a false sense of security. Rather than simplifying the task of management, they have added to its complexity and have placed a high premium upon administrative ability. Research in the behavior sciences has further extended the responsibilities of the police administrator in the application of sound preventive techniques. The expanding role of police administration in the prevention of crime and delinquency now presents an inescapable challenge.

The objectives of modern police service and the approach to them tend to become complex in proportion to the extent to which they are understood. Today, these problems and the procedural decisions that must be made crowd the desk of the police executive on a bewildering scale. Compelled to make decisions, he is also compelled to reckon with the resources that are at his disposal for their execution. An inventory of these resources runs the gamut of police organization and management and requires on the part of the executive a careful evaluation of all the factors, both internal and external, that bear a dynamic relationship to the combat strength or striking power of the organization. Faced at times by a hostile public, and press headlines that call attention to mounting crime rates and traffic fatalities that show no sign of abatement, administration is frequently hard pressed for the answer. The standard explanation in the past, "We are undermanned," is giving way to a more critical view of the police problem and of the requirements for its solution.

Numerical Strength and Striking Power

The numerical strength of police departments has been for many years a matter of acute concern to police administrators throughout the United States. The question has aroused a corresponding solicitude on the part of municipal management in general as well as of the average citizen whose interest in the amount and quality of police service that can be delivered is important to him as a taxpayer. It is apparent that police costs per capita have risen during the past fifty years to a point where further invasion of tax funds no longer appears feasible.

Competent surveys indicate that increases in the mere numerical strength of American police departments is approaching the saturation point.[3] The universal appeal of police administration in the past for more manpower is changing to a demand for better manpower. The erroneous assumption that numerical strength is a commanding determinant insofar as crime rates are concerned is going into the discard. Supporters of this fallacy contend that a high correlation exists between the numerical strength of a police organization and its criminal case

---

3 See bibliography for a list of surveys and reorganizations conducted thus far in the American police field.

load, and point to the need for increased payroll expenditures. There is a general failure to recognize the distinction between numerical strength and absolute strength.

Conscientious police executives know that the mere addition of manpower does not enhance the ability and efficiency of the individual officer and that such additions do not increase to any appreciable degree the over-all effectiveness of the department as a whole. Mere numbers do not make a strong crime fighting organization. The number of men on the payroll of a police department is among the least of several factors that determine the combat power and efficiency of the organization. Military science has long since confirmed this distinction.

The striking force or combat power of a police organization is the measure of ability and thrust toward the achievement of objectives. It may be concerned in one situation with the prompt solution of a murder case through laboratory examination and identification of evidence materials. Such facilities are a part of the potential combat strength of the department that has made them available. In another instance, striking power may be exerted toward the threat of an upward trend in the traffic accident rate, or to an epidemic of automobile thefts or service station hold-ups. It may be further reflected in the amount and quality of police leadership in the community toward crime prevention. Riots, mob situations, disorderly crowds, disaster, parades or athletic events may be the occasion for bringing the combat strength of the department into play.

Within a brief space of time during the night or day the striking power of a police organization may find expression throughout the whole range of human relationships. It may be a show of physical force and even gun-fire in bringing a bank robbery to a socially acceptable conclusion, or in quelling mob disorder. It may symbolize the scientist in the extent to which the arts and sciences are brought into play in crime control and prevention. It may express the language and technique of the statesman in the application of supreme tact and judgment to the case of a neighborhood or family quarrel, or in a patrolman's contact with a youngster on the beat.

Success, mediocrity or failure may describe the end result, depending upon the degree and quality of power that can be put into play. In a modern society, the striking power of a police force is directed toward complex objectives, including the preservation of public order, the protection of life and property, and the suppression and prevention of crime and vice, as well as toward the solution of the manifold problems of traffic administration. As if these were not enough, the growing complexity of the social and economic order has increased the burden of the police by giving them additional duties and responsibilities of a regulatory nature. Some of these have had the effect of greatly reducing the combat strength of the organization for the handling of problems which only the police can deal with effectively.

Based upon strictly numerical considerations, the police force is at a tremendous disadvantage. The number of professional criminals and their amateur brethren, together with random and potential offenders, may outnumber police personnel in any one community by a ratio of from 500:1 to 2,000:1. Add to this the fact that the time and place of criminal attack is known in advance only to the offender, and some idea of the magnitude of the police problem may be gained. In riots, major disturbances and outbreaks, the police force is responsible for the restoration of order, and where mob violence gains the upper hand, deficiency in numbers may make control of the situation difficult if not impossible, unless striking power is decisive in amount and quality. An enormous gap must be bridged over if the power of an incredibly small force is to be amplified to a point where operations will be attended with success. When to these threats to life and property are added the vastly increased responsibilities of the police, such as traffic administration, one begins to perceive in broad outline the dimensions of the problems facing police management today.

Police operations bear some striking resemblances to those associated with military engagements in time of war. Strategy, tactics, logistics, communications, reconnaissance, intelligence, the techniques of patrol and combat and many other basic military principles find their counterpart in the administration of a successful police department, where success is primarily dependent upon the expert use of a limited number of men. The strategy and tactics employed by the police are essentially military in the sense that both police and military operations are directed against hostile forces bent upon an attack against life and property. The theatre of police activities is one of potential combat in which engagements are real, and in which gunfire and loss of life may characterize the day's work.

Rear-Admiral Fiske has shown the distinction between the striking power and numerical strength of two opposing forces. Assume that one force is numerically superior to the other, in the ratio of 1,000 to 500, and that the destructive ability per man, 10 per cent, is the same in each force. In other words, one man will be put out of action by each ten men of the respective forces in each engagement. In the first engagement, the larger force will inflict a damage of 10 per cent of its own numbers, or 100 men, on the smaller; and the smaller will inflict a loss of 50 on the larger. The relative losses and the number of engagements required to annihilate the smaller force, other factors being equal, are shown in Table I.

In the entire six engagements the destructive power of the individual men in each force is exactly the same. If in the smaller force, we introduce an effective program of personnel selection and training, and combine it with more modern equipment and a superior type of supervision and generalship, the destructive power of the individual is greatly increased. If increased from forty to fifty, the smaller force of 500 becomes as powerful as the larger contingent and, beyond that point, complete annihilation of the greater force is a certainty.

TABLE I
EFFECT OF SUPERIORITY OF FORCE

| | Larger force (1,000) | | Smaller force (500) | |
Engagement	At opening of Engagement	Loss	At opening of Engagement	Loss
First	1,000	50	500	100
Second	950	40	400	95
Third	910	31	305	91
Fourth	879	21	214	88
Fifth	858	12	126	86
Sixth	846	4	40	40
Sixth surviving	846		0	

Superiority at the proper time and place is essential in war. It is equally indispensable in police administration. In military operations, the principle of superiority was originally based upon sheer weight in numbers at the critical point. This concept has undergone almost total revision by military experts, as evidenced by their use today of the terms *absolute strength and skill in using that strength.*

Robinson states that superiority embraces much more than mere numbers, as numbers alone, unless overwhelming (in violation of the law of diminishing returns), cannot be accepted as the true measure of superiority.[4] Superiority means superior combat strength or striking power at the decisive place at the decisive time.

Bruce Smith, noted police consultant, expressed his views on this point in unmistakable language:

"No matter how real its influence may be, the mere quantity of police service is not the only factor in successful law enforcement. The quality of

4 Oliver Prescott Robinson, *The Fundamentals of Military Strategy,* U. S. Infantry Association, Washington, D. C., 1928, p. 93. Carl von Clausewitz, *On the Principles of War,* Kegan, Paul, Trench, Trubner & Co., Ltd., 1911, p. 192.

See also, V. A. Leonard, *Police Communication Systems,* Berkeley, California, University of California Press, 1938, p. 473.

that service is of even greater importance. The basic unit of any police force is the policeman. The manner in which he performs his duties—often far from the critical eyes of his superiors—can go far towards securing an impressive record for the force he represents, or it can offset a considerable part of the efforts put forth by even the most vigorous and enlightened leadership. If the policeman is carefully selected and thoroughly trained, if official discipline is applied to him fairly and firmly, and if his morale is maintained by adequate salary scales, satisfactory working conditions, and open road to promotion and a sense of security both during his active employment and his years in retirement, the prospect is brightened for an effective handling of the difficult problems with which the police must deal.

"*On the other hand, if many of these features are lacking in any marked degree, there is a corresponding deterioration in the quality of police service for which even greatly increased numbers cannot altogether compensate.* Some of the best police forces in this country operate successfully with a numerically inferior strength; some of the worst—and that can be very bad indeed—are endowed with a generous financial support, an abundance of manpower and the latest and most expensive gadgets." [5]

Thus, in police operations, the numerical strength of a police department is not a true measure of the combat strength of the organization. The intelligence, education, professional training, mental health and career interests of the individual officer combine with expert organization and management superimposed from above to amplify the combat power of a police organization far beyond the point attainable by sheer numerical strength alone.

The formula for modern police service is not simple. The elements in both the staff and line that condition the line performance of a police organization require constant reappraisal and improvement, for it is operating strength in the line that very largely determines the measure of success or failure in the delivery of police service. The components of line power, their content and application to the police enterprise in terms of performance merit detailed analysis, and in the following pages an attempt is made to present a synthesis of procedures which have been used with successful results in this branch of the public service.

[5] Bruce Smith, *The Baltimore Police Survey*, Institute of Public Administration, New York, 1941, p. 28.

Chapter 2

THE CLIMATE OF POLICE ADMINISTRATION

A study of the dynamics of police efficiency emphasizes the importance of organizational structure. Among the factors that condition the striking power or combat strength of a police department, the external and internal factors which determine control of the force and condition its performance, merit careful scrutiny.

Administrative Controls

Police administration does not operate in a vacuum. As one of the principal line agencies of government it must be located at some point in the organizational structure of government, either at the federal, state or local level. The nature of the controls exercised over the police differs with the level of government at which police duties are performed. In a democratic society the question assumes considerable importance.

The possibility of a national police force has been mentioned on occasion. The extraordinary efficiency demonstrated in recent years by federal law enforcement organizations has brought into sharp relief some of the deficiencies of decentralized control at the local level of government and has prompted some observers to explore the possibilities of a federal police force. One alternative advanced by proponents of greater centralization is patterned after the English ideal of police administration, which may be described as a system of local control coupled with national supervision, with the powers and functions of the central government steadily increasing.

In theory, all police forces in England, with the exception of the London Metropolitan Police (under direct control of the Home Office), are administered locally. Actually, however, the Home Office has a large measure of indirect control over them through its power to inspect these forces and formulate regulations prescribing their organization, equipment and discipline.[1] The organization pattern tends toward

[1] Sir Edward Troup, *Police Administration, Local and National;* London Police Journal, Vol. 1, p. 5, 1928.

Also, A. L. Dixon, *The English Police System,* the Annals of the American Academy of Political and Social Science, Vol. CXLVI, p. 177, Nov. 1929.

uniformity of administration throughout England. A further advantage of this close alliance is the cooperative working relationship that pervades the entire system. County or borough forces, for example, may call upon the highly specialized facilities of Scotland Yard in difficult cases, and these services are furnished without charge. Centralized record controls located at Metropolitan Police Headquarters in London provide an effective answer to mobile criminal operations.[2] Furthermore, the salutary effect upon the county or borough chief constables of pressure from the upper levels of government is also not to be overlooked in explaining the efficiency of the English police. English government follows a unified pattern in contrast with our federalism; hence, the same observations would be applicable to public health, education and other governmental functions as well as police administration.

In the United States where the principle of local autonomy reigns supreme, state, county and city police forces function in a state of comparative independence. Although the city and county are creatures of the state under state constitutions, these local jurisdictions operate with little or no interference from above. In fact, it may be said that police administration in the United States is only rarely exposed to any serious pressure above that of the local appointing authority, such as the Mayor, City Manager or Director of Public Safety, etc. In this country, we operate largely under the principle that Main Street has the intelligence and resources to meet its problems, and that suggestions from the state capital or from either end of Pennsylvania Avenue are out of order.

This has not prevented some federal assistance. Especially notable are the splendid services of the Federal Bureau of Investigation in the operation of the national fingerprint bureau, organization of in-service training programs and the availability to local police forces of its outstanding laboratory crime detection facilities. A wholesome spirit of cooperation pervades the relationship between local police forces and federal law enforcement agencies, including not only the Federal Bureau of Investigation but the Secret Service, Postal Inspectors, Customs Inspectors, Border Patrol, Military Police, Shore Patrol and

---

[2] Essentially the same result has been achieved in the United States through the activity of professional police associations. Recognizing the indispensability of a national clearinghouse for criminal records and information, the International Association of Chiefs of Police developed the idea of a national fingerprint identification bureau and arranged for its operation by a federal agency, the Federal Bureau of Investigation. Under the superb management of the Bureau, this important facility has been developed to the point where it would be difficult to measure its value to criminal justice administration in this country.

others. This is particularly true in those cases where suspects may be reached under federal statutes.

However, local independent police forces are costly, ineffective and a barrier to uniformity and standardization of administration in the United States. We may urge, and we may expect, administrative centralization in the American police field up to county organization, as a part of the trend toward consolidation of city and county governmental functions and the elimination of extravagant duplication of services.[3]

Closely associated with these developments is the trend toward a centralized records and communication system on a state-wide basis, made possible by technological advances in electronic data processing. It is not likely that the American tradition will countenance a degree of centralization that goes very far beyond the foregoing possibility. Altogether remote is the possibility that local police administration will ever be subjected to any form of supervisory control, direct or indirect, from the national level. The answers to the problems of American police administration lie in other directions. It may safely be contemplated that the line delivery of police service in the United States and its control will continue to be, as it has in the past, largely a function of local government. Any theory of police organization and administration must, therefore, be devoted primarily to the problems of the municipal police services. The professional up-grading of these thousands of local forces, both small and large, upon which the American people place their chief reliance in the preservation of law and order, is the central concern of the present inquiry.

Paradoxically, despite the American emphasis on local autonomy, the inauguration of state control of local police forces in the larger cities accompanied the introduction into this country of Peel's concept of a professionalized police organization. State controlled police departments were to be found in New York, Chicago, Boston, Detroit, Cleveland, Baltimore, Cincinnati, St. Louis, New Orleans, and Kansas City, among others. In each instance, a police board, with its members appointed by the governor or elected by the legislature, was placed in complete control of the municipal police establishment. The removal of the police from local control was attributed to the alleged failure of city authorities to maintain proper standards of order but it soon became apparent that a desire on the part of state politicians to extend the range of their patronage activities was the real reason. This was a phase of the typical distrust and hostility between rural-

---

[3] See Chapter 5—*Administrative Alternatives.*

dominated state legislatures and the developing metropolitan governments of the nineteenth century. It was not conducive to efficiency in meeting local problems of crime control. Urban disapproval and opposition increased until state control was subsequently abolished in all of these cities, with the exception of Baltimore, St. Louis, Kansas City, and Boston. Generally speaking, the experience thus far does not argue for any further expansion in the experiment.

On April 5, 1962, the Governor of Massachusetts signed a bill enacted by the Legislature with which the state abdicated control of the police in Boston and returned to the Mayor the power to appoint the Commissioner of Police. Only twelve cities now remain in the state control category; these are Baltimore, Maryland; Kansas City, St. Louis and St. Joseph, Missouri; and Berlin, Claremont, Dover, Laconia, Manchester, Nashua, Portsmouth and Somersworth, New Hampshire.

The interest of political party organizations and other pressure groups in the spoils of public office, combined with resentment to invasion of local home rule, make impractical any full reliance on state control of local police administration. The resulting descent of responsibility from the state to the municipal level brings into focus the nature of the local administrative controls which condition for good or for bad the conduct of police administration in this country.

Influence of Governmental Patterns upon Police Service

The organization of American police departments has passed through several stages in an evolutionary process which was characterized in the beginning by a plurality of official controls. This administrative pattern early took the form of a committee of members of the city council which supervised the police. By diffusing responsibility and mingling it with the councilmen's interests in other matters it encouraged corrupt political controls, favoritism, and extravagance. The inefficiency which it produced soon led to the appearance of a separate police board somewhat independent of the council. Members of this body were appointed by the mayor or elected by popular vote, in some cases on a non-partisan basis. Whether by-partisan or non-partisan, both plans violated a basic principle of organization by placing executive control in a plural agency. The motives of those in control often were not in the best interests of the public service, and for the most part they were unfamiliar with the techniques of management in general and with the technical aspects of modern police operations in particular. Neither an army nor a police force can deliver effective service under plural leadership, or under the leadership of a committee.

Recognition of the need for unity of command and centralized executive control over the police mounted with the realization that the work of maintaining law and order in a city, large or small, is a highly complicated and difficult enterprise, which cannot be successfully performed by a group of well-intentioned citizens who give only their spare time and thought to the task. Operating a police department is altogether different from maintaining a public library or a school system. Experience both in Europe and in the United States has demonstrated the indispensability of the single executive possessing final authority and accepting undivided responsibility for the administration of a crime fighting organization. Police administration, one of the major line agencies of government, operates in a climate of emergency, which calls for strict discipline in order to meet the demands for prompt and direct action. A definite location of authority in the hands of a single individual forms the foundation for such discipline.

A gradual implementation of this basic principle of organization in the American police field is closely related to the evolution of municipal government itself. It may be best understood within the frame of reference of the three major forms of present-day municipal organization, the Mayor-Council plan, the Commission plan, and the Council-Manager plan. The position of the police department in the administrative pattern is of the greatest importance, for without sound administrative structure at the top, no police organization can be administered and controlled efficiently and honestly. The type of administrative climate in which the police find themselves compelled to function may cripple the effective line power of the organization, or may foster a high degree of competence and efficiency.

The Mayor-Council Type

The traditional pattern of municipal organization is the Mayor and Council form. Under this plan the members of the Council are elected. They represent the political aspect of local government and in a democracy provide the opportunity for the flow of control and responsibility between government and the electorate. The Council constitutes the chief legislative and policy making body. Through its ordinance power, subject to constitutional and statutory provisions, including the city charter, the Council carries out its legislative functions; when within its authority, its enactments have the force of law and are binding upon both administration and the electorate. In addition to legislative and policy making functions, the Council in common with most legislative bodies, holds the purse strings and exercises control over appropriations.

Under the principle of separation of politics and administration, within the framework of government, the power to determine public policy is vested in one group of men, while the function of carrying policy into execution is given to another. Representation of the people is what is wanted in one case; administrative skill and efficiency in the other. Executive power is vested in the Mayor, who may be chosen by the City Council from among its own members or elected directly by the people. Theoretically, the Mayor has all administrative powers and responsibilities and he may have authority to veto ordinances passed by the legislative body. Upon the Mayor is also conferred the power of appointment and removal of the heads of administrative departments, including the police, subject in most instances to the approval of the City Council.

Ideally, the head of each department whom the Mayor appoints should be an expert in those functions over which he has jurisdiction. He should also possess the administrative talents required for a highly technical job of management. There are instances where the office of Mayor is held by a man with a strong personality, endowed with those qualities of leadership, integrity and vision which are necessary for the administration of a large business enterprise. Under these conditions capable leadership may be reflected in the competence of the police executive and other municipal department heads. Unfortunately, however, such a happy condition is a rare occurrence. The history of police administration in the United States is largely an account of the failures of the Mayor-Council form of municipal government. As often as not, the Mayor is a figurehead while the line departments of government are dominated and even corrupted by legislative interference.

The Mayor as an elected official is a politician who must depend on the political campaign for retention of his office. Yielding first to one pressure group and then to another, his office too often becomes headquarters for the dispensing of patronage, favors and gratuities which undermine the administration of line departments and reduce public service to the level of graft and incompetence. Police administration is the first to suffer in this type of situation. Morale and discipline experience a decline; sound personnel administration becomes an impossibility and the quality of management deteriorates to such a point that public officers are unworthy of their responsibility. It was under such conditions of incompetence in local government that new forms of municipal administration were born.

The Commission Plan

In 1900, Galveston, Texas, was one of the most miserably governed cities in the United States. Enjoying a low tax rate, operations were financed largely through increasing the bonded indebtedness. Department heads were elected and municipal government was run largely for personal profit. Then in that year, came the great tidal wave resulting in great loss of life and destruction of property. It was a tremendous crisis demanding brains and energy; municipal officials could furnish neither.

A group of business men drew the blueprints for a new form of municipal government—the Commission Plan—and moved it through the legislature for approval. The distinguishing feature of the Commission Plan was that it combined both the legislative and administrative functions of government in an all-powerful body of five members chosen by popular election. As a group, the Commission constituted the legislative and policy-making body of local government; singly, each Commissioner was the administrative head of one or more municipal departments. Thus, the Commissioner of Public Safety exercised administrative control over the Police and Fire Departments.

The plan had the initial advantage of making a clean break with traditional political ties; in an atmosphere of emergency it put a new concentration of powers in new hands. Perhaps the challenge of the task, as much as the change in forms, accounted for the early success of the plan in Galveston. The public debt was reduced; the budget was balanced and salaries increased. Steps were taken to prevent a repetition of the disaster of 1900 through the construction of an enormous sea wall. Almost overnight Galveston became one of the best governed cities in the nation. Featured in the public press, the commission form of municipal government was hailed by students of municipal affairs as the reform that would bring light out of darkness and end the dominion of the professional politicians. This was good news for police administration. By 1909, twenty-eight other American cities adopted the Commission Plan, and by 1917, the total number of commission-governed cities had reached five hundred.

However, the Commission plan possessed fatal defects inherent in its original structure, which became apparent after the first impact of emergency or reform was gone. In recent years it has been rapidly losing ground. The combining of basic legislative and administrative functions in a small group foreordained it to ultimate extinction. The useful distinction between legislative and administrative functions was almost totally lost. Government by commission has proved to be government by amateurs, as no provision is made for drawing "career" men into the municipal service as heads of department. Each department head is elected by the people. The records reveal that the individual commissioner usually is not a trained administrator.[4] Able technicians are seldom brought into the public service by the way of the ballot box. The commissioners are elected and inevitably they have become politicians who must depend upon the political campaign to produce the votes that will put and keep them in office.

Although the Commission plan held forth considerable promise for a new era in police administration at the beginning, subsequent events exposed it as a new device for corrupt exploitation. The dual role of the individual commissioner as both legislator and administrator opened wide the door for illegitimate influence and pressure, and made police administration more vulnerable than ever before to the sinister forces in the community whose interests are opposed to those of the public.

Of even greater significance, however, it restored plural command over the police force, which had been previously demonstrated to be a violation of sound organizational procedure. Among other responsibilities of the Commissioner of Public Safety, this individual presides over both the police and fire departments. As a principal feature of the Commission form of local government, he appoints the Chief of Police and although charter provisions may vary in detail from one city to another, both are responsible for the proper administration of the department. It is inevitable, therefore, that the Chief of Police must share control of the force with the Director of Public Safety and unless the latter official exercises extraordinary discretion unified command becomes a physical impossibility. Police organization under conditions of dual control tends to become a divided house with a part of departmental personnel devoted to the interests of the Commissioner and other members of the department directing their allegiance toward the Chief of Police. In either case, the tradition of loyalty to the public service suffers.

Where does the authority of the Chief of Police leave off and that of the Director or Commissioner of Public Safety begin? The answer in this type of situation has never been clear, with the result that administrative confusion is unavoidable. Theoretically, the Director or Commissioner depends on the Chief of Police to exercise exclusive control up to the point where the Director himself makes the really important decisions. The point at which the Director may elect to "make the

---

[4] Harold Zink, *Government of Cities in the United States*, The MacMillan Company, 1939, p. 312.

really important decisions" is necessarily ambiguous in this pattern of plural control. The end result may be demoralizing interference with the administration of the department by extending lower the point at which decisions by the Director are made, or demoralization by raising the point of decision when it is politically expedient to do so. Fosdick held that the whole scheme is admirably suited to the favorite game of "passing the buck"—an especially useful game when public criticism is involved.[5]

Both the Mayor-Council and the Commission plans of city government were shortly to be challenged by a new pattern of control in the administration of municipal affairs in the United States—the Council-Manager or City Manager plan—under which new developments in the professionalization of police service have occurred.

The City Manager

The Council-Manager plan was originally devised and promoted by the National Short Ballot Organization, of which Woodrow Wilson was president and Richard S. Childs was secretary, as a part of its effort to make government more responsible by reducing the number of elective offices. This organization had been promoting the Commission Plan, but when Mr. Childs read of the success of a "general manager" in Staunton, Virginia, in 1908–11 under a mayor and bicameral council, he argued that the concentration of administrative authority in such an appointive official under a single commission would remedy the weaknesses of the commission plan. The Short Ballot Organization drafted a charter for Lockport, New York, in 1911, but the first city to adopt its "commission-manager" or Council-Manager plan was Sumter, South Carolina, in 1912, and the first large city to do so was Dayton, Ohio, which put the plan into effect in 1914. In 1919 the Organization and its program merged with the National Municipal League.[6]

Although the Manager plan actually originated in Staunton, Virginia, in 1906, and was later adopted by Sumter, South Carolina, in 1912, it remained for Dayton, Ohio, to launch the new idea on a substantial basis in this country. A tidal wave swept the Commission plan into Galveston. Thirteen years later a flood on the Miami River confronted the citizens of Dayton with a tragedy of major dimensions and a grave crisis. The Dayton Bureau of Municipal Research had previ-

---

[5] Raymond B. Fosdick, *American Police Systems*, New York, The Century Company, 1916, p. 115.

[6] Charles M. Kneier, *City Government in the United States*, Harper and Brothers, New York, 1934, p. 364.

ously referred to the government of that city as "government by deficit." In the ten-year period 1903–1913, the municipal debt increased from $26.37 per capita to $46.13, or an increase of 76 per cent. In 1913, 47 per cent of the total income was spent in the liquidation of maturing bonds and interest. As in Galveston, bonds were being issued to pay for current operations. The flood crisis brought out into bold relief the incompetence of existing local government and revealed its inability to deal with either the crisis or the routine responsibilities of municipal administration.

As a result of this emergency situation, a committee of five, under the leadership of John H. Patterson of the National Cash Register Company was appointed by the local Chamber of Commerce to study the possible application of the City Manager plan to the management problems of Dayton. The committee reported favorably on the plan and it was subsequently approved by the voters by a vote of two to one.

The new pattern provided an outstanding demonstration of efficiency in the administration of public affairs. Other cities soon followed the example of Dayton in the march toward better government. By the end of 1917 council-manager government was operating in 81 cities; by 1922, in 240 cities; by 1927 in 348; and by 1933, there were 429 council-manager cities in the United States, 13 in Canada, 3 in Ireland and one in Puerto Rico. The cities ranged in size from Polk City, Florida, with a permanent population of 22, to Cincinnati with a population of 451,160.[7] As of 1968, there were 2,318 cities and 26 counties in the United States operating under the Manager plan of local government.

Municipal government is the largest single business enterprise inside the city limits; the City Manager plan borrows its methods of organization from modern business. Under this arrangement, the City Council functions in much the same manner as the board of directors in a corporate enterprise. The Council determines public policies and chooses the city manager to carry them out. The manager is a technical expert in the field of management who is placed in charge of every phase of municipal administration. Once chosen, he is given wide administrative control with authority to select his subordinates, including the executive heads of the departments of municipal government. The City Manager plan has served to produce trained administrators for a supremely technical job of public management and has given American city government its first professional touch. Among its recommenda-

[7] *Questions and Answers—About the Council-Manager Plan and the City Manager Profession*, International City Managers Association, Washington, D. C., 1968.

tions is the fact that the plan has from the beginning been consistently opposed by the professional politicians and pressure groups whose interests are not in harmony with the development of high standards in the public service.[8]

While an efficient police service can be developed within the framework of the Mayor-Council or the Commission Plan, it is patent that the City Manager form fosters professionalization in the various municipal departments. A professional administrator with full administrative power and responsibility would by the very nature of his training and position endeavor to place at the head of each department the most capable individual available. Hence, the City Manager would obviously be interested in the appointment of a Chief of Police qualified for the delivery of a professional grade of management, and then delegate to this subordinate executive the powers and responsibilities required for the proper exercise of the functions of this important position.[9]

External control of the force is thus turned into legitimate channels, with the police chief executive responsible directly to the City Manager alone. With the complete separation of the legislative and administrative functions of government provided by this pattern of municipal organization, political interference with police administration is reduced to a minimum. Under this form of administrative control police administration finds itself in a professional atmosphere where it is less likely to be burdened by the inhibitions which in the past have retarded the professionalization of this branch of the public service. It is significant that City Managers have uniformly sought for the position of police chief executive men who were professionally qualified for the task, and that they have in most instances based their selection on the professional qualifications of the candidate rather than upon political and other extraneous considerations that too often have governed appointments to this position in the past.

Most of the major universities have graduate programs in public administration, and some of them grant special degrees in this field. An average of 75 young men each year who obtain a master's degree in public administration seek to become city managers. A young man with university training normally starts out as an intern for six months to a year in a manager's office. Some universities require an internship as part of the work toward a master's degree. Following the internship, he serves as an administrative assistant to the manager in the same city

---

[8] Also see Charles M. Kneier, City Government in the United States, New York, Harper and Brothers, revised edition, 1947 and *Public Management*, Journal of the International City Managers Association.

[9] *The Municipal Yearbook*, International City Managers Association, 1963.

or in another city for two or three years. Many managers believe that this background topped off by experience in the manager's office is a good way to prepare for a career in city management.

Any pattern of government may be successfully prostituted to the ends of corrupt elements in the community, as is aptly illustrated by the Kansas City spectacle of 1928.[10]   The illegitimate forces that play upon the officials of local government in their efforts to achieve control are constantly alert.   Stamina, sagacity and integrity on the part of administration and eternal vigilance on the part of intelligent public opinion in a community are called for if these corrupters of government are to be blocked in their invasion of the public service.   Control of the police force is constantly at stake, and where corrupt controls are impressed upon police administration, the process of professionalization is seriously retarded.   These threats to organized government may be understood only in terms of the external control of the force which may be exercised by various interest groups in the community.

Pressure Groups

It is a basic principle of democratic government that administration must be responsive to public control.   This is especially true of police administration because of the unique powers with which it is entrusted. Basic, also, is the fact that such control must find expression through formal channels of governmental structure, descending vertically from the people by way of the ballot box through the legislative body to the appointing officer, and through him to the police chief executive.   It is likewise essential that responsibility flow vertically upward from the police to the appointing authority, and then from him to the legislature and finally to the people.   These controls should be out in the open where they are exposed to observation and appraisal.

Violation of this fundamental principle of organization is undoubtedly responsible for many of the ills and growing pains that have afflicted local government in general and police administration in particular.   Violations take the form of pressures and controls generated by special interest groups; they are usually brought to bear upon the weakest point or points in the organizational structure.   The point of vulnerability may be the patrolman on the beat, the "gold braid" of the department, the police chief executive, the Mayor, the City Council, or a combination of two or more of these officials.   Depending somewhat upon the form of local government, it is usually the case that when

---

[10] Walter Matscheck, "Kansas City, Where the Manager Plan Has Failed," p. 62. *The Annals of the American Academy of Political and Social Science,* September, 1938.

illegitimate controls are effectively exercised upon police administration, one or more members of the legislative body are parties to the illicit operation.

It is a necessary characteristic of corrupt controls that they operate under cover due to the fear of exposure. This alone is sufficient to place the public service and the people it serves on guard. Of the greatest concern, is the devastating effect of these informal controls upon morale, discipline and the effective combat strength of the organization.

All men in public life, from the Congressman, the Legislator, on down through the hierarchy of government to the Mayor, City Council, and the Police Chief and the members of his force, are influenced by the pressure and activities of special interest groups. They constitute a sort of phantom fourth branch of government. In every type of government, pressure groups are a normal part of the social and political process. They offer to a considerable extent, effective avenues for the expression of public opinion. In a dictatorship, a major effort is made to suppress their activities. In a democratic society characterized by representative government, together with freedom of speech and expression, they have the almost unbridled opportunity for full play.

Police administration is surrounded by a constellation of social forces in the community that may approach from any point of the compass to influence policy and administrative decisions. It is appropriate, therefore, to explore the nature and objectives of these special interest groups and their potential impact on the police enterprise.

Although the strength of political party organization varies considerably from one city to another, the political machine continues as a corrupter of government and as a direct threat to sound public management in many American municipalities. This is not so much an indictment of the so-called "machine" as it is a reflection of failure on the part of responsible citizens to exercise a participating interest in the affairs of local government. The inevitable result is that a small minority gains control.[11] Generally bankrupt on issues, political party organization in many cities depends for cohesion and loyalty upon the number of positions in the public service at its disposal for distribution to the faithful. In fact adherents of the spoils doctrine point unashamed to the contributions of the patronage system in maintaining party discipline and as a means to aid in financing the elaborate party machinery that seems to

---

[11] See Edward J. Flynn, *You're the Boss*, The Viking Press, New York, 1947; 244 pp.

be necessary under our form of government. "It is sometimes argued," states Pfiffner, "that there must be some patronage for the political officers to dispense to their campaign workers; that American democracy relies upon the party system, which in turn relies upon the spoils of office to keep it going. This is a fallacy which should be blasted before its cancerous growth goes farther on its malignant way. If American democracy is based on loot, its foundations are dangerously weak. It has been proved quite definitely that citizens actuated only by the highest civic motives can organize in the interests of professional public administration." [12]

There are "old timers" still in police uniform in American cities who can recall the days of the "suitcase parade," when the inauguration of a new Chief of Police following an election was the signal for a clean sweep at the City Hall to clear the way for the appointment to the force of friends, relatives and political henchmen. Although the political neutralization of police personnel administration through the device of civil service reform has eliminated the suitcase parade, appointments to the force, promotions and general policy continue to be unduly influenced by political and personal factors in many American cities.

The inroads of the spoils system in the past into police organization are linked closely with the operations of other pressure interests whose influence upon police policy and administration probably will survive the elimination of patronage in the American police services.

Houses of prostitution, gambling places ranging all the way from palaces to dingy quarters in the rear of a tavern, receivers of stolen goods, narcotic peddlers, racketeers, and gangsters cannot operate long without detection. All of them must depend upon a certain amount of protection in order to continue their operations. Operators of gambling casinos and houses of ill-fame want protection from police raids, and they must arrange for protection or close their doors.

Gambling operators and prostitutes may constitute a potent pressure group even in the smaller cities. The situation is not limited to cities in any particular population class nor to any particular section of the country. In every community, regardless of size, are to be found those whose standards are in the marginal zone of morality, and who are constantly on the alert for the relaxation in enforcement pressures which will permit them to open the doors for business. Their policy is not altogether one of watchful waiting; discreet but nonetheless aggres-

[12] John M. Pfiffner, "*Municipal Administration*," The Ronald Press Company, New York, 1940, pp. 31–32.

sive effort is constantly exerted upon officials at the various levels of local government by individuals and interest groups in this category to weaken the dikes that resist corrupt invasion of the public service.

In the metropolitan centers, the criminal population includes in addition, racketeers, gangsters, professional thieves and organized crime in its various forms. As Zink states:[13]

"The aim of these people is almost always that of protection; they want to be let alone by the police and the city authorities. Few pressure groups have as simple a program or on the surface ask as little; yet in the case of gangs and organized crime rings at least, few pressure groups constitute as great a public menace.

"In contrast to the simple desires of the underworld, the techniques employed are quite complex. The traditional method is of course, the paying of protection or hush money to the police and other officials. Houses of ill fame—they pay every week or every month a certain sum of money to the policeman on the beat. Where this money goes after it is received by the roundsmen, it is always difficult to ascertain. City officials frequently say that it goes no further than the roundsmen and that a certain amount of dishonesty among such inferior employees is to be expected, in view of their small salaries and large opportunities. Some of these officials maintain that the only realistic way to handle the situation is to recognize legally the existence of sporting houses and gambling palaces.

"There is considerable doubt among observers whether the claims of the city officials are well founded, for there is much reason to believe that the money finds its way to almost the top if not the very top, of the police department. There is some evidence that other officials and departments are involved. . . . If it is true that this corruption involves the entire police department of large cities, possibly the higher-ups of the political organization which controls the city government, and even the city administration itself, then the situation is bad indeed. Certainly in the case of the gangs and racketeers that have preyed on such cities as Chicago during recent years it is almost too much to believe that they pay only local police patrolmen and enjoy such a high degree of immunity. Higher-ups must connive at their crime, else there would be more arrests and convictions."

The extent to which the criminal underworld may become a factor in political changes in the United States has probably occurred to few American citizens. Crime is a corrupter of government. The rise to power of the crime-spawned political (Pendergast) organization in

---

[13] Harold Zink, *Government of Cities in the United States*, The MacMillan Company, New York, 1939, pp. 242–243.
Also see: The President's Commission on Law Enforcement and Administration of Justice, *Task Force Report: Organized Crime*, U. S. Government Printing Office, Washington, D. C., 1967.

Missouri is but one of many warnings that should be heeded by the American people. Carr takes an even more somber view, with the comment:[14]

"In some parts of the nation it is actually a question whether thugs or decent people are sovereign in the community. Certainly a forced 'tax' by crookdom each year of more than orderly government can raise for education makes one wonder what sovereignty amounts to if it cannot protect its own people against such tribute."

When police administration finds itself operating under corrupt external controls, law enforcement becomes a mockery. Police operations become defensive in character. The primary concern of the police and their confederates is to "prevent the heat from being turned on." Sporadic vice raids are properly arranged and given wide publicity in order to appease moralists and give the impression that all is well. Outbreaks of major crime are vigorously investigated; even corrupt administration is embarrassed by the robbery and murder of law-abiding citizens because it is fully aware that there are limits to public tolerance. But a relaxed administration attracts to the community more than its share of criminal parasites and spawns increased criminal activity on a menacing scale. The system fosters high crime rates and soon the officials are confronted with epidemics of sex attacks upon women, outbreaks of armed robbery and steady up-swings in burglary and larceny as the situation gradually moves out of control. Morale and discipline are at a low ebb; police organization is demoralized and helpless. Fighting power and combat strength are decimated under such conditions and the department can no longer discharge its functions in protecting the citizens of the community against criminal attack. Community sentiment becomes aroused. Even a corrupt press may be unable to stem the advance of reform.

Recent years have witnessed considerable gain in the elimination of corrupt external influence on police administration. Expert observers know, however, that few American police departments can claim complete freedom from illegitimate pressures.[15] Every competent survey of municipal police organization and administration has revealed

---

[14] L. J. Carr, *Delinquency Control*, Harper & Brothers, New York, 1941, p. 35. Also see Craig Thompson and Allen Raymond, *Gang Rule in New York*, Camden, 1940; and current reports of the Chicago Crime Commission.

In order to become convinced that organized crime and the underworld are not the product of a capricious imagination on the part of the fiction writers, the reader should examine carefully—The President's Commission on Law Enforcement and Administration of Justice, *Task Force Report—Organized Crime*, U. S. Government Printing Office, Washington, 1967.

[15] See list of police surveys and reorganizations in bibliography.

their presence and on occasion their influence upon the administration of police affairs. Symptomatic of this pathological condition are the short tenure and frequent replacement of the police chief executive, low quality of management, defective organization, departmental cliques, substandard personnel resources, and a general failure to ascertain and apply the tested tools and procedures of modern police administration.

Interference with local police administration expresses itself in many different forms. Occasionally it is well-intentioned but frequently it is ill-conceived and misguided. Chambers of Commerce and the constellation of service club organizations that characterize the American scene in every city may affect the quality of police administration for good or for evil. These organizations, as a rule, exert a constructive influence in municipal affairs, but they are not infrequently short-sighted, and may even be prostituted to the selfish ends of an individual or a group. Most service clubs attempt to remain politically neutral. They should also remember that political neutrality is an absolute prerequisite of successful police organization. Service clubs and organizations can do much to promote civic pride and civic improvement by demanding of the City Council that the conditions for a professionalized police service be made available.

The churches in a community represent a potential pressure group of considerable proportions. If their members are aroused their influence can be a controlling factor in administrative policy determination. The voting power of the active church members in an average American city is more than sufficient to elect or defeat council members. However, churches are rarely able to mobilize their effective strength and present a united front. Furthermore, church membership includes a fair cross-section of most interest groups in a community, which complicates any effort to pool their resources on issues that are other than neutral in character.

Nevertheless, the influence of churches in municipal affairs should not be underestimated. A man's thinking can be shaped by the impact of the principles enunciated by the Man of Galilee, and a transformation in viewpoint on the part of an individual may have important implications at the ballot box. Furthermore crusading ministers have not infrequently stirred communities to action by messages from the pulpit. Where economy in government and a low tax rate form the basis for current issues, churches will not ordinarily become too greatly concerned. However, if vice is rampant and corruption the rule, and if these conditions are quite apparent, churches may take a definite stand.

Organized labor has attempted penetration of police departments in many sections of the country. With the growth in cities, police departments became employing units on a substantial scale. Naturally their members became intensely interested in conditions of service, including adjustment of working hours, pension and retirement benefits, protection of tenure, wage increases and other benefits. Members of police forces came together early in fraternal societies or clubs, and through this medium exchanged information, carried on social activities for themselves and their families, and established benefits to aid fellow officers or their dependents. Such social or fraternal clubs exist today in many jurisdictions. In some departments they have accomplished much good and have contributed greatly to the morale of the force. In other departments, they have been used to accomplish the selfish ends of malcontents in the organization and have left in their wake dissension and wreckage of departmental morale and efficiency.

With the phenomenal development of labor union organization in industry since 1900, police personnel in a number of departments where administration was weak and ineffective sensed the possibility of applying union mechanisms to their problems. Labor organizers also saw in the police forces of the nation new sources of revenue and an opportunity for a new extension of power and influence. They probably were not unmindful of the advantages that would accrue from control of the force during clashes between labor and management in industrial disputes.

Fundamental issues, including the security of government itself, appear to be involved in the question whether unionized police forces should be permitted to affiliate with national unions. For this reason legislative restrictions on police unionization have been generally sustained.

Within recent years, the effort to organize police unions has received increased impetus, but the movement has met with comparatively little success. Of 27 state police and highway patrol agencies replying to a questionnaire circulated in 1956 by the International Association of Chiefs of Police, but one, Wisconsin, reported its personnel belonged to a union. Members of the Wisconsin State Patrol are organized in the State Traffic Officers Local 55, a unit of the Wisconsin State Employees Association and the Council of State Employee Locals, affiliated with the American Federation of State, County and Municipal Employees (AFL).[16]

Of 742 municipal police departments in cities over 10,000 population replying to the questionnaire, 44 reported they had police unions. Of these, two (Seattle and Spokane, Wash.) have since disbanded.

---

[16] International Association of Chiefs of Police, *Police Unions*, p. 74, revised edition, August 1958.

The Municipal Yearbook 1953, reported 58 cities in 23 states had locals of the American Federation of State, County and Municipal Employees (AFL) comprised exclusively of police officers. Of the 58, at least six—Tuscaloosa and Mobile, Ala.; Baltimore, Md.; Youngstown, Ohio; and Seattle and Spokane—have disbanded and one—Augusta, Ga.—is inactive with but 12 members, and new members prohibited from joining by a 1954 General Assembly Act.[17]

At the 1957 Conference of the IACP in Honolulu, Mr. A. S. Reile, as the "prime target" for police unionization. Late in 1958, the head Industrial Organizations, told Conference delegates there were unions in 65 police departments in villages and cities over 10,000.

From the above three sources of statistics, covering the years 1953 to 1957, the number of police unions, therefore, is not more than 65 and not less than 39.

There is little question that union organizers view New York City as the "prime target" for police unionization. Late in 1958, the head of the Teamsters Union announced his intention to unionize all of the police forces of this country and that he would begin with the largest force of all, the New York City Police Department. The strong stand of municipal officials convinced the Teamsters Union that it would not be wise to picket New York police facilities. The resolution to organize all of the nation's police forces appeared to have been broken before New Year's Day.[18]

The questionnaires returned in 1956 by 742 police departments in cities over 10,000 population throughout the United States revealed that there is no formal union organization of police in 698 of the cities, that there is a police union under AFL affiliation in 41 cities, and under CIO affiliation, 3 cities.

Of the cities reporting no police union, 114 stated there was no expressed or implied policy prohibiting police unions and no formal

---

[17] These cities were Tuscaloosa and Mobile, Ala.; Hot Springs, Little Rock, North Little Rock and Pine Bluff, Ark.; Denver and Pueblo, Colo.; Bridgeport, Hartford, Middleton, New Britain and New Haven, Conn.; Augusta, Ga.; Aurora, East St. Louis, Joliet, Kankakee, La Salle, Ottawa, Springfield, and Streator, Ill.; Fort Madison and Keokuk, Ia.; Hutchinson, Kans.; Alexandria, Bogalusa, Monroe and Shreveport, La.; Baltimore, Md.; Duluth and St. Paul, Minn.; Meridian, Miss.; Hastings and Omaha, Neb.; Irvington, N. J.; Asheville and Durham, N. C.; Massillon and Youngstown, Ohio; Portland and Salem, Ore.; Columbia, S. C.; Chattanooga, Tenn.; Portsmouth, Va.; Bremerton, Pasco, Port Angeles, Puyallup, Renton, Seattle, Spokane, Tacoma, Vancouver and Yakima, Wash.; LaCrosse and Madison, Wis.; and Sheridan, Wyo.

[18] The International City Managers' Association, *The Municipal Yearbook,* 1959.

ruling or court decision banning unions. 78 cities indicated a "neutral" position on the question of police unions, while 166 reported an expressed or implied policy against police unions. 340 cities did not reply to the question about policy.

Only 50 of the 742 police agencies replied affirmatively to the question, "Has there been any move to organize a police union in your city?" Of these, 26 indicated the approach had been made before 1950, 17 between 1950 and 1954, 5 in 1955 and 2 in 1956. Only a very few did not reply to this question, with the great majority replying with an unqualified "No."

From a review of the IACP questionnaires and the accompanying comments by police officials, as well as further contacts with some police departments since the questionnaire was circulated in 1956, it may be concluded that:

1.   There is renewed effort from time to time by union organizers to bring law enforcement officers into unions with AFL–CIO affiliation.

2.   The great majority of police officers throughout the country are loyal to the highest ideals of impartial and unbiased police service to the community they serve and are therefore willing to forego some of the personal prerogatives open to other public and private enterprise employees.

The United States Supreme Court in effect upheld the decision of the supreme court of Mississippi, City of Jackson v. McLeod, 199 Miss. 676, 24 So.2d 319, that refusal of city policemen to renounce their intention of joining a labor union, in line with a city regulation prohibiting such membership, was an act of insubordination and valid cause for dismissal.[19] Of important collateral interest is State Lodge of Michigan Fraternal Order v. City of Detroit in which the Court in effect upheld the decision of the Michigan Supreme Court (318 Mich. 182, 27

[19] 328 U.S. 863, 66 S.Ct. 1368, 90 L.Ed. 1633. See Municipal Yearbook, 1950, p. 387.

Also see People v. Crane, 214 N.Y. 154–161, 108 N.E. 427, L.R.A.1916D, 550, Ann.Cas.1915B, 1254 (1915); Kemp v. Division No. 241, 255 Ill. 213, 99 N.E. 389, Ann.Cas.1913D, 347 (1912); Railway Mail Association v. Murphy, 180 Misc. 868, 44 N.Y.S.2d 601 (1943); Raycraft v. Harrison, 108 Ill.App. 313 (1903); Coane v. Geary, 298 Ill.App. 199, 18 N.E.2d 719 (1939); Carter v. Thompson, 164 Va. 312, 180 S.E. 410 (1935); O'Kelly v. Collins, 281 Ill.App. 604 (1935); Goldstine Realty Co. v. City of Chicago, 306 Ill.App. 556, 29 N.E. 2d 283 (1940); Petrucci v. Hogan, 27 N.Y.S.2d 718 (Sup., 1941); Seattle High School Chapter No. 200 v. Sharplies, 159 Wash. 424, 293 P. 994 (1930). In addition, there have been rulings of Attorneys General and Corporation Counsels holding that the sovereignty of the people and their government cannot be trespassed upon by the obligations of union membership.

N.W.2d 612) upholding Detroit's commissioner of police in forbidding police from joining a named fraternal order.

Judicial decisions have denied the application of the union mechanisms of collective bargaining, the closed shop, the check-off system and the strike in the police forces of this country. When by law or by mutual consent the union is denied the most fundamental of the traditional instruments for achieving its purposes, the strike, there is very little advantage offered to police officers by membership in national unions. Nationally by 1948 there were few places where police personnel newly affiliated themselves with national labor unions. The movement seemed to have come to a halt and reversed itself in some places for the reason that such affiliation is incompatible with the public interest and the tradition of independence of action necessary for the police. (See the Municipal Yearbook, 1949, p. 388.)

But the question cannot be disposed of merely on grounds of constitutional or statutory right. Its implications involve the pathology of police administration itself. Like an individual, a social institution may become sick. Through inadequate leadership and ill-conceived policies, it may become incapable of coping with its internal problems or with its major social responsibilities. The unionization of a police force usually can be traced to inadequacies of management. In the majority of cases where union penetration of police forces has occurred, it has been a measure of desperation on the part of personnel faced with intolerable conditions of service for which they could secure little redress from indifferent city officials. A vigorous administration will spare no effort in gaining for its personnel all the privileges and benefits consistent with the integrity of operations in terms of compensation, days off, sick leave, vacation, hours of duty, pensions and other conditions of service. Indeed, it has been demonstrated that under this type of administrative policy employees find no occasion to look elsewhere for assistance in the solution of their problems. As professionalization of the police services gains its stride, with a corresponding improvement in managerial ability, it is likely that the need for employee organization will diminish and tend to disappear. Until that time, management will be compelled to face the challenge of police unions and other forms of employee organization, and the compromise in morale and line performance which they entail.

In a studied approach to *The Legal Status of Municipal Police Employee Organizations,* by Harvey A. Juris and Kay B. Hutchison, the authors conducted a survey of the police in all cities over 50,000 population in the 50 states, and a one-in-five sample of cities between 10,000 and 50,000. They found that the largest cities are most likely to have police employee organizations. The following Table shows the type and distribution of police employee organizations by city size: [20]

TABLE II
TYPE OF POLICE EMPLOYEE ORGANIZATIONS BY CITY SIZE

Affiliated with:	City Size (000's)							Total
	10– 25	25– 50	50– 100 a	100– 250 b	250– 500	500– 1000	1000 Plus	
Fraternal Order of Police	12	7	19	17	8	5	1	69
Police Benevolent Association	4	1	7	7	0	0	1	20
AFSCME *	1	2	1	3	0	0	0	7
ICPA **	0	0	0	1	1	0	1	3
State Organization	6	3	14	4	0	1	0	28
Local Independent	13	7	21	7	1	6	1	56
Joint	11	12	39	27	12	5	2	108
Total	47	32	101	66	22	17	6	291
Column total as a percent of returned questionnaires	(66)	(86)	(87)	(92)	(96)	(85)	(100)	

a In addition one city reported affiliation with the Teamsters.

b In addition one city reported affiliation with the International Union of Operating Engineers.

* Union-affiliated in some states (AFL–CIO)—The American Federation of State, County and Municipal Employees.

** The International Conference of Police Associations.

The authors observe that of the several standard objections to the unionization of police forces, the strike and the question of dual allegiance, may well be as great a problem with non-affiliated as with affiliated organizations.   They recommend that before any new legislation is drafted by local and state governments, careful consideration of the following questions is urged:

1.   Does affiliation with a labor organization compromise the loyalty of police officers?

2.   Are police-only organizations free from this criticism.

20 Juris, Harvey A., and Hutchison, Kay B., *The Legal Status of Municipal Police Employee Organizations*, Working Paper Number 3, Center for Law and Behavioral Science, University of Wisconsin, Madison, Wisconsin, June 1969.

3. Can we justify prohibiting affiliation as an officer but allowing membership in the union which has jurisdiction in the officer's moonlight employment?

4. What has been the experience where strikes, sick-calls, and other job actions have occurred?

5. In addition, researchers might consider the definition of an appropriate bargaining unit, the nature of and experience with grievance procedures, and other substantive issues relating to the structure and process of collective bargaining.

In regard to the first item listed above, it should not be necessary to go far afield to learn that divided allegiance is heavily involved in the case of a union-affiliated police force.

There is an even more somber aspect of the problem which merits recognition. Despite the best efforts of many capable and honest labor leaders, allegations are widespread that communistic interests have infiltrated the ranks of labor organizations in this country. If this is true even to a limited degree, union affiliation of police forces opens the way for invasion by subversive interests of this primary instrument for the preservation of the social order. History and the events of recent years reveal that high on the agenda of those who would overthrow government are well ordered plans to undermine and gain control of the police. This alone is enought to place everyone on guard.

Conscientious police administrators will welcome the day when women's organizations may become more articulate in matters which concern the standards of local government. It is a serious mistake to underestimate the potential power of women in the realm of public affairs, particularly when the welfare of their children is at stake. It is equally hazardous to assume that women's organizations will be content to confine their efforts to embroidery contests and book reviews when environmental hazards and other forces in the community continue as a threat to youth welfare. Prophetic of the role of women in the community affairs is the observation that among the most devastating things that could happen to mar an otherwise pleasant day for the average city hall official would be the announcement by his secretary that a delegation of women awaited him in the reception room.

The power of the press has not been underestimated. The newspapers of a community or city can "make or break" a police department. Among the external controls that condition police administration the press plays a commanding role. Front page stories, or editorials or cartoons—occasionally all three—may be published with the hope that pressure will convince the city officials that something must be done. Diversions of police manpower and equipment, not infrequently in flagrant violation of sound principles of organization and administration, often result. The police feel that they must placate the newspapers. But matters first in importance should receive first attention. In determining the order of priority, the police are compelled to rely in large part upon the penal code. Murder, usually punishable by death, necessarily takes first place. Kidnapping, rape, robbery, and burglary follow in the order named. However, local prejudice and press releases modify the order of priority in many instances, and cause a shift of police emphasis among these different assignments so that some are given attention out of all proportion to their importance.

Police headquarters is one of the most prolific sources of news in any city or community. In the larger communities and cities, newspapers may maintain one or more police reporters at headquarters on a 24 hour basis. Police-press relationships are important. It has been demonstrated over and over again that through a mutual policy of confidence and cooperation, the ends of both news reporting and police administration can be served in a most effective manner. It is seldom that a newspaper reporter has violated the confidence of a Police Chief in, for example, a sensitive case where premature publicity could prejudice or disrupt the investigation.

Police management and its personnel have a tendency on occasion to ignore the good effect of the press and the results that can be achieved through a sound policy of cooperation with the press. The editorial policy of every newspaper supports good law enforcement. Usually, the men who write editorials have had broad experience in dealing with the police. Most of the nation's successful editors have served as police reporters at one time or another and many have never forgotten the experience. One editor has suggested that if they were not newspapermen, many of them would be police officers.

The news media throughout the nation has consistently supported such things as:

Improved criminal procedures.
Improved police facilities.
Improved police management techniques.
Better police equipment.
Increases in manpower.
Better selection and training procedures.
Increased compensation for police officers.
Improved traffic management.
Intelligent and well-conceived enforcement policies.
Improvements in the judicial system.

Minority groups are a potent and viable pressure group in many communities throughout the nation. Historically they have had minimal influence, but in recent years they have become an important aspect of the political and social processes of community life. This ethnicity is quite apparent and is a specific manifestation of America's race problem. With increasing frequency, minority groups are demanding more citizen participation in the governance of our cities as indicated by the tendency in some communities for neighborhood control of the police or the demand for a police review board. It is a strong movement in certain cities; police administrators must be prepared to deal with demands from Blacks, Chicanos, Puerto Ricans and other ethnic groups.

Militant activists and agitators can also be described as a pressure group and while there is considerable confusion about the goals or purposes of far left groups such as the Students for a Democratic Society (SDS), they certainly have had an impact on our society that is proportionately far beyond their number. Alienated from society, members of such groups make unrealistic demands on our nation. The diverse elements of the far left, typified by the alienated young, expound a special understanding of America's problems; however, their only solution seems to be destruction rather than a resolution of the problem. Some of these radicals pose a special law enforcement problem because rhetoric has been replaced by destructive action, with the assassination of police officers, and the bombing of government buildings.

The external pressures that play upon the forces designed to protect law and order complicate enormously the problems of modern police organization and administration in the United States, and place a high premium on executive ability. An undue emphasis has been placed on popular control of administration, as necessary to insure democratic operation of the public services. Americans have blocked the professionalization of their police forces by almost insurmountable barriers. Demoralized organization, dissipated striking power and diminished efficiency follow unwise external interference with police administration and foster an unfavorable public opinion which further retards professionalization. The problem of the present moment is to release the forces of law and order from the shackles, including some recent U. S. Supreme Court Decisions, that have prevented their effective operation.* Responsibility for the successful achievement of this objective is a challenge to police administration itself.

It has been said that in a democracy, "A city gets the kind of police service that it deserves, because it can get any kind that it wants."

---

* See V. A. Leonard, *The Police, the Judiciary and the Criminal,* Springfield, Illinois, Charles C. Thomas, Publisher, 1969.

The statement is misleading because it assumes that the people know what to want, which was not the case either in England in 1826, or in the United States today.

The people of England did not know what they wanted in 1826 during the period of social chaos and upheaval except relief from their tribulations. The man in the street and the average citizen were in the dark as to the means to be employed. It remained for administration itself to take the initiative and formulate the means and the method which turned in such a creditable performance on this occasion. Approval of the administrative formula was the next step, and it came quickly. Given all the facts by courageous and responsible leaders, the people can be entrusted with the final decision.

It is undoubtedly true that the people of the United States do not know what to want in terms of police service. They know they want relief from the tremendous costs of the administration of justice, from crime and the criminal, and from the huge social and economic losses that follow in the wake of traffic accidents, retarded traffic flow, parking, and congestion. That was the sort of language the British people could understand in their dilemma of 1826. But like the British, the American people are necessarily confused as to the means and the method to be employed.

There has been a general failure in America to recognize the basic principle that formulation of means and method is not a responsibility of the people. They can approve or disapprove. But the average citizen has no time for an intensive study of police science and administration. It is stupid to expect of him an interest in government that would go to any such lengths. He must rely upon administrative talent in this professional field to initiate and put in motion those agencies and procedures which will produce results. Bruce Smith states: [21]

"Police administration has become a complex and highly technical calling. The problems of law enforcement can be satisfactorily described and made real only to persons who have had some experience with public administration or who have themselves known the complexities which surround the business of handling and directing large numbers of men.

"In other words, the task of law enforcement is now a problem of management, and lies beyond the comprehension of those who are not experienced in it. Such experience is possessed by relatively too few members of a popular electorate to provide a sufficient backlog of informed and understanding public opinion."

It may be stated, then, that the quality of American police service is a direct responsibility of police administration and is not predeter-

[21] Bruce Smith, "Politics and Law Enforcement," *The Annals of the American Academy of Political and Social Science*, Vol. 169, September, 1933, p. 72.

mined, as is generally assumed, by public opinion. The responsibility rests squarely upon the shoulders of police administration. Too often, either through incapacity or indifference, it has failed to interpret its problems to the people, and has failed to formulate and present to them for their approval an organization and program equal to the demands of a modern social order.

A virile administration is called for, capable of presenting to the people the specifications of modern police service. Until the people know what to want, until they can visualize the possibilities of a scientific police administration in terms of lowered crime and delinquency rates and lowered unit costs, they never will get the kind of police service they deserve. Those who believe in democracy are convinced that once the people are in possession of the facts, they can be depended upon to support the kind of administration to which they are entitled. In those few American cities where administration has performed this missionary work, the people are enjoying an experience in modern police service altogether unknown to other sections of the country. In those few instances, police administration operates in an atmosphere of mutual confidence and respect, proving that it can be done in the United States as well as in England.

The nature of the police task places an extraordinary premium upon administrative ability and emphasizes the importance of adequate professional preparation for this technical job of management. Our English friends choose their administrators with extreme care. From the beginning of organized police service, England has recognized that the success or failure of any police organization is largely dependent upon the head of the force. A man who possesses the various capacities required of a successful police executive is not easily found, and the English authorities are correspondingly cautious in their selection of an individual for this key position in the public service. The appointment of the Commissioner of the London Metropolitan Police, for example, is regarded as being among the most difficult upon which Ministers have to advise the Crown.[22] In making the first appointment in 1829, it is interesting to note that Peel decided that anyone who applied for the job would be *ipso facto* ineligible. The English have from the start preserved a healthy independence in their appointments so that all considerations other than merit would be ruled out of the selection process. They have made the position of police executive one of great honor and distinction. The police commissionership of an English city is a career of prominence which attracts the best talent that the universities or the

[22] J. F. Moylan, *Scotland Yard and the Metropolitan Police*, Putnam and Company, New York, 1934, p. 33.

government service can produce. Many police executives are chosen from among retired high officers of the armed services.

The critical importance of the executive as an organizational determinant of line performance suggests a more detailed treatment of the qualifications for the top administrative position and the mechanics of selection by which men are brought into this office.

Chapter 3

THE POLICE EXECUTIVE

NO greater responsibility confronts the appointing power in American cities than the choice of the individual who is to be given control of police administration. Leadership is the most important single factor in the success or failure of police operations. Invariably in observing a successful police organization one finds a strong executive who has been the driving force in elevating the level of performance. Conversely, where mediocrity or failure characterizes the work of a police organization, it generally can be traced to incompetence in management. The fundamental basis for the success of a police enterprise is to be found in the ideas and efforts of the police chief executive.

Too frequently, radio patrol cars, crime detection laboratories, traffic investigation units and other observable expressions of performance are looked upon as the beginning and the end of police service. True, they are component parts of great importance, but back of all these is an intricate job of management performed by the executive who guides and controls the far-flung operations of a metropolitan police organization, or those of a smaller department, and without whom the enterprise would become shapeless and inoperative. The leader is a dynamic force in the actual work of organization and operation. The value of his service cannot be expressed in dollars and cents on the balance sheet, but his effort or lack of it is clearly reflected in the success or failure of the police in the community they serve. As one goes up the scale of supervisory and command personnel in a police department from the sergeant through the lieutenant, captain, inspector and deputy to the chief executive, emphasis is placed increasingly on judgment, self-reliance and resourcefulness. The scope of duties gradually broadens and planning in advance expands in importance until one comes to the chief executive who is the chief strategist and the one who is responsible for the operation of the entire enterprise.

Qualifications of the Police Executive

Generally speaking, top management in the police field has not kept pace with technological improvements at the periphery of the enterprise. Amazing progress has been made in the United States in the application of scientific method to the laboratory examination and identification of materials involved as evidence in criminal cases. The bio-

39

logical and physical sciences and other scientific tools have been harnessed effectively to the processes of criminal investigation and they have introduced into the field of criminal justice administration important economies through shortening of the investigative trail. Motorization of the force and radio communication have amplified the potential mobility and striking power of the force to the point where the arrest almost has been synchronized with the depredation. Unusual strides have been made in procedures for the selection of personnel and improved training methods have been adopted. These gains, however, are more apparent than real due to the fact that advances in technical proficiency have not been paralleled by equal progress in the techniques of management. Police science has been advancing faster at the bottom of the enterprise than at the top; great effort has been devoted to the improvement of the patrolman and the detective, but relatively little attention has been given to the development of competent police executives.[1]

Too frequently, it is assumed that the man who has the longest service or if several are approximately equal on this point, then the man with the best record as a policeman may confidently be expected to be successful in the management of the department as its chief. The fallacy of this procedure is demonstrated by its failure in many American cities. The administration of a police department is a technical undertaking, requiring not only successful experience as a policeman, but also special talent and a number of peculiar skills that are not acquired in the course of ordinary police training and experience. Fosdick was among the first to make this observation and he came to the conclusion that:[2]

"The police executive should be chosen from outside the professional ranks. The management of police business demands as able an administrator as can be obtained. Indeed, in a city like Cleveland, and in many cities of lesser size, the task of police administration is so great that the best man obtainable is none too good, and in an endeavor to find him, no search can be too thorough. That such a leader can be found in the ranks of a police force is in the highest degree improbable. The officer who has walked his 'beat' as a patrolman, investigated crime as a detective and managed the technical routine of station house activity as lieutenant or captain, is not fitted by this experience to administer the complex affairs of a large police department.

"The chances are rather that he is unfitted for the task. Lacking in administrative experience, with scant appreciation of the larger possibilities

---

[1] The International City Managers' Association, *Municipal Police Administration*, 1943, p. 52.

[2] Raymond B. Fosdick, "Police Administration," Part III of the Cleveland Foundation Survey of Criminal Justice in Cleveland, 1921, pp. 16–17.

of the position, and often indeed without imagination or resourcefulness, he has little chance of success, and it would be unwise and cruel to saddle him with the responsibility. If police management were merely a matter of assignments, promotions, and discipline; if it had to do only with the ordering of a well-defined routine, any capable man who himself had been through the mill might be well adapted to handle it.

"But the task, particularly in large cities, is so much broader than routine, and involves activities of such vital consequence that only a high order of creative intelligence can cope with it. The executive must deal with community problems in the large. He must be familiar with the underlying social forces which are responsible for the need of police service. Constantly before him must be the conception of the department as an agency for the prevention of crime, and the consequent relationship of his work to all activities, social, economic, and educational, operating to that end. He must be able to interpret public opinion, to be a community leader, and above all, he must be qualified to inspire a great force of policemen. In addition, he must have a thorough understanding of the principles of administration. These qualifications are not readily found in the uniformed force, nor, indeed, are they easily found in any walk of life."

Fosdick was eminently correct in interpreting the magnitude of the problem of management in the police services but even he failed to anticipate collateral developments that were to occur in the decades following the publication of his study in 1921. It also probably is true that he was influenced by his observations of selection procedure in European countries, where it has long been common practice to go outside the department for executive material.[3] Barristers and high ranking military officers have been chosen in many instances to fill the top position in European police departments.

This method of selection may be understood when observed against the background of the peculiar conditions which existed in Europe. During an inspection of the Belgian police services in 1947, the author learned that in the police department of Brussels not only the police chief executive, but all supervisory and command personnel above the rank of sergeant were recruited from outside the department! The men employed for patrol service had to abandon all hope of promotion. It was explained that the altogether inadequate salary scale for patrolmen and the resulting low quality of personnel recruited into the patrol services precluded any possibility of having in the patrol ranks individuals who were qualified for promotion. The head of the Brussels police training school expressed the view that when salary structures were adjusted to attract to the patrol services a higher type of individual, external recruiting for higher posts would be abandoned. These officials

---

[3] Raymond B. Fosdick, *European Police Systems,* The Century Co., New York, 1914, pp. 100–149.

recognized that their policy was unsound because the introduction of inferior personnel into the patrol ranks did irretrievable damage to this important branch of departmental operations in preventing the development of a career service.

At the time Fosdick made his observations, recruiting standards in the American police services were low. The quality of personnel secured for patrol service did not afford an ample number of qualified men for promotion within the department to the higher administrative positions. The situation has now changed materially with the widespread elevation of recruiting standards and qualifications and by improved salary scales. The type of individual now being recruited into American police departments is far superior to the patrolman of thirty-five years ago.

Appointment of an American police chief executive from outside the department would lead to many difficulties. A man with no police experience or training would function under a heavy handicap even though he might be a person of superior administrative ability. His executive abilities in the successful control of large numbers of men would carry him only so far as the basic principles of organization and administration would apply to group undertakings in general. Beyond that point he would be confronted with administrative decisions which require a thorough command of the technical procedures and techniques peculiar to this profession, decisions which he could not delegate altogether to technically trained subordinates. It is not at all likely that the personnel of a police organization, themselves familiar with the technical aspects of police service, would accord to such an executive the respect and confidence which are necessary for effective executive control. There are few instances in American police history of laymen being appointed as chiefs of police. Notable among these has been the occasional appointment of a ranking military officer as head of a state police organization. The comparative success of such men in positions of police management is understandable because of the close parallel between military and police operations.

Lay management of a police organization with its inherent limitations may be observed where administrative control of both police and fire departments is lodged in a commissioner of public safety, as in the commission form of municipal government, and in some cities under the mayor-council plan where a director of safety controls both departments. These officials seldom have had either experience or training in the police field, with the result that in addition to the evils of plural command, inexperience and professional incompetence paralyze the efficiency and striking power of the crime fighting organization.

Basic, then, among the indispensable qualifications of the executive is an extended and successful police experience characterized preferably by service at every rank in the department. The knowledge gained first hand concerning the problems of the patrolman, the sergeant, the lieutenant, the captain, the inspector and the deputy or assistant chief add immeasurably to the capacity for management of the police enterprise. If experience includes periods of service in each of the major functional divisions and bureaus of the department, including patrol, detective, vice, traffic, crime prevention, records, communications and personnel, the chief will be even better prepared to assume the responsibilities of his new position. Armed with a technical knowledge of the functions and problems of these various staff and line units of police organization, he is in a position to weigh their relative importance in the equation of crime control, to exercise intelligent budget controls and to integrate their joint effort toward the immediate and long-term objectives of police organization.

But the foregoing qualifications—experience and training—are of little avail unless the individual possesses administrative capabilities and the attributes of executive leadership. Above all other considerations, the police executive must be a leader of men.

Leadership.

Organization alone is an inert, inanimate thing until it fuses with leadership to become a dynamic force with a compelling thrust toward the achievement of objectives. There is much more to police service than the headquarters building, patrol cars, radio communication, police records and all the other material elements of a modern police system. There must be present *leadership* to control, plan and direct the involved activities of a police organization.

The fire of inspired leadership is a contagious thing. It usurps the role of command and leads men to go on beyond the call of duty to new levels of performance. Many books have been written on the psychology of leadership. They are to be found in every library and await their use by those interested in improving their capabilities in this important area of the profession. What is an executive? What is leadership? Why do some men fail miserably in positions involving the supervision and command of personnel while others seem to meet such responsibilities with confidence and comparative ease? The answer is not simple; the formula of successful leadership is yet to be derived. No satisfactory set of rules ever has been developed which will insure success as an executive. However certain traits and manners of conduct predominate in effective leadership. Some of these appear to be innate, while others may be developed.

As Cornell points out:[4]

"Some persons never could become executives. Some few individuals appear destined to be leaders from their youth because of the wealth of executive qualities with which they are endowed. Between these two groups is a great middle group composed of persons who have the desired qualities but in varying degree. It depends upon themselves whether such men become executive or remain among the ranks of routine workers. If they make the most of their abilities and bend every effort to overcome or compensate for their shortcomings they may in the end surpass those who from youth appeared destined for leadership. It is a compensation of nature that those with the greatest natural gifts sometimes rest too heavily upon them and thus permit those less fortunately endowed to stride past them."

Whatever the diagnosis of leadership may be, the executive must be an acknowledged leader of men, capable of inspiring them to carry on until the set task is accomplished. This type of leadership leads instead of drives, in contrast with the approach which depends upon fear. An intelligent group of men will not respond when driven, whereas, there is almost no limit to the sacrifices which men will make under inspired leadership.

The complexity of relationships between the executive and his men requires a peculiar insight into human nature with all of its strength and all of its weaknesses. A high order of intelligence and good judgment is called for, with a measure of common sense which will permit discrimination and decision as to the relative importance of things and the selection from among several possible lines of action the one which will yield the most favorable return. Strength or power of personality, intangible and indefinable though it may be, is a common denominator of successful leadership and will always be found transmitting its impulses to the men in an effective organization. Another quality which appears strongly essential is a scientific turn of mind. The executive is constantly facing problems which yield most readily to the analytical approach of the scientifically-minded thinker.[5] The technical problems involved in coordinating the work of a group of men, materials, and equipment in such a way as to achieve maximum amplification of the line power of an organization are often exceedingly complex.

In a survey of opinion regarding the qualifications of an executive, Davis listed fifty-six different characteristics and traits regarded as es-

[4] William B. Cornell, *Organization and Management*, The Ronald Press Company, New York, 1936, p. 67.

[5] Erwin Haskell Schell, *The Technique of Executive Control*, McGraw-Hill Book Company, Inc., New York, 1942, p. 11.

sential.[6] He pointed out, however, that it would be quite improbable that all of them would be possessed by any one individual in any high degree, and offered the following list of basic traits required for executive success with no indication of their relative importance:

1. Intelligence
2. Experience
3. Originality
4. Receptiveness
5. Teaching ability

6. Personality
7. Knowledge of human behavior
8. Courage
9. Tenacity
10. A sense of justice and fair play.

A follower of the Taylor philosophy [7] of organization and administration, Davis emphasizes the importance of intelligence, experience and originality as requisites for executive success in most situations. The primary functions of the executive are planning, organizing, and controlling the activities of people in the undertaking for which he is responsible. It is uniformly characteristic of the police day that situations are constantly changing. A local management-labor dispute holding potentialities for strike and riot, the unexpected death of a prisoner in a jail cell, a sudden upsurge in the volume of automobile thefts or other crimes, an increase in traffic accidents, a change in the density distribution of police hazards, the development of new suburban residential areas and business districts, and the activities of pressure groups represent but a few of the new situations which may confront the police executive from day to day. He must possess the intelligence and originality to relate his previous background and experience to planning of operations and the solution of new problems.

Audacity tempered with fine judgment and discrimination characterizes most successful executives. Much of their work is concerned with planning for unforeseen emergencies and the removal of interference with the execution of those plans. There are times when a great deal of mental courage is required to initiate action in situations where there is a possibility of failure. The line of least resistance is to play safe, as for example, when there is opposition within the department itself to plans whose adoption the executive believes are sound and necessary. The executive is responsible for accomplishing results, and the fact that he may yield to the pressure of others will not relieve him of his responsibility in the event of failure. He needs a considerable degree of mental courage, together with the strength of character and ability to follow through with plans in the face of opposition.

[6] Ralph Currier Davis, *Industrial Organization and Management*, Harper and Brothers, New York, 1940, pp. 32–33.

[7] See Frederick W. Taylor, *Shop Management*, Harper & Brothers, New York, 1911.

The true executive possesses an innate interest in, and affection for people. Executives are moulders of human stuff. They know the possibilities and capabilities of those associated with them and endeavor to build them into better instruments for the accomplishment of the objectives of the enterprise. They also know that increased professional stature of their men increases the quality of departmental performance and that this in turn reflects credit upon the head of the organization. This trait was among those that contributed to the successful leadership of August Vollmer during the years he was Chief of Police in Berkeley, California. Chief Vollmer encouraged the individual to reach for the highest rungs on the ladder of achievement in his chosen profession. As a matter of fact, under his expert supervision, the Berkeley Police Department became the nation's training school for police chiefs and more than twenty of his officers subsequently became police chief executives in other American cities.

Tenure of the Police Executive

Continuity of administration is an essential condition to the effective expression of the qualities of leadership. It represents a principle which has not yet invaded the American public services to any marked extent. The indefinite and usually long tenure of English police executives looms large in any explanation of the professional standing and success of police administration in England. Uninterrupted tenure makes possible continuity of policy and administration, an indispensable prerequisite to successful management. The English view is, "Why introduce a new man to the position? What is wrong with the incumbent? Our chiefs have too much valuable experience accumulated over years of effective administration. We cannot afford to change." [8] The changing of police chiefs with every shift in the political fortunes of local government is completely foreign to English procedure. Even Prime Ministers come and go without affecting in the least the continuity of administration at New Scotland Yard. Buttressing the English example is the long tenure of J. Edgar Hoover, Director of the Federal Bureau of Investigation, and heads of the Secret Service and other federal law enforcement agencies in the United States. The sterling performance of these organizations is a matter of common knowledge. The average tenure of the Chief of Police in the United States is slightly over four years in cities under 300,000 in population and is less than two and one-half years in cities over 500,000 in population.[9]

[8] Raymond B. Fosdick, *European Police Systems*, The Century Company, 1915, p. 169.

[9] Bristow, Allen P., and Gabard, E. C., *Decision-Making in Police Administration*, Charles C. Thomas, Publisher, 1961.

The chief of police in American cities is too often appointed on the basis of political considerations. Further, since the American chief of police rises universally from the ranks, prevailing entrance requirements for patrolmen and limited training facilities still serve to limit seriously the area of selection. Police executive talent in this country is not impressive. To combat this weakness, it will be necessary to effect a marked elevation in police entrance qualifications and to provide effective pre-entry and post-entry training programs,[10] or to be more broadminded about the sources of police chiefs.

The American police department continues as a center of political attack and a shift in the balance of political power in the community or a change in the complexion of the city council often results in replacement of the chief. Retirement of the chief with the administration which appointed him is practically a foregone conclusion in many American cities.[11] Some of America's foremost police administrators have passed through this disheartening experience.

The police executive is subjected to various pressures from those wielding political influence in the community and from miscellaneous interest groups. These have produced an instability of tenure that endangers administrative efficiency. With frequent change in the head of the police department there can be no continuity of policy. More important, demoralization usually follows a change in leadership, and this is especially true in police organization. Men who are friendly to one administration are penalized when a new administration gains control. There is thus set up in the department a number of cliques that function for their own welfare and individual interests rather than for those of the department and the community. No executive, however strong he may be, can command the absolute obedience and cooperation of his subordinates as long as they know that he is a political puppet and that he will pass out of office at the next election.[12]

The constructive results of stable tenure in England provide an important lesson. Once appointed as Chief of Police a man should be permitted to remain in that position for as long as he can deliver a high grade professional performance. The position must be neutralized politically and removed from the vagaries of local politics and the pressure mechanics of special interest groups who seek to prostitute police administration to their own selfish ends. This is a difficult task. As the first

10 See Chapter 6.

11 Bruce Smith, *The State Police*, The MacMillan Company, 1925, p. 92.

12 August Vollmer, *The Minneapolis Police Survey and Reorganization*, 1930, p. 52.

important step, it is necessary that informed public opinion understand that low efficiency and extravagant costs accompany short tenure. Toward that end, the interpretation of the problem to the people in the community is a responsibility of police administration itelf.

The greatest single factor contributing to the short tenure of American police chiefs is the concept that the terms of department heads should be coterminous with that of the political chief executive, a heritage of the Jacksonian administration. Under this arrangement, the terms of department heads end with that of the mayor or other appointing authority, and the new head of city government replaces them with new department executives. It is held by those who continue to support this procedure that a newly elected mayor, for example, should have the whole-hearted support of his principal subordinates at the outset, and that they should be individuals who are in sympathy with his outlook and aims.[13]

A number of American cities are paving the way toward the solution of this problem through charter amendments which provide for indefinite tenure of the police chief executive. There is a growing recognition that the health officer, the city engineer, the chief of police and other municipal department heads should be professionally qualified. It is becoming equally apparent that professional talent will not expose itself to the hazards of political selection at short intervals. Gradually, the public services are coming to be manned to a higher degree by a professionalized personnel animated by the ethical standards of a profession.

In some jurisdictions the police chief executive has been placed under the classified civil service. Pfiffner believes that there is little reason why municipal department heads should not be chosen and hold their offices under merit system rules. He came to this conclusion after observing the application of the merit system to department heads in Los Angeles County government over a period of years.[14] There all executive officials, excepting three elective officers, are in the classified civil service. Professional and student observers frequently remark at the high order of professional attainment, administrative competence and integrity demonstrated by department heads of Los Angeles County.

---

[13] John M. Pfiffner, *Municipal Administration*, The Ronald Press Company, New York, 1940.

[14] John M. Pfiffner, *ibid.*, *supra* note 14, at p. 31.

On the other hand, there are those who hold that permanence of tenure in high administrative police positions does not guard the community against corrupt controls by political and other pressure groups in the community. There must be something more than continuity of incompetence in office. Fosdick, one of the principal spokesmen for this point of view, states: [15]

"Politics can get around any artificial system. On the other hand, with public opinion on the alert, politics can be kept in control without any system at all. . . . Continuity of service based on freedom of choice, has real meaning, but a continuity based on the inherent difficulties of removal through a civil service trial nullifies responsibility and stultifies the work of any administrator, however enterprising.

"What every police force needs is leadership—one official to whom the community can say, 'Thou art the man!' and who has power corresponding to his responsibility. We shall never solve the police problem in America until we give honest and effective leadership an opportunity to show what it can do. Some time or other, we have to make a beginning of trusting our public officials. Checks and balances to curb and minimize possible abuses of power have gotten us nowhere. Complex systems to prevent bias and unfairness have brought nothing but confusion. It is time to take off a few of the yokes that have made public administration an impossible task, and put a new emphasis on positive qualities. The problem before us is not how to build up a structure that will circumvent the dishonest and incompetent official, but, after finding a competent and honest official, to surround him with conditions in which he can make himself effective."

Insulating the position of police chief with civil service protection might be sound public policy in one jurisdiction, whereas, in another, the results would be disastrous. The question pivots largely on the character of personnel administration in the city concerned. If it is based throughout upon the merit principle there is some justification for placing the position of chief of police in the competitive classified service. On the other hand, if, as in many jurisdictions, civil service is merely a beautiful theory, no useful end would be served by applying the dead letter to a high administrative position.

The protection of tenure is one thing; the protection of incompetence in office is another. Unless the character of personnel administration is such that it will bring into office persons with a high grade of administrative ability, a spoils system may be preferred. Before giving the position of police chief executive protected status, the officials of the city concerned should retain the services of an unbiased personnel expert from the outside to inventory local personnel methods and meas-

---

[15] Fosdick, "Cleveland Survey," *ibid.*, *supra* note 2, at pp. 20, 21.

ure their worth against the standards of modern public personnel administration. Failure to take this precaution is almost certain to invite disaster.

Assuming the presence of a sound personnel system, the fact still remains that expert opinion in the police field is not unanimously in favor of protected status for the position of chief. It has been demonstrated that continuity of administration and high quality administration can be achieved without legally permanent tenure. During his thirty-two years as chief of police in the police department of Berkeley, California, August Vollmer was able to develop a sound system of police administration without tenure protection for himself or for his men.

Salary

The salary structure of a police organization must provide for the chief executive such compensation as will attract to this position the necessary talent and ability. In general, police salaries continue to lag behind those of industry and the commercial world. The police are compelled to compete at a disadvantage for high quality personnel. Among municipal administrative officials, city managers and superintendents of schools are the highest paid positions, except in the largest cities (where mayors replace city managers since there are no council-managers cities over 500,000). In the largest city group, the mayor, school superintendent, attorney, and director of public works are the top four, in that order. In each of the other population groups the city manager has the highest average salary, the superintendent of schools comes second, the attorney third in cities from 250,000 to 500,000, the mayor third in cities 100,000 to 250,000 and 50,000 to 100,000, and the engineer third in the two smallest city groups. The director of public works holds fourth position in the three smaller population groups, and is sixth and ninth respectively in the 250,000 to 500,000 and 100,000 to 250,000 population groups. Other officials among the six highest paid positions are controller, auditor, health officer, personnel officer, and police chief.

Fire and police chiefs rank between sixth and twelfth in all groups. But for a few minor exceptions, the salaries of all administrative positions in every population group of cities followed the trend in other occupations and have risen consistently since 1942. Except in the case of city managers and engineers, the greatest average salary increases were experienced by officials in cities in the two smallest population groups, with the percentage of increase declining as the city-size group became larger. Police chiefs' salaries, although generally higher than those of the fire chiefs', were not raised quite to the same extent. The following table indicates the salary paid for police leadership in cities of various population groups.

TABLE III
SALARY RANGE OF THE CHIEF OF POLICE
IN THE UNITED STATES

1962

Population group	Lowest	Highest
Over 500,000	$10,920	$30,000
250,000 – 500,000	8,832	19,248
100,000 – 250,000	6,775	16,794
50,000 – 100,000	3,000	15,600
25,000 – 50,000	4,977	14,700
10,000 – 25,000	3,492	14,232

Municipal authorities may well ponder the relative yields on the investment to be gained by attaching to the position of chief police administrator a salary sufficient to attract to this responsibility the best man available. Some method of measurement is indicated which would make it possible to evaluate the social significance of crime and vice in all of their categories, of traffic delay and congestion, traffic accidents and the inadequacy of parking facilities. In a scheme of social accounting there must come eventually a scientific determination of the relative social importance of the various municipal activities if there is to be an intelligent distribution of emphasis in terms of budgets and salary structures. The time is now at hand to undertake the necessary research which will provide a scientific basis for this important aspect of municipal management and eliminate the necessity of making these determinations upon a strictly empirical basis. When that study is completed, it seems clear that the role of police administration as an agency of social control will be revealed in the light of its true importance and that this branch of the public service will be accorded fiscal recognition on a more rational basis.

Method of Selection

The method of selection by which the police chief administrator is brought into office has an important bearing upon the quality of management.

The cornerstone of public personnel administration, or any personnel program for that matter, is the process of selection. It is precisely at this point that the course of events is determined for years to come in terms of the calibre and the quality and quantity of police service.

In view of the qualifications demanded of the Police Chief Executive, it is appropriate to inquire into the methods by which men are selected for this important position. As will be noted, new trends are observable in the development of a screening process through which the necessary talent, and capability can be brought into serve in this top command post.

The appointing authority in municipal government is the Mayor, or in the City Manager form of local government, the City Manager. In some jurisdictions under the Mayor-Council plan, the appointment of the Chief of Police requires the confirmation of the City Council. This is unwise, since it opens the way for Council interference and the exercise of political influence in the affairs of police administration. One of the major attributes of the City Manager system is that it gives to this professional administrator exclusive power to appoint his department heads, including the Chief of Police.

The method employed in selecting a new Chief of Police is usually provided for in the City Charter. Conventional procedure until recent years has been to base the selection on rank, performance record and personal standing among the members of the department. Appointments have been made generally from the rank at the next level below that of the Chief of Police, usually from the rank of Captain in the average department.

This method, essentially empirical in nature, is unsound since it amounts to little more than "sizing up a man" on the basis of experience and observation. It has little predictive value in terms of later performance on the job.

Performance record is obviously important; the rank of Captain would indicate under a merit system that the individual had qualified for promotion on one or more occasions. To be held in high esteem generally by members of the department, would give us the picture of a man who was affable, socially adjusted, who got along well with people and whose public relations were good.

None of these, however, establish the presence of executive and administrative ability for the job of top management, and appointments made on this basis court mediocrity and failure at a vulnerable point in organization where nothing should be left to chance. The rank of an officer may have pivoted on considerations altogether foreign to the requirements of this high position. Performance records can on occasion be misleading; moreover, there is no assurance that a good criminal investigator or a good thief catcher is blessed with any great amount of executive capability. Getting along well with people is an acceptable personal attribute, but a popularity contest is hardly the arena in which to make such a critical appointment.

The American police services must now turn to modern personnel administration for a more valid method of selecting the Police Chief Executive. All the evidence points convincingly to a competitive selection procedure that merits as far as possible the stamp of scientific sanction.

Business and industry have long since begun to move away from the rule-of-thumb and "across the desk" appraisal of men for executive positions. A recent study by the United States Navy of personnel practices in fifty-three major industrial concerns revealed that approximately one-half reported the use of a series of tests in their search for executive talent.

If business and industry are turning to the competitive examination as a method of selecting executive material, police administration should and is moving toward the adoption of this procedure. It is standard practice in the American police field to fill the positions of Patrolman on through the ranks of Sergeant, Lieutenant and Captain through the use of the competitive examination. The opinion is unanimous that it functions with a high degree of success in the selection of qualified individuals for promotion to supervisory and command positions. That being true, it is equally applicable to the top position of Chief of Police.[16]

The competitive examination for the selection of the Police Chief offers the following advantages:

1. It is a democratic method.
2. It is based upon the merit principle.
3. It rewards merit.
4. It fosters morale.
5. It opens up the channels of promotion on a strictly competitive basis to the highest position in the organization.
6. It fosters the elimination of politics, favoritism and prejudice in the selection process.
7. It is an honest and valid attempt to select the best man available for one of the most important posts in the field of public management.

Some authorities hold to the position that we need to know more about the qualities that make for executive success and how to test for them. Others present a convincing case for the view that there are

---

[16] V. A. Leonard, *Guide to the Study of Police Organization,* Washington State University Press, 1965.

fairly clear guide posts to those aspects of aptitude and proficiency that are most likely related to leadership success, and that there are available standardized procedures by which these qualities can be tested and scored. Actual experience confirms this point of view, notably in the Police Departments of Berkeley, Pasadena, Long Beach and Los Angeles in California, and Columbus, Ohio, among others, where today, the man who is directing the affairs of police organization and administration was selected through a competitive examination.

Examination Procedure

1. The Search for Candidates. A competitive examination for the position of Chief of Police may be restricted to departmental personnel or opened to candidates on a state or national basis, with no residence requirement. A search for candidates on a nation-wide basis is recommended and the trend appears to be in that direction. No Police Chief selected on a merit or career basis is a stranger to any professional policeman anywhere. The highest paid top police executive in the world, Superintendent O. W. Wilson of the Chicago Police Department, was brought in from the outside.

2. Announcement of Examination. In preparation for an open competitive examination for this position, it is necessary to prepare a printed announcement similar to the example shown in Appendix A, for national distribution. Appropriate application forms accompany the announcement—see same Appendix.

3. Audit of Application. The screening of applications serves to eliminate those candidates who obviously do not possess the necessary qualifications. In the Seattle competitive examination, eighty-seven applications were received, with only fifty-six qualifying for the written examination.

4. The Written Examination.

a. *Aptitude and Proficiency Tests:*

Leaders must possess above average intelligence. They must have intellectual ability sufficient to cope with the problems they are required to solve. However, experience indicates that an extremely high IQ invites a critical emphasis on the emotional stability of the individual. Proficiency tests include those designed to measure administrative judgment. They evaluate the candidate's ability to get the right answers to questions involving hypothetical supervisory situations. Word fluency and verbal manipulation ability characterize most leaders and these qualities, among others, are measured in the aptitude test.

Sources for these tests include the Bureau of Educational Measurements, Kansas State Teachers College, Emporia, Kansas; World Book Company, Yonkers-on-Hudson, New York; Test Division of The Psychological Corporation, 522 Fifth Avenue, New York; and Stanford University Press, Palo Alto, California.

b. *General Written Test:*

This test involves formulating solutions to an extended series of problem-solving situations at the level of top management. The calibre of this test should be such that it proves to be an exacting experience for the candidate.

All written tests should be administered and scored by an individual familiar with test administration.

5. *Personality Testing:* In measuring basic personality traits and factors, written tests and so-called personality inventories have not proved too successful. Opinion favors the use of the structured oral interview for this purpose. Candidates who have passed the oral examination are admitted.

The oral examination or interview consists of two phases:

a. Non-stress interview.

b. Stress interview.

In the Non-stress Interview, the candidate enters and is seated facing the members of the Examining Board. The questioning is conducted at a leisurely pace, with all examiners taking a friendly attitude toward the candidate. He is asked about his age, interests and experience. Reasoning, character and technical questions may be presented to him. The basic purpose of the Non-stress Interview is to give the examiners an opportunity to observe the candidate in a relatively relaxed state. His base norm for stability and poise is observed and evaluated as a standard for comparison with his reactions in the Stress Interview.

In the Stress Interview which follows, the examiners gradually move from a friendly attitude toward the candidate to one of challenge and opposition, bordering on hostility. The approach is negative; doubt is openly expressed concerning his qualifications; his character is questioned.

The Stress Interview shows the candidate's emotional arsenal and control when placed on the defensive. The objective is to confuse the candidate and observe how he behaves under pressure, "under fire". Of significance here are:

a. The degree of tension the situation produced in the subject.

b. The degree of mastery he maintained in the situations.

c. The degree of poise.

d. How rapidly he responded in the conversational situations.

e. Rate of psychological and physiological recovery following the removal of stress.[17]

6. *Medical Report.* Upon completion of the Oral Examination, passing candidates are given a thorough physical examination by a licensed physician.

7. *Background Investigation.* A complete background investigation is then required in the case of each candidate passing the Oral Examination. In addition, each candidate should be fingerprinted and a copy sent to the Federal Bureau of Investigation in Washington, D. C., for a search of their fingerprint files. In the Background Investigation, particular attention should be given to any business interests, connections or income outside of police service.

The following weights may be assigned to the foregoing phases of the examination: Aptitude–20; Proficiency–20; General Written Examination–30; Oral Interview–20; Medical Report–5; Background Investigation–5. The names of the three candidates making the highest combined grade are then submitted by the Examining Board to the appointing authority.

The Examining Board may consist of five persons, three in the Department and two from outside the Department, all of whom exercise supervisory or command responsibility. In addition, the services of an experienced psychologist should be retained for the Oral Interview.

The City of Seattle, on a consultant's recommendation,[18] amended its charter and in 1946 held a national open competitive examination for the position of chief of police. The elimination of residence require-

---

[17] Sergeant F. C., RA 19593526, HQ MACU (SOG), APO San Francisco, 96222, has directed the attention of the author to the possible usefulness of the Polygraph during the stress interview.

[18] V. A. Leonard, *Survey and Reorganization of the Police Department in Seattle, Washington,* 1945.

See Appendix A for copy of Examination Announcement and Application Form which were given national-wide distribution.

ments and abolition of tenure coterminous with the mayor operated in attracting to the competition men of demonstrated ability. Forty-six candidates, representing some of the best administrative talent in the American police field, competed in the examination. The outstanding record of the Seattle Police Department under Chief George D. Eastman's administration more than vindicated the decision of the people in that city to select their police chief executive by open competitive examination. The official announcement of the examination and the application form shown in Appendix A give convincing evidence of a new trend in the selection of police administrators.

An increasing number of American cities in various population groups are now following this tested procedure in the selection of their Chiefs of Police.[19] The competitive examination should not be limited to personnel in the department concerned. In order to extend the field of selection, examination announcements should at least be distributed throughout the state in which the city or community is located or preferably, distributed on a national basis. It should be noted that the police in the smaller communities and the people they serve also stand to make important gains in the quality of police service through the use of this method. If considered necessary, the cooperation of police personnel officers in nearby cities or in the State Police in developing examination materials and examination procedure, would be available for the asking.

In recent years a number of police executives have been selected by a technique identified as "résumé analysis." This has been utilized by a number of federal agencies such as the U. S. Air Force, Office of Special Investigation when selecting key personnel for specialized positions.

The application form serves as the basic screening device; the Examining Board reviews all completed papers then selects the best-qualified candidates. A precise evaluation of all aspects of the applicant's background is undertaken with particular stress upon education and supervisory experience. After initial screening, a preliminary background investigation of the remaining applicants is conducted. Candidates who successfully pass the above phases are then requested to appear for an oral interview whereupon the most capable applicant is selected for the position.

The standard duties of an American police executive throw additional light upon the qualifications that should be possessed by the in-

[19] See *Lateral Mobility of Police Personnel*, p. 180.

dividual confronted with the responsibilities of this office. They include the following:

1. Carry into effect the provisions of the plan for police organization.
2. Manage the affairs of the police department and direct its operations.
3. Develop long-term plans for the department.
4. Prepare and submit budget proposals.
5. Supervise departmental expenditures.
6. Concern himself with the care and welfare of the men.
7. Instill the ideals of police service in departmental personnel.
8. Prepare rules and regulations governing the force and cause these rules and regulations to be revised from time to time.
9. Provide suitable training for the members of the force.
10. Hold weekly staff conferences.
11. Make semi-annual inspections of the department.
12. Make intermittent inspections and spot audits of departmental personnel, equipment, buildings, and operations.
13. Analyze and measure the accomplishments of individuals and units within the organization.
14. Investigate carefully charges made concerning the inadequacy of any branch of the organization.
15. Fix departmental standards for entry into the department for all employees.
16. Insist upon rigid discipline throughout the entire department.
17. Seek improved police procedures.
18. Direct through his assistants the activities of the line divisions and staff services.
19. Refer suggested procedural changes to his assistants for analysis and recommendation.
20. Require that an annual report be prepared that will adequately present police problems and police activities.
21. Maintain suitable relationships between the police department and other governmental agencies and private organizations, especially those concerned with traffic control, crime prevention, and the administration of justice.
22. Develop and maintain sound public relations.

It is probably a far simpler task to measure the effectiveness of executive leadership in a police department than to state a precise formula of qualifications for the position. Obviously, the test of an executive's success is his ability to get results. The following criteria for measurement of the executive are suggestive not only to permit a qualitative appraisal of leadership but also to clarify further the qualifications for this position: [20]

1. The degree of voluntary enthusiastic cooperation within the organization.
2. The nature and degree of discipline.
3. Evidence of a mutual understanding and confidence between executives and subordinates.
4. A general knowledge and understanding throughout the organization of the functional relationships between executives, their responsibilities and their authority.
5. The use of positive rather than negative methods of leadership.
6. The quality of the executive's subordinates.
7. A low rate of turnover in the executive, in supervisory and command positions, and in departmental personnel as a whole.
8. The soundness of the principles and methods used in the solution of police problems.
9. The presence of satisfactory facilities and methods for the detection of emerging situations, the forecasting and anticipation of police problems and preparation of plans for their solution.
10. Definite written plans based on sound objectives and police ideals.
11. The extent to which plans are based on verified facts related to factors in the "equation of the situation."
12. The extent to which the organization achieves its objectives.

Executive Development Programs

The individual charged with the responsibility of managing the police enterprise has an increasingly difficult role to fulfill as the chief executive officer. The complex societal, behavioral and administrative problems of our dynamic society demands a constant and continuing search for new and better ways to achieve administrative excellence.

The police executive must develop the expertise that will allow him to respond to his responsibilities in a positive manner. An executive development program should provide a frame of reference moving from the conceptual to the applied, and simultaneously constructing a management philosophy providing the chief executive with the tools and methods needed to deal with the myriad of management problems.

A program for police executives must emphasize a broadening of individual perspectives, enhancement of the ability to anticipate and re-

20 Adapted from Ralph Currier Davis, *op. cit. supra* note 7, at p. 37.

act to problems, and the acquisition of skills to continue independent study for self-improvement.

Executive development programs must be structured in a manner to accomplish the following objectives:

1. Development of an understanding of the role and function of the executive.

2. Development of a management philosophy.

3. Development of a managerial style.

4. Construction of an intellectual frame of reference from which to anticipate, analyze, and solve organizational problems.

5. Development of an ability to understand the behavioral problems in organizations and the effects of managerial styles and techniques on organizational effectiveness.

6. Development of an awareness of the numerous internal and external pressures which modify the role of the police executive.

7. Familiarization with research methods and data analysis.

8. Development of an awareness of the assets and liabilities of computers and other hardware.

9. Familiarization with contemporary and new trends in police management.

Colleges and universities are best equipped to provide executive development training. Outstanding programs have been developed by numerous institutions of higher education such as the University of Southern California and San Jose State College.

However, technical qualifications and leadership ability can go only part of the way in effecting the delivery of a professional grade of police performance. In addition, sound internal organization must be present if the executive is to bring about the effective translation of policy into action.

Chapter 4

INTERNAL ORGANIZATION

FEDERAL and state laws, the City Charter and the Rules and Regulations of a Police Department impose multitudinous and very important duties upon the Chief of Police. Obviously, in the average police department, no one person could possibly perform all of the assigned responsibilities without considerable assistance from others. In order to achieve the objectives of the position, as set forth in the preceding pages, it is imperative that the police chief executive delegate some of his powers, responsibilities and duties to others. However, when he does delegate such authority to subordinates, he cannot escape responsibility for their actions. Since he cannot perform all of the prescribed duties, the Chief of Police must of necessity confine his sphere of activities to broad general management and control of the work of his immediate subordinates.

In order that the executive may accomplish the ultimate delivery of police service, there must be a systematic arrangement of a wide variety of functions and functional tools. Such arrangement has for its main purpose the extension in reach of the executive in order to facilitate the accomplishment of the tasks assigned to him. This is the simple fact of organization, too often ignored. Organization on any scale is, in fact, organization of the executive.

It is a fundamental premise that organization must be geared directly to goals and objectives. The functions and objectives of police service include the protection of life and property, the prevention and suppression of crime and vice, preservation of the public peace and order, and the regulation and control of traffic.

In order to carry out these important functions and objectives, the police enterprise requires organization on a sound and effective basis. Experience tends to confirm the view that a Chief of Police with superior qualifications would be handicapped with structural defects in the organizational pattern, and that high calibre personnel would be thwarted in their best efforts by faulty organization. Such being the case, no structural aids to good management should be overlooked.

Organization stated simply, is the assignment of work to people who are placed in a structure of authority so that the total operation may be coordinated by orders of superiors to subordinates, reaching from the top to the bottom of the enterprise. *Work* may be looked upon as the carrying out of assigned responsibilities for the achievement of results, goals and progress toward objectives. *Work to be done* occupies the center of the stage in organization.

The accepted patterns of police organization follow rather closely those to be found in military service. This appears to be a very logical development since a police organization is essentially semi-military in character. In both a police department and military service, personnel are in uniform; in both cases, they are arrayed against an adversary and again, in both cases, gun-fire and loss of life may characterize the day's work. The presence of the ranks of Captain, Lieutenant and Sergeant, among others, offers still another parallel in the approach to discipline and the control of operations. In mob, riot and other combat situations, the patterns of operation are virtually identical.

The ultimate unit of organization is a group of operations that can be performed directly by one individual and which constitute a satisfactory work load for him. This is called "a position." In a small community with a population of from one to two thousand inhabitants, the basic police functions may be performed successfully by one man. The work load in this instance would not exceed the capacity of a single individual. However, all of the major functions of police service to be found in the more complex organization of a large city are represented on a small scale in the one-man department, and even here, organization is necessary. The town marshal, as the sole representative of law and order, must organize his time, energies and the available facilities if his work is to be effective.

As the size of a community increases, expanded work loads create a need for the services of more individuals. There are more crimes, more traffic accidents to investigate and an increase in the volume of general services to be rendered. One man is no longer able to do all the work by himself. He must have others to assist him and work under his direction. He is now a Chief of Police with one or more officers under his command to carry out his orders and instructions during the day and during the night. The executive is unable to do everything himself; hence, the necessity of extending his reach and capacity for achieving goals by delegation of functions to a subordinate or subordinates. An extension in the organization of the executive is thus indicated, accompanied by creation of lines of authority and responsibility through which executive control may find expression in the coordination of work by orders from superiors to subordinates. The larger the police organization and the community it serves, the more involved these controls become, with an increasing necessity for attention to sound organizational structure. In a metropolitan police department, the organization of the executive tends to become complex with five or more administrative levels between top management and the individual policeman and with a need for a high degree of coordination from the top to the bottom of the organizational structure. The far-flung operations of such an organization require administrative controls and coordination of a very superior order.

In the evolution from a one-man department to large scale organization, functional specialization appears. As the complexity and volume of operations increase, the need for specialists to handle certain functions becomes evident. One by one these functions are differentiated from the original functions, and specialized units are created for their execution. In the process of organizational growth and development, for example, the time arrives when the investigative work load of the department may justify the establishment of the post of detective, so that one or more individuals may concentrate their energies and time exclusively on the investigation of criminal cases. Subsequent increases in this phase of departmental operations lead to assignment of additional detectives to this work and the establishment of a detective division as a major administrative unit. At a later stage in the evolution of police organization, crime volume in the various offense classifications may expand to the point where the need is recognized for functional decentralization of the detective division by creation of special details or squads who give their undivided attention to investigation of crimes in a single category, such as homicide, robbery, burglary or automobile thefts.

At this juncture, it may become economical for the department to provide itself with laboratory facilities and a laboratory technologist for the scientific examination and identification of questioned materials involved as evidence in criminal cases. The presence of patrol, traffic, records and crime prevention divisions, as well as other administrative units such as personnel, communications, transportation and property control in a police department provide additional examples of functional specialization.

It should be noted here that specialization has made serious inroads upon the line power of American police forces. Admittedly, as a department grows, some degree of specialization is necessary and desirable. However, heavy emphasis must be placed upon eliminating as far as possible, the sacrifice of personnel, usually from the patrol force, in order to strengthen the shift toward specialization. This important matter is reserved for later treatment in detail.

During the growth and development of a police department, together with the increase in every phase of police operations, there appears the need for supervisory and command positions. Within this frame of reference, the first appointment is usually to the position or rank of Sergeant. The sequence then continues with the appearance of the rank of Lieutenant, followed by the rank of Captain.

The question then arises as to when the establishment of a supervisory or command position is justified or necessary. Is it possible to determine on a rational and sound basis how many or how few, and where they should be assigned? The answers to these questions flow from the *law of the span of control*, to be discussed presently in some detail.

The arrangement of units of work in the organizational structure is a matter of critical importance. From a functional point of view, the activities of a police organization fall into certain well defined categories. They are here first enumerated without respect to proper arrangement and relationship in the structure of organization:

Criminal investigation	Patrol
Personnel	Budgetary control
Criminal identification	Purchasing
Communications	Crime prevention
Traffic regulation and control	Transportation
Planning	Property control
Police records	Follow-up control

In order to implement executive control from the top to the bottom of the enterprise, these activities should be systematically arranged. But, as Bruce Smith states, in the American police field,[1]

"The problems of administrative structure are largely ignored, despite the fact that certain broad principles of organization have won wide acceptance in military, commercial, and industrial undertakings and are readily adaptable to many of the problems arising in connection with such governmental functions as police protection. The failure of police forces to take advantage of the knowledge which organization techniques now place at their disposal is probably due to two causes. In the first place, nearly all police agencies, even the largest of them, have sprung from small beginnings and have only gradually acquired those complex structural features which are now so common. From mere lapse of time various stopgap and temporary devices have come to be accepted parts of the police organism, and procedures have grown up around them which resist all but the most vigorous efforts at uprooting.

---

[1] Bruce Smith, *Police Systems in the United States*, Harper and Brothers, New York, 1940, pp. 251–252.

"A second underlying cause of defective police organization may consist in the fact that only in the rarest instances have American police forces been led by men with prior experience in large-scale operations or by men who have enjoyed a sufficient background of general knowledge and administrative performance to make them even aware of the existence of a problem of organization."

Experience in the field of public administration tends to confirm the view that even a superior executive cannot overcome structural defects in the organizational pattern and that high-class personnel will be thwarted in its best efforts by faulty organization. Administrators will rarely be supermen and organization must be geared, not to the exceptional executive, but to ability which may at times descend to the mediocre.[2] Such being the case, no structural aids to good management should be overlooked.

Unity of Command

Foremost among the indispensable prerequisites to successful organization is unity of command. This principle has been discussed previously with reference to the plural executive and external controls of the force, and it requires little additional comment at this point. Subordinates there can and must be, but command is singular, whole, indivisible. At the top level of management the police chief executive should be responsible to one superior and only one. The same principle should find expression from the top all the way down through organization to the bottom of the enterprise. A police officer subject to orders from several superiors will be confused, inefficient, and irresponsible, while an officer subject to orders from but one superior may be methodical, efficient and responsible. "The significance of this principle in the process of coordination and organization must not be lost sight of. In building an organization structure it is often tempting to set up more than one boss for a man who is doing work which has more than one relationship. The rigid adherence to the principle of unity of command may have its absurdities; these are, however, unimportant in comparison with the certainty of confusion, inefficiency and irresponsibility which arise from the violation of the principle." [3]

---

[2] John M. Pfiffner, *Public Administration in the United States,* New York, 1936, p. 50.

[3] Gulick and Urwick, "Papers on the Science of Administration," Columbia University, New York, 1937, p. 9.

Line and Staff

Among the contributions that military science has made to organization and administration is the concept of staff and line. The distinction between maintenance and operations is a fundamental one and possesses many implications. It necessarily follows that the two major administrative areas of activity in a police organization are line operations and staff services. Recognition of the concept of line and staff is the first step toward the arrangement of related functions under unified supervision and command. The chief value of this distinction is that it gives proper location and status to the two major functions of police organization—preparation for the delivery of police service, and the delivery of police service. Within this frame of reference, the staff services the line, supplying it with, among other services, qualified trained personnel, records, data, communication facilities, transport and materiel, so that it may operate efficiently in the discharge of its functions. The terms "housekeeping functions" and "auxiliary services" have been applied by some observers to staff activities in what would seem to be inadequate recognition of the importance of the staff function. The line translates plans and policies into action in the field; it is the point at which the discharge of police service is made. The ultimate delivery of police protection and the maintenance of law and order is the responsibility of the line.

The accepted classification of staff functions and line operations in police organization follows:

1. Planning.
2. Inspection.
3. Personnel administration.
4. Police records system.
5. Statistical operations.
6. Follow-up control.
7. Identification services.
8. Property control.   Staff
9. Communication system.   Functions
10. Budgetary control.
11. Purchasing.
12. Transportation.
13. Jail administration.
14. Supply.
15. Crime detection laboratory
16. Public relations.

1. Police patrol system.
2. Criminal investigation.
3. Vice investigation.   Line
4. Traffic regulation and control.   Operations
5. Crime prevention.

The foregoing elements lend themselves easily to orderly arrangement in the structure of a police organization. Charts A and B portray the organization of a police department. In Chart B, it will be noted that Staff Services are under one command and Line Operations under another, with both, including the function of Inspection, reporting directly to the Chief of Police. This is the military type of organization; it has been tested in the fire of combat on the battlefield over the centuries and has been found not wanting. Here, there is no question concerning the lines of authority and the chain of command.

It should be noted again that all of the elements shown on the Chart are represented on a small scale in the one-man department and even here, organization is necessary. The Town Marshal or Constable, as the sole representative of law and order in the community, must organize his time, energy and the available facilities if his work is to be effective.

Although administrative separation of these two broad phases of police organization and management is essential, examination of the organizational structure of American police departments reveals a frequent lack of a clear distinction between line and staff functions. Staff services often are to be found under direct line supervision and in an organization where this situation prevails, it is also likely that one or more line functions are directly controlled and supervised by a staff agency. Under this faulty arrangement, coordination is frustrated through interruptions in the normal flow of authority and control and the effective line power of the organization is reduced.

Chart A shows the organization of a police department in one American city of 500,000 population and illustrates the extent to which this basic principle of organization is occasionally ignored. The arrangement of staff and line functions in accordance with accepted principles of organization is shown in Chart B.[4]

The organizational defects portrayed in Chart A are remedied in the proposed plan of reorganization. The suggested arrangement provides an increased opportunity for specialization and is produc-

---

[4] V. A. Leonard, *A Theory of Police Organization and Administration*, Doctoral Dissertation, Ohio State University, 1949, pp. 62 and 63.

tive of enhanced efficiency in management. Staff functions may deal exclusively with the activities of planning in cooperation with the line, preparation and maintenance, upon which the line must depend for the success of its operations. Line organization, freed from the problems of maintenance, may devote its energies to the accomplishment of line objectives, which in the last analysis is the ultimate goal of organization. Thus, a clear distinction should be made between (1) those divisions and bureaus in a police department which furnish services, not directly to the people, but indirectly by servicing those functions that do, and (2) line organization upon which the responsibility for the ultimate discharge of basic police functions depends.

Span of Executive Control

The executive of any enterprise can personally direct the activities of only a few persons. As a result, he must depend upon these to direct others, and upon them in turn to direct still others, until the last man in the organization is reached.[5] There is some difference of opinion concerning the number of subordinates who can be effectively supervised by any one supervisor, but all agree that there is a limit to the span of managerial contacts that can be accommodated by a single individual.

It has long been known that one of the surest sources of delay and confusion is to allow any superior to be directly responsible for too many subordinates. Armies have observed this principle for centuries. Based upon what is known to psychologists as "the span of attention", the number of separate items to which the human brain can pay attention at the same time is strictly limited. Just as the hand of man can span only a limited number of notes on the piano, so the mind and will of man can span but a limited number of managerial contacts.

This limitation on supervisory capability is further accentuated by cross-relationships involving the supervisor and the supervised. If A supervises B, C and D, there is much more involved than the direct relationship between A and each one of his subordinates. The cross-relationships between B and C, between C and D and between B and D, with all that this can mean, must be accommodated by the supervisor's span of attention. It is generally accepted that as one moves upward through the levels of organization to the top of the enterprise, the number of subordinates supervised should be progressively reduced.

Congestion results when decisions are too highly centralized. In his attempt to keep up with routine demands, the executive may neglect

---

[5] Gulick and Urwick, *ibid.* supra note 3, at p. 7.

planning and policy matters of much greater ultimate importance, simply because the detail has to be settled while the planning can wait. His decisions made at long range, may overlook or wrongly evaluate important considerations whose importance would have been appreciated at once by a man on the ground. Excessive centralization of decision wastes the resources of the organization. In the average American police department today will be found the ability at the several levels of organizational structure to handle routine matters. By delegating the responsibility for decisions the interest and initiative of the subordinate are increased.

Although it is impossible to lay down any fixed rule as to the number of subordinates who should report directly to the chief of police, it is clearly preferable that the executive load should be kept within the range where this official can give proper attention to the duties of his position. Experience indicates that the number of such subordinates should not be less than three nor more than seven. The evidence seems to show that when the chief of police attempts to supervise directly the activities of more than seven individuals, his office tends to become a bottleneck and a place of confusion which impedes the work of the entire organization.

The general structure of a police organization lends itself easily to the observance of reasonable limits in the span of executive control. In recent years capable observers in the American police field have reached the conclusion that even the largest police structure can be set up so that its head exercises direct supervision over only six or seven divisional commanders. The same general principle will apply to supervisory and command personnel generally, such as assistant chiefs and captains, since the size of any office unit or field force should not be greater than can be adequately supervised. Some recognition must be given, however, to gradual contraction in the effective span of control as one moves from the subordinate to the top level of management, since ordinarily the complexity of the matters to be settled between supervisor and subordinate, and hence the amount of time to be spent in conference, increases at the higher levels.

In general the executive span of control should, if possible, be limited to the direct supervision of three individuals, the subordinate in charge of staff services, the officer responsible for inspectional services, and the officer who is in command of line operations. This reduced distribution of responsibility for the supervision of subordinates is graphically shown in Chart B.

Chart A.

PRESENT ORGANIZATION
1945

BASED ON POLICE DEPARTMENT RECORDS

MAYOR and CITY COUNCIL

CHIEF OF POLICE

Secretary

SERGEANT City Jail

CHIEF CLERK

Records — Property Room

Printing — Accounting

Purchases

DIRECTOR Junior Safety Div.

Missing Men — Juveniles

INSPECTOR Detective Division

Details
Auto Theft
Checks
Pawnshops
Narcotics
Post Office
Morals

Squads
Homicide
Robbery
Burglary and Larceny
Bunco

Superintendent Identification Bureau

FOREMAN Garage-Radio

COMDG. OFFICER Nat. Def. Det'l.

SERGEANT Investigator

ASSISTANT CHIEF

INSPECTOR Traffic Division

Captain Enforcement

Captain Investigation

Sergeant Office-Records

CAPTAIN (F) Womens Division

Vice Squad

Womens Division

Missing Women

DIRECTOR Police Training

Laboratory

School

Captain Combat Training

SERGEANT Dance Supr.

Drill Team

INSPECTOR Patrol Division

Captain Precinct 3
Captain Precinct 2
Captain Precinct 1

Captain Precinct 4
Captain Precinct 5
Captain Precinct 6

Patrol

Booking Office

Emergency

Radio Telephone

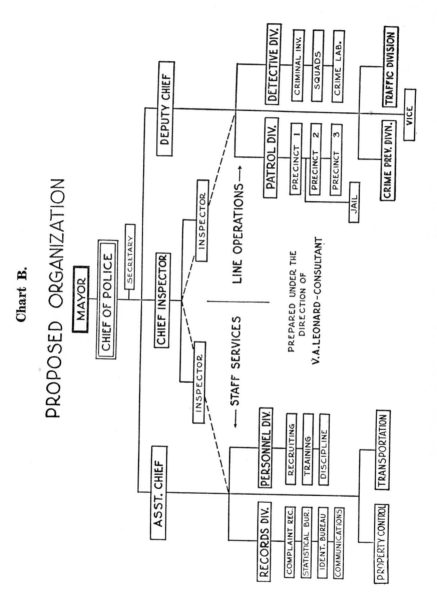

Chart B.

PROPOSED ORGANIZATION

PREPARED UNDER THE DIRECTION OF V.A. LEONARD - CONSULTANT

There is some difference of opinion concerning the location of the jail facility and the crime laboratory in the organizational structure. Chart B shows both of them in the Line. Actually, both units service the line and a strong case can be made for placing them under staff supervision.

Related Elements of Organization

Within the structure of organization, it is necessary to arrange for the distribution of the work load according to some logical plan. Fundamentally, this involves the grouping of related functions into administrative units for economical and effective supervision and control. In the determination of those functions or activities which are sufficiently related to justify location under unified supervision, a number of factors will influence the decision. These include the major purpose of the activity or function, the process or method to be employed in achieving its immediate objectives, the nature of the clientele with which it must deal, the geographical distribution of operations, and the time element. Most of these factors operate simultaneously in determining the organizational pattern of a police department and they come together in complex combination in the larger department which requires careful attention to structural arrangement.

Organization by Major Purpose

The purpose of an activity or operation is an important determining factor in organizational relationships. In municipal government, for example, organization by major purpose, such as water supply, crime control, or education, furnishes the basis for bringing together in a single large department all of those who are concerned with the rendering of a particular service. The divisionalization of a police department is largely the expression of the need for effective division of labor in the organization of the enterprise. Thus, because of its peculiar function and the comprehensive character of the patrol operation, patrol services are assembled in the police organizational structure under unified supervision. The crime prevention division is distinguished in major purpose from all other administrative units by virtue of the specialized attention it gives to the prevention of delinquency and crime through the casework approach to behavior problems encountered by the police. Unified control over personnel engaged in this highly specialized activity makes more certain the accomplishment of the purpose of bringing under a single command the departmental operations which lie within this frame of reference. It clarifies objectives for a large group of workers drawing upon their energies and loyalties to give focus and drive to one of the most important of all police roles.

The same considerations apply to the traffic division, where the major purpose or objective is directed toward a reduction in the social and economic losses occasioned by retarded traffic flow, traffic congestion, traffic accidents and parking problems; and to the detective division in its specialized approach to the problems of criminal investigation.

Similarly, the major purpose of the records division is to receive, assemble, digest and analyze the data concerning the police problems of crime, delinquency, vice and traffic, and thereby afford an intelligent point of departure in administrative planning for their solution. Economy and efficiency in organization demand that all operations related to each of these functions be located under single command and supervision as a basic principle of sound organization.

Organization by Major Process

Application of the principle of major process serves to bring together in a division or other administrative unit of police organization those who make use of a special skill or technology. Major process finds expression in the crime detection laboratory of a police department where facilities and scientific skills are concentrated for the technical examination of evidence materials. Thus, functional specialization in police service brings with it specialized facilities, methods, procedures and techniques which may be properly grouped in the organizational structure with respect to both major purpose and major process. Workers in the police records division are confronted with tasks that are altogether different in nature from those of any other division in the organization and which require distinctly specialized training and skills if competence is to be attained. Major process finds expression in the crime prevention division of a modern police organization through specialized training in the behavior sciences required of qualified workers in this important field and in the specialized techniques which must be used in the successful approach to behavior problems. In fact, it would be difficult to identify any unit of activity or any operation in a well ordered police department which does not reflect the influence of the concept of major process in the structure of organization. Such an arrangement promotes the most efficient utilization of technical skill through the concentration of work load in a particular category, and for this same reason, flow of work in the organization as a whole and effective supervision are expedited. Organization by major process also lends momentum to the development of a career service through the appearance of professional specialization in the various units and the stimulation of professional standards and pride.

Organization by Clientele

Superimposed upon purpose and process as they condition the structure of organization is the influence of the type or class of persons served or dealt with. For example, the nature of police work brings organization and personnel into contact with a relatively large volume of potential and actual offenders at the juvenile level each year, in addition to those whose behavior patterns are much further advanced in the direction of delinquency and crime. Intelligent attention at an early stage in the development of a delinquent or criminal career is the principal thesis of crime prevention. The youngster represents a very special type of clientele and within recent years the crime prevention unit has become a standard feature of police organization in this country. This development represents an attempt to gear organization to the needs of a specific clientele so that trained workers may bring to the individual case the clinical resources of the community for diagnosis and treatment. Functional specialization within the detective division is to a considerable extent the expression of organization by clientele. The establishment of homicide, robbery, burglary, check and automobile theft details is in recognition of the gains to be made through the highly specialized study of the operational characteristics and modus operandi of a particular type or class of criminal offenders. Foreign language and racial clusters such as the Chinese in San Francisco, Italians in New Haven, Mexicans and Filipinos in Los Angeles and Negroes in Birmingham, etc., may likewise warrant separate recognition in police organization.

Organization by Area

The line delivery of police service requires a territorial decentralization of operations. In no other way can the police organize to reach the people who are to be served or who are to be controlled. A universal feature of police organization and administration throughout the civilized world is the sub-division of the area policed into small units, known as patrol areas or patrol beats. The police patrol beat is the ultimate unit of organization in the police structure; it may be regarded as a geographical area of operation in which the demands for police service constitute a work load which does not exceed the capacity of a single patrolman, or two patrolmen where double-officer patrol is employed. The selection of the beat as the basic unit in all police operations conforms to the fundamental principles involved in all military and police strategy—breaking the total problem into its smallest divisions and attacking each one singly. The existence of the beat is based upon the conviction that effective patrol service is the foundation of police organization. The individual patrolman is society's first line of defense against the criminal.

In large cities, the overwhelming number of police beats and the extent of the problem of supervision has led to the grouping of these patrol areas into precincts. Each precinct is in charge of a commanding officer who directs police operations in his prescribed area and who is directly responsible to headquarters.

The presence of the precinct in the structure of police organization gives rise to serious problems of management. In addition to the burden on the taxpayers which they represent in many instances, they foster a breakdown in executive control. American police experience indicates that too often these precinct stations, isolated geographically, tend to insulate themselves from central headquarters control and become more or less independent entities moving in an orbit of their own. The precinct station comes to be looked upon by the people in the territory it serves as the symbol of police service while central headquarters is regarded as a foreign agency too remote from the local picture to be taken seriously. The usual practice in the past has been to equip such stations with independent telephone facilities and to encourage people residing in a given precinct area to direct all calls for the police to that station. The records reveal that the net result in many instances has been a deterioration in the lines of central executive control over operations in the precinct area. Wherever additional levels of supervision and command are inserted in the structure of organization, there is an increased need for the strengthening and multiplication of administrative controls.

Sound organization requires that where men are on permanent assignment in any one functional division, their work be subject to the supervision and review of a superior officer in that functional division at headquarters.

Such officers as are detailed to the area commander will report to him as the immediate source of command, and will be subject to his review in matters of discipline and routine performance, but the ultimate responsibility of these officers is to their superiors in their functional division at headquarters. A detective working out of an area station will be under the immediate supervision of the area commander, and his assignments and reports may clear through this officer, but his superior in the detective division at central headquarters will be responsible ultimately for his assignments and for the appraisal of the quality of his investigations.[6]

The need for the existence of numerous precinct stations is being questioned and subjected to careful scrutiny in many jurisdictions today. Motorization of the force and two-way radio communication between headquarters and line personnel have made possible intensified control of the force and have increased its mobility and maneuverability. These technological improvements have in many instances rendered obsolete and extravagant the maintenance of sub-stations and in many

---

[6] International City Managers' Association, "Municipal Police Administration," 1943, pp. 95–96.

jurisdictions their number has been reduced if not eliminated altogether. Characteristic of the trend in this direction, the reorganization of the Seattle police department in 1945 provided for the abandonment of three of the five precinct police stations.[7]   It was found that continued operation of these three stations represented an unnecessary waste of manpower, departmental resources and public funds, and it was recommended that steps be taken to close them forthwith.   It was estimated by those possessing an intimate knowledge of the operation of these stations that their closing would represent a saving of between $75,000 and $100,000 per year in police expenditures.   The savings in terms of personnel strength and in terms of increased police efficiency could not be expressed in dollars and cents.   Motorization of the police in this American city of a half million population and the use of two-way radio communication facilities had accelerated the control and mobility of the force to the point where these precinct stations were no longer necessary.

Organization by Time

The police conduct an around-the-clock operation which creates the necessity for chronological distribution of the personnel resources of the department.   Most police organizations operate on a three-shift or three-platoon basis, each platoon having an eight hour tour of duty. Distribution of the manpower of a police department on a three-shift basis is something more than dividing three into twenty-four, or dividing three into the number of men available.   The amount and nature of the demands for police service are not the same on all of the three shifts.   When this fact is combined with the basic principle that in a crime fighting organization, maximum manpower must be made available at the time and place of the greatest demand for police service, it becomes apparent that chronological distribution of staff services and line power is a matter of considerable importance and difficulty.   Expert studies of police organization and management reveal that the case load peak for a twenty-four hour period occurs as a rule between 9:30 P.M. and 11:30 P.M.   The normal excess of manpower assigned to the 4:00 P.M. to 12:00 midnight shift in most jurisdictions is intended to accommodate this increase in the volume of police activity; however, the trend is toward greater flexibility in distribution of combat strength with provision for a fourth shift in the line power organization of the department during these peak load hours, with respect to both crime and traffic.

Thus, it is so, that when organization by major purpose, process, clientele, time and area are brought into play in thinking through the

---

[7] V. A. Leonard, "Seattle Police Survey and Reorganization," 1945, p. 47.

structure of police organization, the project is brought into sharper focus and the basis strengthened for the delivery of effective police service to the community.

Functional Distribution of the Force

There is still another matter of high administrative importance to challenge the ingenuity and ability of management. The formula for the numerical distribution of men among the various divisions and units of a police organization is as yet unknown. The administrator of a police department is constantly confronted by the demands of divisional heads for increased personnel strength in their respective units, and these petitions are usually well supported by impressive statistical data. The competition for manpower occasionally becomes critical in nature and the chief executive is hard-pressed to weigh the relative importance of the various requests. Will the addition of two men to the traffic division secure better results in protecting life and property than the addition of two men to the detective division, or to the patrol division, or to the records division? Or, would the addition of a trained social worker to the staff of the crime prevention division prove ultimately of greater value? Again, would the establishment of a crime detection laboratory in the department and the employment of a laboratory technologist transcend in importance all other requests for personnel increases? Since the chief executive must work within well-defined fiscal limits, he is compelled to give some sort of answer to these questions.

What, for example, is the relative social significance of preventing one case of juvenile delinquency, one death due to a traffic accident, one adult case of robbery in which a citizen is brutally clubbed, one murder, or one 10-year old girl from being attacked by a degenerate? These are the subjective, qualitative determinations that the chief executive must make in balancing the competing demands for manpower that are presented to him. He can, to be sure, take into account operational costs, case load and the frequency of various types of crime as are available to him. He will be influenced to some extent by Beccarian criteria still prominent in the criminal law and expressed in terms of a scale of penalties as a measure of the relative gravity of the various offense classifications. His judgment will also be shaped by public sentiment prevailing at the moment. It is apparent that the problems presented by functional distribution of the force will challenge the best executive talent available.

Dominance of an Idea

Organization is necessary but it will not take the place of a dominant central idea as the foundation of action and coordination of all parts of the enterprise. Among the most important tasks of an important executive, the Chief of Police, is the development of the desire and will to work together for a purpose in the minds of every man in the organization.

Individuals are tied together by ideas rather than coercive authority and control. Their capacity for productive and creative work, loyal self-sacrifice and enthusiasm for the job, knows no limits when the whole man—body-mind-and-spirit—is thrown into the program. Administration by objectives rather than command, fosters initiative, discretion and self-development. It is the men and not the organization chart who do the work.

In addition to the kinetic drive of a dominant central idea and closely associated with it, is the opportunity for personal achievement and success. It can be kept in mind that the police field is a career service where the individual officer may move on upward on a merit basis through the channels of promotion to higher positions and higher responsibilities. Although the opportunity for promotion may be somewhat limited in the smaller department, the gradual development of lateral mobility or lateral entry as a part of police personnel policy,[8] offers the greatest of promise for the future.

Organization of the Executive

Since the police chief executive cannot perform all of his prescribed duties, it seems sensible for him to confine himself to those matters of general management that presumably no one else can do as well. In order to do this in the larger organizations he normally will divide the major tasks of the organization into three major administrative branches:

1. Staff Services.
2. Line Operations.
3. Inspections.

The chief executive must then appoint a head for each of these major units, define his duties, establish the jurisdiction and authority of each, co-ordinate his activities, eliminate friction incident to their relationships and give to these administrative heads such moral and physical support as may be required for the satisfactory performance of their respective duties.

Staff services refer to personnel, materiel, planning, research, public relations and the maintenance of equipment and buildings. Staff services strengthen line operations so that the latter may be more productive. Line operations constitute the field activities which are more immediately

[8] Leonard, V. A., *Police Personnel Administration*, Charles C. Thomas, Publisher, Springfield, Illinois, 1970.

directed toward achieving the objectives for which the department is organized. The inspectional branch, as the word implies, is that division of the administrative unit which evaluates performance in the staff and line in the discharge of their responsibilities. It also inspects the members of the organization, plant and materiel.

Because the economical and efficient administration of the police organization rests upon all three of these administrative branches, it is imperative that the most competent men in the department be selected as the executive heads of these major units. The sole purpose is to distribute the executive load of the head of the department in a fair and equitable manner and according to accepted administrative principles. These branch chiefs are not intended to deprive the chief executive either of his authority or powers because nothing that any one of them could do, could be done without his implied approval. The addition of managerial aids to extend the reach of the executive does not contradict the principle of unity of command. They act only by and through the authority of the chief executive. In organization, the aids become just so much additional executive capacity for planning and for supervision.

In order that the authority of the chief may be properly established and recognized by subordinates, it is necessary for him to direct his orders and directives through his immediate subordinates—the assistant chief, the deputy chief and the chief inspector. This is also important in establishing the responsibility and authority of intermediate subordinates. A collateral purpose of this procedure is to prevent members of the department in positions below that of the administrative group from taking up his valuable time unnecessarily with minor matters that should be settled by subordinates. A wise chief will learn how to insist on this as a general rule without closing his door, or his ears, to communications from subordinates further down the line who have good reason to think that their problems can be settled only by the chief executive.

Triple extension of the executive is thus achieved through subordinate command of the three major administrative units of organization—staff services, line operations and inspection. It must be kept constantly in mind that the end result sought for is line power, intelligently controlled and directed toward police objectives. This is the essence of police organization and management. A police department may boast of an outstanding crime laboratory, an excellent training school, a merit system, superior communication facilities, a crime prevention division, a traffic division, a record system and all the other trappings of modern police service but all of these will be of no avail unless they can be and are translated into line power. Too often this basic principle is obscured and even forgotten in the confusion of activities that characterize the average police department. It is the measure of striking power at the point where the line delivery of police service occurs that determines the extent to which a police organization is capable of achieving its objectives. Thus, organization of the executive through staff services, line operations and inspection has for its major purpose one end result, and only one—line power. The manner in which this result may best be achieved and applied constitutes the central thesis of the present work.

Organization for Line Power

The necessity for a clear distinction in organization between line and staff functions has been emphasized previously. Implementing this principle, consolidation of staff functions under single, unified command is a first prerequisite to the development of efficiency in both staff and line operations. It follows that any staff activity or function, whatever its nature may be, which does not serve to enhance the line power of the organization should be dropped, reorganized or restaffed. The sole justification for the allocation of funds to any activity or function in a police department is the amplification of the line power or combat strength of the department. There is no other criterion.

Duties of the Chief of Staff Services

The Chief of Services is charged with command of that administrative branch of the police department referred to as Staff Services. He has the responsibility of managing police affairs that have reference to personnel and materiel for the men engaged in field operations. Included are administrative duties associated with the selection, training, disciplining, and management of personnel; equipment, materiel and supplies; housing and maintenance. He also has directive control over the records division, the communication system, the property custodian and the departmental accountant and the crime laboratory. The primary function of services is to implement operations and when these duties are well performed, line operations will receive the right type of men, materiel, communication facilities and the statistical data needed to plan and carry to a successful conclusion the general and special operations of the department

Control of Line Operations

The existing line organization of too many police departments is similar to that of an army in which the infantry, artillery, cavalry and engineers each operate as an independent unit with no single leadership imposed from above upon their combined operations. Under such conditions of disorganization, operations could not be integrated and the arrangement would court disintegration and surrender. Military organization cannot afford to take such chances with failure and a premium is placed upon leadership at top command levels where the responsibility for the direction of combined operations is lodged. Neither can police management ignore this basic principle of organization. The police operation is inherently semi-military in character and most of the basic principles of military science find their counterpart in the efficient management of a crime fighting organization.

Technological advances and a pronounced tendency toward specialization in police work have produced organizational hazards which tend to violate this cardinal rule and dissipate combat strength. New activities and functions are accorded special recognition by the creation of new administrative units and details, accompanied by a disposition to treat each once as something separate and apart, with a separate personnel acting under special supervision, and each moving in a semi-independent orbit.

For example, the appearance of traffic regulation and control as a major police function brought about the establishment of the traffic unit in police departments throughout the country. Some police departments became "traffic-centered," with the result that a disproportionate percentage of personnel and equipment were assigned to this function. In such departments the extreme emphasis on traffic matters tends to obscure the approach to other major police problems of equal if not greater importance, and to throw the organization out of balance. The necessity for accommodating this emphasis by transfers of personnel to the traffic division has played no small part in the depletion of patrol strength in American police departments. Bruce Smith expressed the view that, "When to traffic squads, vice squads, special divisions and detachments are added other special details and assignments which are parcelled out with a liberal hand, one is struck by the thought that unless this tendency is checked, the uniformed patrol force performing general police duty may soon become a vanishing institution." [9] More important, however, is the semi-independent status which is usually accorded the traffic division in its approach to a specialized problem. Overmanned as a rule and over-emphasized, it tends to hold itself aloof from contact with any police problem outside the restricted realm of traffic administration and seems surprised if called upon to assist in meeting other police problems.

[9] Bruce Smith, *The State Police*, The MacMillan Company, New York, 1925, p. 203.

Likewise, the divisional lines which set it apart in exclusive control of all operations dealing with traffic control and regulation tend to bar the invasion of the traffic function by any other individual or unit in the organization. Members of the patrol division come to ignore even the most flagrant traffic infractions on the theory that these are the exclusive concern of the traffic division. Divisional competition for departmental budget funds and the position of the traffic unit generate interdivisional rivalry and are destructive of morale and coordination. In this manner, the total line power potential of the organization is disintegrated into a number of semi-independent parts, each serving its own selfish interests.

Similarly, in many American police departments, the detective division has developed unwarranted power and in many instances, dominates the organization. The tyranny of detective domination leads to unhealthy rivalry among the various divisions of the department and weakens the combat power of an organization.

Functional specialization increases the need for administrative controls and coordination. It is futile to expect a number of semi-independent divisions to function together as a unit unless they are placed under single, unified command. There is no alternative. Organizational efficiency depends upon consolidation of command at one point. Only in this manner can the effective personnel strength in the various divisions of the line be coordinated and directed intelligently in time and place toward the complex problems of crime, vice, and traffic, which confront the police.

It is essential, therefore, that all operations of the following line units be placed under the single, direct command of the Chief of Operations:

1. Patrol Division
2. Detective Division
3. Traffic Division
4. Crime Prevention Division
5. Vice

The commanding officer in charge of line operations will have as his immediate subordinates the heads of all divisions of the line. These commanding officers report to the Chief of Operations and not to the Chief of Police. They are accountable to him for the honest and proper performance of their duties, and he, in turn, is responsible to the Chief of Police. Except in extreme emergencies, all orders by the Chief of Police are directed to the division heads through the office of Chief of Operations.

The Chief of Operations will play, and should play, an important role in the administration of police affairs. He must possess very superior intelligence and must be a competent, outstanding leader as demonstrated by his experience and performance record. The Chief of Police must use the utmost care in the selection of the man for this position. The administrative abilities of the chief executive can be largely measured by the judgment he exercises in making the appointment to this important post.

Merging the combined personnel strength of line divisions under one command makes possible definite lines of control and responsibility. It locates power and authority, and fixes the lines of responsibility. Reorganization of line operations under a single command paves the way for the elimination of much of the friction and petty jealousy which generally characterize the relationships between divisions, and which are destructive of morale and efficiency.

Equally important, it increases flexibility of management in concentrating various sections of the force at points and at hours where records data indicate the need is greatest. Furthermore, it implements the intelligent planning of operations because with control of personnel strength located at one point, the total line power of the force can be maneuvered with precision and certainty of control when and where that power is needed.

Inspections

Executive control must provide itself with the means for evaluating the quality of work. It is the function of inspection to see that the quality of performance is at all times in agreement with the standards of the department. Inspection does not create quality but it does control quality, in that it provides the means for measuring personnel, materiel and operational performance. It embraces preventive measures which may be invoked to prevent failure and raise the probability of success. Quality control is the function of insuring that personnel, materiel and performance conform to the prescribed standards. With the gradual but steady professionalization of the police, the public is becoming accustomed to a higher standard of quality in police service and this has imposed increased responsibility on the function of inspection. There must be provision for a measuring agency to prevent deviations from departmental standards, and to initiate through the Chief of Police the necessary action when these violations are observed. Inspection is the examination and evaluation of procedure, performance and the implements of performance measured by departmental standards. Independent periodic inspection of methods and performance is indispensable to a high degree of efficiency in both staff services and line operations. Supervision of men and department materiel must be consistent and according to a well-developed plan, so that nothing will be overlooked. Forms should be developed for this purpose so that inspectors on their tour of duty will be sure to check every detail.

The end-result sought for in the inspectional function is the maximum development of the combat strength of the department. All other considerations are tributary to this single purpose. It inspects Staff Services to determine whether staff functions are being discharged efficiently in providing the department with the implements of line power, including personnel, materiel and equipment. It inspects line operations to evaluate the extent to which these tools are being properly applied to the attainment of police objectives. It is itself inspected to determine that the inspectional function is being efficiently exercised as a tool of executive control.

Intelligence

The intelligence function of a police department is fulfilled by gathering information concerning the activities of individuals engaged in organized criminal activities. While such criminal matters are primarily a phenomenon of larger cities the strangling tentacles of organized crime defy geographical boundaries thus reaching communities of all sizes.

Criminal cartels participate in any illegal activities that offer maximum profit at minimum risk of law enforcement interference. They offer goods and services that millions of Americans desire even though declared illegal by law-makers. These illegal activities include gambling, loan sharking, illegal narcotic activities, and other forms of vice. Unfortunately organized crime, with its profits from illegal ventures, has infiltrated legitimate business and is deeply involved in labor racketeering.[10]

Essentially, efforts to curb the growth of organized crime have not been successful. The problems involved in combatting criminal cartels include: [11]

   1.   Organizational insulation makes it difficult to obtain live witnesses and collect documentary evidence.

[10] For excellent studies of organized crime see: Donald R. Cressey, *Theft of the Nation*, Harper and Row, New York, 1969, and Ralph Salerno and John S. Tompkins, *The Crime Confederation*, Doubleday and Co., Garden City, New York, 1969.

[11] The President's Commission on Law Enforcement and Administration of Justice, *Task Force Report: Organized Crime*, U. S. Government Printing Office, Washington, 1967, pp. 14–15.

2. Local law enforcement agencies are inadequately staffed in order to deal with the problem of breaking down criminal organizations.

3. Limited coordination between law enforcement agencies.

4. Failure to develop strategic intelligence information on criminal cartels.

5. Insignificant punishment of offenders who engage in illegal activities such as gambling, which is the greatest source of revenue for organized crime.

6. Lack of public and political commitment that are essential if organized crime is to be effectively combatted.

Any program that is to have any degree of success must be based upon the pooling of resources and the exchange of information. The unwillingness of departments to exchange intelligence has seriously impeded effective local or joint action.

One of the more successful attempts at improving interdepartmental relations occurred in 1956 with the formation of the Law Enforcement Intelligence Unit. This organization was formed by twenty six police and sheriffs' departments in seven western states; its membership has increased to 152 different agencies including state police, sheriffs' departments, metropolitan police, prosecutors' offices and other investigative units.[12]

The unit was organized for the purpose of exchanging confidential information on individuals and organizations. The California Bureau of Criminal Identification and Investigation serves as a clearinghouse for criminal intelligence information accumulated by LEIU. Membership is limited to individuals affiliated with permanent law enforcement intelligence units.

LEIU conducts its business through an executive board composed of three elected members plus four geographical region chairmen. The unit has no investigative authority, but has been highly successful as a unifying program for the exchange of intelligence information.[13]

In recent years there has been increasing evidence of greater local cooperation in disseminating intelligence information; for instance, the New England State Police Compact in which six states are eligible for membership. One of the organization's expressed purposes is to

12 *Ibid.*, p. 13.

13 *Ibid.*

provide close and effective cooperation and assistance in detecting and apprehending those engaged in organized criminal activities.[14]

Another development includes the New York State Identification and Intelligence System (NYSIIS) which, when fully operational, will serve as a records exchange center with files including criminal intelligence information.[15]

The federal government has responded dramatically to the challenge of organized crime by establishing "strike forces" in major metropolitan areas throughout the nation. These special units, composed of special U. S. Attorneys and investigators from all major federal law enforcement agencies, have shown great promise in developing tactical and strategic intelligence on organized crime.

Presently, well-developed organized crime investigation units exist in only a handfull of local jurisdictions. Some of the larger cities, such as New York, Los Angeles and Chicago, have had active intelligence units for a number of years. For example, in Los Angeles an intelligence division was established in 1950 that is responsible for gathering information pertinent to all aspects of organized crime. In accomplishing this task the intelligence division, having a fifty-one full-time man assignment, makes extensive use of physical surveillance as a means of developing information and preventing hoodlum contacts or illegal activity.[16]

If organized crime is to be positively confronted, police departments must universally acknowledge its existence and develop an adequate organizational response.

Internal Investigation

The chief executive of a police department is responsible for the discipline and control of the members of his agency. His command responsibility can seldom be accomplished without some type of formal machinery for the investigation of complaints concerning police activity or employees. Corruption or police misconduct must be dealt with forcefully by each department, having a planned program that insures departmental integrity.

---

[14] V. A. Leonard and Harry W. More, *The General Administration of Criminal Justice*, The Foundation Press, Inc., Mineola, N. Y., 1967, p. 143.

[15] The President's Commission on Law Enforcement and Administration of Justice, *Task Force Report: The Police*, U. S. Government Printing Office, Washington, 1967, p. 79.

[16] The President's Commission on Law Enforcement and Administration of Justice, *op. cit.*, p. 12.

In small departments, the chief, or his designated representative can perform internal investigations, but in medium-sized and larger police departments there is generally a sufficient case load to warrant the creation of an internal investigation unit.

Many police departments have recognized this need, but there are still departments with inadequate programs. A nationwide survey by the National League of Cities indicated that 90 percent of the police departments surveyed require an investigation of all citizen complaints, but that many agencies did not have a special unit to deal with such problems.[17] A survey conducted in California indicated that 33 percent of the responding cities had some type of special unit for processing complaints, and that 44.4 percent had a written complaint procedure.[18]

These statistics clearly reflect the need for some departments to develop an organizational response to complaints in terms of clear-cut procedures and policies.

When developing a complaint procedure the following factors should be considered.[19]

1. Every police officer is aware that complaints are an occupational hazard. As long as the police continue to restrict people in their activity, prevent people from doing illegal acts, grand or petty; and engage in other control or authoritative activity which at its best causes inconvenience or resentment, citizen complaints can be expected.

2. A police department must actively inquire into the possibility of dishonest, excessive use of force, and other misconduct on the part of police officers. It is not sufficient to merely react to complaints from without.

3. A police department must investigate all complaints, even if the complaint does not appear to be justified at the time it is received.

4. A police department procedure and policy for handling complaints should be written and explicit and detailed. The procedure should be standardized and execution of the policy mandatory.

5. The written directive establishing the policy and procedure for the handling of complaints should seek to compel and exercise the responsibility at each level of the supervisory and command echelons.

[17] The President's Commission on Law Enforcement and Administration of Justice, *op. cit.*, p. 195.

[18] Lee P. Brown, "Handling Complaints Against the Police," *Police*, Vol. 12, No. 5, May–June, 1968, p. 78.

[19] *Ibid.*, p. 79.

6. The Chief should either supervise the entire procedure himself or delegate supervision to an immediate subordinate who reports directly to him.

7. Police officers must be protected from dishonest or mistaken complaints.

8. While innocent officers must be protected from both the direct and indirect onus of wrongful charges, the guilty officer must be punished.

9. Except for extreme cases involving the discharge of an officer, the penalty should be assessed with the intent of improving the future conduct of the employee disciplined.

Misconduct will occur in any law enforcement agency, however, it is imperative that the department establish machinery that can respond adequately by insuring the agency's integrity and publicly demonstrating appropriate standards of fairness and impartiality.

Civilian Review Boards [20]

The subject of civilian boards to review the activities of the police, particularly in matters concerning police contacts with members of minority groups, is one that has received a great deal of attention during the past five years, both from proponents and those who are strongly opposed to the civilian review board concept. The chief proponents of the civilian review board appear to be the American Civil Liberties Union and the National Association for the Advancement of Colored People, with the former demonstrating the most vocal outcry.

Melnicoe concludes his study of the subject with the view that the installation of civilian police review boards provides no solution to any of the problems concerned with police-minority group relations. In fact, he observes that they would be quite likely to generate more of the type of behavior they are supposed to control. He stated that, in effect, the review board would create more problems than it would solve.

The ultimate solution lies in the development of trust and understanding by the police of minority groups and conversely by the minorities of the police. The author concludes that this can only be accomplished by opening the channels of communication between the two groups and establishing a complaint and grievance procedure that is palatable to all concerned.

O. W. Wilson, Superintendent of the Chicago Police Department was asked recently, "Do you think a civilian board to review police action

---

[20] See Melnicoe, William B., *Police Review Boards*, Sacramento State College, Sacramento, California, 1969. This paper includes a meaningful bibliography on the subject.

in cases where brutality is charged would help the situation?" He replied, "I think it would destroy discipline in the Chicago Police Department if we had one. Discipline is a function of command. This is my responsibility. I recognize a tendency of police officers to close in around an officer who is charged with some irregularity. I have the machinery and determination to penetrate the 'blue curtain' as some people call it, and take suitable action where we find an officer has been remiss. If we have a civilian review board, that board then creates a situation where I, as the head of the police department, am confronted with an adversary group which the entire department will tend to unite against. Therefore, if we had a civilian review board, my discipline would be less effective than it is today."

The American police field appears to be unanimously aligned against such proposals and every major police organization, including the International Association of Chiefs of Police and the California Peace Officers Association, has authored resolutions taking an unalterable position against review boards.

The broad civil rights movement in this nation, in addition to its essential purposes, has served to focus more attention than ever before on the vital nature of the process of criminal justice. The pre-trial phase of the process—that in which the police are most directly involved—has been singled out for special critical appraisal. Police activities are both conspicuous and dramatic. They are the most obvious example of the established order. Their nature makes those who engage in them convenient targets for all sorts of allegations—some valid, some completely false, and a great many in between. At times some policemen engage in willful misconduct. Some make mistakes because of inadequate preparation for the task at hand, incompetence, unrealistic or improper attitudes or inept leadership. A great many complaints against police activities are shown to be caused by public misunderstanding or confusion about the police task. Some are the result of deliberate provocation or falsification by the complainants.[21]

Rather than directing their energies toward solving the underlying problems, some elements of our society advocate the establishment of super agents or extra agency committees to receive complaints, conduct investigations, hold hearings and recommend action in cases where police are alleged to have acted improperly or exceeded their authority. There are a number of things wrong with this solution and the IACP firmly opposes it.

The concept in substance is commonly called a "Police Review Board." Such panels are composed of citizens from field of employment and interest unrelated to law enforcement. Unlike elected or appointed boards or commissions which serve to establish and maintain basic police personnel policies and be responsible for their proper execution, review boards are answerable

[21] *Police Community Relations Policies and Practices—A National Survey;* International Association of Chiefs of Police and United States Conference of Mayors, Washington, D. C., November 1964; 11 pp.

to no one but themselves. They represent a form of control which is entirely alien to the American concept of democratic process.

It is recognized in most quarters that the development and expansion of governmental services have increased the need for specially trained personnel to solve the difficult administrative and technical issues that are interwoven with basic policy questions. The virtual demise of popularly elected functional executives or "commissioners" and their replacement with trained professional administrators are indicative of this trend. Popular control is still retained, however, through elected representatives who define policy, promulgate the general objectives of the government and appoint the administrators. The maintenance of public safety is a general objective and a fundamental reason for the existence of constituted government. Technical competence, awareness of the problems and professional interest in resolving threats to public safety rest principally with those who deal with them daily.

When this combination of authority, responsibility and competence is properly placed, an outside review board of even enlightened citizens is superfluous at best. Its presence merely adds another to an already abundant number of agencies beside the police which have authority to receive and consider complaints against police personnel and take proper action. Its supporters deny the ability of governmental officials to investigate complaints objectively. The review board solution, however, is a narrow, restrictive one. It is one of reaction rather than planned management. The underlying causes of events coming to the attention of such a board would go unresolved. It would be impossible for the board to consider symptomatic cases of police misconduct which are uncovered and immediately corrected by alert departmental supervisory and command personnel. Minor rule infractions are warnings of the development of more serious delinquencies. The ability and desire of police leaders to cope with personnel problems at the minor level would necessarily diminish were they to be relieved of or superseded in the responsibility for more aggravated incidents.

Far greater benefits will be achieved by detecting and preventing incipient misconduct rather than waiting for it to grow in magnitude and then treat it after the fact. Police executives must acknowledge and correct mistakes. They must investigate all complaints thoroughly to correct a legitimate grievance, or equally as important, to protect the reputation of an innocent officer. Competent police administrators are in the best position to do these things; moreover, they and the political leadership of a community are the repository of constituted authority to protect the public safety. It is difficult to see how that responsibility, or any part of it, legitimately can be assigned elsewhere. Where such authority and machinery do exist and disciplinary action is still lacking, the defect is one of management. The cure is the removal or discipline of the defective administrator and replacement by a competent administrator. Where the communities' executive leaders fail to act against an incompetent police leader, the public must seek leadership that will act.

Since the police review board concept focuses mainly on the civil rights arena we are obliged to offer alternatives to the solution proposed. A recent national cross-sectional survey has revealed the absence of continuing formal community relations programs in more than two-thirds of 165 cities in the United States that have:

(1) A population of over 100,000; or

(2) More than 5 percent non-white population.

The same study also disclosed that more than half of the police departments serving these cities are being charged by racial groups with brutality and/or differential treatment.

Poor communications between the police and those at variance with them underlie most of the pronounced differences. It seems vital, therefore, to open and maintain a high quality and quantity of continuous communications between the police and the public, and more particularly, between the police and minority groups. That the police and communities as a whole have not yet done this effectively is indicated by the aforementioned survey.

The police must make every effort to improve the degree of public understanding and sympathy for the police role in their lives. So, too, the police must become both knowledgeable and responsive to the yearnings of those in the community who have previously been denied a proper role in their government.

Formal machinery within every police department for the investigation of complaints against police activities or employees is an absolute necessity. Police departments should endeavor to inform the complainant of the results of its investigation and the disposition of the complaint. If the complainant remains dissatisfied, there are numerous sources of appeal outside the police department: the local prosecutor, elected officials, the courts, the Department of Justice, and various civil rights commissions. These are well-established, competent and authorized institutions of legal redress.

Enlightened citizens who share the professional police executive's desire to provide the highest caliber of law enforcement service are not likely to accede to short-range expediencies. The problems exemplified by citizens' complaints against police agencies will not be cured, nor even revealed in their entirety, by a panel of citizen-judges concerned only with the aspects of a case at hand.

The following statement clearly indicates the position of the IACP with respect to Civilian Review Boards:

RESOLUTION
by the
International Association of Chiefs of Police

Whereas, there is a movement current in the United States to establish so called "Civilian Review Boards" by groups and persons some of whom have been noted for their expression of anti-law enforcement sentiments; and

Whereas, among the stated purposes of these boards is to confer the power to judge the propriety of acts of law enforcement officers in the performance of their duties and to take or recommend disciplinary action against them; and

WHEREAS, an aggrieved citizen, believing a law enforcement officer has used excessive force, abused his authority, or infringed on his rights and liberties, has recourse to the established civil and criminal processes of justice, including civil suit, complaint to district, county or state attorneys, the Federal Bureau of Investigation, the criminal courts, as well as to the powerful and diligent news media; and

WHEREAS, the law enforcement profession knows that the most efficient and effective discipline comes from fellow members of the profession, as in the case of the professions of law and medicine; and

WHEREAS, attempts by pressure groups and some well-meaning individuals to superimpose "Civilian Review Boards" by any name or under any guise which departs from the present duly constituted orderly processes of law will lend itself to the impairment of professional law enforcement through the harassment, weakening and usurpation of legal law enforcement procedures, as well as materially endangering efficient and effective police performance; now, therefore, be it

RESOLVED, that the International Association of Chiefs of Police, in convention assembled at its 73rd annual conference in Philadelphia, Pennsylvania on October 6, 1966 states that as a matter of policy, it is unalterably opposed to the establishment or maintenance of any type of so-called "Civilian Review Board"; and be it

FURTHER RESOLVED, that any member of the Board of Officers, the Executive Committee, and the Executive Director, be and is hereby authorized to enunciate this policy on behalf of the International Association of Chiefs of Police at any hearing called by a duly constituted governmental agency, legislative committee, or at other appropriate forums.

Community Relations

An additional staff function receiving increased attention from the police executive is community-relations. The need for strengthening police relationships with the community is becoming increasingly critical, as pointed out by the President's Crime Commission.[22]

An effective and enlightened community relations program must be a long-range, full-scale effort to acquaint the community and the police with each other's problems and to stimulate action in order to solve the problems.[23]

---

[22] The President's Commission on Law Enforcement and Administration of Justice, *The Challenge of Crime in a Free Society*, U. S. Government Printing Office, Washington, 1967, p. 100.

[23] *Ibid.*

A Michigan State University study listed six purposes of police-community relations programs: [24]

1. To encourage police-citizen partnership in the cause of crime prevention.

2. To foster and improve communication and mutual understanding in the relationship of the police with the community.

3. To promote interprofessional approaches to the solution of community problems, and stress the principle that the administration of justice is a community responsibility.

4. To enhance cooperation in the relationship of the police with prosecution, the courts and corrections.

5. To assist police and other community leaders in an understanding of the nature and causes of complex problems in people-to-people relations, and especially to improve police-minority group relationships.

6. To strengthen implementation of equal protection under the law for all persons.

While community relations is definitely the business of the entire department, many chiefs have found it necessary to create special units to plan and supervise a community-relations program.

Experience has dictated that if such units are to be successful they most assuredly must have prestige and authority. Responsibility must be placed at the highest level possible and the unit must be commanded by a high-ranking officer or a qualified civilian who is directly responsible to the chief. Personnel of the unit should be involved in the decision making process of all activities of the department with particular emphasis on recruitment, training and field operations. The unit should represent the department with all civil and community organizations and constantly evaluate and assess attitudes toward, or conflicts with, the department.[25]

Public Information

A neglected but vital aspect of contemporary police management is providing information to the public. Failure of administrators to acknowledge the importance of positive information can be traced to a prevailing belief, by many governmental officials, that such activities are not a legitimate administrative function.

---

[24] Michigan State University, *A National Survey of Police and Community Relations* Field Surveys V, U. S. Government Printing Office, Washington 1967, pp. 7–8.

[25] The President's Commission on Law Enforcement and Administration of Justice, *op. cit.*, p. 103.

This barrier is slowly crumbling as evidenced by the increasing number of departments developing comprehensive public information programs. In small departments the chief of police performs this function, however, as the size of the agency increases it must be accomplished by one or more staff members.

A public information officer is responsible for obtaining community support for police policies. This phase is particularly important as cooperation is essential to the success of any police program. This objective can be accomplished by: [26]

1. Evaluating public opinion and attitudes in relation to the policies, methods, and personnel of the department.

2. Advising the chief in regard to the public relations aspect of new or revised department programs, policies, procedures, and activities.

3. Planning and implementing programs aimed at keeping the public informed of police activities.

4. Staff supervision of all police activities that may influence public support.

Successful performance of these duties will result in a broad gauged program that will promote public support.

Informal Organization

In recent decades an ever increasing body of knowledge questioning the logic of traditional organizational theory has developed. The classical approach to management has been to emphasize its structure. Leonard D. White stressed this approach when he stated: [27]

A system of administration, viewed from the special aspects of its structure, is then an interrelated aggregate of positions and incumbents. It is relatively stable, existing usually for the purpose of fulfilling permanent and continuing needs of the community. It is rational, not intuitive or haphazard. It is based on general, not personal, considerations. Personalities come and go, but the organization maintains a life of its own; many are now ancient, and short of catastrophe or collapse, they will persist indefinitely. In all their parts, organizations are based on purpose and function. Their backbone is the hierarchy and the acceptance of the superior-subordinate relationship in mutual arrangements of authority, responsibility and obedience.

[26] California State College at Los Angeles, *Effective Police Organization and Management*, A Report Submitted to the President's Commission on Law Enforcement and Administration of Justice, Volume 5, California State College at Los Angeles, Los Angeles, 1966, pp. 570–571.

[27] Leonard D. White, *Introduction to the Study of Public Administration*, The MacMillan Co., New York, 1955, p. 42.

The above statement reflects management's school of thought stressing principles. Initial orientation can be traced to such leaders as Heri Fayol,[28] the famous French industrialist who is responsible for initiating the scientific study of administration. Others who identified traditional approaches to organization include Weber,[29] Taylor,[30] Mooney,[31] and Seckler-Hudson.[32] In general, the classical school has emphasized hierarchy, structure, formal authority, planning, staffing, directing, coordinating and budgeting.

The human relations school renounced the principles of management concept, its inception being traced to the Hawthorne experiments [33] showing that human beings were not merely extensions of machinery. These studies disclosed that an individual's productivity was not a "simple mechanical procedure of muscular motions but a complex socio-psychological process springing from the inner sanctum of the human psyche and the complex grid of man's social setting." [34]

The human problems of administration were noted by a number of social scientists who directed their attention to a study of management as a social system conditioned by society.[35] These initial studies quickly broadened into a wide range of behavioral research emphasizing numerous approaches such as the small group being the basic unit of organization; [36] decision-making as the model of the organization; [37] or-

---

[28] L. Urwick, "The Functions of Administration," in L. Urwick and Luther Gulick, *Papers on the Science of Administration*, Institute of Public Administration, New York, 1937, pp. 117–130.

[29] Max Weber, "The Essentials of Bureaucratic Organization: An Ideal-Type Construction," in Robert K. Merton, *Reader in Bureaucracy*, The Free Press, Glencoe, Illinois, 1952.

[30] Frederick W. Taylor, *Scientific Management*, Harper and Brothers, New York, Publisher, 1947.

[31] James D. Mooney, "The Principles of Organization," L. Urwick and Luther Gulick, *Ibid.*, pp. 91–98.

[32] Catheryn Seckler-Hudson, *Organization and Management: Theory and Practice*, The American University, Washington, 1955.

[33] F. S. Roethisberger and W. J. Dickson, *Management and the Worker*, Harvard University Press, Cambridge, 1939.

[34] Nicholas G. Nicolaidis, *Policy-Decision and Organization Theory*, John W. Donner Fund Publication No. 11, University of Southern California Bookstore, Los Angeles, 1960, p. 5.

[35] For a detailed analysis of this approach see: Peter M. Blau, *The Dynamics of Bureaucracy*, University of Chicago Press, Chicago, 1955, and Philip Selznick, *Leadership in Administration*, Row, Peterson, Evanston, 1957.

[36] Dorwin Cartwright and Alvin Zander, *Group Dynamics, Research and Theory*, Harper and Row, New York, 1953, and Hubert Bonner, *Group Dynamics: Principles and Applications*, The Ronald Press Co., New York, 1959.

[37] Herbert A. Simon, *Administrative Behavior*, The MacMillan Company, New York, 1958.

ganizational equilibrium based upon a system of cooperative action; [38] organization as a social phenomenon with an emphasis on cultural differences and ecology; [39] and formal organizations and human beings integrated by the "fusion process." [40]

This research focuses on the importance of the individual in all the activities of any enterprise. Most police organizations today base their standard operating procedures and practices on classical organizational theories. These theories rely on basic assumptions made by executive officers and reflect the organizational principles that practitioners have deemed essential in managing an organization. Today, the art of management can be based on data derived from rigorous, quantitative research.[41]

In general, the present approaches of the new organizational theory include the following: [42]

1. A more explicit recognition of the place and effects of values.

2. Much more attention to methodology.

3. A changing conception of jobs or positions.

4. A recognition that civil servants are individuals who work (a) as members of a group and (b) in organizations that must be defined as social institutions.

There is a distinct need to reconcile the numerous approaches to management by retaining the best elements of each organizational theory.

John M. Pfiffner emphasized this when he pointed out that, "orthodox tenets of organization and management are useful and essentially valid, but they must be viewed in the light of what we now know about informal social organization." [43]

Many practitioners, acknowledging the presence of informal organization, view it as irrational; however it does exist and arises spon-

[38] Chester I. Barnard, *Organization and Management*, Harvard University Press, New York, 1948.

[39] Bronislaw Milinowski, *The Dynamics of Culture Change*, Yale University Press, New Haven, 1945.

[40] E. W. Bakke, *The Fusion Process*, Yale University Press, New Haven, 1953, and Chris Argyris, *Understanding Organizational Behavior*, The Forsey Press, Inc., Homewood, Illinois, 1960.

[41] Rensis Likert, *The Human Organization: Its Management and Value*, McGraw-Hill Book Company, New York, 1967, p. 1.

[42] John M. Pfiffner and Robert Presthus, *Public Administration*, Fifth Edition, The Ronald Press Company, New York, 1967, p. 200.

[43] John M. Pfiffner, *The Supervision of Personnel*, Second Edition, Prentice Hall, Inc., Englewood Cliffs, New Jersey, 1958, p. 4.

taneously from the sentiments, sympathies, traditions and belief stereotypes of employees.[44]   The manifestations of informal organization are subtle and usually are not subject to orderly prescription.   The social organization reflects such factors as ethnic or language differences, economic status, value systems, educational attainment, and personal likes and dislikes.[45]

The table of organization reflecting the structural interrelationships of positions within a department becomes, in reality, a very rough approximation.   The social organization conditions and reconditions the formal organization.   The ingredients of the informal organization are the result of certain universal phenomena that prevail wherever people work together:[46]

1.   People band into informal groups that may or may not correspond to hierarchical groupings.

2.   Growing out of this tendency is the informal or indigenous leader.

3.   An informal status system assigns roles to individuals.

4.   An underground communication system is rapid and subtle.

5.   A belief system exists that often runs counter to management logic and seems irrational to the management mind, but is nevertheless very real.

6.   The formal theory of hierarchy is often modified in practice by a pattern of internal conflict characterized by personal antagonism, factionalism and struggle for power.

In police departments the social characteristics of the informal organization are evident in: rivalry between deputy chiefs; the conflict between specialized units such as patrol and investigations; the tension produced by conflicting goals of officers working in internal affairs or community relations; and the officers who form cliques or the secretary who exercises administrative authority.

The positive aspects of the informal organization are numerous and include the indispensable function of communication.[47]   The "grapevine" is commonplace in most organizations and while in some instances it serves as a vehicle for rumors, it can also serve in the facilitation of official communications.[48]   A second function is cohesive

---

44 *Ibid.*, p. 133.

45 White, *op. cit.*, p. 27.

46 Pfiffner, *op. cit.*, p. 138.

47 Chester L. Barnard, *The Functions of the Executive*, Harvard University Press, Cambridge, 1938, p. 42.

48 Pfiffner, *op. cit.*, p. 136.

maintenance of the formal organization, accomplished by regulating the employees willingness to produce. An additional function is the maintenance of the individual's integrity, self-respect and independence of choice.[49]

There is evidence that formal organizations create informal organizations;[50] it remains the responsibility of a departments executive officer to acknowledge its existence and channel social efforts in order that employees may maintain their identity and the department may attain its objectives.

The Reserve Force Concept

Many conscientious police administrators recognize the tactical advantage of a reserve force to supplement the line power resources of the department in emergency situations. Circumstances may arise where the available personnel strength of the department is inadequate to cope with the problem and the availability of a well organized and trained reserve force may provide the difference between success and failure.

Known generally as Auxiliary Police Units, these supplementary forces are recruited from among the responsible citizens in the local community. Their duty assignments may involve traffic regulation and control along parade routes, at athletic events and other community functions, crowd control, assisting in surveillance, civil disturbance control, service under disaster conditions, road block operations, Civil Defense, routine patrol and other functions. In some instances, air squadron units, Scuba diving units, boat flotillas and rescue squads have been organized as a part of auxiliary police activities.

Admittedly, auxiliary police units must be recruited, organized and trained under the closest supervision by regular officers in the department who possess the necessary capabilities for this important assignment. The Sheriff's Department of Alameda County, (Oakland) California, operates eight platoons of male reserves; two platoons of female reserves; two underwater rescue platoons; fire units; rescue units; a posse; and an air squadron. More than 1,200 people have been trained a minimum of 90 hours, and advanced proficiency training has been continuous since 1954.[51]

---

[49] Barnard, *op. cit.*

[50] For excellent works on contemporary management see: Philip B. Applewhite, *Organizational Behavior*, Prentice-Hall, Inc., Englewood Cliffs, 1965; Robert H. Guest, *Organizational Change: The Effect of Successful Leadership*, The Dorsey Press, Homewood, Illinois, 1962; James L. Price, *Organizational Effectiveness*, Richard D. Irwin, Inc., Homewood, Illinois, 1968; and Douglas McGregor, *The Professional Manager*, McGraw-Hill Book Company, New York, 1967.

[51] King, Everett M., *The Auxiliary Police Unit*. 215 pp.. Charles C. Thomas. Publisher, 1960. The reader will find this volume helpful in financing

Opinion concerning the desirability of these reserve forces varies somewhat among police administrators. Chief Jacob A. Jessup of the Department of Public Safety in Sunnyvale, California, conducted a survey among a number of American police departments and concluded that the formation and use of a police reserve in Sunnyvale would not be in the best interests of the public and the police service.[52] In the final analysis, however, the best course of action may be tempered by local conditions and circumstances.

A novel variation in the auxiliary police concept has been developed in Highland Park, Michigan. An unusual increase in juvenile crime prompted officials in that city of 38,000 to organize a Citizens' Night Patrol, consisting of five radio-equipped cars with from two to three men in each car. On duty from 8:30 P.M., to midnight, they exercise no police power and engage in no police action of any kind whatsoever. Their function is "prowl", observe and report any unusual or suspicious activity by radio to headquarters, whereupon one or more uniformed patrolmen take over the situation. Members of the Citizens' Patrol are unarmed and do not leave their cars under any circumstances. Radio-equipped cars of other city departments which would otherwise be in the garage for the night are used on the Citizens' Patrol. The essence of the plan is that it doubles the observation power of the patrol force and officials of Highland Park report a sharp reduction in the number of incidents involving juveniles.

The Departmental Rules and Regulations

The Departmental Rules and Regulations are a standard feature of virtually every police organization. They will vary somewhat in format and content from one police department to another, but the purpose served is always the same—to provide a framework and fixed guide lines within which police activities and operations may function smoothly and in an orderly manner.

The Rules and Regulations prescribe the standards, procedures and policies of the department. They outline the authority, responsibility and duties of every rank in the organization. Among other things, they cover uniforms, equipment, the use of firearms and set forth disciplinary proceedings. A typical set of Departmental Rules and Regulations for

and staffing, organizing, training, equipping and administering an auxiliary police unit.

[52] Jessup, Jacob A., *A Study of the Use of Police Reserves or Auxiliaries*, Police, January–February 1960, pp. 26–29.

a medium-sized police department will be found in Appendix B.* In the larger departments, the Rules and Regulations may run to two hundred pages or more.

* V. A. Leonard, *The Police Enterprise,* Springfield, Illinois, Charles C. Thomas, Publisher, 1969, p. 68.

Chapter 5

ADMINISTRATIVE ALTERNATIVES

I N recent years, several alternatives to the conventional police department have appeared on the scene, and they have proven of particular interest to the police and other officials in the smaller communities and cities of this country. Each one of them appears to serve the interests of both efficiency and economy, and with no sacrifice on the part of professional growth. In fact, the professional stature of the police is being enhanced by these developments.

Metro-Planning

The growth and proliferation of metropolitan areas in the United States has created new police problems of the first magnitude. The mobility of the criminal population and an increase in the volume of criminal activity altogether out of proportion to the increase in population, presents to police administration a compelling challenge to re-examine organizational patterns.

By 1960, almost 117 million people, about seventy percent of the nation's population, resided in America's 18,000 cities. Of these, almost 113 million persons resided in the 212 areas designated by the United States Bureau of the Census as *standard metropolitan statistical areas*. The heavy concentration of population in SMSA's is revealed when one notes that these areas cover only 8.7 percent of the nation's land area, and yet 63 percent of America's 180 million people resided in these SMSA's in 1960. As of 1970, the population concentration is certainly greater in these areas than in 1960.*

America's 212 SMSA's offer the spectacle of 18,422 units of local government, including 313 counties and 4,144 cities. The urban mosaic then, comprises a fragmented multiplicity of coterminous, contiguous and overlapping jurisdictions, with all this means in terms of an astronomical duplication in costs to the taxpayer. The net result is confusion of bewildering dimensions and complexity and accompanying functional bedlam throughout these metropolitan areas.

One bright spot on the horizon is a growing trend toward the merger of police operations on an area basis.[1] Among the results of such

---

* U. S. Bureau of the Census, 1970.

[1] V. A. Leonard, *The Police Detective Function*, Springfield, Illinois, Charles C. Thomas, Publisher, 1970, p. 91.

101

consolidations are increased financial capability, increased purchasing power and increased personnel resources.

Five administrative alternatives to the conventional police department have appeared on the scene, and they have proven of interest to the police and other officials in the communities and cities of this country. They are:

1. The metropolitan police authority.
2. The federated police system.
3. Integrated fire and police services.
4. Contract law enforcement.
5. City-County consolidation.

The Metropolitan Police Authority

It is frequently the case that responsibility for the delivery of police service in large metropolitan areas is fragmented among a constellation of local law enforcement agencies, each operating in its own orbit and in a state of almost complete independence. There is little opportunity or incentive for operational planning on an area basis. In some instances, a system of informal cooperation has developed in a futile attempt to meet the problem.

As an alternative, and in terms of metro-planning, it has been suggested that a single metropolitan police authority be created to discharge the law enforcement function on an areawide basis, replacing the plurality of local police departments. Admittedly, this would serve a number of constructive purposes, including a unified organization, a centralized police communications system, uniform police service throughout the area, amplified police training facilities, a centralized police records system, continuity of policy, and added financial capacity and administrative capability. It is entirely possible that the American flair for local autonomy can be adjusted to accommodate this form of approach and the advantages it appears to offer.

The Federated Police System

The continued existence of a multiplied number of semi-autonomous law enforcement agencies in a single metropolitan area would seem to be incompatible with any reasonable concept of efficient police organization and administration. A federated system of police protection may prove to be an acceptable alternative. Under this arrangement, a metropolitan police agency would join with local departments in an integrated operation designed to possess the advantages of a single metropolitan police authority and yet not do violence to the principle of local autonomy.[2]

The metropolitan agency would be responsible for certain staff services needlessly duplicated at considerable cost to the taxpayer among the various local jurisdictions. These would include a centralized police communications system, centralized police training and crime detection laboratory facilities, and a centralized police records system. This arrangement would afford an appropriate vehicle for areawide planning and operation in criminal emergency situations. It should also prove effective in carrying out certain line functions, including the control of arterial traffic. Decentralized routine patrol operations, municipal traffic regulation and control, together with certain other functions, would remain a responsibility of local departments.

Examples of a merger of police operations under one form or another and the opportunity it affords for a more economical and efficient police service include metropolitan Dade County in Florida, metropolitan Nashville-Davidson County in Tennessee and the metropolitan Toronto Police Department in Ontario. As an illustration, the metropolitan Toronto Police Department provides police protection for the entire Toronto metropolitan area, which includes 241 square miles, nearly 2 million people and 13 incorporated municipalities, including the city of Toronto. There are no independent policing agencies in metropolitan Toronto.

Integrated Police and Fire Services

Another type of merger of police operations involves the integration of police and fire services into one department—the Department of Public Safety, with a number of modifications or variations in this basic concept.[3]

There is no single pervasive reason why integrated protective service should be adopted. However, it is apparent that a number of elements will certainly encourage additional city administrators to consider unification as a potential solution to their public-safety problems.

---

[2] *Metropolitan Services: Studies of Allocation in a Federated Organization*, by Director Winston W. Crouch of the Bureau of Governmental Research, University of California at Los Angeles. Part II of this study, *The Police Function*, was prepared by Richard D. Yerby in consultation with personnel of the California Highway Patrol, the Los Angeles County Sheriff's Department, the Los Angeles Police Department, the San Diego Police Department and other jurisdictions.

[3] Harry W. More, Jr., *The New Era of Public Safety* (Springfield: Charles C. Thomas, Publisher, 1970), p. 195.

First, public employees engaged in protective activities constitute a major portion of all those engaged in municipal operations; therefore, a large share of the average city budget is directed toward the support of public-safety service. Proposals for additional police-fire mergers are in various stages of study and development in a substantial number of other communities.[4] Police and fire protection are usually the two largest items in municipal budgets outside of the retirement of bonded indebtedness, and the resulting economies of integration have attracted the interest of taxpayers and public officials alike.

In Sunnyvale, California, which has had a combined department, the Department of Public Safety, since 1957, the City Manager estimated that the unification of the two forces was saving the city more than $300,000 per year in comparison to what it would cost to maintain two separate departments. Although most of this saving comes from greater efficiency in the use of manpower, some of it is the result of not having to maintain two communication systems, two sets of buildings and two records facilities, as well as freedom from the duplication of other services.

Since 1959, the number of protective-service employees in all cities has increased by .2 of a percent annually, and from all indications, this rate of growth will increase substantially in the years ahead.

From these facts it may be deduced that municipalities have already observed, and will continually encounter, increasing expenditures for salaries and wages, shorter work weeks for municipal employees and a constantly pressing urgency for supplemental employees to provide adequate municipal services. These intensified requests are certainly justifiable.

The public pressure for improved protective services, and the increasing militancy of public-safety employees are more evident today than at any time in our history. The "blue flu," "work slow-downs" and state compulsory arbitration laws for public-safety employees will all contribute to greater expenditures for salaries and fringe benefits. It is also surmised that fire departments will continue their requests for shorter workweeks, which will increase personnel expenditures.

Secondly, during the last decade the hazards generated by criminal acts and fires have posed a serious threat to the well-being of many citizens, and the frequency of these hazardous occurrences has increased at an alarming rate. Today, crime and fire represent major social problems in this country, and an analysis of all available statistics would seem to indicate their continuing upward trend. Certainly, the under-

---

[4] *Police-Fire Integration—A Survey*, Cleveland Bureau of Governmental Research, November 15, 1961.

lying causative sources of crimes and fire are eclectic in origin, thereby rendering them unamenable to a simple solution; but it is also clear that the traditional means of efficiently and effectively regulating these social problems have proven to be, for the most part, fallible. Unification has merit as an alternative to the present method of providing protective service because it maximizes the utilization of personnel.

Although most of this saving comes from a greater efficiency in the use of manpower, some of it results from not having to maintain two sets of buildings, two communications centers, two record systems and freedom from the duplication of other facilities.[5]

Other factors encouraging integration include the circumstance that the integrated department requires fewer men than the more conventional dual forces. This results from utilizing the individual's capabilities and time to the fullest extent. Actual fire-fighting accounts for approximately one percent of a fireman's time. It is the remaining 99% of his time that is put to more productive use through the unified force. In terms of personnel and morale, higher salaries and better working conditions have followed in the wake of the additional skills and responsibilities demanded of the individual public safety officer.

Third, a barrier that it has been necessary to hurdle before a unification of police and fire services could be attained, has been a break with the past by transgressing the traditional principle of separate service groups.

While custom has been a factor difficult to overcome, the historical gap between the two has slowly been closing as a result of improved communications systems, fire departments placing greater emphasis upon prevention, and improvement in the more traditional areas of cooperation such as traffic, crowd control and arson investigation. Accordingly, this barrier is not as significant as it has been in the past and is no longer considered to be an impenetrable obstacle.

Fourth, in recent years an indisputable reality has been that officials in cities and towns throughout the nation have been confronted with an intensified clamor for improved public-safety services. The public is demanding better protection, especially from crime and the criminal. Public officials are now obliged to evaluate their total safety program, the goals of which are proving difficult to accomplish within the confines of progressively severe budgetary limitations.

In a recent study it was determined that a total of 129 municipalities have adopted one of the models of public-safety unification. Statistical

---

[5] Cleveland Bureau of Governmental Research, Inc., *A Survey of Police-Fire Integration in the United States and Canada,* October 1961.

analysis of the departments identified in a nation-wide survey indicated that they constituted a sample percent of 23.7, and that the standard error of the sample percent was 2.6.   At the 95 percent confidence interval for the population, it was found that there would be, as a minimum, 672 or as a maximum, 962 combined police-fire departments out of the 3,613 police departments surveyed.[6]

To clearly understand the concept of integration it is essential to be aware of the fact that there are five distinct types of consolidated police-fire services: consolidated services, partial consolidation, selected area consolidation, functional consolidation, and nominal consolidation.

Of all the degrees of unification, functional consolidation merits the most serious consideration by city administrators.   There would seem to be little justification for perpetuating a system whereby protective employees are not required to do a day's work for a day's pay.   Firemen can be productively employed by being required to perform tasks which by custom are police duties, such as operating the complaint desk or fingerprinting prisoners.   And likewise, police officers can be assigned fire duties, such as conducting inspections.   This degree of consolidation offers the closest alignment with the usual separation of the police and fire services, and if implemented with care and prudence, can be inaugurated in any size city; it is especially adaptable to the smaller community.

Partial consolidation represents a method of utilizing "generalists" as members of a special police-fire unit in an organizational relationship that retains the integrity of the two protective services.   The public-safety officer positions are filled with men from the police or fire services (who have voluntarily taken the duty), or by newly recruited personnel.   This method seems to enhance the potential outlook for currently employed personnel because they have the option of continuing to perform their customary duties, or they may accept the newly formed dual-duty position.   This type of consolidation represents an accommodation of the customary separation of the protective services and the assignment of selected personnel to positions where they can be more effectively utilized.   Of those surveyed, it has worked in communities as small as 10,261 population and as large as 112,007.

Selected area consolidation exemplifies a degree of unification whereby the two protective services can function separately except for the operation of specially trained police-firemen throughout a limited geographical area of the community.   This system has the same advantages as those described under partial consolidation.   It is a means of

6 *Ibid.*, p. 32.

providing fire-police patrols in newly annexed areas and demonstrates the versatility that can be achieved in combining protective services to meet the needs of expanding municipalities; in this instance the consolidation application has no community-size limitation because emphasis is placed on implementation in newly acquired territories.

Consolidated service represented a complete departure from conventional means of providing protective services. With the majority of the members functioning as "generalists" (by performing both police and fire duties), emphasis can be placed upon intensified patrol and preventive activities. This degree of consolidation is best suited to smaller communities and will, in all probability, be implemented most easily in rapidly expanding or newly created communities.

Nominal consolidation, as presently practiced, represents an attempt by city administrators to group into one agency a number of bureaus which perform functions related to safety. The more effective means of utilizing protective employees are perhaps exhibited by any of the other four types. By virtue of the fact that such a department of public safety is administered by a single director, it would seem that there is a structural relationship between the two protective services that could serve as a springboard toward unification, but this study did not perceive any movement in this direction.

In established communities, the creation of a unified public-safety service could be accomplished with a minimum of friction by organizing a functionally consolidated department. Then after a period of successful operation, the program could be extended to partial consolidation or directly to consolidated services. This procedure would allow the organization, the personnel and the community ample opportunity to adjust to the new system.[7]

It is explicitly evident that the varying degrees of unified protective services have worked effectively in varying sizes and types of communities in all parts of the nation. It is also apparent that successful unification in communities has proven to be the result of careful planning and implementation. The decision to inaugurate some degree of coordinated police-fire services must be made with the acknowledgment that a panacea is not expected; of prime importance in attaining this goal, however, is the detailed study of the community prior to the actual installation. If the survey indicates that the protective services should be consolidated, the new organization should be tailored to meet the needs of the particular community.

Undeniably, unification can prove to be a method whereby a community may fulfill its obligation of providing adequate protective serv-

[7] *Ibid.*, pp. 195–197.

ices; but it must be properly supported by positive leadership, sufficient personnel, an adequate training program, modern operating procedures and ample equipment.

Neither the police field nor the fire services are in complete agreement concerning the merits of the integrated police-fire system. Opposition has been strong in some quarters. Opponents point out that policemen do not relish the idea of becoming firemen and vice versa; that the patrolman is already over-loaded and that the addition of firefighting responsibilities would neutralize his efficiency in both areas; that the two services are so radically different in character and nature; that consolidation is incompatible with sound administrative practice and procedure; and that the failure of integration in some communities is strong evidence that the plan is basically unsound and inadequate.

Actual efforts to unify municipal protective services or even to consider the possibility, have, in almost every instance, resulted in immediate opposition. Adversaries of consolidation are numerous, and in many instances have welded themselves into well-organized resistance groups, demonstrating the capacity to rise to any challenge in their efforts to avoid or discourage proposals for consolidation.

The opposition has, in actuality, presented no evidence to substantiate their position to the effect that when consolidation is instituted, police and fire services deteriorate rapidly. In fact, this study has clearly established that such is not the case. Unified public-safety services, when properly planned, implemented and supported have very definitely provided adequate protection of life and property with a reasonable expenditure of public funds.

The International Association of Fire Fighters (AFL–CIO), the most adamant of the opposing groups, has emphasized its conviction that proponents of consolidation are motivated by a hostility toward organized labor and that the consolidation movement offers a real threat to many of the members as well as to their continuance as trade unionists. While this union advances these beliefs as sound trade-union reasons for opposition, it is clearly an attempt to involve unionism as an issue when in actuality it has never been a relevant point in any consolidation. This approach is most unfortunate and should be labeled for what it is— emotionalism and not fact.

While the prospect of opposition from fire unions and professional fire associations is a contentious element, it is not insurmountable. With an adequately prepared proposal for unification coupled with a public demand for improved protective services, such a recommendation can stand on its own merits. All too frequently these two influential constituents have been missing in the past, but it can be anticipated that both of these components will be prevalent in a greater number of communities in the future.

The size of the community has been an important factor in past efforts to unify. It is evident that the greater the population of a municipality and the larger the separate police and fire services, the greater the difficulty of implementing any degree of consolidation. The larger protective services exhibit the principal characteristic of being self-contained entities with a strong emphasis on separatism and functional specialization, and a larger number of the protective employees have affiliated with unions or professional associations. All of these factors have worked and will continue to work against unification, but it is evident that partial, selected area and functional consolidation are especially adaptable to a city of any size.

The majority of unified protective services (89.6 percent of those considered in this probe) were found in communities with populations under 50,000. Therefore, the combined police-fire services are basically a phenomenon of these communities in the United States. Accordingly, it may be surmised that the greatest growth will occur in smaller communities, especially those with a population under 50,000.

The smaller-sized municipalities have limited sources of revenue; hence, in an effort to fulfill their responsibilities to the community while reducing personnel expenditures and attempting to fully utilize protective personnel, they are more apt to adopt some type of consolidation. In all probability, consolidation plans will meet with a lesser degree of resistance in smaller municipalities because the number of full-time fire officers is usually less or because fire protection is provided by volunteer personnel.

In addition to size, other factors will influence the growth of unified services. Communities that are primarily the residential type seldom have the revenue sources that will provide adequate budgetary support for separate protective departments; consolidation represents a suitable method whereby these services can be provided.

The population of many municipalities that are located in the suburbs of major metropolitan areas is increasing at a rapid pace. Faced with this population explosion, administrators in these communities will, of necessity, consider alternate means of providing public-safety services. New communities will undoubtedly review all methods by which protective services can be provided, and it is anticipated that some will adopt unification. The remaining type of community that will benefit tremendously from a consolidated type of safety protection is the established municipality that is expanding due to the annexation of residential areas. The previously mentioned influencing factors will undoubtedly prompt increasingly frequent unification of protective services.

Hypothetically, the type of community that will most likely adopt unified services will have the following characteristics: a population under 50,000, an above-average growth rate, a predominance of family dwellings, an enlightened city administration and a public demand for adequate protective services.

The unification of protective services is not espoused as a cure-all; nor can it be considered a simplified solution to the public-safety problems of our nation's municipalities. The successful implementation of one of the types of combined protective services represents a method whereby a community can deal with the hazards to life and property that have increasingly occurred in communal living, while simultaneously furnishing a means of more effectively utilizing public-safety personnel. Consolidation provides a community with the long-range opportunity of reducing expenditures when compared to budgetary support required for two separate protective services. It is a design whereby, in selected communities and with a reasonable expenditure of municipal funds, the public can be provided with effective and efficient public-safety service.[8]

At this writing, the evidence appears to indicate that it is here to stay and may likely experience continued growth and development. It is the general concensus of opinion that the negligible number of failures may be traced to faulty administration and lack of an adequate appraisal of physical and social factors, as well as other conditions in the community, rather than the system. City Managers, Mayors and City Councils confronted with serious fiscal problems may do well to look into the potential advantages of integrating their police and fire services into a single operation, with due regard for local conditions and realizing that the plan has been eminently successful in some communities, and that it has failed in others.[9]

---

[8] *Ibid.*, pp. 199–202.

[9] A typical example of an Ordinance providing for the integration of police and fire services may be obtained by addressing the Department of Public Safety, Oak Park, Michigan.

TABLE IV

DISTRIBUTION OF MUNICIPALITIES
BY DEGREE OF CONSOLIDATION AND
PERCENTAGE OF POPULATION

Degree of Consolidation	No. of Cities	Percentage of Cities	Population	Percentage of Population
Consolidated	24	18.6	228,044	6.7
Partial Consolidation	10	7.7	476,877	14.8
Selected Area Consolidation	2	1.6	155,487	4.5
Functional Consolidation	77	59.6	822,237	27.5
Nominal Consolidation	16	12.5	1,492,346	46.5
Total	129	100.0	3,174,991	100.0

Note: U. S. Bureau of the Census: *U. S. Census of Population: 1960, Volume 1, Characteristics of the Population*, Part A. Number of Inhabitants. Washington, D. C., U. S. Government Printing Office, 1961. Cited by Harry W. More, Jr., *The New Era of Public Safety*, (Springfield: Charles C. Thomas, 1970) p. 37.

TABLE V

DISTRIBUTION OF MUNICIPALITIES WITH CONSOLIDATED POLICE–FIRE SERVICES BY GEOGRAPHICAL AREA AND PERCENTAGE OF POPULATION

Geographical Division	No. of Cities	Percentage of Cities	Population	Percentage of Population
New England	4	3.3	66,765	2.1
Middle Atlantic	32	24.8	922,758	27.1
East North Central	40	31.0	1,463,700	40.0
West North Central	14	10.8	166,420	4.9
South Atlantic	18	13.9	457,786	16.3
East South Central	—	—	—	—
West South Central	8	6.2	162,432	4.8
Mountain	5	3.8	60,839	1.8
Pacific	8	6.2	104,201	3.0
Total	129	100.0	3,174,991	100.0

Note: U. S. Bureau of the Census: *U. S. Census of Population: 1960, Volume 1, Characteristics of the Population,* Part A, Number of Inhabitants. Washington, D. C., U. S. Government Printing Office, 1961. Cited by Harry W. More, Jr., *The New Era of Public Safety,* (Springfield: Charles C. Thomas, 1970) p. 37.

TABLE VI

DISTRIBUTION OF MUNICIPALITIES WITH CONSOLIDATED POLICE–FIRE SERVICES BY POPULATION GROUPINGS AND PERCENTAGE OF POPULATION

Population Group	No. of Cities	Percentage of Cities	Population	Percentage of Population
Group I (Over 250,000)	2	1.5	1,106,882	33
Group II (100,000 to 250,000)	4	3.7	546,262	19
Group III (50,000 to 100,000)	5	5.2	329,681	10
Group IV (25,000 to 50,000)	12	11.1	428,993	13
Group V (10,000 to 25,000)	30	22.2	445,992	13
Group VI (Under 10,000)	76	56.3	339,791	12
Total	129	100.0	3,174,991	100

Note: U. S. Bureau of the census: *U. S. Census of Population: 1960, Volume 1, Characteristics of the Population*, Part A, Number of Inhabitants. Washington, D. C., U. S. Government Printing Office, 1961. Cited by Harry W. More, Jr., *The New Era of Public Safety*, (Springfield: Charles C. Thomas, 1970) p. 37.

Contract Law Enforcement

A unique police development in recent years has been the appearance of Contract Law Enforcement. Under this arrangement, a municipality dissolves its local police force and enters into a contractual relationship with the county or state for the delivery of police service.

In Los Angeles County by May of 1963, the Sheriff's Department was operating under contracts with twenty-seven incorporated cities within the county, to perform all of the law enforcement functions of a police organization. Allocated to the twenty-seven cities were a minimum of eighty-five radio patrol car units, consisting of thirty-two on the day shift, thirty-three on the evening shift and twenty on the early morning shift. The units are manned by a minimum of 124 officers, of which thirty-two are on the day shift, fifty-four on the evening shift and thirty-eight on the early morning shift. If needed, city assigned radio patrol units will respond to render emergency assistance to other patrol units in unincorporated areas. The reverse is true with unincorporated units assisting those assigned to contracting cities where necessary in emergency situations.[10]

A survey indicated that opinions differed somewhat on the question as to whether Contract Law Enforcement was a temporary, intermediate or ultimate development in the Los Angeles metropolitan area. The majority of officials expressed the view that as long as Contract Law Enforcement works as it presently does, it will continue. Supporters of the plan feel that it offers the following advantages:

1. Economy—police service is delivered at a lower cost than would be the case where the city maintains its own police force.

2. Professionally trained personnel on the job.

3. The immediate availability of emergency re-enforcements at no additional cost, permits a city to pay for only the minimum necessary level of protection, while having the advantages of necessary emergency strength being available.

4. Radio patrol cars are completely equipped.

5. Unbiased, non-partisan service—people who might have sufficient political influence to obtain special favors from a local police agency are unable to obtain them from the Sheriff's personnel. There is complete freedom from local pressures and local ties.

6. Availability of a crime laboratory and technically trained personnel in the investigation of criminal cases.

7. As stated by one City Manager, "At first, I was skeptical. The more I see of the operation, the more I am converted. The Sheriff's Department far exceeds the advantages of a local police department. There are no personnel problems; no capital outlay is necessary."

Following a similar pattern, in at least one state, municipalities may contract with the State Police for the delivery of police service. Known as the Connecticut Resident Police System, the plan concerns small towns without full time police protection. As late as 1963, a Connecticut State Trooper was on duty in thirty-five towns in that state,

---

[10] Howard H. Earle, *Contract Law Enforcement Services by the Los Angeles County Sheriff's Department*, a Master's Thesis, University of Southern California, June 1960.

under contract with the Connecticut State Police to carry out all of the functions of police service.[11]

The towns pay approximately one-half of all costs. This includes salary, automobile expense, telephone, maintenance and clothing, amounting to about $4,200.00 for each contracting community. The officials of one typical town stated that the annual per capita cost for its resident officer was sixty cents. This becomes significant when it is noted that *The Municipal Yearbook* for 1959 shows per capita expenditures for police protection in cities of 10,000 to 25,000 population to be $9.36.

Observers of the Connecticut Resident Police System unanimously agree that it is working well. Townspeople involved are impressed with the fact that for a nominal sum, the services of the professionally trained and well equipped Connecticut State Police are readily available.

Equally deserving of attention is the trend toward consolidation of city and county governments, which would bring to an end the needless duplication of services, facilities and costs. All of the foregoing administrative alternatives to the conventional police department move the police into a prime position for the delivery of a professional grade of police service.

As a part of professional growth in the American police field, the consolidation or merger of police operations on an area basis can be expected to continue on an accelerated scale. All of the evidence points in that direction. The taxpayer and his representatives in local government are becoming more and more aware of the reduction in public expenditures that result from curtailing the duplication of facilities and costs through merger and consolidation.

The metropolitan police authority, the federated police system, integrated police and fire services, contract law enforcement and the consolidated city and county government—all five—offer important administrative alternatives to the conventional police department. Each one fosters a professional grade of police service and merits consideration by the officials of local government in this country. In an era of high taxes and increasing governmental costs, eliminating the duplication of services at the local level invites close scrutiny.

[11] James H. Ellis, *The Connecticut Resident State Police System, POLICE,* September–October 1960.

See Appendix C for copy of contract between Connecticut State Police and municipalities for the delivery of police service; also copy of Special Order covering instructions to Troopers on municipal assignment. Also see same Appendix for specimen copy of contract between Los Angeles County and the municipality.

*

Chapter 6

POLICE PERSONNEL SELECTION

THE caliber of police service is almost completely determined by personnel policy, and very largely at the intake by recruiting standards. From the point of view of the tax-payer personnel policy in the American police field invites close scrutiny in terms of costs and quality of service rendered. Furthermore, the increasing tendency to measure police administration against the standards of modern social service marks personnel policy as a problem of the first magnitude. In terms of the total municipal budget, the cost of police protection generally is second only to appropriations for retirement of bonds and liquidation of other public obligations.[1] Of this amount, between EIGHTY and NINETY percent is accounted for by the single budget item of police salaries! This percentage is in agreement with the distribution of the police budget in most American police departments. If for no other reason, the mere fact that the major share of the cost of law enforcement is to be found in the monthly payroll, merits inquiry into the soundness of the principles upon which these expenditures are made.[2]

The personnel resources of a police department are its greatest asset. All the way, from the top to the bottom of the enterprise, the calibre of personnel sets the stage for standards of performance in the delivery of police service. The degree of intelligence, zeal, determination and devotion to duty that a police officer brings to roll call as he prepares for his tour of duty, is determined in advance by police personnel policy with respect to recruiting standards.

Fundamental to successful police service is the individual police officer, selected with care and well-trained for the job. The patrolman of today is the Sergeant, the Lieutenant, the Captain, the Chief of Police of tomorrow. Thus, the character of police service is almost completely determined by personnel policy and very largely at the intake by recruiting standards. Police Chiefs and other officials of local government are recognizing this basic principle and as a result, recruiting standards are moving upward in order to attract to police service career-minded young men and women.

But there are other factors which suggest the propriety of an inventory of police personnel resources in the United States. Tech-

[1] See current issue of *Statistical Abstract of the U. S.*

[2] International City Managers' Association, *The Municipal Yearbook*, 1963.

nological advances and the application of scientific disciplines to the police field have created major personnel problems. Today, most of the arts and sciences find important expression in this branch of the public service with a progressive multiplication in the tools and procedures that must be employed for the delivery of police service. Personnel standards of yesterday fail to meet the test of an emerging profession which almost overnight has become an exceedingly technical and complex undertaking. Effective line power in a modern police organization is dependent upon an array of qualifications in the individual officer that would have seemed strange indeed, fifty years ago.

Conscientious police executives know that the quality and quantity of line power is not exclusively a function of numerical strength, and recognition of that fact is bringing the problems of police recruitment and training into sharp focus. Management in the police field is becoming personnel conscious. The measurement of personnel resources relates not merely to numerical strength, but also to the intelligence, ability, skill and "know-how" that are available in the organization for the execution of plans and operations. Recruiting standards must be adjusted to attract a higher type of individual, and training facilities are an essential part of the administrative program.

Unfortunately minimum entrance qualifications and selection techniques in too many American police departments are sub-standard and are not designed to recruit the kind of personnel that the nature of modern police service demands. Furthermore, it is too often true that after induction there is no provision for a satisfactory training program that will give to or develop in the new recruit the skills and information that he must possess if he is to meet the exacting responsibilities of police service. Survey reports covering police reorganization projects in the United States have repeatedly called attention to these deficiencies.

Police Entrance Qualifications

A satisfactory personnel program in any enterprise requires the establishment of entrance standards that will bring into the service men and women equipped to meet successfully the tasks they will be called upon to perform. The most critical stage in police personnel administration is that of recruitment, for it is at that point that the caliber of the police force is determined. This concept received early recognition in the organization of state police systems and in all probability explains their frequent superiority to municipal police forces. The first state police executives were military leaders. These men were trained to the belief that the proper selection of a man for a given job was fundamental, and they carried this idea over into their methods of choosing men for the state police force.[3]   The fear in which characters of the underworld hold state police forces, and the respect in which these officers are held by the general public, is a tribute to the careful selection and training which these units have received.[4]

Prevailing entrance requirements in the municipal police services of this country can be stated in general as follows:

Age .... 21 to 31
Height .... 5'8" to 5'10" (in stocking feet)
Weight .... 150 or more
Education .... Grammar school to high school, or equivalent
Physical Condition ..... Good health and freedom from any major physical defect
Character .... No previous criminal record
Residence .... Applicant must be a bona fide resident of city concerned

The above requirements will vary somewhat from one department to another but may be regarded as a cross-section or average of entrance qualifications in the American police services today.   Some departments are less exacting in this respect than others, and wherever this is true, the people of the communities they serve suffer a corresponding reduction in the quality of police protection.

At the other end of the spectrum in police personnel administration is one American police department where it has proved more difficult to gain admission than it would be to register at West Point.   The entrance standards were high, as exemplified by the fact that a university education or its equivalent was considered desirable, if not necessary before being admitted to the entrance examination room.   Only a very superior type of individual could hope to qualify in this examination which required from two to three days.   The results in this case speak for themselves.   With this type of personnel, Chief August Vollmer was able to present to the citizens of Berkeley, California, the lowest crime and delinquency rates of any city in its population class in the United States (85,000 to 150,000).[5]   The odds under which he achieved this record are revealed by the fact that Berkeley is located in the center of a dense metropolitan area, immediately adjacent to Oakland, San Francisco, Emeryville, and San Leandro, where it is exposed to unusual crime hazards.   In addition, he developed a police system

[3] Vollmer and Parker, *Crime and the State Police*, Berkeley, 1936, p. 105.

[4] Norman M. Yoder, *The Selection and Training of Public Safety Employes*, Ph.D., Thesis, Ohio State University, 1942, p. 113.

[5] See Uniform Crime Reports.

costing less per capita than in any other American city in Berkeley's population class; this, despite the fact that the salary scale for his officers was higher than could be found in any other comparable department.

It is little wonder that the Vollmer system of police administration, one of the major contributions of the century to crime control, attracted international attention. The Vollmer police system is complex and involves many factors, but leading them all in importance are the high entrance standards that were established to recruit into the department only those individuals possessing superior intelligence and ability. Confirmation of this policy is to be seen in the splendid record of the Federal Bureau of Investigation, where entrance standards are superior to those of any other law enforcement agency on earth. In the early 1930's, with a force only one half the size of the San Francisco Police Department, Mr. J. Edgar Hoover conducted a nation-wide operation with a degree of outstanding success that aroused national admiration. This record of achievement may be traced almost exclusively to the high quality of personnel recruited into that organization.

Based upon the complex tasks that the police are now called upon to perform, it would seem that the following minimum requirements should be established for induction into the American police services:

1. *Intelligence.* Admittedly, the person possessing an absorbing interest in the police service may be able to overcome intellectual defects; advocates of interest tests assert that a consuming interest in any field cannot fail to bring success to its possessor. It is extremely doubtful, however, that there ever was a *successful* policeman who was not unusually intelligent. In some positions a person with limited mental equipment who is greatly interested will make a good showing, but in the police service there appears to be a level beyond which a policeman cannot go unless he has superior mental equipment. Interest, initiative, and dynamic personality may carry some persons up the promotional ladder, but it does not follow that they have the capacity to fill their positions adequately after they have reached the higher levels.

The misinterpretation of these and similar qualities as intelligence has greatly retarded the progress of police service. The highest degree of intelligence available is none too good for the trying tasks that daily confront every police officer. The organizational chain is no stronger than its weakest link, and the stupid, blundering individual, who by his acts can bring discredit upon an entire organization, becomes the public's measuring stick for the whole department. One inferior man who fails to rise to an emergency can ruin the reputation of an otherwise excellent police force.

Rapid and accurate thinking is an essential quality of the police officer. He must decide in split seconds matters that may affect his own life or that of several persons. He must reach decisions concerning the application of the law without delay, and he must make no errors in arriving at his decision because the public is always the "second guesser." A New York City police officer made a decision on one occasion and it later took the State Supreme Court six months to decide whether he was right or wrong. His perceptive powers, his imagination, his ability to concentrate his attention upon the tasks that are before him, his memory—visual and auditory—and his reasoning and judgment must all be of the best; otherwise, the individual must fail when confronted with some of the crucial tests that are the lot of every police officer. Furthermore, a high order of intelligence is necessary if the new recruit is to absorb readily the material submitted in the training programs, preliminary, intermediate and advanced.

Police entrance standards must provide for the selection of men possessing a superior degree of intelligence in order to assure satisfactory performance in positions to which the candidate may later advance. The patrolman of today is the potential Sergeant, Lieutenant, Captain or Chief of Police tomorrow. The influence, therefore, of recruiting norms upon administrative standards for years to come is readily apparent.

According to a recent study underwritten by the U. S. Justice Department, the average intelligence quotient of recruits entering the New York City Police Department in 1969 were the lowest in a number of years. The average score of the 2,075 men recruited into the department in four classes during the year was 98.20, with one class of 358 men averaging 93.19. The average was 107.7 in 1962, 107.28 in 1964, and 105.75 in 1967. Some departments, such as the Los Angeles Police Department, report that they will not consider applicants with an IQ under 110, according to Dr. Nelson Watson, Director of the Professional Standards Division of the International Association of Chiefs of Police.*

A minimum intelligence quotient of from 110 to 112 is recognized by leaders in the field for entry into police service. With the trend toward a minimum educational standard of two years preparation at the university and college level, the minimum IQ is virtually set automatically. An individual with less than this rating would experience difficulty in completing course work at the university level. Since entrance requirements in colleges and universities are being raised continuously, it is possible that a minimum intelligence quotient of from 115 to 120 may eventually become the standard for entry into police service.

* The Spokesman-Review (Spokane, Washington), July 24, 1970.

2. *Education.* Educational requirements in American police departments vary from the ability to read and write to high school graduation with the trend definitely toward a university degree in the police major. Accidental infiltration of men with university training into the police services has escaped the attention of most observers. As early as 1945, in one metropolitan police department with a total personnel of 628 men and women, there were 84 individuals possessing from two to eight years of university training.[6] The head of one division in this department was a holder of the Phi Beta Kappa key. This may be attributed in part to the rise in average educational levels among the total population but it is undoubtedly true that the complex nature of modern police service and the trend toward professionalization have operated as factors in challenging the interest of college trained men and women. The presence of men with a university background is no doubt largely responsible for an ascending average intelligence level among the personnel of American police forces today. The following table portrays the distribution of scores in eight metropolitan police departments where the Alpha Army Test was administered to personnel under controlled conditions.

TABLE VII

COMPARATIVE PERCENTAGE SCORES OF EIGHT METROPOLITAN POLICE DEPARTMENTS [7]

Percent of Group

Rating	Score	Kansas City (1928)	Cleveland (1922)	Minneapolis (1930)	Los Angeles (1925)	Syracuse (1943)	Dallas (1944)	Seattle (1945)	Portland (1947)
A	135 to 212	5	4	8	10	11	23.7	37	55
B	105 to 134	13	13	19	17	16	24.8	31	23.6
C plus	75 to 104	24	28	29	30	37	28.1	17	12.4
C	45 to 74	33	34	26	29	27	17.5	12	5.4
C minus	25 to 44	15	17	11	12	7	5.9	3	2.7
D	15 to 24	6	3	3	1	0	0	0	0.4
D minus	0 to 14	4	1	4	1	2	0	0	0.5 [8]
		100	100	100	100	100	100	100	

It can now be said that more than 10% of the total personnel in metropolitan police departments of the United States possess from one to four years or more of university training! This infiltration, although

[6] Seattle Police Department, also see *Spring 3100*, official organ of the New York City police, and Annual Reports of other metropolitan police departments.

[7] Kansas City, Cleveland, Minneapolis, Los Angeles, Syracuse, Dallas, and Seattle police surveys.

[8] Army Alpha Test.

proceeding for the most part unnoticed, marks a significant turning point in American police history. The performance record of these men is paving the way for formal elevation of educational standards in the police service and has directed attention to the need for the establishment of professional curricula in universities and colleges affording specific training of men and women for entry into this branch of the public service.

3. *Character.* The character and reputation of a police officer must be unassailable. Examination procedure includes the taking of three sets of fingerprints from the candidate; one set is retained for the departmental personnel files, one is forwarded to the State Bureau of Identification, and the third to the National Bureau of Identification at Washington, D. C. This is a highly important phase of the recruiting process, as police departments—first of all—should assure themselves that they are not employing persons with criminal records. It is a sad commentary on the American police services that there are instances where known felons have worn a police uniform.

In addition, inquiry is made of persons mentioned as references in the candidate's application form. It should be noted and emphasized that references, as such, given by the applicant constitute the weakest source of information concerning his character and that the greatest reliance should be placed upon other methods of investigation. An estranged or divorced wife, for example, might be a prolific source of information concerning the character traits of the applicant. A detailed report should be secured from the police department in the applicant's home town if he has resided elsewhere. These measures will uncover important information concerning the candidate's relations with friends and previous employers, his credit standing, and his reputation with persons qualified to judge his honesty and reliability.

All inquiries should be conducted by capable investigators and every effort expended to obtain all the information possible concerning the applicant's life history and habits. This stage of the screening process should be considered as qualifying only, and there should be no hesitation in rejecting applicants whose previous reputation for character is not of the highest type. All border line cases should be resolved against the applicant.

4. *Physical Qualities*

A. *Height*

An examination of many qualification schedules in American police departments reveals a height range from 5 feet 5 inches to 6 feet 6 inches. It is obvious that those departments permitting an excessive maximum in height do not give any consideration to the strong possibility in such cases of glandular disfunctions, with their negative effect on personality. Giantism is often the result of a hyper-functioning gland. The small man is invaluable at times in the police service, but there is a psychology that goes with the larger man in the control of people, singly or in groups, that is generally not overlooked. Most departments have arrived at the average of 5 feet 10 inches in height. Obviously, there is little or no correlation between height and intelligence, which leads all other factors in qualifying for police service.

B. *Weight*

Where formerly 200 pounds of brawn constituted the primary requirement for service in a police uniform, the weight factor now possesses only a nominal significance. The requirement today will vary somewhat from one department to another, but most departments agree upon a minimum of 150 pounds. Variation of as much as 30 pounds either way, however, is noted in some instances. From a glandular standpoint this is entirely unsafe. A reasonable and safe procedure is to consider weight in proportion to height, and for this purpose the United States Army physical examination standards at West Point provide the answers that have survived the test of experience. There is an observable and justifiable tendency among American police departments to place greater emphasis upon physical and mental health than upon height and weight.

C. *Physical and Mental Condition*

The candidate must possess robust physical health in every respect, as determined by a competent doctor of medicine, aided by the facilities of a medical laboratory and laboratory technicians. Equally important, accurate determinations must be made with respect to mental health, personality, nervous condition, glandular functioning, temperament, social intellect, habits and ideals. These evaluations can be made only by a competent and qualified psychiatrist, neurologist, endocrinologist and psychologist.

The time and cost involved in appraising physical and mental condition may seem out of proportion to their importance. But experience has proved otherwise in those few departments where the exercise of rigid precautions in this respect has lowered personnel turnover and brought about other economies in administration which more than offset this additional expense. On the credit side of the ledger also is the enhanced personal performance on the job of men who can meet these standards.

The same considerations which dictate a rigid physical examination for all candidates suggest the necessity for annual physical examinations of all departmental personnel. In addition to personal incentives evoked by this procedure, it offers definite advantage to the individual officer. From the standpoint of preventive medicine, incipient difficulties may be discovered and proper remedial measures taken at a time when they can produce the best results. Such examinations serve the interests of both the officer and the department in connection with retirement procedures. If for no other reason, annual physical examinations would be justified on the ground that it would be difficult for a department to inventory its striking power or combat strength without reliable information concerning the health and physical condition of its personnel.

Recruits in doubtful health should be rejected. In addition to the liability of sub-standard performance, he may become a pensioner in a short time with the necessity of replacing him, and with the result that two men are carried on the payroll for the rest of their lives rather than one. Days lost on account of sickness in American police departments continue as a serious drain on effective personnel strength and add tremendously to the cost of police protection in this country.

Equally disastrous is the neurotic individual who becomes irritable and brings the department into disrepute by his actions and who is frequently the subject of disciplinary action. Because of poor coordination he is often injured either on or off duty. The mentally unstable person may take life unnecessarily, become brutal and commit other abnormal acts which may subject the department and the city to damage suits and other forms of embarrassment. The glandular type, although he may have the intelligence, sees nothing, hears nothing, and does nothing. He may be found asleep on duty and loses much time off duty as a result of factors traceable to his condition. The temperamental individual makes trouble in the ranks and among the citizens. He is destructive of both morale and public relations, and must eventually be replaced.

D. *Physical Strength and Agility*

Both physical strength and agility should be required to a superior degree and at least equal to that of the average individual.

5. *Age.* The prevailing age limits for induction into police service were for many years from 23 to 35. There has been a discernible trend during the past few years toward a reduction in both limits. A large number of jurisdictions have reduced the minimum to 21, and the maximum to 31. However, in 1929, Chicago raised the age limit from 21 to 23 on the grounds that the young man does not reach the age of reason until he is 23; that at the age level of 21, he is something of an adventurer and, therefore, not as reliable as the older candidate. It is further argued that police service demands men of more mature years in

order to assure the exercise of discretion and settled habits. The foregoing statements are consistent with the low standard of police service endured by the people of Chicago for the past century, and up until Superintendent O. W. Wilson took command of that metropolitan police department in 1961.

Appropriate habits and discretion can be acquired and directed under discipline in the police school and the service. Young men are more flexible and, therefore, more easy to mold to the aims, ideals and accepted practices of the department. They learn easier in the police school. They possess more vigor, energy and alertness than the older men and are not likely to have had their initiative stifled by some previous job failure. From the standpoint of personnel turn-over, if the officer has not already firmly established himself in some trade, he is less likely to leave the department when industrial production is at its peak and jobs are plentiful. The career-minded man is the young man. Insistence upon youth in recruiting police officers is generally found wherever effective police departments are maintained.

The age of 21 is widely considered as the absolute minimum limit for induction into police service on the questionable basis that this is the age at which the young man first attains legally the status of manhood. There are some who relate this to voting and say that it is a relic of the spoils system. So far as police objectives and the means for achieving them are concerned, mental age is of far greater importance than chronological age, and it offers a more scientific basis than minimum age requirements. It is not at all unlikely that this concept ultimately will prevail.

There is strong testimony for fixing the maximum age limit no higher than 25. There is strong evidence to indicate that men between 21 and 25 make the best material for policemen. They learn quicker and make better records in the Academy than do men who are past 25. It is the belief also, that the younger man after a few years of experience is a far better police officer than an older man with the same amount of experience. Young men are more readily trained than are men of 30 or over. Furthermore, failure to take police action has been found to be due not so much to lack of maturity as to lack of experience in similar situations. It is experience in the exercise of the type of judgment required of police officers that counts the most, and not the general maturity attaching to age. In addition, it is of the greatest importance to observe that the more nearly the age of the applicant approaches 30, the more likely it is that he has failed at everything else he has tried.

6. *Residence Requirements.* An important obstacle to career service in the police field is the "home talent" tradition in American cities.

This expresses itself in the local residence requirement for appointment to the force. Much public education will be required in order to overcome this pernicious requirement and to replace it by a broader and more enlightened public policy. Any gain will be worth the effort.

However, as recently as 1961, a survey by the International Association of Chiefs of Police revealed that nearly 75 per-cent of the responding departments had pre-service residence requirements, varying from six months to five years. Since nearly all police departments are experiencing difficulty in filling positions up to authorized strength, these restrictions interfere seriously with attempts to improve the quality of police personnel.

The local residence requirement denies the police and the community they serve the opportunity to recruit promising candidates who may, in some instances, provide a superior grade of qualifications that may be lacking among local applicants. The police and local officials in the community should take steps to abolish the local residence requirement and should also encourage the removal of state residency requirements, if they exist.

Every effort should be made to overcome the pernicious requirement of local residence and replace it with a more enlightened policy that would be more nearly in the public interest. It is noteworthy that in recent years, an increasing number of cities and communities have abandoned the residence qualification and require only that the candidate be a citizen of the United States.

7. *Aptitudes.* Exceptional personal qualities are necessary for the satisfactory performance of police duty. Many of them are quite fundamental and should be present to a degree beyond that of the average individual. Among the qualities which have proved especially significant are the following:

Initiative	Judgment
Alertness	Adaptability
Observation	Curiosity
Ideation	Imagination
Speed of thought	Resourcefulness
Self-confidence	Reasoning power
Self-assertion	Power of concentration
Freedom from gullibility	Persistence
Visual memory	Endurance
Auditory memory	Perception
Physical courage	Energy
Moral courage	Patience

Tactfulness

Forcefulness

Self-reliance

Speed of movement

Economic intelligence

Ability to work under distraction

Accuracy of thought

Organizing ability

Systematizing ability

Flexibility

Cooperativeness

Oral expression

Vocabulary

Written expression

Discretion

Discrimination

Diligence

Ability to follow directions

Vigor

Wide range of interests

Wide range of information

Assembling ability

Arithmetical reasoning

Mathematical capacity

Social intelligence

Vollmer stated the situation accurately when he said that the average citizen expects the police officer "to have the wisdom of Solomon, the courage of David, the strength of Samson, the patience of Job, and leadership of Moses, the kindness of the Good Samaritan, the strategy of Alexander, the faith of Daniel, the diplomacy of Lincoln, the tolerance of the Carpenter of Nazareth, and finally, an intimate knowledge of every branch of the natural, biological and social sciences. If he had all these he might be a good policeman." [8]

Mechanics of Selection

1. *The Search for Candidates.* Following the establishment of adequate entrance standards, the next and perhaps the most essential step of the whole recruitment process is an active search for qualified candidates. The best selection procedure that can be devised will be ineffective if not applied to as outstanding a group of men as can be attracted to the examination. A thorough canvass should be made of all possible sources of likely candidates. Appropriate publicity concerning forthcoming police entrance examinations can be planned and executed with telling effect.

There is a certain fascination in police work that is characteristic of no other profession and which can prove useful in attracting candidates. Men in all walks of life are intrigued by the detective mystery thriller, the crime buster radio programs and front page stories of major crimes, despite the fact that all of these present for the most part an inadequate image of police service. Any police officer will certify that these presentations, dramatized against a backdrop of murder and graft for the benefit of the gullible reader or listener, are seldom in agreement with the

[8] August Vollmer, *The Police and Modern Society*, University of California Press, 1936, p. 222.

facts and fail to portray the challenging dimensions of police work in modern society. Police service is infinitely more interesting than the year's best mystery thriller. Nevertheless, this widespread popular interest has not yet been properly exploited in the recruiting process.

The search for candidates should not be confined to persons who happen to be unemployed at the time the examination is announced. An effort should be made to attract the most able young men obtainable, which means that police service enters a highly competitive market in the search for talent and ability. Needless to say, this involves the establishment of a salary structure that will enable this branch of the public service to compete with industry and business in attracting to the police services high grade human material. The average tax-payer should be delighted to know that this can be done without any material increase in the expenditure of public funds. It has been demonstrated that *scientific police administration can reduce crime and delinquency rates without a major increase in prevailing police budget figures, and at the same time establish salary scales sufficiently high to bring into the service a high quality of personnel.*

Coordinated Recruiting. Police departments and police associations in each state should take the initiative and pool their resources in the establishment of a coordinated state-wide recruiting program. This would be especially helpful to the smaller and medium-sized departments, where the field of potential candidates is limited. A coordinated state-wide recruiting program offers the following advantages:

1. It makes possible a more widespread recruiting effort.

2. More sophisticated advertising of openings is justified.

3. It provides the opportunity to conduct recruiting and selection programs under the leadership of professional personnel officers.

4. The applicant has the opportunity of taking a single examination for openings in several jurisdictions.

5. Potential candidates would be informed of all vacancies in police departments throughout the state.

6. More extensive budgets could be appropriated for recruiting at substantially less cost than would necessarily have to be incurred by individual departments acting alone.

7. Uniform procedures in applying for positions in all departments could be formulated.

In those states where Commissions on Police Selection and Training Standards have been established, the Commission is in an excellent position to organize and administer a coordinated state-wide recruiting program.

2. *Preliminary Interview.* Interested applicants should be required to appear first at the office of the Personnel Officer of the Police Department for a preliminary personal interview. It is possible at this time to screen out those who, for one reason or another, are obviously not suited for police work. Badly impaired vision, a nervous spasm occurring at regular intervals during the interview, physical defect, gross mannerisms and other disqualifying characteristics that can be detected empirically without difficulty, should remove the applicant immediately from further consideration. If the applicant passes the inspection of the Personnel Officer during the preliminary interview, he is provided with a Personal History Questionnaire and Application Form.[9]

3. *Audit of Applications.* A perusal of the Application Form and the Personal History Questionnaire will reveal a tremendous amount of information that the applicant is compelled to give concerning himself. None of these items is unimportant or ambiguous. Each one has a specific and well-defined purpose. Those individuals whose applications clearly indicate that they do not meet the entrance requirements should be rejected at once and notified to that effect. There would be no purpose in loading examination procedure with individuals who can be eliminated on the basis of other disqualifying information. It should be noted parenthetically, that the usefulness of the Application Form and Personal History Questionnaire does not end at this point. They also provide leads for the later investigation of the applicant's character and reputation. Following appointment to the force, these documents, together with examination papers and examination scores, are filed in the applicant's personnel folder for future reference.

4. *Competitive Examination.* All applicants who apparently meet the minimum standards set up by the department, as indicated by oral interview and their application forms, are admitted to the examinations. This is a crucial point in the selection process.

The means for improving selective methods in police personnel procedure are now ready at hand. With the employment of carefully validated and standardized tests, there is as much difference between se-

---

[9] The Personal History Questionnaire and Application Form developed by the Police Department in Berkeley, California, is probably the most thorough and comprehensive of its kind in the nation. Over the years they have played a major role in promoting the high personnel standards that prevail in that department. Copies may be obtained by addressing the Chief of Police in Berkeley.

lection on the basis of their results and haphazard selection as between the purchase of an automobile "sight unseen" and its purchase after careful trial. Where such tests are not a part of the screening process at the intake, selection and replacement are necessarily uncertain matters. The myth of the man who can correctly judge character or ability at a glance has been exploded by an extended array of psychological experiments. The intelligent use of tests and examinations, now accepted as a part of standard procedure in the best American police departments, will go far toward reducing the element of chance in the process of selection, placement and promotion.

Psychiatric Screening of Police Applicants

Any written examination has both its usefulness and its limitations. It may not expose the neurotic individual who becomes irritable in stress situations and who brings the department into disrepute by his actions and who is frequently the subject of disciplinary action. Because of poor coordination, he is often injured either on or off duty.

The mentally or emotionally unstable person may take life unnecessarily, become brutal and commit other abnormal acts which may subject the department and the city to damage suits and other forms of embarrassment. The glandular type, although he may have the intelligence, sees nothing, hears nothing and does nothing. He may be found asleep on duty and loses much time off duty as a result of factors traceable to his condition. The temperamental individual makes trouble in the ranks and among the citizens. He is destructive of both morale and public relations, and must be eventually replaced.

The emotional stability to withstand the stresses of police work must of necessity, be a primary requirement of police personnel. Officers must be prepared to cope rationally wtih violence, verbal abuse, resentment and emergency situations. The emotionally unfit cannot meet these stress situations. One incompetent officer can trigger a riot, permanently damage the reputation of a citizen, or alienate the community against a police department. Police service operates within a context of danger and emergency, and the emotionally unstable person is no match for the exacting demands that police duty will impose upon him.

Although a comprehensive character and background investigation may eliminate some socially maladjusted individuals, personality defect in some of the applicants will be latent and not easily discernible. Hence, the necessity for psychiatric screening in order to protect the department against the danger of moving an acute personality problem into the ranks. Its extreme usefulness as a screening tool in exposing those personal traits which are incompatible with service in a police uniform, has been amply demonstrated.

Psychiatry as a personnel screening tool is beginning to receive the police recognition that it deserves. Its cogency and extreme usefulness in exposing those personal traits which are incompatible with service in a police uniform, become readily apparent in the following comment of Dr. James H. Rankin, Psychiatrist for the Los Angeles Police Department: [10]

The movement to utilize psychiatric techniques as an aid in the selection of police applicants had its inception at Berkeley, California, a number of years ago. There, the late Dr. Douglas Kelley, Professor of Criminology at the University of California and a recognized psychiatrist, began screening applicants for the Police department in the City of Berkeley.

Initial psychiatric screening of cadets in the Police Training Academy of the Los Angeles Police Department began on June 1, 1953. Since that time, no applicant has graduated from the Academy without being exposed to a psychiatric examination.

In this metropolitan police department, in one year, there were four thousand two hundred thirty-nine persons who filed for the entrance examination. Of this group, one thousand nine hundred eighty-nine passed the written Civil Service Examination, approximately forty-seven per cent. Of this group, one thousand two hundred ninety-two passed the Physical Agility Test. Of this remaining group, only six hundred twenty-nine passed the oral examination, less than fifteen per cent of those who originally filed. By the time the medical examinations were completed, there were only one hundred eighty-eight persons still surviving.

Of these, one hundred sixty-one took the psychiatric examination. Of this small group, twenty-five failed, 15.6 per cent. One hundred nineteen men went into the Police Academy for thirteen weeks of basic training. Of this number, only one hundred and three men put on uniforms and went to work "in the field" out of four thousand two hundred thirty-nine who filed for the examination, a percentage of 2.4!

Between June 1, 1953 and July of 1957, seven hundred sixty applicants were given the psychiatric screening test. Of this number, eighty-six or 11.3 per cent were rejected as not meeting acceptable psychiatric standards. Fifteen per cent of this group were classed as Inadequate Personalities; clinical judgment and testing pointed to their being generally inept, inadaptable and lacking in judgment and emotional stamina. Twenty-two per cent were diagnosed as Schizoid Personalities. Fourteen per cent were diagnosed as having either Cyclothymic or Paranoid personalities. Thus, over half of the rejected applicants, forty-four individuals, were considered borderline psychotics.

---

[10] James H. Rankin, M.D., *Preventive Psychiatry in the Los Angeles Police Department*, *POLICE*, Charles C. Thomas, Publisher, Vol. 1, No. 6, July–August 1957, pp. 24–29.

It is all too easy to visualize the potential trouble such individuals could cause when given the authority of a police uniform and badge.

Thirty-nine per cent of the non-acceptable applicants were grouped under the heading of Personality Trait Disturbance. The *A. P. A. Statistical Manual* describes this group as persons who are unable to maintain emotional equilibrium and emotional independence under stress because of disturbance in their emotional development. This group includes both those who have personality fixations and distortions and those whose behavior is due to regression under stress. Two-thirds of the personality trait disturbances were the Emotionally Unstable Personalities. Their judgment under stress is undependable. Their relationship with other people fluctuates widely because of poor control over their emotions. Anxiety, guilt and hostility are manifest. The balance of the Trait Disturbances included the Aggressive Personalities and those excessively rigid, brittle compulsive personalities who cannot meet new and changing situations. Only ten percent of failures were classed as Sociopathic Personality Disturbances. These persons are always in trouble, and do not profit from experience and discipline.

From the standpoint of efficient police service and governmental economy, no device should be neglected which will obtain the best human material available.[11]

The intelligent use of tests and examinations, now accepted as standard procedure in the best American police departments, will go far toward reducing the element of chance in the selection of police personnel. In the case of smaller police departments, contact with the police personnel officer in nearby cities and the State Police will prove very fruitful in connection with the content of the written examination. It should include at least one recognized intelligence test, such as the Army Alpha, the Otis Self-Administering Test, and the Henmon-Nelson Test of Mental Ability.[12]

The extent to which civil service may contribute to sound selection procedure is yet to be determined. L. J. O'Rourke of the United States Civil Service Commission has rendered yeoman service in the development of police selection techniques. At the local level in a few cities, civil service as a staff agency of municipal government is delivering an outstanding performance in the selection of police personnel. In too

[11] See Harold E. Burtt, *Principles of Employment Psychology*, Harper and Bros., 1942; this work sets forth the principles and the procedures which must ultimately be applied in the formulation and validation of testing instruments for police personnel selection.

[12] Information concerning personnel tests and testing materials may be obtained from World Book Company, Yonkers-on-Hudson 5, New York; Bureau of Educational Measurements, Kansas State University, Emporia, Kansas; Educational Test Bureau, 720 Washington Avenue, S. E., Minneapolis, Minnesota; and the U. S. Civil Service Commission, Washington, D. C.

many others, it constitutes an impediment to professionalization in the police field. At its worst, it recruits mediocre men and then protects their tenure.

Whenever, and wherever, civil service actually operates as a merit system with emphasis upon its positive role of elevating personnel standards and with its negative role of tenure protection relegated to a background position, it can be serviceable to police administration. Personnel work is a technical undertaking and unless there is included on the staff of a civil service commission at least one person professionally trained in personnel administration, this formula is not likely to be satisfied. It is to be remembered that merit systems are now operating successfully in the police field without the trappings of civil service. A good police administrator may provide for all the contributions that a civil service system can offer and more. What is wanted, in any event, is a merit system.

Collateral Elements of the Examination Process

1. *Qualifying Oral Interview.* The oral interview is the final stage in the initial recruitment process. The interview should be conducted by the personnel officer in such a manner as to appraise the traits of personal appearance, ability to meet others, social intelligence, ability of the candidate to express himself and ability to fit into the departmental organization. Generally speaking this interview may aid in determining appearance, likeableness, affability, attitude toward work, outside interests, forcefulness, conversational ability and disagreeable mannerisms. The total score is computed for qualifying candidates and they are ranked on an eligibility list in the order of their final grades.[13] Since selection must be based upon merit, the applicant with the highest total score is qualified for the first vacancy in his position classification.

The foregoing selection procedure will produce the best possible police recruits, but no recruiting process is so perfect that it will not occasionally pass candidates who will fail when tested by the actual per-

---

[13] *Veterans' Preference* may influence favorably the final score of the individual candidate, although it must be conceded that the allowance of extra grade points on this basis is in conflict with the merit principle. *Veterans' Preference* is obviously a question of politics and outside the pale of sound personnel administration. In approaching this problem, governmental agencies must decide how far they are willing to go in compromising the merit concept. It should be emphasized at this point that military experience is definitely an asset to a career police officer; however, if credit is given, it should be variable and based upon an evaluation of the extent and character of military experience rather than mere status as a veteran. *Veterans' Preference* as presently understood and applied in most jurisdictions is basically unsound.

formance of police duties.[14]   There are many men of intelligence, character and ability who never under any circumstances can become good police officers; they may work hard, long, loyally and faithfully and yet prove incompetent.   In the interest of the service as well as for their own good, such men should be eliminated at an early date.

2. *Probation.*   A probationary period is thus an indispensable part of the examination process.   A probationary period of not less than one year, preferably two, is recommended during which superior officers may give close attention to the candidate's actual ability to do police work before the tenure protection becomes absolute.

There are many undesirable traits that can be and will be kept under control by the new recruit for short periods.   Even a periodic drunk might not be discovered, or an epileptic might escape notice.   The lazy person would naturally speed up while he was without tenure protection and the temperamental person would be able to keep himself under control for short periods.   However, it would be rare indeed, if competent supervision were provided, adequate training courses were established, frequent ratings were taken and carefully scrutinized and work performance studied monthly over a two-year period, that the potentially unsatisfactory employees whom the examinations failed to detect, would remain in the organization.

This check on performance is concerned with the probationer's capacity to understand and execute directions, his alertness and the rapidity with which he learns the techniques of a patrolman's job, his ability to fit into the organization harmoniously, his loyalty to the force and to the municipal government, his aptitude in comprehending the fundamentals of criminal law and procedure and his skill in performing police duties.   He can be dismissed without the filing of charges and without hearing at any time during probation.

It is quite natural for a probationer to put his best foot forward and to cooperate in every way with the educational program, which should be more or less continuous during this period.   He will in the majority of cases attempt to conform to the rules for conduct, matters of policy, standards of practice, and standards of quantity and quality of work performed.   If the period is sufficiently long, the probationer will form habits which are in agreement with departmental standards and which he is not likely to abandon in the future.

---

[14] It is interesting to note that there are instances where men who were rejected by rigorous police entrance examination procedures have gone on to distinction in other professional fields.   Obviously, no selection process is perfect; examination techniques are necessarily in a state of flux and will be undergoing continuous revision.   Here is a field of high promise for psychological research in the police arts and sciences.

No probationer should be given the rank of patrolman until the end of the probationary period and only upon the specific recommendation of his superiors. It is too often the case that rank and tenure are acquired by default. The only safe practice is to drop summarily all probationers who do not demonstrate something above the minimum ability, for once given rank, it is more difficult to eliminate incompetents. The Department should be given the benefit of the doubt in all borderline cases.

3. *Rating of Police Personnel.* Some form of rating system by which superior officers may at periodical and regular intervals appraise the desirable and undesirable qualities of the new recruit is an indispensable part of modern personnel management. Personnel rating systems have in recent years been subjected to greater criticism than they deserve. This important tool of police personnel administration has been permitted to become inoperative in many departments.

Just as no line is perfectly straight, no board perfectly smooth and no circle perfectly round when scrutinized closely, neither is any measurement or appraisal of a human being perfect, because it is impossible to eliminate entirely the factors of personal judgment and bias. However, any measuring device which will yield results within reasonable limits if placed in skilled hands, is better than none at all, providing that it is developed to measure qualities called for in the qualifications.

Why have rating systems? [15]

First: For the same reason that we have examinations to determine the applicant's degree of intelligence and adaptability.

Second: To determine his efficiency on the job.

Third: To assist him in increasing his efficiency and thereby the efficiency of the organization.

Fourth: As a basis for determining his fitness for promotion or salary increase.

Fifth: As a basis for determining what branch of the service he is best fitted for.

Sixth: To stimulate and keep alive the personnel spirit.

Seventh: To make supervisory officers more analytical in their judgments of the men under their supervision.

Eighth: To rate by use of the rating scheme the ability of the person doing the rating and his success in building up the efficiency of his subordinates.

---

[15] Adapted from an unpublished manuscript by the late J. A. Greening, Chief Division Deputy, Sheriff's Department, Oakland, California, and former Chief of Police of Berkeley, California.

Ninth: To discover the reason why men who have previously done good
            work go into a slump, and to help them overcome the difficulty.
Tenth: To eliminate probationers that the examination failed to detect
            as inadaptable, or who are adaptable but who will not apply their
            abilities.
Eleventh: Order of layoff.

It is generally conceded that a rating scale is just as valid as its design and the degree of intelligence, judgment, honesty and understanding of the rating instrument, exercised by the raters. Men on the same
intellectual level will vary somewhat in their ideals; their degree of honesty may differ slightly, but as a general rule, aside from personal idiosyncrasies, their judgment and understanding of the design and purpose
of the rating instrument and knowledge of human nature will reduce
the element of error. Aided by personnel experts, the United States Defense Department and the State Department have done important work
in the development of a Forced Choice Performance Report for the rating of personnel. It is reported that the validity coefficient (cross-
validated) of the completed scale is 0.63. A considerable amount of
technical work preceded the development of this rating scale and it is
designed to eliminate over-rating and bias as well as to detect irresponsible reporting on the part of the rater.[16]

If a rating scheme does not try to embrace too many qualities under
one heading, its validity will be higher than if each individual quality is
rated separately, because it calls for more analytical judgment and does
not permit personal bias to enter to any great degree. There is evidence
to support the belief that there should be five different grades of rating
scales used in the police department regardless of whatever "cover-all"
system might be in use by the Civil Service for the entire city.

First: For recruits covering a two-year period, with short period
            ratings being made.
Second: For detecting those qualities which merit promotion.
Third: For sergeants to cover qualities necessary for supervision, and
            some of the qualities of leadership that should be present in
            lieutenants, together with qualities that indicate detective abil-
            ity.
Fourth: For detectives showing their success in this division qualitative-
            ly and quantitatively combined with leadership ability demon-
            strated.

---

[16] Inquiries concerning this rating scale may be addressed to Richard-
son, Bellows, Henry & Company, 224 East Thirty-Third Street, New York 16,
N. Y.

Fifth: For lieutenants showing leadership ability and administrative qualities.

Sixth: For captains, covering qualities necessary to point out presence or lack of executive ability and administrative accomplishment.

If it points out the highly adaptable,
If it points out the leaders,
If it points out the energetic workers,
If it points out the drones,
If it points out those with special abilities,
If it points out the temperamentally unfitted,
If it points out the morale tone of the individual,
If it points out the defects in the organization,
If it aids in morale development,
If it speeds up the organization,

then the rating scale is *decidedly worth while* and justifies all the time and effort necessary to administer and analyze it.

There are no short cuts to the selection, training, or rating of personnel. Some of the abbreviated methods that have been tried are responsible for a large percentage of the failures. A rating scale condensed to save time at the expense of accuracy is of little use and should be avoided if the best results are to be obtained.

The sum total of:

> *Examination results,* plus
> *Training school records,* plus
> *Concrete evidence of acts performed,* plus
> *Work load carried,* plus
> *Success in satisfactorily disposing of the load,* plus
> *Annual examinations,* plus
> *Rating scale average*—equals

Efficiency Records

> *Training,* plus
> *Counseling,* plus
> *Study and aiding to improve low averages in traits and performance,* plus
> *Restoration of morale,* plus
> *Removal of factors causing it*—equals

Efficiency of Supervised and Supervisor

Rating procedure thus becomes integrated with the probationary period as a continuing part of the elimination process. Those individuals who cannot or do not measure up to departmental standards or performance need to be eliminated at as early a stage as possible.

The Police Cadet System

A relatively prosperous and continually expanding economy has placed the police in a serious competitive position with commerce and industry in recruiting personnel. Elevated entrance requirements and higher selection standards have further complicated the problem. The typical yield in recent years in terms of qualified personnel has averaged about 8% of the total number of applicants. Recruiting has become a major problem.

The problem is compounded by the circumstance that police regulations in most cities seldom permit individuals to qualify for police work until they have attained at least the age of twenty-one. By the time they have reached this age, most young men have either completed all or most of their college work in another area of interest or have become well established in some other occupation.

An increasing number of police departments are turning to the police cadet system as an important partial solution to a critical police recruiting problem.

Under this plan, the police cadet enters police service as a civilian employe immediately upon graduation from high school, usually at the age of eighteen. They are selected through a regular competitive police entrance examination. Requirements relating to character, intelligence, emotional stability, aptitude, height, weight, vision, strength, agility and general health are usually identical with those required by the department for its regular patrolmen. Upon attaining the age of twenty-one, the cadet is promoted to the rank of patrolman and becomes a uniformed police officer.

Cadets are usually assigned to the performance of clerical duties and generally are rotated to the various divisions and units of the department in order to observe and learn police methods and procedures. They have no police powers. In addition to their work assignments, they are required to attend departmental training schools and in some instances, they may be encouraged or required to work toward a university or college degree in the police science major. As a general rule, the cadet's maximum salary averages about 75% of the average maximum salary of patrolmen and ranges from $250.00 per month to a maximum high of $400.00 per month in one department.

The advantages of the police cadet system appear to be clearly well established. First of all, it provides the police with a new and added recruiting mechanism, reaching young men before their interest in other vocational areas has become well developed. The period from eighteen to twenty-one is regarded as probationary in character and affords the department an excellent opportunity to observe and evaluate the cadet's performance on the job.

In addition, by the time he is appointed as a patrolman, the cadet has already had the advantage of extensive police training. From the standpoint of the individual cadet, he is provided with an immediate job opportunity on graduation from high school and is given the chance to develop and cultivate an interest in police service as a career and to develop the attitudes and outlook essential to successful performance as a professional police officer.

The police cadet does not automatically become a patrolman upon attaining the age of 21. At that time, he must take and pass the same tests that every applicant for the position of patrolman takes—written, physical, medical and character. They take the same open competitive examination as other applicants; no special treatment or credits are given.

In New Zealand, eighty members of the police cadet wing answered a questionnaire in which they were asked what had influenced them in selecting the police field as a career. Following are the results:

Advertisement in a national newspaper .... $2\frac{1}{2}\%$
Advertisement in a local newspaper 5%
Suggestion by vocational guidance officer 15%
Meeting, knowing or association with
    members of the force 45%
Own idea .... $13\frac{1}{4}\%$
Seeing a police display at shows, etc. .... $3\frac{1}{4}\%$
Suggestion from relative or friend .... $12\frac{1}{2}\%$

The police cadet system is now operating in the following jurisdictions: Alabama State Police; Baltimore County Police, Maryland; and in the police departments of New York City, N. Y.; Cincinnati, Ohio; Detroit, Michigan; Fresno, California; Hamilton, Ontario; Toronto, Ontario; Honolulu, Hawaii; Milwaukee, Wisconsin; Philadelphia, Pennsylvania; Rockford, Illinois; San Diego, California; Seattle, Washington; Aiken, South Carolina, and Berkeley, California, among others.

Personnel Record Controls

A single file folder should be maintained for each officer in the Department which will include among other items, the following: [17]

1. A copy of application form (as illustrated in the appendix) with all the information that it contains concerning the officer's history prior to appointment as a member of the department.

2. Results of character investigations.

3. Scores made on all phases of the entrance examinations together with examination papers and other data pertaining thereto.

4. Record during probation.

5. Scores made on Rating Scales.

6. Evaluation by Police Training School Director and results of Training School examinations.

7. Performance record on duty, including such matters as percentage of cases cleared, etc.

8. Letters of commendation received concerning the officer.

9. Communications and letters of complaint received concerning the officer.

10. Citations for distinguished service in line of duty.

11. Record of all disciplinary measures addressed to the officer, including reprimands, warnings, suspensions, dismissal, etc.

12. Telegrams, letters and other communications inquiring about the officer.

13. Record of equipment issued to the officer.

14. All other information which combined together in one file will furnish a complete personnel biography of the individual officer.

The value of a well ordered personnel record system to the Chief Executive and his Personnel Officer is not to be underestimated. During promotional examinations, as well as on all other occasions where the personnel factor is involved, it is indispensable.

The Police Salary Structure

It has been previously emphasized that the character and calibre of police service for years to come are determined largely at the intake today. This is the fact of life and it carries with it important implications in terms of the police salary structure.

---

[17] Personnel records are usually held on file in the office of the civil service commission or central personnel agency. Most departments, however, find it expedient to maintain a supplementary personnel record system of their own.

One of the major administrative errors of local government has been to handcuff the police salary structure to that of the fire department. This mistake is based upon the illusion that police and fire protection are functions of much the same nature. Superficially, there may be some resemblance. Both police officers and firemen are engaged in the protection of life and property. But there the analogy ends. The day-to-day problems of the two departments have little in common. The police deal almost wholly with human relations while the work of the firemen is largely related to physical property.

Fosdick stated as early as 1921: [18]

"The problems of fire extinguishment are physically definable and the work of fire prevention is highly specialized and easily reduced to mechanical standards; the uniformed force of the fire division deals with material elements. The police force deals largely with human relations; its problems are to a certain extent intangible. Firemen work in groups under the immediate direction of their superior officers; they respond to a fire in their properly assigned places and employ chemicals and other equipment as they are ordered by their officers in charge. The policeman's work is done largely on his own initiative, prompted by his own judgment.

"Policies affecting fire administration relate almost entirely to the financial aspects of providing equipment and men that are necessary in the light of definitely known insurance rates and fire hazards. Policies of police administration involve social and moral needs which are far removed from such factors as the storage of inflammables, hose and water pressure and building regulations. There is no divided opinion about the desirability of putting out fires; there is considerable room for division of opinion to how much money the city should pay for the intangible returns of crime prevention to be achieved through an enlarged and better equipped police force, or even as to how far the police may go in curbing individual liberties in their efforts to prevent crime. Thus, although these two forces are similarly organized, the objectives of their work are found to be wholly different and their methods of procedure widely dissimilar, while the values of their work are appraised on entirely different bases."

Public support for relative equality in police-fire compensation rates is often influenced by:

1. Both are uniformed services.

2. The public image of both services is good, except that the police exert more control and therefore irritate more people than do firemen.

3. In many of the larger cities, the policemen and firemen have been closely associated in their requests for improved wages, fringe benefits, working conditions and similar matters.

[18] Raymond B. Fosdick, *Police Administration*, Cleveland Foundation Survey of Criminal Justice in Cleveland, 1921, p. 15.

Danielson found in a study of police-fire salary structures in Berkeley, California, that a patrolman should have a higher pay rate than a firefighter. He held that the impetus for breaking the traditional equality of patrolman-fireman salaries frequently comes from the greater difficulty in selecting and retaining qualified police applicants. It is common for municipalities to find a smaller percentage of police applicants who are successful in all phases of the examination process, as compared with fire applicants. Admittedly, if this difficulty in recruiting were true for firefighters and not for police officers, the argument would then support a pay differential in favor of firemen.

Police selection standards include rigid physical requirements, intensive background investigation and penetrating oral and written examinations. Therefore, Danielson concludes, entrance pay and incentive increases must be sufficiently high to attract large numbers of well qualified applicants to the police entrance examination room.[19]

A 1964 survey of 129 Michigan municipalities over 4,000 in population by the Michigan Municipal League, disclosed 36 communities with a pay differential between patrolman and firefighter. Twenty-eight cities have a higher pay maximum for patrolman, two have a higher maximum for firefighter, and six have starting rates which differ but the maximums are the same. Since the special salary adjustment for patrolmen in Berkeley in 1963, other California cities have instituted police-fire salary differentials. In Fresno, San Diego, San Jose and Santa Monica, salaries for patrolmen and for higher ranks were increased from 2.5 percent to 5.4 percent above that of firemen. In Phoenix, Arizona, the police officers salary was increased in 1955 5 percent above the firefighter's compensation.

It is undoubtedly true that this linkage of police and fire compensation plans has embarrassed the development of police administration in the United States. Based upon a comparison of the duties and responsibilities of the two services, one comes to the conclusion that personnel resources equal to the complex demands of modern police service are unobtainable at the salary levels prevailing in fire departments. Fosdick's suggestion of the differences in functions and responsibilities in the two areas clearly indicates the inequity of any attempt to associate these two branches of the public service within the same salary structure. As professionalization of the police proceeds and the means for measurement of municipal activities are perfected, the professional distance between the two services may be expected to increase.

[19] Berrodin, Eugene F., *Should Policemen and Firemen Get the Same Salary?*, PUBLIC MANAGEMENT, January 1965.

The technical nature of every phase of police service is such that police administrators must be in a position to compete with business and industry for the best human material. This means very simply and very directly that the police salary structure must be competitive. It must be sufficiently high to attract candidates to the entrance examination room who are qualified to meet the exacting demands of police service in a modern social order.

In recent years, police salary structures have moved generally upward. In sixteen typical American cities, the average starting salary for a patrolman was $564 per month in the late 1960's. The average salary after three years of service was $658 per month. Police salaries are higher in those departments noted for their professional standards of performance. In cities along the Pacific Coast, police salaries have advanced more than in other sections of the country. However, the trend toward improved compensation is clearly observable throughout the United States.

The foregoing considerations have important implications for the police in every city and community, regardless of size. The mobility of the criminal population today means simply that the exposure to criminal attack has increased on a scale that merits serious concern. This, together with the growing complexity of the traffic problem, places a high premium on the quality of police personnel and police performance.

The officials of local government would do well to re-examine their thinking in this respect with the view of adjusting police salaries upward to the point where they will be consistent with the quality and quantity of work to be done. Mounting crime rates, together with the growing demands of traffic management, are grounds for sober reflection on the part of these officials. They are under obligation to the community and its security to see to it as the first order of business that the personnel resources of the police are equal to the urgent needs of our time.

Chapter 7

THE POLICE TRAINING FUNCTION

In-Service Training

Even after police candidates are selected by scientific methods, the police structure will continue to remain unsound as long as it is generally assumed that a person with any type of training or with none at all, is qualified to perform police duties. An in-service police training school, staffed by the most competent officers available and operating continuously the year around, is an indispensable feature of every modern police department. Especially is this true in view of the fact that the police recruit must for some time to come be accepted in the raw, unprepared for the rigorous and exacting responsibilities of police service. Unlike workers in health, engineering and other professions, he must be trained on the job at public expense.

In-service training has found expression in the American police services in a wide variety of forms. Until about 1915, the old American concept that there is "more law in the end of a nightstick than in all the law books," was the operating criterion of the police officer. Any idea that a policeman should "go to school" would have been received with both astonishment and skepticism. However, the police began to feel the impact of new and unexpected forces. The appearance of Fosdick's notable work [1] directed attention to the difference between the efficiency of the European police and the obsolete methods of our police forces. The stress that he placed upon personnel and training in accounting for this disparity placed a new emphasis upon police problems in the United States. There was no city of importance in Europe that did not provide some form of systematic training for police recruits. Continental police schools were well staffed and equipped. The police recruit in Vienna was sent to school for two years, and his responsibilities after training were insignificant when compared with those of the American policeman. The training school for the police of Rome, with its facilities for scientific and technical instruction was second to none.[2] Fosdick's influence was supplemented by changes in the character of police service which began shortly after the turn of the century to place a premium upon talent and ability in the performance of police duties.

[1] Raymond B. Fosdick, *American Police Systems*, New York, The Century Company, 1916.

[2] S. Ottolenghi, *The Italian Police Upper School and Its Technical Services*, Polygraphic Institute of the Italian State Library, Rome, 1933.

Preparation for police service, like that in other professional fields, had its beginnings in a form of apprenticeship. Without previous training of any kind whatsoever, the new recruit was instructed to don a uniform and a gun and go to work. The formalities were quite simple and elementary. As a freshman in the school of experience, he began to learn what he could at public expense through a process of trial and error, with the errors predominating. Personal instruction began when it became the practice to send the recruit out with an experienced policeman. In an increasing number of departments the new officer was detailed for duty with a veteran as a sort of conditioning process. This procedure adapted itself nicely to the almost universal system of double officer patrol. The length of this apprenticeship varied from a few days to several months, and the recruit was then considered a trained man.

It is safe to say that at least 85 percent of American police officers today are the product of this form of training program. Let no one underestimate the value of experience. Regardless of training, it has no substitute. The few outstanding police officials in this country today are graduates of on-the-job training. On their own initiative, these men of superior talent and ability supplemented their meager training by intensive study and application to the job, rising to the top of their profession through a natural process of selection. This is the training history of those few men who have achieved distinction in the American police field, and it explains why they can be numbered on the fingers of the hands. The contributions which these same men, as well as others, could have made if they had received adequate training challenges the imagination and suggests the dimensions of the police training project today. The voices of these same individuals, denied the opportunity for career preparation, can be heard distinctly today urging that professional training requirements be recognized in the police field.

As early as 1931, the Wickersham Commission found in a survey of 383 cities that only 20 percent conducted police training schools for the new recruit.[3] In the majority of cities, particularly the smaller communities, there was not even a pretext of training. In the counties, and smaller cities and communities, the Commission reported that the assumption of badge, revolver and the authority of the law, had no prerequisite whatsoever, in terms of police training and police experience.

Inspired by the Federal Bureau of Investigation, which dramatized the need, set standards and provided curricula and instructors, the police have made significant strides during the past thirty years in the wide-

---

[3] National Commission on Law Observance and Enforcement, *Report on the Police*, U. S. Government Printing Office, 1931, p. 19.

spread development of formal recruit training programs.   As late as 1965, a survey of 1,352 cities conducted by the International City Managers Association, found that 1,135 police departments were operating some type of recruit training program for their officers.

A recent survey of 269 police departments by the National League of Cities, conducted in 1966, reported that 97 percent of the departments surveyed were engaged in formal police recruit training.   But another survey of 4,000 police departments in 1965 by the International Association of Chiefs of Police revealed that 85 percent of the officers appointed were sent into the field prior to their recruit training.[4]

The Departmental Training School

Today, it is taken for granted that in every police department, provision should be made for:

1. The organization and establishment of a police training school within the Department under the immediate supervision of the staff commanding officer and his subordinates.

2. Organization of the faculty from among the most competent officers of the department, in addition to enlisting the services of lay experts in specialized fields of knowledge.   The mature experience of veterans in the department should not be overlooked, whether ranking officers or not.

3. Continuous operation of the school and the formulation of a compulsory attendance schedule.

4. Establishment of an organized curriculum, supported by textbooks, outlines, syllabi, lectures, discussions and demonstrations with scheduled examinations, followed by posting of grades to personnel records.   Courses of instruction should cover the full range of police duties, responsibilities, methods and techniques.

5. Establishment of a police library.

In-Service Training Curricula

Experience has shown that it is necessary to provide an in-service instructional program at five different levels:

1. Recruit training (required of all new appointees)
   a. Beginning
   b. Intermediate
   c. Advanced

[4] The President's Commission on Law Enforcement and the Administration of Justice, *Task Force Report, the Police*, U. S. Government Printing Office, 1967, p. 138.

2. Refresher

3. Divisional

    a. Patrol Division

    b. Detective Division

    c. Records Division

    d. Crime Prevention Division

    e. Vice Division

    f. Traffic Division

4. Supervisory and command officers

5. Administrative officers

Recruit Training

It is important that all new appointees to the department be put through the recruit training program. The beginning phase is a period of indoctrination. It includes instruction in the origin and nature of police work, general police responsibilities under the federal and state constitutions, federal and state laws, and the city charter. Attention is directed during this period to the history of the police and the elements of police organization and administration. The ideals of police service and the ethics of the profession should be given strong emphasis. The new recruit learns the importance of public relations in this branch of the public service. The line power concept of police operations and the patrol system are analyzed, and careful instruction is given in the techniques of patrol, as well as in patrol strategy and tactics. He must know what to do and how to do it in all types of dangerous situations. Tested procedures in the approach to an armed criminal under a great variety of circumstances, transportation of criminals, handling of crowds, gatherings, parades, disorderly crowds and mobs, disaster operations, raids, surveillance and other related subjects are presented in detail.

The recruit becomes acquainted with the art and science of criminal investigation and comes to understand something of the potential evidence resources of every crime scene. The services of the laboratory and the expert are explained so that he will know how and when and where to request the assistance of these technicians in the solution of cases assigned to him for investigation.

It is essential that all new appointees to the department be exposed to the recruit training program. The course content of this program is a matter of the greatest importance. It is now widely accepted that the following course subjects should be included in the recruit training school:

Required Courses

1. Classroom Notetaking.
2. The Role of Law Enforcement.
3. Police-Community Relations.
4. Police Ethics.
5. Racial and Minority Groups.
6. Laws of Arrest, Search and Seizure, Constitutional Guarantees.
7. Code of Criminal Procedure, Criminal Law.
8. Vehicle and Traffic Law.
9. Traffic Control.
10. Traffic Accident Investigation.
11. Laws of Evidence.
12. Evidence Resources in a Criminal Case, including the Crime Scene Search.
13. Collection, Care, Identification and Preservation of Evidence.
14. Court Organization and Procedure.
15. Courtroom Demeanor and Testifying.
16. Basic Criminal Investigation.
17. Notetaking and Report Writing.
18. Interviews, Interrogation, Admissions, Statements.
19. The Patrol Function.
20. Care and Use of Firearms.
21. Defensive Tactics.
22. Techniques and Mechanics of Arrest.
23. Emergency Aid to Persons.
24. Recognition and Handling of Abnormal Persons.
25. Juvenile Offender Laws, Juvenile Court, Handling of Juveniles.
26. Field Notetaking and Crime Scene Recording.
27. Crowd and Riot Control.
28. Use of Police Radio and Teletype.

Elective Courses

1. Special Investigative Techniques—Gambling, Narcotics, Prostitution.
2. Driver Training.
3. Care and Maintenance of Police Equipment.
4. Administration of Criminal Justice.
5. Fingerprint Identification.
6. Jail Procedures.
7. Jurisdiction of Other Law Enforcement Agencies.
8. The Police Records System.
9. Powers and Duties of the Sheriff.
10. Raid Techniques, Stake-Outs, Surveillance.
11. Scientific Aids—The Crime Laboratory.
12. Police-Press Relations.
13. Transportation of Prisoners.

The basic elements of criminal law and procedure, together with the law of arrest and the law of evidence are an important part of this phase of the neophyte's training program. The general administration of justice and its pattern of organization are presented. He learns that the police record system is the mainspring of the police department. Through an analysis of its functions and facilities he becomes familiar with its value to the department and to him as an individual officer in the discharge of his duties. He also learns at the same time why it is important that his reports be accurate, if the collected data of the records division are to be significant.

Also included in the recruit's training is a study of the police communication system as the nerve center of a crime fighting organization. The complex nature of traffic problems and the police approach to their solution occupy an important place. Further, the aspiring young officer discovers that the night stick is no longer the first resort of the police and he is acquainted with the shift in police emphasis from enforcement to prevention as the major strategy in crime control. This list represents only a fractional part of the total training that must be administered to the newcomer before he can be entrusted with the discharge of any form of police duty.

The recruit training program through the beginning phase requires at least three months full time, eight hours per day and six days per week. At the end of this period each recruit should be assigned to an experienced patrolman under the immediate supervision of a Patrol Sergeant, and he should accompany the patrolman on his regular tour of duty for a period of three months, during which time he should begin attending classes in the intermediate phase of the recruit training program. At the termination of this conditioning period on patrol, he should undergo rotation at approximately one-month intervals to the Record Division, Detective Division, Traffic Division, Crime Prevention Division and other functional units in the organization. The rotation plan also should include assignment to the administrative offices for a short period.

Approximately one year after his conditional appointment, the new recruit may be a candidate for divisional assignment if he has survived the rigorous training program and has received satisfactory ratings by superior officers. It should be remembered that the recruit training period is a part of the entrance examination process. The recruit is on pobation during this time and he may be "screened out" if he fails to meet the standards of the department in any way. The recruit training period provides an excellent opportunity to discover disqualifying characteristics that escaped detection during previous stages of the examination. The reasons for elimination at this point are as numerous as there are individuals. Domestic discord in the home, dishonesty, insubordination, infidelity, lack of interest and enthusiasm for the job, critical attitude toward superior officers, appearance of undiscovered temperamental defects, drinking, lack of punctuality, inability to get along with associates and poor attention to personal appearance are typical of traits whose degree and permanence are difficult to measure on any form of entrance examination test thus far devised. However, it would be difficult for the recruit to conceal these defects for a period of one year, while working under pressure and under the close scrutiny and observation of superior officers.

The new officer should enter upon his assignment to a division with a comprehensive grasp of the department and its program as a whole. In addition to formal training of rigorous proportions, the opportunity has been presented to him to become familiar with the functions, procedures and problems of all the organizational units in the department. If he has passed all these tests he is in a position to become a member of a winning team. Immediately following divisional assignment, he is automatically enrolled in the "refresher" phase of the department's training program, which provides for review and amplification of subjects previously studied, as well as the presentation of new developments in police procedure. Since he can never hope to master completely even a fractional part of the field and its procedures in an in-service training program, the recruit's enrollment in the refresher school is continuous until retirement from the service. The refresher schedule of instruction can be presented on a less intensive schedule than in the case of the recruit training program.

Divisional assignment involves the necessity for specialized training beyond that provided in the recruit training period; it is concerned with the facilities, functions, procedures and techniques peculiar to a particular division. The necessity for divisional instruction can be appreciated when the functions and procedures of a particular division are analyzed. Thus, workers in the Police Records Division are confronted with tasks that are altogether different in nature from those of any other division in the organization. They require distinctly specialized training if any degree of competence is to be attained. The ordinary qualifications of a skilled clerk or typist fail completely when measured by the nature of the work to be performed in this important division.

The necessity for specialized training is equally apparent upon assignment to the Patrol Division. A recruit training program limited to one year could not possibly prepare a man for competent service in this division. It therefore becomes necessary to superimpose upon this preliminary period of instruction, thorough specialized training covering the skills and information that are peculiar to this important branch of the service, and to it alone. The situation is the same when the new recruit is assigned to the Traffic Division, Crime Prevention Division, Detective Division, Communications Division, or to Vice Operations. Divisional instruction on an intensive basis is an indispensable part of a police in-service training program.

Supervisory and Command Officers

The operation of the law of the span of control makes it mandatory upon the chief executive to delegate responsibility and power to subordinates in a heirarchy of several levels of authority. In police organization, the arrangement provides in a descending scale for Captains, Lieutenants and Sergeants. The size of the work load in the larger departments and the need for another level of administration calls for a further division of the executive at higher levels by the introduction of one or more ranks above that of Captain. The top administrative ranks immediately below that of the chief executive are referred to variously as Assistant Chief of Police, Deputy Chief of Police, or Inspector of Police.

For in-service training purposes, supervisory and command officers include Captains, Lieutenants and Sergeants and it is necessary to provide for these officers a specialized program of instruction dealing with the principles and techniques of command and supervision. Instruction of supervisory and command personnel should be conducted by the conference technique as distinguished from the classroom method employed in recruit training.

The content of the instructional program should be based upon the qualifications and duties of Captains, Lieutenants and Sergeants; job analyses covering these positions; nature of leadership, psychology and conditions of effective leadership; the functions and techniques of leadership and supervision, and the elements of personnel administration, all presented in their relation to the problems of police organization and administration. Army manuals will prove invaluable in this phase of the in-service training program and the departmental faculty should be supplemented by the frequent appearance at those conferences of supervisory and command officers from the United States Army. These arrangements can be easily made. Military authorities have always shown the police the highest degree of cooperation. A number of recent works dealing with the selection and training for foremen in industry also afford an excellent basis for this program of instruction.[5]

Departmental administrative officers should participate personally in the training of supervisory and command officers. They should be supplemented by lay experts in other fields who can be invited in as instructors. Emulating the methods developed by the Army War College, tactical field problems and their solution should occupy an important position in the supervisory and command curriculum.

General Pershing when asked to identify the most important rank in army organization replied without hesitation—the Sergeant! The same can be said with reference to police organization. No administration can achieve its objectives without effective supervision of men and their performance. Every person is as lazy as circumstances permit. Intelligent supervision activates the constructive drives in the individual; there is no known substitute for it. The rank of Sergeant is the point at which direct supervision of the officer occurs, and the grade of supervision delivered by him exercises an important influence upon the efficiency of the department. Hence, it is necessary that a large part of the supervisory and command training be focused upon the preparation of Sergeants for their work.[6]

---

[5] For example, see Harold B. Maynard, *Effective Foremanship*, McGraw-Hill Book Company, New York, 1941; Charles R. Allen, *The Foreman and His Job*, J. B. Lippincott Company, Philadelphia, 1922; Glenn Lion Gerdiner, *Practical Foremanship*, Industrial Education Series, McGraw-Hill Book Company, New York, 1925; A. L. Kress, *Foremanship Fundamentals*, McGraw-Hill Book Company, 1942.

[6] See B. W. Gocke, *Police Sergeants Manual*, O. W. Smith Book Company, Los Angeles, 1943. This work will prove indispensable in this phase of the departmental training program.

Administrative Officers

Training is no less important for the highest administrative officers in the department than for the first line supervisors. There is no human effort more complex and technical than organization and administration, whatever the enterprise may be. The chief executive of a police department is confronted with a technical job of management requiring a very high order of intelligence and administrative ability. But to this must be added a high order of administrative training. It is absurd to assume that, given leadership qualities and an extended experience in the department, a Captain suddenly elevated to the position of chief will meet his new responsibilities with any degree of success. The expenditure of every dollar in a police budget where it will yield the greatest social return requires not only intelligence but executive training as well. There is a wide gap between mere leadership ability and administrative "know how" that must be bridged. The best authorities are not in complete agreement concerning the techniques of successful administration.[7] It is hardly possible, therefore, that the police chief executive can expect to measure up to his responsibilities without some mastery of the known principles that have been developed and tested in the field of organization and administration.

As in the case of supervisory and command officers, this phase of the in-service training program is presented by the conference method or on a consultation basis. Again, military commanding officers whose training and experience in the management of men on a large scale place them in a position to counsel with the voice of authority, are especially valuable for the purpose. Almost every cardinal principle of organization and administration has been tested by Military Science under operating conditions. The principles of strategy, tactics, patrol, command, organization, span of control, combat, communications, and intelligence are among the contributions that police administration has inherited from military science. Successful heads of business organizations also can make important contributions to this phase of the program.

An attempt has been made in the foregoing pages to formulate the specifications for an ideal departmental in-service training program, which would approach as far as possible the needs of the service. Unfortunately, if these recommendations were implemented in full by any but the largest American police departments, the costs in terms of man-

---

[7] Gulick and Urwick, *Papers on the Science of Administration*, Institute of Public Administration, Columbia University, 1937. Also see Waldo, Dwight, *The Administrative State*, The Ronald Press Company, New York, 1948, p. 227.

power, time and equipment would be prohibitive and altogether out of proportion to the results. However, anything less would fail to make impressive gains in the effort to prepare untrained personnel for duty. Experience has shown that even four years of specific preparation at the university level, with the total resources of a major educational institution geared to the task, represent too short a time in which to prepare a man for entry into police service. Hence, with the best in-service training facilities obtainable, it would be impossible to impart to a man more than a fractional part of the skills and information that he must have as the indispensable tools of the profession. The limitations of the departmental training school, therefore, argue against placing sole reliance upon it as a total solution to the police training problem.

Regional In-Service Training Schools

The almost total lack of any departmental training program in smaller cities and the failure of some larger departments to inaugurate adequate training programs have prompted the organization in scattered instances of in-service training schools on a regional basis. Occasionally, metropolitan police departments have extended their training facilities to members of the smaller police forces in suburban areas as a measure of self-defense. It was realized that the crime rate of a large city is affected to a considerable extent by crime in the surrounding territory; mobility of the criminal population suggests the expediency of a common program. A centralized school where police personnel in a given area are exposed to the same pattern of instruction is an important step in this direction. It also serves the purpose of promoting coordination in blockades and other operations which involve large scale cooperation over an extended area in the emergency. Under this arrangement, a few selected officers attend the metropolitan police school from communities within a radius of from fifty to one hundred miles. The sessions usually are of from three to six days' duration.

The Federal Bureau of Investigation has for a number of years placed at the disposal of local law enforcement agencies the superb training facilities of that organization. Under the name of the National Police Academy, this program is available to selected officers from police departments in every part of the United States. The objective of this school is to train selected men of special ability and promise as instructors, so that they may return to their respective organizations and impart the training that they receive to their associates. The police officer fortunate enough to attend the National Police Academy is exposed to a comprehensive curriculum requiring residence of three months in Washington. The Federal Bureau of Investigation also has conducted a series of regional law enforcement conferences in all of the states, which are in the nature of short training schools for police personnel. Such conferences usually are scheduled at central points and officers attend them from the surrounding area. These sessions usually require three days in addition to the officer's travel time. Some state police organizations have also made their training facilities available to local law enforcement officers through the organization of regional training schools.

The resources of the state have also been applied to police in-service training through other channels. Texas Agricultural and Mechanical College, Pennsylvania State University, Iowa State University, University of Oklahoma and other educational institutions have made notable contributions in the organization of in-service training facilities on a zone or regional basis. In California, a state-wide peace officers training program has functioned vigorously for a number of years under the auspices of the Bureau of Trade and Industrial Education of the California State Board of Education.

In practically all state-projected in-service programs it is significant to observe that the training resources of universities and colleges have been brought into play on an expanding scale. Of unusual interest in this respect is the program at the University of Louisville. Financed by grants from the General Education Board of the Rockefeller Foundation and the Carnegie Corporation of New York, Southern Police Institute at that institution offers three twelve week terms a year in the fundamentals of police procedure to police officers of the southern region of the United States. Students selected receive a stipend covering living expenses and a travel allowance. The course of instruction includes such subjects as investigation, identification, patrol, communications, records, administration, law, crime prevention, human relations, and police problems of the South.

In the state of Washington, the University of Washington, Washington State University, the Washington State Patrol and the State Board for Vocational Training, pooled their resources toward the organization and administration of a state-wide police training program designed to reach every police officer in the state. The program contemplated a central training school for new police recruits, a series of zone schools scheduled to blanket the state, a school for specialists, a school for supervisory and command personnel, administrators' conferences and other related activities. But a change in administration at the University of Washington brought these plans to an untimely end. A faculty committee took over the reins of administration at that institution in the interim pending the selection of a new President.

One of the policies adopted by the committee was to abolish activities of the university that were not strictly academic in nature, in order to divert budget funds into salary increases for the faculty. The projected police training program was one of the casualties.

In general, regional in-service training schools have not measured up to the results anticipated by their sponsors and their failure to meet the training needs of the police becomes increasingly manifest. The short sessions of from three days to three months are inadequate. It is physically impossible to cover more than a small fraction of the field within such a short time limit. Furthermore, "graduates" of these regional schools have occasionally returned to their respective departments to encounter sales resistance as the reward for their industry. Few departmental schools have been established as a result of the teacher training program. The added prestige of the returning officer was in some instances regarded by the Chief and his immediate subordinates as a potential threat to their positions, with the natural result that further constructive developments were stymied. By the normal process of selection, however, many of these enterprising young officers have ascended the promotional ladder to administrative positions.

The Limitations of In-Service Training

In-service training in the American police field is on trial. Thus far, it has failed to train policemen just as it failed to meet the training requirements of pharmacy, medicine, law, engineering, and the other professions. Despite twenty years of experience, it is estimated on the basis of personal observation, that less than one per cent of the personnel of American police forces has been exposed to any form of in-service training worthy of the name. Members of this comparatively small group have received only a very limited and abridged instruction. The *school of experience* is still the training ground for the American policeman.

In-service training is costly. In one American police department the investment in training plant and equipment totaled $11,500, and the annual cost of training operations was approximately $30,000.[8] The training program was an extremely limited one. If it were expanded to meet the standards set forth in the foregoing pages, the annual cost of training operations would approximate $50,000, in addition to increases in capital investment. Between eighty and ninety per cent of the American police budget is already traceable to personnel—

[8] Includes salaries of instructional personnel, supplies and general operating expense, loss of on-duty time while attending school sessions and estimate of increase in property losses as a result of reduced personnel strength.

salaries alone. Under the law of diminishing returns there would seem to be a point beyond which we cannot go in training men at public expense for the public services.

In-service training for the police as presently conceived is not likely to survive. Projected to overcome mistakes made at the recruiting stage, it was called upon to accomplish a task for which it was never designed. In-service training was never intended, nor can it be expected to train a man professionally for a given field. The fact that it yielded some measure of success in the trades suggested the assumption that it was the answer to the training needs of the police profession. The basic function of in-service training is to keep professionally trained men abreast of new developments in a field. To expect more is to court continued failure. The experience of the police with apprenticeship and in-service training is not a singular one. As previously indicated, other professions endured the same growing pains in the early period of their development before university standards of preparation were established.

At best, in-service training in its present form can serve only as a temporary stop-gap during a period of transition in which other solutions are gradually beginning to appear. Neither the health officer, city engineer or prosecuting attorney asks the state or the city to pay him a salary while he is attending a training school in preparation for his work; he acquires the desired education in advance and at his own expense.

But, there was good news for police training in the offing. The facilities are potentially available for an effective police training program in this country and the police field itself, is in general agreement concerning the curriculum content of an in-service training program. The problem is—how to organize it and bring it to the doorstep of every police officer in the nation. The answers appear to be coming into focus and at an accelerated tempo during the past two decades.

A New Era

The American police service has now entered a new era in terms of its most vital resource—personnel. Escaping the attention of most observers, the time is now close at hand when the best in police practice and procedure will be brought to the doorstep of every police officer in the nation.

The new era finds expression on two major fronts—*legislation at the state level prescribing minimum selection and training standards for entry into police service, and the emergence of professional police training curricula in the universities and colleges of this country.* Both developments sharpen the focus on the American police field as a career service.

Mandated Pre-Service Police Training

There is a definite trend toward the passage of legislation at the state level establishing mandatory minimum training standards for entry into police service. The New York State Legislature in 1959, enacted into law the *Municipal Police Training Council Act,* which established a Council to formulate and put into operation a mandatory municipal police training program. This new State program has been coordinated with the police training effort previously supported for several years as a cooperative program of the New York State Sheriffs' Association, the New York State Association of Chiefs of Police and the Federal Bureau of Investigation. Eight public officials with professional experience in law enforcement were appointed by Governor Nelson A. Rockefeller to the State's municipal Police Training Council as an advisory and policy-making body.[9]

The Council completed the necessary study and research for an 80-hour minimum Basic Training Course consisting of seventeen separate subjects. Thereafter, as specified in the Municipal Police Training Council Act, all police officers appointed from the date of July 1, 1960, would be required to satisfactorily complete the Basic Course as a condition of permanent appointment. The first year of operation saw the completion of thirty-five Basic Schools of Instruction throughout the state and the awarding of certificates to eight hundred twenty-two municipal police officers. It is significant that these eight hundred twenty-two graduates are employed by two hundred sixty-seven different municipalities or agencies within the State, indicating that the benefits of this police training program have been broadly dispersed throughout every area of New York State. Many departments had but a single graduate while some of the larger departments had as many as 45, 49 and 78 police officers completing the course.

At least one school was held in each of the twelve training zones outside of New York City during the first year of operation, thus making the Basic Training Course available to new police officers every-

[9] See *Municipal Police Training in New York State,* 1961. Copies may be obtained by addressing Orrell A. York, Executive Director, Municipal Police Training Council, 155 Washington Avenue, Albany 10, New York.

where in the State. According to the provisions of the enabling legislation, allowance was made for the exemption of cities of one million or more population when, in the opinion of the Council, their standards of police training are higher than the minimum requirements of the statewide program. All other municipal police agencies are covered by the provisions of the Act.

It will be noted that the minimum police training standards program in New York is mandatory. In other words, an applicant must complete satisfactorily a basic police training course before he can enter police service. It is *mandated* police training, by state mandate.

As of October 23, 1960, legislation passed by the California State Legislature under the title, *Law Enforcement Standards Training Act,* went into effect. The Act establishes minimum police training standards for California peace officers and provides for the certification of schools where this training may be obtained. The program is not mandatory; it is organized on a voluntary basis. The governing Commission on Peace Officer Standards and Training will allocate to cities and counties which voluntarily agree to adhere to the Commission's standards for hiring and training, moneys from the Peace Officers Training Fund, covering one-half of salaries of peace officers who participate in this training program, in addition to certain living expenses.

Significantly, the individual applicant may substitute for the prescribed basic training course, satisfactory completion of a minimum of 60 credit hours in an undergraduate police science major leading to a degree at any university or college certified by the Commission.

Today, in California, police training that meets the standards of the Commission is state-wide; it blankets the state and exceeds by far any to be found elsewhere in the nation, with the exception of the state of New York. In California by 1966, 98 percent of the population in that state was being served by police departments which adhered to the required minimum standards for police training.[10]

As of June 3, 1961, state legislation became effective in New Jersey, prescribing minimum training standards for entry into police service. The training is undertaken during the probationary period of one year and prior to permanent appointment as a police officer. The program is organized on a voluntary basis. Similarly in Oregon, state legislation was passed, effective June 1, 1961, creating an Advisory Board on Police Standards and Training, recommending minimum physical, emotional, intellectual and moral standards, and minimum

---

[10] The President's Commission on Law Enforcement and Administration of Justice, *Task Force Report: The Police,* 1967, p. 217.

police training standards.   Here again, the participation of police agencies in the program is on a voluntary basis.   However, the Board received in a comparatively short time favorable responses from half the police departments in the state, indicating they either (1) already had in effect standards equivalent to or higher than the minimum requirements recommended by the Board, or (2) highly favor the recommendations of the Board and will make every effort to voluntarily comply.[11]

In 1963, Oklahoma joined the expanding list of those states where minimum police selection and training standards have been adopted. By 1969, legislation at the state level prescribing minimum police selection and training standards had been enacted in nine states.   In a number of other states, similar legislation is under consideration.   It is now apparent that this development in the American police field marks a new milestone in police in-service training.   Apparently, it is just a matter of time until every state in the nation will have established minimum standards for the selection and training of police officers. This means that police best practice and procedure in the training of personnel is on the way toward making total contact with the field, including especially the smaller police departments of this country.

As an important step in this direction, in 1966, a Model Police Standards Council Act was drafted by the Advisory Council on Police Training and Education, and the Professional Standards Division of the International Association of Chiefs of Police.[12]   It offers to the states a legislative model or pattern which can be followed in the establishment of minimum standards for the selection and training of police personnel.

Police departments and state police associations in those states where such enabling legislation has not yet been passed, should make strong and effective contact with the members of their legislatures and call their attention to these developments.   Such action will accelerate the day when police personnel in police departments throughout the nation will have the benefit of adequate police selection and training facilities.

It should be emphasized at this point that the recruit training period is an integral part of the entrance examination process.   The recruit is on probation during this time and he may be "screened out" if he fails to meet the standards of the department in any way.   The recruit train-

---

[11] Copies of legislation passed by the foregoing states may be obtained by addressing the Office of the Governor in each state.

[12] See Appendix B—*Model Police Standards Council Act Drafted by the International Association of Chiefs of Police.*

ing period provides an excellent opportunity to uncover disqualifying characteristics that escaped detection during previous stages of the examination.

The foregoing comments have been concerned primarily with the development of police recruit training schools. The same state-sponsored facilities can also be addressed to refresher training, the training of supervisory and command personnel and administrative officers. Where personnel strength is large enough to justify the operation of a departmental training school, much of this training may be delivered within the framework of the organization itself.

Roll Call Training. This type of training is presented during the roll call period at the beginning of a shift and just before the officers go out on duty. Roll Call training was originally developed in the Los Angeles Police Department, where the opinion is unanimous that it has proved to be an effective training device. It does not replace the rigorous program of the Los Angeles Police Training Academy. In implementing this program, the Roll Call period was extended from 15 to 30 minutes in order to set aside 15 minutes for the Daily Roll Call training period.

The training or orientation is presented by supervisory and command officers. However, this does not rule out regular staff and line officers who by virtue of their special assignment, experience or qualifications, may have important contributions to make to the program. Following are a few typical subjects presented at Roll Call training which illustrate the wide range of problems that can be discussed and analyzed: [13]

How to use the telephone.
How to use the field notebook.
How to advise citizens on crime prevention techniques.

[13] Under the title, *Roll Call Training Bulletins*, the Los Angeles Police Department has published in two volumes a complete presentation of its Roll Call training program. They may be obtained from Charles C. Thomas, Publisher, 301–327 East Lawrence Avenue, Springfield, Illinois.

Note—The Professional Standards Division of the International Association of Chiefs of Police has made available TRAINING KEYS—A SEMI-MONTHLY PUBLICATION, an invaluable aid in police training programs. They are loose leaf training bulletins prepared by the IACP that may be used for roll-call training, formalized classroom instruction or individual study. The various issues cover such subjects as recent Supreme Court decisions, current patrol and investigative techniques, principles of organization and management, and many other important subjects. The effectiveness and general acceptance of this program is demonstrated by the rapid growth of the service. Presently, over 2,000 law enforcement administrators in the 50

How to testify effectively in Court.
Lie detector tests and preliminary interrogation.
Care and use of firearms.
Combat shooting.
Operation of mobile radio equipment.
How to respond to a "459 There Now" call.
How to proceed with a preliminary burglary investigation.
How to answer an "ADT" call.
Current criminal emergencies.
How to handle calls involving dead bodies.
How to recognize stolen vehicles.
How to work a stake-out.
How to apprehend prowlers.
How to make vagrancy arrests.
How to determine intoxication.
How to handle mentally ill persons.
Techniques in the use of tear gas.
Disaster operations.
The use of force.
Self-defense tactics.
How to preserve evidence at the scene of a crime.

Teaching Methods. Whatever the form of police training, qualified instructors with demonstrated teaching ability are a prerequisite. In the presentation of technical subjects, it is excellent practice to go outside to the professions and nearby universities and colleges for special instructors. The Federal Bureau of Investigation has long used civilian instructors in the National Police Academy as a part of its visiting faculty. For example, in a typical year (1966), the following civilian instructors taught in this outstanding training program: a professor of psychology, a sociologist, a chief clinical psychiatrist, four judges from various levels of the Court system, a professor of history, a physicist, a chemist, a superintendent of schools, and a representative from the news media.

Most training courses are taught almost exclusively by the lecture method although professional training directors and educators recognize

states and in four Canadian provinces are ordering the Training Key for all of their sworn personnel. The Catalog number of this publication is 70–50.
The IACP also made available in August of 1970 Catalog number 70–100 POLICE FILM CATALOGUE, the first comprehensive catalogue of films which relate to law enforcement. Over 500 films produced in the last ten years are described in terms of content, effectiveness and availability. Categories of films included are those on police procedures, criminal justice, community relations, highway safety and narcotics control.

that this method does have some limitations. In a police training program, as in any training program, it is necessary to keep in mind some of the basic elements of the learning process.

Learning is in large part a communication of ideas from one person to another. Consequently, the senses of the learner must be brought into play. The decision on which method of instruction to use is somewhat simplified by the fact that of all the senses, sight is by far the most effective. Hence, it would appear that a pattern of presentation which combines showing and telling—the lecture-demonstration approach, takes advantage of this variation in the learning potential of the several senses of perception.

The Police Library. A first prerequisite to a police in-service training program is a good departmental library. The literature of the police field has expanded rapidly during the past quarter century. Today, reliable texts, reference works and manuals are available in every area of police operations, including: police organization and management, police personnel administration, the police records system, the police communications system, criminal investigation and identification, police patrol organization, the police detective function, traffic regulation and control, and police crime prevention.

It is now possible to organize and shelve a well-rounded police library with adequate texts and reference works to support a sound in-service training program. Depending on the size of the department, it may be wise to make available in the library from six to twelve copies of certain standard texts in order to meet the circulation demands of departmental personnel. Many departments follow this practice. Supplementing the departmental library, an increasing number of individual police officers are accumulating their own personal police libraries.

Need for an Adequate Recruiting Formula

The police training problem in the United States is now at a stage where universities and colleges must recognize their responsibility to the public service and bring their superb resources to bear upon the training requirements of the police profession. Police service is an undertaking as technical as the other professions, and there should be no further delay in according it the same academic recognition. Until such time as career-minded young men and women can be given the opportunity of preparation at the university level for this branch of the public service, the selection and training of police personnel in the United States will continue an unsolved problem.

Based upon the expert studies of American police service made by Vollmer, Wilson, Greening, Harrison, Smith and others, it is clear that the success of police administration depends upon the quality of personnel from the top to the bottom of the enterprise. It is the determining factor in the performance level of management, supervisory and command personnel, on down to the last man in staff and line. Since, in American police service, administrative as well as supervisory and command positions are filled by promotion from the ranks, the implications of recruiting standards and procedure are self-evident. The application of university police training and research to the immediate problems of police administration can have far-reaching results in this important area of social control.

Experience has shown that the establishment of a professional curriculum in police administration at the university level is a comparatively simple academic operation. Every major university and college already includes in its offerings more than 90 per cent of the subject materials that should be geared into a professional police curriculum leading to the Bachelor degree. It remains only to superimpose upon these courses in a four year undergraduate program the necessary technical police subjects, following the pattern that has proved successful in the other professions. Furthermore, this can be done within the framework of the highest existing academic standards and at negligible cost.

The application of university facilities for instruction and research to the immediate problems of police administration is a matter of considerable social significance. The impact of higher education on this branch of the public service can be understood to advantage in terms of the responsibilities of a modern police organization. Most of the arts and sciences are directly involved in the problems that confront modern police service and adequate preparation for a professional grade of work in this branch of the public service must of necessity include the study of academic subjects which bear upon police problems and their solution. Political science, public administration, sociology, psychology, biology, chemistry, physics and mathematics, among others, are basic artillery pieces of the modern police officer and are an essential part of his training for career service in the police field.

It is now evident that preparatory work in the social, biological, natural and physical sciences is essential to the caliber of police performance demanded by the dimensions of the police problem today. The universities and colleges of this country are thus presented with the opportunity for extending their pattern of leadership into another scientific field. It is believed that they could make no greater contribution to the science and art of government. The implications of high level training for this branch of the public service in terms of sound public policy, lowered police costs and increased performance efficiency, cannot escape the attention of municipal authorities and the tax-payer; nor can university and college administrations long postpone recognition of the training service they are so superbly equipped to give this arm of government.

It has been stated that police service is an undertaking equally as technical as medicine, engineering, pharmacy, law and the other professions and it follows that the only point at which men and women may prepare adequately for career service in this field is in the classrooms and laboratories of the university and college.

Promoting Police Education at the University and College Level

Initial support for police education was expressed by the father of modern police administration, August Vollmer. Some thirty-five years ago he pointed out the need for providing Criminology programs in colleges and universities. Unfortunately his recommendation was heeded by few and the development of such programs has been slow and laborious.

Impetus for the creation of such programs occurred in 1964 when the Ford Foundation funded the International Association of Chiefs of Police. This grant provided for a staff of consultants who undertook the task of encouraging law enforcement education. Assistance was provided in curriculum planning and the development of degree programs in colleges and universities. Simultaneously, the consultants involved police executives in their local academic institution through local advisory councils and executive development programs.*

Starting in 1966 the Office of Law Enforcement Assistance, U. S. Department of Justice, awarded developmental grants to fifty colleges and universities in order to establish law enforcement education programs. Consequently, curriculums were established in areas of the United States previously unserviced by such educational programs. This limited infusion of federal funds stimulated the development of additional law enforcement curriculums thereby constituting a tremendous increase in the number of criminal justice education programs. In 1968 all but ten states offered either a 2 or 4 year law enforcement education program.*

---

* Thompson S. Crockett and James D. Stinchcomb, *Guidelines for Law Enforcement Education in Community and Junior Colleges*, American Association of Junior Colleges, Washington, 1968, p. 31.

* Thompson S. Crockett, *Law Enforcement Education 1968*, I.A.C.P., Washington, 1968, p. 1.2.

Additional private funding has also been important as indicated by a Kellogg Foundation grant to the American Association of Junior Colleges. Operating under the assistance of this grant a national advisory council, representing law enforcement and education, created a curriculum guideline for two year law enforcement degree programs that must be considered a land mark for the establishment of standards.**

Education for police officers and correctional personnel received additional support as the result of the creation of the Law Enforcement Assistance Administration by the Omnibus Crime Control and Safe Streets Act. This program provides funds for college degree studies; during the second half of the 1968–69 academic year a total of $6.5 million was given to 485 colleges and universities. Approved courses include those offering degrees or certificates in police science, criminology, criminalistics, police administration, law enforcement, technology, criminal justice, public safety administration, corrections, penology and correctional administration. Loans up to $1,800 per academic year are available for full-time study and grants of $300 per semester can be used for full or part-time study.***

Today, the universities and colleges of this country are bringing their resources for training and research into contact with the personnel needs of the American police field. It is now possible for a high school graduate to prepare for a career in police service at the university and college level in exactly the same manner as the doctor, lawyer and engineer. In any field, it goes without saying, the individual with a university background has the advantage. This is especially true in police service. In terms of professional advancement, the university graduate has a strong foundation on which to build a successful career in this branch of the public service.

As of 1970, in excess of three hundred universities and colleges in the United States were offering academic programs in preparation for career service in the police field, criminology and corrections. Of this number, more than seventy were in the state of California. The

---

** Crockett and Stinchcomb, *op. cit.*, pp. 16–18.

*** Law Enforcement Assistance Administration, *First Annual Report of the Law Enforcement Assistance Administration*, U. S. Government Printing Office, Washington, 1969, p. 6.

following table provides a partial list of institutions of higher learning in this country now offering police science programs.

UNIVERSITIES AND COLLEGES OFFERING ORGANIZED INSTRUCTION AT THE ACADEMIC LEVEL IN POLICE SCIENCE AND ADMINISTRATION

(AA—Indicates a Junior College; otherwise, the institution offers a four-year undergraduate program in the Police Science major leading to the Bachelor degree)

Antelope Valley College,
Lancaster, California. (AA)
Arizona State College,
Flagstaff, Arizona.
University of Arizona,
Tucson, Arizona.
Bakersfield College,
Bakersfield, California. (AA)
Brooklyn College,
Brooklyn, New York. (AA)
Broward County Junior College,*
Broward County, Florida. (AA)
University of California,
Berkeley, California.
Central Missouri State College,*
Warrensbury, Missouri.
Cerritos College,
Norwalk, California. (AA)
Chaffey College,
Alta Loma, California. (AA)
Citrus College,
Glendora, California. (AA)
Contra Costa College,
San Pablo, California. (AA)
Diablo Valley College,
Concord, California. (AA)
El Camino Junior College,
El Camino, California. (AA)
Elmira College,
Elmira, New York. (AA)

Florida State University,
Tallahassee, Florida.
Fresno State College,
Fresno, California.
Fullerton Junior College,
Fullerton, California. (AA)
Glendale College,
Glendale, California.
Imperial Valley College,
Imperial, California. (AA)
University of Indiana,
Bloomington, Indiana.
State University of Iowa,
Iowa City, Iowa.
Long Beach City College,
Long Beach, California. (AA)
Long Beach State College,
Long Beach, California.
Los Angeles City College,
Los Angeles, California. (AA)
Los Angeles Harbor College,
Wilmington, California. (AA)
Los Angeles State College,
Los Angeles, California.
Los Angeles Valley College,
Van Nuys, California. (AA)
Michigan State University,
East Lansing, Michigan.
Monterey Peninsula College,
Monterey, California. (AA)

* Being organized.

Mt. San Antonio Junior College, Walnut, California. (AA)

New Mexico State University, University Park, New Mexico.

City College of New York, New York, New York.

New York University, New York, New York.

Northeastern University, Boston, Massachusetts.

Oakland City College, Oakland, California. (AA)

Oceanside-Carlsbad College, Oceanside, California. (AA)

University of Oklahoma,* Norman, Oklahoma.

Orange Coast College, Costa Mesa, California. (AA)

Riverside City College, Riverside, California. (AA)

Sacramento State College, Sacramento, California.

St. Petersburg Junior College,* St. Petersburg, Florida. (AA)

San Bernadino Valley College, San Bernadino, California. (AA)

San Diego Junior College, San Diego, California. (AA)

San Jose City College,

San Jose, California. (AA)

San Jose State College, San Jose, California.

Santa Ana College, Santa Ana, California. (AA)

Santa Rosa Junior College, Santa Rosa, California. (AA)

College of the Sequoias, Visalia, California. (AA)

Seton Hall University College, Newark, New Jersey. (AA)

Shasta College, Redding, California. (AA)

University of Southern California, Los Angeles, California.

Santa Monica City College, Santa Monica, California. (AA)

Southern Illinois University, Carbondale, Illinois.*

Texas A & M College, College Station, Texas.

Vallejo Junior College,* Vallejo, California. (AA)

Ventura College, Ventura, California. (AA)

University of Wichita, Wichita, Kansas.

Washington State University, Pullman, Washington.

Note: Since the date this book was set in type, a complete listing of law enforcement degree programs as of 1970 has been received from the International Association of Chiefs of Police. It is presented in a *Supplement*; see page 518.

Recently, the International Association of Chiefs of Police, parent organization of the police field, with the aid of a $400,000.00 grant from the Ford Foundation, threw the full weight of its power and prestige behind police training at the university and college level. It can be expected with complete certainty that within a comparatively short time, university police training will blanket the nation with a plurality of programs in every state.

As recently as 1941, there was openly expressed skepticism concerning this new development in the police training field and in the

* Being organized.

field of higher education.   Today, the police recruiters are on the campuses of the nation seeking out candidates for the entrance examination.

Many police departments now offer extra credit on the examination where the candidate possesses a degree in the police science major. An increasing number of departments have established a minimum education requirement of two years of college work in police science and administration.   In some departments already, the candidate must present a Bachelor degree in the police major in order to gain admission to the entrance examination room.

Based upon experience in organizing a four year curriculum leading to the Bachelor degree in police science and administration at Washington State University, the author can certify to at least one thing.   The establishment of a professional curriculum in the police major at the university level is a comparatively simple academic operation.

The extent to which the American police have become training conscious is typified by Bulletin No. 13 released by the New York City Police Department on February 24, 1969.   It indicates in convincing terms the extent to which personnel in that department are now involved in training programs, both in-service and at the university level.   The Bulletin stated: [14]

New York City policemen put in more than one-third of a million student-hours of in-service advanced and specialized training during 1968, Police Commissioner Howard R. Leary disclosed today.

A total of 31,081 Patrolmen and superiors attended forty Police Department training courses conducted during the year.

In addition, the largest number of police recruits and trainees in the history of the Department took their recruit training in 1968.   The Police Academy registered 3,210 Probationary Patrolmen and Policewomen and 800 Police Trainees in its 18-week recruit training program during the year.

In many respects both the in-service and recruit training programs of 1968 represented improvements and additions to courses introduced in 1967.

For both groups, recruits and veterans of the force, there was increased emphasis on human relations and community problems.   All members of the force attended intensified one-day courses on these subjects at the Academy during the year to supplement their precinct unit training programs.

For recruits, training in "The Police Role in Human and Race Relations" was expanded during the year from 44 to 65 hours.   This training included lectures, workshop discussions, problem-solving seminars, films, and human relations research projects.   Among the areas covered were "The History of the American Negro" and "Puerto Rican Culture and Customs."

One particularly important area in which Police Department training has expanded, Commissioner Leary noted, has been in the experimental

[14] V. A. Leonard, *Police Personnel Administration*, Springfield, Illinois, Charles C. Thomas, Publisher, 1969, p. 48.

college program introduced in 1967. In that year, 35 members of a recruit class that completed its Academy training were selected to attend John Jay College of Criminal Justice (of the City University of New York) on one of the five days of their regular work week. There they took courses in the field of human relations and earned six college credits for the year's work. In 1968 the program was expanded by the addition of 21 additional Academy graduates.

The ultimate objective of this experiment is to expand the college training program to include all recruits and make it an integral part of the Department's recruit training.

Another facet of the Department's commitment to higher education was the granting of leave, with pay, to three members of the force who had won scholarships or fellowships for advanced degrees. A Sergeant is working for his Master's Degree in Criminal Justice at the state School of Criminal Justice, in Albany, under a State University of New York scholarship. Two other men are studying under fellowships provided by the Federal Office of Law Enforcement Assistance. One, a Lieutenant, is working toward a Master's Degree in Police Administration at Michigan State University. The other, a Detective, is seeking a Masters Degree in Criminology at the University of California.

During 1968, a total of 1,342 members of the force were enrolled in the John Jay College of Criminal Justice in undergraduate courses. Another 127 were enrolled in the graduate program of John Jay and six were taking graduate work at the Baruch School, another unit of the City University of New York.

In addition to training Patrolmen, the Police Academy stepped up its instructional courses for Precinct Unit Training Sergeants—the superiors responsible for in-service training of Patrolmen in their own precincts. In a 35-hour method-of-instruction course, the training Sergeants were equipped to improve the level of their on-the-job training, carried out in conjunction with the Police Academy's unit training program. This program utilizes the facilities of WNYC–TV, the city's television station.

A special command course given prior to promotion to men on the Sergeant's eligibility list, which was expanded to three weeks in 1967, was lengthened to six weeks during 1968. Major improvements in course contents and teaching methods were part of the change. Lecture time has been decreased and the prospective Sergeants are now doing more of their training in seminars, role-playing and carefully supervised field training. New areas covered include anticipatory guidance, handling the mentally ill, and special training in providing security for individuals and residential and business premises.

Another broad area in which Police Department training has been expanded is in the management development program. Particular emphasis is given to development of the student's understanding of people and his ability to communicate effectively. The career development course, essentially a study for promotion, has been expanded and special emphasis is given to the development of discretion and judgment in crisis situations.

In the area of field training, an innovation has been the establishment of practical courses in disorder control. Utilizing the facilities of the 69th Regiment Armory and unused streets and unoccupied buildings on Welfare Island, more than 5,000 Patrolmen and superiors have been trained to provide better protection for life and property in various disorder situations. In addition, all superior officers with the rank of Captain and higher have attended conferences in preparation for a series of command post exercises being carried out this year in conjunction with an operational plan for mobilizing trained precinct personnel at any hour of the day or night in disorder situations.

Other improvements and innovations in department training included the development of an orientation program for newly inducted civilian personnel and the development of a series of training brochures including guides to specialized libraries of particular interest to police researchers and of management periodicals of special interest to police administrators.

Over 1,000 detectives attended specialized courses in criminal identification and new methods of developing fingerprint evidence.

As early as 1964, the Police Commissioner of New York City announced that 156 members of the Department had, during the year, received university and college scholarships and awards with a total value in excess of $48,000. These scholarships and awards were donated by civic-minded individuals, organizations and educational institutions to career-minded officers who have demonstrated aptitude and leadership potential.

A formidable group of present and former officers in the New York City Police Department are now serving on police science faculties at higher institutions of learning, including the University of California at Berkeley, University of Southern California, Los Angeles State College, Sacramento State College, Michigan State University, Indiana University, University of Louisville, Western Reserve College, Northeastern University, the City College of New York, State University of New York, Fordham University, New York University, Rutgers University and New Haven College.

As of September 21, 1970, the New York City Police Department announced the introduction of formal university and college level education as a regular required component of the Recruit Training Program of the Police Academy.

As of 1970, Chief Jerry V. Wilson of the Metropolitan Police Department in Washington, D. C., reported a new upsurge in the number of university and college graduates coming into the Department. Thirty Princeton students recently took the initial entrance examination and about the same number of students from Amhurst took the test, as did a group from Harvard. Out of the current force of 4,571, there are 138 officers with college degrees. About 800 officers, including Chief Wilson, are enrolled at American University in police administration. The city pays nine-tenths of the tuition. Six men are receiving their regular salary while enrolled full time; two are working toward the Master's degree.

It is not difficult to perceive that in the foreseeable future, a minimum educational requirement for entry into police service will be a Bachelor degree in the police science major. But that is not all. Police administration may be expected to follow in the footsteps of the other professions in another important respect.

The lawyer, doctor, pharmacist, engineer and even the beautician and barber are required to pass a qualifying state board examination before being admitted to practice. It is interesting to note, for example, that the states began to pass legislation providing for the state board examination and licensing of barbers as early as 1893. In the early 1900's, a standard textbook of some 501 pages appeared for use in barber training schools which today, involves a minimum of eleven months intensive preparation.[15] Among other things, the text included orientation in the history of barbering, personal hygiene, bacteriology, anatomy, physiology, nervous and circulatory systems and chemistry.

Surely, the work and responsibilities of a police officer and the clientele with which he deals—human beings and human personality, even life itself—are as important as a haircut. We may confidently look forward to the time when the individual will, in addition to a Bachelor degree in the police science major, be required to pass a qualifying state Board examination before he can move into a police uniform.[16]

Institutional Leadership

The time is now at hand to give to police administration the same academic recognition accorded other professions. University and college administrations are now confronted with this challenge and opportunity. Tax-supported in the main, these institutions have an inherent responsibility to lead the way in bringing their training resources into contact with the needs of this branch of the public service.

[15] American Barber College, *Practice and Science of Standard Barbering*, 501 pp., about 1910.

[16] Leonard, V. A., *Police Personnel Administration*, Charles C. Thomas, Springfield, 1970, p. 49.

University training for the police services has long since passed beyond mere speculation. It is an established fact. Over two hundred universities and colleges now offer organized courses of instruction at the academic level in the law enforcement major, with from forty to fifty providing the opportunity for work toward the Bachelor degree in police science and administration, a substantial number offering in addition, the Master's degree, and two where the Ph.D., is available. The number is steadily increasing each year. These programs serve three general classes of students: [17]

Those students who wish to acquire an understanding of the police role in society as part of a broad general university education: The police power of a nation, particularly the manner in which it is exercised is a matter of concern to every citizen. The university campus has traditionally been the source of a large majority of the nation's future community leaders. Today, with the ever-growing problem of reaching a compromise between a maximum of personal liberty and the restraints which must be imposed by a complex society, there is a special need for an understanding by future leaders of the role that law enforcement administration plays in our social structure.

The successful exercise of police power in a community almost always reflects the amount of concern, interest, and understanding of the nature of the police problem by its leading citizens. There is perhaps no better place to inculcate the concepts of preserving peace within our social order in future community leaders than within the university. It is here that the student in pursuit of a liberal-arts education may gain insight into the nature of this important area.

The specialized student who wishes to prepare himself for a professional career in the police field: Persons planning to enter police service must be provided training that will prepare them for future positions of leadership. It is not a primary objective to train police

[17] Based in part on the remarks of Professor Robert F. Borkenstein, Chairman of the Department of Administration, Indiana University, at a Police Science Administrators' Conference held at Washington State University May 9, 10, 11, 1963, to discuss among other things, the standardization of university curricula in police science and administration.

Among those present, in addition to Professor Borkenstein, were Professor John P. Kenney, Head of the Law Enforcement Training Program at the University of Southern California, Los Angeles, California; Professor G. Douglas Gourley, Chairman of the Department of Police Science and Administration, Los Angeles State College, Los Angeles, California; Professor Edward Farris, Head of the Police Science Program at the University of New Mexico, Albuquerque, N. M.; Professor D. F. McCall, Chairman of the Department of Police Science and Administration, Washington State University, Pullman, Wash.; Professors F. M. Fabian, Harry W. More Jr., and the author, of the same institution.

officers or to equip young men and women with the skills to perform the many tasks required of the working police officer. The principal objective of police training at the university and college level is to provide a liberal education with sufficient emphasis on subjects in law enforcement administration to give a broad perspective of the functioning of police power within society. There is, however, a real shortage of people who have sufficiently broad vision to deal effectively with police problems at the decision and policy-making level. It is here that the university has a real responsibility.

Those students who seek to prepare themselves for advanced study at the graduate level in police organization and management: The installation of a four-year undergraduate curriculum in police science and administration should be regarded by educational administrators as a preliminary step to the inauguration of opportunities for study and research at the graduate level leading to the Master's degree and ultimately to the doctorate. Few if any procedures in the field of criminal justice administration today merit the stamp of scientific sanction, nor will they until the findings of research are adequately developed and applied. August Vollmer takes the dim view that our present day system for the administration of criminal justice is making criminals rather than curing them.[18]

The existence of graduate programs in the police arts and sciences would bring within the sphere of advanced study an overwhelming number of problems now awaiting research attention. There is an urgent need for specific texts and manuals in police organization and administration, police tactics, police statistical procedure, criminal investigation and identification, police psychiatry, patrol organization and procedure, traffic administration, delinquency and crime prevention. Through the research facilities of educational institutions, a strategic service can be performed in developing new techniques and procedures in delinquency and crime prevention, crime detection, judicial and correctional administration, police communications, record systems, personnel methods, traffic administration, and in disseminating this information to the profession. Projected research programs should include the translation into English of important police works now available in many languages. French, German, Spanish, Italian and Russian scholars, among others, have been prolific contributors to scientific police literature. Graduate programs would also serve the important purpose of introducing into this professional field practitioners with the additional maturity of preparation made possible by the requirements and opportunities of work at the graduate level.

---

[18] August Vollmer, *The Criminal*, Foundation Press, Inc., 1949.

The dimensions of the challenge to educational institutions is revealed when it is recognized that degree programs in police science and administration should be paralleled by comparable curricula in penal and correctional administration, and in parole and probation. Only then can it be said that American society has taken the first intelligent steps toward the problem of crime and the criminal.

Professional Opportunities for Graduates

There is an increasing demand for trained men and women in the police field. Those who have an inclination toward this type of work should not hesitate to begin their undergraduate preparation for it. Within the police field, conditions are rapidly becoming adjusted to accommodate the professionally trained person. Salaries are being scaled upward in order that police service may compete with industry in attracting the highest type of men available. Appointment and promotion on the basis of merit, security represented by tenure of office under modified civil service, and the opportunity for a distinguished career of service and achievement mark the police field as a wise choice for the ambitious young man. Starting their service at the bottom of the enterprise, the gradual infiltration of these men into the key posts of police administration, where they can influence policy portends a new era in this branch of the public service and reveals the true implications of university and college training for the police profession.

Significantly, it is now the general pattern for police departments to encourage their personnel to enroll as degree-seeking students in the police science major where educational institutions are conveniently available offering these programs. On a typical day, one hundred and eighteen members of the New York City Police Department were awarded degrees by the City College of New York at commencement exercises on June 12, 1963.[19] The highest ranking officer to receive a degree was Deputy Chief Inspector William P. McCarthy, commanding the Civil Defense Bureau of the Police Department. He was awarded a Bachelor of Business Administration degree with specialization in Police Science, magna cum laude. Others to receive degrees magna cum laude included Captain Rudolph Blaum, Queens Communications Bureau, and Sergeant William Devine, Emergency Service Squad #1.

In addition to Chief McCarthy, 9 captains, 17 lieutenants, 15 sergeants and 76 patrolmen received degrees in the joint police higher education program sponsored by the Baruch School of the City Col-

---

[19] See Appendix C Professional Code of Ethics Promulgated by the International Association of Chiefs of Police.

lege in cooperation with the New York Police Academy. The degree of Master of Public Administration went to 16 members of the force, that of Bachelor of Business Administration to 22, and the Associate in Applied Science degree, representing completion of a two-year course, to 80 officers. Currently, 1,300 members of the New York City police force were enrolled in this program, as of 1963.

Police officers in Virginia are being reimbursed by the state for tuition costs of college courses in law enforcement. The measure was recently approved by the Virginia legislature and sponsored by the International Association of Chiefs of Police. Officers participating in the program apply to the State Department of Education after being accepted by a state college or university for work in an accredited course for a degree or associate degree. The application must be accompanied by evidence of satisfactory completion of such a course. The officer is then paid 50 percent of the tuition cost of the course, not to exceed $40. If the officer continues to serve as a law enforcement officer for one year after completing the course, the state pays the remaining 50 percent of the cost of the course, not to exceed a total cost of $80. It is to be noted that a number of other states are following the same procedure.

Fairfax, California, has instituted an educational and incentive pay program for public safety personnel aimed at increasing the professional level of its police and fire employees. Personnel with $3\frac{1}{4}$ years experience who earn an associate of arts degree in either law enforcement or police science, receive a 5 percent salary increase above the maximum rate for their position. Personnel who complete 30 accredited units in either approved police science or fire science courses, receive a $2\frac{1}{2}$ percent increase. In either case, employees are expected to continue attending college classes to further their professional and educational training. All employees take courses on their own time. However, the city pays all tuition and text book costs.

Of the 5,000 men in the Los Angeles Police Department, one holds the doctor's degree; fifteen have the master's; fifteen possess the LL.B; 280 the B.A., or B.S.; 388 have earned the certificate of Associate of Arts; and 370 other certificates of academic accomplishment. Looking at it further in terms of college background, 709 had one year; 517 two years; and 179 the three or more years of college work; 477 the second year, and 628 are registered in the first year college courses. The Los Angeles Police Department places a premium upon a college education.

In order to meet the increasing need for better trained, educated and professional police officers, the Davis, California, City Council unanimously adopted a management formulated educational incentive program. Patrolmen and sergeants with five years service and thirty approved college semester units are eligible for the program. In order to maintain eligibility, personnel must successfully complete at least fifty approved hours or three college units during the fiscal year. A 5% per-cent salary increase above the top step is given to those who qualify.

Eligibility must be maintained each year in order to receive this increase. All time spent in preparation for eligibility must be off-duty time and entail no expense to the city. Since the implementation of the program, over 80 percent of the qualified members of the force are participating.

Under an incentive pay for education plan, members of the police department in Oceanside, California, in the ranks of Patrolman, Sergeant and Lieutenant receive additional pay upon completion of prescribed study courses at the college level. The plan provides that any member of the force who may be in one of these three ranks, who has satisfac-torily performed his duties, and who has completed a prescribed course of study leading to a certificate of completion in police science is given one additional increase in compensation amounting to an advance of 5 percent.

Indicative of the mounting professional stature of police person-nel, on June 10, 1968, thirteen members of the New York Police De-partment's legal bureau were admitted to practice before the United States Supreme Court. They included Lt. John J. Sullivan, Lt. Joseph F. Lynch, Sergeant Francis J. Coyne, Sergeant Francis G. GaNun, Detective Edward C. Ciffone, Detective Thomas J. Flanagan, Detective Patrick J. Healy, Detective Jerome A. Isoldi, Detective Matthew C. King, Detec-tive John J. Maguire, Detective Mary J. McDonnell, Patrolman Leroy D. Willis and Patrolman Joseph F. Crowley. The new admissions were sponsored by another staff member, Detective William T. Johnson, who was admitted to practice before the High Court in 1966.

University Police Training v. In-Service Training

Police training at the university and college level reduces to a very marked degree the load on in-service training, *but does not take its place.* Both are necessary. Each one supplements the other. The objectives of university police training are:

1. To give the future police officer a broad liberal arts education, in conjunction with intensive professional training for the police and other investigative services.

2. To give the future police officer a thorough command of those tools in the arts and sciences which are essential to the successful delivery of police service in a modern social order.

3. To provide a strong foundation for a career in this professional field.

4. To develop the qualities of leadership and executive potential.

5. To provide a reservoir or personnel reserve from which to draw police administrative talent for tomorrow.

6. To give a long range perspective of the role of the police in modern society.

7. To foster the ideals of professional achievement in this branch of the public service.

On the other hand, the objectives of in-service training are more immediate in nature. They include orientation in such typical areas as the following:

1. Departmental policies.

2. Departmental Rules and Regulations.

3. Established police practices and procedures, vocational in nature, which are normally not included in a university police training program.

4. Development of on-the-job skills in all phases of the police operation.

5. Local police problems.

6. Refresher training.

Thus, it can be easily seen that the two training areas, although entirely different in nature and objective, are both essential to the effective delivery of police service. Both play important roles in preparing the individual officer to meet the complex demands of police service today.

It is to be observed that there is some variation in the content of the police curriculum from one institution to another. At one end of the spectrum will be found a sharp emphasis on vocational skills such as gunnery, for example. At the other end, the educational philosophy is one of training for leadership.

There is a definite movement among university police training officials to standardize curriculum content. The International Association of Chiefs of Police has expressed a strong interest in this direction. The task is made less formidable by the circumstance that approximately the same basic "core" curriculum will be found at most institutions. The problem, therefore, involves primarily a fringe operation. If a prediction could be ventured, it would indicate a reduction in the emphasis on vocational skills.

SUPPORTING ELEMENTS IN POLICE
PERSONNEL MANAGEMENT

Lateral Mobility of Police Personnel

The horizontal movement of personnel, particularly at the supervisory and command levels, among police departments has not yet been widely accepted in the United States. However, in business and industry, lateral mobility or lateral entry is commonplace and has been for many years. This would appear to indicate to them that the procedure is an attractive one, both for management and personnel. The apparent advantages of this personnel mechanism for the police field invite closer scrutiny.

Promotional opportunities in the small and medium-sized police departments, and even in the larger departments, are somewhat limited. The number of supervisory and command positions is relatively small when compared to the total personnel strength of the department. This circumstance tends to freeze personnel in the lower ranks for extended periods of time, resulting in the exposure of the department to possible loss of morale and incentive.

With the increasing emphasis on the police field as a career service and the growing influx of college trained personnel into the police uniform, this problem is now pressing forward for attention. The risk of frustration because of the lack of movement upward through the channels of promotion has important implications for police management.

The trend toward lateral mobility or lateral entry of police personnel is one bright light on the horizon which stands to offer an approach to this problem. For some years now, an increasing number of cities and communities have been selecting their Chiefs of Police through open competitive examination, not limited to members of the department concerned. It has become very common practice in Southern California, for example, for a new Chief of Police to be imported from some other department, and frequently from some other part of the country. A recent study indicated that at least forty California cities with populations of 10,000 or more, had selected Chiefs from outside the department.

And it is increasingly the case where supervisory and command positions are being filled on an open competitive basis. Several police departments in California have recently held open competitive examinations for the rank of Captain, which were open to any law enforcement officer with the proper qualifications. These qualifications included five years experience as a police officer plus three years as a police

Lieutenant, or a Police Sergeant with at least one year of college level training in police science or related subjects.

Our foreign contemporaries in general support the lateral mobility concept. The British favor a plan whereby specially selected and trained officers of senior rank would be given the opportunity of seeking employment as and when vacancies occur in the senior ranks of other forces, as a promotion policy.

One school of thought in high official circles is that good officer material in some of the smaller forces is often wasted because of the lack of opportunity for promotion in those forces, where the number of higher ranks in the organization is small and vacancies in them are few and far between. It is felt that appointments in the higher ranks of all police forces should be made on an open competitive basis from selected applicants recruited from forces in all parts of the country.

In a recent survey of the extent to which lateral mobility was being practiced by police departments in the United States, questionnaires were mailed to departments in 234 cities. Of the 234, 88 or 38% of the questionnaires were returned.[20] The returns showed that lateral entry was being employed in ten departments. One California Chief of Police observed, "I believe that the lack of lateral entry is an *important obstacle* to professionalization in the law enforcement field."

Some of the apparent advantages of lateral mobility or lateral entry are:

1. It opens up the channels of promotion.
2. It fosters initiative and enthusiasm for the job with the knowledge that the opportunities for advancement are greater than before.
3. It enhances police morale.
4. It encourages a career service.
5. It widens the field of candidates for supervisory, command and administrative positions in the police service.
6. Police service becomes more attractive to the police candidate and the new recruit when he knows that the channels of promotion are open and that his chances for promotion are amplified.

On other shores, the interchange of New Zealand and Australian detectives introduced in 1962, has met with encouraging success. Of-

---

[20] Scott, James C., *An Analysis of Lateral Entry as a means of Obtaining Municipal Police Supervisors and Administrators in the United States*, a Master's Thesis, Washington State University, 1965.

ficials state that the interchanges have proved worthwhile in view of the large number of criminals moving between the two countries.

Conditions of Service

Promotion. What has been said concerning lateral mobility, in terms of opening up the channels of promotion, speaks for itself. Promotion is one of the most important mechanisms in the entire field of personnel management. It serves two major purposes in organization—through the avenue of promotion, supervisory and command personnel, and administrative officers are selected. Secondly, it gives expression to the opportunity for personal achievement and success, with all that can mean in terms of morale and initiative.

In the American police field, it is now standard practice in virtually every department to award promotion on the basis of merit, as determined by competitive examination. This examination should include, in addition to written tests, the following:

1. The officer's prior performance record.

2. The results of rating by superior officers.

3. The officer's educational background.

4. Demonstrated qualities of leadership potential and the ability to assume greater responsibility.

5. Contents of the officer's personnel folder, with respect to complaints, commendations, and other related matters.

The fringe benefits in police service today are competitive with business and industry. The forty hour work week is now standard throughout the country. Some departments provide compensation for overtime, but this is the exception rather than the rule.

It is the practice in virtually every police department to accumulate sick leave at the rate of one day for each month of service up to a maximum of six months, exclusive of Saturdays and Sundays, or other regular days off. It must be observed at this point that the effective personnel strength of too many departments is depleted by time lost due to illness. As previously indicated, this can be drastically reduced by the use of extreme care in the recruiting process. An annual vacation of at least two weeks, exclusive of regular days off, is now standard practice in the American police field.

Coupled with the foregoing conditions of service, provision for the retirement of police personnel is a regular feature of police departments throughout the country. Pension plans, of course, vary from one department to the other. One thing is certain—a department should determine through those competent to judge that its pension program is actuarially sound.

In order to foster the development of lateral mobility and for other important reasons, a nation-wide police retirement system is now mandatory.[21]   There is ample precedent for a national police retirement program.   For example, the Teachers Insurance and Annuity Association of America blankets the nation's academic system with a retirement and pension program second to none.   A member of a university or college faculty may transfer his retirement credit at will from one educational institution to another.

[21] The President's Commission on Law Enforcement and Administration of Justice, *Task Force Report: The Police*, U. S. Government Printing Office, 1967, p. 142.

*

Chapter 8

POLICE RECORDS ADMINISTRATION

I N military service, planning and operations depend on intelligence. In the theater of war, unless accurate information has been obtained and analyzed concerning the strength and disposition of the enemy's troops and equipment, his morale, his lines of communication and other factors affecting his striking power and probable movements, operations are stalemated. Likewise, in the police field, the dimensions of the problem must be known before plans can be made for the most effective use of personnel and physical resources. Failure to recognize the strategic role of intelligence in the field of police organization and administration continues to be a serious handicap to police performance in this country.

Of considerable import in the project of crime control and prevention is departmental intelligence upon which administration must rely as one of the most indispensable tools of management. It is derived from organized information available in the Police Records Division, which concerns the nature, size and distribution of the police problems of crime, delinquency, vice and traffic. The extent to which police records are properly maintained and processed is directly related to administrative performance and is a principal determining factor in the quality of police service delivered to the community.

The maneuver of military power in the theater of operations is predicated upon estimates of the situation, which in turn are based upon accurate intelligence. From the estimate of the situation ensues the decision and plan of operation. For illustration, preceding the decision for a surprise attack in force upon the enemy's left flank at 3:00 o'clock in the morning there must be a prodigious effort at the planning stage if the operation is to be successful.

With the objective of the projected flank operation being an effort to sever the enemy's lines of communication, the commander must have complete, accurate information with respect to the opposing force in the combat area, including the strength of his intelligence, his air power, nature and amount of light and heavy artillery, missile weaponry, numerical strength and disposition of that strength,

185

length and character of lines of communication, nature and location of supplies, amount and availability of reserve power, front line zones where his forces are concentrated and those where light disposition of strength may make penetration possible, possible offensive and defensive strategy of the enemy, morale of the opposing forces and many other factors which enter into an estimate of the situation. In addition, the estimate equation must take into consideration the topography of the combat area, accidents of the ground, meteorological data, reserves, and striking power of the attacking force. These basic principles of planning have long since been confirmed by military science. They were used by Alexander and by the German forces immediately preceding the Belgium Bulge during World War II.

A successful business enterprise invokes the same principles and procedures. Railroad systems prepared exhaustive estimates of the situation before conversion from coal burning locomotives and steam power to Diesel engines. Balance sheets, comparative costs in terms of investment and operations, operating efficiency, nature and extent of expendable funds, congested schedules, personnel implications, extent and character of fuel supplies, required changes in maintenance operations, analysis of freight and passenger traffic volume curves, and public opinion were among the factors that would lead to a decision for or against conversion. A vast documentation and complex data are involved in the process of arriving at an estimate of the situation.

Likewise, the intelligent planning and execution of police operations must of necessity be predicated upon critical estimates of the situation, involving expert statistical interpretation of records data. It has been previously emphasized that in complex undertakings performed by many men, precision and certainty in action and control over far-flung operations can be achieved only with the assistance of scientific record controls. In the detection and analysis of emerging situations and in the identification of the points where the preventive work of the department may be focused, the strategic position of the police record system again becomes apparent.

Functioning in an area of social control where short-term and long-term planning could be productive of far-reaching results, police management must make use of basic intelligence procedures founded on its own information and records as one of the basic devices of administration.

All authoritative works in the field of public administration place a strong emphasis upon the importance of an adequate system of records and reporting as a basis for the planning and execution of operations.   Further, there is no lack of agreement concerning the principles to be applied in providing management with these professional tools of control.   As instruments of sound administrative practice, they serve the public interests in two important areas.

1. *The Basis of Democratic Control.*   Intelligent records and reporting constitute the only sound basis for democratic control.   It is a maxim in democratic government that administration must be responsive to public control.   Through an honest records and reporting procedure, control patterns are brought out into the open and a rapport is established between administration on the one hand and public opinion on the other.   "One of the reasons," states Kneier,[1] "why democratic government has not functioned more intelligently in our cities is because the ordinary men and women have found it difficult to secure information about the government of their city.   The electorate cannot be expected to pass judgment upon administration, to perform an audit of governmental affairs, without having facts on which to base the decision.   Public reporting seeks to give public opinion a sound basis on facts.   It should prevent the misrepresentation of the conduct of government, which is inevitable with the lack of an authentic record and report."

Munro [2] early came to the conclusion that the great majority of annual reports of city departments represented a gross waste of time and printing.   No one reads them; no one would understand them if they did.   Walker is equally emphatic in his opinion that most public reports tend to be either dry compilations of figures and facts without interest to the citizen reader or personal advertising so colored as to reflect credit upon officers who are seeking continuance in office.   Small wonder that citizens customarily ignore or distrust much of the information which comes to them from public sources. "One of the primary requisites of successful democratic government," states Walker [3] "is the building up of a tradition of accurate, reliable and interesting reporting and wide-spread citizen use of the material so presented as the basis for intelligent political action."   Munro adds that "The reorganization of administrative departments must

[1] Charles M. Kneier, *City Government in the United States,* Harper & Brothers, revised edition, 1947, p. 302.

[2] William Bennet Munro, *Principles and Methods of Municipal Administration,* The MacMillan Company, New York, 1916, p. 7.

[3] Harvey Walker, *Public Administration in the United States,* Farrar & Rinehart, Inc., New York, 1937, p. 298.

surely bring an end to this profitless parroting of miscellaneous information which informs nobody. No distribution of municipal reports in their regular form will bring the facts home to the citizen in such a way as to make him use them as a basis for forming an independent opinion. Publicity pamphlets which try to give voters the entire story on the eve of an election will not do it."

Zink [4] observed:

The neglect of city administrations in informing the citizens of the work, the expenditures and the current problems confronting the city government is almost beyond belief. Some city officials make no effort at all to acquaint the people with what is going on; some of them go so far as to resent inquiries from interested persons who take the trouble to ascertain facts. They may pretend ignorance, shift the burden to some other official or department, maintain that they are too busy with public duties to be bothered with questions, and at times even refuse outright to furnish information on the ground that it is no one's business. In many cases, they are willing enough but simply do not themselves know what the facts are. If reports are issued at all, they are usually so involved, so uninteresting, so incomplete that they defy the ordinary citizen, if he ever sees them.

Cities in the United States, large and small, may reasonably be expected to furnish their citizens at the close of each municipal year a consolidated report which will cover in some detail the conduct of municipal affairs during the preceding year. Such a report requires careful preparation. Above all, it must not be an ill-assorted conglomeration of hastily assembled more or less meaningless formal reports of the "Dear Mr. Mayor: I have the honor to submit herewith the Annual Report" variety. Instead of complicated jumbles of figures, which mean little to anyone other than an accountant, this consolidated report might wisely make generous use of charts and diagrams to set forth the distribution of funds, the prevalence of disease, crime and other appropriate items.

Police administration should be among the first to give the public a frank accounting of its problems and achievements. Only in this manner may public confidence be stimulated and retained. However, a perusal of contemporary annual reports of police departments justifies the criticisms quoted above. There is general failure to furnish a thorough-going, intelligible analysis of police problems and performance.

Most annual reports contain basic information concerning major offenses, including murder, robbery, burglary and automobile thefts, but little or nothing concerning the field of misdemeanors, the under-

---

[4] Harold Zink, *Government of Cities in the United States*, The MacMillan Company, New York, 1939, p. 594.

graduate level from which the major criminal is recruited. The report may be primarily a pamphlet containing arrest statistics, in deference to the ill-conceived notion that the number of arrests affords a clue to the size of the problem and to the success of the police in coping with it.

It must be concluded, therefore, that information concerning police administration at the present time is not generally accessible to intelligent public support or public control, since the only basis upon which intelligent public opinion can be formulated is not adequately available. This situation is not only a liability so far as the public interest is concerned, but also operates as a barrier to successful police management.

2. *Administrative Planning.* From an administrative point of view, a plan of operations is a synthesis of various plans: annual, long-term, short-term, and special. The need for a plan of operations is recognized by all, but the practice of providing one is not yet general. Planning is the working out in broad outline of the things that need to be done and the methods for doing them in order to accomplish the purpose set for the enterprise. It involves a forecast of the future problem and a scheme for meeting it. Police problems involving crime, delinquency, vice and traffic occur and reoccur in time and place with such a high degree of regularity that administrative predictions are possible. The curves of yesterday and today can be projected into tomorrow in terms of what and how much is going to happen, when and where. Accurate estimates of the situation can be prepared and from them short-term, long-term, and special plans can be formulated.

With proper records and reporting it is possible to forecast with great accuracy what will happen, and when and where in the field of crime and delinquency. Where the records are properly administered and analyzed, exceedingly reliable predictions can be formulated in statistical terms concerning the number of persons who will be killed and injured in traffic accidents, and when and where they will be killed and injured. Burglary operations can similarly be forecast in advance in terms of hour of day, day of week, month of year and in terms of geographic location throughout the city. Likewise, robbery, automobile theft, assaults, larceny and other crimes, as well as the demand upon police time and manpower by miscellaneous services, are amenable to accurate prediction in terms of amount, hourly, daily and seasonal variation, and in terms of geographical distribution. With this type of information it becomes possible to deploy equipment and personnel resources with great economy and effectiveness. In this manner, administration moves into its problems on a scientific basis, supplanting guesswork and haphazard methods of management.

A competent administrator appreciates the indispensability of the police record system in the intelligent control of operations, services and inspections, and makes use of this important facility in the diagnostic approach to the manifold problems presented to his department for solution. ·This type of administrator knows that he must have the facts concerning the character, extent and distribution of crime, delinquency, and other police problems in the community before operations can be intelligently planned and executed. He discovers that adequate records data constitute an accounting system for the police business, and that they are a prerequisite to successful management and the measurement of departmental performance.

Perhaps one reason for the lack of planning in the field of police administration is the great effort required and the lack of managerial ability to sustain such effort; another is the fact that the basic data necessary for estimate and planning may be inadequate or not available at all. The extent and quality of police intelligence or administrative data depend upon the character and administration of the police record system. Expert surveys of police departments in the United States reveal a wide range in the character of police records administration.

The Records Division is more than a mere depository for routine records. A police record system is not a question of bookkeeping but is rather a form of accounting for the police business. It is not concerned with the mere recording of events as an historical record so much as with the intelligent planning and control of operations, with the measuring of the result of those operations and with the study of the problems which confront the police. Just as the records and accounting office in any corporation is the tool upon which the management must rely in deciding questions of policy in distributing its men, and in eliminating wasteful operations, so too, the police records system may provide the police chief executive with one of his major tools of administrative control. The most successful police departments have been those which have based their administrative actions upon facts in the form of reports and analyses prepared from basic data covering the nature and distribution of police problems referred to the Department for investigation.

The Record Division serves in the first instance as a control over the police business. It is the mainspring of police administration and unless the records are correct and the information concerning offenses and complaints is properly filed, tabulated, and chartered, the head of the police department is helpless. He cannot know the who, where, when, what, why, and how of police work, and unless he does, it is impossible for him or his assistants to cope with the situation. A modern police records system equal to the standards set forth by the International Association of Chiefs of Police constitutes one of the principal needs in the field of police administration at the present time.

Among the important purposes served by a police record system are the following:

1. *Determining the nature, extent and distribution of the police problems of crime, delinquency, vice and traffic.*

2. *Determining the size and distribution of the force.*

3. *Control over crimes committed and their investigation.*

4. *Apprehending criminal offenders through a study of their Modus Operandi or method of operation.*

5. *The analysis of traffic accidents with a view toward prevention and selective enforcement.*

6. *Control over arrests and their disposition.*

7. *Making administrative predictions in terms of what, how much, when and where is going to happen with respect to crime, vice, traffic accidents and other demands upon police service, with all this can mean in the deployment of the force.*

8. *Revealing unusual problems and the detection of emerging situations.*

9. *Selecting the best men for particular assignment and for promotion.*

10. *As a tool of criminal investigation and as a source of investigative leads.*

11. *Determining the amount, nature and distribution of police equipment.*

12. *Through projecting the crime and traffic accident experience of yesterday and today into tomorrow, administrative predictions can be made concerning what, how much, when and where—is going to happen.*

Specifications of a Police Record System

The minimum standards for a police record system have been made available to the profession from reputable sources, including a number of American police executives whose achievements in the police field have been accorded national recognition.[5]   They include: [6]

1. Consolidation of all record functions into one division, the Records Division, under one head responsible to the Chief of Staff Services, affording a centralization of responsibility and control.

2. Integration of police operations through the inauguration of a standard police complaint record system and reporting procedure as recommended by the International Association of Chiefs of Police.[7]

The location of the records function in a police organization is a matter of prime importance.   A crime records system can never attain its greatest effectiveness so long as it is operated by a line agency.   The maintenance of records is a staff function, and the current audit of police operations, which they facilitate, can be effectively conducted only by a staff unit.   (See Chapter III, Internal Organization) Operating the Record Division is not a routine clerical duty but an administrative task of the highest order.   It is the focal point of all police administrative controls.

The Police Complaint Record System

The proper organization of the police record system is contingent upon the establishment of approved record and reporting procedure. All complaints and reports received by the Department for investigation, involving violations of city ordinances, state, and federal laws, should be typewritten on standard complaint record forms.   Each complaint should be given a consecutive serial number in the order of its receipt, regardless of classification so that there will be no question concerning the integrity of the records or the accuracy of the total number of complaints that are received.   Such numbers should be stamped in the space provided for that purpose on the complaint record form.   They may extend from 1 to 99,999 and then in alphabetical sequence A–1 to A–99,-999, etc.

The reports should be recorded immediatetly after receipt of the original information.   Failure to record properly any matter referred to the Department for investigation should constitute a violation of the Departmental Rules and Regulations.   After being so recorded, each item is entered on the Daily Bulletin in numerical sequence.   The Bulletin should be typewritten for duplication and at the end of his tour of duty, copies should be furnished the various departmental units so that

5 August Vollmer, *Survey of the Police Department of Minneapolis, Minnesota*, 1930, p. 92.

6 See list of police surveys in bibliography.

7 O. W. Wilson, *Police Records and Their Installation*, International Association of Chiefs of Police, *Uniform Crime Reporting Manual*, Washington, 1930, pp. 73–137; R. Weldon Cooper, *Municipal Police Administration in Texas*, University of Texas, Austin, 1938, pp. 184–200.

the entire force may be kept informed concerning criminal happenings, stolen, lost and found property and persons wanted.

With the exception of the Desk Sergeant's Office, each unit should maintain a file of Daily Bulletins in chronological order for the preceding thirty days. The Sergeant's Office should bind each thirty days' business and file these reports as a permanent record.

Complaint Record Forms and Routine Procedure

Separate record forms must provide for two distinct steps in recording and compiling of offenses. There must be:

1. Records for the original entry showing that a crime has been committed (offense report forms).
2. Reports of investigations and results secured (supplementary reports of the investigating officer).

The offense report is for the original entry of facts about a crime when brought to the department's attention. It serves as the first formal record of the offense and as the fundamental basis for headquarters' control of the investigation. It is important that all "on view" arrests be transferred to offense reports, otherwise the offense record will be grossly incomplete.

The following legend explanation covers the primary classes of information provided for on the offense report forms:

Where committed: Location where offense was committed, or where incident occurred.

Date and time committed: Day of month plus year, and time of day that offense was committed, or when incident occurred.

Persons Attacked: The number of victims should be shown, their sex, whether adults or juveniles, race and, insofar as possible, their occupations. This is important because some criminals operate against a certain sex, grown persons or juveniles, certain races, certain types of professional people, etc.

Property Attacked: The type of premises in which the offense was committed should be stated. If a bank were held up, the property attacked would be a bank. Stores are described as to type of business, and whether independent or chain. Where a building is used for a number of purposes, specify first the purpose for which the particular room entered is used, and after that the general use of the building. For instance, a grocery store under apartment; dentist's office in front of residence; or conversely, sleeping quarters in rear of grocery. Buildings are described as to the number of families living therein, and the type of building, as bungalow, apartment, club, etc.

How Attacked: Refers to the way in which the person or property was attacked. In burglary, property is attacked by breaking in. The point of entry, as rear door, first floor, side window, first floor transom, should be given. In case of robbery, state whether victim was strong-armed, slugged, threatened, choked, beaten, etc. In worthless checks, drafts, notes, forgeries, etc., state if by passing, forging, or raising, or if fictitious or fraudulent checks, drafts, or notes. In larceny, specify the place from where the property was stolen, i. e., cash register, clothesline, desk, kitchen, etc.

Means of Attack: Refers to the instrument, tool, device, trick or method by which the person or property was attacked. In burglary all tools should be described briefly but specifically. In the case of robbery, give the best possible description of weapon used. In larceny, the means may be merely by carrying away, or climbing adjoining premises, fence, fire escape, ladder, porch, rope, driving away, shoplifting, or with any instrument.

Object of Attack: It is not necessary at this point to give details of the articles taken but rather the general class to which they belong. The objects of attack of one criminal may be money, overlooking other articles of real value. Others will take money and jewelry or certain types of clothing, or silverware, etc. In crimes against the person, not involving property, the object of attack will be the motive rather than a material thing, i. e., illicit love affair, insurance plot, etc.

Trade-Mark: List the personal idiosyncrasies or peculiar methods of operation which may serve to distinguish the crime from other crimes committed in much the same fashion. Some men commit a robbery with no fuss and very little conversation, while others make a great deal of noise, commotion and conversation. Some men turn on house lights in a burglary, while others burn matches or use flashlights. Some invariably raid the ice box, whereas others will take food into the premises. A man who gains entrance to a house by representing himself as an inspector from a gas or electric company is an old type. Such items as committed during funeral parade, party, assaulted occupant bathing, malicious damage to premises, poisoned dog, cut telephone wires, pretended to be blind, left sarcastic note, re-arranged furniture, etc., are all examples of the trademark. The more unusual, the more queer, strange, or peculiar the trademark is, the greater its value in identifying the perpetrator of future crimes, or of connecting a suspect with past crimes.

Vehicle Used: A brief but complete description of vehicle, if used in the commission of the crime is entered here.

Illustrated on the following page is a typical master complaint record form for recording the crime of robbery. Identical forms are used for all other crime classifications.[8]

---

[8] It is not the function of this volume to illustrate all of the principal record forms required in a police record system nor to treat police records procedure in detail. These matters are adequately presented in O. W. Wilson, *Police Records and Their Installation*, Public Administration Service, Chicago, 1942. The present chapter is concerned more with the application of the record system as a tool of police management than with the procedural details involved.

Jan. Feb. Mar. Apr. May June July Aug. Sept. Oct. Nov. Dec.
1 2 3 4 5 6 7 8 9 10 11 12 13 14 15 16 17 18 19 20 21 22 23 24 25 26 27 28 29 30 31

ROBBERY   **Class**   **B**

Victim _____ Investigators _____

Address _____ Ph. _____ Re-assigned to _____ Date _____

Where Committed _____ C P B

Person and Prop. Att. Owner☐ Friend☐ Empl.☐ Insured☐ Locked☐ Unlocked☐   Suspects or responsible M F Age

How Attacked _____ Previous Record _____

Means of Attack _____

Time of Attack _____ Day

Object of Attack _____ Warrant Issued _____

Trademark _____ Arrested by _____ Date _____

Similar M. O. _____

Auto Used _____ Gun Used _____

Reported by _____ Other reports _____

Address _____ Ph. _____

Reported to _____ Prop. rec. by _____ ☐ Partial ☐ Complete

Time reported _____ Where rec. _____ Date _____

How Reported: Phone☐ Person☐ Let'r☐ Telgr'm☐ Telet'p☐ Light☐ Radio☐   Dispn. Code _____ by _____ Date

Beat Off. notified by: Sta.☐ Citzn☐ Bultn☐ Wrnt☐ Out. Dp.☐ On vw.☐ Box☐   Other officers detailed as follows:

Outside Departs. notified by: Radio☐ Phone☐ Wire☐ Teletype☐ Contact

Cancelled by: Radio ☐ Phone ☐ Wire ☐ Teletype ☐ Contact ☐

Date _____ By Officer _____ Remarks: _____ Date _____

Bulletin Cancellation by _____ Date _____

Card Mailed by _____ Date _____

Record to Dist. Atty. by _____ Date _____

P.S. 7-5c-1-43

In any case where it is known that the offense was committed by a juvenile, or where such information becomes known, the word "JUVENILE" should be typed above the serial number in order that this information may be properly tabulated. Copies of such reports should be transmitted to the Crime Prevention Division, as the central office for the handling of the problems of juvenile offenders.

Any letter, telegram or other communication requiring investigation by the Department should be transferred to an offense report immediately upon receipt, the classification being usually determined by the content of the communication. Where such communication originates with another law enforcement agency, the word "OUTSIDE" should be typed above the serial number. If in written form, it should be attached to the original offense report copy and routed to the Record Division. Copies of such communications may be typed for the investigating officer on request, but no original communications or any part of the master complaint record should be removed from the Record Division Office except in rare situations where the circumstances so indicate, and in such cases authority for removal of the record should be obtained from the head of the Record Division and a receipt signed therefor.

Supplementary Reports of Investigation

The offense or complaint report provides for the original entry of facts about a crime when brought to the attention of the department, but if record procedure should terminate at that point, the means for control would still be missing. Through the requirement that the investigating officer assigned to a case must promptly file a written report covering the results of his investigation, the means for control is established. The supplementary offense report is used for recording the results of the investigation. It is prepared by the officer assigned to the case. It may also be used by other officers who have occasion to enter certain facts in addition to those appearing on the offense report.

It follows from this that there may be several supplementary offense reports concerning a single offense, falling under one or more of the following categories:

1. Statements by investigating officers on the progress of the case. These should be submitted at regular intervals while the case is under investigation; when special developments occur; or upon request of the supervising officer.

2. Statement by investigating officers that the report of the offense appears to be unfounded. A case should not be declared unfounded until this conclusion is approved by the commanding officer.

3. When the investigating officer has not been able to make substantial progress and recommends that the case be declared "inactive" (not cleared). In such event, the recommendation should carry the approval of the commanding officer. A case, therefore, remains open until the commanding officer countersigns the officer's recommendation that it be declared inactive or until the case is closed by an actual final disposition, such as arrest of offender, recovery of property, etc. In this manner, active investigation is not discontinued without a review of the case by the commanding officer in charge. The investigating officer should be required to state fully his reasons for dropping the case. A large proportion of cases declared inactive would not be a desirable feature of the performance and personnel record of an individual officer.

4. When additional facts concerning the case come to the attention of the investigating officer or any other member of the Department.

If the complaint or incident is not fully disposed of as a result of the first investigation and the submission by the investigating officer of the preliminary report, he is required to make subsequent reports on follow-up report form blanks provided for that purpose. It should be an inviolable rule that follow-up reports be submitted in all open cases within three days following the date of the preliminary report and weekly thereafter until the case is closed. This follow-up report is used by the officer to report progress on the case, additional details, descriptions of new suspects, persons apprehended, property recovered, proposed changes in the classification of the offense report, and other action taken. The report may also be used by the officer to indicate that no substantial progress appears possible and that the case should be declared inactive (not cleared). Since it has already been suggested that "on view" arrests are to be transferred to offense report forms, the arresting officer is required to submit such supplementary and follow-up report forms on them also, as may be indicated by the nature of the case.

If the investigating officer has not submitted the reports indicated above, the Record Division will automatically, through its follow-up system (to be presently described), note this failure and report the matter to the commanding officer. The case is kept open until the necessary reports are submitted. The other divisional commanders need to give full cooperation to the Record Division in this matter. A considerable amount of supervision is required upon the inauguration of this procedure, if the officers have not been accustomed to the preparation of such reports.

Report Writing

Report writing is an art and one that is essential to the orderly and prompt conduct of police business. Some officers write more fluently than others and for them, the preparation of an investigation report presents no problem at all. Other officers find the writing of a report to be somewhat difficult at times. It can be said that any officer, with some thought and practice, can develop proficiency in the writing of a report that will convert the task into a pleasant experience.

If at all possible, the report should be typewritten. The heading of the report calls for the name of the victim in the upper left hand corner, in the center—the date the case was reported to the department for investigation, and in the upper right hand corner, the case number.

The body of the investigation report is introduced with a brief résumé which will permit the reader to determine in a general way the subject matter of the report that follows by reading the first sentence. This technique is followed universally by newspaper reporters. An inspection of any newspaper article will reveal that the first sentence, even the headline, tells the whole story.[9]

This is followed by a detailed account of everything that the investigating officer did or learned about the case that he has not reported at some previous time. This information is presented clearly and concisely, and in sufficient detail so that the report explains exactly what has happened, what has been done, and what has been learned. A cardinal rule is that an investigation report which must be supplemented by a verbal explanation has not been properly written.

Careful attention must be given to the spelling of names and the recording of sex, color and marital status so far as it affects the name. The given name by which a person is known and an initial is considered sufficient except in the case of common names such as Smith or Jones, and in such cases, the full name should be spelled out.

This part of the report includes facts as observed by the investigating officer, facts as reported to him by witnesses and in some instances, the opinions of citizens whom the officer may have interviewed in connection with the case.

More often than not, it also includes descriptions of property and it is here that complete accuracy is essential. Property description includes:

1.   Name of the article.

2.   Trade name.

3.   Material.

---

[9] See Hazelet, John C., *Police Report Writing*; Dienstein, William, *How to Write a Narrative Investigation Report*; Gammage, Allen Z., *Basic Police Report Writing*, all published by Charles C. Thomas, Publisher, Springfield, Illinois. These books should be in every departmental library.

4. Form.

5. Physical measurement.

6. Sensory description.

7. Design.

8. Identifying marks (letters, serial numbers, etc.).

9. Condition (including age).

10. Value (cost and present value).

More than one criminal offender has made his way to the penitentiary because of a search the officer made in the property files at headquarters.

The description of a person is one of the chief investigative tools at the disposal of the police and the greatest of care should be exercised in obtaining the original information and recording it accurately in the investigation report. Personnel description includes:

1. Name, and alias or aliases.

2. Sex.

3. Color.

4. Eye color.

5. Height.

6. Weight.

7. Age.

8. Build.

9. Hair color.

10. Complexion.

11. Occupation.

12. Nativity.

13. Beard.

14. Dress.

15. Identifying marks (scars, tattoo, etc.).

The investigation report should include a description of the Modus Operandi of the offender wherever this can be developed.[10]

[10] The system of modus operandi analysis was developed shortly after the turn of the century by Colonel L. W. Atcherley, in charge of the Yorkshire West Riding Constabulary in England, and its success in that country led to its adoption by a number of American police departments. It is based upon a conclusion, consistent with our present knowledge of behavior, that the criminal in his defensive position develops individual techniques and

The investigation report closes with the conclusions and recommendations of the investigating officer. The end of the report is marked by the date, hour of writing, and the signature of the investigating officer.

If the complaint or incident reported to the department for investigation is not fully disposed of as a result of the preliminary investigation and the submission by the investigating officer of the supplementary report, he is required to make subsequent follow-up reports covering his continued investigation of the case on follow-up report blanks provided for that purpose. It should be an inviolable rule that follow-up reports are to be submitted on all open cases within three days following the date of the supplementary report and weekly thereafter until the case is closed.

Processing Reports in the Record Division

It is fundamental to sound police record procedure that an accurate index and cross-index system be established. This reduced to its simplest terms means that ALL offense reports should be indexed by:

1.   Name of complainant or injured party.

2.   Name of person arrested or suspected.

3.   Name of investigating officer.

4.   Names of all witnesses and other persons mentioned in either the offense report, supplementary report or follow-up reports.

5.   Crime classification.

In addition to the above general cross-index required for all types of offense reports, certain crime categories require additional entries in

methods which he considers conducive to safety and success and, further, that a fairly high degree of persistence of certain factors will be found in the operating pattern of any given individual. Within a given criminal specialty, such as burglary or worthless check operations, for example, Colonel Atcherley determined through analysis of thousands of crimes, that each criminal followed an identifying pattern of operation in committing his crime, and that astute investigation at the scene of the crime would reveal the characteristic delineations of this pattern. He found that often the operating pattern included small, irrelevant acts which had no relationship to the actual commission of the crime, and which could be accounted for only by the personality characteristics and general behavior pattern of the individual.

This particular phase of crime detection offers a prolific field for research. The interested student should consult W.P.A. Projects No. 7042, *Modus Operandi*, by the Police Department of Wichita, Kansas, a scholarly inquiry into the modus operandi system conducted under the supervision of Chief O. W. Wilson, now Superintendent of the Chicago Police Department.

Also see "Catching Thieves on Paper," a manual employed for the instruction of new personnel assigned to the modus operandi section of New Scotland Yard.

an expanded cross-index system. This distinction applies particularly to all forms of theft, including robbery, burglary, automobile theft, worthless checks, crimes committed by fraud, false pretense, imposture, etc. These additional cross-index facilities include the modus operandi system and property indices.

In the modus operandi system the method of operation, through index classification, is broken down and factored into its component parts as an investigative aid in the identification of a crime series, and as an aid in the identification of the offender. These index divisions include in part:

1. Crime classification.
2. Where committed (location index; spot maps, etc.).
3. Time of attack.
4. Person or property attacked.
5. How attacked.
6. Means of attack.
7. Object of attack.
8. Trade-Mark.

The necessity for consolidation of property control in the Department has already been mentioned. The property index is one of the most important of all files in the Record Division. This file should include cross-index facilities for all property reported stolen, lost, or found. The serial number of all articles bearing serial numbers serves as the first classification under that particular type of article. In case such serial numbers are not obtainable from complainants, the cards are filed by the make or maker's name or by other identifying marks. Musical instruments, watches, cameras, tools, typewriters, bicycles, and most mechanical contrivances bear serial numbers. Initials, monograms, and other special marks serve as additional index divisions.

Diamond-set articles, except rings (if unmarked) are filed according to the number of diamonds and next according to design. Other stone-set pieces are filed first according to type (for example, an emerald ring, or diamond ring), next by design, as Tiffany, Belcher, Gypsy, etc., and lastly, by size of stone. Clothing is classified as male or female, then by type of article; next by color; then by maker's name. Even though articles may carry serial numbers, they should also be indexed by other distinguishing features, such as monograms, make, or design. This file properly maintained and checked against local pawn shop activities leads to a considerable increase in property recovered and case clearances.

All complaint reports should be kept currently indexed to 7:00 A.M., each day.

The Follow-up Control System

Supplementary offense reports are connected to the master offense report by serial number in the Record Division, and all cases not cleared are held in a pending file under the supervision of the follow-up officer. Simply stated, the follow-up system is a plan whereby every complaint report or other matter reported to the Department for investigation is inspected by the Record Division to determine whether proper and timely action is being taken. Until a case is properly closed and finally filed away, its progress is constantly checked by the follow-up officer. Upon the follow-up officer rests the responsibility for checking, approving or rejecting and questioning all the reports submitted to the division. His job is not to interfere with the actual work on the case, only to take up with the officer or his commanding officer if necessary, instances of incomplete reports, failures to follow prescribed rules in handling various types of cases and to suggest further steps, if needed, prior to final disposition. No case should be permitted to be permanently filed until every investigation is complete and until every effort has been made to clear the case.

The follow-up officer is concerned primarily with the knowledge that the required work has been performed by the officer assigned to the case. Deviations from the departmental standards of procedure are to be recognized at once and steps taken to rectify them and prevent their repetition. The evidence of this performance appears in the officer's written supplementary and follow-up reports, through which the follow-up system maintains its check on cases under investigation by the Department.

The mechanics of the follow-up system consist of the making out of a 3 x 5 index card on every complaint report, arrest, request for information, inquiry requiring an answer, or other matter *which is not completely disposed of at the time of the original report*. These cards are placed in a small file case on the desk of the follow-up officer and arranged according to the days on which the follow-up action is to be taken. Thus, the index cards for this file are set up according to months and subdivided into days of the month.

All reports filed by officers investigating a complaint are checked by the follow-up officer with a view to locating any delinquencies in the investigation and reporting these to the proper superior officer. The request for follow-up action is issued by the follow-up officer and is directed to a superior officer. This official, on receipt of follow-up request on a case to which a subordinate officer is assigned, should:

1. Immediately call the matter to the attention of the subordinate officer and request report from him at the end of his tour of duty.

2. Retain possession of the request until he has received a proper report from the subordinate officer if such report is necessary.

3. Upon such receipt he initials the request, clips the two reports together, and routes them to the Record Division.

The work of the follow-up officer is a staff function. He does not exercise any direct control over investigation. His primary duty is to check, not to supervise. Direct control of investigations is the duty of the commanding officer of the primary division involved. The duties of the follow-up officer place a premium on tact and diplomacy. He must be careful to keep within the limits of his jurisdiction, and should be responsible to the Captain of the Record Division. These considerations, however, should not be permitted to cause any relaxation in the general objective of moving cases through to final disposition as rapidly and accurately as possible.

Procedure for Reporting and Controlling Persons Charged by the Police

The recording of persons charged is a simpler task but as important as the offense procedure. In scope it covers every step from the initial booking to release or court sentence. Every system for recording persons charged by the police should provide for:

1. A formal record of every person charged by the police or proceeded against within the police jurisdiction. Such person may be arrested (taken into custody), summoned directly by the court, or notified (cited) by the police to appear in court. The nature of the offense charged is an indispensable part of the record.

2. Means of identifying the person charged.

3. Certain social facts concerning the offender. This is required both as an aid in determining the proper disposition of the offender and for statistical purposes.

4. Knowledge of how the offender's case terminated in court. The police need to know the whereabouts of criminals and the results obtained in their prosecution.

5. Some convenient means by which these records may be compiled, such as tally sheets, master sheets or tabulating cards.

This record is not only the department's primary record of the offender, but it also controls the case until final disposition. This form is made out in duplicate at the time of booking and bears the case number of the offense report which it concerns, and the arrest or blotter number. The original is routed to the Record Division where it is attached to the proper offense report and forms the basis for follow-up action pending final disposition of the arrest. Transfer to the county jail is not a disposition, nor is release on bond.   Not until a disposition of the charge pending against the offender has been made by the court can the case be considered closed.   The filing of a report of final disposition of arrest is a responsibility of the arresting officer, regardless of who may have been assigned to the investigation of the original offense.   This responsibility arises in part from the individual civil liability of the arresting officer in making an arrest.

The duplicate copy of the arrest card is held on file by the Jail Booking Office until the prisoner is released or transferred from the City Jail.   Hence, the file of duplicate arrest cards in the Booking Office is at any one time, an index to the jail population and affords a continuous audit in this respect.   Upon release of the prisoner, the duplicate arrest card is routed to the Record Division, where it is filed alphabetically by name.

The following General Order recommended in one city and providing for the installation of a centralized police records system is quoted below.   It affords additional insight into the organization and mechanics of a police records division.[11]

GENERAL ORDER

Effective, as of this date, all offense, arrest, identification, communication, property, correspondence, personnel and fiscal records of the _____ Department, are hereby consolidated into one division to be known as the Records Division.   The Records Division shall be under the direct control of the Superintendent of Records, and he shall be responsible to the Chief of Staff Services and the Chief of Police for carrying out the terms of this order.

As of this date, all complaints and reports received by the _____ Department for investigation shall be typewritten by personnel on duty in the Central Complaint Room, and on standard offense record forms provided for that purpose.   Each offense or complaint report shall be given a consecutive serial number in the order of its receipt, regardless of classification, such number to be stamped by the numbering machine in the space provided for that purpose in the upper right hand corner of the offense report.   The offense report shall be filled out in duplicate or triplicate and a copy routed to the division or divisions concerned.   The original is to be held on file temporarily in the Central Complaint Room.

Said reports are to be recorded as described above immediately after receipt of the original information.   Failure to so record any matter referred to the Department for investigation, whatever its nature, shall constitute a violation of this order.   Report clerks in the Central Complaint Room shall be sup-

---

[11] V. A. Leonard, *Survey and Reorganization of the Seattle Police Department*, 1945, p. 187.

plied with memorandum offense report forms to facilitate obtaining complete information necessary for typing the original offense report.

All "on view" arrests, regardless of the charge, shall be transferred to proper offense report forms by personnel on duty in the Central Complaint Room. Requests for investigation from outside agencies received by letter, telegram or otherwise, shall also be recorded in the manner described above on proper offense report forms, and the original letter, telegram, photographs or other documents so received, shall be attached to the original copy of the complaint record on file in the Records Division. Copies of such documents shall be made for the division and investigating officer concerned when necessary.

No letter, telegram, warrant, photograph, or other document shall be detached from the original offense report record and delivered to any investigating officer until he has signed a receipt therefor, on the form prescribed for that purpose. Such receipt shall be issued only by the Superintendent of Records or by an assistant authorized by him, and said receipt shall be attached to the original offense record form which it concerns.

A blank offense report form with the case number stamped thereon may be issued to any commanding officer on request by Central Complaint Room personnel. In all such cases the offense report shall be stamped in duplicate and the commanding officer shall receive the duplicate copy. Only the name of the commanding officer and the date may appear on the original and this information, together with the case number, shall be entered on the Central Complaint Room Bulletin, as outlined below for all offense reports. The foregoing procedure shall be followed in recording reports of subversive activities and occasionally certain types of vice complaints where operations must be attended with some measure of secrecy pending final disposition of the case.

The original copy of such report serves the Records Division as an instrument of control over the case to the end that the records of the Department may, for administrative purposes, accurately reveal the total amount and nature of work being performed by the Department. Upon final disposition of such cases, the division concerned shall furnish the Records Division with information necessary for recording the case on the original blank numbered case report. In rare instances following disposition, detailed records and information of a highly confidential nature bearing upon the case may, if necessary, be retained by the division concerned on the authority of the Deputy Chief of Police, but such records must be attached to the duplicate copy of the case report on file in that division and be subject to inspection by the Superintendent of Records.

Authorization for the retention of such supplementary records shall be granted only in exceptional cases and such authorization, together with an enumeration of documents so retained by the division concerned shall be attached to the original case report on file in the Records Division. No case shall remain silent for a period exceeding thirty days from the date the blank numbered case report is issued to a commanding officer, except on authorization of the Deputy Chief of Police. Such authorizations shall be attached to the original case report on file in the Records Division.

It is the full intent of this order, both expressed and implied, that no case involving a violation of city, state or federal laws, nor any other case, report or complaint, shall be investigated by any member of this Department except under the authority of a case number issued by the Central Complaint Room.

After being recorded as previously outlined, each offense report, regardless of classification, shall be entered in numerical order on the Central Complaint Room Bulletin. Immediately prior to the end of each eight-hour tour of duty, this bulletin shall be mimeographed in sufficient quantity to supply a copy to each officer then reporting for duty, to administrative, supervisory and command personnel, and to each division and unit.

A file of Central Complaint Room Bulletins for the immediate thirty-day period shall be maintained in the Assembly Room for the convenience of officers, and a similar file shall be maintained in the Central Complaint Room. The Records Division shall maintain a Bulletin file in unbroken sequence from the beginning.

As of the date of this order, each automobile patrolman shall be held responsible for all offenses, regardless of classification, originating during his tour of duty in the area he patrols. Final disposition of felony cases shall be the responsibility of members of the Detective Division. Final disposition of misdemeanor cases shall be the responsibility of the automobile patrolman. At the end of his tour of duty, the automobile patrolman shall report to headquarters or to his precinct station and file a preliminary report, on forms provided for that purpose, covering the investigation of each offense originating in his patrol area during his tour of duty, such report to bear the headquarters case number appearing on the original offense record form. This responsibility shall be discharged for the automobile patrolman by a foot patrolman with respect to each "on view" arrest made by the latter, and in those instances where the foot patrolman initiates the investigation.

Since the automobile patrolman shall be held responsible for the disposition of all non-felony cases originating during his tour of duty in the area patrolled by him, he shall file at regular intervals a follow-up report covering his continued investigation of any uncleared case pending its final disposition. This procedure shall continue until the case is disposed of or until the patrolman's commanding officer permits the case to be declared inactive. Any uncleared case shall be considered as a direct charge against both the patrolman and his commanding officer. The Superintendent of Records shall institute the necessary follow-up procedure for control purposes to the end that the Record Division may have on file current investigative reports evidencing continued attention to uncleared cases. The foregoing procedure shall also apply to those members of the Department charged with the disposition of felony cases, and to foot patrolmen in misdemeanor cases where the investigation is initiated by them.

At the end of each tour of duty, all offense reports and officers' reports shall be routed to the Records Division where they shall be assembled and processed in accordance with special instructions covering this phase of records procedure. It shall be a responsibility of the Superintendent of Records to maintain the highest degree of accuracy in meeting the requirements of Uniform Crime Reporting, and it shall also be his responsibility to compile a daily consolidated report, monthly reports, annual reports, and particularly, special studies and analyses dealing with present or emerging situations for the administrative use of the Deputy Chief of Police in charge of line operations.

All arrests shall be recorded, in addition to the offense report record, on the conventional blotter by personnel on duty in the booking office, and on an arrest card form in duplicate, provided for that purpose. The duplicate shall be routed to the Records Division where it will furnish a control over disposition of the arrest. The original copy of the arrest card shall be held on file in the booking office until the individual concerned is no longer a prisoner in the city jail. At that time, the date of release is entered on the original copy of the arrest card, and it shall then be routed to the Records Division. Hence, the arrest cards on file in the booking office provide a continuous inventory of the jail population.

Further implementing this order, all telephone trunk lines into precinct stations are ordered disconnected, and all calls for police service to be rendered by this Department shall arrive at the Central Complaint Room at Police Headquarters. Where the request for police service is presented in person at a precinct station, precinct personnel shall record the information on memorandum offense report form, previously mentioned, and promptly communicate the complete report to the Central Complaint Room so that the procedure above outlined may be followed.

Further, the operation of all communications facilities shall be under the direct supervision of the Superintendent of Records. It is also the intent of this order that all records procedure covering the control of prisoners' property, found property, recovered propety, impounded property and evidence shall be under the supervisory control of the Superintendent of Records.

This order requires no change in records procedure in the Traffic Division, with the exception that the branch switchboard now located in the Traffic Division and public counter shall be regarded as extensions of the Central Complaint Room and shall be under the control of the Superintendent of Records. Personnel on duty at the traffic switchboard and public counter in the Traffic Division shall clear with the Central Complaint Room for case numbers.

The term "Offense Report" used in this order refers to any violation of city, state, or federal laws, exclusive of minor traffic violations, or any other case report or complaint referred to the Department for investigation.

The Records Division shall remain open for business twenty-four hours per day, including Sundays and holidays.

All records procedure heretofore employed which is in conflict with this order, is hereby countermanded.

_____

Chief of Police

Date _____

In the foregoing General Order, it will be noted that the respective jurisdictions and responsibilities of patrolman and detective are redefined to some extent, with a substantial increase in the responsibility of the patrolman. This is in agreement with an observable trend in the American police services today although prevailing practice generally too often, still conforms to the obsolete principle that the investigative function should be located exclusively in the detective division. The future course of police administration in the United States is substantially involved in the solution of this question. It is reserved for more extended treatment in the chapter which follows.

Departmental Statistician

In the larger organizations provision should be made for the employment of a professional statistician and facilities provided for the mechanical tabulation of statistical information from offense reports and from the records of persons charged. A number of police departments in cities have long ago installed this feature of successful police management. Effective police control today demands a vast number of facts marshalled accurately, quickly, and economically together. Incomplete and inaccurate results, tardy figures, excessive administrative costs, and little, if any, control data are the results of continuing in use methods and equipment declared obsolete long ago. The police business has expanded to embrace more manifold objectives and more diverse fields of activity, requiring the development of a high degree of administrative technique and method in the management and use of records data for the proper employment of the available resources of manpower and equipment.

The need for compiling and analyzing offense reports and persons charged by means of tabulating machines increases with the size of the city. In the large department it is the only practical method of analyzing the facts of crime as embodied in the offense report and of analyzing the social characteristics and dispositions of the thousands of arrests made by the police. If full advantage is to be taken of the record system, the information on all offense and arrest records must be transferred to tabulating punch cards. Even though master sheets may serve as temporary makeshifts, many of the desirable analyses are either very difficult or too complex to make without tabulating machinery. Except in crude form, modus operandi analysis is almost impossible. Further, it is a difficult matter to analyze the various social facts and dispositions of persons charged unless tabulating machinery is employed.

The first step in the mechanical tabulation and compilation of statistical data is the coding of this data and its complete transfer to the tabulating cards in coded form. Through the assignment of numerical code values to the various classes of data, the transfer of a vast amount of classified information becomes possible. This physical transfer is accomplished through the use of the automatic key punch machine. The principles are so well known as to require no detailed description.

The facts of crime are thus quickly determined. Grouping of like data is quickly accomplished through the automatic sorter and counter. Suppose, for example, it became necessary to know the number of burglaries committed over the weekend in District No. 4 during the past six months in which the burglar used matches, entered by prying open a bedroom window, rifled drawers and threw contents on the floor (disorderly worker), cut telephone wires, helped himself to food in the refrigerator, wore tennis shoes, and stole only money and gold jewelry, passing up other valuables. The automatic sorting machine and tabulator sorts cards and prints the results at the rate of 400 or more per minute. Thus, it would be possible to start with 5,000 ungrouped cards and obtain the information within 30 minutes. Suppose there were 15 such cases. The column at the left of the tabulating card indicates the serial number of the offense report and from this, the reports themselves may be pulled from the files for detailed study.

Mrs. Rhoda Cross, until recently chief statistician of the Los Angeles Police Department, has pointed the way for American police administration in the application of automatic tabulating machinery and statistical method to the solution of police problems. Through the rapid mechanical search of police records she makes possible the clearance of the type of cases that often frustrate detectives and which may apparently baffle solution. The persistence of the modus operandi pattern in the operations of the individual criminal offender is effectively exploited. For example, during one three-month period, twenty-eight burglaries were committed by a thief who used matches instead of a flashlight and always drank milk from the refrigerator during his nocturnal raids.

These traits linked all twenty-eight crimes, but the officers still lacked any description of the suspect. When they turned to Mrs. Cross, she ran the code cards on burglary for the past decade through the automatic sorter, and finally reported: "The man you want is named Joseph Cyriakowski. Here is his description and home address." The officers called on Cyriakowski, found stolen goods from these burglaries and obtained a prompt confession. Mrs. Cross had solved the case by searching records of burglaries for the past decade. She quickly narrowed the hunt to three different burglars who followed the same pattern of operation. Two were then in prison. The third had just been released on parole. Parole records revealed his address in Los Angeles, and a speedy clearance of a series of twenty-eight burglaries followed.

The application of this method is also useful in the preparation of administrative reports and analyses, upon which ultimately police management and administration must depend in the planning and measurement of operations.

Administrative Reports and Analyses

Since the Chief of Police or his commanding officers cannot personally supervise every act of every member of the force or visualize the sum total of departmental operations, they must utilize systematic controls and administrative reports. The mere recording of information on record forms is not enough. The records must be tabulated and analyzed so that informative summaries of crime conditions and the work of the Department may be submitted daily, weekly, monthly, and annually. Only in this way can the department realize the objectives of police administration. These summaries should include complete information on crime conditions, results obtained from investigations, persons arrested and their disposition, distribution of personnel, and of police problems in general. Without a picture of both the problems of crime and the effectiveness of the department in solving them, police administration can be little more than a haphazard and casual affair.

In preparing statistical reports, the standards set forth by the Committee on Uniform Crime Records of the International Association of Chiefs of Police in *Uniform Crime Reporting* and the *Guide for Preparing Annual Police Reports* should be adhered to.

The Consolidated Morning Report

Each morning the Chief of Police, Chief of Services, Chief of Operations, and Inspectors should receive a consolidated report which shows the crime and police personnel conditions for the preceding twenty-four hours. With information at hand concerning the amount, nature, and distribution of crime on the one hand and the strength of the force on the other, personnel can be detailed and distributed according to immediate crime demands. The consolidated morning report is compiled in the Record Division from the offense reports, records of persons charged, accident reports, and daily personnel reports received during the previous twenty-four hours. The tables in this report are standard and can be obtained from the International Association of Chiefs of Police.

(Standard Form of the Committee on Uniform Crime Records of the International Association of Chiefs of Police)
(Copies available at Federal Bureau of Investigation, Washington, D. C.)

CONSOLIDATED DAILY REPORT

POLICE DEPARTMENT

CITY OF ....

For 24 hours ending 7 A. M. ...., 19......

NUMBER OF OFFENSES KNOWN TO THE POLICE (Includes on-view arrests)				UNIFORM CLASSIFICATION OF OFFENSES	PERSONS CHARGED (Includes arrests, summons, and notices)			
Past 24 hours	This month to date	Last month to date	Same month last year to date		Past 24 hours	This month to date	Last month to date	Same month last year to date
				PART I CLASSES				
				1. Criminal homicide:				
				(a) Murder and nonnegligent manslaughter				
				(b) Manslaughter by negligence				
				2. Rape				
				3. Robbery				
				4. Aggravated assault				
				5. Burglary—breaking and/or entering				
				6. Larceny—theft (except auto theft)				
				7. Auto theft				
				TOTAL, Part I classes				
				PART II CLASSES				
				8. Other assaults				
				9. Forgery and counterfeiting				
				10. Embezzlement and fraud				
				11. Stolen property; buying, receiving, possessing				
				12. Weapons; carrying, possessing, etc.				
				13. Prostitution and commercialized vice				
				14. Sex offenses (except 2 and 13)				
				15. Offenses against the family and children				
				16. Narcotic drug laws				
				17. Liquor laws				
				18. Drunkenness				
				19. Disorderly conduct				
				20. Vagrancy				
				21. Gambling				
				22. Driving while intoxicated				
				23. Violation of road and driving laws				
				24. Parking violations				
				25. Traffic and motor vehicle laws (except 22-24)				
				26. All other offenses				
				27. Suspicion or held for investigation				
				TOTAL, Part II classes				
				GRAND TOTAL				

TRAFFIC ANALYSIS

Persons charged	Past 24 hours	Month to date	Same month last year to date
1. Speeding			
2. Reckless driving			
3. Illegal parking			
4. Improper or defective lights and brakes			
5. Nonobservance light or sign			
6. Improper registration or license			
7. Violation by pedestrians			
8. All other violations			
9. TOTAL			
Traffic accidents (total No.)			
Injuries in			
Deaths in			

7—9246

[*Reverse side:*]

PERSONNEL REPORT	Total	Chief's office	Records bureau	Uniformed force	Detective bureau	Traffic bureau		First relief	Second relief	Third relief
Numerical strength										
Total absent										
Temporary details										
Effective strength										
CAUSE OF ABSENCE:										
1. Sick										
2. Injured										
3. Vacation										
4. Day off										
5. Leave										
6. Suspended										
7. A. W. O. L.										

U. S. GOVERNMENT PRINTING OFFICE   7—2305

Major events, brief details of outstanding crimes, etc.:

The Monthly Report

The most important record from the standpoint of general police administration is the monthly consolidated report. This report shows crime tendencies and conditions and the effectiveness of the department in coping with them. It is an up-to-the-minute appraisal of the police work and police problems, including personnel, results of investigations, accidents and miscellaneous services with sufficient comparisons to point out trends. The monthly report serves as a very valuable aid to the Chief in administering the force. For example, a large decrease in the number of burglaries cleared by arrest may indicate faulty distribution of the force, lack of training, improper discipline, or inadequate personnel. The figures may indicate the need for special analyses. In fact, this is the major function of these administrative reports. The monthly report is as significant to police administrators as the monthly operating financial statement is to a large industrial corporation. Many of the tables in the monthly report find their counterpart in the *Guide for Preparing Annual Police Reports*. Thus, the monthly reports build up the materials for the annual report, making its preparation a relatively simple matter.

(Standard Form of the Committee on Uniform Crime Records of the International Association of Chiefs of Police)
(Copies available at Federal Bureau of Investigation, Washington, D. C.)

CONSOLIDATED MONTHLY REPORT

POLICE DEPARTMENT

City of ....   Month of ...., 19......

TABLE 1.—DISTRIBUTION OF PERSONNEL

	NUMERICAL STRENGTH		AVERAGE DAILY ABSENCE		PERCENT DAILY ABSENCE		AVERAGE DAILY TEMPORARY DETAILS		AVERAGE EFFECTIVE STRENGTH		
	End of this month	Same month last year	This month	Same month last year	This month	Same month last year	This month	Same month last year	This month	Last month	Same month last year
Total personnel..											
Chief's office......											
Records bureau..											
Uniformed force.											
Detective bureau.											
Traffic bureau....											
....											
....											
First relief........											
Second relief......											
Third relief......											

TABLE 2.—CHANGES IN PERSONNEL

1. Present for duty end of last month.............. ....
2. Recruited during month.............................. ....
3. Reinstated during month.......................... ....

     Total to account for............................ ....

·4. Separations from the service:

     (a) Voluntary resignation ....

     (b) Retirement on pension...................... ....

     (c) Resigned with charges pending................. ....

     (d) Dropped during probation.................... ....

     (e) Dismissed for cause.... ....

     (f) Killed in line of duty.. ....

     (g) Deceased.................. ....

     Total separations...................... ....

5. Present for duty at end of month.............. ....

TABLE 3.—DAILY AVERAGE PATROL STRENGTH

	This month	Same month last year
1. Total number of patrolmen...............		
2. Less permanent assignments (public offices, clerical, chauffeurs, etc.)......		
3. Less details to special squads or bureaus (traffic, vice, park, etc.)........		
4. Average daily absences of patrolmen assigned to patrol duty owing to: (a) Vacation, suspension, rest days, etc..		
(b) Sick and injured.................		
(c) Temporary details................		
Total average daily absences.................		
5. Available for patrol duty..........		

TABLE 4.—NUMBER AND DISPOSITION OF OFFENSES KNOWN TO THE POLICE

UNIFORM CLASSIFICATION OF OFFENSES	OFFENSES KNOWN TO THE POLICE					PERCENT OF OFFENSES CLEARED BY ARREST (Includes exceptional clearances)		
	Reported or known this month	Unfounded	Actual offenses this month	Actual this year to date	Actual last year to date	This month*	This year to date	Last year to date
PART I CLASSES								
1. Criminal homicide: (a) Murder and nonnegligent manslaughter								
(b) Manslaughter by negligence								
2. Rape								
3. Robbery								
4. Aggravated assault								
5. Burglary—breaking and/or entering								
6. Larceny—theft (except auto theft): (a) $50 and over in value								
(b) Under $50 in value								
7. Auto theft								
Total, Part I Classes								

*Includes offenses reported not cleared other months, cleared this month.

TABLE 5.—VALUE OF PROPERTY STOLEN AND RECOVERED
(Automobiles not included)

	This month	Last month	This year to date	Last year to date
1. Total value property reported stolen				
2. Total value stolen property recovered				
(a) Recovered through property identification records				
(b) Recovered by police officers				
(c) Recovered by other jurisdictions				
(d) Recovered otherwise				
3. Percent of stolen property recovered				
4. Value of property recovered for other jurisdictions				

TABLE 6.—AUTO THEFTS AND RECOVERIES

	This month	Last month	This year to date	Last year to date
1. Number automobiles reported stolen in city				
2. Total recovered (stolen in city)				
(a) Recovered by auto squad				
(b) Recovered by other police officers				
(c) Recovered by other jurisdictions				
(d) Recovered otherwise				
3. Percent of stolen cars recovered				
4. Automobiles recovered for other jurisdictions				

7—2206

TABLE 7.—ANALYSIS OF PERSONS CHARGED BY THE POLICE

UNIFORM CLASSIFICATION OF OFFENSES	Released by police (no formal charge)	PERSONS CHARGED THIS MONTH			FOUND GUILTY THIS MONTH		PERCENT FOUND GUILTY	
		Arrested	Summoned or notified	Total	Of offense charged	Of lesser offense	This year to date	Last year to date
PART I CLASSES								
1. Criminal homicide:								
(a) Murder and nonnegligent manslaughter.								
(b) Manslaughter by negligence								
2. Rape								
3. Robbery								
4. Aggravated assault								
5. Burglary—breaking and/or entering								
6. Larceny—theft(except auto theft):								
(a) $50 and over in value.								
(b) Under $50 in value								
7. Auto theft								
Total, Part I Classes								
PART II CLASSES								
8. Other assaults								
9. Forgery and counterfeiting								
10. Embezzlement and fraud								
11. Stolen property—buying, receiving, possessing								
12. Weapons—carrying, possessing, etc								
13. Prostitution and commercialized vice								
14. Sex offenses (except 2 and 13)								
15. Offenses against the family and children								
16. Narcotic drug laws								
17. Liquor laws								
18. Drunkenness								
19. Disorderly conduct								
20. Vagrancy								
21. Gambling								
22. Driving while intoxicated								
23. Violation of road and driving laws								
24. Parking violations								
25. Traffic and motor vehicle laws (except 22–24)								
26. All other offenses								
27. Suspicion or held for investigation								
Total, Part II Classes								
GRAND TOTAL								

7—2205

TABLE 8.—ANALYSIS OF TRAFFIC ACCIDENTS

CLASSIFICATION OF THE NATIONAL SAFETY COUNCIL	NUMBER OF INJURY ACCIDENTS			NUMBER KILLED (All ages)			NUMBER INJURED (All ages)			NUMBER ACCIDENTS (Property damage only)		
	This month	This year to date	Last year to date	This month	This year to date	Last year to date	This month	This year to date	Last year to date	This month	This year to date	Last year to date
A. Motor vehicle accidents—total												
1. M. V. with pedestrian												
2. M. V. with motor vehicle												
3. M. V. with R. R. train												
4. M. V. with electric car												
5. M. V. with bicycle												
6. M.V. with horse vehicle												
7. M. V. with fixed object												
8. Noncollision operating accidents												
9. Other M. V. accidents												
B. Public accidents—total (not with M. V.)												
10. R. R. accident												
11. Electric car												
12. Other vehicle												
13. Airplane												
14. Other public accidents												

TABLE 9.—MISCELLANEOUS SERVICES AND INCIDENTS

	This month	This year to date	Last year to date		This month	This year to date	Last year to date
1. Lodgers cared for				10. Arrests for other jurisdictions			
2. Persons assisted				11. Insanity cases handled			
3. Doors found open and reported				12. Suicide cases investigated			
4. Persons reported missing				13. Sudden deaths investigated			
5. Persons missing, found				14. Wagon service runs			
6. Fires discovered				15. Ambulance runs			
7. Lamp outages reported				16. Licenses issued			
8. Noncriminal complaints investigated				17. Reports made of conditions affecting other departments			
9. Nonvehicular accidents							

U. S. GOVERNMENT PRINTING OFFICE   7—2206

The Annual Report

Just as the morning and monthly reports are indispensable in studying police activities over a short period of time, so the annual report is essential in presenting the picture of police problems and operations for the year. Its dual function as a means for implementing democratic control and as an aid to management has been discussed earlier.

Special Studies and Analyses

The consolidated morning report, the monthly and annual reports need to be supplemented by intensive, specialized studies of records data bearing upon specific police problems.   Such studies facilitate effective planning and lead to economic use of departmental resources in a professional approach to problems and situations that press forward continuously for attention and solution.   These problems may be operational or administrative in nature.   A high traffic accident or burglary rate may command attention at the moment.   Competent traffic administration is predicated almost completely upon the application of statistical analysis to factors involved in traffic accidents, congestion, retarded traffic flow and other problems.

Crime in all of its categories can be attacked successfully only upon the basis of painstaking records analysis.   Personnel problems, organizational changes, budget requests, design of a new headquarters building, distribution of the force by function, time, and area are representative of an almost endless succession of problem situations which require analytical attention if they are to be met effectively.   Consolidated morning reports, together with monthly and annual reports, merely reveal problems; they do not furnish solutions.   The method of attack or the procedure to be employed can only be determined through special study and analysis of raw data to be found available in a well administered police records system.   The strategic role of records administration in amplifying the striking power of a police organization becomes more evident in the following chapters.

The Research and Planning Unit

As police service becomes more and more sophisticated, the more pronounced the trend toward exploring and exploiting the tools of management that have proved effective in successful business enterprise. A characteristic development has been the emergence in recent years of the Research and Planning Unit in the structure of police organization.

In a recent survey of the extent to which the Research and Planning Unit was being utilized in the American police services, questionnaries were sent to police departments in seventy-six cities in four population brackets: over 1,000,000; 500,000 to 1,000,000; 250,000 to 500,-000; and 100,000 to 250,000.   Forty-five departments responded for a total return of 59%.[12]

---

[12] Colliton, Patrick H., *The Evaluation of the Research-Planning Function in the American Police Services*, a Master's Thesis, Washington State University, 1962.

In analyzing the returns, it was found that 44% of the departments reporting had established formal Research and Planning Units. Five per cent were organized between 1930 and 1940; ten per cent were established between 1940 and 1950; fifty-five per cent between 1950 and 1960; and thirty per cent were organized or in process of being organized since 1960.

The appearance of the Research and Planning Unit in the American police services reflects the sharpened recognition being given to the function of decision-making in police administration.[13]   There must be preparation for the decision if it is to be adequate, and research and fact-finding are basic to such preparation.   The Research and Planning Unit is specifically organized for a systematic and intelligent approach to the study of police problems and emerging problems, together with the recommendation of plans and procedures for their solution.[14]

It may address its attention to a wide variety of problems in several critical areas, including organization and management, general and special operations, and general departmental procedures.   Following are typical research projects that have been undertaken by this unit in various police departments:

A work-load study of the beat patrolman.
The use of dogs in police patrol service.
Report writing procedures.
A study of police records and reporting forms.
The blockade-quadrant system.
Special M. O. and crime pattern bulletins.
Patrol beat survey and beat construction.
The mobile tactical unit or task force.
Increasing the investigative responsibility of the uniformed force.
Manual for the care and preservation of evidence.
Renting police vehicles vs. purchasing them.
Approaching suspicious vehicles.
Handling of aircraft emergencies.
Operating procedure in regard to road blocks.

---

[13] See *Decision-Making in Police Administration*, by Allen P. Bristow and E. C. Gabard, 118 pp., Charles C. Thomas, Publisher, 1961.

[14] As of 1962, Research and Planning Units were reported in the Police Departments of Buffalo, New York; Chicago, Illinois; Columbus, Ohio; Des Moines, Iowa; Detroit, Michigan; Fresno, California; Houston, Texas; Kansas City, Missouri; Long Beach, California; Los Angeles, California; New Orleans, Louisiana; New York, New York; Oakland, California; Philadelphia, Pennsylvania; Portland, Oregon; St. Louis, Missouri; Sacramento, California; San Antonio, Texas; San Francisco, California; and Spokane, Washington.

Microfilming Police Department records.
Civilian employee needs in a Police Department.
Evaluation of promotional examinations.
The Police Cadet System.
Personnel performance rating.
The roll call training program.
Handling of explosives.
Use of safety belts in police vehicles.
Use of aircraft in enforcement.
Pre-disaster police planning.
Detection of the emerging situation and operational planning.
A study of the performance record of university trained personnel.
Inauguration of command-level training classes.
Research into sonic alarm device for burglary apprehensions.
An evaluation of vice control activities.
Revised mug photo—3 views on one negative, using two cameras.
Job analysis and development of duty manuals.
Operational planning based upon records analysis.
Reduction in the number of special details.
Police policy on labor-management relations.
The "Oddity File".
Review of Departmental Rules and Regulations.
Projecting police needs in relation to planned annexation.
Patterns of reports and analyses for administrative planning.
Application of IBM facilities to the police problem.
Detective audit system.
Use of civilians in certain positions for release of uniformed personnel to patrol service.
Policing special events.
Field dictation of investigation reports.
Departmental vehicles—cost analysis and performance study.
Modus Operandi as an investigative tool.
The control of property—departmental, prisoner's, evidence, impounded, etc.
Study of existing office lay-out.
Police Headquarters design.
Police needs in relation to urban renewal development.
One-man car vs. two man car.
One-man car training procedure.
One-man car operation.
Dispatching procedure in the one-man car operation.
Radio calls—calls requiring the service of two or more cars.
Hold-up road block system.

The police pension system.

Use of women for parking meter enforcement.

Motorcycle accident costs.

Report writing manual.

Policy with respect to fingerprinting juveniles.

Police ambulance procedure.

Departmental reorganization.

Organization and use of the mobile reserve or tactical unit.

Undercover expenditures.

Emergency equipment in police vehicles.

The importance and usefulness of the research and planning function is not limited to the larger cities. Police departments in communities under 100,000 population, regardless of size, would do well to consider making the same systematic approach to problem solutions. In the smaller departments, this function might well be assumed by the Chief of Police or some qualified person in the department delegated by him to undertake this responsibility.

The Criminal Identification System

Closely associated with the police records and almost universally a part of it in the organizational structure is the criminal identification system.

One of the most indispensable tools at the disposal of the police in criminal investigation is a method for identifying criminal offenders. It is absolutely essential that the police have some positive method for identifying persons who have been arrested. Such a system is equally necessary for identifying persons wanted for crimes but who may not as yet have been taken into custody.

The Bertillon System. Prior to 1900, the police throughout the civilized world, including the United States, used for this purpose what is known as the *Bertillon System* of criminal identification. It was developed in Paris, France, by Alphonse Bertillon, a famous French criminologist. In a building in Paris known as the Palace of Justice, which houses the French Criminal Identification System, can still be seen the laboratory where Bertillon worked and developed this new identification technique.

Bertillon was born in Paris in 1853, the son of an eminent anthropoligist. For several years, he was employed by the French police in a minor capacity. His superiors soon recognized his talents and ability, and in 1882, he was placed in charge of the French Police Identification Bureau. He early perceived the need for a positive system of identification which the police could use in cataloging criminal offenders.

After some experimental work with prisoners in the La Sonte Prison in France, Bertillon came to the conclusion that certain bony structures of the human body which could be easily measured would offer the basis for a reliable method of identification. The Bertillon Identification system employed the following measurements:

1. Measurements based on the entire body.
    a. Standing Height.
    b. Arm reach (outspread).
    c. Sitting height.
2. Measurements based on the head.
    a. Length of head.
    b. Breadth of head.
    c. Length of right ear.
    d. Breadth of right ear.
3. Measurements based on the extremeties.
    a. Length of left foot.
    b. Length of left middle finger.
    c. Length of left little finger.
    d. Length of left cubitus (elbow to tip of extended middle finger.

He developed for this purpose several types of calipers with which these measurements could be easily taken. As the measurements were made, they were recorded on a printed identification card form. The next step was to classify these measurements into a formula. Since no two individuals would have exactly the same measurements, no two individuals would have the same formula. Yet any single individual would carry the same formula throughout most of the years of his adult life. The Bertillon card formula was then searched in the Bertillon files to determine if an arrested person possessed a prior record of arrests or criminal activity and then filed by the formula, rather than the name.

The Bertillon system is no longer used by the police. It had certain basic defects, which included:

1. The bony structures of the human body change somewhat over a period of years. It is obvious that this would cause a change in the formula of an individual and make a search of the records difficult if not impossible.
2. It required a considerable period of time to take the measurements of an individual. In large cities where many persons are arrested each day, the Bertillon system proved very time consuming.

3. Then there were occasions when errors occurred in taking these measurements. Such errors would result in a formula that was not correct. With an incorrect formula, an effective search of the Bertillon files would be out of the question.

Nevertheless, the criminal identification system developed by Bertillon served the police throughout the civilized world very well indeed, and for a period of years. But a new and more effective identification system was about to be introduced and made available to the police.

The Fingerprint Identification System. Near the turn of the century, Sir E. R. Henry of Scotland Yard made a study of fingerprints as a possible means of criminal identification. As a result of his study of fingerprint patterns, he developed a rather simple system by which the ten fingerprints on the human hands could be classified into a formula. In 1808, a committee was appointed by the English Parliament to consider the possible adoption of the fingerprint identification system by the police. The committee turned in a favorable report and in 1900, the new system went into operation in Scotland Yard, replacing the Bertillon system.

It proved so efficient and successful that its use soon spread to other English cities. The fingerprint system of criminal identification is now employed by the police everywhere throughout the civilized world. Today, even the smallest police departments use this method for the identification of criminal offenders.

There are very sound reasons for the rapid adoption of the fingerprint system. They include:

1. If all the millions of people on earth were fingerprinted, it is safe to say that no two fingerprints would ever be found alike. Galton working with the theory of probabilities, found that by using the patterns of all ten fingers, the chances were 64,000,-000,000 to 1 that no two human beings would ever possess fingerprints exactly alike.[15]

2. It is a very simple operation to take the fingerprints of an individual, and it requires only a very few minutes.

3. As indicated before, fingerprints lend themselves to a very simple system of classification by which a fingerprint formula is derived. Since the fingerprints of an individual do not change throughout life, the fingerprint formula of each person remains the same from birth to death.

---

[15] Vanderbosch, Charles C., *Criminal Investigation*, Professional Standards Division, International Association of Chiefs of Police, Washington, D. C., 1968, p. 131.

4. As an unequaled advantage to the police—under most conditions, on everything a person touches, he leaves his fingerprints. Many a criminal offender has found his way to the penitentiary through latent fingerprints he left at the scene of his crime.

The fingerprint identification system or file is today a characteristic feature of virtually every police department. Even the smallest police department should proceed to establish such a facility, if it has not already done so. Also, the desirability of setting up a single fingerprint classification system on known burglars and automobile thieves, as well as on those who have been handled for robbery should be given favorable consideration.

As is well known to police officers, it is usually the case that not more than one or two latent fingerprints, most likely the thumb, index or middle fingers, are recovered in a single criminal case.[16] Since the presence of all ten fingerprints is necessary for a search in the conventional fingerprint file, the search of a single latent fingerprint found at the scene would be out of the question unless a single fingerprint classification system is maintained. Police departments employing this system report a high yield in terms of the number of identifications or "raps" made, particularly in juvenile burglaries.

Arrested persons who are photographed are given a consecutive whole identification number, such as 3845, for example. If a photograph is not made of an arrested person who has been fingerprinted, immediately following photograph number 3845, his identification number would be 3845–D–1, indicating that one person had been fingerprinted only since the last photograph was taken. If eleven more arrested persons were fingerprinted but not photographed before the next photograph was taken, the identification number of the twelfth prisoner would be 3845–D–12.

The Criminal History File. Since it is possible to record only a limited amount of information in terms of criminal record on the reverse side of a fingerprint card, it is necessary to maintain a Criminal History File. Each criminal history contains the known criminal record of an individual offender and it is given the same identification number that appears on his fingerprint record; it is filed by this number. As new

---

[16] The author was involved in the investigation of a series of burglaries extending over a period of three or four years. The offender invariably drank milk "on the job", with the result that over a period of time, a complete set of latent prints from milk bottles was obtained with the exception of the left little finger. Yet, the search was a monumental task due to the number of reference classifications that had to be taken into consideration.

arrests of the offender occur or come to the attention of the department, they are posted to his criminal history file.

When a person is arrested and fingerprinted by the police, at least three sets of fingerprints are taken. One set is classified, searched and filed in the local police fingerprint files. The second is sent to the State Bureau of Criminal Records and Identification in the capital city of the state. All law enforcement agencies in every state, including the Sheriff's Department and the State Police, follow the same procedure.

As a result, each State Bureau has on file many thousands of fingerprint records of known criminal offenders. In this manner, it functions as a state-wide clearing house for criminal records and information. In the State Bureau, when a set of fingerprints is received, it is classified and searched by the formula. If an identification is made, a copy of the record or "rap" sheet is sent to the department which originally forwarded the fingerprints to the Bureau.

The third set of fingerprints is sent to the Federal Bureau of Investigation in Washington, D. C. Here again, all law enforcement agencies throughout the United States and its territories, follow the same procedure.

As in the State Bureau, fingerprint experts in the FBI classify the third set of fingerprints and search them by formula. In the event an identification is made, a complete copy of the criminal record is sent to the department which originally forwarded the prints to the Bureau, and a copy to the State Bureau in the state where the department is located. Where the criminal record of an offender shows an arrest or arrests by other departments, a copy of his criminal record is also sent to the department or departments involved.

As of 1970, more than 50,000,000 standard ten-finger criminal fingerprint cards were on file in the Fingerprint Section of the Federal Bureau of Investigation. The Bureau also maintains a special single fingerprint file on a selected group of notorious criminals. The prints in this file are classified under a special system which makes it possible to search for duplicates of a single finger impression. When, for example, a single latent fingerprint is developed at the scene of a crime, it is this file to which the fingerprint expert refers in his efforts to identify the source of the print.

A high speed facsimile fingerprint identification network has been installed throughout the state of New York by the New York State Identification and Intelligence System. After a suspect is arrested and fingerprinted, the fingerprint card is then transmitted via the New York State network to Albany where the central file section maintains records of all persons previously arrested. If the subject has a past criminal record, it is then transmitted back to the arresting law enforcement agency. Law enforcement agencies throughout the state can now identify a known criminal in less than half an hour.

The foregoing is society's answer to the mobility of the criminal population. Wherever the criminal offender may operate—California, Texas or Pennsylvania, or even across international boundary lines—his shadow faithfully follows him immediately behind. There is no escape.

*

Chapter 9

PATROL—MAJOR COMPONENT OF LINE POWER

I N the attack upon crime and other police problems, patrol service is at once the most important and at the same time, one of the most neglected phases of police management. The patrol or uniformed division is the basic element of line power in a police department. It carries out in police service the functions performed by the combat services in military operations. It represents the front line where policies and plans are translated into action, including the prevention and suppression of crime, preservation of law and order, and the protection of life and property.

Since the combat strength of a police organization is almost entirely a measure of the striking power of the patrol force, all the tools of management and managerial procedures should be directed toward maximum accretion of patrol line power. Any organizational function which does not serve this end represents lost motion and wasted resources and should be abandoned forthwith as a matter of sound administrative policy.

Since the work of the patrol force includes all police functions, the more effective the patrol division, the less need there is for the other, more specialized operating divisions and units. Although it is impossible for the patrol force to be one hundred per cent effective in the discharge of all police functions, the other operating line divisions are necessary only to the extent that the patrol division falls short of this ideal.[1] It is axiomatic, therefore, that any attempt to improve or strengthen other divisions at the expense of the patrol division serves to pyramid the case load not only for the unit that has prospered through personnel transfers but for all other divisions and units in the department. A balanced organization is one in which the various units have been developed in accordance with the relative importance of their contributions to the total line power of patrol service.

All other line units in a police organization, including detective, traffic, and crime prevention, are secondary and collateral to the patrol division and are only extensions of that division. Failure to recognize

[1] "Municipal Police Administration," The International City Managers' Association, Municipal Management Series, second edition, 1943, p. 248.

227

this relationship results in an unbalanced organization. Wherever this is true, depletion of the line power of the patrol force is occasioned by transfers of personnel strength to meet the demands of collateral divisions and units for manpower.

Size and Distribution of the Patrol Force

Amplification of patrol line power by every means possible should be a managerial objective of the commanding officer in charge of line operations, and a major concern of the chief executive. Determination of the amount of patrol power required and its distribution are among the gravest administrative problems confronting police management.

The problems involved in determining the size of the force are complex. Obviously, with unlimited funds, it would be possible to provide police officers in sufficient numbers to deal promptly and effectively with virtually every public emergency within the jurisdiction of the police. No community would be willing to make expenditures on this lavish scale. In addition, the law of diminishing returns would argue against it. The alternative is to underwrite a less numerous force and to tolerate a certain amount of crime which *might* be suppressed were a larger number of men employed. The average police executive is tempted to think in terms of the improved service he could render if he had additional personnel at his disposal; this leads almost invariably to a demand for more manpower.

It is questionable that there is a permanent relationship between the number of police officers employed by a city and the amount of crime in that city, despite statistical data which tend to support this conclusion. It was indicated in a previous chapter that the number of men on the payroll of a police department is among the least of several factors that determine the combat efficiency of the organization. The intelligence, education, professional training, mental health and career interests of the individual officer combine with expert management to amplify the combat power of a police organization far beyond any point attainable by sheer numerical strength alone. Qualitative factors are a commanding determinant in the equation of personnel strength and must condition any estimates of the size of the force required.

Furthermore, crime rates are influenced by social and economic factors, some of which are beyond the immediate control of the police. Composition of the population, economic status and activities of the population, social character of neighborhoods and districts possessing a high crime potential, community tolerance of environmental hazards, civic consciousness; educational, recreational and religious facilities, standards of local government, attitude of the public toward law enforcement problems, industrial concentrations and the impact of war and post-war psychology on behavior patterns, all play important roles in determining the amount of crime in a community.[2]

The complex nature of crime control becomes even more apparent when it is realized that the crime rate of tomorrow in any American city will be determined largely by the number of developing behavior problem cases now in the primary and elementary grades and the type of attention that is being given the child who is socially, mentally or physically different. The killers, prostitutes, stick-up men, burglars, drug addicts, automobile thieves, thugs and other members of the criminal gentry the police will be chasing tomorrow are now in the schools of the land. Crime control is something more than a matter of police raids, arrests, criminal court procedure and penitentiaries. As in preventive medicine, so in the field of criminology, prophylactic measures must be applied upstream if we are to make substantial social gains in the control of crime.

The foregoing circumstances complicate determinations with respect to the size of the force, but they in no way diminish police responsibility. In fact, the responsibilities of police administration are thereby increased and its sphere of operations expanded enormously. Operating under a moral and legal mandate to achieve crime control, police administration has no alternative but to supplement its enforcement activities by a positive merger with those constructive forces in the community that may prove useful in the prevention project.

Other factors enter into the determination of the size of the force, including area, topography and geographical characteristics of the municipality; relative location of schools, churches and hospitals, number and direction of streets as well as the general lay-out of the street system, and even climatic factors. The age distribution of the citizenry bears weight also, for the incidence of crime is greater among certain age groups. Even the proportion of males to females in the population and the percentage of married and single persons may affect the police problem.

The factors influencing the crime rate illustrate the dilemma confronting the police executive in supporting his request for an increase either in quantity or quality of personnel. On the one hand, there is no precise formula available for determining total personnel strength; on the other, he is faced with the necessity of justifying current and contemplated expenditures for police protection. In this situation many

---

[2] See E. L. Thorndyke, *Your City*, Harcourt, Brace and Company, 1939, p. 62, for a penetrating discussion of these factors in which this respected research investigator attempts to formulate a measuring scale for determining the desirability of any given community as a place in which to live.

chiefs have in the past taken the unsatisfactory middle course, applying the rule-of-thumb standard which prevailed in American police service for a good many years—one police officer for each 1,000 population. This standard is, of course, now obsolete.

On the hypothesis that other operating divisions are necessary only to the extent that the patrol division fails to achieve its objectives, it follows that the size of the patrol force determines the size of its supporting elements, including staff services and other operating line units. Application of this principle delimits the problem to a determination of the amount and quality of patrol line power required, which in turn resolves itself into an analysis of the requirements and specifications of the individual patrol area or beat. As stated earlier, the ultimate unit of organization is a group of operations that can be performed directly by one individual and which constitute a satisfactory work load for him. Vollmer, Wilson, and other leading American police experts emphasize the police beat as the fundamental unit in the structure of police organization. It is safe to say that not only the size of the force but the development of a scientific police administration in all of its aspects depends upon the derivation of a valid formula for beat construction, with all that it implies. This critical subject is reserved for later treatment.

Distribution of the Force. The effective distribution of the personnel resources of a police organization occurs simultaneously in three directions—by function, by area and by time.

Functional Distribution

The distribution of the available personnel strength by function involves a determination of the number of individuals to be assigned to the Records Division, Patrol Division, Detective Division, Traffic Division, Crime Prevention Division, and other administrative units in the department. It is here that organization by major purpose, by major process, and by clientele enter the picture to influence the divisional assignment of manpower. It has already been noted that the size and performance of the Patrol Division will determine the personnel strength of the various units in the staff and line; hence, the importance of strengthening the patrol services with every available resource.

Mistakes in the functional distribution of the force are frequent. The most common defect in the average American police department is a patrol force which has been depleted to satisfy the demands for more manpower by specialized operating divisions and details, and even by staff services. The records of the Seattle Police Department revealed in 1945 that there were 429 men in the organization with the rank of patrolman. Of this number only 209 were actually engaged in patrol

service.[3]   Earlier, Vollmer observed in Minneapolis that point duty
either at school crossings or at other specially designated places, and
special duties including money messenger protection, protection of banks,
churches, weddings, funerals, athletic events, special details, and many
other assignments not related to police duty, took up a disabling percentage of the time and attention of the patrol force of the city.[4]   In
Cleveland an attempt to meet the problems of traffic regulation and control was made by sapping the department's resources for coping with
crime.[5]   Bruce Smith found in New Orleans that unnecessary precinct
commands absorbed in their administration the partial or entire energies
of a considerable operating personnel that was maintained at full strength
regardless of the depletion of the patrol force by other factors such as
sick leave, furloughs, court appearances, and similar demands on manpower.[6]   In addition to these drains upon combat strength many men
were assigned to public offices and private enterprise, and to various other types of special duty where their usefulness in keeping the peace and
enforcing the law was limited.   The inevitable consequence was inadequate patrol service.   It was found that 36 New Orleans police officers,
ranging in rank from captain to patrolman were assigned to the mayor as
chauffeur, to the city hall, city treasurer's office, recorders courts, commissioner of public utilities, board of health, war manpower board,
social security agency, office of price administration, and other similar
points.   In addition, there were 42 assignments of officers ranging in
rank from lieutenant to patrolman, to such locations as banks, railway
terminals, public utilities, hotels, bus stations, various educational institutions, a chain store, and a construction company.   Twelve provi-
sional policewomen were engaged for special duty in night clubs.

A similar situation prevailed in Baltimore, where the patrol force
functioned as a reservoir of manpower from which personnel was
drawn for a wide variety of temporary assignments.[7]   While conceding
that some of these special details were concerned with essential tasks, it
was pointed out that such assignments as the following should not be the
concern of the police under any circumstances: three patrolmen detailed

[3] V. A. Leonard, "Survey and Reorganization of the Seattle Police Department," 1947, p. 129.

[4] August Vollmer, "Survey and Reorganization of the Minneapolis Police
Department," 1930, p. 80.

[5] Raymond B. Fosdick, "Police Administration," Part III of the Cleveland Foundation Survey of Criminal Justice in Cleveland, 1921, p. 5.

[6] Bruce Smith, *The New Orleans Police Survey*, 1946, p. 10.

[7] Bruce Smith, "The Baltimore Police Survey," Institute of Public Administration, New York, 1941, p. 121.

to the state attorney's office; one patrolman detailed at the Bureau of Receipts in the Municipal Building; one patrolman detailed to the attorney general as chauffeur; two lieutenants detailed at the State House in Annapolis during legislative sessions. (It was reported that it was an unwritten law that the men so detailed should belong to the political party having majority control of the legislature.)

Commenting on the depletion of patrol line power in the Dallas Police Department, Vollmer stated: [8]

"Specialization should never, under any circumstances, be permitted by the Chief of Operations until every other possible method of controlling the need has been completely exhausted. All requests for special duty and for diversion of manpower from the patrol division to other operating units should be denied unless it can be proved that there are aggravating or dangerous circumstances which compel special consideration. These calls for special services, despite their compelling nature, must always be weighed against the loss of the patrolman's time which follows his detachment from the patrol force."

It is a responsibility of the Chief of Operations to maintain a continuous inventory of the relative requirements of the several line units with the view of protecting patrol power. Special details of every type and kind should be given careful scrutiny and any doubt should be resolved in favor of the maintenance of the patrol division at full strength.

Geographical Distribution

The basis for geographical distribution of the patrol force is the individual patrol area or beat, the ultimate unit upon which the structure of police organization is reared. It may be described as a circumscribed area to which one or two officers (depending upon departmental policy which respect to single or double officer motor patrol) are assigned, and within which the officer is held responsible for the prevention and suppression of crime and vice, traffic duty, preservation of law and order, and the protection of life and property. All of the line functions of police service are discharged largely within this frame of reference.

The selection of the beat as the point of attack in all police operations conforms to the fundamental principle of decentralizing the total problem into small units and attacking each one individually under a coordinated plan; it is based upon the conviction that effective patrol service is the foundation of police organization. It has been said that

---

[8] August Vollmer, *Survey and Reorganization of the Dallas Police Department*, 1944, p. 100.

the individual patrolman is society's first line of defense against the criminal; he also carries the thrust of offense strategy and tactics in a modern police service which no longer places its chief reliance upon defensive operations.

The geographical distribution of the patrol force serves a number of strategic purposes:

1. It decentralizes a total problem into small units, making it possible to attack each one individually under a coordinated plan. The beat approach is based upon the conviction that systematic, effective patrol service is the foundation of police organization. It has been said that the individual patrolman is society's first line of defense against crime and the criminal.

2. It gives the criminal offender and the non-criminal alike the impression that a uniformed police officer may appear unexpectedly at any time and at any place. As Sir Robert Peel observed in 1829 upon the organization of the London Metropolitan Police, later to become known as Scotland Yard,

    "The influence of a large, well composed and efficient police will be more powerful than all the law which the sagacity of man can devise. Separate the officers in feeling and in interest from the criminal; let them feel the public interest to be their own and send them forth. *They cannot be everywhere, but they may be expected anywhere."*

3. Geographical distribution of the patrol force by patrol area or beat provides the opportunity for an equitable distribution of work load. Thus, through a tabulation and study of criminal offenses, traffic accidents, police hazards, inspection responsibilities, and other demands on a patrol officer's time, by existing beats, it becomes possible to restructure beat boundaries and to equalize work load.

4. It distributes patrol strength throughout the area in such manner as to equalize response time on calls for the police.

5. It provides the individual patrol officer with the assurance that if help is needed, it can be quickly mobilized by radio communications contact with fellow officers on adjoining beats.

6. It places line power where the action is; distributing the patrol force geographically in accordance with the need as indicated by the records, deploys patrol power in point of time

and place when and where the need for police service is most
likely to occur.

7. Closely related to No. 6, it locates suppressive patrol in those
areas where the presence of a police officer is most likely to
give its highest yield.[9]

How to distribute the patrol force equitably and strategically on the
basis of sound beat construction has given conscientious police executives concern for many years.   This must be accomplished if every
patrolman is to carry his share of the total load and if each section of
the community is to receive its share of police protection.   Executives
have recognized first, that if the patrolman is overloaded with work, he
becomes dissatisfied and inefficient, and if he is not given enough to do,
he becomes lazy and dodges his responsibilities;   second, that if the distribution is uneven, the lawless element quickly discovers the weakness
and plan their depredations accordingly;   and finally, that an ill-balanced
plan ultimately draws complaints of discrimination from the force and
brings down the wrath of the people on the head of the unfortunate
police executive.   The individual beat must be constructed on sound
principles, or the entire organization will be structurally weak and will
cease to function effectively as an agency for the protection and safety
of the public.

In the beginning it was the custom to take a map of the city and
divide it into a number of patrol areas of equal size, the number corresponding to the number of patrolmen available.   Later, patrolmen
were distributed according to population density, the ratio being one
patrolman to approximately one thousand inhabitants.   Still later, additional factors came to be considered.   The value of property, volume
of vehicular and pedestrian traffic, crime and vice conditions, character
of buildings and of inhabitants were taken into account.   The method
of patrol in American cities today is based more or less definitely on the
principle that patrol officers should be distributed by areas in proportion to the amount of work to be done.   In recognition of this principle,
the size of the beat in most cities gradually increases from the center
of the city outward toward the perimeter, due to the ecological pattern
of decreasing density of offenses, police hazards, and other work-gener-
ating factors.

In the formulation of beat boundary lines, special attention must
be given those particular parts of the area where crime is a chronic
condition, or where potential emergencies are indicated.   There may
be within the boundaries of a beat potentialities for riots, rendezvous

---

9 See, p. 240, *Effective Police Manpower Utilization* by Allen P. Bristow.

for criminals and prostitutes, low rent areas, concentration of foreign elements, restricted sections for colored people and transition areas inhabited by transients. A study of such hazards must supplement the analysis of the geographic origin of offenses, arrests, and miscellaneous calls for police service in order to determine properly the most effective distribution of the available manpower and equipment.

Furthermore, these criteria must be applied at intervals of not more than five years for revision of beat boundaries as a continuing policy of intelligent management and control. There are many instances where beats, once star contributors to the city's crime total, take on the air of a peaceful and respectable neighborhood. Social life and organization are in a constant state of flux. Changing population density and nationality, shifting business areas, changes in the character of suburban residential districts, appearance of new hotels, banks, theaters, jewelry stores, and other mercantile establishments render existing beat distribution obsolete. Beat boundaries often are maintained long beyond the time when the conditions that first determined their limits ceased to exist.

Some police authorities, long in the service and respected for their ability, hold that no universal method of beat construction can be developed because of the infinite number of variables encountered. Others insist that a few simple principles can be formulated and that these may be of service to cities within a particular country but are likely to be useless in other countries where conditions are fundamentally different. A few believe that a universal formula can be derived and that it can be used in any part of the world.

A small minority of professionally trained police executives in the United States are conscious of the administrative necessity for derivation of a formula that will serve as a basis for the scientific distribution of the force. For the most part, however, the significance of this administrative problem is not widely recognized and understood.

Proportional distribution of the patrol force was conceived as early as 1909, when Chief August Vollmer assigned the force (which then was bicycle-mounted and in 1911 became auto-borne) to two 12-hour shifts and to beats which were laid out in accordance with the number of calls for the police anticipated in each part of the city. Some officers worked very large beats and some patrolled areas far smaller, where calls were more highly concentrated.

Following Vollmer's innovation, Elmer Graper and Raymond Fosdick elaborated on the distribution concept. This in turn led to the more sophisticated approaches developed by Bruce Smith and O. W. Wilson. The success inherent in distributing uniformed personnel in accordance with the need for their services was noted as early as 1926 in the *Missouri Crime Survey* in language that is equally valid today:

> . . . Several police forces are faced with the fact that under their present scheme of distribution, uniformed patrols are inadequate in number. Rising police costs render personnel increases inexpedient and undesirable. But this survey shows that the effect of a substantial increase can be secured if outworn schemes of distribution are abandoned, and the patrol force distributed and administered not according to conditions which existed a generation ago, but in line with conditions existing today.

In the United States, Chief Vollmer of Berkeley, California, paved the way for a systematic approach to beat construction analysis, and his pioneering work in this area of police management has inspired others to undertake further investigations.[10] In addition to insisting on a determination of the amount of police service required in particular areas, he also demonstrated that standard time units can be developed and applied to the routine operations of patrol. In other words, it should be possible to allocate patrol duty quantitatively so that no patrolman will have an impossible task to perform and all patrolmen will have definite minimum duty requirements.

Basically, in the distribution of the patrol force by beats and in the determination of the size and boundaries of patrol beats, case load patterns, inspectional services and the distribution of police hazards are the major factors to be considered. The sociological characteristics of the area are not to be ignored; however, where they are of unusual police significance, they find expression as police hazards in one form or another and are, therefore, automatically taken into account.[11]

It is thus necessary as a first step, to tabulate by hour of day and by existing beat boundaries, the number of Part I and Part II offenses, miscellaneous reports, accidents and number of arrests for the preceding six months period. Since inspectional services are an important patrol function, the number of business establishments must be included in the tabulation. This is, of course, a police matter of major importance between the hours of 5:00 P.M., and 7:00 A.M.

---

[10] August Vollmer, "The Police Beat," Proceedings of the Fortieth Annual Conference of the International Association of Chiefs of Police, 1933, p. 304.

[11] A police hazard is any person, place, situation or thing possessing a high potential for criminal attack or for the generation of any other type of police problem creating a demand for police service.

See Appendix D for a Classification of Police Hazards.

But this is not enough. Vollmer early perceived that it would be necessary to translate work into time units or man hours in order to have a common denominator with which to compute existing work load distribution and to project necessary changes in work load distribution. The average time spent in case investigation varies from one crime classification to another. In terms of man hours, the investigation of a traffic accident and a worthless check investigation may present two entirely different situations. Likewise, so far as the inspectional services are concerned, man hours invested in this function are subject to variation with a sharp increase between the hours of 5:00 P.M., and 7:00 A.M. The man hour picture will vary from one department to another, depending upon recruiting and training standards, departmental policy with respect to assignment of the investigative function, quality of the investigation, morale and a number of other factors. Hence, it would be impractical at this juncture in the development of the American police services to attempt to establish norms which would be applicable to every department. Each department must take its own measure.

The conversion of work into time units or man hours is not a difficult operation. It is merely a matter of each investigating officer making a systematic and accurate record over a reasonable period of time, of the amount of time spent, for example, in the investigation of a traffic accident, a burglary investigation, a car theft case, a robbery investigation, or a case of vandalism, etc. Averages are then obtained from the reports of all investigating officers and a time factor thus established for each category.

In this manner, each work unit is *weighted*. It is then not a difficult matter to compute the percentage distribution of work load by existing beat lay-out and by platoon shifts. At this point, solutions suggest themselves. Patrol beat boundaries may be adjusted, on a rational and sound basis, thus effecting an equitable distribution of work load by patrol beat. Since the number and size of patrol beats vary from one platoon shift to another, the foregoing procedure also offers an effective basis for the organization and distribution of patrol beats by platoon shifts.

As of 1969, the police department of Oakland, California, and a number of departments in other jurisdictions, were employing the *consumed time* concept in the geographical distribution of the patrol force by beats. In addition to the conversion of work into time units, these units are then weighted. All types of police service, including the various crime classifications, are placed in four categories—those requiring more than one hour, those requiring forty-five minutes to one hour, those requiring thirty to forty-five minutes, and those requiring less than thirty minutes. Weights are then given to the various types of police activity, as follows: [12]

1. More than one hour .... Weight 4.
2. Forty-five minutes to one hour .... Weight 3.
3. Thirty minutes to forty-five minutes .... Weight 2.
4. Less than thirty minutes .... Weight 1.

The weighted data is then tabulated for each sub-census and the percentage of the total patrol work load computed for each sub-census area. The weighted work load and the percentage of the total patrol work load is then calculated for each beat. In this manner, through the shifting of reporting districts or sub-census areas, the size and boundaries of patrol beats can be effectively adjusted to permit an equitable adjustment of work load for each beat.

Several departments with computer capacity have inaugurated a continuous statistical assessment of patrol work loads and deployment. The St. Louis Police Department is actively engaged in implementing a program that not only will predict the police field problems for the forthcoming tour of duty but will also monitor the crime picture as it emerges, and adjust the predictions as changes develop. Although this is a highly sophisticated application and is practical for a limited number of departments, any department regardless of size can engage in a continuing manual reassessment of patrol areas through a manual tabulation and study of records data.

In the smaller department, even with a personnel strength of only a few men, patrol officers can be advantageously allocated on a need-for-service basis. In this manner, the power of a relatively small force can be amplified up to a point equivalent to the addition of more manpower. It only remains to have available an efficient police records unit where the manual tabulation of the necessary information can be produced as a basis for the effective deployment of patrol personnel.

The Fluid Patrol System

A unique method for the deployment of the patrol force has now made its appearance, under which the conventional beat system is abandoned. Known as the *Fluid Patrol System*, it completely replaces the patrol beat concept and provides for the shifting of patrol personnel hour by hour into sections of the community where and when current records

---

[12] The President's Commission on Law Enforcement and Administration of Justice, *Task Force Report: The Police*, U. S. Government Printing Office, 1967, p. 52.

data indicate the greatest demand for police service is most likely to occur.

Originating with the Aberdeen Plan and later, the Salford Plan, in England, the implementation of the Fluid Patrol System concept in the United States has led the police to combine some of the features of these two plans with the Tactical Unit or Task Force operation discussed in Chapter 11.

Probably the most notable application of the Fluid Patrol System is in the Police Department of Tucson, Arizona. As of 1965, the thirty patrol beats covering an area of 72 square miles, were abolished and replaced with the new patrol system.

The city is divided into small grids or reporting districts of approximately one-quarter mile in area. Crime data and data concerning other demands for police service are tabulated by grids, from which special reports are prepared by the police records division and made available to the patrol commander at the beginning of each tour of duty. The platoon is divided into squads, each under the command of a field sergeant.

The city was separated into four sub-sectors, with a sergeant and his squad assigned to each sub-sector. He may require one or two of his six or seven officers to report for duty in plain clothes for a stake-out; he may assign two or more officers to patrol the entire sub-sector; or he may keep two or more officers with him for saturation patrol of two or more "hot" grids—all depending on the flow of reports and information from the police records division and what they have to say about the current situation.

Under certain circumstances, the radio dispatcher may direct all broadcasts to the sergeant and he in turn, assigns his men accordingly. This arrangement represents a special type of situation in which, for the duration of the emergency, radio control is temporarily vested in the field subject, of course, to the receipt of additional instructions and information from headquarters. From the standpoint of police records administration and investigative responsibility, when a member of a squad becomes involved in a case, he carries it through to final disposition. As an alternative, one or more officers may be assigned exclusively to follow-up case investigation.

The Police Department of Oakland, California, among others, is considering the installation of the Fluid Patrol System. They contemplate the possibility of hourly reports from the police records division, making possible the shifting of patrol personnel hour by hour into sections of the city where and when current records data indicate the greatest demand for police service is most likely to occur.

The police records unit or division is the life-blood of the Fluid Patrol System. The mainstay of the system in Tucson is the computer and the machine tabulation of statistical data based upon the grid or reporting area.

It is strongly recommended that departments, even those with a personnel strength of from one to seventy-five officers, make a conversion to the grid system of tabulating criminal offenses, traffic accidents and other calls for police service. Whether the department moves toward the fluid system of patrol deployment or remains with the conventional patrol beat concept, the grid system will expedite a sound determination of patrol areas based upon the crime and traffic accident experience. In this connection, two books are recommended for every departmental library—*Effective Police Manpower Utilization,* by Allen P. Bristow, Charles C. Thomas, Publisher, Springfield, Illinois; and *Police Patrol Readings,* by Samuel G. Chapman—by the same publisher.

Chronological Distribution

Since the police conduct an around-the-clock operation, the force must be efficiently distributed by hour of day in accordance with the crime, delinquency, vice and traffic accident experience, as shown by the records. The need for police service is the determining factor in the chronological distribution of the force. Most American police departments follow a plan, known as the three platoon shift, in which the line power of the department, particularly the patrol force, is divided into three shifts of eight hours each, as follows:

First Platoon—8:00 A.M. to 4:00 P.M.

Second Platoon—4:00 P.M. to 12:00 Midnight

Third Platoon—12:00 Midnight to 8:00 A.M.

The exact time for platoon relief or change may vary slightly from one department to another, but the general schematic arrangement is now an almost universal characteristic of American police service.

But the question cannot be disposed of quite so simply. On what basis can it be said that platoons should change at 8:00 A.M., 4:00 P.M., and 12:00 Midnight, respectively? Would 9:00 A.M., 5:00 P.M. and 1:00 A.M., or some other variation more appropriately meet the operating demands that are placed upon a police department? Furthermore, what should be the exact distribution of the available patrol strength among the three platoons? The answers to these questions cannot be provided by rule-of-thumb methods or speculation but depend upon painstaking analyses of data that should be made available by the record division of the department concerning the distribution of the need for police services by hour of day. It is obvious here in the approach to an important administrative problem that a good police records system is indispensable.

The variation in need for police service from hour to hour throughout the day follows a pattern that is fairly consistent, so that the distribution of the force by hour of day presents no serious statistical difficulties where a police records system is properly maintained and the necessary statistical reports and analyses are provided and used. Whether it be Chicago, San Francisco, or Kansas City, the case load of a police department usually reaches a peak for the twenty-four hour period between 9:30 and 11:30 in the evening. Hence, it is during the period from 4:00 P.M., until Midnight that maximum personnel strength must be maintained. Statistical studies confirm the general soundness of the traditional three platoon system, and the change-over hours commonly used; however, they also point up the need for special assignment of patrol power to meet the requirements of certain short peak load periods.

Since the police case load for a twenty-four hour day does not arrange itself categorically by eight-hour periods, special deployment of patrol power superimposed over the regular shifts is being accepted by an increasing number of police administrators as the answer to case load peaks which occur within an hour to a three-hour interval. Where this procedure is based upon careful analysis of case load as indicated by records data, it represents a desirable refinement in the selective distribution of manpower.

The foregoing considerations apply to the basic distribution of the patrol force to achieve the objectives of General Operations. It is not to be assumed as a fixed, inflexible pattern, however. The police calendar is a succession of emergency situations, frequently with a time distribution that does not follow the general twenty-four hour pattern, but requires a special disposition or deployment of line power. Sound police administration requires the existence and availability at all times of a tactical unit or mobile task force which can be concentrated in any quarter of the city, and at whatever hour or hours the circumstances may dictate, as indicated by the records. This special administration of line power resources is reserved for extended treatment in a later chapter.[13]

---

[13] See Chapter 12, *The Tactical Unit.*

The Determination of Patrol Beat Responsibility

Police service, basically, is patrol service. Specialization has made serious inroads upon the line power of the patrol force. The compelling requirement or prerequisite for the elimination or modification of this special deployment of patrol personnel resources is a determination of policy by police management with respect to *patrol beat responsibility*. Everything pivots on this determination.

Once the amount and the most effective distribution of patrol power have been determined, it still is necessary to locate the individual partolman in the organizational structure where he will operate with maximum efficiency. Under accepted administrative practice, the individual patrol officer is assigned to a given patrol beat and is held directly responsible for handling police problems in that circumscribed area. This serves to focus responsibility upon a given individual for the accomplishment of a given unit of work. Upon the successful application of this principle rests the fate of the police department and its administrators.

But the problem is not so simple. The important question arises immediately—where does the work and responsibility of the patrolman end and that of the detective begin? This basic question and its answer should be high on the administrative agenda of every police department. If it is not the most important, it is among the most important of all administrative problems in the American police services. Police administrators will do well to ponder its significance in the attainment of police objectives and re-examine their patterns of operation in the line.

Policy in regard to this important matter, which is among the most important of all problems presented to police management, will vary from one department to another. At one end of the administrative spectrum, detectives are charged with total investigative responsibility. The patrolman merely responds to the radio call, makes an arrest, if perchance this is possible, and protects the scene until the detectives arrive to launch the investigation.

Under this ill-advised policy, the detective division usually finds itself overloaded with uncleared cases in every category, with the result that major crime fails to receive the attention that it deserves, and the patrolman has relatively little to do. It is difficult to escape the observation that under this arrangement, the department experiences a tragic waste of manpower because of the unused resources of the patrol division—this despite the sobering fact that patrol salaries represent the largest single item in the police budget.

One problem generates another. The comparative idleness of the patrolman no doubt played a major role in the macabre police scandals that have in recent years rocked Chicago, Denver and other jurisdictions. Clothing the patrolman with substantial investigative responsibilities and imposing upon him case follow-up pressures from headquarters would bring into play additional elements of supervision which would prove wholesome and constructive in this respect, in addition to other important advantages to be considered presently.

There follows in succession those departments where the patrolman is held responsible for the preliminary investigation of cases originating on his beat and the filing of a report covering his investigative activities on the case. The follow-up investigation and final clearance are a responsibility of the detective, except perhaps in minor cases. In an increasing number of other departments, the investigative responsibilities of the patrolman are even greater.

At the other end of the spectrum is the department operating under a policy where virtually total case investigation and case clearance responsibility are assigned to the officer on the beat. Under this concept, the officer is responsible for the investigation and clearance of all cases originating on his beat, regardless of classification.

He is geared to the total delivery of police service, which means that he is held responsible for the robbery rate, the burglary rate, the automobile rate, the amount of grand and petty larceny, the extent of juvenile delinquency, the number of traffic accidents, traffic congestion, and all other police problems that originate within the limits of the patrol area to which he is assigned. All uncleared cases represent a direct charge against the efficiency of the individual patrolman concerned, and provide a fair index to his general performance record. Not only that, as pointed out above, he is responsible for the case investigation and its final disposition in all of these categories. Referred to by some as the "all purpose patrolman" and by Bristow as the "Generalist",[14] he is totally responsible for the case investigation and its final disposition in all of these categories.

The following significant paragraph appears in the General Information Bulletin for Applicants furnished by one police department to potential candidates for the position of patrolman, before an application form is issued:

"A patrolman is responsible for all crimes or reports arising on his beat. The officer reports off his beat after completing his tour of duty, and is then required to write reports on all cases handled by him. This may take

---

[14] Bristow, Allen P., *Effective Police Manpower Utilization*, Charles C. Thomas, Publisher, 1969, p. 18.

only a few minutes, or it may take several hours, depending upon the nature of the reports handled and the ability of the individual. Patrolmen are held responsible for the investigation of all complaints regardless of seriousness and regardless of the fact that detectives or supervisory officers may assist and counsel in the investigation."

Obviously, the individual officer cannot discharge these manifold duties and responsibilities without considerable assistance; hence, he has at his disposal the entire resources of the department. The facilities of the detective division or in any jurisdiction where the position of detective has been abolished—experienced patrolmen in plain clothes, are available to give the necessary aid in the investigation of felony cases, and in other instances where the case investigation would take the officer beyond the boundaries of his beat. Experts in the traffic division are at his disposal in meeting the various situations and problems associated with the regulation and control of traffic in his area. In the smaller departments where specialization and the appearance of specialized units have not developed, one or more patrolmen in plain clothes may furnish this assistance.

Members of the crime prevention division likewise come to his assistance in the solution of problems connected with the prevalence of juvenile delinquency in the area to which he is assigned. Similarly, the facilities of the crime laboratory, the records division, the vice squad, and all other administrative units in the organization assist the individual patrolman to keep his beat clean. But regardless of the type or volume of assistance he may bring into play, he cannot "pass the buck;" the responsibility for the delivery of police service in that area to which he is assigned belongs to him.

Such a system requires a superior man in police uniform, superior recruiting standards, and a superior training program, together with a salary structure that will attract this type of personnel.[15] Today, this is the calibre of manpower that is being recruited on an increasing scale into the American police services.

The Patrolman-Detective Combination

In cities of 150,000 population and under, perhaps higher, the presence of a detective division would seem to be a waste of departmental resources. In such jurisdictions, there appears to be no sound reason for not lodging total investigative responsibility in the patrol division.

In those cases where the patrolman needed special investigative assistance or where the investigation would take him beyond the boundaries

---

[15] Leonard, V. A., *A Theory of Police Organization and Administration*, Ph.D., Dissertation, Ohio State University, 1947.

of his beat, the necessary number of experienced patrolmen operating in plain clothes and under the control of the Patrol Commander, should be able to perform this function effectively. Patrolmen should be selected for this assignment on the basis of demonstrated aptitudes for the different types of case investigations.

In addition to the economy in money and manpower, this arrangement would eliminate split-division responsibility for case investigation, with the added advantage of concentrating the total investigative function under the control of one man—the Patrol Commander. It would further serve to enhance the combat strength of the Patrol Division, with all that implies.

In at least one known instance, this improvement has been made; there are undoubtedly others. The Police Department of Port Arthur, Texas, a city of 66,676 population, has abolished the position of detective. Responsibility for all criminal case investigation has been assigned to patrol personnel.[16]

Supervision

Since every individual is at least tempted to be as lazy as circumstances will permit, it is necessary in any group undertaking to apply the pressures of supervision in order to insure that performance takes place in accordance with instructions and in conformity with the standards of the department.

There is no substitute for supervision and inspection in organization. In both police and army organization, its indispensability has been demonstrated time and again. Important in any accounting for the extraordinary quality of the English police services is an effective structure of supervision and inspection that reaches from the top to the bottom of the enterprise. English police officials have recognized the importance of these administrative tools to a far greater degree than have the American police. The superiority of the English police in this respect is explained by the intensive training that is given in the preparation of officers for supervisory and command positions.

Supervision is concerned not only with the detection of deficiencies in performance but with inducing men through motivation and training to do the best possible job. It involves analysis by field observation and by examination of records data to reach a fair appraisal of each man's performance, and the adoption of incentives which induce maximum effort. This implies the existence of standards by which individual per-

---

[16] International City Managers' Association, *The Municipal Yearbook*, 1962.

formance can be judged, and these must be understood by both the officer and his supervisor.

In the absence of vigorous supervision, lines of control and responsibility weaken and disintegrate, and an organization tends to dissolve into an inorganic collection of semi-independent parts, wholly lacking in coordination and devotion to a common purpose. It is in this type of climate that the departmental politician thrives. In the hazy atmosphere of poor supervision, he becomes concerned with the achievement of his own personal objectives and toward this end proceeds with the formation of cliques among the men in the department, spreading dissension at every turn. Many a police department has gone down to ruin because of this form of sabotage. A firm executive control is called for, with direction and supervision reaching down through all ranks in the organization to the last man at the periphery of the enterprise.

The special problem of supervision in police work is due to the nature of police duties which require men to work alone and for substantial periods of time beyond the eye of an immediate superior. In this respect, the nature of patrol service creates the need for a high order of supervision. Combined leader, commander, instructor, administrator, tactician, disciplinarian, trouble-shooter, and builder of morale, the patrol sergeant is the one man upon whom the responsibility for supervising the line delivery of patrol service largely depends. No organization can rise higher than the quality of its supervisory personnel, and for this reason the department should include in its in-service training program special provision for the selection and training of men for supervisory positions. The ability of these men is reflected directly in the grade of performance delivered by their subordinates.[17]

In a well-managed department, the function of patrol supervision is usually accomplished by combining up to six patrol beats under the supervision of a patrol sergeant, whose duty it is to see that the patrolmen in his charge perform their duties in a faithful and effective manner. He constantly visits his men, sees that reports are properly prepared, checks on follow-up cases, inspects their clothing and equipment, notes the way in which they go about their duties, and instructs them in the responsibilities of their office. The sergeant is expected to get the work out of his men. That is his job. If he exacts anything less than full and honest performance from them, he is negligent of his own duty.

---

[17] See B. W. Gocke, "Police Sergeants Mannual," O. W. Smith, Los Angeles, 1944; this important publication should be on the desk of every police executive and in the personal library of every police officer.

Live, alert, and competent supervisors lead their men and set the pace for them so that the task is never too easy but always a challenge calling for more and better work.

Motorization of the Force

Motorization amplified enormously the line power of the patrol force through increased mobility, maneuverability and speed of movement. As early as 1947 of the 855 cities reporting the extent to which the police force was motorized, 38 cities did all police patrol work with motor vehicles; 813 used both motor vehicles and patrolmen on foot, while four cities (all below 25,000 population) did not use any motor vehicles for patrolling. Ninety-five percent of the 38 cities using completely motorized patrols were in the 10,000 to 25,000 population group. Every city above 100,000 used both men on foot and men in patrol cars. Only one city between 50,000 and 100,000 used completely motorized patrols. In 1950, of the 903 cities reporting the extent to which the police force was motorized, 27 cities do all police patrol work with motor vehicles, 875 use both motor vehicles and patrolmen on foot, while one city (below 25,000) does not use any motor vehicles for patrolling. Twenty-three of the 27 cities using completely motorized patrols were in the 10,000 to 25,000 population group. Every city above 100,000 used both men on foot and men in patrol cars. Only two cities between 50,000 and 100,000 employed completely motorized patrols.[18]

Motorization of the force does not mean that the work formerly performed by the foot patrolman is discontinued. In fact, it has been demonstrated that a motorized patrolman travels an average of thirty-five miles during his tour of duty in addition to walking as far as he did as a foot patrolman.

Single Vs. Double Officer Motor Patrol

In the past, motor patrol has been carried on in American police departments largely with two men in each car. Vollmer early came to the conclusion that in the interests of both economy and efficiency, this costly practice should be discontinued. For more than forty-five years, the city of Berkeley, California, has been policed by single-officer motor patrols. The record speaks for itself. It has now been demonstrated over this period in Berkeley, Wichita, and in other cities, that one man in the patrol car is more efficient than two. As a general rule, when two

---

[18] "Municipal Police Administration," The International City Managers' Association, Chicago, second edition, 1943, p. 262.

men are placed in a car, both become lazy and indifferent; experience shows that one man in a car must, of necessity, keep on the alert.

The use of one man in a car makes possible a much broader and more intensive patrol of the city by releasing men for additional patrol. Twice as much patrol service is thus provided; a police car gives twice the attention to the area; a given police hazard is inspected during a tour of duty twice as many times as it would be if there were only half as many units. Further, the factor of safety of the individual officer is increased by the availability of a larger number of patrol units.[18] Not only does the use of the one-man car extend the range of patrol coverage, but it also discourages the inattention to police duty which often is the result of two men fraternizing together or engaging in non-police activities.

The adoption of two-way radio communication facilities to police patrol operations has eliminated the last substantial argument against the single-officer motor patrol. Thus, any one beat becomes the nucleus of a larger patrol unit; the patrol cars on adjacent beats constitute a reserve force instantly available and capable of being massed or concentrated in the affected area at a moment's notice. In an emergency situation, as many officers as are available can be moved quickly into the scene of operations.

An officer patrolling by himself in a car is actually safer than when accompanied by a brother officer. During a nine-year period prior to 1928 in Wichita, Kansas, nine policemen lost their lives as a result of gunfire, an unusual record for a city of slightly over 100,000 population. In practically every case the officer was one of a pair of officers. In only two instances did the second officer succeed in killing or apprehending the assailant. In the twelve years following 1928 Wichita patrolmen operated alone in cars, and during that time only one patrolman was killed as a result of gunfire, and he was a foot patrolman killed in a rooming house.[19] Similar experiences are reported in Berkeley, California, where Vollmer first introduced the practice of single-officer motor patrol and in other cities which have recognized the economy and efficiency of this procedure.

By 1939, 28 major American cities had made the conversion from double to single-officer motor patrol. One hundred sixty-one other cities were in process of transition, using both one-man and two-man cars

18 "Municipal Police Administration," The International City Managers' Association, Chicago, second edition, 1943, p. 262.

19 "Motorized Police Patrol—One-man or Two-man Crews?", Report No. 140 of the American Municipal Association, Chicago, 1940, p. 10.

at that time. The following table indicates the extent to which American police departments had adopted single-officer motor patrol by 1944:

TABLE VIII

ADOPTION OF SINGLE–OFFICER MOTOR PATROL BY AMERICAN POLICE DEPARTMENTS

Data as of January 1, 1944

CITY	Per cent motorized	Per cent single-officer motor patrol
San Francisco	31%	79%
Birmingham	53%	23%
Cincinnati	31%	61%
Denver	59%	47%
Houston	76%	19%
Oakland	57%	45%
Providence	51%	87%
Rochester	51%	80%
San Antonio	84%	100%
Seattle	38%	0%
Toledo	63%	36%
Charlotte	59%	20%
Chattanooga	55%	19%
Duluth	47%	20%
Erie	33%	100%
Grand Rapids	56%	24%
Hartford	56%	100%
New Haven	23%	89%
Omaha	49%	37%
Reading	100%	100%
South Bend	63%	67%
Syracuse	77%	77%
Austin	64%	100%
Berkeley	100%	94%

Based on data contained in the Municipal Year Book as of January 1, 1944.

By 1946 a total of 151 cities over 10,000 population, or 18 per cent of the 840 cities reporting, used one-man cars exclusively; 384 cities, or nearly 46 per cent of the reporting cities, used both one and two-man patrol cars; while 305 cities, or 36 per cent, used only two-man patrol cars. Three-fourths of the 151 cities using one-man cars exclusively were in the 10,000 to 25,000 population group. Of the 92 cities over 100,000, four used one-man cars exclusively; 35 used both one and two-man cars; and 48 used only two-man cars. It is noted that in 1946, 64 per cent of the 840 reporting cities were making use of one-man patrol cars on a more or less extensive scale. The following table indicates the distribution of one-man and two-man patrol car operations by 1962:

TABLE IX

MANNING OF POLICE PATROL CARS IN CITIES OVER 10,000: 1962 [20]

Population Group	Number of Cities Reporting Motorized Patrol	Two-Man Patrol Cars Only		One-Man & Two-Man Patrol Cars		One-Man Patrol Cars Only	
		No.	%	No.	%	No.	%
Cities over 500,000	19	2	11	16	84	1	5
250,000 to 500,000	28	3	11	20	71	5	18
100,000 to 250,000	74	3	4	52	70	19	26
50,000 to 100,000	151	11	7	86	57	54	36
25,000 to 50,000	319	14	4	180	57	125	39
10,000 to 25,000	751	52	7	374	50	325	43
All over 10,000	1,342	85	6	728	54	529	40

Use of Dogs in American Police Departments

The use of dogs in police service to supplement patrol activities appears to have gained increasing acceptance throughout the police field. By 1961, police departments in 120 cities were making use of the dog in patrol service, in addition to their expanding use in the Armed Forces.[21]

Police departments in thirty cities used only one dog; two dogs were used by the police in twenty-two cities; in fifty-one cities, from three to ten dogs were in service; eight police departments were using from eleven to fifteen dogs and in nine cities, from sixteen to seventy-five dogs were being used in police work. The Metropolitan Police Department of Washington, D. C., was highest on the list, with seventy-five dogs in active service on patrol. The prevailing favorite breed of dog for police use in this country is the male German shepherd.

---

[20] International City Managers' Association, *The Municipal Year Book*, 1963.

[21] Trained dogs, primarily the German shepherd may now be found on duty at American military installations throughout the world. In 1960, the Army planned the procurement of 1,000 additional dogs for security patrol at missile bases within the country.

Typical of the American police use of dogs is the K–9 Corps in the Police Department of Baltimore, Maryland, with a population of 921,363 and a policed area of 79 square miles. In that city the police began recruiting dogs for police work in December 1956. In 1957, fifteen officers and fifteen dogs completed a basic training course and went to work on patrol on a limited basis. Later that year the K–9 Corps officially became a line unit of the Department. By 1960, Baltimore's police dog operation involved forty-five dogs and their handlers.[22]

Police departments were finding dogs of particular value with officers patroling the waterfront, railroad yards, transportation terminals; factory, warehouse and industrial areas, back alleys, parks, business districts, low rent areas and other high hazard locations, particularly during the night. Their usefulness appears to be well demonstrated in the following situations: [23]

Psychological advantage and reduction of risk to the officer in hazard and potential hazard situations.
Protecting an officer under attack.
Preventing and curbing crimes of stealth and violence.
Searching for and holding criminal suspects.
Searching a building.
Indicating to the officer the presence of a suspicious person.
Crowd control.
Guarding police vehicles.
Deployment to those areas in the city where the records indicate crime is most prevalent.
Open country searches, where the dog is trained for tracking.

Police departments planning to initiate canine corps programs should confer in advance with departments where the use of dogs has extended over a substantial period of time. It is advisable to study carefully the need, the cost, impact on the officer's work patterns, and to ascertain the details of program administration.

---

[22] Among other users of police dogs were the police departments of Salt Lake City, Utah; St. Louis and Springfield, Missouri; Richmond, Virginia; St. Paul and Minneapolis, Minnesota; Houston, Texas; Pittsburgh and Philadelphia (Fairmount Park Police), Pennsylvania; Atlanta, Georgia; Wilmington, Delaware; Newport News, Virginia; Kansas City, Missouri; Alexandria, Virginia; Hennepin County, Minnesota; Rochester, New York; Stockton, California; Pennsylvania State Police; Washington, D. C.; Buffalo, New York; Birmingham, Alabama; and Providence, Rhode Island.

[23] Samuel G. Chapman, *Dogs in Police Service*, Public Administration Service, Chicago, 1960. A Summary of Experience in Great Britain and the United States. This publication also contains an excellent bibliography of the rather extensive literature now available on the use of dogs in police service.

Since the use of dogs is now being accepted by the police throughout the country, police departments will do well to explore their value and usefulness in the patrol services. In addition to routine patrol, they would seem to be particularly well adapted in certain types of situations for use with the Tactical Unit or Mobile Task Force.[24]

Some Legal Aspects of Patrol Service

The criminal law usually finds expression in the penal codes of the several states and in the federal codes, where criminal offenses are classified, defined and specific penalties are prescribed for each classification. The determination of the nature and extent of criminal liability in any given instance is altogether a different matter. In actual practice, the approach to this problem is largely through the application of *stare decisis* or prior case decisions to the facts presented in the individual case. Prior legal precedents may be cited during the original trial of the case in criminal court, or on appeal before appellate courts up to, and including, the United States Supreme Court.

Hence, the criminal law in operation is, to a considerable extent, the operation of case-decision law flowing from interpretations and decisions handed down by the courts in a given set of circumstances. In fact, a formal course in *criminal law* at any accredited law school is largely a study of case decisions. The companion course in the law of evidence, which implements the criminal law, is likewise dominated by a study of case decisions. Together, the criminal law and the law of evidence offer to the police a working blueprint for the important function of criminal investigation, the marshaling of evidence, and the presentation of the case in court by the prosecution.[25]

If case decisions have illuminated the criminal law and the law of evidence, as well as the law of arrest, search and seizure in promoting the administration of criminal justice in this country, they have also on occasion embarrassed the process of criminal investigation and placed roadblocks ahead of the police in discharging their basic function of crime control and suppression.

In the American legal system, a convicted person may appeal his conviction to the appellate courts at the state and federal levels. If the

---

[24] See Chapter 12.

[25] See, for example, Perkins, Rollin N., *Cases and Materials on Criminal Law and Procedure*, 3rd ed., Brooklyn, The Foundation Press, Inc., 1966; also, McCormick, Charles T., *Cases and Materials on the Law of Evidence*, 3rd ed., St. Paul, West Publishing Co., 1956.

outcome is adverse to his interests, or if he is denied a new trial by an appellate court, he may appeal his case to the highest court in the land, the United States Supreme Court. The judgment of this Court is final except for a possible change by a constitutional amendment; even here, the Supreme Court could have the last word by declaring the amendment unconstitutional.

The United States Supreme Court has shown no lack of devotion to its responsibility in the review of cases adjudicated in the lower courts and in the review of legislation. Thus, its decisions have, from time to time raised questions in some quarters concerning the separation of powers in a federal system of government.

As early as 1932, Louis B. Boudin noted the continuous and gradual encroachment of the United States Supreme Court upon the legitimate and constitutionally based rights of the legislature, the executive branch and the people. He also observed at the same time that the Judges of the Supreme Court have become superior not only to the legislative and executive branches of the federal government but to the Constitution itself, since the Constitution is what the Judges say it is.[26]

During the past thirty years, and particularly the last ten years, the United States Supreme Court has handed down a series of decisions affecting the police which virtually set up a new constitutional code of rules in the processing of criminal cases. It has been said that these decisions will undoubtedly have a greater impact upon the police, the legal profession and the general administration of criminal justice than any other series of judicial precedents in the history of criminal procedure.[27]

The profound effect of these decisions upon the law enforcement field has brought into sharp focus a central issue of the present era: the interests of individual civil liberties versus the security of the community. There has been considerable anxiety across the American police field concerning the apparent philosophy of the Supreme Court and what may still lie around the corner in terms of further judicial opinions. The point where crime and the ends of justice come together for a rationale —the appellate court decision—has produced serious problems for the police in carrying out their sworn duty and responsibility for the control of crime and the criminal.

[26] Boudin, Louis B., *Government by Judiciary*, New York, William Godwin, 1932.

[27] James B. James, the Institute of Continuing Education, *Constitutional Limitations on Evidence in Criminal Cases*, Ann Arbor, Dean Hicks, 1966.

In recent years, the Supreme Court has handed down decisions which seriously impede police operations in ten key areas of the investigative process:

1. Restrictions on arrest and detention.
2. On-the-street detention and questioning.
3. Police interrogation of a criminal suspect.
4. Self-incrimination.
5. The right to counsel.
6. The confession.
7. The search for and seizure of evidence.
8. Wiretapping and electronic surveillance.
9. Arraignment.
10. Police use of the informer.

The restrictions imposed by the Supreme Court in these ten vital areas of the police operation and their impact on police operations are treated in detail in a book by one of the present authors—*The Police, the Judiciary and the Criminal.*[28] Under the leadership of Honorable Earl Warren, until recently Chief Justice of the United States Supreme Court, recent decisions of this tribunal have imposed disabling restrictions upon the investigative process and telescoped the opportunity for the police to make any appreciable gains in the approach to the problems of crime in this country.

In an editorial under the title, *The Rights of the Guilty,* the conservative Wall Street Journal had the following to say in its April 26, 1965 issue:

> Debate on crime is starting to move beyond the usual exchange between "bleeding hearts" on one side and "vigilantes" on the other. Perhaps we will even get some illuminating discussion of a serious paradox in criminal law: that just as crime rates are soaring, courts are stepping up enforcement of strict procedural rules which make it more difficult to convict criminals. Indeed, Walter Lippman, seldom counted among the vigilantes, put the situation nicely, "The fact of the matter is, I think that the balance of power within our society has turned dangerously against the peace forces—against governors and mayors and legislatures, against the police and the courts."
>
> Certainly, it is only fair to apply the same justice to all (the indigent and the wealthy) both in theory and in practice. The confusion arises when sympathy for the unfortunate merges into favoritism for the criminal. The line can get very fine. A judicial system exists not only to exonerate the unjustly accused, but to convict the guilty."

---

[28] For a complete analysis of these decisions and their impact upon the American police services, see V. A. Leonard, *The Police, the Judiciary and the Criminal*, Springfield, Illinois, Charles C. Thomas, Publisher, 1969. This work also covers the leading case decisions on the use of force by a police officer.

An all-time high in United States Supreme Court decisions affecting the police adversely, occurred on June 13, 1966, in the case of *Miranda v. Arizona*.[29] In the manner of "government by judiciary", the decision spells out in unmistakable detail the procedures that must be followed by the police as they approach the interrogation of a criminal suspect who has been taken into custody. Mr. Chief Justice Warren authored the opinion of the Court in this case:

Our holding will be spelled out with some specificity in the pages which follow but briefly stated, it is this; the prosecution may not use statements, whether exculpatory or inculpatory, stemming from custodial interrogation of the defendant unless it demonstrates the use of procedural safeguards effective to secure the privilege against self-incrimination. By custodial interrogation, we mean questioning initiated by law enforcement officers after a person has been taken into custody or otherwise deprived of his freedom of action in any significant way. As for the procedural safeguards to be employed, unless other fully effective means are devised to inform accused persons of their right of silence and to assure a continuous opportunity to exercise it, the following measures are required: Prior to questioning, *the person must be warned that he has a right to remain silent, that any statement he does make may be used as evidence against him, and that he has a right to the presence of an attorney, either retained or appointed.*

The defendant may waive effectuation of these rights, provided the waiver is made voluntarily, knowingly and intelligently. If however, he indicates in any manner and at any stage of the process that he wishes to consult with an attorney before speaking, there can be no questioning. Likewise, if the individual is alone and indicates in any manner that he does not wish to be interrogated, the police may not interrogate him. The mere fact that he may have answered some statements on his own does not deprive him of the right to refrain from answering any further inquiries until he has consulted with an attorney and thereafter consents to be questioned.

As a result of this decision, it is now mandatory on the part of the police that they observe the following instructions of the Court before the interrogation of a criminal suspect begins:

1.   At the outset, if a person in custody is to be subjected to interrogation, he must first be informed in clear and unequivocal terms that he has the right to remain silent.

2.   The warning of the right to remain silent must be accompanied by the explanation that anything he says can and will be used against him in court.

3.   An individual held for interrogation must be clearly informed that he has the right to consult with a lawyer and to have the lawyer beside him during the interrogation.

---

[29] *Miranda v. Arizona*, 284 U.S. 436, 86 S.Ct. 1602, 16 L.Ed.2d 694 (1966).

4. It is necessary to warn him not only that he has the right to consult with an attorney, but also that, if he is indigent, a lawyer will be appointed to represent him.[30]

A tragic sequel to the Miranda decision occurred recently in a New York Courtroom. New York Supreme Court Justice Michael Kern had before him a man who had admitted slaying his five children, ranging in ages from 11 months to five years, and his wife. The man had signed a full confession after being arrested. But seven months later, after the Miranda decision had been handed down with all its implications, he decided to retract the confession and plead not guilty.

With no other evidence than the inadmissible confession, Justice Kern had no other alternative but to turn him loose. In freeing this man, Justice Kern observed to those in the courtroom, "This is a very sad thing. It is so repulsive that it makes one's blood run cold and any decent human being's stomach overturn to let a thing like this out on the street."

In a strong criticism of the *Miranda* decision, Justice Robert C. Finley of the Washington State Supreme Court, referred to it as a tidal opinion washing away much of the debris deposited on the shore by previous decisions. Like other tides, it is a combination of forces, winds and currents that have increasingly troubled the waters of criminal justice. Indeed, the debris deposited by *Escobedo* has been, for the greater part, swept away, but the potential erosive effects upon the efficient administration of justice resemble the aftermath of a hurricane rather than a mere tide.[31]

Commenting still further upon the entire series of Supreme Court decisions affecting the supervision and regulation of local police administration, Justice Finley observed that they "may have to be characterized by future commentators as the most ill-founded, unrealistic, and costly judicial social experimentation in our time."

The eminent John Henry Wigmore, dean of the law of evidence, took a dim view of the mounting restrictions on the right of the police to interrogate a criminal suspect:

(1.) In the first place, an innocent person is always helped by an early opportunity to tell his whole story; hundreds of suspected persons every day

---

30 See Dahl, Raymond A., and Boyle, Howard H., *Arrest, Search and Seizure*, Supplement, Milwaukee, Hammersmith-Kortney, 1967, p. 6. This book gives a suggested statement format to be signed by the suspect as proof that the pre-interrogation instructions of the Court have been carried out. Also see Penofsky, Daniel J., *Guidelines for Interrogation*, Rochester, Jurisprudence, 1967. This book is devoted to the obtaining and proving of a valid waiver of rights under the Miranda decision.

31 Finley, Justice Robert C., Washington State Supreme Court: "Who is on trial—the Police? the Courts? or the criminally accused?" *J Crim Law, Criminal Pol Sci*, 57 (No. 4): 401, December 1966.

are set free because their story thus told bears the marks of truth. Moreover, and more important, every guilty person is almost always ready and desirous to confess, as soon as he is detected and arrested. This psychological truth, well known to all criminal trial judges, seems to be ignored by some Supreme Courts.

The nervous pressure of guilt is enormous; the load of the deed done is heavy; the fear of detection fills the consciousness; and when detection comes, the pressure is relieved; and the deep sense of relief makes confession a satisfaction. At that moment, he will tell all, and tell it truly. To forbid soliciting him, to seek to prevent this relief, is to fly in the face of nature.

It is natural and should be lawful, to take his confession at that moment —the best one. And this expedient, if sanctioned, saves the State a delay and expense in convicting him after he has reacted from his first sensations, has yielded to his friends' solicitations, and comes under the sway of the natural human instinct to struggle to save himself by the aid of all technicalities.

(2.)   In the case of professional criminals who usually work in groups, there is often no hope of getting at the group until one of them has "preached", and given the clues to the police. The police know this, and have known it for generations in every country. The only ones who apparently do not know it are some of the Supreme Court judges. . . . To forbid this (interrogation) is to tie the hands of the police. The attitude of some judges towards these necessary police methods is lamentable. . . . To disable the detective police from the very function they are set to fulfil is no less than absurd. Let the judges who sit in judgment on crime look a little into the facts. Let them not sit up aloft and dictate a rule which ignores the well-known facts of criminal life and hampers the needful methods of justice.[32]

Under the *Miranda* decision, one criminal suspect after another in virtually unbroken succession will be advised by his lawyer to remain silent and answer no questions propounded by the police. As Mr. Justice Jackson stated in a dissenting opinion in *Watts v. Indiana*:[33]

To bring in a lawyer means a real peril to solution of crime, because, under our adversary system, he deems that his sole duty is to protect his client— guilty or innocent—and that in such capacity he owes no duty whatever to help society solve its crime problem. Under this conception of criminal procedure, *any lawyer worth his salt will tell the suspect in no uncertain terms to make no statement to the police under any circumstances.* (The italics are those of the author.)

Judge Madden, writing for a unanimous panel in *United States v. Wilson*, stated:

It is not an evil thing for one accused of crime to voluntarily admit his guilt. It is a good thing. It removes his crime from the list of unsolved crimes and

---

[32] Wigmore, John Henry: *Evidence in Trials at Common Law*, 3rd ed., Boston, Little, 1949, vol. 3, 851 at 319.

[33] *Watts v. Indiana*, 338 U.S. 49, 50, 69 S.Ct. 1347, 1348, 93 L.Ed. 1801 (1949).

enables the police to get about the task of solving other crimes on the list. It enables the Criminal Courts and their juries to reach decisions free from the uncertainties which trials involving principally circumstantial evidence involve. It brings down upon the accused no worse than is his due, the punishment prescribed by law for his crime.

But, there may be changes around the corner. Chief Justice Warren has retired and the Honorable Warren E. Burger has been appointed by President Nixon as Chief Justice of the United States Supreme Court. There are those who anticipate that this change in the complexion of the High Court may be reflected in some change in judicial philosophy which could prove to be more favorable to the police.

As a step in that direction, the U. S. Department of Justice recently took steps aimed at prompting the Supreme Court to soften its controversial *Miranda v. Arizona* decision. Attorneys for the Department have been instructed that they may offer confessions as evidence in court, even though the suspects were not informed of their rights to silence and to counsel, as required by the *Miranda* decision. This action on the part of the Justice Department will no doubt return the confessions controversy to the High Court for reconsideration, this time with Congress firmly on record in opposition to the Miranda decision's rigid curbs on police questioning of a criminal suspect.

The new policy of the Department is based upon a section of the Omnibus Crime Control Act of 1968 known as Title II. It states that confessions shall be admissible as evidence in federal prosecutions if the trial judge finds that the confessions were voluntarily given. Under the statute, failure to warn a suspect of his rights is only a factor to be considered in deciding if his confession was voluntary.

An editorial in the *Spokesman-Review* (Spokane, Washington), on July 29, 1969, seemed to express the reaction of much of the nation to this move on the part of the Department of Justice. It stated in part:

There is little question that the Warren Court decisions have been controversial, and that the public's protection from crime suffered as a result. Many citizens have felt that the offender got more than an even break; he seemed, indeed, to have an advantage over law officers.

What may happen is that convictions obtained via the new Justice Department plan may be challenged, bringing the confessions matter back before the Supreme Court.

Earl Warren is gone now, and Warren E. Burger has succeeded him as Chief Justice. The complexion of the Supreme Court may have changed enough so that reversals of some of the permissive crime rulings may occur. Most ordinary citizens, tired of crime throughout the country, can hope so.

The Use of Force.   Also included within the purview of the legal aspects of patrol service is the use of force, more particularly, the use of
firearms.   A police officer may exercise only that amount of force which
he reasonably believes is necessary to effect an arrest; but there are important additional limitations.   Most courts have subscribed to the
proposition that it is "better to allow one guilty only of a misdemeanor
to escape altogether than to take his life." [34]   Under certain circumstances, officers have been found guilty of murder for shooting the
driver of a car,[35] and guilty of manslaughter when death followed a
disabling of the vehicle by gunfire.[36]

The importance of the subject is such that all Departmental Rules
and Regulations include specific instructions concerning the use of firearms.   The following excerpt from the Rules and Regulations of one
department is typical:

> An officer may use his revolver or other firearm to save his own life
> or to protect himself from a felonious assault, and that which he is authorized
> to do in his own defense he is authorized and required to do in the defense of
> any prisoner, citizen or other officer.

> An officer may use a firearm to effect a felony arrest when the use
> of such weapon can be justified in accordance with the laws of arrest, and
> then only when all other efforts have been unsuccessful.   Officers shall be
> ever mindful of the seriousness of the offense for which the person is being
> arrested and shall use discretion in determining the necessity for using a fire-
> arm.

> An officer shall never fire on a person fleeing from him on the mere
> suspicion that the person may have committed a felony, or on one who runs
> a blockade unless known to be the wanted suspect, or solely because the person
> fails to stop on the officer's order.

> Under NO circumstances can the use of firearms be justified in effecting
> an arrest on a misdemeanor charge or a person fleeing from such a charge.

The case of *Commonwealth v. Duerr* [37] illustrates some of the
conditions under which an officer may be acting at his own peril
in the use of his gun.   In this case, the Court stated:

> The notion that a peace officer may in all cases shoot one who flees
> from him when about to be arrested is unfounded.   Officers have no such
> power except in cases of felonies and there, as a last resort, after all other
> means have failed.   It is never allowed, where the offense is only a misde-

34 *Reneua v. State,* 70 Tenn. 720, 721 (1879).

35 *Hill v. Commonwealth,* 239 Ky. 646, 40 S.W.2d 261 (1931).

36 *People v. Klein,* 305 Ill. 141, 137 N.E. 145 (1922).

37 *Commonwealth v. Duerr,* 158 Pa.Super. 484, 45 A.2d 235 (1946).

meanor, and where there is only a suspicion of felony. The officer is not warranted in treating the fugitive as a felon. If he does this, he does so at his peril, and is liable if it turns out that he is mistaken. An officer may lawfully arrest upon a suspicion of felony, but he is only warranted in using such force in making the arrest as is allowable in other cases not felonious.

The generally recognized rule is that an officer endeavoring to make an arrest in cases of felony may use all the force necessary to overcome resistance, even to taking the life of a resisting offender. However, even a felon cannot be killed in an effort to arrest him without criminal responsibility, unless he cannot otherwise be captured: *Commonwealth v. Micuso,* 273 Pa. 474, 477; 117 A. 211. The right to kill an escaping offender is limited to cases in which the officer knows that the person whom he is seeking to arrest is a felon and not an innocent party.

Mere suspicion that a felony has been committed will not justify the killing to prevent the escape of one suspected of the crime. The officer in that event acts at his peril and he will be liable if it is shown that no felony was in fact committed: 4 Am.Jur.Arrest, Sec. 80; 6 Am.Jur.Homicide Sec. 235.

One of the leading cases, and with facts similar to those before us, is *Wiley v. State,* 19 Ariz. 346, 170 P. 869, L.R.A.1918D 373; Wiley, a deputy sheriff, was patrolling the highway with another deputy looking for persons who had committed a robbery at a nearby amusement park. They saw a car down the road turn around and proceed in the opposite direction. They pursued and fired shots bringing the car to a halt. One of the shots killed the driver's wife, who was sitting beside him on the front seat. A verdict of murder in the second degree was affirmed by the Supreme Court. The Court held there was no justification for an officer killing a person who fled from him when the officer was acting on suspicion and no felony had in fact been committed.

On the other side of the fence are the sometimes ominous perils confronting a police officer in his line of duty, perils not too quickly recognized and appreciated on occasion by the people they serve and by the courts. That gunfire may characterize the day's work of the man in uniform is shown by the fact that there were 64 law enforcement officers killed by criminal action in 1968. This number was below the record high of 76 set in 1967, and raised the toll of these tragic deaths to 475 for the years 1960 through 1968. The 64 deaths exceeded the yearly average of 51 for the eight-year period, 1960–1967.

In 1968, the trend established in prior years continued in that more law enforcement officers met death by criminal action when attempting arrests than from any other cause. Twenty of the 64 officers were attempting to make an arrest when they were killed. In 1968, seven officers were killed when their weapons were seized and used against them. These deaths demonstrate a misplaced trust on the part of the officer with respect to the occasional and unpredictable violent nature of human behavior.

Twenty-five percent of the officers met death by robbers whom they interrupted during the commission of their crime or while in pursuit of these criminals. In 1968, 16 percent (or 10) of the officer victims were killed by mentally deranged individuals or shot from ambush with no warning given. Eleven percent of the officers killed met death when answering disturbance-type calls, such as family disputes, man with a gun, etc., and 13 percent were killed while handling, transporting, or through contact with custodial prisoners. Another 3 percent met death while pursuing or attempting to apprehend burglary suspects, and 2 percent lost their lives while investigating suspicious persons or circumstances.

In terms of type of assignment, the patrol officer is the most vulnerable. The officer on car patrol is constantly faced with tense situations demanding instant decisions and response. He is usually the man first on the scene in answer to most calls for police service and during his routine patrols he is often confronted with the need to question suspicious persons on foot and in autos. He is the one most apt to come face to face with the burglar, robber, and other felons caught in the act of committing a crime and hurriedly fleeing the scene. As a result of these confrontations, each of which is unique, the officer riding in a patrol car most often becomes the victim of the police killer.

Forty-one officers on car patrol duty were killed in 1968 and fifteen others were detectives or officers assigned to special duties. Technically, six were off-duty officers, and two were officers on foot patrol. Due to the fact that a law enforcement officer under his oath of duty must take action at any time when he observes a crime being committed, the six men off duty sacrificed their lives when they attempted to prevent the commission of a crime occurring in their presence. Since 1960, 313 or 66 percent of the deceased officers were assigned to car patrols at the time they met their death.

During the eight-year period, 1960–1968, 475 law enforcement officers have been murdered in the line of duty. Among the 626 persons who were involved in these police killings, 65 percent had prior convictions on criminal charges, and of this group, two-thirds had been granted leniency in the form of parole or probation on at least one of these prior convictions. It is significant to note that almost three of every ten of the murderers were on parole or probation when they murdered a police officer. Sixteen or nearly 3 percent of these individuals involved in a police killing had been convicted on some prior occasion with an offense of murder.

Over the eight-year period, seventeen females have been involved in the murder of police officers and in all but one instance, these females were with male companions at the time of the murder. Considering the race of police killers, 381 or 61 percent were white and 245 or 39 percent were Negro.

It should be noted that of the 626 individuals responsible for police murders, 72 were killed at the scene of the crime or soon thereafter by other officers, sixteen committed suicide shortly after the police murder, and four died from other reasons while in custody.

Persons involved in police murders ranged in age from a boy of thirteen to a man of seventy-three, with a median age of twenty-six. Over the eight-year period 1960–1968 there have been forty-two juveniles (6.7 percent) under the age of eighteen arrested for the murder of a police officer. Almost one-half of the murderers were in the twenty to thirty age bracket with the age twenty-five appearing most frequently.

1969 brought forth a record high of 86 law enforcement officers killed by felonious criminal action. This is a 34 percent increase over 1968 when 64 law enforcement officers were murdered. This raised the toll of these tragic deaths to 561 for the years 1960 through 1969. The 86 deaths exceeded the average of 53 murders a year for the period 1960–1968.[38]

Police Chief Herbert T. Jenkins of Atlanta, observed recently that the police across the country will continue to be on the receiving end of shootings, bitings, slugging, and kicking. Their job, he said, always a dirty and dangerous one, appears to be getting dirtier and more dangerous by the day.

[38] Federal Bureau of Investigation, *Uniform Crime Reports*, 1969.

Chapter 10

PATROL POWER—SUPPORTING LINE ELEMENTS

SINCE the work of the patrol force includes all police functions, the more effective the patrol division, the less need there is for the more specialized operating divisions and units. It has been shown that, although it is impossible for the patrol services alone to be one hundred per cent effective in the discharge of all police functions, the other operating line divisions are necessary only to the extent that the patrol division falls short of this objective. It follows, as a corollary, that all other line divisions or units in police organization, including detective, traffic, crime prevention, and vice, are to be regarded fundamentally as supporting elements of patrol power, although not subordinate to it in the organization structure. Consolidation of all line operations, including the patrol division, under a single, unified command provides the necessary coordination and proper distribution of emphasis.

The Detective Division

The primary function of the detective is to apprehend those offenders who escape arrest at the hands of the patrol division and the recovery of stolen property. In the growth of a department, the necessity arises for a specialized investigational unit of one or more men when the uncleared case load of the patrol force reaches a point where departmental efficiency demands specialized assistance. Numerous offenses come to the attention of the police which require extensive investigation both in time and place for their solution. The number of these offenses and the grave character of many of them may make necessary the organization of a separate division in the police department manned by persons assigned exclusively to criminal investigation. The duties of the detectives supplement those of the patrol division, and the coordination of the work of these two units is among the most important of all problems confronting the police chief executive.

Organization

Since it performs one of the primary functions of the police, the detective division in the larger cities occupies a place in the structure of police organization similar to that of patrol, with the head of this division or unit reporting directly to the Chief of Operations. The size of the division should be flexible; its numerical strength is determined by the number of cases which are escaping solution by the uniformed patrol force. Since the patrol force is the backbone of the department and its most numerous unit, it should be utilized to the utmost in the final disposition of as large a proportion of the total case load as possible. Every case which can be disposed of by the uniformed force should be so handled. In police departments where this policy is followed, primary responsibility for the investigation and disposition of all cases, whatever their nature, originating on a given beat, is given to the patrolman assigned to that particular area.

Structuring the Detective Function

Criminal investigation is the keystone of police service. The detection and apprehension of the criminal offender and the production of evidence against him, all depend upon it. It is the point at which society brings the forces of law and order into sharp focus in its approach to the problems of crime and the criminal. The detective function—*criminal investigation*—is a basic feature of modern police service.

The role of the detective operation includes the primary objectives of apprehending those offenders who escape arrest at the hands of patrol service, and the recovery of stolen property. As in the case of traffic control and regulation, in order to structure the detective function under sound principles of organization and management, it is first necessary to consider the commanding role of patrol service in a police organization.

It has been previously noted that numerically, it is at once, and should be, the largest single unit in both the staff and line of a police department. In terms of work and performance, it carries out in police service the functions discharged by the combat elements in military operations. The patrol force marks the point in police organization where planning, strategy and police are translated into action in the field, in the approach to the major objectives of police service:

1. Protection of life and property.

2. Prevention and suppression of crime and vice.

3. Apprehension of criminal offenders.

4. Recovery of lost and stolen property.

5. Preservation of the public peace and order.

6. Regulation and control of traffic.

All other line units in a police organization move in orbit about the patrol force and are secondary to it. Since the work of the patrol force includes all major police functions, the more effective patrol service is, the less need there will be for the more specialized operating units, including the detective function. In cities and communities of 150,000 and under, perhaps even higher, the presence of a detective unit or division would seem to be a waste of departmental resources. In such jurisdictions, there appears to be no sound reason for not locating total investigative responsibility in the patrol force.

In at least one known instance, this improvement has been made; there are undoubtedly others. The police department of Port Arthur, Texas, with a population of 66,676, has abolished the position of detective. The responsibility for all criminal investigation has been assigned to the patrol force. In those cases where the individual patrolman is in need of specialized assistance or where the investigation might take him beyond the boundaries of his beat, experienced patrolmen operating in plain clothes if necessary and under the control of the Patrol Commander, should be able to perform this service effectively. Patrolmen can be selected for this assignment on the basis of demonstrated aptitudes and capabilities for the different types of case investigation. In addition to the economy in money and manpower, this arrangement eliminates split-division responsibility for case investigation, with the added advantage of placing the total investigative function under the control of one man—the Patrol Commander.

The compelling requirement for the elimination of this special deployment of patrol personnel resources to a separate administrative section—the detective unit or division—is a determination of policy by police management with respect to *patrol beat responsibility.*[1] Everything pivots on this determination. Policy in regard to this critical decision will vary from one department to another. At one end of the administrative spectrum, the detective is charged with total investigative responsibility. At the other end, with variations in between, the individual patrolman is charged with the total delivery of police service, including the investigation and disposition of cases in all categories originating on his beat.

It is fundamental that tasks ordinarily assumed by specialized divisions that can be satisfactorily performed by the patrol division should be reserved for patrol in order that its manpower may be increased and the force of the special unit decreased. This basic principle of police

[1] See page 242.

management is not widely followed. Too frequently detective divisions are observed handling a large volume of petty cases which should be carried through to final disposition by the patrolman. Thus, departmental policy with respect to patrol responsibility is a highly important factor in determining the personnel strength of the detective division.

When because of case load, the patrol force cannot discharge this responsibility with maximum efficiency, it must have specialized assistance of the detective. But this does not diminish the responsibility of the patrolman. An uncleared case originating on his beat remains as a direct charge against his operations. The detective division should be regarded only as a supporting element available to him in meeting his responsibilities as the person charged with the delivery of all the line functions of police service on his beat. Adherence to this form of patrol policy results in maximum employment of manpower in the largest administrative unit in the organization, and wherever it has been applied, it has reduced the volume of uncleared cases that must be referred to the detective division for investigation and clearance.

Specialization in a detective division permits the investigator to concentrate his time and energies in the investigation of a particular type of criminal activity and through continuous work in a specific criminal area, he gradually builds up a fund of skills and information that is indispensable to departmental efficiency. He comes to know personally the offenders who operate within the specific criminal specialty which constitutes the functional area assigned to him for investigation; he becomes familiar with their methods of operation, their habits, friends, relatives, and close associates. Not infrequently an experienced detective is able to narrow the investigation and search down to a single individual after a careful study of the crime scene and recognition of the salient features of the modus operandi.

As a result of the yield from specialization in criminal investigation, detective divisions, particularly in the larger cities, are decentralized functionally into special details, such as the homicide, robbery, burglary, automobile theft, worthless check, bunco, and other squads. Case load will determine the necessity for the creation of a special squad. Such units should be created only in response to a real need and liquidated or consolidated with another unit when the need has passed or ceased to be acute or continuous.

What has been said previously with respect to single-officer motor patrol applies also to members of the detective division. Condemning the almost universal custom of detectives working in pairs, Vollmer stated: [2]

"Contrary to the prevailing practice, team work should be the rare exception and not the rule. It seems the height of absurdity to detail two strong robust men to conduct an inquiry where larceny, burglary or robbery has been committed. One man would, unquestionably, do the work better than two. The Federal Government and a number of police departments observe this practice and there is no reason why it should not be the custom here. A plain clothes team is never any better than its poorest member because the weakest member pulls the better one down to his level. Most of the work now being done by teams can be accomplished to better advantage by an individual. Notable exceptions are when dangerous suspects are being apprehended or interviewed, or where corroborative evidence is essential."

It has been amply demonstrated that more and better work will be done when detectives work alone rather than in pairs. Under this arrangement, furthermore, it is much easier to place the credit or the blame for the quality of work performed.

Selection and Training

Extraordinary care must be used in recruiting detectives. They may possess the qualities necessary to patrol beats or supervise patrolmen, but they must have other personal qualifications which peculiarly fit them for specialized investigative services. A deep interest on the part of the investigator is essential for this phase of police work, and this interest must be supplemented by an intimate knowledge of the arts and sciences applicable to a particular field of investigation, plus an acquaintance with and personal knowledge of criminals who specialize in particular types of offenses.

Like the patrolman, the detective must have energy, persistence, courage, resourcefulness, initiative, intelligence, imagination, alertness, discriminating observation, memory, and judgment—only to a greater degree. Contrary to popular impression, a criminal case—whether it be murder, robbery, burglary, or automobile theft—is seldom solved by miraculous sleuthing powers or by the methods exploited in detective mystery thrillers, but by persistent, intelligent hard work.

The selection of competent criminal investigators for assignment to detective work presents a difficult problem. Some police authorities hold that competitive written examinations, as a prerequisite to assignment to detective duty, fail to accomplish their purpose; they point out

---

[2] August Vollmer, "Survey and Reorganization of the Police Department of Dallas, Texas," 1944, p. 58.

that experience generally has proved that formal tests cannot finally determine detective aptitude or capacity. Nevertheless, in the selection of men for transfer to the detective division, some criteria must be applied. No measuring device, whether written examination or other forms of tests, should be overlooked in the effort to select men who are best qualified for this type of work.

If promotional examinations possess validity at all, their use is certainly suggested in the attempt to identify men in the department who possess the qualities needed in successful detectives.[3] Assignment to the detective division should be contingent upon a weighted superior score based upon written examinations and previous performance record in the department. Such assignment should be on trial-and-error basis at the probationary level. Even after permanent assignment, a noticeable decline in effectiveness should result in immediate return to the patrol force and the discontinuance of increased compensation.

The prevailing practice in American police departments is to draw personnel for the detective division from the patrol force. This practice would appear to be sound. The nature of the duties imposed upon the patrol division is such that they constitute an effective proving ground for a successful detective. This is especially true where departmental policy places investigative responsibility upon the individual patrolman for the clearance of cases originating on his beat. Where proper records are kept, it is a simple matter to evaluate with a high degree of accuracy the investigative aptitudes of the patrolman and in many instances to identify the presence of specialized abilities in the investigation of certain types of criminal cases. This type of information is priceless in the process of selecting men for work in the detective division.

After applying the foregoing standards to selection of detective personnel, the odds are against the efforts of the probationer being attended with any marked degree of success unless he is given some form of specialized training which will prepare him to meet the demands of his new assignment. All that has been said previously with respect to divisional training applies with special force to members of the detective division.[4] It is necessary to superimpose upon the in-service training received by the embryo detective as a patrolman, thorough specialized instruction in the techniques of detective operations. There is little or

---

[3] Rollin M. Perkins, "Police Examinations," The Foundation Press, 1947, see *Detective Examinations*, pp. 299–325. Also B. W. Gocke, "Police Sergeants Manual," O. W. Smith, 1944, *Promotional Examinations*, pp. 171, 275.

[4] See Chapter 7.

no provision in the programs of American police departments for this form of divisional training. In too many organizations, the men are assigned to their new duties as if no training or special aptitude were necessary at all. Training is generally limited to on-the-job experience accumulated during a period of apprenticeship in which the detective recruit is assigned to plain clothes duty with retention in the detective division depending somewhat on their performance during this time. This is admittedly an unsatisfactory procedure.

American practice is in marked contrast with the system followed in European countries, where detective schools and courses often are maintained as an integral part of the police training program. In Vienna before the war, divisional training for detectives involved two hours a day in lectures and recitations and covered a period of six months. In Paris, detectives are required to attend a series of lectures each year in connection with their work.

The English have in recent years come to realize the basic importance of specialized training for the various branches of police service. The divisional aspect of their total training program is well exemplified in the highly specialized training provided for detectives. As a guest of Scotland Yard officials during the summer months of 1947, the author was given the opportunity of visiting the Metropolitan Police Detective Training School at Hendon. Intensive training was provided not only for the detective recruit but also for supervisory and command personnel in the Criminal Investigation Division.

Control over Detective Performance

It is necessary for management to know the extent to which the detective division is being properly supervised and whether it is fulfilling its functions adequately. Achievement of this objective requires some method which will aid in the appraisal of detective operations as a whole, in an estimate of the work of special squads or details and, more especially, in an evaluation of the performance and accomplishments of the individual detective. In fact, the first two depend upon an accurate inventory of the work of the individual detective. The familiar blotter or assignment record used as a chronological tabulation of offenses reported to the detective division and showing the squad or officers to whom the complaint was referred is altogether inadequate for this purpose. Any effort to examine the record of an individual detective is made doubly difficult and time-consuming by the necessity of searching in detail through all complaints received.

DETECTIVE ASSIGNMENT REGISTER

Name of Detective

Case Number	Date Assigned	Time Assigned	Name of Complainant (Title of Case)	Offense	Suspect Known	Date Closed or Declared Inactive	Unfounded	Not Cleared	Cleared by Arrest	Property	Recovered	Dates of Investigation Reports

Institute of Public Administration, New York City, 1941

In addition to the foregoing record, it is necessary that a detective assignment register be employed similar to the illustration. This record provides the head of the detective division with a continuous summary of the work of each detective and, in addition, affords an intelligent basis for distribution of the case load among investigators. It is in effect a continuous report of progress on all assigned cases and constitutes a measuring scale by which the scope and effectiveness of the work of each individual detective may be appraised. In the assignment register form illustrated above, it will be observed that it shows not merely the serial numbers and the names of cases assigned, but also the results secured. It serves as an index to the case reports, thus facilitating a continuous and systematic review.

In recommending the installation of this control device in the Baltimore Police Department, Bruce Smith pointed out that while it may not provide conclusive evidence of adaptability or of the effort put forth by a detective, it does serve as a guide to that end, and is a necessary first step towards securing a more frequent and more penetrating examination of individual detective operations than has been available in the past.[5] He cautioned that from that point on, it is a question of following up the progress of all investigations from day to day—not merely those eliciting great popular interest—of bringing additional resources to bear on cases that require them, and of continually appraising the work of individuals both as a current matter and also against a long-range record of performance. He properly held that if these things were persistently done, more cases would be pursued to a successful conclusion, both because of the greater effort put forth by detectives, and because those who are not well fitted for the work may be assigned to less exacting duties, and their places taken by others who are better qualified.

Time studies, similar to those recommended for job analyses in the patrol division, should be conducted in order to establish time units for the various types of investigations performed by members of the detective division. Such studies make possible a more adequate appraisal of the performance of the individual detective and also provide a basis for distribution of work load. Combined with the data on personal performance revealed by the follow-up system of control [6] over all cases reported to the department for investigation, the means is provided for a continuous check upon the effectiveness of the detective division as a whole.

[5] Bruce Smith, "The Baltimore Police Survey," Institute of Public Administration, New York, 1941, p. 82.

[6] See Chapter 8.

It has been appropriately indicated in police surveys that without some objective means of evaluating the individual performance of each operative, hidden abilities and weaknesses are too apt to go unnoticed, and needed adjustments within the division are apt to be disregarded. It has been proved repeatedly that an officer may be a failure in one branch of criminal investigation but successful in another. Clash of personalities may also cause failure on particular assignments. Further, some men after years of police service relax their efforts and "coast," while others continue to gain wider knowledge, sustain their interest, and render superior service. The freedom of movement, both in time and place, which is characteristic of the detective function, places a premium on the man who can withstand the temptation and opportunity to relax, and apply himself vigorously to the task at hand. Vollmer has been heard to refer to the detective division as "the old lady's home," and it is probably true that he had in mind this tendency on the part of some detectives to regard their position as a sinecure. In his various reorganizations of American police departments, he has emphasized the necessity for revitalization of this branch of the organization.

Coordination of Patrol and Detective Divisions

One of the most difficult problems of coordination confronting police management is the integration of the activities of the detective and patrol divisions. Where their respective functions are not clarified, undue importance often is attached to detective operations, with the result that detective-dominated police departments are common. The status of the detective division in the larger departments has prevented the profitable exchange of information between detective and uniformed personnel, and has been instrumental in elevating the detective division almost to the level of an independent department.

Another factor conducive to jealousy is the higher pay of the detectives and the greater freedom of action accorded them in their work. A feeling that long service in the patrol ranks is indicative of lack of ability in police work is commonly held by detectives.

One notes an unwholesome rivalry between the patrol and detective divisions in many sections of the country. The basic cause is the tendency in many departments toward a rigid line of demarcation between the duties of the detective and patrol divisions which excludes the uniformed patrolmen from conducting the investigation of any cases other than those which can be undertaken and disposed of by immediate action. This policy neutralizes the prestige and effectiveness of the patrol force and paves the way for detective domination of the department, destructive rivalry, dissension, and lowered morale within the organization. A collateral, but more important, result is the curtailment and weakening of the line power of the largest operating unit in police organization, the patrol division.

The opening up of the investigative field to patrolmen and the coordination of the activities of these two divisions under unified command undoubtedly would institute a more positive relationship between patrolman and detective. The commanding officer in charge of line operations is interested in each division only to the extent that its growth and expansion contribute to the total line power of the department, and within this frame of reference patrol power and responsibility is the basic point of departure. He will utilize the detective division under strong central direction in carrying out his plans for meeting the problems to which line operations are addressed and will hold the head of that division strictly accountable for the quality of its performance.

The Investigative Process. If selected with care and adequately trained for police service, the individual patrol officer is in a strong position to undertake the responsibilities of case investigation. It is important to observe that the exposure of the officer to investigative responsibility occurs on two fronts:

1. In those departments where the patrolman is held responsible for the total delivery of police service, including the clearance of all cases orginating on his beat, criminal investigation is an integral part of the day's work.

2. Where the case load of the patrol force or other circumstances dictate the use of a patrolman or patrolman in plain clothes, the day or night on this assignment is devoted exclusively to criminal investigation. In both 1 and 2, the detective function is structured within the patrol services. Again, in both 1 and 2, by the very nature of the task, the officer finds himself in a training environment which offers strong preparation for the discharge of the detective function.

Webster defines investigation as *observing or studying by close examination and systematic inquiry.* Criminal investigation involves four specific objectives:

1. *Establishing the fact that a criminal offense has, in fact, been committed.*—the *corpus delicti* or the body of the crime, which embraces all of the facts related to the commission of a particular criminal offense, and the fact that it was committed by a human agent.

2. *Identifying the elements of the offense.* Pinpointing the major components of a crime frequently reveals important

leads in the investigation of a criminal case. These components include:

a. Name and address of victim.
b. Where committed.
c. Person and/or property attacked.
d. How attacked.
e. Means of attack.
f. Time of attack.
g. Object of attack.
h. Trademark.

3. *Detection and apprehension of the offender.*
One of the major objectives of criminal investigation is to establish the identity of the offender and to bring about his apprehension.

4. *The production of evidence against him.*
This important phase of criminal investigation is concerned with the development of proof sufficient to sustain a conviction of the offender in a criminal court proceeding.

Equipment of the Investigating Officer. All that has been previously said concerning the selection and training of police personnel comes into sharp focus at the threshold of a criminal case investigation. Here—intelligence, skill, enterprise, initiative, perseverance, patience, ingenuity and an insatiable curiosity, in addition to a rational method or procedure, are among the essential prerequisites to investigative success.

It has been said that one of the most effective weapons the officer has against the criminal is his *notebook.* An important place for the notebook is in the courtroom when the case comes to trial. On the stand, it is altogether appropriate for the officer to consult his notebook to refresh his memory. As a matter of fact, the notebook is admissible in evidence. Full, complete and detailed notes should be made of every step in the investigation, and of every fact or bit of information developed in the case. Furthermore, it is fundamental that all notes be recorded with a pen rather than a pencil. The fact that defense counsel may be permitted by the court to examine the officer's notebook, indicates the need for extreme care and accuracy in all notebook recording. It is important to observe that the notebook contains the raw material from which the investigation report is ultimately prepared.

In actual practice in the field, the officer will find some form of investigation kit to be very functional and useful because of the wide variety of tools and aids that may be needed during the course of a case investigation. Such kits are available on the market and are obtainable from police supply houses. However, they can be easily made by the investigating officer at relatively little expense. The dimensions of one designed and made by the author were 22″ x 18″ x 8″. Consisting of two hinged sections, the portable case contained [7] some fifty items, including a camera. In one sense, the investigation kit is a portable laboratory. Every department, regardless of size, should be equipped with at least one investigation kit.

It has long been recognized that *sources of information* are an important part of the equipment and reserve support of the investigating officer. In fact, the value of a police officer to his organization can be measured to an important degree by the nature and extent of his lines of information.

The Informer. The detective function as it is generally understood today, first found expression in the use of informers by the Courts in England and France during the sixteenth and seventeenth centuries. Magistrates charged with the suppression of crime in that day recognized the need for advance information concerning the activities of criminal offenders. The circumstances suggested the advantage of buying information from informers who themselves on occasion, lived outside the pale of the law. Today, the informer continues to play an important role in the investigative process.

The motives for revealing information to a police officer run the entire spectrum of human nature. They include vanity, civic-mindedness, fear, repentance, avoiding punishment, gratitude or gain, revenge, jealousy and remuneration.

The list of potential informants useful to a police officer has no end. They include responsible citizens, barbers, bartenders, beauty shop operators, club and association secretaries, dry cleaners and laundry delivery men, employment agency personnel, garagemen, grocers, gunsmiths, hotel managers, bellboys, telephone operators, household servants, insurance investigators, janitors, window cleaners, locksmiths, milk delivery men—in fact all home delivery persons, money lenders, neighbors, newspaper carriers, parking lot operators, postmen, prostitutes, public utility employes, race track employes, bookmakers, rental agencies, restaurant employes, entertainers, tailors, waiters, waitresses, and individuals with a known criminal record.[8]

In order to protect this vital source of intelligence, both the police and the informer have an understandable interest in shielding the iden-

---

[7] See V. A. Leonard, *The Police Detective Function*, Springfield, Illinois, Charles C. Thomas, Publisher, 1970.

[8] See Harney, Malachi L., & Cross, John C., *The Informer in Law Enforcement*, Springfield, Illinois, Charles C. Thomas, Publisher.

tity of the latter.   In an effort to cooperate with the police and in the interests of public safety, the United States Supreme Court has developed a rule of evidence known as the *informer's privilege* against the disclosure of his identity.   But the rule and the privilege are limited, and disclosure or nondisclosure of identity pivots on the circumstances of the particular case.   On the one hand, the Court is interested in protecting these lines of information; on the other, the Court is also interested in providing the accused with a fair opportunity to defend himself.[9]   It can be said, however, that the basic interest of the Courts in protecting this vital flow of confidential information has tilted the scales somewhat in favor of the police.

There are unlimited sources of information available to a police officer other than the services of an informer.   For a complete, classified inventory of these sources, the reader is referred to the excellent work, *Fundamentals of Criminal Investigation,* 2nd ed., published by Charles C. Thomas, Springfield, Illinois.[10]   This book should be in the library of every police department.

Care and Preservation of Evidence.   Evidence is that which sustains proof, or denies it.   It includes testimony on the witness stand, records, documents, objects, scientifically established facts and other data that can be legally presented during a criminal trial for the purpose of assisting the court and jury in arriving at a determination concerning the truth of the issue involved.

Evidence falls into two major classifications—direct and circumstantial.   Direct evidence is the testimony of an eye witness and is the weakest and most unreliable of all types of evidence.   It can be perjured and is subject to all of the frailties of human memory and the senses of perception.

Circumstantial evidence, the most reliable of all, is concerned with a scientifically validated fact which speaks for itself, such as the identification of a bloody fingerprint on a butcher knife, or a laboratory determination that a fatal bullet recovered from the body of the victim was fired from a revolver which was in possession of the suspect at the time of his arrest.   The total yield from a crime detection laboratory qualifies as circumstantial evidence.

In certain categories of crime, including all crimes of violence— homicides, assaults, robbery, burglary and certain other forms of theft— the search of the crime scene can easily prove to be among the most im-

---

[9] See Leonard, V. A., *The Police, the Judiciary and the Criminal*, Springfield, Illinois, Charles C. Thomas, Publisher.

[10] Charles E. O'Hara, *Fundamentals of Criminal Investigation*, Springfield, Illinois, Charles C. Thomas, Publisher, 1970.

portant phases of the investigation. Wherever there has been an impact of the offender upon the crime environment, the crime scene search becomes a matter of major importance.

It would be extremely difficult for an individual to merely walk into and out of a room without leaving some evidence behind that he had been there and without taking some evidence with him that he had been there. The criminal impact is such that the chances for this displacement of matter, whether large or microscopic, is multiplied many times. The evidence resources of the crime scene are such that a thorough search is mandatory. Techniques of the crime scene search are fully described in a number of important works that are now available to the police.[11]

The Police Laboratory. Every police department, regardless of size, even the smallest, should have at least a rudimentary police laboratory. Even though the equipment may be limited and no highly trained specialists present with degrees in the laboratory sciences, even the smaller police department can easily and with relatively little expense, develop an elementary laboratory facility that can serve very important purposes.

The nucleus of such a laboratory is a photographic darkroom and basic camera equipment. The Eastman Kodax Company and other suppliers of photographic equipment will gladly furnish any department with detailed plans for the darkroom. In order of importance, the basic elements of a simple police laboratory include the following:

1. Photographic darkroom.
2. A view camera with flash attachment.
3. Elementary lighting equipment.
4. Latent fingerprint camera.
5. Investigation kit (see page 274).

The view camera is a multi-purpose piece of equipment. It serves for the photography of crime and traffic accident scenes and for the "mugging" of arrested persons, in those instances where the departmental budget will not permit the purchase of more sophisticated equipment for this purpose. Mounted on a tripod, it is also useful in photographing latent fingerprints on articles and objects that have been brought in to headquarters from the scene, and in photographing other types of evidence.

---

[11] See Gerber, Samuel R.; Schroeder, Oliver, *Criminal Investigation,* W. H. Anderson Company, 1962.

O'Hara, Charles E., *Fundamentals of Criminal Investigation,* Springfield, Illinois, Charles C. Thomas, Publisher.

Scott, Charles C., *Photographic Evidence,* Vernon Law Book Company, 1955.

As is well known, the fingerprint camera is designed primarily for field use in photographing latent impressions on objects that cannot conveniently be taken to headquarters. There are occasionally situations where the fingerprint camera cannot be used because of the contour of the surface on which the print has been developed. In such cases, the view camera can be used effectively for this purpose. The author has made it a practice to "lift" a latent fingerprint impression only as a last resort.

In the smaller department, from the standpoint of personnel, the identification officer is usually the man in charge of laboratory work. A police officer with an enthusiastic interest in scientific crime detection and with elementary equipment can make important contributions to the investigative process and to the reputation of his department. As Wilson observed, whenever he searches for, develops and photographs latent fingerprints, photographs the scenes of crimes and serious accidents, and makes casts of footprints and performs other work in the development of evidence materials, he is engaged in *scientific crime detection.*

In addition to its value in the processing of evidence materials, the presence of such a laboratory facility cultivates a scientific attitude on the part of police personnel generally and sharpens the approach in the search for evidence, and its care and preservation. In the larger departments, the police laboratory is a standard feature of police service. Supplementing local police laboratory installations are state crime laboratories and the incomparable scientific crime detection laboratory of the Federal Bureau of Investigation in Washington, D. C.; the services of both are available to local law enforcement agencies on request.

Collateral elements of the investigative process include *Modus Operandi*, among the most important investigational tools at the disposal of the police. In the United States, an increasing number of police departments are making effective use of the Modus Operandi system. In the larger departments, on all theft cases reported to the police—robbery, burglary, larceny, worthless checks and automobile theft—the elements of the Modus Operandi or operational profile in each case are punched out on tabulating code cards, searched and placed on file. A Modus Operandi search of thousands of these M. O. cards requires only a few minutes.

The M. O. in an uncleared burglary case, for example, is coded and programmed on the automatic sorting machine. M. O. cards on file are then run through the sorting machine and all cases with the same or similar M. O. are automatically selected. The operation serves two investigative purposes:

  1. On uncleared cases, it brings together offense reports with the same or similar Modus Operandi, with the probability that

all or most of these cases were committed by the same individual.

2. By running through the automatic sorting machine cases cleared in the past with the same or similar M. O. as currently unsolved cases, it may indicate to the police who they are looking for.

Metropolitan and state police computer installations offer unlimited opportunities in the Modus Operandi identification of criminal offenders. Through the use of the computer, the verdict is virtually instantaneous. In the smaller police departments, the same operation can be conducted effectively through the use of index cards. Through cross-index classification, the M. O., on each case of theft, can be broken down and factored into its component parts as an investigative aid in the identification of a crime series, and as an aid in the identification of the offender. These cross-index divisions are:

1. Crime classification.
2. Person and/or property attacked.
3. Where committed (location index, spot maps, etc.).
4. Time of attack.
5. How attacked.
6. Means of attack.
7. Object of attack.
8. Trademark.

Each main index division will have a number of subdivisions. Time of attack, for instance, would be broken down by hour of day, day of week, week of month, and month of year. As these index files build up and through cross-indexing and searching in the M. O. file of current cases reported to the department for investigation, important identifications can be made, with a corresponding increase in the quantity and quality of police performance.

Interrogation. In the general administration of criminal justice, *information* at the investigative stage in a criminal case is the most vital element in the total process. *Sources of information* available to the police, and their wide range and diversity, have been previously considered. However the greatest source of direct information bearing upon guilt or innocence is obtained through the interrogation of criminal suspects, and through interviewing witnesses and others who may possess relevant information concerning the case under investigation.

The line of distinction between an interview and an interrogation is very thin. Both involve questioning and more important, *listening*. An interview can be regarded as a formal consultation with a person who may have knowledge that is of official interest to the investigating

officer.   On the other hand, an interrogation is the *systematic* questioning of a criminal suspect or of a person who is reluctant to disclose information in his possession which is pertinent to the investigation.

Much has been written concerning the techniques of interrogation
and it would be idle to involve the reader in any detailed discussion of the
subject at this point.   Since interrogation is one of the most important
investigative tools at the disposal of the police, every police officer should
spend much time and effort in studying the works in this area that are
now available.[12]

In the interrogation of a criminal suspect, it is well to keep in mind
that the suspect labors under a psychological complusion to tell everything that he knows.   The observations of that eminent authority on evidence, John Henry Wigmore, bear repeating:

In the first place, an innocent person is always helped by an early opportunity to tell his whole story; hundreds of suspected persons every day
are set free because their story thus told bears the marks of truth.

Moreover, and more important, every guilty person is almost always
ready and desirous to confess, as soon as he is detected and arrested.   This
psychological truth, well known to all criminal trial judges, seems to be ignored by some Supreme Courts.

The nervous pressure of guilt is enormous; the load of the deed done is
heavy;   the fear of detection fills the consciousness;   and when detection
comes, the pressure is relieved;   and the deep sense of relief makes confession
a satisfaction.   At that moment, he will tell all, and tell it truly.   To forbid
soliciting him, to seek to prevent this relief is to fly into the face of nature.

It is natural and should be lawful, to take his confession at that moment
—the best one.   And this expedient saves the State a delay and expense in
convicting him after he has reacted from his first sensations, has yielded to
his friends' solicitations, and comes under the sway of the natural human
instinct to struggle to save himself by the aid of all technicalities.[13]

---

[12] See O'Hara, Charles E., *Fundamentals of Criminal Investigation*,
Springfield, Illinois, Charles C. Thomas, Publisher, 1956, pp. 79–114.

Inbau & Reed, *Lie Detection and Criminal Interrogation*, Williams & Wilkins Company, Baltimore, 1953.

Vanderbosch, Charles G., *Criminal Investigation*, International Association of Chiefs of Police, 1968, pp. 196–209.

Dudycha, George J., *Psychology for Law Enforcement Officers*, Springfield, Illinois, Charles C. Thomas, Publisher, 1955.

Grace, Richard C.; Coffey, Alan; Eldefonso, Edward, *Principles of Law
Enforcement*, New York, John Wiley & Sons, Inc., 1968, pp. 215–217.

Clift, Raymond E., *A Guide to Modern Police Thinking*, Cincinnati, W. H.
Anderson Company, 2nd ed., 1965, pp. 132–143.

Gerber, Samuel R.; Schroeder, Jr., Oliver., *Criminal Investigation and
Interrogation*, Cincinnati, W. H. Anderson Company, 1962, pp. 247–306.

[13] Professor Wigmore is here referring to restrictions placed by the United
States Supreme Court on the police interrogation of criminal suspects.

In the case of professional criminals who usually work in groups, there is often no hope of getting at the group until one of them has "preached", and given the clues to the police. The police know this, and have known it for generations in every country. The only ones who apparently do not know it are some of the Supreme Court judges . . .. To forbid this (interrogation) is to tie the hands of the police. The attitude of some judges towards these necessary methods is lamentable . . .. To disable the police from the very function they are set to fulfill is no less than absurd. Let the judges who sit in judgment on crime look a little into the facts. Let them not sit up aloft and dictate a rule which ignores the well known facts of criminal life and hampers the needful methods of justice.[14]

Police Surveillance. Surveillance is the covert or secret observation of persons, vehicles, places or situations where the identity of the observer must be protected. It is distinguished from undercover work by the circumstance that in this form of surveillance, the investigator discards his real identity, assumes another role or identity, and makes a direct personal contact with the person, place or situation.

In the extended police literature that is available today, the reader will find that the techniques of surveillance, both moving and fixed, have received excellent treatment. Every police officer should consult these works and give them careful study.[15]

Among the tools of criminal investigation potentially available to the police under a rather confusing array of limitations is the interception of communications, generally referred to as wiretapping. Developments in the field of communications engineering have made the interception of any form of communication a relatively simple matter. A confusing array of decisions have been handed down by the United States Supreme Court on wiretapping and electronic surveillance by the police. The reader is referred to *The Police, the Judiciary and the Criminal* by one of the present authors, for a detailed analysis of this problem.[16]

[14] Wigmore, John Henry: *Evidence in Trials at Common Law*, 3rd ed., Boston, Little, 1940, vol. 3, 851 at 319.

[15] O'Hara, Charles E., *Fundamentals of Criminal Investigation*, Springfield, Illinois, Charles C. Thomas, Publisher, 1956, pp. 160–176; for undercover assignments, see pp. 177–186.

Eldefonso, Edward; Coffey, Alan; and Grace, Richard C., *Principles of Law Enforcement*, New York, John Wiley & Sons, 1968, pp. 218–221.

Gerber, Samuel R.; Schroeder, Oliver, *Criminal Investigation and Identification*, Cincinnati, W. H. Anderson Company, 1962, pp. 21–32.

[16] Leonard, V. A., *The Police, the Judiciary and the Criminal*, Springfield, Illinois, Charles C. Thomas, Publisher, 1970.

Use of the Polygraph

The polygraph or lie detector is now standard equipment in most American police departments in cities of 50,000 population and above. As of 1959, a survey revealed that police departments in 199 American cities and the State Police in 48 states were making use of the polygraph. The inquiry further indicated the extent to which the polygraph is being employed in the armed forces, including the U. S. Air Force, the U. S. Marines and the Military Police. The polygraph training program at the Provost Marshal General's School at Camp Gordon, Georgia, is conceded to be among the best and most comprehensive programs of this type in the entire United States.[17]

For more than forty years, the polygraph has proven its worth to the police in declaring the innocent and exposing the guilt of the criminal offender. As an aid to interrogation in the early stages of case investigation, it has shortened the investigative trail to a point where, from an economic point of view and increased police efficiency, its use is now mandatory. Some departments follow the policy of examining on the polygraph virtually all persons arrested, including those in the "suspicious character" category. Where this is done, the number of uncleared cases in the files of the department is materially reduced.

The use of the polygraph is also now well established in the screening of police applicants. It has proven to be effective in discouraging patently unqualified candidates from even applying for a position in the department. In addition, there is its obvious value in disclosing important information unreported on the application form, such as prior criminal participation in unreported or unsolved crimes, abnormal sexual tendencies and other unfavorable information.

The conservative *Wall Street Journal* featured on the front page of its October, 1961 issue an article on the expanding use of the polygraph by business and industry in the screening of personnel. On the roster of known users of the polygraph were major companies in steel production, copper refining, automobile manufacturing, meat packing, food processing, oil refining, electronics manufacturing, mail order retailing and wholesale drug concerns. Lloyd's of London recognizes the worth of the polygraph by granting insurance premium reductions on embezzlement and other forms of theft where the company or business in question processes its personnel periodically on the polygraph.

Inventory shrinkage across the nation is big business, amounting to a total annual loss nationally of between one and two billion dollars.

---

[17] Gootnick, Louis, *A Survey of Police Use of the Lie Detector*, a Master's Thesis, New York University, October, 1959.

The Director of Security for one wholesale drug concern, who is a trained polygraph examiner, observed that at the time he became associated with the company, they were experiencing an annual inventory shrinkage of between three and four million dollars. It is estimated by security personnel that of every $10.00 loss, $1.00 may be attributed to shoplifting and other forms of outside theft, and $9.00 to employe or employe-related theft. The important role of the polygraph and its associated techniques in the approach to this problem, is thus self-evident.

In a few states, attempts have been made to pass legislation prohibiting the use of the polygraph in the screening of personnel on the grounds that it invaded the privacy and rights of the individual. This is totally unacceptable. The polygraph examination performs exactly the same function as the application form and background investigation in revealing information concerning the applicant to a prospective employer. No objection to the application form and background investigation has as yet been heard.[18]

The polygraph is a diagnostic instrument and functions as an aid in the diagnosis of truth or deception. The technical aspects of the polygraph examination and the interpretation of the results require the presence of a well trained and experienced examiner. This is no place for the novice or amateur. There is a definite trend among the states toward a qualifying State Board Examination and the licensing of polygraph examiners. Kentucky in 1962 was the first to take this desirable step with Senate Bill No. 63, and similar bills have been under consideration by Legislatures in other states, including New York, Illinois, Wisconsin and California.[19]

---

[18] As a former president of the Academy for Scientific Interrogation, a national organization of polygraph examiners, the author is of the opinion that the motives of persons interested in this type of legislation should be carefully examined.

[19] It is to be noted that in August of 1966, the American Polygraph Association was formed, merging the entire polygraph field into one parent organization. In connection with the movement toward the licensing of polygraph examiners, the Association has drafted a *Model Polygraph Examiner's Act* to expedite the passage of enabling legislation at the state level. Copies of the Act may be obtained from the Secretary of the Association, C. B. Hanscom, 2030 University Avenue, S. E., University of Minnesota, Minneapolis, Minnesota—55455.

There are four classes of membership in the American Polygraph Association—Member, Intern, Affiliate and Honorary.

A. *MEMBER*

In order to qualify as Member an applicant must meet the following requirements:

1. The applicant must have completed a course of formal instruction in polygraph instrumentation and techniques totaling at least 200 hours of classroom instruction at a school approved by the APA.

Research directed toward further improvements in instrumental design and examination techniques may be expected to continue. Much of this research, and that is considerable, is being undertaken by Medical

2. The applicant must have completed at least 200 cases within a three year period following the completion of formal instruction.

3. The applicant must have demonstrated proficiency in the conduct of polygraph examination.

4. The applicant shall possess as a minimum a degree at the baccalaureate level from a college or university accredited by the Regional Accreditation Board.

5. The fee for membership shall be $25.00 per annum, due and payable at or on 1 January, but no later than the annual seminar of the APA.

B. *INTERN*

Applicants for membership as intern members shall be admitted to membership during the period of their formal training or internship as polygraph examiners, provided:

1. These applicants for intern membership meet requirements for educational level cited above.

2. That such intern memberships shall not be extended past three years from the date of entering into intern membership, except upon approval of extenuating circumstances by the Committee on Membership.

3. That the fee for intern membership shall be $15.00 per annum due and payable 1 January, but no later than the annual seminar of the APA.

4. Interns shall be eligible to attend and participate in functions of the APA but shall not represent themselves as being members of the APA. Interns shall have no vote in matters before the APA.

C. *AFFILIATE*

Persons who have a sincere interest in the polygraph field, but who are not themselves polygraph examiners, shall be eligible for membership as Affiliates of the APA. This will include manufacturers of polygraph instruments, personnel involved in research in polygraph instrumentation and techniques, and other persons who have a valid and professional interest in the polygraph field. Annual dues for Affiliate members shall be $25.00 per annum. Affiliates shall be eligible to attend and participate in functions of the APA but shall not represent themselves as being members of the APA. Affiliates shall have no vote in matters before the APA.

D. *HONORARY*

Those persons who shall have been nominated by a two thirds majority of the Board of Directors and approved by the majority vote of the membership of the APA as having made significant and outstanding contributions to the polygraph field may be elected as honorary members of the APA. Such persons shall be entitled to participate in all functions of the APA, but shall not vote as members of the APA.

E. *WAIVER OF MEMBERSHIP REQUIREMENTS*

In recognition of the fact that highly capable, competent, professional and ethical examiners, currently practicing their profession, may not meet all of the requirements for members of the APA, the following provisions are established for a waiver of strict membership standards:

1. At the time of establishment of the APA, all members in good standing of the merging organizations shall be accepted as members of the APA without regard to the provisions of Paragraph A above.

2. During the period August 1966 through December 31, 1967, the requirements for a degree at the baccalaureate level and for formal instruction at an approved school may be waived at the discretion of the Membership

Schools and their Departments of Psychiatry throughout the country, in connection with the study of the emotions.

Vice Detail

Those who entertain the mistaken view that crime does not pay should examine the balance sheets and the income tax returns of the individuals and interests in every American city who control and profit from vice operations. Syndicated vice is one of the biggest and most lucrative business enterprises in the United States. When representatives of a Chicago gambling syndicate appeared in Dallas, Texas, a few years ago and offered a newly elected sheriff $40,000 per month for the protection of their projected operations in that area, they had no misgivings about the return on this investment.[20] The Four Horsemen—prostitution, gambling, narcotics, and the illegal liquor traffic—prolific breeders of crime in all of its categories, continue as a major problem in this country.

Placing with the police department responsibility for the enforcement of laws for the regulation and control of vice has contributed enormously to the demoralization of the police in many sections of the country. On the one hand, police officials are criticized and unsupported by many of the best citizens in their attempts to control vice. On the other, there are steady demands for police "shake-ups" and elimination

Committee, to demonstrate satisfactory proficiency in the conduct of polygraph examination.

3. During the period of 1 January 1968 through June 30, 1970, the requirement for a degree at the baccalaureate level may be waived at the discretion of the Membership Committee, provided that the person meets one of the following educational standards:

a. Completion of two years of education at an accredited college or university representing at a minimum the completion of 60 semester hours of work and acceptance to standing in the junior class.

b. An associate degree from an accredited junior college representing the completion of two years of college work.

c. In the case of former military personnel a G.E.D. certificate representing second-year college level.

4. Following June 30, 1970, applicants for membership shall be required by the Membership Committee to meet all of the requirements of Paragraph A above.

[20] The sheriff in this instance did not surrender to the temptation. Following the first contact made with him, he arranged for a conference several days later with these gentlemen at his home. In the meantime, he reported this information to the Texas Department of Public Safety, and arrangements were completed for the installation of microphones and recording equipment in the sheriff's home. During the conference with these Chicago men, the entire conversations were recorded, and the records were subsequently admitted as evidence against them during a criminal trial in which they were convicted.

of the incumbent administration if the city is not made chemically pure. The police are denounced regardless of the type of action they take.

There is no one method of controlling vice. It is not a question of police manpower. The chief impediment in the attack upon these problems is that vice has until quite recently been considered an individual problem rather than a crime against society. Repression of base human appetites cannot be achieved by law. Vice actually is an illegal business enterprise which cannot be conducted except in such a manner that reasonably well informed persons are aware of its presence. Yet, there is no effective support for its repression. It should be increasingly apparent to every thoughtful citizen that police administration can focus against vice only that degree of enforcement pressure which the community will tolerate. It cannot long ignore the will of the majority, if that majority takes the time and trouble to find effective expression for its opinion. Civic organizations, women's organizations, and other public spirited groups in any city can play a dynamic role in this sphere of social control, but their efforts must be well directed and sustained with unremitting energy over long periods.

The policy determining body in local government is the City Council, and the police have no alternative but to function in accordance with policies laid down by this group of elected municipal officials. If prostitution and gambling are rampant in a city, responsible citizens are entitled to the reasonable assumption that members of the City Council have adopted general policies which permit these conditions. Surely, no one is stupid enough to believe that a City Council would tolerate a police administration which failed to carry its policies into execution.

Constructive interest groups in the community should obtain from City Council candidates prior to election, clear, unequivocal statements which declare their views on these problems in unmistakable language, and these statements should be given thorough-going publicity in the press, in the pulpit, and on the radio and television. Political candidates dislike specific commitments on these issues, but if they fail to comment, they have failed in the discharge of the first responsibility of public office. Due partly to the basic responsibility of the City Council in these matters, Vollmer has suggested the possibility of removing vice control from the police altogether and placing the execution of policy under the joint direction of the legislative body and the Mayor, or City Manager.

The demand for the services of the prostitute and the demand for gambling, narcotics, and other vices are widespread; the patronage which supports these highly lucrative enterprises and which balks at the thought of control or repression comes from every social and economic level in American communities.[21] Those directly interested include, in addition to patrons and vice over-lords, many erstwhile respectable and influential citizens who own property which yields exorbitant returns through rental or lease to operators of these nefarious enterprises. These gentlemen smugly send their own sons and daughters to Sunday School, speak at service clubs, and exhibit a high degree of civic virtue while perpetuating tragedy and failure in the lives of others. When these individuals, or the real estate agencies or investment companies they represent, are approached by municipal officials or others, they present the standard evasion that income from these properties would scarcely meet taxes and other fixed charges, let alone yield a return on the investment, if their present use were discontinued. The dollar sign is given a high priority in this business, with social values still far in the background.

There is some encouraging evidence that community tolerance of vice operations, particularly with respect to prostitution, is gradually diminishing, and as tolerance limits recede, enforcement policies can be amended accordingly. This development is traceable to a shift in emphasis from prostitution as a moral issue to prostitution as a problem in public health. World Wars I and II brought this new approach into clear focus. There was less venereal disease per thousand men in the first American Expeditionary force than in any other army engaged in the struggle. This was because General Pershing established and enforced strict repression of prostitution in areas adjacent to concentrations of American troops. Even then, the American army lost 7,000,000 man-days because of venereal infection—the greatest single cause of noneffectiveness except for wounds sustained in battle, which cost a total of nearly 17,000,000 man-days. The tribute to prostitution was equivalent to 19,000 men—more than one entire division—continuously absent from duty.[22]

During World War II the Federal Government took effective steps to prevent a repetition of this damage to the combat power of an army. The Federal Security Agency, emphasizing the problem as a medical issue and working through local Boards of Health and police departments, delivered a body blow to commercialized prostitution during this period.[23] Nor can it be said that with the relaxation of controls in the

---

[21] August Vollmer, "Survey and Reorganization of the Dallas Police Department," 1944, p. 19.

[22] Frederick D. Stricker, M.D., Oregon State Health Officer, "The Professional Prostitute is Hitler's Agent," Portland Oregonian, April 12, 1942.

[23] Federal Security Agency, Division of Social Protection, "The Program of Division of Social Protection," Bulletin issued November 14, 1941, by Region XII, San Francisco, California.

postwar period, prostitution has returned to the status quo, although its controlling interests in every city are laboring to regain their former power and income.

Police Organization for Vice Control

The satisfactory control of vice is among the most difficult of all police problems. Those officials who determine policy in municipal government have a grave responsibility in this matter. A city cannot have "wide open" policy toward vice and an effective police administration. Furthermore, community tolerance limits which condone the presence of vice to a limited degree, depress to that extent the integrity and efficiency of police administration. It is necessary then to discuss police organization for vice control in terms of a policy of absolute repression of vice operations. No half-way measure or concession is compatible with good police administration. It has been demonstrated that where the people of a city lend their support to this type of policy, police administration can carry out its functions in this area with an extraordinarily high degree of efficiency. Vice-free communities in this country are not altogether unknown.

The point of departure in police organization for vice control, as in the discharge of all other police functions, is the individual patrolman. However, the time arrives in the growth of a city and its police department when the nature and volume of case load is such that the efforts of the patrolman must be reenforced by the specialized assistance of a vice unit in the attack upon these problems. The presence of such a unit in a police organization does not in any way diminish the responsibility but rather improves the effectiveness of the patrol force in this area. A vigorous and sustained patrol policy and participation by the patrol force in the control of commercialized vice reduces the personnel needed in the vice unit; it increases the efficiency of this unit and conserves the time and energy of its members, thus permitting them to focus their attention on the more important violations, and on the well organized and deeply entrenched operators.

Through close cooperation, members of the patrol division are in a position to supply the vice unit with important information concerning the existence and location of vice operators on their respective beats. Through the work of the individual patrolman, vice operations may be discovered early, and the more flagrant violations may be eliminated immediately. He may investigate and dispose of the less serious vice complaints. Where the responsibility for vice control is shared by the patrol force and the vice unit, the likelihood of graft is considerably reduced. It is then impossible for a single division to be in a position to grant protection to vice operators, and the larger number of officers involved makes the corruption of the police a very expensive business.

The patrol force and the vice unit should, therefore, have a joint responsibility for vice conditions in the community, and each should be held accountable. The patrolman should be responsible for the eradication of vice operations on his beat and should report conditions with which he is unable to cope, so that the vice unit may give them special attention. The existence of a vice detail cannot excuse the patrol division for failure to control vice conditions, and the vice unit cannot offer in defense of its failure to eliminate vice operations the fact that the responsibility also belongs to the patrol division. Vice control operations, therefore, should not be the exclusive province of the specialized unit but should be shared by all other divisions in the department, and especially by the patrol division.

The vice detail should operate as a separate unit with full power of independent action and should be concerned solely with the problems of commercialized vice. As a line agency, it reports directly to the commanding officer in charge of line operations, and this official holds the members of this unit accountable for the quality of performance in the discharge of this specialized function. In smaller departments, the vice unit should be attached directly to the office of the Chief of Police. Under no circumstances should its control be vested in the chief of detectives or any other divisional commanding officer. Because of the political implications connected with the enforcement of vice laws and the moral hazards involved, it is necessary that a rigid supervision be maintained over this work by the Chief of Operations. For these reasons also, the number of men required for vice duty should never be very large, and there should be a rapid turn-over in the personnel assigned to this operation. With the function of vice control attached to the office of the Chief of Operations, it becomes possible for this officer to give aid to the vice unit when required; through his control of all line divisions he is in a position to divert the necessary striking power for the completion of raids and other line operations in this particular area of police activity.

Vice operations differ from the usual types of crime in that they are continuing offenses, are usually conducted at fixed places of business, and require some public support to exist. The most effective police control results from the prosecution of persons who manage, or otherwise control, vice operations, rather than the individual participants. Vice over-lords who control all vice in a particular field, but who cleverly conceal evidence of their connection with these enterprises, are to be found in all cities. If the police are to control commercialized vice, they must curtail the activities of these persons rather than limit their attention to individual gamblers, prostitutes, and narcotic addicts. Ample secret service funds should be allocated to the Chief of Operations and made available through him to the officer in charge of the vice detail. Paid informants are indispensable to successful investigation in this area of the underworld.

Traffic Administration

Development of Land Transportation. From the beginning, man's evolution through the various stages or levels of civilization has been geared closely to the development of a means of transportation. It is a far cry from walking as the original mode of travel to landing on the moon and contemplated expeditions into planetary space.

Since the dawn of history, man has faced a traffic problem of one kind or another in his efforts to go from one place to another. When two men first passed each other on a narrow path in the jungle, the question of right of way came into the picture. Who was to move to one side so the other could pass, and should he pass to the right or the left? The first traffic fatality in the history of the world may have occurred as one of them met death in the course of settling the dispute.[24]

Ladd points out that the caravan routes of the ancient world were the first highways and Mesopotamia is said to have laid out the first real roads in about 1900 B.C.[25] One of the first important camel routes of the time ran from the city of Damascus to the Euphrates River.

Then came the invention of the wheel and a new mode of transportation as man began to reduce both time and distance. Military operations generated the need for substantial road systems. In the days of the Roman Empire, a great highway system was built to accommodate the chariots, carts and other similar vehicles. Twenty-nine great roads totaling more than 50,000 miles, led into every part of the Empire. They were built primarily for movement of the Roman legions to points of conquest, rebellion or insurrection.

The heavy flow of traffic coming into and out of Rome increased congestion on the streets and made the movement of men, chariots and other vehicles exceedingly difficult. As a result, the Caesars created the one-way street. Regarded as a twentieth century development, the idea actually is almost 2,000 years old. The first control of parking

[24] Leonard, V. A., *The Police of the 20th Century*, Mineola, New York, The Foundation Press, Inc., 1964, p. 93.

[25] Ladd, Walter D., *Organizing for Traffic Safety in Your Community*, Springfield, Illinois, Charles C. Thomas, Publisher, 1959, p. 5.

also occurred in Rome. It is thought that the Romans also built the first sidewalks and the first crosswalks for pedestrians.

The potential of the steam engine occurred to man as early as 130 B.C. But the idea was to be forgotten on through the Middle Ages and up until the eighteenth century. The first contrivance in history that could be called an automobile was developed about 1770 by a Frenchman, Captain Nicholas Joseph Cugnot. It could travel only about a hundred feet at a time and then it was necessary to stop in order to generate more steam. It was a large unwieldly steam device, steered by chains fastened to the single front wheel.

Cugot built three steam powered vehicles, said to be the forerunners of a 150-year line of steam cars which ended in 1929, when the Stanley Steamer Automobile Company in the United States went out of business. The economy and efficiency of steam power are such that one wonders why the steam-powered vehicle was never able to gain any headway on the American scene. Perhaps this problem will one day challenge the interest of some researcher.

Rise of a new social problem. It was in 1885 that the German Daimler appeared, the first such vehicle to be propelled by a high speed internal combustion engine. The stage was gradually being set for the development of the modern automobile, and from 1900 a number of improved cars appeared in America. Because they were expensive, only persons of substantial means could afford them; and because they were hard to operate and prone to break down miles from help, only able-bodied men with a talent and proclivity for the repair of machinery drove them. World War I saw the introduction of mechanized field operations and this, together with the advantage of large scale movement of men and materiel in the theater of war, gave added impetus to the effort of automotive engineering.

Subsequently, with the introduction to industry of the mass production line by Henry Ford, the Model T, originally costing $850, was scaled down steadily in price until in 1926 it sold for $310 at Detroit, placing the automobile within reach of the common man; said Mr. Ford, "I will build an automobile that will be structurally sound, economical in operation and in a price range where it can reach every family in the country." He did. Other manufacturers recognized the desirability of widening their markets through the production of low-priced cars and followed his lead. In the ensuing years motor vehicle registration in the United States pyramided at an incredible rate to impose upon street systems and highways, originally designed largely for horses, buggies, and bicycles, a transportation load they were not prepared to accommodate. In 1939 there were 30,750,000 motor vehicles registered in this country, and by 1946, despite the interruption in automobile production occasioned by conversion to a war economy in the intervening years, the figure had increased to approximately 34,000,000. The 1961 registration of motor vehicles reached an all time high of 63,488,000 passenger cars, in addition to 12,519,000 trucks and buses!

Man had a new social problem of unusual dimensions on his hands and he still has it today. Increased population, spreading highway networks, together with vigorous advertising and sales campaigns by car manufacturers, have placed more cars in service than ever before in history. Eighty-two million vehicles were registered in 1963; the nation's highway system totaled over four million miles in 1965; and the number of licensed drivers in the United States is expected to reach a total of 139 million by 1980.[26]

While the reader is moving over this page, someone in this country will be killed by an automobile. Today death stalks the highway. As a killer, the lethal efficiency of the automobile compares favorably with the planned destruction of modern warfare. The automobile has snuffed out more lives than all the wars in which this country has been engaged. Traffic deaths in 60 years of automobile use have claimed the lives of approximately 1,300,000 people. Deaths of U. S. Military personnel in eight conflicts over 185 years of the nation's existence, totaled 1,128,000. But this includes not only battle deaths but deaths from all causes, including sickness, while in military service.

The gun and bludgeon of the criminal deal out death to less than half the number of people who draw their last breath in an automobile accident. In one year, 16,450 Americans died in crimes of violence. During the same year, 40,000 Americans answered the last call in a traffic accident. As of 1970, the picture looked even more gruesome—more than 50,000 people paid the supreme sacrifice on the streets and highways of this country. Most of these accidents, strangely enough, occurred under virtually ideal driving conditions—on a straight well paved road, dry pavement, in daylight on a clear day with the car in good mechanical condition.

Add to the toll of the grim reaper the number of persons injured, many of them permanently disabled, and the staggering economic loss represented by people off the job and in hospitals, property damage and the costs of traffic congestion, retarded traffic flow and inadequate parking facilities. It all totals up to multiplied millions of dollars each year.

During the early history of motor car development, only the larger cities were affected by traffic problems to any important extent. To-

---

26 Weston, Paul B., *The Police Traffic Control Function*, 2nd ed., Springfield, Illinois, Charles C. Thomas, Publisher, 1968, p. 3.

day, however, the unequalled development of the automobile, the price range and the pyramiding number of automobile owners and drivers, no longer limits the problem to metropolitan areas.[27]   In addition to inherently local automobile traffic, freeways, major arterials and other features of a modern highway system, together with the increased mobility which this affords the general population, have increased the exposure of cities and smaller communities alike, to the demand for effective traffic control and regulation.

The location of the police traffic control function in a police organization is a matter of major administrative importance.   All that has been said previously with respect to structuring the detective function applies with equal force to the traffic function.   (See page 264).

Weston points out that it is a possible administrative error to believe that the patrol force is incapable of performing the traffic control function because of the lack of training, administrative skill and competent, interested supervision, and that the problem of traffic control should be attacked through the use of small specialized traffic units.[28] He further observes that a major realignment of police departments is indicated to put the full force of every uniformed officer on patrol behind the traffic control program.   He emphasizes that calling on the patrol force for the performance of duties common to traffic serves the additional purpose of pointing up the importance of traffic work and gives it the stature necessary to secure the same degree of attention from the patrol force that is now given to crime and delinquency.

It has been previously indicated that the traffic problem is not limited to the larger cities.   The officials of local government in towns, communities and the smaller cities have long since been confronted with the necessity of facing up to the problems of a smooth flowing traffic stream, the matter of life and safety, traffic accidents, parking and congestion.   It would be extremely difficult to find a community, no matter how small, that is not presented with a traffic problem in some degree.   Traffic regulation and control in small and medium-sized communities has now become big business.   By 1970, the problem has been compounded to the point where the application of the principles of sound traffic management is now mandatory.

It is now apparent that the problems generated by automotive transportation can never be alleviated by amateurs.   There is a need for experts trained in the dynamics of modern high-speed and heavy-volume traffic control.   Although many of the factors that are respon-

---

[27] McCracken, Dwight, *Traffic Regulation in Small Cities,* Municipal Administration Service, 1932.

[28] Weston, op. cit. p. 156.

sible for this tragic annual toll are known to specialists, few of them are eliminated by the men who are directly responsible for the regulation and control of traffic.   Without scientific training and without the application of synthesis and analysis by the men engaged in the approach to these problems, it is futile to hope for any material reduction in the tribute we now pay for the use of the automobile.

As these problems began to press forward and gain the attention of municipal authorities everywhere, highway officials and the public alike turned almost mechanically to the police for their solution under the illusion that enforcement offered the answer.   The American propensity for legislation rather than social adjustment and reform again found expression in the multiplicity of traffic ordinances that were enacted by every city, town, and hamlet in the country.   Lacking uniformity, these ordinances ranged the entire length of the legal spectrum in nature and content.   Since laws imply enforcement, this new-born social problem found its way to the door of police administration, bringing with it a new type of clientele generally non-criminal in character.

The salutary effect of this new assignment upon the police themselves and its influence in raising the general standards of police service in this country have escaped the attention of most observers.   The police control of criminals has been based on firm treatment; experienced police officers hold to their belief that the professional criminal understands no other.   In dealing with regulatory problems concerning the general public, it was natural for the police to apply the techniques and procedures employed in dealing with the criminal offender.   Great harm was done before the police realized that the regulation of the average citizen required an entirely different kind of control.   Progressive police administrators soon recognized the function of public relations in developing favorable public opinion and in gaining public confidence in the ability and integrity of the police department.   The net result has been a gradual reinterpretation of police administration to the people and a growing recognition by the public of police service as a professional undertaking.

Police Organization for Traffic Control

As suggested earlier, the function of traffic regulation and control is basically a responsibility of the patrol force.   However, the necessity appears very early in the growth of a police organization, when the traffic case load exceeds the capacity of the patrol force, and provision must be made for specialized assistance and the assignment of one or more officers to full-time duty for studying traffic problems and formulating plans for their solution.   From such a beginning, the specialized traffic unit has become a conventional fixture in the average American police department.

The creation of a traffic unit in police organization paves the way for specialized attention to a highly technical problem and provides the means whereby management can bring into clear focus responsibility for plans and operations in this specialized area. Properly manned by individuals possessing the necessary skills and information, it can lead to the formulation of a police traffic program that will approach the problems associated with traffic accidents, traffic flow and congestion. Through intelligent studies and analyses, it provides the basis for operational plans involving application of the entire line resources of the department to the solution of these problems.

As in the case of the detective division, specialized traffic units or divisions are usually manned by transfers from the patrol division, with resulting depletion of the patrol force. It is important, therefore, to establish some criteria as a basis for determining the personnel strength of the traffic division. With the increasing interest, both nationally and locally, in this problem, a tendency is observable in many jurisdictions to over-emphasize the traffic division and to misinterpret its role in police organization. In no small number of instances, police departments have become "traffic centered," with the result that unpardonable transfers have been made from the patrol division to raise the personnel strength of the traffic division up to "standard."

In fact, it has become traditional practice to meet the traffic problem by building up expensive traffic divisions. There are those who hold that, based upon property losses, insurance rates, and similar criteria, 25 per cent of the total police problem is traffic in nature, and that a corresponding percentage of the department's personnel and material resources should be assigned to the traffic division. It would seem extremely hazardous to conclude that one-sixth, one-fourth, or one-third of the total police problem in any city was traffic in nature, for the reason that there are few instances, indeed, where anyone is in a position to know the true dimensions of crime and vice in his community.

Even though it were possible to assume that 25 per cent of the total police problems in a given city could be accounted for by traffic accidents, parking, congestion, traffic flow, etc., it would still be an erroneous and ill-conceived policy to assign 25 per cent of departmental resources to the traffic function. Furthermore, it is a costly administrative mistake to assign to any one division exclusive responsibility for meeting this important problem. It is more than a question of arithmetic. The traffic problem is too great for any one division to cope with alone. There is a trend toward acceptance of the line power idea, with the total line resources of the department available for meeting traffic problems where and when the records indicate this is necessary.

Although located in the line, the traffic unit should be regarded primarily as a planning agency. It is an administrative error to give it large field strength and to clothe it with exclusive responsibility for carrying its plans into execution. Such administrative action is the function of the commanding officer in charge of line operations. As a planning agency in the line, it must be staffed with persons with police experience and educational background who are trained in the application of statistical disciplines and engineering procedures. In the smaller communities the officer in charge of traffic regulation and control may seek the assistance of the city engineer. His technical ability combined with the professional experience of the officer will make possible the intelligent formulation of plans for meeting local problems. In larger cities the services of a full-time traffic engineer supported by a statistical analyst and a staff of trained workers will be needed.

The technical aspects of the approach to the problems of traffic regulation and control have prompted an increasing number of cities to retain the services of traffic consultants. At the request of local authorities, experts from the Field Service Division of the International Association of Chiefs of Police, the Traffic Institute of Northwestern University and the National Safety Council have rendered a professional service in an increasing number of instances through competent traffic surveys and recommendations.

The functions and work of the traffic unit of a police department should be devoted primarily to statistical analyses of data made available by the records division, traffic field studies and surveys directed toward the solution of traffic problems, the detection of emerging situations, and subsequent formulation of operational plans for submission to the chief of line operations. This commanding officer with the total line resources of the department at his disposal is then in a position to bring to bear upon the problem or problems a degree of line power altogether impossible where the traffic line function is exclusively a responsibility of one division.

The personnel strength of the Patrol Division is a major asset of the Chief of Operations in carrying operational plans into execution. Properly trained, the personnel of this line division will constitute his chief reliance in translating plans into lowered accident rates, improved traffic flow and reduced traffic congestion. Thus, through adequate use of the total field strength of the department, the Chief of Operations can reduce the field strength of the traffic unit proper to a minimum.

Closely associated with this question is the function of traffic accident investigation and its proper location in the organizational structure. Over-specialization is observable in many American police departments where, within the traffic division, special traffic accident investigation squads have been established. These squads usually are manned by transfers from the personnel strength of the patrol division. Commenting on the highly specialized assignment of men to accident investigation, as well as the special motorcycle units in the traffic division of the Dallas Police Department, Vollmer stated:

"Further reductions in the patrol force were made when men were detached from patrol duty and assigned to accident investigation. Originally, accident investigation was a highly specialized type of work; however, this is no longer true, since the principles underlying accident investigation have been transmitted to all members of the force.

"What actually has happened is that the uniformed patrol force has been decimated to the point where it is utterly impossible for the members of that division to do the work for which they have been appointed and are being paid. Taking men for the motorcycle and accident investigation functions from the uniformed patrol force, then placing these officers on special duty in the same districts covered by automobile patrolmen and sergeants produces much duplication of effort and an enormous wastage of man hours that should be available for general police duties.

"Such intensive specialized duties as those performed by the motorcycle squad and the accident investigators have contributed in no small degree to the rapid deterioration of the quality of regular patrol service found throughout the United States. So far as the evidence is concerned, there are no facts that have as yet been presented to prove conclusively that the functions performed by these specialists have compensated for the loss suffered by their severance from regular beat patrol. This intensive patrolling of the beats is indisputably the primary function of every police department. Moreover, just as long as the regular patrol functions are reduced quantitatively and/or qualitatively, just so long will the traffic, detective, and other divisions be overwhelmed with unfinished tasks." [29]

That a similar situation prevails in most cities is indicated by other American police surveys. In Seattle it was recommended that,

" . . . the existing eight traffic accident investigation cars be converted into mobile crime detection laboratories for dispatching to *the scene of major crimes as well as the scene of traffic accidents*. The additional equipment necessary is comparatively inexpensive. The importance must be understood of the need for intensive training of officers in the search for evidence at the scenes of both crimes and accidents, and in the care and preservation of evidence. Whether the scene of the investigation involves a traffic accident or a burglary, robbery or sex attack, its evidence resources should be scientifi-

[29] Vollmer, op. cit. p. 20.

cally explored to the fullest extent. The operation of these eight cars as recommended would, in fact, represent a field extension of the Crime Laboratory proper, now located in the Seattle Police Training School." [30]

It is not to be assumed that traffic accident investigation squads have not been successful in carrying out the highly specialized tasks assigned to them. The reverse is true. Bruce Smith observed in Baltimore that since the establishment of the traffic accident investigation squad in the police department of that city, it has maintained a highly satisfactory level of performance.

He stated that, while it was impossible to classify and weigh all the influences contributing to the success of the accident investigation squad, it was probable that the largest single factor was the specialized training accorded to its members. Thirteen of them had the benefit of formal instruction in accident investigation either at the Northwestern University Traffic Officers' Training School,[31] or at the various sessions conducted under the auspices of the University of Maryland. Several of them had attended one or more retraining courses. "Hence," he stated, "the squad was more thoroughly trained for a specific task than any other unit in the police department." [32]

It is important to observe, however, that there is nothing particularly occult about the investigation of a traffic accident. Given the intelli-

---

[30] V. A. Leonard, *Survey and Reorganization of the Seattle Police Department*, 1945, p. 132.

[31] Bruce Smith, "The Baltimore Police Survey," Institute of Public Administration, New York, 1941, pp. 98–99.

[32] The Traffic Institute at Northwestern University in Evanston, Ill., has for a substantial number of years conducted a superior training program in Traffic Police Administration for the benefit of selected municipal, county and state police officers. Students are carefully screened and selected on the basis of competitive examinations and personal interviews.

Law enforcement officers who complete the nine-months Traffic Police Administration Program, take back valuable staff and administrative skills to their departments. The training is concentrated in two major areas— General Management Functions, and Supervision of Traffic Operations; it finds expression in four areas of study and preparation—Highway Transportation, Traffic Police Functions, Police Service Management, and General Educational Background. As of 1960, 900 officers had successfully completed this professional training program since its inception twenty-seven years ago. Graduates are to be found in top command positions in municipal, county and state law enforcement agencies throughout the United States and in several foreign countries.

In addition to the nine-months training program, the Traffic Institute conducts a series of unit courses for command and staff personnel, Chiefs of Police annually send about 1,000 selected officers to receive unit course training. The Institute also extends its services into the field in the programing of police traffic courses and conferences at the local, county, state and regional levels.

gence and training, it matters little for the end result of a traffic accident investigation whether the patrolman is in a special accident investigation car at the time of the emergency call or in a patrol car on his beat. With proper recruiting and training standards for patrolmen, the necessity for specialized accident investigation squads is eliminated. It is of no avail to raise the performance levels of a traffic division and perpetuate the status quo in the patrol division. Under such a policy, regardless of the nature of improvements in the traffic division, it can be assured of a constantly increasing case load.

At the time the author was called to conduct a survey of the Seattle Police Department, it was found that a competent, professional survey of the traffic division in that department had been completed two years previously. The way was prepared through this study for a scientific approach to the traffic problems of parking, traffic flow patterns, congestion, and traffic accidents by statistical analysis and the application of selective engineering, educational and enforcement techniques. It was discovered also that provisions of the recommended traffic reorganization had been carried out at the expense of other divisions in the department, with considerable damage to the over-all efficiency of a metropolitan crime fighting organization. More important, it was observed that the proposed traffic reorganization had been delayed, if not completely stalemated, because the report failed to provide for bringing other units and divisions in the police department up to the same standards of efficiency.

The formula for successful traffic administration can be stated as the identification and analysis of present and emerging problems by the traffic unit, formulation of operational plans, and their execution under the direction of the Chief of Operations through the application of the total line power resources of the department. The three E's have been previously mentioned—Engineering, Education, and Enforcement. Engineering merits first place in any order of priority. In terms of a long range program, the educational approach is probably the most important. Based upon any criteria, enforcement is of the least significance, not only in traffic administration, but in every phase of police organization and administration.

There must be superimposed upon Engineering, Education, and Enforcement three additional E's: Evidence—scientific analysis of the data relating to traffic problems in all of their various categories as a basis for the formulation of plans by which the methods of engineering, education, and enforcement may be intelligently and successfully applied; Execution—implementation of plans under unified command of line resources; Evaluation—scientific measurement of results. The reciprocal roles of engineering, education, and enforcement in the total program of traffic regulation and control are matters of considerable importance.[33]

Engineering

The engineering study of a traffic problem is a prerequisite to its solution. In the field of traffic administration the least regulation possible is the best regulation. If a stream of water flowing along its natural course is dammed up, it is sent out in other directions, creating two or more additional problems of control. Too often, the ill-advised installation of a traffic signal device or the assignment of an officer to regulate traffic at a given intersection causes cascading changes in the characteristics of the traffic stream at intersections within a radius of ten blocks of the point at which this control is administered. Communities are now learning at considerable cost that no regulation of any kind should be applied to traffic flow until competent traffic engineering studies and analyses have been made to determine the need for such regulation and the type of regulation that should be imposed.

Webster's definition of engineering is not overwhelmingly helpful, but it will serve as a point of departure—"A science by which the properties of matter and the sources of energy in nature are made useful to man." Robinson states that engineering is the use of energy and material for the benefit of mankind. More specifically, he points out that traffic engineering is that phase of the general field of engineering which deals with the planning of streets and highways and the movement of traffic thereon in terms of the safe, convenient and economic transportation of persons and goods.[34]

Traffic engineering deals with transportation. The traffic engineer is concerned with the question of where people and goods want to go, and how they are going to get there. He plans new roads or highways and improvement of old ones, how wide they should be and permissible speeds adapted to each traffic situation. Determinations are

---

33 It is not the function of this book to present the details of a police traffic program. Appropriate information in this respect will be found in: Harold F. Hammond, *Traffic Engineering Handbook*, Institute of Traffic Engineers, New Haven, Conn., 1950; *Traffic Accident Investigator's Manual*, Traffic Institute, Northwestern University, Evanston, Ill., 1957; and Henry K. Evans and Franklin M. Kreml, *Traffic Engineering and the Police*, National Conservation Bureau, New York, and International Association of Chiefs of Police, Evanston, Ill., 1946.

The reader is also referred to Walter D. Ladd, *Organizing for Traffic Safety in Your Community*, Charles C. Thomas, Publisher, 1959.

34 Robinson, Carlton C., *Traffic Engineering*, Universal Publishing and Distributing Corporation, New York, 1966.

made with respect to the need for bridges or clover leaf inter-changes, and whether channelization and traffic signals are indicated in order to promote a smooth flowing traffic stream. Traffic signs and pavement marking are a part of the traffic engineer's assignment. He measures the efficiency with which these installations serve their purpose and engineers the necessary changes where recurring accidents or congestion come into the picture.

The study of traffic problems is fundamentally a task for the trained traffic engineer. Furthermore, his effort pivots largely upon a study of traffic accidents, because the traffic accident is a symptom of conflict in the traffic stream whether due to poor organization of traffic flow, volume and speed, the human factor (driver or pedestrian), or any two or more of these factors combining to produce the result.[35] Where the police records system is properly administered, it is possible to predict with a high degree of accuracy where and when and how many accidents will happen. Accident location files and spot maps are indispensable to this phase of the work. With the aid of statistical data assembled from reports, accident prone locations are identified and steps taken to modify or eliminate the factors which have given these locations an unfavorable accident history.

Corresponding studies must be made of driver observance of stop signs and other types of traffic signs and signals, as well as the type, density and distribution of those moving violations which contribute heavily to the traffic accident rate. Pedestrian volume, density and distribution, and pedestrian observance of traffic signs and signals must also be properly studied and analyzed. In addition, traffic studies and surveys must take into account the identification of major route congestion, motor vehicle volume and density, traffic origin and destination, transit facilities and passenger volume, street and off-street parking,

---

[35] Dr. John F. Edlund, Forensic Pathologist and Toxicologist at the University of Missouri, has stated that vehicular suicides may be more common than the records show. He was of the opinion that an appreciable percentage of traffic fatalities may be actually caused by suicidal drivers, stating that it appears to be socially acceptable to die in a traffic accident whereas, there is a stigma attached to dying by one's own hand. Speaking within the general area of traffic accident pathology, Dr. Edlund observed that there is no way to determine how many traffic fatalities are so motivated.

However, he reported on a special study of 11 Kansas City accidents resulting in 13 fatalities, all of which were listed as accidental. All 11 drivers and two passengers died. No suicide notes had been left, but three drivers had threatened suicide before departure. Four of the drivers had past histories of suicidal threats or attempts. Of the 11 fatal crashes, four were off bridges, cliffs, six were against stationary objects, and one was a sudden left turn into oncoming traffic on the crowded freeway. With one exception all of the fatalities followed quarrels with wives, sweethearts, other family members, or employers.

parking lot facilities and other factors which affect either favorably or unfavorably the efficiency of the traffic stream.

The objective of traffic engineering is to " . . . achieve an efficient, free and rapid flow of traffic, yet at the same time, to prevent traffic accidents and casualties." [36] On the other hand, the objective of police traffic control is to "secure compliance with the law, expedite the flow of traffic and promote the safety of motorists and pedestrians." [37] The basic objective of police traffic control is the movement of traffic with safety. This is also the objective of the traffic engineer, but he is also concerned with the planning and geometric design of streets and highways and with the safe, convenient and economical transportation of persons and goods over these facilities.

Weston observes that traffic engineering offers an effective approach to three elements of street and highway traffic—the road user, the vehicle and its load, and the road itself. Through the improvement in the design and operation of roads, the traffic engineer curtails the accident potential inherent in any street or highway situation. Although traffic engineering and police traffic control have much in common, major physical changes in the street and highway system are the domain of the engineer.[38] In small and medium-sized police departments, it is pertinent to observe that *consultation regarding the administrative set-up that will be best adapted to the special conditions in any community is available from the Traffic Engineering Bureau of the National Safety Council, 425 North Michigan Avenue, Chicago, Illinois.*

It would not be irrelevant to indicate at this point that attractive career opportunities lie ahead for qualified young men in the field of traffic engineering. A high school student considering the possibility of a career in traffic engineering should remember that the standards and requirements for admission into and graduation from engineering colleges is high. He should evaluate his aptitudes in the natural and physical sciences, especially mathematics—*the language of engineering*. In addition to a four or five-year curriculum leading to the Bachelor degree, work at the graduate level is strongly recommended. A year of graduate work offers the opportunity for additional specialized course work and a chance to move into research. In addition to the opportunity for graduate work in engineering schools, a number of universities

---

[36] Matson, Theodore M.; Smith, Wilbur S.; and Hurd, Frederick W., *Traffic Engineering*, New York, McGraw-Hill, 1955, p. 3.

[37] Brody, Leon and Stack, Herbert J., *Highway Safety and Driver Education*, New York, Prentice-Hall, 1954, p. 124.

[38] Weston, Paul B., **The Police Traffic Control Function**, Springfield, Illinois, Charles C. Thomas, Publisher, 1968, p. 100.

have developed advanced programs with a traffic engineering emphasis and orientation. These include:

> *Yale University Bureau of Highway Traffic.*
> *University of California Institute of Transportation and Traffic Engineering.*
> *University of Illinois Highway Traffic Safety Center.*
> *Northwestern University Transportation Center.*
> *Texas Transportation Institute, A & M College of Texas.*

In Toronto, Ontario, a new and novel communications system automatically controls 500 traffic signals in the city's congested business district. The heart of the system is a digital computer which acts on information fed from vehicle detectors buried in the pavement. One thousand detectors measure traffic volume at 500 intersections and send the data over leased wires to the central computer.

The computer takes an even broader view of traffic flow than to consider only the volume of cars in each lane at each of the 500 intersections. It also takes into account the amount of traffic shown by nearby detectors to be approaching from every direction. This data is integrated by the computer with information stored in its memory system with respect to the number of seconds each light has been in its present phase—red or green, the time it takes for traffic to clear the crossing after a change of signals, and the probable patterns of traffic at various times of day. The computer makes its decisions almost instantaneously.

In Los Angeles, fifty intersections have been guarded for several years by stop-go signals controlled by a computer. It is said that this has led to a 15% improvement in the capacity of the street system. Even the most crowded streets have unused capacity that can be used if traffic flow is better organized. However, this can only be accomplished with the speed and flexibility that only a computer can offer.

Education

Consideration also must be given to the human element involved. Educational processes must be employed to produce within the individual pedestrian or driver an awareness of danger that exists on the streets and highways, as well as a conscious responsibility for the more courteous use of these thoroughfares. There is a need for the development of ethics and good sportsmanship behind the wheel.

Law, if it is effective, is reflected public opinion. Traffic legislation turned this fundamental principle topsy-turvy. Under the pressure of the emergency, laws were passed first and then the attempt was made to mold public opinion accordingly. Traffic law enforcement campaigns have proved futile and are objectionable, both from the standpoint of the officer and of the public. The function of arrest and punishment in traffic administration is gradually being superseded by education in normal behavior.

Safe use of the streets by drivers and pedestrians is a matter of correct attitude and habit. While it is true that most people will react correctly to hazards which are obvious to them, the development of proper habits of walking or driving insures safety from injury during those times when danger appears unexpectedly—and this is when it usually appears. The records reveal that the great majority of traffic accidents, which took a toll of human lives during an average year, occurred under apparently ideal driving conditions.

There is need for sustained educational effort which will inculcate so deeply in the citizens' minds the elementary rules of safety and good sportsmanship that they become attitudes and habits. Traffic safety is not yet fashionable. It has not yet taken its proper place in the code of etiquette.

An important approach to building a safe driving attitude is to make it a part of social manners; to make people realize that the boor on the road is more offensive than the boor in the drawing room because the latter irritates only the sensibilities whereas the reckless driver is a menace to life and limb. It is altogether a significant matter that Emily Post has included in her masterpiece on etiquette a chapter on automobile driving. The profound influence of this woman in civilizing human relationships may extend itself with important results toward the development of good driving manners and become an influential factor in the reduction of the traffic accident rate and the promotion of an efficient traffic stream.

The educational effort of the police should make effective use of every available avenue of publicity in the promotion of safety education, including the newspapers, radio, television, panel discussions, dramatics, public addresses, posters, motion pictures, essay contests, and the many other devices. Data from the traffic records of the department will provide dramatic materials for this important work.

The principles of selective education should be exploited to the fullest extent. The analysis of traffic accident statistics will reveal certain groups of people who appear to be accident prone and who are involved in more than their share of such accidents. With this type of information, as well as data concerning the types of accidents and violations which are most prevalent, the educational effort can be oriented toward specific remedies. Spot maps showing residence of accident victims may coincide with definite population areas. In one city it was discovered that the rate was high in a Mexican district. Such patterns mean that broadside education has escaped these people. A study of accident statistics will reveal their ages, time and place of occurrence, together with all the other details necessary for an intelligent educational project. Special clinics and training facilities for the accident-prone driver have been instituted in a number of cities with outstanding success.

High on the agenda of the educational program are educational institutions, including the public schools and universities. Children who are taught at an early age to understand and respect traffic regulations are least likely to be offenders as adults. Furthermore, the public schools provide an excellent opportunity for reaching a large group with a program of traffic education.

Wilson holds that for each dollar expended, public education offers greater immediate results in preventing traffic accidents than either engineering or enforcement.[39] This holds not only for educational programs in the schools but for educational effort directed toward the general public with the objective of promoting public understanding of police traffic problems and support of the police program, policies and methods used in their solution, and improving habits of safety among individual drivers, pedestrians and school children.

Safety education began in the elementary schools and the movement grew rapidly until today it is common practice in schools throughout the nation. Here, a rare opportunity is presented to integrate instruction in traffic safety into regular course materials. An increasing number of schools at the elementary level have developed specific courses dealing with the problem of traffic safety. Supporting these efforts are effective visual aid materials, including film strips, motion pictures and other educational devices adapted to the needs and interests of the younger generation. Full information concerning these resources may be obtained from the National Safety Council.

At the high school level, there has been a mass approach to driver education. Today, most high school officials accept driver training as an important function of public education. In many instances, credit is allowed for the course in driver training. It should be a standard requirement for graduation in every high school. Ladd estimates that about thirty-two percent of high school students now receive driver training before graduation.[40] He joins with others in observing that this is in-

[39] Wilson, O. W., *Police Administration*, New York, McGraw-Hill, 1950, p. 142.

[40] Ladd, Walter D., *Organizing for Traffic Safety in Your Community*, Springfield, Illinois, Charles C. Thomas, Publisher, 1959, p. 37.

adequate coverage. At the present rate of increase in driver training programs, it will require another fifteen years before such training is given to all students. In any community where driver training is not offered in high school, the police should join with other interested persons and groups in insisting that such a program be inaugurated without further delay.[41]

The role of the university in the traffic program is in the field of instruction and research. Gradually, these institutions of higher learning, tax-supported in the main, are coming to recognize their responsibility to the public service and are beginning to bring their superb training resources into contact with the professional training requirements of the police. An important part of this professional program of preparation will be concerned with the training of men for career service in the field of traffic administration.

As previously noted, legislation found expression in a multiplicity of traffic ordinances that were enacted by every city, town and hamlet in the country. Lacking uniformity from one community and city to another, these ordinances ranged the entire length of the legal spectrum in nature and content, resulting in a maze of confusion for the driving public.

The need for uniform traffic legislation has now been met at the state and local levels by the adoption of *Uniform State Vehicle Code* and a *Model Traffic Ordinance*, (both revised in 1968) by the National Committee on Uniform Traffic Laws and Ordinances.[42] In the same connection, the National Safety Council, in collaboration with the American College of Surgeons and the American Association for the Surgery of Trauma, made available in 1970, a *Model Ordinance Regulating Ambulance Service.*[43]

This ordinance is applicable in situations where an independent business firm, such as a funeral home, is licensed to provide ambulance service to the community. Many police departments operate their own ambulance services, usually manned by personnel in the records unit or division. This arrangement has two distinct advantages so far as the police are concerned. First of all, it means prompt reporting of all in-

---

[41] See Appendix F for suggested scope and content of an instructional program in safety and driver education.

[42] National Committee on Uniform Traffic Laws and Ordinances, *Uniform Vehicle Code* and *Model Traffic Ordinance*, the Mitchie Company, 1968.

[43] The National Safety Council, *Model Ordinance Regulating Ambulance Service*, 1970.

Copies of the *Model Traffic Ordinance* and *Model Ordinance Regulating Ambulance Service* may be obtained by writing to the Field Service Department, National Safety Council, 425 North Michigan Ave., Chicago, Illinois. 60611.

cidents resulting in injury or death which obviously, are of prime interest to the police. In the second place, it puts the police first at the scene with all that this can mean in terms of the recovery, care and preservation of evidence pertinent to a case investigation, criminal or otherwise.

Enforcement

The problems of traffic administration cannot be left to engineering and education alone. There will always be nonconformists who understand no language but that of enforcement. For their own welfare and in the interests of public convenience and necessity, these people must feel the hand of the law. Economy of forces demands a policy of selective enforcement under which attention is concentrated on those points of greatest traffic danger as shown by accident records.

Analysis of accidents and congestion, according to time, place, and nature, form the basis for selective enforcement procedures and makes possible the application of the line resources of the department when and where the need is greatest, and where they will accomplish the best results.

The judicial process also is involved in the enforcement phase of traffic administration. The failure of the courts to keep pace with problems created by the rapid growth of automotive travel has resulted in a general disrespect not only for traffic laws, but for law in general. Enforcement will not be effective unless the courts follow through. Inadequate functioning of the American traffic court system as a corrective agency in meeting the problems of traffic control, has prompted a number of important studies in this area.[44] The trend toward specialization in the legal system generally has been accompanied by the appearance of specialized traffic courts and the establishment of Violations Bureaus, designed to eliminate the pernicious results of "ticket fixing" and to expedite the judicial process in the handling of a tremendous volume of traffic violation cases.

The Point System. Upon conviction for a traffic offense in a court of law, the state concerned records this event upon the record of the violator. With subsequent convictions on traffic offenses, the process is repeated until a point is reached where the driving record of the individual suggests suspension or revocation of the driving privilege. In this effective system for driver control, the state licensing authority maintains a central file of all resident drivers.

---

[44] "Traffic Courts on Trial," National Committee on Traffic Law Enforcement, Trenton, 1941.

Where a driver who loses his license in one state moves to another, his shadow continues to follow him. Today, a central national file contains the names of all licensees whose driver's license has been suspended or revoked and this information is available to all cooperating states through the Federal Driver Register—of problem drivers—in Washington, D. C. Under the point system, numerical values are attached to each conviction for a serious moving traffic law infraction; the system penalizes the hazardous driver and rewards the good one.

The New York State Department of Motor Vehicles recently revised its point system and weighted traffic convictions in accordance with the following table: [45]

Violation	Points
Speeding	3 points.
Reckless driving	3 points.
Following too closely	3 points.
Failure to yield right-of-way	3 points.
Inadequate brakes	2 points.
Any other moving violations	2 points.

Following convictions for these violations, the Motor Vehicle Bureau may take three types of action—four or five points within eighteen months will result in the driver receiving a warning letter; six or eight points within the same period may warrant rehabilitative or clinical action; on the accumulation of nine or more points within eighteen months or twelve or more within twenty-four months, the driver will be summoned to a formal hearing by the Department of Motor Vehicles. In the event a driver receives four or more points within eighteen months or twelve or more within twenty-four months after the formal hearing, he is summoned to a second hearing and at that time, his driving license is subject to suspension or revocation.

In California, the point system provides for the allocation of either one or two points for a violation and one point for an accident. Suspension or revocation of a driver's license to operate a motor vehicle is warranted when the total points accumulated are more than four, six or eight violations in one, two and three years respectively.

The Enforcement Index. Wilson holds that an arrest index, which is the ratio of traffic citations to injury accidents, is useful in maintaining a suitable level of enforcement and assuring its uniform application at the locations and during the hours as indicated by the records.* The number of citations divided by the injury accidents, gives the enforce-

---

[45] Weston, Paul B., *The Police Traffic Control Function*, Springfield, Illinois, Charles C. Thomas, Publisher, 1968, p. 43.

* O. W. Wilson, *Police Administration*, New York, McGraw-Hill Company, Inc., 1950, p. 169.

ment index. Weston states that an enforcement index of 20:1 is a balancing point and indicates that some areas and their accident problems may warrant more activity and that in others slightly less than 20:1 may be satisfactory.**

The seriousness of the traffic problem generally has prompted action at the federal level. In 1924, Secretary of Commerce Herbert Hoover called the first National Conference on Street and Highway Safety. The major contribution of this Conference was the Uniform Vehicle Code, a model document incorporating the best and most workable traffic laws and based upon experience in the various states. This was a major step forward in establishing uniform national standards in the field of traffic legislation.

In 1946, President Truman called the White House Conference on Highway Safety. Two thousand delegates representing all parts of the nation, every possible interest and all applicable fields of experience, attended this important Conference. Out of this impressive fund of knowledge, talent and competence came the ACTION Program for Highway Safety. Active compliance with the principal recommendations of the ACTION Program has been urged upon all states and localities. They are as follows:

1. Enactment, by every state and community, of sound, uniform traffic laws and ordinances.

2. Fair, firm and impartial enforcement of these laws and ordinances by properly trained and adequately equipped state and local police.

3. Traffic courts that dispense fair and impartial justice, fostering respect for the law and support for its enforcement.

4. Development, by all states and communities, of adequate and uniform accident reports, and use of this information to determine needs and corrective actions.

5. Stimulation of construction of new highways, and rehabilitation and maintenance of those now existing, using the best engineering techniques to insure maximum safety.

6. Periodic inspection of all motor vehicles.

7. Nationwide instruction of young people in driving practices and attitudes.

8. Progressive improvement of motor vehicle design and construction to afford greater ease in safe operation and greater protection for occupants.

** Paul B. Weston, *The Police Traffic Control Function*, Springfield, Illinois, Charles C. Thomas, Publisher, 1968, p. 53.

Crime Prevention Division

The Problem. When the history of the American police is written, the past three decades will be recorded as the era of scientific crime detection. During this period almost unbelievable advances have been made in the application of scientific disciplines to investigative procedure. Prompt case solutions have become a matter of routine with the increased range of skills and information possessed by the officer and detective. All of the arts and sciences have been brought into play in the detection and apprehension of the criminal, and the production of evidence against him. At the convenient disposal of the investigator are the miracles of physics, chemistry, the microscope, the metalloscope, photography, microspectroscopy, photomicrography, and other tools in the physical and biological sciences for the laboratory analysis and identification of questioned materials involved as evidence in criminal cases. Circumstantial evidence has come into its own.

The trained police officer and detective, supported as they are today by the technical resources of the laboratory, present an almost invincible combination in the investigation of crime. The era of scientific crime detection has witnessed the virtual extinction of the so-called crime mystery. From the records we are compelled to conclude that the American police have been doing a commendable job of law enforcement.

In fact, the police have been catching adult and juvenile offenders, and processing them at such a high level of efficiency that our public institutions now are crowded far beyond their capacity. The judge of one Juvenile Court reported recently that he had two hundred youngsters, tried and convicted, awaiting admission to the state training school. The fact that institutional facilities are lacking in this country is beside the point. The conclusion remains that police administration in the United States has established an unparalleled record of performance in the application of enforcement as an instrument of crime control.

Enforcement Alone Not The Answer

With the total resources of the administration of justice geared to the punitive function, the American people are becoming aware of the utter futility of this approach to a major social problem. Enforcement has been given a fair trial! It has not produced the results anticipated by a society that has worshipped at the shrine of punishment as the major strategy in combating the crime problem. Police administrators know that despite their best efforts, no appreciable reduction has been noted in crime. In fact, if we accept the criminal case-loads of police departments and commitments to prison as a guide in measuring criminality in the United States,[46] we are forced to the conclusion that crime

---

[46] *Statistical Abstract of the United States,* Bureau of the Census. *Uniform Crime Reports,* United States Department of Justice.

has been increasing at a consistent rate far greater than the rate of population increase.

This discouraging fact has prompted the police to look in other directions for more effective measures of control. In casting about for a solution, there has been an increasing recognition in police circles that the present system of arrest, prosecution, conviction, and punishment is not effective. The criminal offender either escapes successful prosecution or goes to prison to renew criminal contacts and emerge eventually with a sharpened grudge against society and a delightfully polished aptitude for new criminal activities. The true ends of justice are defeated in both directions.

It is obvious that crime detection and the apprehension of criminal offenders must go on. A bank is robbed; a child is kidnapped; a citizen is murdered. Immediate action is imperative. The thug must be caught; the kidnapper apprehended, and the murderer taken into custody. No intelligent person can question the necessity of this immediate program in which the police, the prosecutor, the judge, and prison officials all play a vital and fundamental part. In this and succeeding generations there will be defective individuals for whom there is no alternative but protective confinement.

But the insanity of the man-hunt is apparent to every experienced police officer. After thirty-two years as America's outstanding Chief of Police, August Vollmer stated, "I have spent my life enforcing the laws. It is a stupid procedure and has not, nor will it ever solve the problem unless it is supplemented by preventive measures." [47]

The failure of enforcement and the shift in emphasis to preventive and correctional measures mark the beginning of a new approach to the problems of crime control. As a working hypothesis, it has been assumed that if the causes of crime and delinquency could be ascertained and then, either modified or eliminated altogether, a steady decline in the number of delinquents and criminals could be expected. The voluminous literature of criminology is very largely an account of the prodigious effort that has been expended in this direction.

It is not within the province of this volume to consider the etiology of delinquent and criminal behavior. It is pertinent to note, however, that although there are still many unknowns in the riddle of human behavior, research workers in the biological and social sciences have paved the way for the application of preventive techniques and procedures which bear the stamp of scientific validity. While actual practice trails far in the wake of the available knowledge in this area of

[47] August Vollmer, *Community Coordination*, Coordinating Councils, Inc. March–April, 1939.

social control, states and communities are gradually implementing these procedures as the foundation for a more enlightened policy in criminal justice administration.

For example, prison administration in recent years has made professional gains of a high order. Research in the behavior sciences has shed new light on the diagnosis and treatment of behavior difficulties, and these advances herald the appearance of a new penology based upon scientific sanctions. Institutional administration is gradually emerging as a distinctly professional undertaking; with the increasing use of professionally trained personnel and the emphasis on program, the controlled environment is actually becoming an asset rather than a handicap to the process of rehabilitation. Associated with professionally administered probation and parole systems, these developments hold significant implications in the reduction of recidivism.

The problem of crime prevention is further concerned with the offender and potential offender before the need for institutionalization appears. Studies have shown that in the majority of cases, the adult criminal offender was once known to the police as a juvenile delinquent. That the young delinquent is the forerunner of the adult criminal has now been proved by the analysis of thousands of criminal careers. The cpinion is now generally accepted that it is much better to attempt reform of the juvenile delinquent than to postpone action until the individual reaches maturity as a confirmed adult offender.

At the age level of juvenile delinquency the personality, temperament, and behavior traits are still somewhat in the formative stage and are more responsive to therapeutic measures than the fixed behavior patterns of the adult criminal offender. Modern juvenile court administration operates under the thesis that the child and the state have much in common and that the interests of both will be served by intelligent effort in helping the youngster to solve his problems. The increasing application of diagnostic facilities to the individual problem case and the parallel emphasis on probation as a therapeutic device are in deference to the role of prevention in the project of crime control.

The results of the approach to the problem thus far at the age level of juvenile delinquency, however, are far from impressive. After the home has failed; after the school has failed; and after the church, neighborhood and community have failed, the police are called in to make the arrest and somehow in a punitive scheme of things to effect a dramatic change in the direction of a life pattern. The enforcement process fails and subsequently the youngster becomes involved in more serious infractions and is sent to the reformatory where society once again expects the miracle to be performed. Despite determined efforts at reformation, the young offender here accumulates the necessary credentials and is later ushered into the penitentiary.   The futility of depending upon a miraculous transformation of personality at this level of desperation in the individual's life is shown by the records.

As early as 1937, Warden James A. Johnston of the Federal Penitentiary at Alcatraz, speaking on the functions of the modern prison concluded, "Prisons have important work to perform.   I want to see them bettered, improved, modernized and humanized.   But when all is said and done, the finest prison that we can build will stand as a monument to neglected youth." [48]   Walter Dunbar, Director of the California State Department of Corrections, observed, "We are trying to help the offender after his criminal pattern has developed.   This is almost like waiting until a youth is crippled by polio to give him vaccine." [49]

The evidence is conclusive in showing that where behavior problems are permitted to develop unattended up to the point where the youngster knocks on the door at police headquarters for admission, the cause is virtually lost.   In fact, his presence in jail or the detention home for the first time is but a formality, the most recent of a chain of events in a conditioning process that has led inevitably to the end result.

The police in a leading city had searched for an experienced criminal ring.   They arrested 40 children.   Sixteen were boys 15 years of age; fourteen were 14; five were 13; one was 12; two were 11; and two were 10.   It is at this juncture in the development of a criminal career that society first springs heroically into action, and it is at this point that the enforcement and correctional cycle officially begins its record of failure.

It is to beginning deviations and the determining conditions which induce them, that the police and community agencies must now address their attention.   In the past we have been dealing with the end result rather than with the conditioning factors that produce the delinquent and the criminal.   General policy even today, in the project of crime control is reminiscent of the housewife who was so busy swatting the flies in the kitchen that she failed to notice the garbage can outside the window where they were breeding by the thousands.   As Carr stated,[50]

---

[48] Warden James A. Johnston, Federal Penitentiary at Alcatraz; *Functions of the Modern Prison*, quoted in an address delivered by Henry W. Wichofen, U. S. Assistant Attorney General, *The Police and Crime Prevention*, at the University of Illinois, June 17, 1937.

[49] Walter Dunbar, California Youth Authority Quarterly, Vol. 16, No. 1, Spring 1963.

[50] Lowell J. Carr, *Delinquency Control*, 1938, p. 181.

"It is not enough to treat. Inefficient as the actual procedures in the correctional cycle may be, there seems to be little prospect that they can ever be made efficient enough to do the whole job that is needed. Back behind the personality that has broken the law there is always an earlier phase of that same personality that has just begun to deviate."

The Hawthorne Study, the Bodin Study, and other research investigations have pointed out that delinquency and crime stem usually from early life maladjustments and that delinquent juveniles and adult criminals display in almost every case a history of early behavior difficulties.[51] Among other things the foregoing studies reveal that from two to three per cent of the public school population in the average American community are children with problems, sufficiently severe to warrant special attention. This vast army of children who are today serious deviates in mental, physical, or temperamental traits, soon represents a major segment of the adult population with which the machinery of law enforcement must spend its time and energies. A veteran jurist stated recently,

"Messrs. Police Officers, Sheriffs and State Patrolmen: Do you want to meet the young killers, rapists, stick-ups, automobile thieves, burglars and others you will be chasing in a comparatively short time. If you do, go to the schools and look at the records that show the following information: chronic tardiness, persistent truancy, scholastic progress below mental ability, poor citizenship, unwillingness to accept correction and lack of interest. These records among others are red-flag warning signals of delinquency and crime and will point you almost unerringly to your man." [52]

Addressing further comment to the teaching profession, he said,

"Mr. and Mrs. Schoolteacher: Would you like to do something for the public health of your community in the field of sick conduct? Then, heed your records. Under your very eyes are developing the symptoms of infection that will develop into the ruptured appendix or organic collapse of good citizenship. The attendance record alone is enough to put us all on guard."

The philosophy of crime prevention stems from the conviction, now confirmed by research, that the burglar, killer, prostitute, automobile thief, and thug do not become that way suddenly. The records

---

[51] August Vollmer, *Pre-delinquency*, Journal of Criminal Law and Criminology, XIV, 2, Aug. 1923, pp. 279–283; Nathan Bodin, *Do Problem Children Become Delinquents and Criminals?* Condensed from a Master of Arts Thesis, University of California, Journal of Criminal Law and Criminology, November-December, 1936, pp. 545–559; E. K. Wickman, Children's Behavior and Teacher Attitudes, Commonwealth Fund Division of Publications, New York, 1928, pp. 232–233.

[52] Honorable William G. Long, Judge of the Seattle Juvenile Court, *The Relation of Juvenile Courts to Other Agencies*, Proceedings of the Fifth Pacific Northwest Law Enforcement Conference, State College of Washington, Pullman, 1944, p. 26.

show that in the majority of cases, they start their abortive development in early childhood and progress by almost imperceptible degrees into confirmed criminal offenders. Early discovery and diagnosis of the physically, mentally, and socially different child is gradually opening the door to opportunities for the prevention of delinquency and crime which now overshadow the man-hunt and the penitentiary.

The police occupy a commanding position in these new approaches to the crime problem. Police administration has the machinery and the methods to focus the community's attack on crime at the source. The police conduct an around-the-clock operation. They have a mobile personnel which moves rapidly and as a matter of routine into areas where other agencies would find unhampered movement difficult. They have the power of the state behind them.[53] Due to the nature of their work, the police are more familiar than any other organized group with crime hazards in the community that play their part in the needless wreckage of human life. They are in a position to understand the criminal and the forces which result in his development. They have in their files the basic data concerning crime and delinquency that are necessary for an intelligent plan of attack. Because the police and the schools are generally the first to have official contact with a problem youngster, theirs is an opportunity not presented to any other branch of government. Developing delinquency cases and the conditioning factors that produce them come under their observation long before other social agencies are aware of them. Basically important, also, is the fact that the police operate under a mandate from the people to achieve crime control, a circumstance which carries with it something of the obligations of leadership.

Police Organization for Crime Prevention

The prevention of crime is a fundamental responsibility of the patrol force. The preventive role of the individual patrolman is a basic element of modern police service. The mere presence of a properly organized and efficiently operating patrol force is conceded to be one of the greatest crime deterrents thus far developed by organized society.

The efficiency of the individual beat patrolman is reflected in large measure by the amount of crime and delinquency reported in the patrol area to which he is assigned. A point is reached in the growth of a community and its police department when, due to increased juvenile case load, the preventive role of the patrolman must be supplemented by specialized assistance. In recognition of this principle, the crime

---

[53] Graphic Survey, March, 1944.

prevention or juvenile unit has become a standard feature of American police organization and practice.

The establishment of a new service unit for such a purpose in the department requires a determination of its personnel strength and involves drawing upon the personnel of an existing unit, usually the patrol division, or recruiting from the outside. A minimum of five per cent of the departmental strength is generally recommended for assignment exclusively to crime prevention work. This means that the police administrator with a force of twenty men should assign at least one to work primarily on juvenile cases. In smaller departments where such specialized assignment is unjustified, the responsibilities of the task must be assumed by members of the patrol force.

The crime prevention or juvenile unit should have status in the organizational structure equal to that of other divisions, and as a line agency should be located under the direct control of the commanding officer in charge of line operations. The elementary functions of a police department and its crime prevention unit include discovery of the case and its investigation. Beyond this point, two general types of operations are observable in modern police practice. The distinction is determined largely by the procedural patterns employed in the disposition of juvenile cases. In the first type of operation the police function primarily as an agency of discovery and referral.[54] Juvenile cases are referred to the juvenile court, to the welfare department, or to some other social agency or agencies in the community and the disposition of the case rests with them.[55]

Wherever this type of operation prevails, the police have very largely abdicated their obligations and responsibilities in the project of delinquency and crime prevention.

In a more professional and enlightened approach, the police juvenile unit assumes responsibility for the disposition of a substantial number of juvenile offenders and beginning behavior deviation cases that come to the attention of the department. Here, the law enforcement function is augmented by a clinical approach to the adjustment of behavior difficulties.

In processing an individual case, the preliminary factual investigation is followed by diagnostic procedures in an attempt to identify those factors in the individual and his environment that have contributed to

---

[54] *Peace Officers' Manual on Juvenile Control,* California State Department of Justice, 1944, p. 11.

[55] This is mandatory in some jurisdictions. In the State of Washington the juvenile automatically by law becomes a ward of the juvenile court at the moment he is taken into custody by any peace officer.

the end result. The clinical resources of the community, including medical, psychological and psychiatric services, may be brought into play in behalf of the youngster. Their findings are integrated with the social case history of the individual as developed through investigations of the police case worker. Together, they offer the basis for an intelligent determination of the type of action that should be taken in the individual case.

The circumstances may warrant placing the offender in the detention home and referral of the case to the juvenile court. The factual investigation and diagnostic data in the great majority of cases will not warrant such referral, yet the youngster may require help in the solution of his problems if he is to escape later frustration and tragedy. Based upon the case diagnosis, the worker in the juvenile unit assigned to the case proceeds to bring into contact with the needs of the youngster those procedures and those community resources which the diagnosis indicates will be of the greatest therapeutic value in bring about a favorable adjustment. As in medicine, the unit of practice is the patient.

In the larger departments, the juvenile unit should be staffed with trained social workers who are graduates of an accredited Graduate School of Social Work, and who are schooled in the application of casework skills and techniques. In smaller departments where the caseload would justify the assignment of only one or two officers to this work, the Chief himself or someone in the department designated by him, may assume this responsibility. He will generally be able to arrange for technical assistance from others in the community, where this is indicated.[56]

In the early twenties, when Police Chief August Vollmer established the first crime prevention division of its kind in the United States, he stated:

"The woman police officer in charge of the Crime Prevention Division of the Berkeley Police Department, as well as each additional policewoman who may be appointed later, shall be a trained social worker, preferably with the stress laid on the psychiatric and psychological training, as evidenced by a certificate of a recognized school of social work, or the equivalent of such a certificate from a school of the first class, and she must have had some

[56] This is the position taken in the first and second editions; it stands in the third.

Among those who support the thesis of police participation in the diagnosis and adjustment or treatment of young behavior problems, in addition to the late Chief August Vollmer, is retired Superintendent O. W. Wilson of the Chicago Police Department, formerly Dean of the School of Criminology at the University of California, Berkeley, Calif. See his *Police Administration,* 2nd Edition, McGraw-Hill, 1963, pp. 321–353.

practical experience with executive responsibility in work with individual delinquents." [57]

There are those who disapprove of police participation in the treatment phase of delinquency prevention. Group work agencies have tended to resent the intrusion of the police into what they consider their field, and some judges disapprove of the exercise of quasi-judicial power by the police. Social agencies have failed to recognize the distinction in functions. The juvenile division is not an intruding and competing new welfare agency, but a police unit with a social welfare point of view. There is an element of treatment involved in every police contact prior to, as well as after, the arrest, and it is a police responsibility to make these contacts beneficial rather than harmful. Regarding the exercise of quasi-judicial power, no police officer can be divested of discretionary power in determining the advisability or inadvisability of arrest.

Modern police practice recognizes the principle in dealing with juvenile problems that the arrest is to be invoked only as a last resort; it is obvious, therefore, that the discretionary power of the police in this respect cannot be safely undermined. In fact, it is in the prearrest period that the police may play their greatest role in the project of crime control and prevention. In that vast zone of police activity preceding arrest, patrol officers come into contact with thousands of emerging behavior problems annually. An unprecedented opportunity is presented here for constructive police work. Intelligent attention at this stage to the development of constructive behavior patterns hold the greatest of promise in making the ultimate arrest unnecessary. It is here that "unofficial" police activity may yield important dividends. In a letter to Mrs. Lossing prior to her appointment as head of the Berkeley Police Crime Prevention Division, Chief Vollmer stated,

"The policewoman's work in Berkeley will consist largely in dealing with pre-delinquency problems. Primarily it is intended to harmonize the agencies that are here in an effort to concentrate these forces that deal with the health, education and morals of the children upon the problem child *long before he reaches the police station.*"

In addition to the case work approach to individual behavior problems, an efficient police force seeks to depress the crime rate by encour-

[57] The appointment was given to Mrs. Elizabeth G. Lossing—B.S., Mills College; summer study in psychiatric social work and criminology, University of California; awarded Child Psychology Fellowship, New York School of Social Work (field work experience at Institute of Child Guidance, New York); also took courses in psychiatric social work at the University of Michigan and at New School for Social Research, New York City; practical experience with San Francisco Associated Charities, Berkeley Health Center, Berkeley Commission of Public Charities, and as policewoman; contributor to *The Journal of Delinquency.*

aging merchants, banks, jewelry stores, and other high hazard locations to install burglary and hold-up alarm systems wired directly to police headquarters. The installation of improved locking devices to promote greater security of buildings against attack; increased illumination of buildings from within and without; proper handling of cash and high-value merchandise; and the education of the public in self-protection against criminal attack, all constitute activities intended to repress crime by eliminating the opportunity. Modification or elimination of environmental hazards in the community inimical to youth welfare fall also in this category.

Based upon the statistical data produced by the Records Division, the Chief of Operations will be in a position to focus the work of the Crime Prevention Division when and where it will yield the greatest immediate results. Armed with factual data, he can direct emphasis in those areas and upon those factors that are productive of criminality and delinquency, using not only the personnel of the Crime Prevention Division, but the line resources of the Patrol Division and other units throughout the department. Again, the significance of single, unified command over all line operations is this ability to apply the combined power and resources of the department where and when they are needed.

*

Chapter 11

IMPROVEMENT OF APPREHENSION CAPABILITY

PROMPT arrest following the commission of a crime serves five very important purposes in the administration of criminal justice:

1. It removes the offender from circulation temporarily, for an extended period of time, or on a permanent basis, thus reducing the criminal threat to the community.

2. It reduces the delay in bringing an offender to the bar of justice where he must answer for his deeds.

3. Basic to the concept of deterrence is the assumption that to increase the threat of apprehension raises the risk in committing the crime, and so reduces the likelihood of a criminal offense being committed. Projecting that threat of apprehension is a primary objective of police field operations.

4. Prompt arrest shortens the investigative trail with a resulting economy in police effort, together with a reduction in police costs and the cost of criminal justice administration in general.

The Police Communications System

The police communications system holds a key position in the apprehension process.

The evolution of American police administration in its present form is geared directly to the emergence of the police communication facilities. The history of their development is not a long and continuous one, for the ancient Greeks and Romans communicated with as great facility as did George Washington. It was not until 1829 with the organization of Scotland Yard, that police organization became coherent enough to make use of formal communication facilities. The smartly uniformed police officer to be seen on the street today is the symbol of an organized police service that is little more than a hundred years old.

If the mobility, maneuverability, and flexibility of control made possible by motorization are to be translated into striking power, there must be unfailing lines of communication between the elements of command in police organization, and they must be properly organized. The phenomenal development of communication facilities during the past thirty years is a matter of record. The police have been reasonably prompt in applying these devices to the problems of operational control.

The appearance of the telegraph as a means of communication marked the first advance in the development of police communication systems. It was first used in the larger cities for communicating between police headquarters and the precinct stations. Departments employed trained telegraph operators who were capable of sending and receiving messages through the use of the Morse code. The "telegraph key" became the symbol and the instrument of communication between headquarters and the precinct station and to a limited extent, between police departments from one city to another.

However, the problem of communication between headquarters or the precinct station, and the patrolman on the beat received little attention until the 1880's. Shortly thereafter, the development of telegraphic fire alarm boxes installed at strategic locations throughout the community, soon led to the installation of similar equipment on the police beat for one-way communication beteen the individual patrolman and the precinct or police headquarters.

Subsequently improved, largely by the Gamewell Company, the apparatus made it possible for the patrolman on the beat to transmit a variety of signals to his quarters station. An ordinary duty or "reporting in" call, which he was required to make every hour, could be sent by merely opening the box with a specially constructed key. This automatically registered the number of the box and its location, together with the time, on a tape in the terminal apparatus at headquarters. Other signals such as wagon calls, ambulance calls and calls for help, were sent by opening the inner door of the box, setting a pointer at the required call, and pulling the release mechanism.

Thus, the introduction of the telegraphic call boxes on the beat ended the isolation of the patrolman and enabled him to bring into play the entire resources of the department wherever necessary, in the performance of his duty. It did not, however, enable his headquarters to communicate with him. Two-way communication between the individual patrolman and his headquarters or precinct station awaited the invention and commercial introduction of the telephone. The appearance of the telephone exchange switchboard opened wide the door for a rapidly expanding police use of the telephone system on five fronts:

1. It established for all time two-way voice communication between police headquarters and the individual patrolman on the beat.

2. It gave the general public speedy access to police service. "The police are as near to you as the telephone" had become a reality.

3. Accessibility of the police by means of the telephone gave police management a tremendous advantage in terms of an

increase in the volume of incidents and criminal offenses reported in to headquarters.

4. The telephone offered an ideal means for inter-office communication, including contact with precinct stations in the larger cities.

5. The telephone system provided for immediate voice contact for inter-departmental communication between cities. Among other things, this fostered coordination of the police effort on an area basis in emergency situations. The road block was now on its way.

One major police communication problem remained—the development of some means by which headquarters could initiate communications contact with the individual partolman on the beat. Known as the Police Recall System, in various cities, semaphores, electric light signals or bells were installed on the top of police signal boxes or on lamp posts. When headquarters found it necessary to transmit a report or order to a particular patrolman, it could notify him by turning on the signal lights or other form of signal. As soon as the patrolman noticed the signal, he called headquarters from the nearest police call box to receive his instructions.

He could be informed quickly of any matter on the beat requiring his attention. The flexibility and coordination of police operations were increased enormously, for by use of the Recall System, headquarters could initiate almost instantaneous contact with the members of the dispersed force in the field.

Police Recall Systems became more and more sophisticated with engineering improvements in their design and installation. Soon, the red light recall signals were now suspended above strategic street intersections where they could be observed by the officer from four different directions. An appropriate control system at headquarters permitted the desk sergeant to flash the recall signal, usually the beat number, on a single beat, on two or more adjoining beats, or over the entire area. A steady burn indicated an emergency, criminal or otherwise, requiring fast and immediate action.

Following the introduction of the teletypewriter, the police were not slow to take advantage of this new form of communication. Teletypewriting is typewriting by wire. It combines the speed of the telephone with the authority of the printed word. The distance, whether a few feet or the width of a continent, makes no difference; the results are the same—accurate, fast and reliable transmission of orders and information from one point to another. It offered the promise of a means for rapid communication between headquarters and precinct stations in metropolitan police departments, and for the solution of many territorial communication problems which confronted the police. County and state police teletype networks were not long in developing, once the efficiency of this new communication facility was demonstrated.

Police Radio Communication

The emergence of radio as a practical means of human communication occurred at 11:30 A.M., one day in 1901 when the huge induction coils of Marconi's radio transmitter in the British Isles went into action and radio signals spanned the Atlantic Ocean for the first time. The apparatus Marconi had at his disposal was very crude when compared to modern radio equipment. At that time there were no vacuum tubes, no amplifiers, much less transistors and other radio engineering refinements that are so well known today.

Gigantic induction coils and other high voltage equipment of the day were employed. On the day of the test, the operator pressed the sending key with a lever of wood to escape electrocution. Sparks leaped from the knobs of the huge Leyden jars, illuminating the room like lightning flashes with a deafening sound like the clatter of a Thompson machine gun. Subsequent developments in the field of radio communications engineering are well known.

The introduction of the automobile into patrol service completely transformed the tactical operations of a crime fighting organization. It gave the force mobility potential, with the capability of rapid movement from one point to another. Following the appearance of efficient automobile receivers, the number of police radio installations increased at an incredible rate. By 1950, the use of radio communication was universal in the American police services, and radio installations were to be found even in the smallest departments.

At first, full advantage of the capabilities of the automobile in police service could not be realized. The recall system was still the only facility at the disposal of the police for initiating communication contact with the individual patrolman as the first step in getting him on the way to the scene. Studies indicated that under ideal conditions, headquarters could establish contact with the beat patrolman in an average time of approximately 3 minutes and 57 seconds. This interval was computed from the moment that the signal control mechanism was set in motion at headquarters until the officer lifted the receiver from a beat telephone and reported in for instructions. In other words, from the moment headquarters was in possession of the report or information, a time interval averaging from 4 to 7 minutes passed before the officer was under way to the scene of the emergency. The situation was further complicated by the additional time employed by the officer in traversing the distance from the telephone on the beat to the scene of the incident or disturbance.

Under ordinary conditions, the offender found in this period of free time his margin of safety; within this time interval, he could escape to comfortable seclusion four or five miles from the scene. Loss or destruction of valuable evidence, the disappearance of material witnesses and apprehension failure were frequent results of this delay. Radio changed all that and provided the answers.

Innovation, however, is occasionally slow and tortuous. It is not surprising that openly-expressed skepticism met the first proposals to experiment with radio as a device for police communication. To persons not versed in the technique of radio, it seemed a complicated and even impossible undertaking, but to those who understood this modern instrument of communication, it was a smooth-running machine of great potential usefulness in the suppression of crime and the upholding of law and order. However, many municipal authorities believed that the expense involved would not be justified by the results. As late as March, 1927, the following editorial appeared in a conservative police journal:

RADIO NOT FOR THE POLICE

One of the bright prospects which appears to have become a disappointment is that of the use of radio as an auxiliary to police work. Yet it is not certain that the failure is a permanent one and the lack of results up to this time may prompt some genius to bring out an idea that will turn a failure into success. . . . Despite some very valuable instances of crime apprehension through radio alarms, the fact remains that the more profitable use of radio is still a standing police problem.

In 1926 the present author presented to the executives of one of the largest radio manufacturing concerns in the United States a plan for engineering a police radio system in Berkeley, California, and was told that "There is no future for radio in police work." Returning to work and with the assistance of a young engineering student, Reginald Tibbetts, spare radio parts were combined with two copper coils from a confiscated whiskey still in the construction of a 75 watt Hartley transmitter and in that year the police of Berkeley went on the air with what was probably the first police owned and controlled radio system in the country.

The years 1926 to 1928 represented a significant period in the history of police radio communication. Almost simultaneously, the police in various parts of the United States began to experiment with whatever apparatus was available. At the same time that tests were being conducted in Berkeley, the police of Detroit were moving ahead with experimental installations, and soon police departments of other cities became actively identified with the movement.

The development of police radio systems on a substantial scale, however, awaited a solution to the problems of automobile reception. The operation of a radio receiver in a moving automobile presented an entirely original problem. Little or no technical material had been written or published on this phase of radio reception, and progress was, in large part, a process of trial and error. Road shock, constant change of position, interference originating in the electrical circuits of the car and from outside sources, fading of signal, and other problems arose. Satisfactory transmitters were available long before the automobile receiver became practical.

In 1930 commercial manufacturers of radio receiving equipment entered the field of automobile radio, and with the appearance of efficient automobile receivers, the number of the police radio systems increased at an almost incredible rate. Radio communication facilities are now standard police equipment throughout the United States. By 1946 all police patrol vehicles were radio equipped in 88 per cent of the 858 reporting cities above 10,000 population. Some patrol vehicles were equipped with radios in 5 per cent of these cities, while none had radios in the remaining 7 per cent. All but one of the cities above 25,000 population had at least some radio-equipped patrol cars, and nearly 96 per cent of these municipalities had all their cars radio equipped. With one exception, all the non-radio-equipped vehicles were in the 10,000 to 25,000 population group where 11.6 per cent of the cities had no radio equipment. The following table reveals the extent to which radio facilities were being used by the police by 1948.[1]

---

[1] The Municipal Year Book, 1946, p. 384, and 1949, p. 406.

TABLE X

PATROL VEHICLES WITH ONE, TWO, AND THREE–WAY RADIO: 1948

Population Group	Patrol Vehicles					Motorcycles			
			Per Cent With					Per Cent With	
	No. of Cities Reporting	Total No. Patrol Vehicles With Radio	One-way Radio Only %	Two-way Radio Only %	Three-way Radio Only %	No. of Cities Reporting	Total No. of Motorcycles	One-way Radio Only %	Two-way Radio Only %
Cities over 500,000	13	2,290	27.3	72.5	.2	13	1,094	49.6	0
250,000 to 500,000	20	1,624	22.8	71.2	6.0	21	737	20.2	3.1
100,000 to 250,000	48	1,313	8.8	73.5	17.7	49	791	44.1	5.2
50,000 to 100,000	97	1,225	13.7	70.8	15.5	97	748	42.2	8.2
25,000 to 50,000	195	1,226	3.6	70.1	26.3	194	660	43.2	6.1
10,000 to 25,000	494	1,329	8.8	63.9	27.3	479	627	28.4	5.4
All cities over 10,000	867	9,007	16.0	70.6	13.4	853	4,657	39.1	4.3

As of 1963, the use of radio communication facilities by the police is virtually universal, even in the smallest communities.

Technological development is a two-edged sword. The police department must be equipped to meet the criminal who utilizes in his nefarious calling many of the achievements of science and modern civilization. Fast automobiles left conveniently unlocked at the curb by careless or trusting motorists or purchased outright with an illicit income, have solved his transportation problems. Networks of improved highways favor his safe retreat unless the police are able to close every avenue of escape without delay. Given five minutes, the fugitive is from three to five miles away from the scene of his crime. Under the protecting cover of darkness he can be completely lost by the following morning.

Today, the police are superbly equipped with the most advanced communication facilities. Maximum advantage must be taken of this important tool through pre-emergency operational planning. This means the preparation of tactical plans in advance for emergency operations within the city limits. These should be supplemented by the preparation of operational plans on an area or regional basis so that in the emergency, road blockades can be established quickly and effectively.[2]

2 See page 341.

Radio communication combined with motorization of the force to usher in a new era in the history of the American police. Mobilization of the force had become a reality. Through the instrumentality of radio, headquarters was provided with the means for rapid communication with the deployed mobile units of the patrol force. The decentralized field strength of the department could now be called into action almost simultaneously with the receipt of the report at headquarters. The time interval of response by the patrolman on the beat was reduced to zero and members of the dispersed patrol force could be informed at once of any request for police assistance. Turning a new milestone in the delivery of security and protection to the community, the individual patrolman could now traverse his beat on patrol and yet be available instantly to police headquarters at all times for emergency calls.

On the pages of police communications history, there followed in turn two and three-way radio communcation, the radio teleprinter, telephoto, radar, television and the development of other pathfinding communication facilities. The police enterprise, more than any other branch of the public service, is peculiarly adapted to bring to bear upon its problems the gear of science and technology.

Some departments have inaugurated what is known as *Police Call,* under an arrangement which permits police dispatchers to cut into commercial radio stations and broadcast pertinent information concerning serious crimes just committed. The Fort Worth Police Department reports, for example—"the plan has produced unusually good results and has led to the arrest of several armed robbers and the recovery of stolen cars. At any given time, there are about 30,000 car radios turned on in the Fort Worth metropolitan area. Thus, if every station participates, we have 30,000 more observers than we had to start with. It offers a real increase in the policing capabilities of the force. We have strengthened the department at no additional expense to the public."

Two-Way, Three-Way Radio Communication

Since the introduction of police radio communication, the apparatus has been much refined. Transmitters have been reduced in size and weight, and their operation so improved that portable equipment can be operated successfully in the field. As a matter of engineering, two and three-way radio patrol communication presents no difficulty at present, and manufacturers now have available portable transmitting equipment specifically designed for police-patrol communication.

These improvements presage a new era in patrol technique and operation. As a tactical instrument, it represents a radical increase in the available channels of communication between headquarters and the dispersed patrol force, with a corresponding increase in availability of police field strength. Speed of action, flexibility, and mobility of the force are increased through accelerated interchange of information and instructions in emergencies.

Through the ability of the patrol car to acknowledge immediately the receipt of a message, the control-station dispatcher is assured that his broadcast has been properly received, and that the car or cars assigned are on their way to the scene of the emergency. Furthermore, while proceeding to the scene of action, and up to and including actual contact with the emergency, the motor patrolman may report his progress to the central station and to other motor-patrol units in the area. Thus, the patrolman may directly solicit the assistance of other patrol units in the vicinity and not lose valuable time by relaying the request for help through the central-station transmitter. Three-way radio communication thus makes mobilization almost instantaneous by increasing the speed with which patrol strength may be concentrated at crucial points.

Conditions change very rapidly in emergencies. A situation originally reported as a minor disturbance, may suddenly assume the proportions of a felony and require a speedy exchange of information and orders with headquarters and with all mobile patrol units in the area. An officer dispatched to a vacant lot on a report that an intoxicated man is lying there, may arrive to find a man brutally clubbed and left to die. Or, officers arriving at the scene of a reported murder may discover the blood-stained body of a woman lying on the bathroom floor, a victim of a fatal lung hemorrhage. Within the space of a few moments, a simple traffic-accident report may involve the entire patrol force in the search for a hit-and-run driver, wanted for manslaughter. A motor-patrol car detailed to the investigation of three suspicious characters loitering in the vicinity, finds a bank robbery under way. On another occasion, "It is murder, not suicide!" and the manhunt begins.

Examples are legion. The actual facts and circumstances often fail to coincide with the original report of information given the department in a hurried call over the telephone for police assistance. A radio patrolman arriving at the scene of trouble may discover that additional manpower is needed to handle the situation. Through direct conversation, he can mobilize immediate assistance, and later, if necessary, divert the flow of help in his direction to highway control points, at the same time directing the central station to get outside departments into action.

Thus the patrol operating time is drastically reduced, and in a most flexible manner the motor patrol force, either as individuals or as a unit, functions with a minimum loss of time. This arrangement represents a special type of decentralization in which, for the duration of the emergency, radio control is temporarily vested in the field commanding officer, subject, of course, to the receipt of additional instructions and information from the main transmitter at headquarters.

The Police Use of Television and Video-Tape

Television has almost overnight slipped through the barriers that retarded its early commercial development to become a major form of social contact. The police have not overlooked its potentialities as a communication facility and a steady expansion in its use can be anticipated.

On one of the expressways in Detroit, for example, a series of fourteen television cameras each covers a distance of roadway 3.2 miles in length. If an accident occurs, a control officer at headquarters instantly spots it, moves all traffic off that lane by the use of signals, lowers the speed limit in the same manner and dispatches officers to the scene.

Not entirely unrelated to the apprehension process, developments are under way in the use of closed circuit television for traffic control in congested metropolitan areas. A traffic coordinator, seated in front of a bank of television receivers at the central police traffic bureau, can view traffic conditions at any number of intersections. The closed circuit TV system, combined with radio communication, gives him push button control over the timing of the red and green traffic light signals at each intersection.

Closed circuit television is also being employed for the purpose of surveillance in jails and other detention facilities. On the third floor of the Alameda (California) Courts building, a select few watch one of the most unique television shows in the country—actual prisoners awaiting trial.

Mounted on the ceiling inside each of the twelve holding and receiving calls is a closed circuit television camera covering the interior of the cell. The sheriff of Alameda County observed that the cameras have the same effect on the prisoners as one guard constantly looking at them. "And," he added, "the cameras cost much less and are less risky than putting a guard in each of the twelve cells."

The system serves as a deterrent to violence and escape or any other overt action in the cells, in which there may be confined at any time from 20–100 prisoners. The Sheriff stated, "As long as the prisoners know they are being constantly watched, they won't engage in any suspicious activity. If a fight should develop, it can be contained without delay. With the cameras, we have complete surveillance over the cell, even in the 'blind' toilet area."

Only the far reaches of the imagination can contemplate what the future holds forth for the police use of television, in terms of state and national closed circuit police television systems, intercity and interstate show-up of criminal suspects, visual identification of fingerprints, stolen property and evidence, the planting of closed circuit TV cameras at high hazard locations, and other applications of this unique communications media.*

In the city of Olean, New York, the main business street is under around-the-clock closed circuit television surveillance. Olean's police television network, believed to be the first exterior one installed in any American city, has four stationary TV cameras mounted 20 feet high on utility poles along each side of a five-block length of North Union Street. At police headquarters, a bank of eight TV receivers mounted overhead facing the Desk Sergeant provide him with continuous serveillance coverage of a high risk area. Police Chief Michael S. Luty contemplates the eventual extension of the network to more remote areas, including supermarkets, suburban banks and other sensitive locations.

There are many technological advances that have contributed to more effective law enforcement operations; one of the more recent items of equipment that has become an integral part of the police scene is video-tape. Initially the size and weight of such equipment limited its application, however, recent engineering developments have overcome these limitations whereby portable equipment suitable for use by the patrol force, is presently available.

Video-tape cameras and recorders have such numerous practical applications to patrol operations that in many departments it has become an effective tactical instrument. Such equipment has been successfully utilized to record:

1. Actions of drunk drivers as evidence for court.
2. Statements of witnesses, suspects, or victims.
3. Traffic accident scenes.
4. Crime scenes.
5. Civil disturbances and riots.
6. The movement of suspects who are under surveillance.
7. Vehicles that have been stopped for traffic violations.

* See Hansen, David A., and Kolbmann, John J., *Closed Circuit Television for Police*, Springfield, Charles C., Thomas, Publisher, 1970. Between the covers of this book, the reader will find a convincing inventory of the ways in which police departments, both small and large, can make effective use of television equipment and its associated techniques.

Video-tape equipment is expensive, but is certainly a justifiable expense in any police department budget, even if for no other reason than the preservation of important evidence. Visually recorded evidence has tremendous impact in court cases and has been effectively utilized in court trials throughout the nation.

Summary

In building up the combat strength or striking power of the patrol force, two principles of military strategy are at work in modern police service. Separately, they appear to be contradictory and in conflict with each other. Together, with the aid of adequate communication facilities, they have made possible the dual performance of the twentieth century patrolman, namely, that of an agency for the prevention and detection of crime on the beat, and as a unit of reserve strength instantly available for mobilization in an emergency.

The first of these principles, deployment of the force, finds expression as a function of the definite limits imposed upon the personnel strength of a police department by the demands of efficiency and economy. Thus, decentralization of the force has come to be a fundamental principle of police organization, by virtue of which the police beat is the basic unit of operation in the modern police department. The beat patrolman is the final outpost of the crime-fighting organization. While performing the normal routine patrol of his beat, he is also discharging the greater part of the basic functions of police service. Such decentralization permits the maximum employment of the available manpower and equipment.

The second tactical principle is conservation of the reserve strength of the force. It is fundamental in military operations that every field maneuver must be supported from the rear by a reserve force. In police service this provision for reserve strength is equally indispensable. Decentralization of the force of course, is accompanied by a scattering of strength throughout the area policed, and superficially this device seems to imply a disregard of the reserve plan whereby a body of men may be immediately dispatched to the scene of action in an emergency. Two possible alternatives may be considered. A standing reserve force may be held at headquarters, or in police stations, in readiness for concentration in any given quarter. For many years police departments maintained such a force, but as an administrative procedure the practice proved unsound, and it has been almost completely abandoned. The plan was obviously uneconomical and inefficient because of the waste represented by idle manpower and equipment in the intervals between emergency calls.

The remedy has been found in a second alternative whereby through the agency of communication, maneuverability and speed of movement, effective mobilization is possible at a moment's notice. Whether the emergency be the investigation of a reported suspicious character in an outlying neighborhood or response to a major bank alarm, the results are the same, the rapid and intelligent movement of the required strength to the scene of action. Thus, through the simple formula—mass times rapidity of action—the striking power of a numerically inferior body of men is amplified up to a point where they may adequately perform the tasks assigned to them.

The apprehension process may be viewed as an *Operating Time Interval,* and it is defined as the time elapsing between the moment that a crime is committed until the arrival of an officer or officers at the scene.

The purpose of a police communication system is to save time with all that means in terms of increased mobility of the force and amplified combat strength in the field. Its function is two-fold—to expedite the transaction of routine business, and to meet emergencies. It is clear that if the demands of the emergency can be met, the expeditious handling of routine communications traffic will follow as a matter of course. All the technique of modern police communication practice must be directed toward a reduction of the operating-time interval, that is, the interval between the commission of a crime and the appearance of officers at the scene.[3]

This critical period falls quite clearly into four well-defined divisions, each characterized by a specific function; namely, (1) the time between the commission of the crime and the moment when some person lifts a telephone receiver to call the police; (2) the time between the lifting of the receiver and the beginning of actual conversation between the person calling and the police department; (3) the time between this conversation and a broadcast of the report to police radio patrol cars; and (4) the running time of the patrol cars from the point at which they receive the broadcast to the scene of the crime. All four of these time divisions are extremely flexible and amenable to time-reducing methods of operation.

(1) *Time interval between commission of crime and telephone call to police.*—Because of the wide distribution of telephones in all communities, the telephone is the most convenient and most direct means of contact with the police department. The time interval between the commission of a crime and the moment at which a telephone receiver

3 V. A. Leonard, *The Police Communications System,* Berkeley, University of California Press, 1938.
    V. A. Leonard, *The Police Communications System,* Springfield, Charles C. Thomas, Publisher, 1970.

is lifted from the hook is an extremely significant one. It may vary from a few minutes to days or months. Some crimes are never reported to the police. Occasionally, they receive almost instant notification, and in that event, the law-enforcement organization has an opportunity to function effectively.

The late Chief Quinn, of the San Francisco Police Department, commenting on this subject said: "The main difficulty is the human equation represented by the reluctance of the average citizen to communicate with police headquarters after being attacked. . . . If the public can be aroused to the degree that they will immediately, or as soon as possible after the attack, communicate with their police departments, giving full particulars, the results will show great increases in arrests with consequent deterring of those who attempt to commit crime."

A reduction in this time interval may be made to a marked degree through well-directed educational work. The New York Police Department recently issued a pamphlet for distribution in that city, with this purpose in mind. Also, it placed at conspicuous points throughout the city large illustrated posters and placards emphasizing the necessity of telephoning the police without delay. Obviously, the elimination of delay in making the telephone contact is more than equivalent to a reduction in running time of patrol cars, to which attention will be given presently.

(2) *Time interval between lifting of the receiver and actual conversational contact with the police department.*—Generally speaking, it may be said that the second interval of delay is a responsibility of the telephone engineer; it represents the only one of time divisions 2, 3, and 4 over which the police have no control.

Of telephone engineering it can be said that through scientific effort and technical improvement in apparatus, this time interval has been drastically reduced. As late as 1910, the average time required to complete a normal telephone connection between the subscriber and the party called was in excess of thirty seconds. At the present time, telephone traffic engineers use the following approximation of the average intervals elapsing between the moment the customer lifts the receiver until the bell begins to ring at the destination of the call based on national averages:

Multi-Office Exchange

Dial to Dial (up to 7 digits) .... 13 seconds
Dial to Manual (common battery)—Subscriber dials "O" and CB
    operator completes call to local circuit on switchboard multiple 23 seconds
Manual to Dial—Subscriber accesses operator on CB multiple and
    operator completes call to dial multi-office by dialing 5 digits;
       add 3 seconds when dialing full 7 digit number by operator .. 20 seconds

Single Office Exchange

Manual—When call is completed by operator at common battery
    switchboard .... 15 seconds
Dial—   When dialing 7 digits: ABC office code plus 4 digit number 13 seconds
Dial to Toll Switchboard—When subscriber dials "O" and requests
    assistance to a dialable police number .... 23 seconds

In the immediate foreground of telephone engineering are the miracles of "Touch-tone" Dialing and Electronic Switching, which eliminate the forward and reverse movement of the dial. At the press of a button, communication contact is virtually instantaneous. These new improvements are now being installed in various parts of the country. They represent a radical reduction in this time interval.

Considerable publicity has been given to the Telephone Company's announcement of 911 as a nation-wide emergency number. The Bell System has always promoted the use of a back-up universal emergency code, consisting of "0" (zero) for operator. The usefulness and success of "dial zero for operator" is demonstrated by the fact that some 40,000 calls a day are placed through the operator by people desiring to contact the police or fire department, or other emergency services. The operator answers the call, ascertains the location and type of emergency, and then connects the customer to the agency or organization in a position to provide the necessary assistance.

For the past several years, the Bell System has been asked to provide an easy to remember nation-wide telephone number for contacting the emergency services. More recently, the President's Crime Commission, members of the Congress and the Federal Communications Commission have added their support to the move. In addition to being an easy to remember number, it should be easy to dial in a state of panic, for the handicapped and under darkened conditions.

The number 911 is offered by the telephone company to assist local public safety agencies in protecting the life, safety and property of the public at the local level. It is not intended to completely substitute for dial "zero" for the operator. There will always be operator assistance available for emergency calls.

In order to provide one number, community-wide, it is necessary to direct the calls to one answering point in the community. Due to the fact that a high percentage of emergency telephone calls are for the police, it has been suggested that police departments be designated as the point for receiving emergency 911 calls.*

(3) *Time interval between contact with the police and broadcast to patrol cars.*—Delay at this point serves to cripple seriously the effi-

---

* V. A. Leonard, *The Police Communications System*, Springfield, Illinois, Charles C. Thomas, Publisher, 1970, p. 20.

ciency of the entire communication system as well as the line operations of the department. The cause lies usually either in a traffic overload or a lack of a properly organized operating procedure.

It is fundamental in police work that a signal on the exchange board indicative of an incoming call must be answered without delay. At the moment this signal appears, the responsibility of telephone traffic engineers ends; their work is accomplished. At the same moment the police organization should begin to function, but in far too many departments unnecessary delay occurs. Frequently, tardiness in responding to incoming calls is traceable to the physical inability of any one individual to handle properly the volume of incoming traffic. The remedy here is obvious. All functions of the communications bureau must be coordinated and directed toward the elimination of delay and lost motion.

It is appropriate to emphasize at this point that a "busy" signal at police headquarters should be unheard of. It throws the operating time interval down the drain. One survey in a medium-sized city indicated that on an average day, there were 43 times when citizens called the police department and received the busy signal.

Police management should arrange for a telephone engineer to undertake a survey of existing police telephone facilities to determine whether they are fully adequate in this respect. This, the telephone company will do free of charge. Every police department should see to it as a first order of business that there are a sufficient number of trunk lines coming into the police switchboard to accommodate peak telephone traffic loads. There is no place for a "busy" signal in the police business.

In this third time interval we are concerned with the radio-dispatching unit of the police organization upon which rests the responsibility for rapid technique in the delivery of orders and information to cruising radio patrol cars. Between the complainant or person reporting a crime and the operating patrol cars of the department, there must be an intermediate agency for receiving reports and information and for directing the movements of the force to meet the emergency. The complainant is untrained in police technique and at the moment of reporting a crime, particularly a serious one, he is emotionally unstable, and requires skillful and expert coaching in order to get from him without delay the facts of a crime report that are essential for fast and intelligent police action. It is the primary function of the dispatching organization to act as an intermediate or connecting agent between the person or persons attacked and the police field strength which may be dispatched to handle the situation.

The qualifications of the police radio dispatcher are important and are similar to those of the police telephone operator. He should be capable of working at traffic peaks with a cool mind and should possess ability to make decisive judgments that are usually correct. The entire dispatching unit should be organized for rapid movement of the information from the complainant to the patrol force. Direct contact between the caller and the patrol car nearest him is the goal of police communication, and the necessary intervening agencies must, therefore, be reduced to the lowest possible minimum. In some departments this fundamental fact is appreciated, but in others the information may be relayed from two to four times before it finally reaches the input system of the transmitter.

There are three general methods of dispatching in general use. In the first, the functions of operation at the exchange switchboard and of dispatching are performed by the same person; in the second and third, these functions are separated and assigned to different persons, but there is a definite difference between the two in the manner of transferring the information from operator to dispatcher; in the second, a complaint record form is used; in the third, the dispatcher is put into direct contact with the person calling.

In smaller communities incoming calls are received at the police exchange board by the desk sergeant, who also functions as the radio dispatcher. With the microphone and remote-control equipment mounted directly in front of him, he is able to broadcast alarms almost simultaneously with their receipt. The number of intervening and time-consuming agencies between the victim and the patrol car is here reduced to the lowest possible minimum. Such a combination of telephone operator and dispatcher gives a service even superior to that afforded by the more highly refined dispatching systems in the larger cities.

In metropolitan areas the volume of emergency traffic requires special arrangements to accommodate the great flow of incoming calls as rapidly as possible. Dispatching procedure is more involved because of the necessary decentralization of activities in the communication bureau. Here the combination police operator and dispatcher gives way to specialization; functions and duties are divided in order to relieve congestion and to provide maximum speed in handling the individual call for police assistance. Operating and dispatching become separate activities, and each is assigned to a different person or persons.

In the larger metropolitan cities, the radio communication system becomes a complex affair. The Chicago Police Department, for example, in servicing its 3,500,000 people and exercising control over 1,700 police vehicles, uses 27 radio frequencies, 9 base transmitter locations with 3 satellite receiver stations and 56 telephone trunk lines for receiving calls for emergency service.[4]

The radio dispatcher must have at his fingertips the entire resources of the department, and every provision should be made for accelerating their use in the emergency. Maps must be provided, indicating by beats the area patrolled and the distribution of radio-equipped patrol cars. Supplementary devices, either manually or electrically operated or both, should be at his immediate disposal to indicate cars in and out of service on calls, so that the dispatcher may know at all times the number and location of cars available for emergency assignment.

In addition, the dispatcher should have in front of him for fast reference the telephone numbers of all emergency services in the community, including hospitals and doctors available on call, together with ambulance service in the event the police do not operate such a facility. Included on this emergency telephone list also, should be the numbers of certain high risk establishments such as banks, theatres and other locations especially susceptible to criminal attack.

(4) *Running time of patrol cars.*—Running time may be defined as the interval, usually in minutes and seconds, between the time of broadcast and the time of arrival of the directed patrol car at the indicated location. It is the generally conceded opinion of police officials that the running time of radio patrol cars must not exceed an average of three minutes if the communication system is to be considered a paying investment. This opinion, establishing as it does a dead-line operating interval, is fundamentally sound. Where the average running time of any police radio patrol system exceeds a maximum average of three minutes, it may be said that the installation is not providing the service for which it was designed and which it is capable of giving. At the moment that the average running time goes beyond this limit, the investment in radio communication equipment tends to become unprofitable.

The reason for this is simple enough. The investment in radio communication facilities is justified by the radical reduction in patrol operating time. It is through radio communication that the probability of apprehension and the preservation of important evidence and witnesses become a direct threat to criminal operations. The necessity for laborious and costly investigations may be eliminated at the outset by the prompt arrest made possible through reduced running time. Further, preservation of important evidence and immediate identification of material witnesses expedite the criminal-trial process and reduce the costs of prosecution and conviction.

[4] See O. W. Wilson, *Police Administration*, revised edition, p. 509, McGraw-Hill Book Company, 1963.

A three-minute time interval is the extreme maximum limit within which these patrol functions may be discharged with any degree of efficiency.   If that limit is exceeded, the hazard of escape, destruction or loss of evidence, and disappearance of important witnesses becomes almost a practical certainty.   The running-time interval gives to the criminal his chief margin of safety, but it is subject to police control.

It is of the greatest importance to state that any reduction in the running time of patrol cars, even though by seconds, under the established limit, increases to a striking degree the probability of a successful run.   This is an extremely critical period in patrol strategy and operation.   Within the limit of 180 seconds, any fractional reduction produces an increasingly rapid degree of progression from probability to absolute certainty of arrest as the running time approaches zero.

Burglary and hold-up alarm systems wired directly to police headquarters hold a key position in the operating time interval.   There is no lifting of a telephone receiver.   Upon excitation of the alarm circuit, contact with the police is instantaneous.   The first time interval is reduced to zero as the apprehension process moves in for the quarry.

In terms of the protection of valuables, it is interesting to note that the first true safe was introduced in New York in the early part of the nineteenth century, and soon afterward, the race began between the safe builders on the one hand and the safe burglars on the other.   For a half century, safe and vault construction remained almost unchanged in terms of protective strength.   Some modifications were made to offset the introduction of nitroglycerin as a weapon of attack.   Then, the appearance of the cutter burner, the fluxing rod, the electric drill, chisel and hammer, and the oxygen pipe, introduced the need for revolutionary changes in the structural design of these protective enclosures.

In 1920, preparatory to its program of branch bank construction, the Federal Reserve Bank began a series of tests under the direction of Alexander B. Trowbridge, their consulting architect, in an effort to establish the relative resistance to attack of all known types of vault wall and lining construction, and to rate these resistances in terms of cost.

The test walls were constructed by a reputable contractor under careful supervision, and the linings were built and submitted by leading vault manufacturers.   Concrete consisting of carefully graded fine and coarse aggregates and fairly rich cement were found to offer some resistance to all three methods of attack—drills, explosives, and the flame—provided that steel reinforcement extended entirely through the walls and at right angles to the direction of attack.

Further experiments were conducted in the following year and details of vault wall construction were developed which provided increased protection, *but in all of them, penetration was effected under time tests.* It is therefore, a matter of record that the most modern bank vault, representing as it does the ultimate development in protective enclosures, is vulnerable to penetration by the burglar, given the time and the tools.

It isn't necessary to go very far afield in order to discover that burglar-resisting materials can never be more than burglar-delaying materials. If the burglar has time enough—and by that is meant no more than a few hours—and the tools—it is safe to say that no commercially practicable construction is impregnable against him.

Nevertheless, what ingenuity can devise to delay the burglar must be applied. But the mere prolonging of the safe-cracker's task is not protection. This delay must be exploited to the end that completion of the offense is interrupted by apprehension. Therefore, a first prerequisite of burglary protection is an adequate alarm system which will deliver a signal to the principal source of help—the police. With an efficient alarm system, a pasteboard box can be made more nearly burglary proof than a modern bank vault not so protected.

Banks, theaters, super-markets, jewelry stores and other locations which classify as police hazards [5] should be covered with this effective form of protection. Engineering an alarm system is a comparatively simple affair. Many devices are now available that will pass the word quietly to police headquarters that a criminal attack is under way.[6] These include the open and closed circuit triggered by a simple electrical contact, sound sensitive detectors, heat sensitive detectors, the photoelectric cell, radio frequency circuits, magnetic fields, circuited currency trays and cash register drawers, and other devices offer almost endless approaches to the matter of "setting the trap".[*]

[5] As previously indicated, a police hazard is any person, place, situation or thing possessing a high potential for criminal attack or for generating a demand for police service.

[6] In Fort Worth, Texas, the West Side State Bank has designed and put into operation a drive-in banking unit with six tellers who are entirely unexposed so far as a potential holdup is concerned; they communicate with the individual outside in a car via a television screen.

[*] Important sources of security information concerning alarm circuit engineering include the following—Alarmtronics Engineering, Inc., 154 California Street, Newton, Massachusetts 02195; American District Telegraph Co., 155 Sixth Avenue, New York, N. Y. 10013; Babaco Alarm System, Inc., 723 Washington Street, New York, N. Y. 10014; Ruphonics Marketing, 202 Park Street, Miami Springs, Florida 33166; Mosler Safe Company, 1561 Grand Blvd., Hamilton, Ohio 45011; and Pyrontronics, Inc., 2343 Morris Avenue, Union, New Jersey.

Also see Richard S. Post and Arthur A. Kingsbury, *Security Administration*, Springfield, Illinois, Charles C. Thomas, Publisher, 1970.

Police Roadblock Operations

Closely related to the alarm circuit and the apprehension process is the police roadblock operation. A roadblock is defined by Webster as *a road barricade set up by law enforcement officers*. That is exactly what it is. Cases without number demonstrate clearly the value of the police roadblock in bringing to an abrupt halt the activities of a criminal offender. The irony of it all is that altogether too few police departments are prepared to put into operation at a moment's notice in the emergency, this effective tool of apprehension. This is strange in view of the fact, as will be seen later, a relatively small amount of thinking and planning is required.**

As a case in point, in 1946, the mid-west was terrorized at some length by two murderers, Daniels and West, who had been released on parole from the Ohio State Reformatory at Mansfield. After their release, they separated for a brief time and then came back together to launch a series of wanton murders without parallel in the annals of the police. During this time, the highways of the mid-west were virtually deserted.

It all began with the holdup of a downtown restaurant in Columbus, Ohio. During the commission of this robbery, the proprietor attempted to dash through the front door for help, and a bullet from Daniels' gun brought him down with a fatal wound. Realizing that they were now "hot" again, they laid low for a few days. Then, at about 2:00 o'clock one morning, they decided it was time to go out to the Mansfield Reformatory and take care of Red, a guard at the institution who had "hurt their feelings" while they were in custody there.

Fortunately for Red, they were unable to find him. Then they thought of an alternative. They rang the doorbell at the Warden's home outside the walls and when he appeared, Daniels said they were having car trouble and wondered if they could use the telephone. Once inside, Daniels asked the Warden where the rest of his family was and he replied that his wife and daughter were upstairs asleep.

Daniels pulled his gun and ordered the Warden upstairs. All three were marched in their night clothes out to the car. They drove down the highway about four miles and then turned off on a country road, pulling to a stop in an isolated area alongside a cornfield. The Warden and his family were ordered through a barbed wire fence into the field, where Daniels told them to stand up abreast. Daniels spoke

---

** See especially, Schwarz, J. I., *Police Roadblock Operations*, Charles C. Thomas, Publisher, Springfield, 1962. This book should be in the library of every police department.

to the Warden and said, "We want you to go last so that you can see as much of it as you can."

Daniels then asked the girl if she wanted to say a prayer, and then put a bullet through her head. The Mother and then the Warden answered the call and fell to the ground.

After the sixth and seventh murders—a salesman and his wife— they wanted his car, the Ohio State Police pulled a plan from their files and put it into operation—a police roadblock covering parts of five states.

At about 2:30 one morning, with Daniels and West wondering how they could get through the police cordon, they came upon a truck loaded with new cars parked at the side of the road, where the driver was getting some needed sleep. They awakened the driver, ordered him through a fence into a nearby field and shot him in the head. They seemed to prefer the head as their target. The truck loaded with new cars would serve as a perfect disguise in getting through the police roadblock.

In their plans, they failed to reckon with a Sheriff, a former Pennsylvania police Lieutenant, and Sergeant Cohn from a nearby police department, who were manning a roadblock at the intersection of two highways in southern Ohio.

The truck grinding to a halt, the Sheriff walked up to the cab and asked the driver (West) if anyone was with him, and the answer was "No." The Sheriff then instructed Sergeant Cohn to cover West while he climbed up-side to check-out the cars. He found Daniels asleep in one of the top cars with a 45 calibre automatic in his right hand. As they climbed down, the murderer pleaded with the Sheriff, "Please don't kill me."

At that moment, West came out of the cab shooting, a bullet striking Sergeant Cohn in the chest (he recovered later in the hospital). As the Sergeant went down, he pressed the trigger of a Thompson machine gun—it was set on automatic—and a bullet hit West between the eyes. Daniels was later executed in the Ohio State Penitentiary.

During the past thirty days (at the time this is being written— March 1970), three banks have been held up in small communities— population of each community about 1,200—in the Denton, Texas area, with a loss of approximately $75,000. In all three robberies, a successful escape was made.

This is totally unacceptable. By all professional police standards, they should already be well on the way to the penitentiary. These three robberies represent a situation that is all too common throughout the United States. This state of unpreparedness and lack of planning is unpardonable.

The remedy is simple. The basic apprehension area is a single county and the counties that are adjacent to it. The first step is to gather around the conference table—with representatives from the police and sheriff's department in the area and the State Police present. Any town or community large enough to support a bank must be represented at this conference.

The only equipment needed at the moment is a good road map of the area. Through careful study of the map, strategic highway control points can be identified as a part of the roadblock system. It will be a source of some amazement to those present at the conference how few roadblocks need to be established in order to "bottle up" the area. Several years ago, such a study was made of the road and highway system surrounding Detroit. It was found that by manning only twenty-nine control points, there would be a resulting tight blockade of all avenues of entrance to and exit from, the city.

The second step is to install an alarm circuit in each bank wired directly to the local police department. In addition, the circuit should be wired directly to the police department or sheriff's office in the county seat. An effective alternative would be to wire the alarm circuit to the police department or sheriff's office in the county seat of of the county that is the nucleus of the system. Where neither alternative appears practical or in a very small community where there is no law enforcement agency as such, the circuit can be connected to the nearest telephone operator over company lines. Under pre-arranged plans, she would know what to do. In any of the foregoing arrangements, consultation with the officials of local telephone companies will provide the answers to this phase of the problem.

The third step is to plan the deployment of personnel upon the receipt of an alert. Not less than two officers and two cars should be assigned to any one roadblock. In the case of a bank burglary during the night, it would only be necessary in most instances to surround the bank. Details of the total roadblock operation will be found in the book previously mentioned—*Police Roadblock Operations,* by Chief J. I. Schwarz, Charles C. Thomas, Publisher, 301–327 East Lawrence Avenue, Springfield, Illinois, zip code 62733. It should be pointed out here that other high hazard locations in the community, in addition to banks, merit this sure form of protection.

Through the progressive organization of apprehension areas on this basis, the entire state can be covered, up to and including two or more states where the man-hunt over a large geographical area is indicated.

The Indiana Law Enforcement Blockade System has attracted considerable attention. It was devised to coordinate the efforts of all law enforcement agencies in Indiana in setting up police blockades for the apprehension of a fleeing criminal and to prevent an offender from seeking refuge in another section. There are 262 municipal, county and state police agencies who participate in the blockade plan and have predetermined blockade points to cover. The system covers 36,291 square miles.

In establishing a basis for dividing the state into blockade sections, the counties were discarded as being too irregular in shape and size. It was decided that the best approach would be equally spaced horizontal and vertical grid lines (about 17 miles apart), dividing the state into equal areas. The center of each of these areas was designated the center of a blockade plan, given the prefix "X", and numbered consecutively X–1 through X–109. This established 109 blockade plans. The horizontal grid lines were labeled alphabetically "A" through "P" and the vertical lines were labeled "1" through "11".

The intersection of the grid lines was designated the center of a blockade plan and given the letter and number designation of the intersecting grid lines, B–2, G–8, etc. This established 130 additional blockade plans for a total of 239 state-wide. A crime committed anywhere in the state of Indiana is within 8 miles of the center of an established blockade plan.

After establishing the locations that should be covered, such as highway intersections etc., and the police agencies that would cover them, the information was compiled into a Master Blockade Book. There is only one copy of this Book which lists every Blockade Plan and all departments participating in each plan, along with their responsibilities. Each participating agency has a Blockade Book covering only those plans in which they play an active part.

It was necessary to establish a central point from which to disseminate blockade information in a criminal emergency. Because of its central location and access to state-wide police communication facilities, the Operations Center of the Indiana State Police at Indianapolis was designated as the control point. The Master Blockade Map and the Master Blockade Book are kept at the Operations Center.

Electronics and the Patrol Car

Motorization of the force means that the patrol car dominates the police scene. For the officer, it serves as his office, his means of communication, his means of locomotion and pursuit, observation post and as a vehicle for transporting prisoners. More precisely, it is the instrument of mobilization in moving the officer to the scene as the apprehension process gets under way.

Police officials are becoming acutely aware of the need for automotive equipment tailored more completely to police specifications. Involved are a wide variety of practical innovations, including more convenient radio controls, the mobile teleprinter and electronic car locator, in addition to personal radio equipment for the individual officer.

The potential use of mobile teleprinters in patrol cars is of particular interest to the police. Although voice is an indispensable mode of communication for patrol vehicles, it presents a number of problems, including: [7]

1. It is very wasteful of the already over-crowded radio frequency spectrum.
2. It provides no protection against unauthorized interception of official police communications unless expensive scramblers are utilized.
3. It does not provide a set of written instructions or a written record.
4. It is subject to phonetic errors.
5. It cannot be received by an unattended patrol car in the absence of special recording equipment.

In addition to meeting some of the problems of voice communications, two-way teleprinter links could connect the individual patrolman in a car directly to a computer terminal (NCIC), so that he could check without delay for wanted persons, stolen cars and other matters of important investigative interest.

The Walkie-Talkie [8]

The police have long felt the need for a small, inexpensive, lightweight two-way radio for the officer's use when he is out of the car in order to provide uninterrupted communications contact with headquarters. He may need this communications link to report incidents, to call for help, to request instructions, and for other purposes. Leading microelectronics manufacturers agree that microminiaturized versions of currently used police radio equipment would weigh about twelve ounces and could be made available at a reasonable cost. Such equipment would also prove of the greatest value to the conventional foot patrolman.

---

[7] The President's Commission on Law Enforcement and Administration of Justice, *Task Force Report: Science and Technology*, U. S. Government Printing Office, 1967, p. 140.

[8] Leonard, V. A., *The Police Communications System*, Charles C. Thomas, Publisher, 301–327 East Lawrence Avenue, Springfield, Illinois, 1970, p. 34.

As of 1969, an electronic "repeater" system has been installed by the New York City Police Department, which now enables Headquarters to maintain direct walkie-talkie radio communication with every uniformed police officer on duty throughout the city. Every uniformed police officer, whether on foot, scooter, motorcycle, or horseback, as well as those in radio motor patrol cars, will thus be available for emergency calls from the communications center at police headquarters.

The repeater system consists of sixty-five automatic booster stations, located at various points in the city which increase the signal strength of the walkie-talkies and enable them to reach police headquarters. The augmented police communications network was made possible by the purchase of 630 new type walkie-talkies, in addition to the 1,540 of the older type already in use. In addition to uniformed patrol officers, the communications center will also be able to communicate with members of the tactical unit and special events squad, as well as special units of the detective division which are on antimugging patrol.

In the preceding pages, it has been shown that a reduction in the *Operating Time Interval* increases apprehension capability. There are instances where an unnecessarily long running time interval results from the assignment of a patrol car that may not be the closest one to the scene of action. At the moment, a patrol car on an adjacent beat may actually be closer to the scene than the officer on whose beat the case originated. Electronic car locator apparatus has now been developed which would permit the radio dispatcher to identify immediately the patrol car closest to the scene of action. This would effect an important reduction in running time and increases the probability of an arrest. The officer on whose beat the offense or incident originated would remain responsible for taking over the case at that point.

The Indianapolis Police Department recently inaugurated a plan under which police officers assigned to patrol cars take them home at the end of their tour of duty for their own personal use. The only requirement is that whenever the officer is in the car, he must keep the radio turned on and respond to police calls. Said Assistant Chief Spallina, "As a result of this system, we have effected more than 100 felony apprehensions by our off-duty cars. In the past, we only had 110 cars on the street at any one time. Now we are using 450 cars around the clock. We plan to extend the same personal-use system to an additional 60 surveillance cars used by the detectives. That will give us 510 cars on the streets."

In recent years, police transportation management has taken on a new meaning. The costs of automotive equipment are the largest single item in the police budget with the exception of salaries. In terms of the economics of police transportation, the engineering of police vehicles, specification writing, police fleet maintenance and vehicle replacement, it is necessary for police management to approach these problems on a sound, scientific basis.[9]

A large part of police communications with patrol cars is stereotyped in nature. As a result, many standard phrases have been given numerical codes in order to speed communications. The Associated Public-Safety Communications Officers, Inc., (APCO), parent organization in the public safety communications field, has rendered veteran service in standardizing these numbers and they are strongly recommended as the standard for police communications traffic.[10] Known as the APCO

TEN SIGNALS they are as follows:

    *Indicates most used signal

10–0	Caution
*10–1	Unable to copy—change location
*10–2	Signals good
*10–3	Stop transmitting
*10–4	Acknowledgement
*10–5	Relay
*10–6	Busy—Stand by unless urgent
*10–7	Out of service (Give location and/or telephone number)
*10–8	In service
*10–9	Repeat
10–10	Fight in progress
10–11	Dog Case
*10–12	Stand by (stop)
*10–13	Weather and road report
10–14	Report of prowler
10–15	Civil disturbance
10–16	Domestic trouble
10–17	Meet complainant

---

9 See Wynne, G. Ray, *Police Transportation Management*, Coda Publications, Studio City, California, 1965.

10 Associated Public-Safety Communications Officers, Inc., *The Public Safety Communications Standard Operating Procedure Manual*, 1969, p. 47. This Manual should be in the possession of every police department. In addition to the APCO TEN SIGNALS, its Table of Contents include *The Operator, Telephone Techniques, Radiotelephone Voice Techniques, Phonetic Alphabet, 2400 Hour Time, Personal Descriptions, Log Form, Message Form, Complaint and Administrative Forms, The Federal Communications Commission, Law Enforcement Communications, Civil Defense Communications,* and a *Glossary.* Copies of this important Manual may be obtained by addressing Major J. Rhett McMillian, Administrative Assistant, APCO, P. O. Box 669, New Smyrna Beach, Florida, 32069, together with a remittance of $1.25.

*Indicates most used signal

*10–18	Complete assignment quickly
*10–19	Return to _____
*10–20	Location
*10–21	Call _____ by telephone
*10–22	Disregard
*10–23	Arrived at scene
*10–24	Assignment completed
*10–25	Report in person to (meet) _____
10–26	Detaining subject, expedite
10–27	Drivers license information
*10–28	Vehicle registration information
*10–29	Check records for wanted
*10–30	Illegal use of radio
10–31	Crime in progress
10–32	Man with gun
*10–33	EMERGENCY
10–34	Riot
10–35	Major crime alert
*10–36	Correct time
10–37	Investigate suspicious vehicle
10–38	Stopping, suspicious vehicle (Give station complete description before stopping).
10–39	Urgent-Use light and siren
10–40	Silent run—No light or siren
*10–41	Beginning tour of duty
*10–42	Ending tour of duty
*10–43	Information
10–44	Request permission to leave patrol _____ for _____
10–45	Animal carcass in _____ lane at _____
10–46	Assist motorist
10–47	Emergency road repairs needed
10–48	Traffic standard needs repairs
10–49	Traffic light out
*10–50	Accident—F, PI, Pd
*10–51	Wrecker needed
*10–52	Ambulance needed
10–53	Road blocked
10–54	Livestock on highway
*10–55	Intoxicated driver
10–56	Intoxicated pedestrian
10–57	Hit and run—F, PI, PD
10–58	Direct traffic

*Indicates most used signal
*10–59   Convoy or escort
 10–60   Squad in vicinity
 10–61   Personnel in area.
*10–62   Reply to message
*10–63   Prepare to make written copy
*10–64   Message for local delivery
*10–65   Net message assignment
*10–66   Message cancellation
*10–67   Clear to read net message
*10–68   Dispatch information
*10–69   Message received
*10–70   Fire alarm
 10–71   Advise nature of fire (size, type, and contents of building)
 10–72   Report progress on fire
 10–73   Smoke report
*10–74   Negative
*10–75   In contact with
*10–76   En Route
*10–77   ETA (Estimated Time of Arrival)
 10–78   Need assistance
 10–79   Notify coroner
 10–80   Chase in progress
 10–81   Breathalizer report
*10–82   Reserve lodging
 10–83   Work school xing at _____
 10–84   If meeting _____ advise ETA

APCO Ten Signals Interpretation

10–32   Can be used in conjunction with other signals, i.e., 10–10, 10–31,—give location.

10–33   Maximum priority. Should be used on the initial call to indicate traffic pertaining to danger to life or property. All stations or vehicles not involved in the emergency should maintain radio silence until the emergency is over or under control.

10–34   Give location.

10–35   Used to alert all stations or vehicles on the frequency to make themselves available to assist where needed—always followed with maximum information as to the nature of the crime and assistance needed.

10–38   The officer MUST furnish maximum information BEFORE stopping suspicious vehicle. (Color, make, model and license of vehicle. Number of occupants, direction of travel, etc.) Each department should established a time limit for the officer to indicate an "all clear" before all available assistance is sent.

10–39 Can be used to give any other signal an emergency status.

10–40 To be used to indicate haste, while observing all safety precautions and not attract attention.

10–43 Use when asking if any, or supplying information.

10–45 Give location.

10–46 Give location.

10–47 Indicate nature of repairs needed and location.

10–48 Give location.

10–49 Give location.

10–50 F—Fatal—PI—Personal Injuries—PD—Property Damage.

10–53 Give location.

10–54 Give location.

10–55 Give location.

10–56 Give location.

10–57 Give location.

10–58 Can be used to assist funeral procession, highway repairs, etc.

10–60 Give location or area.

10–62 Use when inquiring for, or furnishing, reply to a previous message. Refer to previous number, if any.

10–63 Used to inform a vehicle to park and write down the forthcoming radio message—the officer will not advise the station to "go-ahead" until he is ready to copy.

10–64 Used when the message is not to be relayed by radio but must be delivered to someone in person or by telephone —may require a message in duplicate.

10–65 Used by state nets to obtain the next message number to be assigned.

10–67 Used to capture the circuit and to indicate all units and stations are to copy.

10–68 Used for "attempt-to-locate" messages, etc.

10–69 To inquire if, or state that, a message has been received.

10–70 Give location.

10–73 Used in Forestry Service when smoke has been observed. Give location or coordinates.

10–75 "10–75, 11?" "10–4, 10–75, #11."

10–76 "99 10–76 Jonesville 10–25 #2. 10–77 1600."

10–77 See 10–76 above.

10–82   Used by traveling personnel to request a station to obtain lodging reservations. The station should confirm after reservations have been made.

10–84   To request general information on an intention, or as a specific inquiry regarding a previous request. ("Get with it if you're going to do it.")

10–85   "#2 10–85. 10–77 1630."

10–88   Used to make certain a person is available for a station to station call, where he is at the moment.

10–90   Give location.

10–93   To set up blockade in connection with a crime—to execute an existing blockade plan, or set up a blockade as the situation may require.

10–96   To alert an officer he is dealing with a mental case.

10–98   Follow by detailed information as soon as it becomes available.

10–99   To alert an officer he is dealing with a person who is wanted or who may be driving a stolen vehicle without alarming the suspect.

Phonetic Alphabet [11]

The phonetic alphabet should be used for spelling out unusual names of persons and locations. The names used after each letter have been found to be the most understandable over the air. They should always be given as "A"–Adam, "B"–Boy.... never "A" as in Adam or "B" as for boy, etc. The alphabet is easily memorized.

Standard Alphabet

A	Adam	N	Nora
B	Boy	O	Ocean
C	Charles	P	Paul
D	David	Q	Queen
E	Edward	R	Robert
F	Frank	S	Sam
G	George	T	Tom
H	Henry	U	Union
I	Ida	V	Victor
J	John	W	William
K	King	X	X-ray
L	Lincoln	Y	Young
M	Mary	Z	Zebra

[11] The Associated Public-Safety Communications Officers, Inc., *The Public Safety Communications Standard Operating Procedure Manual.*

Radio Spectrum Limitations

All of the foregoing developments, as well as a more complete use of existing police radio communication facilities, are contingent upon a release from the straight-jacket of radio spectrum limitations. The radio frequency spectrum has finite limits and it is today in a state of crowded congestion.

A recent survey showed that the land mobile services, exclusive of common carrier units, had grown from 60,496 licensed transmitters to over 2,000,000 in 1963.[12] The public safety services accounted for over 490,000 of these transmitters. The necessity for the regulation of this new communications media led to the early passage of legislature at the federal level.

The first recognition of wireless telegraphy in the laws of the United States was the passage of the Ship Act of June 24, 1910 (36 Stat.L., 629), which was made effective as of July 1, 1911. This regulation was directed solely toward better protection of life at sea; it required the installation of wireless equipment on every passenger vessel carrying fifty or more persons, including passengers and crew. Limitations of wireless transmission at that time are reflected in the provisions of the act, which required that the apparatus used should be capable of transmitting or receiving intelligence over a distance of at least one hundred miles. Subsequently, on August 13, 1912, an additional act was passed by Congress dealing with radio apparatus on merchant vessels.

No further legislative action of importance was taken until the passage of a bill, which was approved by the President on February 23, 1927, creating the Federal Radio Commission. The Commission was to possess federal credentials as the original radio licensing authority with the power for radio frequency channel assignments. In June, 1934, a Communications Act was passed abolishing the Federal Radio Commission and transferring its records and functions to the Federal Communications Commission, together with all the duties, powers and functions of the Interstate Commerce Commission relating to the operation of telegraph lines. The Radio Act of 1927, in addition to creating the Federal Communications Commission, codified into an established body of law certain measures for the regulation of radio communication.

Thus, by act of Congress, the licensing of radio transmitters and the allocation of radio frequency channels is a responsibility of the Federal Communications Commission. As a corollary, it has the

[12] Weisz, William J., *The Frequency Congestion Problem, THE APCO BULLETIN*, April 1965.

inherent responsibility or resolving the dilemma of radio spectrum congestion. The Commission is fully aware of the problem in all of its dimensions, and has performed yeoman service to the communications field in policing the airways. Reinforced by further refinements in radio transmission equipment, the police look forward to solutions to the radio spectrum problem which will permit them to harness and put to work the more sophisticated communications equipment that is now being made available.

Consolidation of Police Communication Facilities

One approach to the radio spectrum problem is a reduction in the demand for radio frequency channels. This development is occurring in an increasing number of jurisdictions as a collateral result of merging police operations on an area basis. In this connection, five administrative alternatives to the conventional police department have appeared on the scene. As indicated previously, they are:

1. The federated police system.
2. The metropolitan police authority.
3. Integrated police and fire services.
4. Contract law enforcement.
5. City-County consolidation.

As a part of professional growth in the American police field, the consolidation of merger of police operations on an area basis can be expected to continue on an accelerated scale. All the evidence points in that direction. The taxpayer and his representatives in local government are becoming more and more aware of the reduction in public expenditures that result from curtailing the duplication of facilities through the merger and consolidation.

The merger brings professionally trained police personnel to the job who are in a position to deliver unbiased, non-partisan service to the people and who are well equipped and trained in every respect. Equally important, the merger *fosters the development of centralized police communications* systems, thus reducing the demands placed upon a limited radio frequency spectrum.

The Police and the Computer Sciences

The police are now at the threshold of a new era in which professional gains are beginning to dwarf even the fantastic achievements of the past quarter century in this field. The appearance of the computer and its related technology promises a new renaissance in police affairs of major proportions. Through the communication channels of the telephone, radio and the teletypewriter, it brings police departments, regardless of size, into virtually instantaneous contact with unlimited resources, in terms of information management, and on a state-wide and national basis.

Electronic Data Processing and the Centralization of Police Records and Communications at the State Level. Police problems tend to become complex in proportion to the extent that they are understood. As their complexity is recognized, the greater the need for thinking in depth and for a more scientific approach to their solution. As previously indicated, this involves the presence of adequate data, the processing of these data and the production of administrative reports and analyses upon which management and operational decisions can be intelligently made.

The complexity of police problems and the volume of data to be considered are now reaching the point where the human factor is being challenged and recognition must now be given to the gear of technology. It is now apparent that developments in electronic data processing will have far-reaching consequences in the American police field. The fantastic ability of EDP to handle data invites police administrators to extend their vision concerning its potential usefulness in law enforcement operations. It is conceded that it is in the area of management decision-making that this new tool will have a major impact upon the reach of the police executive and his commanding officers.

Depending on the number of variables present, many decision processes are too difficult for man to execute efficiently because they require that he handle more information than he is mentally equipped to accommodate in a reasonable time. The International Association of Chiefs of Police recently sponsored a study of police manpower distribution in which the computer effectively demonstrated its capabilities in the solution of a complex police problem.[13]

In another area of police interest, electronic data processing promises major advances in electronic files that will hold vast volumes of data. Looking into the crystal ball, the conventional storage of police records in filing cabinets may be exposed to a considerable degree of modification. Manufacturers are now offering equipment that will store in the order of a billion characters of data with access to any set of characters in seconds. In the foreseeable future, almost infinite storage capacity will be available with infinitesimal access time and at sharply decreasing cost.

---

[13] Smith, R. Dean, *Computer Applications in Police Manpower Distribution*, Field Service Division, International Association of Chiefs of Police, February 1961.

This technological capability of storing great volumes of data with fast recall suggests the possibility of still further advances in the centralization of police records administration. In every state at the present time, law enforcement agencies frequently maintain parallel files containing data about the same persons and the same property. Usually, none of these files contain complete information although such central agencies as the State Bureau of Criminal Records and Identification have made strong progress in this direction.

Today, the volumes of data are exceeding the capacity of any suitable information storage and retrieval technique. It is anticipated, however, that electronic data processing will soon make available on a technologically feasible and acceptable cost basis, files of sufficient capacity and magnitude to centralize police records operations on a state-wide basis. This may serve to sharply reduce the scale of the conventional police records system, with a corresponding reduction in local costs. The larger departments may prefer to have supplementary computing and storage equipment, but this would not limit their participation in the system. In the presence of a centralized records facility with virtually unlimited storage capability and fast retrieval of information, it is conceivable that the conventional records system, as such, in local police agencies may undergo considerable change and modification.

The California Police Computer System

California recently began exploratory work in this general direction. In January of 1963, officials representing all levels of law enforcement met in Santa Monica to consider plans for the automation of police records data. The moving force behind the conference was a recognition of the need for a new approach to information control. A resolution was passed recommending that immediate attention be given to the improvement of inter-agency communications facilities as a necessary forerunner to the establishment of an integrated electronic information processing system.[14]

The conference proposed that "information management" be given top priority on a state-wide basis. Among the advantages of a computer-based records and communication system would be rapid access to all outstanding criminal wants, complete warrant information and description of stolen property. It was agreed that the potential benefits of modern storage, processing and retrieval are such that failure to fully explore this concept would be inexcusable in view of

[14] Hearle, Edward F. R., *Can Electronic Data Processing Be Applied to All Police Agencies?*, Logistics Department, The Rand Corporation, Santa Monica, California, *The Police Chief*, February 1962.

its wide use and acceptance in major government agencies, business and industry. An Electronic Data Processing Advisory Committee headed by Director Edward V. Comber of the San Francisco Police Department was appointed to undertake a positive study of the proposal.

It was the general concensus of opinion among those attending the conference that the major problems in law enforcement records and communications are connected with field operations. The patrol officers of the individual city police departments, county sheriff's offices, and California Highway Patrol, require information on wants for specific persons, both criminal and non-criminal; information on stolen vehicles; warrants for the arrest of traffic violators and more serious offenders; identification data for suspicious automobiles and persons encountered in the field; descriptions of stolen property; and records of known criminals. Whenever an officer stops someone on the street and has reason to suspect this person should be detained, he radios his central office for a record check.[15]

As in other parts of the country, the central records and identification units in most police departments and sheriff's offices utilize completely manual systems with inherent time delays and inaccuracies. These manual systems can no longer cope with the rapidly increasing size of files and volume of requests. These are problems that cannot be solved by individual departments alone.

The most severe of these problems is the requirement for rapid information flow from jurisdiction to jurisdiction throughout the state. At the present time, an officer from a small community has to make four separate phone calls to check out a single suspect. He must contact the county sheriff, the Los Angeles Police Department, the State Department of Justice, and the California Highway Patrol. Even then, he is not assured of complete, up-to-date information because of the time lag in processing reports of new offenses, records of stolen property, and wants and warrants.

At present, there is a state-wide teletype system connecting the major law enforcement agencies. There are also microwave radio nets. Unfortunately, the present capacity of these systems is being exceeded by communications traffic demands. For example, despite special efforts to limit the types of messages transmitted through the state teletype system, the traffic increased 39% between 1955 and 1961. This is due to a major increase in the reports of crime throughout the state. Felony offenses, for example, increased 86% in that six-year period. Clearly, this tremendous information problem must be solved, both within the individual departments and on a state-wide basis.

---

15 *System Development Magazine*, Vol. 6, No. 2, February 1963, p. 4.

In outlining operational needs, the group discussed three general categories of problems. First priority was assigned to the field check described above. This is clearly an on-line operation with immediate response time needs.

The second group of problems concerns the follow-up investigator. He is interested in the crime reports themselves; detailed criminal records and arrest reports; modus operandi information; stolen property data; biographical data; corrections, parole and probation data; and a more detailed version of the information required by the field officer.

The third category of problems deals with the command and management functions of the individual jurisdictions, and the statutory requirements for local reporting to the state government. Eleven different types of reports are required by law to be sent from the local jurisdiction to the California State Department of Justice. These cover subjects ranging from motor vehicle accidents and crimes to reports of pawned property. They total hundreds of thousands per month. For the local departments, statistical summary reports of crimes, traffic loads, and distributions provide the commander with information on which he can base deployment decisions and with which he can monitor the effectiveness of his forces.

From their discussion of operational needs, the group concluded that: "Law enforcement can no longer efficiently operate under the present methods of information handling. Communications facilities are inadequate and prevent proper operation under present methods; improvement by means of a centralized electronic data processing system is essential. The problem is state-wide and the complete cooperation of all agencies—city, county and state—is necessary."

The California Department of Justice aided by the Lockheed Missiles establishment drew the blueprints for a state-wide criminal justice information system involving the police, sheriffs, prosecutors, courts, probation, corrections and parole agencies.

The California information system represents a federation of organizational computer centers. The system makes use of computers belonging to the various agencies involved in the administration of criminal justice. The system is coordinated by the state's central information center which serves as a central electronic index and directory of information stored in the files of the participating computer centers, functioning as a switching facility.

Integrated into the system is an RCA computer operated by the State Bureau of Criminal Identification and Investigation, within the California Department of Justice. Current information storage included a firearms file with over 2.6 million records of concealable weapons; daily inquiries—100; law enforcement arrest statistics, including arrests and dispositions—4,000 inquiries per week; narcotic prescriptions by doctor, quantity, patient, type—30,000 inquiries per month.[16]

Also included in the California system is IBM equipment operated by the California Highway Patrol, which provides a rapid communications system for recording and disseminating information on stolen and wanted vehicles. Referred to as the Automatic State-wide Auto Theft Inquiry System, the IBM installation automatically records data fed to it from any of thirty-six terminal locations. These include eight California Highway Patrol offices, twenty-four police departments in California, and four Nevada police departments, serving all together more than 200 police agencies.

To obtain information stored in the computer, a local law enforcement agency simply queries the computer by teletypewriter. Using a coded format, the license or vehicle identification is typed on a keyboard into the terminal equipment; *within one second, the computer responds with all the information on file.*

The New York State Identification and Intelligence System. The development of this sophisticated system grew out of the notorious "Appalachian Meeting" in November 1957, attended by more than 100 members of the nation's organized crime hierarchy. Information was disorganized and inaccessible. Even two years after the investigation began, all of the records on these criminals had not been brought together for study and evaluation. The experience accented the need for a functional criminal justice information system.

On June 14, 1965, Governor Rockefeller signed the bill creating the New York State Identification and Intelligence System. The system is authorized to collect, coordinate, store, process, retrieve and disseminate information concerning the investigation and prosecution of crime, and the general administration of criminal justice. It is designed to bring to some 3,600 agencies of criminal justice—the police, prosecutors, courts, probation, corrections and parole—the miracle of computer science and technology. This split-second access to virtually unlimited information resources challenges the imagination.

A number of local computer installations have been developed by the police, including Alameda County, California; Los Angeles, County, California; Boston, Massachusetts; Chicago, Illinois; Detroit, Michigan; Kansas City, Missouri; Los Angeles, California; New

---

16 Germann, A. C.; Day, Frank D.; and Gallati, Robert J., *Introduction to Law Enforcement and Criminal Justice*, revised twelfth printing, Charles C. Thomas, Publisher, Springfield, Illinois, 1970, p. 283.

York City, New York; Philadelphia, Pennsylvania; and St. Louis, Missouri.

An excellent example of a local police computer installation is the one in St. Louis, where computer operations are quite extensive and also serve law enforcement agencies in the surrounding area. The storage file contains some 900,000 registration records for Missouri drivers who live in St. Louis and the surrounding three-county area. District police stations can update their files instantaneously, and receive current warrant status on wanted persons, together with criminal histories, through stored arrest information data.

The St. Louis Police Department also uses the computer as a tool of management in the distribution of the patrol force. This is done through the projection of crime rates by crime classification, time and geographical location. The commanding officer coming on duty is favored with current information on which he can deploy the force in accordance with the projected need. Plans are under way for the production of maps for use by the patrol force through a computer-plotter technique.

It is to be noted that in most instances, state and local police computer installations are police-based and police-oriented. In some cases, computer installations are designed on a more comprehensive scale to serve the entire field of criminal justice administration, including the police, prosecutor, courts, probation, corrections and parole.

State and local police computer installations already operational provide the foundation for a nation-wide criminal information system. Always pacing the field, the Federal Bureau of Investigation has mounted a computer-based National Crime Information Center at FBI Headquarters in Washington, D. C.

The National Crime Information Center

A new and powerful weapon was conceived for law and order when, in September 1965, the Federal Bureau of Investigation embarked on the development of a national electronic information system to be known as the National Crime Information Center.

The planners visualized an ultimate information network encompassing the entire United States which will make available to each law enforcement agency, *in a matter of seconds,* the facilities of a criminal information file national in scope. No longer will the mobility of today's criminal element afford a sanctuary, even temporarily, as information will be readily available to any participant in the system concerning any criminal or criminal act regardless of geographic boundary.

The logical development of electronic information systems proceeds from local metropolitan computer installations to state-wide systems and then to a national system.   In effect, each succeeding system affords greater geographical coverage.   Mr. Hoover stated:[17]

It is important to avoid any concept that a national information system eliminates the need for systems of lesser geographical scope—metropolitan and state-wide systems must develop to serve local needs which could not be possibly met by any national system.   The ultimate nation-wide information network will not be achieved until such systems develop in each state and the larger metropolitan centers.

As a major step to establishing a nation-wide system, the FBI contracted with the Institute for Telecommunications Sciences and Aeronomy, Environmental Science Services Administration, Department of Commerce, to survey all existing telecommunications networks throughout the United States and to recommend a network that would best support a nation-wide computerized system.

On the operational side, the central computer equipment in Washington, D. C., is capable of furnishing needed information concerning crime and criminals in a matter of seconds, so that the officer on the street has a wealth of information at his command at all times. The individual patrolman in the field and the detective as well, can now make inquiry of stored police information and get a "real time," i. e., up-to-the-minute, answer *in a matter of seconds.*

Information Stored.   Records data in storage at the National Crime Information Center include stolen vehicles, vehicles used in the commission of felonies, stolen engines and transmissions, stolen or missing license plates when all plates issued for a specific vehicle are missing, stolen guns, and other items of stolen property which are serially identifiable, and wanted persons.   The latter category includes all Federal fugitives and individuals wanted on local felony or misdemeanor charges, provided the municipality or state involved will extradite from any point in the United States.

The system is operational 7 days a week and 22 hours a day with limited down time.   Transactions with the NCIC computer, entries and inquiries are approaching 10,000 a day.   This rate, too, is expected to increase materially as operational procedures are developed by NCIC terminals to accommodate larger volumes of inquiries from the patrol cars and officers on the street.   It should be noted that the latter usage is where the real potential of the system lies, that of making the vast

[17] Hoover, J. Edgar, A National Crime Information Center, *FBI Enforcement Bulletin,* May, 1966.

index of information immediately available to the police officer at the scene.

Response times by the NCIC computer to date have more than exceeded expectations. Responses are averaging less than 15 seconds from the time the last character of the incoming message is received until the first character of the reply is on the way back to the transmitting terminal. Actual incidents have demonstrated that an inquiry from the street by an officer over radio or telephone to a dispatcher at an NCIC terminal can be answered back to the street in 90 seconds.

As an illustration of the effectiveness of the system, the following typical cases have been selected. As was anticipated, highly mobile fugitives wanted in one state are "brushing" with the law in other states. In most instances, police agencies in remote states are arresting these individuals for new violations, and through NCIC the agencies obtain immediate information on warrants outstanding in other states. The fugitives are then held for extradition.

In April of 1967, the New Orleans Police Department made inquiry on a number of weapons which had been recovered in connection with a narcotics violation arrest. The NCIC identified three of the weapons as having been reported stolen from Louisiana, Texas and the U. S. Marine Corps.

In June 1967, when the Washington, D. C. Metropolitan Police arrested a woman on an assault charge, they recovered a .22 caliber revolver. A check of NCIC resulted in information that the weapon had been taken in the burglary of a sports store in Maryland on May 1, 1964. As a result of this arrest, the burglary case in Maryland was re-opened and new suspects developed.

The NCIC stolen vehicle file has been successful in identifying stolen motor vehicles moving interstate and intrastate. In connection with a car theft ring between New York City and Knoxville, Tennessee, the NCIC system immediately identified 14 of 23 suspect vehicles as stolen.

Another example of the use of the system occurred in San Antonio, Texas, in April 1967. An automobile dealer in that city, after completing some service on a 1966 Pontiac, called the FBI office, stating that he was suspicious as to the status of the car. An immediate check through the Texas Department of Public Safety to the NCIC identified the vehicle as being registered in Florida, and as having been stolen in Atlanta, Georgia, on November 17, 1966.

In a 1969 case, early one morning 3 pieces of portable radio communication equipment were stolen from a National Park Service ranger station in Yellowstone National Park. Unidentified radio conversations were heard during the morning by various rangers and subsequently 3 persons in possession of these radios were arrested by the rangers for theft of government property. NCIC inquiry on the 1959 Volkswagen in which the 3 persons were traveling revealed it was stolen 2 days before in Merced, California. These persons were confronted with appropriate judicial action.

In February 1969, an inquiry to NCIC through the City of Miami Department of Communications Control terminal concerning a suspicious man observed in a bus depot revealed he was wanted by the FBI in Georgia for desertion from the military. Another inquiry through this terminal on a different man who was arrested for disorderly conduct revealed he was wanted by the Connecticut State Police for larceny. It was this kind of efficient utilization of the system that resulted in this control terminal receiving 21 hits during the first 3½ days of February. The Police Department at Albuquerque, New Mexico, reported that 23% of all stolen car recoveries in 1968 were attributed to hits on their local computerized information system through NCIC.

A man came to the attention of the FBI at Mobile, Alabama, when it was learned he had opened an account at several banks in that city. NCIC inquiry revealed he was wanted by a Sheriff for forgery. The Mobile Police Department was alerted and subsequently, word was received that the man was at a drive-in window of another local bank. On arrival of the Mobile Police, the fugitive hurriedly departed in a 1968 Mercury. Officers, however, quickly apprehended him a block away. Inquiry of NCIC about the Mercury resulted in information that it had been stolen 2 months before in Arkansas.

The Kansas City Police Department reported that it made 80 hits on all files in January of 1969, with 55% of these hits against the Wanted Persons File. One interesting hit involved the arrest of a man in connection with a stolen car investigation with a resulting NCIC check revealing he was a fugitive from Ogden, Utah, where a warrant was outstanding for him on a charge of armed robbery.

During the first three months of 1969, four new central control terminals were added to the NCIC system—Arkansas State Police, Delaware State Police, the Police Department of Dallas, Texas, and the Police Department of Pittsburgh, Pennsylvania.

As of March 1, 1969, the records on file in the computerized National Crime Information Center totaled—823,904, with the breakdown showing 272,788 vehicles, 83,357 license plates, 31,864 wanted persons, 186,667 stolen or missing guns, 150,498 articles and 98,730 securities.

A New Mexico State Trooper observed two men asleep in a car parked alongside the highway near Gallup. He asked for their names and then made a routine check through his headquarters in Santa Fe to the NCIC. In a matter of seconds, the officer received back the information that the two men were suspects in the slaying of four Cincinnati women during a hold-up the week before.

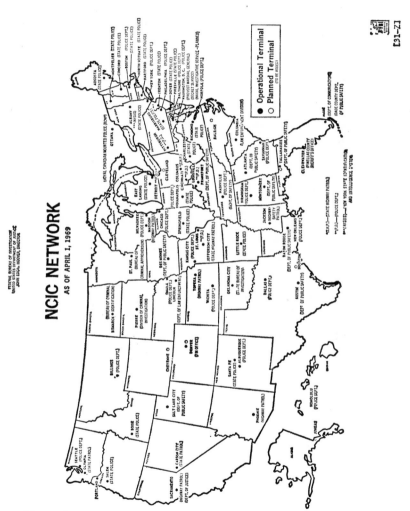

Figure 1 reproduced through the courtesy of the Federal Bureau of Investigation.

The Ultimate User. The ultimate user of the system is the police officer on the street—out on patrol in the field. The objective of the total installation is to expedite case solutions and to increase the risk of detection for the criminal offender. This was well illustrated in the actions of an alert Maryland State Police officer. While on patrol on the Maryland highway, the officer noticed a vehicle with an out-of-state license parked on the shoulder of the highway. Within a mile, the officer observed two youths walking along the highway.

The officer made an inquiry on the car of NCIC through his car radio to Maryland State Police Headquarters. He then approached the two youths and questioned them concerning their identity and reasons for being in the area. While questioning the youths, he received a radio reply from NCIC identifying the vehicle as a stolen car, giving a complete description of the car and the date of theft.

The elapsed time from his initial radio inquiry to receipt of the message was 3 minutes. The officer advised that the radio reply on the stolen car was heard by the youths, and from their reaction it was obvious that they were possibly involved. The officer took the boys to the Maryland State Police Troop Headquarters, where they immediately confessed the theft.

It is of interest to note that communications costs from the NCIC computer to the agency's terminal instrument is borne by the FBI. Thus, the national communications network is federally funded on a continuing basis.

The significance of these portentous developments stirs the imagination, bringing as it does to the individual police officer out on the street the total resources of a national criminal data bank—*and in a matter of seconds!* Thus it is, the march of time in the American police services is the march toward professionalization as police administration recognizes the dimension of its problems and moves forward in a scientific approach to their solution.

Closely associated with the subject matter of this Chapter—*Improvement of Apprehension Capability*—is all the material between the covers of this book, but the following chapter—*The Tactical Unit* or *Mobile Task Force,* is of particular importance.

Chapter 12

THE TACTICAL UNIT

O PERATIONS constitute the field work of a police organization and they should be directed toward securing maximum efficiency with economy of resources in terms of money and effort. The line power of a police organization finds expression in two types of field operations. The first is General Operations, and these are concerned with meeting the normal daily problems associated with crime, vice, traffic, and the miscellaneous activities which are commonly referred to in police circles as general duties. Organization and procedure for achieving the objectives of General Operations have been set forth in preceding chapters. They concern the ordinary stable disposition of personnel resources and equipment in the line.

With trained men, properly distributed and under his central control, the Chief of Operations can address the striking power of the organization in an orderly and effective manner to the routine problems associated with the General Operations of the department. The degree of efficiency with which he achieves this end will determine in large measure the volume of Special Operations and the special assignment of manpower which this entails. However, even in the most efficiently organized and managed police departments, occasions constantly arise requiring special operational planning and execution.

Special Operations

Special operations are limited to the execution of temporary plans for the attack upon specific problems and emerging situations which arise at particular or irregular intervals. They are concerned with the execution of short-term plans designed to cope with critical situations of a temporary nature in order to permit an overwhelming concentration of striking power at a particular time and place to meet a specific problem. In a small department, such situations may develop only a few times during a month; their frequency increases with the increase in the population of a community, and it is influenced also by the composition of the population, sociological and economic characteristics of the community, and all other factors which condition social organization. In an average city of from 100,000 to 200,000 population, these operational crises may follow in comparatively rapid succession during a twenty-four hour period, and require almost continuous provision for special deployment of manpower and equipment. Those departments where proper attention is given to special operational planning and

365

execution can meet these crises as they arise without endangering the General Operations.

Routine duties occupy most of the time of police officers, and when these duties are carefully planned and the personnel properly supervised, they can be discharged with a considerable degree of success. There are times, however, when these daily activities must be interrupted, either briefly or for a long period, for the purpose of concentrating upon some problem which demands immediate action. Criminal emergencies, disasters, conflagrations, riots, mob situations, strikes and many other types of events occur when they are least expected.

Accordingly, plans must be prepared in advance so that the line power resources of the department can be brought into play with dispatch at the time and the place where they are needed. A part of the force or the entire organization may be used to cope with the problem. Parades, meetings where there is a possibility of friction or uprising, visits by the President of the United States or other important personages, athletic events, riots, strikes, fires, disasters of any type, or any unusual or extensive criminal activity or unusual traffic or vice conditions present operational difficulties which require special planning and direction. Increased criminal activities on the part of one or more persons may lead to an emergency situation, which continues until they are apprehended. As a result of their activity, there is created during the hours and in the areas in which they operate a need for police service out of proportion to the year-around average.

These special situations require an orderly diversion of the striking power of the department in sufficient amount to bring about liquidation of the problem. Therefore, implementing the special plans of the Chief of Operations, there must exist and be available at all times a Tactical Unit or Mobile Task Force representing the mobile power of the department which can be concentrated in any quarter of the city and at whatever hour or hours the circumstances may dictate. This Tactical Unit is not to be regarded as a reserve force held at headquarters waiting for something to happen, although headquarters may be its base of operations.

Members of the Tactical Unit are under normal conditions patroling beats, or carrying out the routine work of their regular positions in the detective, traffic or other divisions, but subject to mobilization at a moment's notice for assignment on a special tactical operation. The number of men actually engaged in a tactical operation at any one time may and will vary from one to a hundred or more, depending upon the nature of the problem. In the larger departments, the uninterrupted succession of emergencies may require the maintenance of one or more tactical units or mobile striking forces on a semi-permanent or permanent basis. The entire line strength of the organization may be involved, and in certain types of emergencies in the felony classification, police departments over a large area may be alerted into action where the perpetrator has escaped from the scene of his crime.

Strategy calls for audacity. Deployment of personnel on a tactical operation means a temporary reduction in the strength of beat patrol and other line units for the purpose of dynamic offensive tactics. A skeleton patrol will have to suffice until the objectives are achieved. Obviously, this is attended with some danger, but nevertheless it must be done in certain instances if the police are to fulfill their obligations. It is utterly impossible to assume that the police can solve all the problems presented to them by merely placing the men on beats; therefore, they know that a reasonable amount of ground may be lost while giving attention to one specific problem. By gradually clearing up one after another of these special situations they can, after a period of time, reduce the number of complaints that are received.

It is clear that the routine functions of the police must go on, but frequently this can be managed during limited periods with a comparatively few men where the power of the force is concentrated on some objective which requires immediate attention. The striking power of a police department is amplified in this manner to a degree altogether impossible by routine assignment of personnel. Tactical Unit personnel should be carefully selected on the basis of their personal qualities and performance records. The nature of the work may require moral courage, together with physical courage and endurance of a high order. This unit should be so organized and equipped that it can be moved rapidly from one point to another. Thus, its power may be felt at one place at one time, and then at a different place at another time, whenever this becomes necessary.

The operational pattern of the Tactical Unit is seldom the same on any two assignments, and will depend entirely upon the nature and dimensions of the emergency problem or situation toward which its attention is directed at the moment. Police emergencies classify into two major categories, as follows:

1. Man-made.
    a. Criminal emergencies.
    b. Traffic emergencies.
    c. Vice emergencies.
    d. Jail emergencies.
    e. Riot emergencies.
    f. Mob situations.

 g. Disorderly crowds.
 i. Industrial disorders.
 j. Prison outbreaks.
 k. Press emergency.
 l. Others.

2. Natural.
 a. Earthquake.
 b. Conflagration.
 c. Flood.
 d. Tornado.
 e. Others.

Criminal emergencies command the major share of the attention of the police in the conduct of Special Operations. The number and variety of situations in this category calling for the emergency concentration of police striking power cover the total range of the criminal spectrum.

In the approach to criminal emergencies, the Chief of Operations must have the facts concerning the character, extent, location and time of occurrence of crimes and other incidents requiring police action. With this information available, he can identify police hazards, isolate the particular elements requiring attention, and direct the energies of the force under his command toward a solution of the problems at hand. To combat property losses, for example, he would proceed systematically to determine the types of property subject to most frequent attack. The amount of loss serves as a measure of the relative severity of attacks against certain types of property. Filling stations and drug stores may be found at the moment to constitute more serious police hazards than any other commercial establishments.

Armed with pertinent data supplied by the Record Division concerning the factors (character, extent, location, time, etc.) which the problem involves, the Chief of Operations is in a position to launch programs to lower the crime rate. Effort may be directed at residence burglaries in one section of the community, at car thefts in another, at armed robberies during certain hours of the day, and at rooming-house burglaries during other hours. The particular groups or types of persons who are committing crimes are determined by analyses of the age, race, sex, residence and other characteristics of apprehended offenders. Modus Operandi analysis may establish at once the identity of the individual offender or the "mob" currently responsible for an epidemic of residence burglaries, or business house burglaries, armed robberies or automobile thefts.

A flood of worthless checks descending upon the merchants of the community or a series of sex crimes are of short duration and come to an abrupt end through intelligent special planning on the part of the Chief of Operations. Fluctuations in the need for police service may result from a series of safe burglaries, an unusual amount of car prowling, a sudden increase in the automobile accident rate, a series of robberies perpetrated against a certain class of retail establishments in a certain section of the community, a series of house prowls, or a number of brutal sex attacks.

As in General Operations, the information obtained from the Records Division, maps, and field studies will give the Chief of Operations the facts upon which he can base his plans for Special Operations. He should prepare them according to tested combat principles, and extraordinary care should be exercised to see that the proper person is assigned to put the plan into effect. Following each operation, plans should be checked for defects which have been discovered during the operation and these in turn should be corrected before the plan is filed for future use. Over-preparation as well as too little preparation should be noted and the necessary allowances or additions should be placed in the revised edition.

The data produced by the records division of the Los Angeles Police Department on one occasion revealed that a large number of banks were being held up and further, that these criminal attacks were occurring in a certain area of the city and during a certain period of the day. Therefore, a part of the task was already complete. The tactician knew what type of offense he was going to attack, and he knew the time and area in which he was to operate. It was then necessary to determine how to place the members of the Tactical Unit so that they would be most effective. Each bank where the men were to be located was studied so that he could determine how to place them in order to achieve the purpose of the plan.

These field visits took him to every bank that was to be protected. He studied the surrounding area at each location as a means of anticipating where confederates might be concealed and to prevent the escape of the criminals in the event they happened to get away from the banks and from the officers. Each bank location and its immediate surroundings presented a separate and distinct tactical problem. In addition to other considerations, precautions were necessary in placing the men so that in the event of gunfire (which ensued three days later) bullets from police revolvers would not endanger the lives of innocent people in that particular area.

Similarly, in the attack upon room thieves in that city during the same period, statistics revealed that rooming house burglars constituted a high-frequency hazard and therefore the tactician devoted his attention to that problem. But mere statistical data were not enough. It did show that most of the cheap rooming houses in the downtown area were being attacked and it further uncovered the information that most of the thievery was being committed during the noon hour.

This, of course, was valuable information, but before the plan could be formally drafted it was necessary for the tactician and his assistants to visit every rooming house in which special details were to be placed so that officers could observe without being observed and so that they might be comfortable during the period of observation as far as circumstances would permit. Furthermore, it was necessary to arrange matters so that the offender would have no opportunity to escape once the officers closed in to arrest him. Again, the lives of innocent persons had to be considered because in all activities against criminals there is likely to be gun play. The duty of the tactician here is to provide all the protection that he can for innocent persons in the event shooting occurs. On this particular occasion, the Tactical Unit was detailed for the noon hour only, and 300 men were used in that special operation, which resulted in the apprehension of the leader and his three confederates, identification of "fences" and the recovery of a large amount of stolen property.

In one instance where bungalow burglars operated over a period of a year, investigators were able to determine that two separate organized groups were at work by virtue of the fact that in the operations of one gang, the burglars invariably looked behind the frames of pictures hanging on the wall. This slight difference in the modus operandi made it possible to concentrate the tactical force in a very small area in terminating the operations of one gang. The other required a wide field of operation.

In other cases it may take a considerable force to capture an elusive burglar or hold-up man. The Los Angeles operation involving 300 men has been previously mentioned. During one season in the city of Detroit, two youngsters held up a large number of filling stations. It was necessary to deploy a Tactical Unit for a considerable period before these two young men were finally liquidated. The time of nearly 200 men was involved for almost a month before this case was closed. On the other hand, plans that enable escape routes from the scene of a crime to be quickly blockaded may suffice to solve a hold-up in a few minutes. Bank robberies and payroll robberies justify a more complete and elaborate blockade plan because of their seriousness and because this type of hold-up more usually "cases" in advance the premises to be attacked.

Certain banks, businesses and other establishments of high hazard in the community present unusual opportunities for criminal attack. They should be connected with police headquarters by direct alarm circuits. In addition it is a responsibility of the Chief of Operations to work out detailed plans in advance so that when the report is received that a robbery or other serious crime is in progress or has been committed, the radio dispatcher will know exactly how to proceed in assigning the force effectively and safely. The development of such plans requires a careful survey of the locale, the building plan, the probable point of attack by criminals, and the most likely exits. Search should be made for available cover which will afford maximum safety to the officers and a commanding view of the situation.

In 1969, the New York City Police Department placed in operation an adjunct to the Tactical Patrol Force—the Plainclothes Task Force, consisting of ninety patrolmen operating in plain or civilian clothes in the boroughs of Manhattan, Brooklyn, the Bronx and Queens between 6:00 P.M., and 2:00 A.M., for the purpose of preventing street crimes. Operating both on foot and in unmarked cars, and in disguises as well as street clothes, the unit arrested 68 persons in Manhattan, 25 in Brooklyn, 14 in the Bronx and 6 in Queens in its first week of operation. Most of the arrests made by the plainclothes unit were for serious crimes. Thirty-four were for grand larceny from the person, effected through the use of patrolmen in disguises and appearing to be helpless; they became victims of pickpockets and lush workers. In addition, there were 14 arrests for robbery, 5 for burglary, 3 each for rape, reckless endangerment and possession of dangerous weapons, 2 each for felonious assault and grand larceny of auto, and 1 for criminal tampering. There were 46 arrests for misdemeanors, including the possession of stolen property, possession of burglary tools and dangerous instruments.

Without training, plans are impotent. Without both plans and training, a police department courts disaster. It is a function of police administration to set up training programs for officers in the department and to formulate plans of operation in advance for all types of combat emergencies in order that men may be prepared to meet every situation successfully. This is especially true of the Tactical Unit. Otherwise, there may be needless sacrifice of personnel and discredit reflected on administration because of the lack of preparation. Merely to dispatch a squad or a company of men to the scene of an emergency is to risk the lives of these men and at the same time expose the department to ridicule.

Similarly, plans must be worked out in advance of a possible jail emergency. Police headquarters itself may also be the point of attack, as has been amply demonstrated during the past few years. An attempt may be made to liberate prisoners, or to take custody of them for the purpose of lynching. Police buildings should be designed to withstand such attack, and plans should be developed for assignments and operations in the event of attack. Most police headquarters buildings are far from ideal in this respect and a premium is therefore placed upon preparation in advance for any emergency situation. The importance of advance preparation for all police emergencies cannot be over-emphasized. During the emergency there is no time to develop elaborate plans of action. The police are under a heavy stress at the moment and should be ready for immediate action.

In order to forestall or meet such attack, safeguard firearms, departmental equipment and records, and to prevent the escape of prisoners, it is necessary to maintain maximum headquarters security at all times in all department buildings and offices. Where exterior doors, including roof access points are equipped with an alarm system wired directly to the desk, such alarm system should be tested at least once each month and the desk officer should make an entry on the Police Bulletin of the results of such test. Areas within department buildings which are open to the public should be separated from areas which are designated for the exclusive use of departmental personnel. Public access must be limited to those areas in which police business with the public is normally conducted. Areas ordinarily used only by departmental personnel are to be considered restricted areas to which unauthorized public access is strictly prohibited.

In the field of traffic control, the Chief of Operations will determine through studies made by the traffic unit the engineering, educational or enforcement activities that will solve a particular problem. Analysis of an abnormal rise in the traffic accident rate along a certain thoroughfare may indicate that moving violations are the major contributing cause. The situation may assume emergency proportions and warrant the operation of a Tactical Unit during the time and at the location where these violations are occurring. Supplementing the work of the patrol force by application of intensive enforcement pressures on a selective basis, a concentration of striking power is effected and in this manner the causes contributory to increased accident rates are modified and the situation relieved. The fact must not be overlooked, however, that the results achieved by enforcement are temporary in nature, and that they must be supplemented by strenuous educational effort. With the total line power of the department at his disposal, the Chief of Operations is in a position to address to any traffic emergency, regardless of its nature, the type and strength of operation which the problem demands.

Riot and mob situations represent a direct assault upon the social order and in their threat to civil authority they present a serious challenge to the ability and striking power of police forces.   Thirty-four Americans died, more than one thousand others were wounded in the streets of Detroit and $2,000,000 in property damage was inflicted during Negro-white clashes in the week of June 20, 1943.   Their relatives were fighting and dying on battlefields thousands of miles away in a war for freedom, but the blood of these men and women on the home front was spilled in a senseless hysterical race riot.   Hate-ridden mobs streamed through the central business district, the nearby slums, and even City Hall Square.   They assaulted Negroes at will, derided policemen who were trying to restore a semblance of order and brought admissions from the Mayor that the situation was out of control.   Similar occurrences are a matter of record during recent years in East St. Louis, Chicago, Los Angeles, the Harlem section of New York, Beaumont and other communities throughout the country.   The Harlem riot of August, 1943, killed five, injured 307 including 53 policemen, and destroyed $5,000,-000 worth of property.[1]

More recently, the current movement in this country toward racial desegregation has on occasions without number confronted the police with acute tactical situations.   The reader is referred here in the text to J. E. Curry and Glen D. King, *Race Tensions and the Police,* Charles C. Thomas, 1962; this volume provides constructive suggestions for the handling of racial disorder and outlines preventive measures that may be undertaken.

Riots, mob situations, strikes and other forms of acute social unrest are unpredictable in advance so far as the hour and the scale of disorder are concerned.   On one recent occasion, a sailor became involved in an altercation with a naval patrol officer on the streets of one American city and a civilian came to his rescue.   A crowd gathered and before order could be restored a monumental riot was in progress.

The transformation of a crowd into a mob is an amazing sociological and psychological phenomenon.   A crowd is an assemblage of people. A disorderly crowd is an assemblage of people willing to be led into lawlessness but lacking courage and unity of purpose.   It is usually unorganized, hesitant, uncertain, and vacillating.   Within such assemblage there are usually three well-defined groups—a few determined leaders, many active participants, and a large number of spectators. The majority are spectators, who in the beginning are perfectly harmless. They are drawn to the scene of the disorders desiring excitement, and

---

[1] Alfred McClung Lee, "Race Riot," the Dryden Press, Inc., New York, 1943, p. 2.

hoping for a chance to witness a fight. During the crowd stage, there is much commotion and noise. If the police are present, they may be subjected to verbal abuse and other minor annoyances.

Under the stimulus of intense excitement and swayed by the efforts of agitators, a crowd may rapidly be transformed into a mob. The subtle change from confusion to unity, from the vacillating crowd to the determined mob may occur within a few minutes. A single successful act of violence on the part of a member of the crowd or unfortunate action by an untrained police officer may ignite the emotions and whet the appetite for disorder and destruction.[2] One of the primary responsibilities of the police is to insure that such a transformation does not take place, that crowds are dispersed while they still remain crowds. Once the transformation has taken place, the members of a mob can be brought to their senses only by an overwhelming demonstration of force or by actual use of that force.

Within every community there are potentialities for riot and mob situations, and no police official charged with responsibility for the administration of police affairs is worthy of his position who does not prepare well laid plans in advance for this form of tactical operation. Supplementing these plans, provision must be made for training in the strategy and tactics of riot control for every member of the organization, since a major riot or mob situation is likely to involve the total striking power of the department. The services of commanding officers in the United States Army and in the National Guard, who are usually available in nearby military installations, should be engaged as instructors in such a training program. Their training and their experience will prove indispensable to the success of police plans and operations in this phase of the departmental program. Ample provision must also be made at all times for riot control equipment.

A Tactical Unit composed of specially selected men, intensively trained, should be potentially available as the nucleus for this form of tactical operation. The amount of force necessary to overcome resistance in a specific situation depends on community respect for authority in general and on the amount and character of training the officers have had. The Northwest Mounted Police were so respected that one man could accomplish what would, in some other police forces, require several to do.

Similarly, the traditional performance of the Texas Rangers has captured widespread attention. It is reported that during the oil boom in West Texas a number of years ago, the Mayor of a community in

---

[2] Major Sterling A. Wood, "Riot Control by the National Guard," Military Service Publishing Company, Harrisburg, Pa., 1940, p. 5.

that area telephoned Headquarters of the Texas Rangers at Austin that disorder and riot prompted by a shooting affray had developed on such a scale that local authority was powerless to meet the situation and requested that a company of Rangers be sent immediately. Two hours later, one lone Ranger appeared in response to the Mayor's desperate call for assistance. The latter official stormed about his office and berated the stupidity of Headquarters for sending only one officer. But the Ranger inquired, "There's only one riot, isn't there?" Only one Ranger was needed to restore order on that Saturday evening in a West Texas boom-town. Ruffian, murderer, and thug had a wholesome respect, not for the personal strength of this lone officer, but for what he symbolized. They knew too well that disobedience of his orders would bring down upon them the determination and striking power of a force that never turned back from an assignment until the job was well done.[3]

Equally important as the plan of operation in this type of emergency is *planned prevention*. A professional attitude and professional knowledge on the part of the police and their commanding officers are fundamental. A good department staffed with officers who are professionals in their field will handle racial and other social tensions and will not allow conditions to develop which may lead to riot, mob situations and other forms of acute social disorder. The Chief of Operations should determine that the same kind of law enforcement is administered in minority group districts as among the majority groups. If the lines of information at the disposal of this official are functioning properly, emerging situations will be called to his attention at a time when the most effective work can be done. A properly organized police department is in a strategic position to become cognizant of tensions long before they become a matter of general knowledge in the community. Contact with disorder in its early stages is the best strategy. Conferences with minority group leaders and organizations is helpful in gaining their confidence and in overcoming their unfavorable attitude toward the police. The police can make suggestions to minority group leaders for the education and guidance of their respective groups, and can receive in return suggestions for the improvement of law enforcement work among the minority groups.

Inflammatory movements on the part of irresponsible members of a minority become susceptible to control through co-operation with the responsible leaders of such organizations. Confronted with an emerg-

---

[3] The famous Texas Rangers became an integral part of the Texas State Department of Public Safety in 1936, and in that organization the tradition of high level performance has been perpetuated. Under the leadership of Colonel Homer Garrison, Director, the Texas State Police System represents today one of the nation's most outstanding police organizations.

ing situation, consultation with the press by the Chief of Operations can lead to a constructive policy in the publication of news dealing with social tensions and promote cooperation with the police department. Similar contacts can also be made profitably with representatives of the minority press where there are such papers. A definite and constructive public relations policy is indispensable. A police department which is capable of developing a sound preventive program will be in the best possible position to handle a riot or mob situation, should its preventive efforts fail.

Police departments are usually so busy administering current business that they give little thought to the planning of police procedure for times of disaster or catastrophe, such as earthquakes, fires, floods, or tornadoes, or for times of grave social disturbance. They may function for years without ever being faced by the pressing problems which a great earthquake, fire or flood brings; and this tends to lull them into a false sense of security. But no community can be certain that it will not be the scene of the next disaster. And it is at just these times the police function assumes its greatest importance. Police departments have not yet learned the lesson which military men know well, namely, that effective operations in times of stress and danger require careful and detailed planning beforehand. Disconcerting, for example, is the number of earthquake disturbances that have occurred in the Northwest area since 1930, based on seismographic records. Who can tell us about the intensity of the next shock, to which the half million people of Seattle will be exposed? [4]

Although the great majority of earthquakes in the United States have been mild in nature, eleven of them were major disturbances of the earth's surface, including, one, the New Madrid, Missouri, earthquake of 1811–1812, which ranks as one of the twenty great earthquakes in recorded history. Although it did little damage, because of the unpopulated condition of the territory in which it occurred, it is alarming to speculate upon the tremendous social and economic losses it would have caused had it happened a century later. Three shocks of greatest intensity were felt during December 1811, and in January and February, 1812. Topographic changes occurred over an area of 30,000 to 50,000 square miles and the territory shaken was at least a million square miles in area. The disturbance was felt from Canada to New Orleans and from the head waters of the Missouri to the Atlantic. Over a wide area the ground moved in great rolls; great blocks of the earth were uplifted and others sunk; islands disappeared in the rivers and new lakes were

---

[4] V. A. Leonard, "Survey and Reorganization of the Seattle Police Department," 1945, p. 92.

formed.[5] Earthquakes are not unusual in the United States. As recently as 1948, Helena, Montana reported that it had experienced its 2,888th recorded tremblor since 1935![6]

It is just at such times—times of disaster or catastrophe—that the police function assumes its greatest importance. It is a major responsibility of the Chief of Operations to formulate a pre-disaster preparedness plan. It is inconceivable that the people of a city should be without this protection. The plan should, among other things, provide for the general police duties of maintaining order, protecting life and property, directing traffic and caring for the lost and found. The police are also expected to aid other officials, make preliminary surveys of the extent of the disaster, and cooperate with the Army and the National Guard if these agencies are called upon, and with the Red Cross. All these regular police duties assume unusual and difficult proportions under disaster conditions. Traffic control especially becomes difficult, because of the large number of people who seek to escape from the ruined area and the large number who seek to enter it, either from anxiety for the welfare of friends and relatives or out of mere curiosity.[7]

The protection of property from looting, and especially the guarding of banks and other places where funds and valuables are kept, are duties which the police are called upon immediately to assume. In disasters of major proportions, such as earthquakes or conflagrations, telephone systems and electric power supply sources may be paralyzed at a time when they are most needed. The Chief of Operations, cooperating with the Chief of Services, should make sure that provision is made for an independent auxiliary power supply for the police radio transmitter. Inventories should be made in advance of medical services, hospital facilities, nurses, doctors, ambulances, emergency communication facilities possessed by other organizations, and other facilities, including reserve manpower which may be called upon by the police in such major emergencies. A disaster plan should contain an organization chart with a schedule of duties clearly establishing lines of authority and describing the assignment of responsibilities to each of the community agencies, and to each of the units and divisions of the police department.[8]

---

[5] See Appendix E.

[6] H. N. Heck, "Earthquake History of the United States," U. S. Coast Geodetic Survey, Special Publication No. 49.

[7] See *Operational Manual For Disasters*, Police Department, City of New York, N. Y. 87 pp. 1962. This furnishes an excellent blueprint for pre-disaster police planning.

[8] V. A. Leonard, Police Communication Systems, University of California Press, 1938, Chapter X, *Police Communication Under Disaster Conditions*.

In disasters of major proportions, such as earthquakes or tornadoes, the telephone system may be paralyzed. In the San Francisco earthquake and fire of 1906, all but three of the telephone exchanges were burned and of the 50,000 telephones in operation before the fire, not one was in working order after the fire had been brought under control. Of 83,000 telephones, 1 toll and 19 local exchanges in Tokyo, an earthquake of major proportions destroyed 52,000 telephones, the 1 toll and 15 local exchanges, and the four exchanges not destroyed were put out of commission.

The destruction of power stations and power lines, or the shutting off of power in the devastated area in order to prevent fires and accidents, may cause the total failure of the police radio communications system. Thus, the provision of an auxiliary power supply for central station transmitters should be an indispensable feature of every police communications system. Patrol car mobile transmitters are, of course, operated by a power supply that is independent of any commercial source of electrical power. Central station police transmitters, however, receive their power from the commercial mains and, in the absence of auxiliary power equipment, they would immediately go out of commission in the event either the power plant or transmissions were destroyed or paralyzed.

Civil Defense. The national Civil Defense organization is geared directly to disaster or the threat of disaster, primarily in terms of military attack. Local CD organizations function under the jurisdiction of the State CD Office. State offices, in turn, are structured into Regions, which come together as a national organization operating under the Office of the Secretary of the Army. Each State CD office has a master plan of survival which is related to the Regional plan on the national level and to CD plans at the local level.

Planning and supply are the two major functions of the State offices. Plans at the state level involve the use of the capabilities of state agencies and those at the local level of government. This includes Public Safety communications in general and police communication systems in particular. Section 89.17 of the Federal Communications Commission's Rules reads as follows:

"A station licensed under this part may transmit communications necessary for the implementation of civil defense activities assigned such station by the local civil defense authorities during an actual or simulated emergence, including drills and tests; PROVIDED, that such communications relate to the activity or activities which form the basis of the licensee's eligibility in radio service in which authorized.

Police departments, however, must protect the use of their communication facilities in the discharge of legally defined duties not contained in the Civil Defense plan.

An important Civil Defense responsibility of Public Safety communications is the dissemination of initial attack warnings originating with the North American Air Defense Command. The reader is referred to Section 56–939 of the Federal Communications Commission's Rules concerning initial attack warnings, including the CONELRAD Radio Alert.

Quite apart from the catastrophe or calamity arising from physical causes, a disaster plan worked out in advance may prove of great usefulness in social disturbances, such as prison outbreaks, race riots, industrial disorders and similar man-made emergencies. When such disturbances involve widespread destruction of property, including the destruction or crippling of communications or other essential utilities in the community, the problems facing the police would be identical with those attendant upon destructive flood, earthquake, or fire. The Chief of Operations should spare no effort in drawing the blueprints and outlining the details for such plans of operations. He should communicate with other metropolitan cities in the United States and obtain from them copies of the pre-disaster preparedness plans that have been developed for the protection of life and property in those communities. Similarly, contact with national headquarters of the American Red Cross will tap a prolific source of information concerning the mechanics and procedure of pre-disaster planning.

All of the foregoing situations bring into focus the need for a mobile task force superimposed upon the normal patrol power of a police organization. An increasing number of police departments are now making use of the Tactical Unit or mobile striking force to supplement routine patrol operations in the approach to emerging situations. The number may be expected to continue to increase. The effective results which follow the concentration or saturation of an area or location with striking power sufficient in terms of personnel, training and equipment to assure liquidation of the problem, have now been well demonstrated.

A random sampling survey of forty-seven police departments in the United States in various population brackets, revealed that of the twenty-nine departments responding to a questionnaire, eighteen were using the Tactical Unit as a special phase of their line operations.[9]

[9] Arnwine, Major Henry B., *A Study and Evaluation of Police Tactical Operations*, a Master's Thesis, Washington State University, 1963.

TABLE XI

PARTIAL LIST OF POLICE DEPARTMENTS EMPLOYING THE TACTICAL UNIT IN SPECIAL OPERATIONS

Department	Population of City Served	Personnel Strength of Department	Personnel Strength of Tactical Unit
Oak Park, Michigan	36,000	64	11
Pontiac, Michigan	85,000	112	6
Tampa, Florida	192,000	411	17
Richmond, Virginia	230,000	413	10–20
Portland, Oregon	373,000	646	41
Dallas, Texas	434,000	1,095	29
Ft. Worth, Texas	278,000	585	20–40
Miami, Florida	275,000	613	30
Memphis, Tennessee	396,000	691	22
New Orleans, Louisiana	570,000	994	50
St. Louis, Missouri	857,000	1,844	113
San Francisco, Calif.	725,000	1,742	Variable
Seattle, Washington	557,000	564	23
New York City, N. Y.	7,800,000	24,550	248
Los Angeles, Calif.	1,900,000	4,738	81
Chicago, Illinois	3,600,000	10,317	650
Philadelphia, Pa.	2,071,000	4,670	150
Los Angeles County Sheriff's Department (county)	3,000,000	3,218	41

A Typical Tactical Unit Operation

Under the administration of George D. Eastman, Director of the Police Division of the Department of Public Safety in Pontiac, Michigan, a study of line operations indicated the need for a flexible unit with the capabilities for applying selective enforcement pressures in special crime situations.

Pontiac is a city with an area of twenty square miles and a population of 85,000. The personnel strength of the Police Division is one hundred twenty-four. One-man patrol cars are employed. When the Division staff study clearly demonstrated the need for a special mobile striking force, the Flexible Unit was created, consisting of five experienced patrolmen under the immediate command of a Sergeant. The stated reponsibility of the Flexible Unit was to serve as a compact, mobile and effective operational striking force in given locations at times where the records indicated the need for a special concentration of enforcement pressure.[10]

[10] Eastman, George D., Director of the Police Division in the Department of Public Safety, Pontiac, Michigan, *The Flexible Unit—A Unique Striking Force*, POLICE, July–August 1960.

In order to maintain the Unit intact, it only works five days a week. Due to the variation in need by hour of day, the Unit may go on duty at any time, although it usually begins its work between 7:00 P.M., and Midnight. Depending on the nature of the emergency, the Sergeant and five patrolmen may operate as a compact unit in uniform or plain clothes, or they may work in pairs, or singly. Unmarked cars are used.

At one time, the Flexible Unit, equipped with walkie-talkies, may address its attention to the surveillance of known criminal offenders, or stakeouts at known crime hazards. At another, they may be giving special attention to a series of residential burglaries or, in old clothes, walking a railroad track from which there is ready access for burglars to industrial and commercial installations. The Unit responds to felonies-in-progress reports and renders assistance to the patrol force by closing all avenues of escape from the area. However, it does not answer any call that would be handled by the beat patrolman as a routine matter. When not engaged in meeting criminal emergencies, the Flexible Unit gives its attention to the problem of selective traffic enforcement, with special reference to moving violations. In this manner, the selective application of force by a cohesive, mobile unit, gives the line commander, strong additional striking power without the necessity of adding more men to the force.

Similarly, in Oak Park, Michigan, (integrated police and fire services) the departmental staff decided that one way to improve their capabilities in dealing with disorders and disasters was to organize and train a select group of officers as a Tactical Unit. These men would be the nucleus around which the department would build its emergency capabilities.[11]

A group of chiefs of police in the area had become concerned with the limited ability of the smaller departments to cope with a number of problems. Plans were developed for mutual aid in disasters, disaster identification procedures and in the implementing of area road blockade plans. Officials of Oak Park felt in addition, that impending problems, purely local in nature, might need vigorous tactical police action in reducing the likelihood of disorderly group situations.

Eleven officers are assigned to the squad, with five others in reserve. The Unit is commanded by a lieutenant and is equipped with three shotguns, two rifles, two carbines, three sub-machine guns and one gas gun. Normally, the members of the Tactical Unit are on duty in their regular assignments in the patrol services, but subject to immediate mobilization when the need arises.

---

[11] Leonard, Glenford S., Director, Department of Public Safety, Oak Park, Michigan, *Our Tactical Police Unit*, THE POLICE CHIEF, April, 1962.

In Richmond, Virginia, a city of 230,000 population and a police department with a personnel strength of four hundred twenty-two, it was found advisable to create a mobile, flexible unit to supplement routine patrol operations by having available special striking power capabilities to be used in applying selective enforcement pressures in emerging situations. Training emphasis is placed on crowd control techniques and on meeting the criminal emergency where the records indicate an abnormal increase in crime reports, particularly burglary and robbery.

As in Oak Park, Michigan, the Tactical Unit does not operate on a full time basis but is mobilized for service when the emergency need arises. Tactical operations are conducted on the precinct level, with a Tactical Unit of from ten to twenty officers available to each precinct.

An expanded concept of the Tactical Unit operation has appeared in England, where Area Crime Squads are organized and operated on an area basis in the larger urban complexes. In a typical arrangement, with Manchester (population 686,000) as the control center, seven police forces contribute personnel to the Area Crime Squad, serving an area with a population of approximately 2,000,000 people. Under centralized command, the activities of the Squad are directed toward criminal offenders who operate throughout the area complex and who do not necessarily confine their activities to a single town or city.[12]

[12] A letter dated July 2, 1963, from J. E. Colton, Chief Constable, Salford, England.

Chapter 13

THE AUDIT

WITHIN recent years much effort has been addressed to the task of devising methods for appraising the efficiency of the various departments of municipal administration. In some fields such as public works administration, much research and experiment have been carried on and substantial progress has been made. Police administration has joined with other municipal line services in this significant development. As a means for implementing democratic control as well as a device of management, some form of measurement is indispensable. A number of attempts have been made to develop measuring scales with which an appraisal could be made of police organization and administration.[1] However, the criteria of measurement thus far advanced appear to be generally inadequate. The selection of valid criteria is a matter of considerable difficulty.

Since a police system moves in its orbit surrounded by a constellation of culture traits, human relationships, behavior patterns, attitudes and responses, the existence of certain external conditioning factors which affect police performance and which, in turn, condition the selection of valid norms of measurement, must be accepted. It is necessary, therefore, to maintain the distinction between those norms which would require measurement of the community itself, and those which may be applied to police service as a public enterprise. A brief consideration of a few of the conventional criteria of police performance brings this distinction into sharp relief.

Police Costs Per Capita

The cost of police service per capita is a frequently used statistical device. It is extremely flexible and may be employed to condemn a police department or to extol its efficiency. If the per capita expenditure for police service is high, one might be led to the conclusion that the cost of police protection was excessive. But before such a conclusion is justified, one must know what is being received for the amount

---

[1] Arthur Bellman, "A Police Service Rating Scale," 26 Journal of Criminal Law and Criminology, 1935, pp. 74–114; Spencer D. Parratt, "A Critique of the Bellman Police Service Rating Scale," 27 Journal of Criminal Law and Criminology, 1937, pp. 897–905; Spencer D. Parratt, "How Effective is a Police Department?", The Annals of the American Academy of Political and Social Science, Philadelphia, Vol. 199, September 1928, pp. 153–164; Clarence E. Ridley and Herbert A. Simon, "Measuring Municipal Activities," International City Managers' Association, Chicago, 1938, pp. 1–5.

expended. Two cities of approximately the same size and population may vary widely in per capita costs, since one may have expanded the functions of the police department to embrace activities not included by the other.

The police department in one city, for example, may have realized the wisdom of organizing a Crime Prevention Division, while another has not faced this admitted responsibility. There are other considerations of even greater importance which tend to reduce any existing correlation between police costs and police efficiency. Under a policy of "the least regulation possible," dictated by the interests concerned, direct police costs may actually go down. The fact that the costs of such enforcement policy must be repaid ultimately with compound interest, only serves to further emphasize the dynamic character of the total situation in which police administration functions.

It is apparent that the factors which condition the cost of police protection may, and do, vary from community to community in a manner so far removed as a factor directly related to police efficiency as to reduce its value as a standard of comparison.[2] These considerations assume added significance when we come to consider a second popular method for measuring the efficiency of police administration.

Crime Rates

Although the ultimate purpose of the police is the prevention and reduction of crime, it by no means follows that they are solely accountable for either the increase in or the reduction of the number of criminal offenses.[3] A vast throng of public and private agencies and individuals in the community, including the sheriff's organization, the prosecuting attorney, judges, courts, probation and parole officers, clinics, public welfare and health departments, reform schools, penitentiaries, character-building organizations, public school systems, churches and charitable institutions, expend large sums of money annually with the purpose of preventing crime and delinquency. Because of this vast array of participating social agencies, it is evident that the police must share the credit for crime reduction and the blame for increased criminal activities. With this complex and confused dispersion of responsibility, existing crime rates as an exclusive measure of the efficiency of police administration in a community would hardly be scientifically acceptable.

---

[2] August Vollmer, *Survey of the Police Department of Kansas City*, Missouri, 1928.

[3] R. Weldon Cooper, *Municipal Police Administration in Texas*, Bureau of Municipal Research, University of Texas, 1938, p. 111.

In formulating its approach to crime statistics, the Uniform Crime Reporting Committee concluded: [4]

"At this point another difficulty arises which partially explains the reluctance of some police forces to compile and publish reports showing the number of crimes committed. It is derived from the tendency to charge the crime rate *against the police* rather than *against the community*, and the temptation to draw from such statistics broad generalizations concerning the relative efficiency of various police forces.

"By contrast, the prevailing attitude towards epidemic disease might be cited. During the winter of 1928–1929, a large portion of the United States was visited by an epidemic of influenza. Its appearance in the west and its progress towards the eastern seaboard, was announced by the weekly bulletins of the United States Public Health Service. The prevalence of the disease in various communities was measured by statistical tables. But we have yet to hear of any comparisons of the relative efficiency of local health departments based upon such compilations. The whole subject was viewed as a social misfortune which required the fullest cooperation between the press, the public and the health authorities. Crime, likewise, is a social misfortune, which requires a similar cooperation between public and private agencies if it is to be successfully combated and treated.

"Out of our study of American and European conditions emerge two general conclusions on this subject:

1. Statistics showing the volume of crime when unsupported by other data, do not provide a basis for comparisons of police efficiency.

2. Where such statistics have actually been collected, as in England, any disposition towards unjustified comparisons has long since disappeared."

Thus, any attempt to attach the blame for crime conditions to police inefficiency alone, ignores the community's responsibility. What are the causes of crime? May we not more appropriately ask, what are the dynamics of crime causation? We do not know definitely. Research and knowledge are still pushing forward across new frontiers. A complete synthesis of crime causation is yet to be formulated. Premature theories and ideas concerning the causes of crime come into immediate collision with an extensive array of sociological and biological concepts, all of which must be taken into consideration in any attempt to study personality formation.

Again, the crime rate criterion is weak because no definite amount of crime in its various categories has yet been established as the minimum to which a community should be exposed. To do this would re-

[4] Committee on Uniform Crime Records, International Association of Chiefs of Police, *Uniform Crime Reporting Manual*, Washington, 1930, Sec. 4, p. 4.

quire the accurate measurement of public tolerance, and this varies from section to section, from community to community and even from neighborhood to neighborhood. Is no crime at all the ultimate objective? Is the reduction of crime and lawlessness to a reasonable level a more practical goal? If so, what is meant by "reasonable?"

Adequate definitions are yet to be formulated. Authorities differ with respect to a definition of crime itself. The problem is further confused by the fact that an act classified as criminal under orthodox definitions may actually be socially constructive. The history of social progress is a history of consecutive violation and change in the existing mores, customs, and institutions. The instruments of progress—change, innovation, improvement, reform—must of necessity be in conflict with certain prevailing standards. Social inertia gradually awakens to the impact of new proposals and as the mores change, acts formerly considered criminal may ultimately be recognized as acceptable behavior. Thus, in view of the multiple causation of crime, the wide dispersion of responsibility for its control, and difficulty of definition, it becomes necessary to discard the crime rate as an absolute criterion for the measurement of police efficiency.

Percentage of Cases Cleared by Arrest

The percentage of cases cleared by arrest appears at first glance to be a more discriminating barometer of police efficiency. But here, too, the difficulties and unreliability of comparisons are revealed on reflection. If the police departments in all communities operated under exactly the same external conditions, this means of measurement would doubtless possess more validity. It is only necessary to consider a few of the variables affecting this criterion of appraisal to recognize its weakness. Enforcement policies with respect to crime and vice vary from city to city. The determination of policy is a legislative function, discharged as a rule by the City Council. Social and professional connections of the individual members comprising the personnel of the American city council, the influence of pressure groups and the general cultural level of the community alter enforcement policies to such an extent as to eliminate the degree of uniformity necessary for valid comparison.

One police department may find it advisable to relax its efforts in the control of gambling and prostitution, while another may be permitted to approach these problems both vigorously and intelligently. Similar variations are observable in other crime categories. It follows, therefore, that a police department may, within itself, approach the highest standards of police organization and administration and yet not be permitted to function. The effect of such policy upon the percentage of cases cleared by arrest is so evident and the variables so numerous as to reduce the validity of this factor as a criterion of measurement.

The same criticisms may be addressed to the urbane claim that the total number of arrests is a barometer of police efficiency. The customary publicity given police raids on gambling and other vice haunts is often misleading. Raids without padlocks, or their equivalent, only serve to enrich the professional bondsmen and others in the twilight zone of the legal profession. They miss the issue entirely. The shady rendezvous may be legally barred to minors, but patronized by adults. The juvenile knows they are there and the prohibition energizes mental patterns which anticipate the time when age limits will be a bar no longer.

A large arrest record may defeat its own purpose as a flag of efficiency. Of the greatest social import is the content of the arrest record in terms of human personality.[5] The arrest record may reflect a large amount of police activity, however intelligent. The pertinent question is to what extent arrest procedure followed its normal routine in each case by a dramatization of the offense, the label and the casting of the youngster into a new role as a delinquent and a member of the coming generation of criminals, irretrievably lost to society. The traumatic effect of the first jail experience on a youngster supports the view that in many cases, arrest may be a stupid procedure. These are among the questions that require an answer before arrest totals can be considered other than of embarrassing significance.

Percentage of Convictions Obtained

It is frequently asserted that a high percentage of convictions obtained in police cases is an indication of police efficiency in criminal investigation, the procuring of evidence and the preparation of the case for trial. But there are important variables in this calculation too, which are beyond the control of the police, such as the quality of the District Attorney's staff, his policy in prosecuting cases that are not "open and shut," the skill of defense attorneys, the prejudice of juries in certain types of cases, and the general attitude of the court toward the police and the administration of justice. This criterion should require no further analysis.

Other Contemporary Methods of Measurement

The inaccuracy and unreliability of the standards usually applied are evident in every quarter of inquiry. An attempt is made, for example, to appraise the efficiency of the Traffic Division of a Police Department in terms of the number of traffic accidents and fatalities that occur. A traffic accident is a caused occurrence. The causes, in reality, penetrate deeply into community life. The law observance pattern of a community may be a thing quite apart from any estimate of a police

---

[5] Frank Tannenbaum, *Crime and the Community*, Boston, 1939, pp. 1–23.

traffic division. Carrying the analysis further, it must be conceded that the street systems of most cities were originally designed for the accommodation of horses and bicycles. The engineers of that day could hardly have contemplated the phenomenal increase in motor vehicle registration with its accompanying problems of traffic regulation and control. Another complicating factor is the absence of uniformity in traffic laws and regulations between cities. This has resulted in a degree of confusion and lessened respect for law observance which varies from community to community. Many of these factors are beyond any immediate police control, and to that extent these criteria are not acceptable as a means of measuring police efficiency.

Summary

The flexibility of the statistical method is well known. It may be made to behave in every conceivable manner and to support any claim or hypothesis. A police department is frequently either praised or condemned without taking into consideration the factors that condition police service. The greater the importance of one's statistics for the purpose he has in hand, the stronger becomes the need of determining whether they may be trusted.[6] A police chief addressing a local civic organization may mention only those factors that will tend to entrench him in his position as the Department's chief executive, ignoring those points that would be selected by his critics in an attempt to expose inefficiency. Both approaches are in error, in that both invariably employ one or more of the statistical standards of measurement that cannot meet the test for validity. After the public has been presented with both aspects of the question, it still remains largely in the dark concerning the true character of police organization and administration in the community.

What then, are the standards by which police organization and administration may be measured upon a basis that will meet the scientific test for validity? The difficulty lies in the selection of a frame of reference. As previously indicated, in the past the tendency has been to accept the end results of police administration as a measure of its efficiency, but it is evident that they are not susceptible of scientific appraisal until they have been correlated with all the conditioning factors in the community that have participated in the production of those results. A community may be experiencing a comparatively high crime rate and yet be in a position to say that it possesses a police department that measures up to accepted professional standards in every respect.

In much the same manner, the profit and loss statement of an efficient business enterprise might reflect unfavorable results during a peri-

---

6 W. F. Wilson, *Publications of the American Statistical Association*, Washington, Vol. 14 (N.S.), 1914–1915, p. 418.

od of adverse business conditions. Such a business, even though organized according to the best standards of efficient private enterprise and administration, may experience a severe shrinkage in profits during periods of economic dislocation. It would obviously be an error to measure the efficiency of private administration by profit alone, since there are external forces at work affecting the end result which may be beyond its immediate control.

To qualify for scientific validity, a standard of measurement must, as far as possible, be free of independent and uncontrolled variables. In all fields of research, controlled experiment and observation are the essence of the scientific method.

Professional Standards

Certain attainable standards of excellence are recognized in every profession. A profession is defined [7] as:

1. An organized body of knowledge, constantly augmented and refined, with special techniques based thereon.
2. Facilities for formal training in this body of knowledge and procedure.
3. Recognized qualifications for membership in, and identification with, the profession.
4. An organization which includes a substantial number of the members qualified to practice the profession and to exercise an influence on the maintenance of professional *standards*.
5. A code of ethics which, in general, defines the relations of the members of the profession to the public and to other practitioners within the group and normally recognizes an *obligation* to render services on other than *exclusively economic considerations*.

Professionalization is accomplished through:

1. Prescribed courses of study, standardized and geared to one another in high schools, colleges, and universities.
2. Application of prescribed methods in practice teaching, reading, briefing, etc.
3. Post-graduate courses, prescribed and administered if a specialized field is selected.
4. Interneship for application of theory to practice for the purpose of developing skill.
5. Acknowledgment and acceptance of self-imposed ethical standards of professional practice and personal conduct.
6. Examination to determine fitness to practice and enter the profession.

[7] J. A. Greening, former Chief of Police, Berkeley, California, *Report of of the Committee on Professionalization of Police Service*, Yearbook of the International Association of Chiefs of Police, 1938–1939, Chicago, p. 20.

7. Continuous study and research for improvement and advancement of professional techniques and their application within the profession.

These standards are largely permanent in character, varying slowly from generation to generation and thus providing continuity. At any given time, an organization or individual may be judged by the prevailing standards of a given profession. The accepted principles of organization, or of personnel selection and training, for example, are of the greatest significance to both public and private enterprise, and are universal in application.

Standards of the Police Profession

During the course of its development as one of the major phases of municipal administration, police service has been characterized by the appearance of certain principles of standard procedure which bear the credentials of authority and which are regarded by leaders in the profession as essential to successful police organization and management. These standards are recognized by police experts as being worthy of general application and therefore, constitute a valid frame of reference within which judgment may be passed upon a police department in any city or community.

The Frame of Reference

A police department may be judged and measured by the extent and degree to which it uses the accepted, standard tools and procedures of the profession in the development of maximum line power potential. The following criteria for the measurement of combat strength are advanced as the basis for the evaluation of a police department at any given time:

A. Internal Organization
B. Organization for line power
C. Personnel selection and training
D. Police record controls
E. Patrol system
F. Detective Administration
G. Vice Control
H. Traffic Administration
I. Crime prevention operations
J. Self analysis

The proposed inventory is in essence a recapitulation of the principles set forth in the preceding chapters, so arranged that they may be evaluated in different degrees from zero to best practice. It is not presented as a final answer to the need for some appraisal technique which will enable police administration to measure itself, or be measured. It is held, however, that application of the inventory to a specific police organization should give it a professional rating and provide a reliable answer to the question, *"To what extent does the department measure up to the accepted professional standards of modern police service?"*

The evaluation of a police system is a task for the expert. Therefore, the proposed scale of appraisal will prove of limited value in the hands of anyone unfamiliar with the police techniques and procedures now accepted as standard by the profession. Properly employed, however, it should serve the public interest by pointing the way for both executive and layman toward the development of police organization and administration upon a rational and professional level. It should expose those deficiencies which must be remedied before the community can expect to receive a reasonable return or annual expenditures for police service.

Appraisal Procedure

In the proposed rating scale, each item is rated on a graduated scale embracing five different levels of achievement, from zero to accepted professional practice—columns 0, 1, 2, 3, and 4. The selection of the column in which the rating on a given item should be located is determined by application of the following evaluation criteria:

0 — Problem not understood; see no need to be concerned about it; nothing being done.

1 — Recognize the existence of a problem, but little or no appreciation of its significance; lack sufficient interest to take constructive action; management unfamiliar with the procedure or procedures required; no attempt made to meet minimum professional standards.

2 — Attempting to meet problem in a limited way; chief and commanding officers show some understanding of its nature and extent; substantial progress being made but still marked failure to meet professional standards; present procedure continues as a handicap to line power operations.

3 — Importance of problem recognized and fully understood; management active and moving intelligently toward solution; professional standards being approached, but procedure requires further attention.

4 — Problem solved; established procedure now in agreement with accepted professional standards.

Through the application of these gradations in achievement level, it is possible to examine any given item of the inventory in its departmental setting and arrive at a descriptive evaluation concerning the extent to which it measures up to minimum professional standards. These appraisals offer a valid basis for recommendations leading to improved line performance.

POLICE RATING SCALE

	0	1	2	3	4

A. INTERNAL ORGANIZATION

1. Is there a single chief executive?
2. Is the chief delegated full executive control over the organization?
3. Is he given full powers of appointment, removal, and supervision?
4. Can he require retirement at the age provided in the pension system?
5. Does he require retirement at the age provided in the pension system?
6. Is the executive span of control limited to personal supervision of seven persons or less?
7. Organized decentralization of authority?
8. Related functions integrated into major divisions or units?
9. Lines of control extend downward from top to bottom of enterprise?
10. Adequate supervision at all administrative control points?
11. Clear distinction between staff and line functions?
12. Consolidation of functions through integration of staff services under one command?
13. Consolidation of functions through integration of line operations under one command?
14. Effective organization and supervision of functions within divisions?
15. Coordination of all parts of the system into one integrated, administrative unit?
16. Is the amount of manpower and equipment required actually correlated with work units and work programs, and with the amount and type of work to be performed?
17. Are police operations planned?
18. Is the distribution of manpower and equipment actually correlated with work units and work programs, and with the amount and type of work to be performed?

0 1 2 3 4

19. Does patrol case load justify the existence
    of the following specialized units?
            Detective
            Vice
            Traffic
            Crime prevention
            Crime laboratory
20. Unity of command?
21. Is total work load of department deter-
    mined scientifically by records analysis?
22. Is functional distribution of work load de-
    termined scientifically by records analy-
    sis?
23. Are activities grouped by major purpose
    under unified supervision?
24. Are activities grouped by major process
    under unified supervision?
25. Are activities grouped by clientele under
    unified supervision?
26. Does organization by area adhere to ac-
    cepted standards?
27. Is the number of precinct stations justi-
    fied?
28. Is any precinct station justified?
29. If precinct stations justified, are central
    administrative controls effective?
30. If precinct stations, is administration and
    control of all line divisions centralized at
    headquarters?
31. If precinct stations, is administration and
    control of all staff services centralized?
32. If precinct stations, does central com-
    plaint room have rigid control over case
    record numbers?
33. Is organization by time determined scien-
    tifically by records analysis?
34. Is functional distribution of the total
    force determined scientifically by records
    analysis?
35. Does organization of the executive adhere
    to scientific standards?
36. Is total organization geared to line power
    concept?
37. Has an organization chart of the depart-
    ment been prepared?

0 1 2 3 4

38. Has the line of command under all possible conditions been clearly established?

39. Is the law of the span of control being observed at supervisory, command and administrative levels?

40. Is someone assigned to make regular staff inspections of the entire department and its operations?

41. When responsibility is placed, is commensurate authority delegated?

42. Is there present an intelligence unit or its equivalent?

43. Has over-specialization of the department and its various units been avoided?

44. Do police salaries account for as much as 85% of the total budget?

45. Does the Departmental Rules and Regulations conform to professional standards?

46. Is departmental policy with respect to Civilian Review Boards in agreement with the policy of the IACP?

47. Have the administrative alternatives—federated police system, metropolitan police authority, integrated police and fire services, contract law enforcement and city-county consolidation—been adequately explored?

48. Is there an effective police-community relations program in operation?

49. Officers adequately trained to meet their responsibilities in this area?

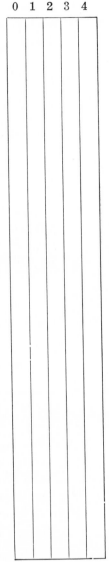

	0	1	2	3	4

B. ORGANIZATION FOR LINE POWER

Staff Services

1. Is the Chief of Staff Services in exclusive command of all staff functions and staff personnel?
2. Has he activated a sound program of personnel selection, training, transfer, rating, supervision, discipline?
3. Has he instituted preparation of Rules and Regulations?
4. Has he caused to be conducted job analyses for the various positions in the department?
5. Has he instituted preparation of a Duty Manual?
6. Are line units properly equipped?
7. Are staff services properly equipped?
8. Has he instituted effective property control?
9. Has he properly equipped and efficiently organized the communications unit?
10. Has he organized and effectively administered a central records and reporting system?
11. Does he cooperate effectively with the Chief Operations?
12. Does he furnish management with the necessary statistical reports, analyses and special studies, properly interpreted?
13. Has he instituted an effective follow-up system for the control of investigations?
14. Is Chief of Staff Services qualified for his responsibilities?

Line Operations

1. Is Chief of Operations in exclusive control of all line divisions and units?
2. Is the department "traffic-centered?"
3. Is there evidence of over-specialization with unnecessary dissipation of patrol power?

0 1 2 3 4

4. Is traffic control and regulation the exclusive concern of the traffic division?
5. Does the patrol force discharge traffic functions?
6. Is the department detective-dominated?
7. Is Chief of Operations qualified for his responsibilities?
8. Is the total line power of the department expendable in meeting all types of police problems, regardless of nature?
9. Does Chief of Operations take advantage of flexibility of control over total line power in the attack upon police problems?
10. Is a clear distinction made between general and special operations?
11. Are operational plans formulated in advance?
12. Are such plans based upon accurate stattistical analysis of records data?
13. Does the Chief of Operations employ the combat principles of strategy and tactics in the use of line power at his disposal?
14. Are operational plans based upon crime and traffic experience?
15. Are the problems of special operations met as emerging situations?
16. Are plans for special operations formulated in advance?
17. Has the Chief of Operations formulated a pre-disaster plan?
18. Could it be said that dynamic offense tactics are applied to the police problems of crime, vice, traffic, and others?
19. Does the Chief of Operations have absolute control over the patrol division?
20. Does he have absolute control over the Detective, traffic, vice, and crime prevention divisions?
21. Has he made arrangements for the organization and use of a Tactical Unit?
22. Is rigid inspection imposed upon all line divisions and units, and upon performance?

                                                    0 1 2 3 4

23. Is rigid inspection imposed upon all indi-
     viduals in all line divisions and units?
24. Are all functions in both staff and line
     oriented exclusively toward increment in
     striking power?

C. PERSONNEL SELECTION AND TRAINING
    1. Chief of Police.
        a. Method of selection
            1) Residence requirement waived?
            2) By competitive examination?
            3) Scientifically validated examina-
                tions administered?
            4) High school education required?
            5) University training required?
            6) Knowledge of American police
                systems required?
            7) Knowledge of accepted profes-
                sional police techniques and pro-
                cedures required?
            8) Knowledge of sociological aspects
                of police administration requir-
                ed?
            9) Independent appointment by City
                Manager?
           10) Non-participation of City Council
                (collectively or individually) or
                pressure groups influencing ap-
                pointment?
           11) Seniority and popularity minor
                considerations?
        b. Tenure on professional performance
            basis?
        c. Average tenure more than five years?
        d. Salary sufficient to attract high order
            of executive ability?
    2. Personnel (General)
        a. Selection
            1) Residence requirements waived?
            2) Absence of political influence in
                appointments?
            3) Absence of nepotism?

0 1 2 3 4

4) High school education required?
5) University training required?
6) University degree preferred?
7) Is time lost by personnel excessive?
8) Is maximum age limit greater than 25?
9) Is maximum age limit greater than 27?
10) Is maximum age limit greater than 31?
11) Is adequate search for candidates made?
12) Is Personal History Questionnaire employed?
13) Is Application Form adequate?
14) Appointment on basis of merit?
15) Integrated examination procedure?
16) Educational tests employed?
17) Standard intelligence tests employed?
18) Army Alpha test employed?
19) Social intelligence tests employed?
20) Social adjustment tests employed?
21) Aptitude tests employed?
22) Adaptability tests employed?
23) Psychiatric screening of police applicants?
24) Will-temperament tests employed?
25) Achievement level tests employed?
26) Observation power tests employed?
27) Personality inventory employed?
28) Rigid character investigation?
29) Fingerprints of applicant cleared through state and national bureaus prior to appointment?

0   1   2   3   4

30) Medical examination equal to that prescribed for entrance at West Point?

31) Neurological examination required?

32) Agility tests employed?

33) Laboratory examination required for
   a. Blood count?
   b. Urinalysis?
   c. Wasserman?

34) All examinations conducted under effective police supervision?

35) Eligibility list employed?

36) Appointment on basis of highest weighted score?

37) Police Cadet System used?

b. Training

1) Minimum probationary period of one year?

2) Continuous police training school within the department?

3) Compulsory attendance of all members of department?

4) Attendance on officers' own time?

5) Full professional police school curriculum, equal to I.A.C.P., standards, in operation?

6) Police school program articulated with institutions of higher learning in vicinity?

7) Is adequate rating system employed?

8) Recruit training?

9) Refresher training?

10) Divisional training?

11) Training for supervisory and command officers?

12) Training provided for administrative officers?

13) Department identified with regional in-service training schools?

	0	1	2	3	4

14) Does department utilize resources of local university or college in in-service training program?

15) Does department utilize lay specialists in in-service training program?

16) Department favors university training for the police profession?

17) Periodical examinations employed and grades posted to personnel records?

18) Roll call training employed?

19) Adequate police library maintained for use of members of the force?

c. Adequate personnel record system employed?

d. Promotion on basis of merit and competitive examination?
 1) Scientifically validated examinations employed?
 2) Seniority a minor consideration?
 3) Absence of politics in promotion?

e. Tenure on professional performance basis?

f. Equitable provision for vacation, day off, and sick leave?

g. Actuarially sound pension system?

h. Semi-annual inspections of personnel and equipment under administrative auspices?

i. Rules and Regulations in printed or mimeographed form, equal to standard specifications?

j. Daily inspections by commanding officers?

k. Duty manual prepared?

l. Job Analysis prepared covering all functions in department?

m. Effective termination process?

0   1   2   3   4

n. Salary scale sufficiently high to compete with commercial field in attracting highest type of young men to the service?

o. Salary scale well integrated?

p. Personnel administration an integral part of the administrative structure and under administrative supervision?

q. Personnel administration under staff supervision?

r. Loyalty, morale, and discipline on a professional level?

s. Absence of politics in removal?

t. Personnel administration offers the attractions of a career service?

u. Affiliation with labor unions prohibited?

v. Coordinated state-wide police recruiting program in force?

w. State Commission on Minimum Police Selection and Training Standards?

x. Department gives credit on entrance examination for two or more years of work at the college or university level?

y. Bachelor degree in police science major required for admission to entrance examination room?

z. Department interested in State Board Examination concept?

D. POLICE RECORD CONTROLS

1. Is public reporting intelligible?

2. Is sufficient concrete data concerning the nature, extent, and distribution of crime available for intelligent formulation of administrative policies?

3. Departmental record functions consolidated into one division?

4. Record Division under staff supervision?

5. Record Division equal in rank to other organizational divisions?

	0	1	2	3	4

6. Police operations integrated through controls exercised by a centralized police record system?

7. Standard complaint record system employed as recommended by I.A.C.P.?

8. Adequate standard cross-indexing procedure employed?

9. Modus Operandi system employed?

10. Detective assignment record employed?

11. Officers required to submit written supplementary reports covering investigations made?

12. Provision for effective follow-up control over investigations and reporting?

13. Rigid supervision over uncleared cases?

14. An uncleared case is a direct charge against the officer assigned?

15. The assigned officer is required to continue submitting supplementary reports on uncleared cases at regular intervals until cleared or declared inactive?

16. A case is declared inactive only upon official sanction of the commanding officer?

17. Record Division audit of all departmental record functions and operations?

18. Standard arrest record procedure, employed as recommended by I.A.C.P.?

19. Effective follow-up control over arrest record procedure pending final disposition?

20. Are arrests transferred to offense reports?

21. Centralized community crime reporting?

22. Mechanical tabulation system employed?

23. Departmental statistician employed?

24. Does the police record system furnish complete data covering the extent, nature, and distribution of crime and deliquency in the community?

0 1 2 3 4

25. Adequate administrative reports and analyses prepared?
   a.   Consolidated morning report?
   b.   Monthly report?
   c.   Annual report?
   d.   Special analyses?

26. Are these reports and analyses used extensively by the executive?

27. Are they employed for the following administrative purposes—
   a.   Control over offenses committed and their investigation?
   b.   Control over arrests and their disposition?
   c.   Determining the effectiveness of the police department?
   d.   Revealing unusual police problems?
   e.   Determining the number of men required on the force?
   f.   Determining proper distribution of the force?
   g.   Selection of the best men for particular jobs or for promotion?
   h.   Apprehending criminals through a study of their methods of operation?
   i.   Ascertaining the proper disposition of offenders and causes of crime?
   j.   Fixing the amount, nature, and distribution of equipment?
   k.   Initiating information useful to concentrating the force on a given problem?
   l.   Analyses of traffic accidents and violations?
   m. Analyses of non-traffic accidents?
   n.   General prevention and detection of crime?

28. Are accurate uniform crime reports forwarded promptly to Washington?

29. Is there a Research and Planning Unit or its equivalent?

0 1 2 3 4

30. Are offense reports made out immediately on receipt of the complaint?

31. Identification records a part of the central records unit or division?

32. Has a job analysis or duty manual been prepared for personnel in the records division?

33. Are monthly accident statistics forwarded to the National Safety Council?

34. Are monthly crime data forwarded to the Federal Bureau of Investigation?

35. Is there an adequate use of spot maps?

36. A criminal history file is maintained?

    a. The Bureau is equipped with a scientific crime detection laboratory?
       1) Questioned document examination?
       2) Firearms identification?
       3) Uses moulage equipment?
       4) Equipped with—

          a) Precision balances?

          b) Wide field low power binocular microscope?

          c) Micrometer calipers?

          d) Precision rules?

          e) Fine measurement glass scales?

          f) Ultra-violet light?

          g) Infra-red light?

          h) Typewriting, watermark, ink, and paper standards?

          i) Comparison microscope?

          j) Helixometer?

          k) Eyepieces for measuring distances and angles?

          l) Reference collection of ammunition and firearms?

          m) Chemical bench and equipment for routine chemical tests?

0   1   2   3   4

      n) Equipment for photomicrography?

      o) Equipment for document Photography?

      p) New photographic mugging equipment purchased within past five years?

   b. One or more members of Bureau are court-qualified experts for delivery of expert testimony covering identification of fingerprints, handwriting, typewriting, papers, inks, firearms, edged tools, impressions, fibre, stains, dusts, and fragments?

   c. Polygraph employed in routine investigation?

Collateral Record Functions

  1. Identification Bureau

     a. A unit of the Central Record Division?

     b. All fingerprint records received are indexed and filed to date?

     c. Standard extension of fingerprint file sub-divisions?

     d. Fingerprint sector file employed?

     e. Latent fingerprint investigation on all theft and felony investigations?

     f. Single fingerprint system employed?

     g. Accumulative arrest and criminal history file maintained on each individual handled by the department?

     h. Adequate property controls.

E. IMPROVEMENT OF APPREHENSION CAPABILITY

  1. Significance of prompt arrest understood and appreciated?

  2. Police communications system meets professional standards?

  3. Police recall system employed?

0 1 2 3 4

4. Modern police radio system?
    a. Under Record Division supervision?
    b. Centralized telephone system?
    c. One-way radio communication on all cars?
    d. Two-way radio communication on all cars?
    e. What per cent single-officer motor patrol?
    f. Department adequately equipped with modern communication facilities?
    g. Are they properly organized?
    h. Is relative significance of operating time intervals understood and applied?
    i. Is dispatching procedure properly organized?
    j. Is running time of patrol cars in excess of an average of three minutes?
    k. Are communication facilities being utilized up to maximum potential in the manuever and application of line power resources?
    l. Emergency communication procedure planned in advance?
    m. Provision for auxiliary power supply?
    n. Chief executive actively participating in promotion and organization of territorial or regional police communication network?

5. Two and three-way radio communication?

6. Police call involving use of commercial broadcasting stations utilized?

7. High hazard locations connected to police headquarters by alarm circuits?

8. Is the significance of the operating time interval and its four components understood and appreciated?

9. Road blockade plans prepared in advance of the emergency?

0 1 2 3 4

10. Adequate number of trunk lines coming into police switchboard to accommodate peak traffic loads?

11. How many times during an average month does a citizen calling police headquarters receive a "busy" signal?

12. Is the central complaint room under the control of the head of the records unit or division?

13. Is the dispatcher assigned to the records unit?

14. Illuminated maps employed indicating cars in and out of service?

15. Plans for the emergency deployment of personnel prepared in advance for each bank and other high hazard locations?

16. Mobile teleprinters used?

17. Walkie-Talkie used?

18. Electronic car locator equipment employed?

19. Police management transportation conscious in terms of the economics of car purchase or rental and maintenance?

20. Are APCO Ten Signals employed?

21. Consolidation of police communication systems in terms of the five administrative alternatives has been adequately explored?

22. Teletypewriter installation?

23. Headquarters tied in with central state computer installation?

24. Adequate use made of the computerized National Crime Information Center in Washington, D. C.?

25. "Hits" average _____ per month?

F. THE PATROL SYSTEM

1. Basic crime data available to govern intelligent distribution of force?

2. Chronological distribution in proportion to work units and work program?

0 1 2 3 4

3. Territorial distribution in proportion to work units and work program?

4. Are all organizational and managerial procedures directed toward maximum accretion of patrol line power?

5. Is the patrol force regarded as the major component of line power?

6. Are all other line divisions and units regarded as supporting units and secondary in importance to the patrol division?

7. Is the distinction recognized between numerical strength and striking power?

8. Is the significance of the difference between quantity and quality of man-power understood?

9. Is determination of total personnel strength based on determination of personnel strength of patrol force?

10. Is determination of personnel strength of patrol force based on maximum work load of one individual?

11. Is the patrol force distributed chronologically on scientific basis by hourly distribution of work load as shown by records analysis?

12. Are line operations based on the concept that lowered patrol efficiency increases case load for all other line divisions and units?

13. Is the individual beat regarded as the basic unit of police organization?

14. Is the size of the beat determined on the basis of the amount of work to be done?

15. Are police hazards classified and evaluated?

16. Have time studies been made of patrol functions in determining individual work load?

17. Do all patrol beats represent approximately equal demands for police service?

0 1 2 3 4

18. Is the individual beat officer held directly responsible for the prevention and suppression of crime and vice, for the arrest of offenders, for the regulation and control of traffic, and for meeting all other police problems originating on his beat?

19. Do all uncleared cases represent a direct charge against the individual efficiency of the patrol officer concerned?

20. Is rigid supervision imposed on the patrol division and upon its members individually?

21. Is full utilization made of the patrol sergeant?

22. Is the patrol force completely motorized?

23. What per cent of patrol force is motorized?

24. What per cent of patrol force represented by foot patrol?

25. What per cent double-officer motor patrol?

26. Size, boundaries and distribution of beats determined by—

   a. Incidence of crime by beats?

   b. Spot maps and statistical charts showing concentration of different classes of crimes by beats?

   c. Classification of type and number of offenses by beats?

   d. Areas of social disorganization and personal demoralization?

   e. Relationship between density of offenses and arrests, and the relative size of beats?

   f. Density and distribution of police hazards in relation to beat boundaries?

   g. Highway and street system patterns?

   h. Traffic conditions and accidents of the ground affecting movement and mobilization of the force?

0 1 2 3 4

27. Conservation of patrol strength effected
    by elimination of—
    a. Foot patrol?
    b. Fixed-point duty?
    c. Special details?
28. Standard professional principles of patrol
    strategy and tactics taught and applied?
29. Patrol operating plans prepared in advance
    of major emergency crime situations?
30. Tactical Unit used effectively?
31. Blockade plans prepared in advance on city
    and area basis?
32. Operational plans prepared in advance for
    jail emergency?
33. Pre-disaster preparedness plan?
34. Single-officer motor patrol?
35. Beat officer engages in traffic enforce-
    ment and regulation?
36. Beat officer is held responsible for crime
    conditions in his district?
37. Beat officer equipped with—
    a. First aid equipment?
    b. Tear gas?
    c. Portable camera?
    d. Emergency arms?
    e. Investigation kit?
38. Has beat officer mapped location of every
    safe and other similar hazards in his dis-
    trict?
39. Are dogs used in the patrol services?
40. Beat patrol officers held responsible for
    the enforcement of moving traffic viola-
    tions?
41. Number of foot patrolmen been reduced to
    lowest possible minimum?
42. All patrol cars conspicuously marked?
43. Is an effective check made on the security
    of commercial establishments?
44. Does the department make use of over-
    lapping platoon shifts?

0 1 2 3 4

45. Establishment of supervisory and command positions based on the law of the span of control?

46. Dominance of an idea concept exploited?

47. Fluid patrol system adequately explored?

48. Grid system of reporting employed?

49. Legal aspects of patrol service thoroughly understood by personnel?

50. Requirements set forth by U. S. Supreme Court decisions being observed?

51. Are frequent changes of beats among patrolmen avoided?

G. DETECTIVE DIVISION

1. Does case load of patrol division indicate necessity for specialized services of the detective?

2. Patrol force assumes investigative responsibility for clearance of all cases?

3. Patrol force seeks investigative assistance of detectives rarely on Part II offenses?

4. Patrol force seeks investigative assistance of detectives in all Part I offenses?

5. Detective function regarded as only supplementary to that of the patrol force?

6. Patrol force still held responsible for case clearances although assisted by detectives?

7. Detective force under direct and exclusive control of the Chief of Operations?

8. Detectives assigned to precincts remain under central headquarters control?

9. Does detective organization provide for complete specialization?

10. Detectives work singly, not in pairs?

11. Detectives recruited from patrol force?

12. Detectives recruited by promotional examinations?

13. Are detective recruits given divisional training?

0 1 2 3 4

14. Is adequate assignment register employed?

15. Does it actually affect control over investigations and performance of the individual detective?

16. Are time studies and job analyses made of detective functions?

17. Is distribution of work load effected scientifically on basis of such studies?

18. Is there effective coordination and lack of friction between detective and patrol division?

19. Does Chief of Operations utilize energies of detective division as an integral part of the total line power of the department?

20. If population of city 150,000 or under, there is no detective division or unit?

21. Do detectives encourage and promote patrol participation in criminal investigation?

22. Are lines of information adequately developed?

23. Services of the informer adequately exploited?

24. Care and preservation of evidence meets professional standards?

25. Considering the size of the department, both large and small, are police laboratory facilities adequate?

26. Are investigation kits employed?

27. Modus operandi as an investigative tool adequately exploited?

28. Interrogation methods effective?

29. Polygraph employed?

H. VICE

1. Does patrol case load warrant creation of a specialized vice unit?

2. Does vice unit report directly to Chief of Operations or Chief of Police?

0 1 2 3 4

3. Individual patrolman held responsible for vice conditions on his beat although provision has been made for vice unit?

4. Does patrol force cooperate with vice unit?

5. Is rigid supervision maintained over vice unit?

6. Is adequate provision made for records control over vice investigations?

7. Are energies of vice unit directed toward vice operations instead of patrons?

8. Does Chief of Operations utilize vice unit as integral part of planned line operations involving total striking power of the department?

9. Are ample secret service funds made available to the Chief of Operations?

10. Is there an intelligence unit or its equivalent?

11. Consistent turnover in vice unit personnel?

12. Is patrolman held responsible for the elimination of vice conditions on his beat?

13. Is vice unit provided with adequate undercover operators and funds?

14. Are undercover funds administered so as to protect the integrity of the operation?

15. Vice records administered so as to assure their secrecy and integrity?

16. Is there present a crime commission in the community?

I. TRAFFIC ADMINISTRATION

1. Is the function of traffic regulation and control regarded as a responsibility of the patrol force?

2. Does traffic-connected case load of patrol force warrant creation of a specialized traffic unit?

3. Department has avoided becoming traffic-centered?

4. Function of traffic unit limited to studies, analyses, and planning?

0 1 2 3 4

5. Less than 10 per cent of personnel strength assigned to traffic unit?

6. Do dimensions of traffic problem warrant services of a full-time traffic engineer?

7. Are services of a full-time traffic engineer provided?

8. If services of full-time traffic engineer unwarranted, does police department utilize effectively the services of the city engineer?

9. Is traffic engineer located in police traffic unit?

10. Is responsibility for traffic engineering delegated to one individual?

11. Department has avoided creation of specialized accident investigation squads?

12. Special investigation cars regarded as extensions of crime laboratory and available for evidence recovery at both crime and accident scenes?

13. One or more traffic officers have been sent to Northwestern University Traffic Institute for specialized training?

14. Is engineering regarded as the basic approach to the problems of traffic regulation and control?

15. Are education and enforcement rated second and third in importance respectively?

16. Does the traffic record system meet adequate standards?

17. Is the traffic record system an integral part of the central police record system?

18. Is automatic tabulating machinery employed in the statistical approach to traffic problems?

19. Does this procedure result in the production of effective studies and analyses as a basis for operational planning?

20. Do these studies and analyses play an important role in operational planning?

0 1 2 3 4

21. Is there a sustained traffic safety educational program?

22. Are the techniques of selective education employed?

23. Have traffic safety units been incorporated into primary, elementary, and high school curricula?

24. Does department assume direct responsibility for administration of junior traffic police in protection of school crossings?

25. Is the punitive effort limited to selective enforcement based upon records analysis?

26. Absence of periodic traffic enforcement campaigns?

27. Chemical tests for intoxication employed?

28. Are special studies and analyses made at sufficiently frequent intervals to provide adequate information with respect to traffic problems?

29. Is police traffic control and regulation a continuous and on-going program rather than occasional campaigns?

30. Has the use of the two-wheeled motorcycle been discontinued?

31. Is the enforcement program developed on a selective basis and geared to the traffic accident experience?

32. Are warnings and non-arrest techniques employed in suitable situations?

33. Are instrumental aids for determining the degree of intoxication employed?

34. Department equipped for taking motion pictures of persons arrested for driving while intoxicated?

35. School boy patrols operated in cooperation with school authorities?

36. Are they properly trained, disciplined and equipped?

37. Is there a well organized safety council in the community?

	0	1	2	3	4

38. Are the resources of the National Safety Council exploited in the approach to traffic problems?

39. Has computer control of traffic signals been considered?

40. Driver training in all high schools?

41. Traffic ordinance conform to the Model Traffic Ordinance?

42. Point system control over traffic violators being utilized?

J. CRIME PREVENTION

1. Is the punitive philosophy still dominant in administrative policy?

2. Are limitations of enforcement appreciated?

3. Are minors detained in jail quarters?

4. Meaningful shift in emphasis from enforcement to prevention?

5. Administrative use of records data in the study of the nature and extent of juvenile delinquency?

6. Extent of operational planning based upon statistical studies and analyses?

7. Significance of delinquent as forerunner of adult offender understood?

8. Significance of the pre-delinquency period understood?

9. Repressive measures understood and applied in modification of the opportunity?

10. More than 5% of personnel strength assigned exclusively to preventive function?

11. Leadership characterizes the preventive role of police administration in the community?

12. Effective relationship established with Juvenile Court?

13. Effective relationship established with major social agencies?

14. Crime prevention unit operates within the framework of a social welfare point of view?

                                          0 1 2 3 4

15. Active participation in community organi-
    zation?

16. Systematic referral of acute cases for diag-
    nosis and adjustment?

17. Effective follow-up routine?

18. Case-work approach to behavior problems
    encountered by the police?

19. Divisional in-service training for workers
    in crime prevention unit?

20. Local social workers, psychologists, and
    psychiatrists retained on training staff?

21. Personnel assigned to crime prevention
    unit university trained?

22. One or more full-time case-workers with
    degrees from reputable schools of social
    work?

23. Training in preventive techniques provid-
    ed for all departmental personnel?

24. Close collaboration of police with proba-
    tion officers in supplying Juvenile Court
    with case information?

25. Social, medical, psychological, and psy-
    chiatric implications of problem behavior
    understood?

26. Environmental risk factors and areas
    being attacked up to limits of community
    tolerance?

27. Significance of the police role in the pre-
    arrest period understood?

28. To what extent are the techniques of un-
    official probation employed?

29. Patrol officers deal intelligently with
    emerging behavior situations?

30. Extent to which patrol force qualified by
    training and experience for preliminary
    contact with beginning behavior devia-
    tions?

31. Extent to which this training and experi-
    ence are applied as routine procedure?

0 1 2 3 4

32. Systematic referral of persistent cases to crime prevention unit?

33. Crime prevention unit cooperates with other social agencies in bringing diagnostic and therapeutic facilities of community into play in individual case?

34. Invocation of arrest as a last resort is a principal feature of police policy?

35. Police administration and public school administration geared jointly to discovery diagnosis and treatment of the socially, physically, or mentally different youngster at the primary and elementary grade levels?

36. Administration has successfully reinterpreted police service to the community within a social welfare frame of reference?

37. Crime prevention unit under central control of commanding officer in charge of line operations?

38. Are all the resources of the community being utilized to the fullest extent in the treatment of the individual?

39. Has a community or coordinating council been organized in the community?

40. Do the police and the schools work together in all delinquency-related matters?

K. POLICE HEADQUARTERS

1. Headquarters building and facilities adequate?

2. Police office locations well arranged?

3. Has the electric company made a survey of the adequacy of illumination within the past five years.

4. Maximum security of police headquarters maintained against possible attack?

5. Exterior doors and roof access protected by alarm circuits?

0 1 2 3 4

6. Public access limited to those areas in which police business with the public is normally conducted?

7. Areas ordinarily used only by departmental personnel considered restricted areas?

L. MEASUREMENT

1. Does management engage in systematic self-inventory as a means for continuous appraisal of organization and administration?

2. Does the central police records system provide adequate data for the measurement of performance of department as a whole, of individual administrative divisions and units, and of the individual officer?

3. Are police problems and police success or failure in meeting them adequately interpreted to public opinion?

4. Is the annual report so organized and presented as to constitute an effective device toward this end?

5. Has management abandoned police costs per capita, crime rates, percentage of cases cleared by arrest and percentage of convictions obtained, as exclusive standards for the measurement of police organization and administration?

6. Are the foregoing criteria used in conjunction with accepted professional standards as a means of self-measurement?

7. Are the results of measurement translated into action by management in terms of organization and procedure?

*

Chapter 14

THE TIDE OF VIOLENCE

WHEN citizens express concern about high levels of violence in the United States, they have in mind a number of different types of events: homicides and assaults, rioting and looting, clashes between demonstrators and police, student seizures of university buildings, violence in the entertainment media, assassinations of national leaders. Foremost in their minds, no doubt, is what appears to be a rising tide of individual acts of violent crime, especially "crime in the streets."

Only a fraction of all crime is violent, of course. Major crimes of violence—homicide, rape, robbery, and assault—represent only 13 percent (or 588,000) of the Federal Bureau of Investigation's Index of reported serious crimes (about 4.5 million in 1968). Moreover, deaths and personal injuries from violent crime cause only a small part of the pain and suffering which we experience: one is five times more likely to die in an auto accident than to be criminally slain, and one hundred times more likely to be injured in a home accident than in a serious assault.

But to suffer deliberate violence is different from experiencing an accident, illness or other misfortune. In violent crime man becomes a wolf to man, threatening or destroying the personal safety of his victim in a terrifying act. Violent crime (particularly street crime) engenders fear—the deep-seated fear of the hunted in the presence of the hunter. Today this fear is gnawing at the vitals of urban America.

In a recent national survey, half of the women and one-fifth of the men said they were afraid to walk outdoors at night, even near their homes. One-third of American householders keep guns in the hope that they will provide protection against intruders. In some urban neighborhoods, nearly one-third of the residents wish to move because of high rates of crime, and very large numbers have moved for that reason. In fear of crime, bus drivers in many cities do not carry change, cab drivers in some areas are in scarce supply, and some merchants are closing their businesses. Vigilante-like groups have sprung up in some areas.

Fear of crime is destroying some of the basic human freedoms which any society is supposed to safeguard—freedom of movement, freedom from harm, freedom from fear itself.

Between 1960 and 1968, the national rate of criminal homicide per 100,000 population increased 36 percent, the rate of forcible rape 65

421

percent, of aggravated assault 67 percent, and of robbery 119 percent. These figures are from the *Uniform Crime Reports* published by the Federal Bureau of Investigation. These Reports are the only national indicators we have of crime in America. But, as the FBI recognizes, they must be used with caution.

There is a large gap between the reported rates and the true rates. In 1967 the President's Commission on Law Enforcement and Administration of Justice stated that the true rate of total major violent crime was roughly twice as high as the reported rate. This ratio has probably been a changing one. Decreasing public tolerance of crime is seemingly causing more crimes to be reported. Changes in police practices, such as better recording procedures and more intensive patrolling, are causing police statistics to dip deeper into the large well of unreported crime. Hence, some part of the increase in reported rates of violent crime is no doubt due to a fuller disclosure of the violent crimes actually committed.

Moreover, while current rates compare unfavorably, even alarmingly, with those of the 1950's, fragmentary information available indicates that at the beginning of this century there was an upsurge in violent crime which probably equaled today's levels. In 1916, the city of Memphis reported a homicide rate more than seven times its present rate. Studies in Boston, Chicago and New York during the years of the First World War and the 1920's showed violent crime rates considerably higher than those evident in the first published national crime statistics in 1933. Despite all these factors, it is still clear that *significant and disturbing increases in the true rates of homicide and, especially, of assault and robbery have occurred over the last decade.* While the reported incidence of forcible rape has also increased, reporting difficulties associated with this crime are too great to permit any firm conclusion on the true rate of increase.

Violent crimes are not evenly distributed throughout the nation. Using new data from a Victim-Offender Survey conducted by a Violence Commission Task Force on Individual Acts of Violence, standard data from the FBI, and facts from other recent studies, we can sketch a more accurate profile of violent crime in the United States than has hitherto been possible. We note, however, that our information about crime is still unsatisfactory and that many critical details in the profile of violent crime remain obscure. Moreover, we strongly urge all who study this profile to keep two facts constantly in mind. First, violent crime is to be found in all regions of the country, and among all groups of the population—not just in the areas and groups of greatest concentration to which we draw attention. Second, despite heavy concentrations of crime in certain groups, the overwhelming majority of individuals in these groups are law-abiding citizens.[1]

The Violence Commission concluded that: [2]

1. Violent crime in the United States is primarily a phenomenon of large cities. This is a fact of central importance.

2. Violent crime in the city is overwhelmingly committed by males.

3. Violent crime in the city is concentrated especially among youths between the ages of fifteen and twenty-four.

4. Violent crime in the city is committed primarily by individuals at the lower end of the occupational scale.

5. Violent crime in the cities stems disproportionately from the ghetto slum where most Negroes live.

6. The victims of assaultive violence in the cities generally have the same characteristics as the offenders: victimization rates are generally highest for males, youths, poor persons, and blacks. Robbery victims, however, are very often older whites.

7. Unlike robbery, the other violent crimes of homicide, assault and rape tend to be acts of passion among intimates and acquaintances.

8. By far the greatest proportion of all serious violence is committed by repeaters.

9. Americans generally are no strangers to violent crime.

Group Violence

We tend to think of group violence as a major aberration in a democratic society, as a sickness that comes only in extraordinary times. A deeper reading of the past belies this notion. In man's political history, group violence has accompanied periods of serious social stress from Homer to this morning's newspaper. Group violence runs through the American experience, as it always has, in varying degrees and manifestations, for every society. Violence has been used by groups seeking power, by groups holding onto power, and by groups in the process of losing power. Violence has been pursued in the defense of order by the satisfied, in the name of justice by the oppressed, and in fear of displacement by the threatened.

At the outset, it must be made clear that group violence has no necessary relationship to group protest, although there continue to be those who decry the one as though it were the other. The right to pro-

---

[1] The National Commission on the Causes and Prevention of Violence, *To Establish Justice, To Insure Domestic Tranquility*, U. S. Government Printing Office, Washington, 1969, pp. 17–20.

[2] *Ibid.*, pp. 20–26.

test is an indispensable element of a free society; the exercise of that right is essential to the health of the body politic and its ability to adapt itself to a changing environment. In this country, we have endowed the right of protest with constitutional status. The very first Amendment to the Constitution protects freedom of speech and the press and "the right of the people peaceably to assemble and to petition the government for a redress of grievances." The Amendment protects much more than the individual right of dissent; it guarantees the right of groups to assemble and petition, or, in the modern phrase, to demonstrate.

Group violence, on the other hand, is dangerous to a free society. All too frequently, it is an effort not to persuade, but to compel. It has no protected legal status; indeed, one purpose of law is to prevent and control it. Nor is group violence a necessary consequence of group protest. The violence of the Ku Klux Klan—the lynching of Negroes at the rate of almost 100 per year from 1890 to 1910—had little to do with protest; if anything, it was more a cause of protest than a response. The same may be said of the harsh treatment of Orientals on the Pacific frontier and the common use of violence to settle property and political disputes among competing groups in the early days of the American West.

It is true, of course, that group protest sometimes results in group violence. Violence may be committed by groups opposed to the aims of the protesters (as in the Southern murders of civil rights workers by groups of white militants); excessive force may be used by the public authorities, as in Selma in 1965; violence may be committed by some within the protesting group itself (as in the case of the Weatherman faction of the SDS). But the widely held belief that protesting groups usually behave violently is not supported by fact. Of the multitude of occasions when protesting groups exercise their rights of assembly and petition, only a small number result in violence.

Thus, the Violence Commission Task Force Report on Historical and Comparative Perspectives reports that over the five year period from mid-1963 to mid-1968, protests or counterprotests and ghetto riots involved more than two million persons. Civil rights demonstrations mobilized 1.1 million, anti-war demonstrations 680,000, and ghetto riots an estimated 200,000. Nine thousand casualties resulted, including some 200 deaths. Ghetto riots were responsible for most of these casualties, including 191 deaths. Almost all other deaths, an estimated 23, resulted from white terrorism against blacks and civil rights workers. These casualty figures are for a five-year period, and apart from the ghetto riots, they are comparatively infinitesimal. While they are not to be condoned, in a country with 250,000 aggravated assaults and

12,000 homicides per year, group protest cannot be considered as accounting for a major part of the deliberate violence we experience.

Do we have a greater amount of group violence today than in earlier periods of our history? While a precise quantitative answer cannot be provided, we may conclude with confidence that, while group violence in the 1960's was at a higher level than in the decades immediately preceding, several decades of American history were marked by higher levels of group violence—in terms of casualties per 100,000 population—than has been true of the decades now ending.[3]

Ever since the Boston Tea Party, occasional group violence has been a recurring—though not a continuous—feature of American political and social history:[4]

1. From 1740 to 1790, Appalachian farmers, protesting against debt and tax collectors from the seaboard centers of political and economic power, engaged in a series of violent disorders, of which the Whiskey Rebellion in Pennsylvania is best known.

2. Southern landowners and northern Abolitionists engaged in a variety of skirmishes, from "bleeding Kansas" to John Brown's raid on Harper's Ferry, that were the violent prelude to the Civil War.

3. During Reconstruction, the Ku Klux Klan and other elements of the defeated white majority in the South conducted a campaign of terrorism against the freed blacks, government officials and Southerners who cooperated with them.

4. So-called "Native Americans" of the original colonial stocks resorted to group violence when they perceived their status as threatened by European Catholic and Jewish immigrants in the East and Orientals in the West; the immigrant groups occasionally engaged in violence such as the New York Draft Riots in 1863.

5. As the freed Negro migrants from the South began settling in border and Northern cities after the Civil War, white residents (including the most recent of the European immigrants) launched occasional attacks on black sections of the city.

6. The growth of organized labor in the half century from 1880 to 1930 was marked by unusually severe episodes of violence in which employers, workers and public authorities were all occasional aggressors. In the three year period 1902–1904, about 200 persons were killed and 2,000 injured in the violence accompanying various strikes and lockouts.

During each of these episodes, most of the community continued to live in peace. The violent episodes themselves were sporadic.

[3] *Ibid.*, pp. 57–59.

[4] *Ibid.*, pp. 59–61.

At any given time they probably involved minor percentages of the total population—certainly not more than a small fraction of the number who were then engaging in various sorts of group protest.

While it is probably true that protest by one or more groups seeking to advance or defend its status in society has been a continuous feature of American life, group violence has not. Indeed, it is group protest, not group violence, that is as American as cherry pie.[5]

Those who engage in group violence as a political tactic advance several reasons to support it. Some of the current justifications have been summarized by the Violence Commission Task Force on Violent Aspects of Protest and Confrontation.[6]

1. Militants argue that the creation of turmoil and disorder can stimulate otherwise quiescent groups to take more forceful action in their own ways. Liberals may come to support radical demands while opposing their tactics; extreme tactics may shock moderates into self re-examination.

2. Militants point out that direct action is not intended to win particular reforms or to influence decision makers, but rather to bring out a repressive response from authorities—a response rarely seen by most white Americans. When confrontation brings violent official response, uncommitted elements of the public can see for themselves the true nature of the "system." Confrontation, therefore, is a means of political education.

3. Militants believe that if the movement really seriously threatens the power of political authorities, efforts to repress the movement through police-state measures are inevitable. The development of resistant attitudes and action toward the police at the present time is a necessary preparation for more serious resistance in the future.

4. Militants state that educated, middle-class, non-violent styles of protest are poorly understood by working-class youth, black youth, and other "drop-outs." Contact with these other sectors of the youth population is essential and depends upon the adoption of a tough and aggressive stance to win respect from such youth.

5. Militants recognize that most middle-class students are shocked by aggressive or violent behavior. In the militant view, this cultural

---

[5] *Ibid.*, p. 61. For conflicting views of civil disobedience see: Howard Zinn, *Disobedience and Democracy*, Vintage Books, New York, 1968, and Abe Fortas, *Concerning Dissent and Civil Disobedience*, Signet Books, New York, 1968.

[6] The National Commission on the Causes and Prevention of Violence, *The Politics of Protest*, U. S. Government Printing Office, Washington, 1969, pp. 81–82. For discussions of revolution see: Lewis M. Killian, *The Impossible Revolution?* Random House, New York, 1968, and Truman Nelson, *The Right of Revolution*, Beacon Press, Boston, 1968.

fear of violence is psychologically damaging and may be politically inhibiting. To be a serious revolutionary, they say, one must reject middle-class values, particularly deference toward authority. Militant confrontation gives resisters the experience of physically opposing institutional power, and it may force students to choose between "respectable" intellectual radicalism and serious commitment to revolution, violent or otherwise.

6. Militants respond to those who point to the possibility of repression as a reaction to confrontation tactics by accusing them of wishing to compromise demands and principles and dilute radicalism. Militants believe that repression will come in any case, and to diminish one's efforts in anticipation is to give up the game before it starts.

Somewhat different arguments are advanced by those among threatened groups to justify defensive private violence and the use of excessive force by public authorities. They believe that the disadvantaged group will cease to exert pressure only if protesters are firmly and decisively repressed and that strong evidence of superior force and willingness to use it will succeed in defending the status quo.

These arguments for group violence—offensive or defensive—are not sustained by history, contemporary reality, logic or law. They are inconsistent with the basic principles of democratic government.[7]

Strategies of Control

Many feel that rioters should be dealt with harshly. At least two-thirds of white Americans, according to one poll, believe that looters and fire-bombers should simply be shot down in the streets.[8] Many believe that even peaceful demonstrators are "agitators" or "anarchists." In a poll conducted for the Violence Commission, 56 percent agreed that "any man who insults a policeman has no complaint if he gets roughed up in return."

As recent history illustrates, the prompt, prudent deployment of well-trained law enforcement personnel can extinguish a civil disorder in its incipiency. But history also demonstrates that excessive use of force is an unwise tactic for handling disorder. To the generalization made earlier, that violence is an always dangerous and sometimes ineffective tactic for dissident groups pressing their demands or for threatened groups resisting those demands, may be added this corollary: the use of excessive and illegal force is an always dangerous and usual-

---

[7] *Ibid.*, p. 65.

[8] National Commission on the Causes and Prevention of Violence, *Law and Order Reconsidered*, U. S. Government Printing Office, Washington, 1969, p. 335.

ly ineffective tactic for authorities seeking to quell unrest. Both in the short and in the long run, the use of excessive force to repress group violence often has the effect of magnifying turmoil, not diminishing it.

It is useful to contrast the official response to the anti-war protest in Chicago during the Democratic National Convention of 1968 and the "counter-inaugural" in Washington on January 20, 1969.[9] These two events were organized by many of the same protesting groups and attended by many of the same individuals, in roughly equal numbers. Yet the results of these events were markedly different. In Chicago, the authorities were restrictive in granting demonstration permits; some of the police, deliberately goaded by verbal and physical attacks of small militant groups, responded with excessive force not only against the provocateurs but also against peaceful demonstrators and passive bystanders. Their conduct, while it won the support of the majority, polarized substantial and previously neutral segments of the population against the authorities and in favor of the demonstrators.

In Washington, demonstration permits were liberally issued. Although there was also provocative violence by some of the demonstrators, the police used only that force clearly necessary to maintain order. As a result, there was little criticism of the police behavior. Our analysis leads to the conclusion that the amount of violence that occurred during these demonstrations and the resulting effects on public opinion were directly related to the kind of official response that greeted them.

In both instances a small number—no more than a few hundred in either case—intended to provoke a "confrontation" with authorities by provocative acts, aimed especially at policemen. A majority of the participants intended to demonstrate peacefully and, in fact, did so.

In response to reports that violence and disruptive conduct would occur, Chicago authorities adopted tight, well-publicized security measures designed to dissuade protesters from coming to the city. To discourage the protesters further, they prolonged the negotiations for demonstration permits and exercised their discretionary powers restrictively. The limited, begrudging dialogue with protesting groups reduced the opportunity of the authorities to assess and separate the component groups in the demonstration (many of which intended to demonstrate peacefully) and to learn the details of their plans. This resistant posture served to discourage more mature and responsible protesters from coming while firing the determination of young militants to attend and confront. To some of the police and some Chicago citizens, the official

---

[9] For detailed discussions see: The National Commission on the Causes and Prevention of Violence, *Rights in Concord*, U. S. Government Printing Office, Washington, 1969.

posture of resistance signified that the protest activities as such were dangerous or illegitimate; they tended to view protesters as trouble-makers and law-breakers, thus failing to discriminate between the small number of radicals seeking trouble and the great majority of peaceful citizens exercising their constitutional rights.

In preparation for the Inaugural in Washington five months later, intelligence reports were carefully evaluated. Genuine threats were sorted from theatric exaggerations. Troublemakers were identified and watched closely, but no attempt was made to interfere with the activities of the majority of peaceful demonstrators. Authorities negotiated conscientiously with protest leaders and arrived at agreements on the scope of permits for parades and meetings that were acceptable to all parties. The protest leaders, impressed with the reasonableness of the government spokesmen, made substantial efforts to cooperate with officials and ensure peace.

As the Chicago and Washington events differed in preparation, they differed in outcome. After minor skirmishes, trouble in Chicago escalated when throngs of demonstrators, having been denied permits to remain overnight, refused to leave Lincoln Park, their main gathering place. Dozens of police attempted to clear the park on three successive nights. In response to serious and deliberate provocations, but without coherent planning, some policemen clubbed and teargassed guilty and innocent alike, chasing demonstrators through streets some distance from the park. Particularly on the side streets, some bystanders who had taken no part in the demonstrations were attacked by police officers. Several media representatives were clubbed and had their cameras smashed. Predictably, tensions and anger rose. Extremists who would otherwise have been ignored began to attract audiences. They urged demonstrators to fight back. The police were exposed to more and more jeers and obscenities and had to withstand heavier barrages of rocks and other missiles. During one of the first nights, fifteen policemen were injured; two nights later, 149 were injured.

In Washington, the cycle of escalating violence never got started. Both verbal and physical provocations by demonstrators were frequently intense, but they were met with restraint. Provocation by policemen was rare; when it occurred it was terminated by police and city officials who intervened quickly to restore discipline. In general, police withstood physical and verbal abuse with great calm. In the end, the behavior of Washington officials and the police won praise in newspaper editorials and from leaders of the demonstrations.

There were some radical leaders, however, who were more grateful for the official response in Chicago, for it appeared to validate their characterizations of government as being "reactionary" and "repressive" and to increase support from other protesting groups. The chaos at Chicago also gave solidarity to the ranks of those who regard all demonstrators, however peaceful, as irresponsible "punks." The overall effect was to increase polarization and unrest, not diminish them.

This comparison between Chicago in August of 1968 and Washington last January can be closed on two encouraging notes. Permits for peace marches in Chicago were sought and granted in October 1969. The marches were organized by the "Weatherman," an extremely militant faction of the Students for a Democratic Society. In the course of the demonstrations, Chicago police had to face four days of intense provocation and wanton violence. This time, however, the police acted with calm and restraint. No injuries to residents, bystanders or newsmen were reported; on the contrary, the police took steps to safeguard bystanders from the violence. As a result of the professional conduct of Chicago police, violence was effectively contained, and blame for damage and injuries that did occur fell squarely upon the violent group among the demonstrators, many of whom were arrested.

The Peace Moratorium Parade and assembly in Washington on November 15 was another example of intelligent and restrained official response. Although the government had reason to expect that some elements among the protesting group were bent on violence, reasonable permits were ultimately negotiated with the responsible demonstration leaders and, ample police and military force were provided to preserve order if necessary. In the largest single protest demonstration in American history, the overwhelming majority of the participants behaved peacefully. Their activities were facilitated rather than restrained by the police. When the few extremists did attempt violent attacks on two occasions, the police responded quickly and firmly but, on the whole, without excessive force. As a result, order was maintained, the right to protest was upheld, and it was possible to judge both the peaceful and the violent aspects of the protest in their true proportion.

Civil governments must, of course, act promptly and decisively against threats to public order. As the National Advisory Commission on Civil Disorders stated: "Individuals cannot be permitted to endanger the public peace and safety, and public officials have a duty to make it clear that all just and necessary means to protect both will be used." [10]

Police manuals recognize that when the police are needed—as in urban riots, demonstrations that threaten violence, and campus disorders

---

[10] The National Advisory Commission on Civil Disorders, *Report of the National Advisory Commission on Civil Disorders*, U. S. Government Printing Office, Washington, 1968, p. 171.

in which court injunctions must be enforced—their behavior must be calm and impartial, however intense the provocation.   Panic, overt expressions of anger, and inflammatory use of force are serious breaches of police discipline.   The FBI riot control manual states that: [11]

A basic rule, when applying force, is to use only the minimum force necessary to effectively control the situation.   Unwarranted application of force will incite the mob to further violence, as well as kindle seeds of resentment for police that, in turn, could cause a riot to recur.

In a survey of 16 major cities, the Violence Commission's Task Force on Law and Law Enforcement found that few city governments had established formal, dependable communication links with dissident groups.   Few had adequate plans for dealing with disorders, and effective planning staffs were rare.   Though all have added riot control to the curriculum of police training, the number of hours devoted to training per man has not increased significantly.[12]

Control of Civil Disorders

The capability of a police department to control a civil disorder depends essentially on two factors: proper planning and competent performance.   These depend in turn upon the quantity and quality of police manpower, the training of patrolmen and police commanders, and the effectiveness of their equipment.

When underlying tensions are present—and they exist in every American city with a large minority population—a minor incident can turn a crowd into a mob.   In the summer of 1967 an appreciable number of incidents were triggered by police actions—some serious such as the shooting of a suspect, but usually by routine activities such as an arrest.

The way policemen approach an incident often determines whether it is contained or develops into a serious disorder.   Experienced police administrators consulted by the Commission on Civil Disorder repeatedly stressed the need for good judgment and common sense among police officers called to the scene of an incident in a neighborhood where tensions exist.   They warned against using sirens and flasher lights in situations that will attract crowds.   They cautioned against over-responding to an incident with too much visible force—riot guns and helmets may only aggravate a tense situation.   Yet they also pointed out that control has sometimes been lost because an insufficient number of police were on hand to control a disorder in its initial stages.   A

[11] Federal Bureau of Investigation, *Prevention and Control of Mobs and Riots*, Federal Bureau of Investigation, Washington, 1967, p. 89.

[12] *To Establish Justice, To Insure Domestic Tranquility*, op. cit.; pp. 70–76.

major lesson of the 1967 disorders was that it takes a seasoned senior officer to make the all-important initial assessments and decisions that will contain an incident.

If an incident develops, and a crowd begins to threaten lawlessness and acts of violence, the police must act promptly and with a sufficient display of force to make clear their intent and capacity to suppress disorder and insure the public safety.

Planning. Effective preparation for disorder requires careful planning. Large numbers of police officers must be mobilized, deployed, and directed by senior officers. They must have adequate logistical support, particularly if extended operations are necessary.

To mobilize enough policemen to handle a riot emergency is difficult, even in large cities. In one major city with a population of more than 1 million, an area of 140 square miles, and a police force of nearly 5,000 men, no more than 192 patrolmen were on duty when a major civil disorder erupted. Of these, only 44 were in the riot area. The difficulties in mobilizing additional men were described by the police commissioner: [13]

It cannot be emphasized too strongly that mobilization is inherently a time consuming operation, no matter how efficient. After a man is notified, he must dress and travel to his reporting point. Once he has checked in and has been equipped, he must be turned around and transported to a command post or an assembly point. There he must be briefed on the situation that exists, the location of the riot area, his duties, and other details required to make him effective once he is deployed. He must then be actually committed to the area of involvement. The time lapse in this entire procedure ranges from $1\frac{1}{2}$ to 2 hours.

By the time sufficient manpower was brought in, the disorder had developed beyond the control capability of the police department.

Adding to this difficulty is the fact that the standard training for police operations is basically different from that required for riot control. Traditional police training seeks to develop officers who can work independently and with little direct supervision. But the control of civil disturbances requires quite different performance—large numbers of disciplined personnel, comparable to soldiers in a military unit, organized and trained to work as members of a team under a highly unified command and control system. No matter how well-trained and skilled a police officer may be, he will be relatively ineffectual in dealing with civil disturbances so long as he functions as an

[13] The National Advisory Commission on Civil Disorders, *Report of the National Advisory Commission on Civil Disorders*, U. S. Government Printing Office, Washington, 1968, pp. 268.

individual. Thus, a major civil disturbance requires a police department to convert itself, suddenly, into a different type of organization with new operational procedures.

To cope with the difficulties of this transition, a police department needs a plan that can mobilize and deploy needed manpower with a minimum deviation from established operating procedures, and with minimum curtailment of essential police services.

A study conducted for the Civil Disorder Commission by the International Association of Chiefs of Police of 30 major police departments found that, while all had some form of written mobilization plan, the quality of the plans varied greatly. Principal defects were in the following areas: procedures for implementing the plan; provision for relief of reserve forces after the plan has been activated; accounting for personnel dispatched to a disorder; predesignation of assembly areas or command posts in the various areas of the cities where trouble might be expected; logistical support of police and other law enforcement officers engaged in control activities; flexibility in planning to cope with disorders of varying nature and magnitudes; and unnecessarily complicated planning that deviated excessively from normal operations.

Operational planning is a necessary complement to mobilization planning. It provides guidance to the police command and the men of the steps necessary to control the disorder, and it includes command and control mechanisms, communication, intelligence, means to combat inflammatory rumors, and tactics.

Whether the shift from normal routine police operations to an emergency basis is smooth and effective depends upon the speed with which the police can provide unified command and control. Under ordinary conditions, a police dispatcher controls the movement of men and equipment from a central position to places where they are needed. In most police departments the system works well enough so long as the demands on the dispatcher are within the capabilities of the man and his equipment.

Many local police departments called upon to control civil disorders have had serious problems in commanding and controlling the large numbers of men required to work together as an effective, coordinated team. The problem has been compounded by the shortage of on-duty supervisors and staff at certain periods of the day. It is one thing to assemble a large force; it is quite another to provide appropriate direction and leadership.

Effective command and control in a civil disorder depends upon communications, and communications is a function both of planning and of equipment. Relatively few police departments have adequate communications equipment or frequencies. Forty-two percent of all police departments studied by the Civil Disorders Commission had no special radio frequency for emergencies.

The lack of emergency frequencies overloads normal frequencies. This may not only preclude effective command and control of police in the area of a civil disorder but may also undermine the ability of the police to provide vital services to the remainder of the city.

The absence of adequate communication facilities is particularly acute with respect to outside police assistance. Approximately 50 percent of all police agencies surveyed had inadequate means to coordinate with neighboring police departments. When local and state police must cooperate with National Guard units, the need for communications coordination is urgent.

Miniaturized communications equipment for officers on foot is critically needed for command and control in civil disorders, particularly if the riot commanders are to exercise effective command and control over police units in control operations. At the present time police officers can generally communicate only to headquarters and only from a police vehicle.

The absence of accurate information both before and during a disorder has created special control problems for police. Police departments must develop means to obtain adequate intelligence for planning purposes, as well as on-the-scene information for use in police operations during a disorder.

An intelligence unit staffed with full-time personnel should be established to gather, evaluate, analyze, and disseminate information on potential as well as actual civil disorders. It should provide police administrators and commanders with reliable information essential for assessment and decision making. It should use undercover police personnel and informants, but it should also draw on community leaders, agencies, and organizations in the ghetto.

Planning is also necessary to cope with the ever present problem of rumors. A rumor collection center will enable police and other officials to counter false and inflammatory reports by giving accurate information rapidly to community leaders and others in troubled areas. Evaluation of rumors can also provide important information about potential disorders.

In one large city, for example, a "Rumor Central" unit established in the Commission on Human Relations has played an important role in averting trouble. When a Negro, after an argument, was shot to death by a white store owner who was placed in custody by the police, a rumor spread through the neighborhood that the white man would not be arrested. This false information was picked up by a radio station and broadcast. But Rumor Central, which received some 500 telephone calls about the incident, obtained the facts from the police and gave those facts to community leaders and news media. This appreciably assisted the police in alleviating tension.

In dealing with disorders, police have traditionally relied on the use of various squad formations and tactics to disperse crowds. These tactics have been of little or no value in some recent disorders marked by roving bands of rioters engaged in window breaking, looting, and firebombing.

Studies made for the Civil Disorders Commission indicate that the police are aware of the deficiency. Many police departments admitted that traditional riot control methods and squad tactics were wholly ineffective or only partially useful in the disorders. But no new and practical response to the recent types of disorders has emerged. Few departments have evolved new tactics against rioters. Even fewer have sent trained personnel to consult with officials in cities that have experienced civil disorders.

When should a mayor or local police chief call for state assistance? The answer is difficult partly because of the problem of determining when outside assistance is actually necessary, and partly because local officials may be understandably reluctant to admit that they cannot control the disorder.

No amount of planning will provide an automatic solution to this problem. Sound judgment on the part of mayors and police chiefs remains the only answer. Yet once the decision has been made, proper advance planning will help speed assistance.

Outside forces will need a relatively long lead time before response. A survey of National Guard capabilities, for example, shows that an average of 4 to 6 hours is required from the time of notification to the time of arrival of an effective complement of men.

Local authorities must not wait until the critical moment to alert a neighboring jurisdiction, the state police, or the National Guard. Outside control forces will then be unable to mobilize and respond on time. All agencies that may be asked to help control a civil disturbance must be alerted at an early stage and kept informed.

The Civil Disorders Commission studies disclosed serious deficiencies in police plans for logistical support. Many of these plans appear to assume that supplies and equipment will be on hand or will be available in the amounts required. The moment of need is too late to find out whether they are.

Regular police vehicles are usually inadequate for transporting and supplying large numbers of police, particularly since the men should be moved in units. Furthermore, a disorder extending over a long period of time will require the resupply of expended items and probably food and shelter for police personnel. In one city, when the failure to plan for these contingencies kept an entire police force on 24-hour duty, physical exhaustion seriously impaired police effectiveness.

A major problem in certain of the 1967 disorders arose from the large number of persons arrested. Facilities to transport, detain, process, feed, and house them were totally inadequate and no emergency or contingency planning had been done.

Training. The Civil Disorders Commission survey on the capabilities and preparedness of selected police departments showed that the most critical deficiency of all is in the area of training. Recruits receive an average of 18 hours of riot-control training; programs range from 62 hours to only 2. Little additional training is provided for supervisory and command officers.

Moreover, although riot control tactics require the work of highly disciplined and coordinated teams, almost all departments train policemen as individuals. Of the 19 departments reporting some post-recruit training for riot-control units, five limit training to the use of firearms and chemicals. In many cases, the training program is built around traditional military formations that have little applicability to the kinds of civil disorders experienced by our cities. Yet 50 percent of all the departments surveyed reported that they were generally satisfied with their training programs and planned no significant changes.

Basic riot control should be taught in recruit school, and intensive unit training should be conducted subsequently on a regular basis. Without this kind of training, police officers cannot be expected to perform effectively in controlling civil disturbances. Training supervisory and command personnel in the control of civil disorders must also be a continuing process.

Emergency plans and emergency operations must be reviewed in the classroom and practiced in the field. Yet few departments test their mobilization and operational plans. As a result, when carefully planned variations from the normal chain-of-command, communications, and unit assignments go into effect at a time of riot emergency, policemen are often unfamiliar with them. The most thoroughly developed emergency plan is useless unless all personnel fully understand it before it is put into operation.

Of the 30 police departments surveyed not a single one reported coordinated training with fire units. Yet recent experience shows a clear need for police-fire teamwork in riots. Even more revealing, only two of the departments surveyed have undertaken coordinated training with other community agencies required in a riot emergency. Only two departments reported coordinating their riot control training with the National Guard and state police.

In order to strengthen police training, the Civil Disaster Commission recomended: [14]

1. Departments should immediately allocate whatever time is necessary to reach an effective level of riot control capability. The need for training in civil disorder prevention and control is urgent.

2. Training must include all levels of personnel within the police agency, especially commanders. Post-recruit riot training must be a continuing process for all personnel which builds upon recruit training rather than duplicates it.

3. Riot-control training must be provided to groups expected to function as teams during actual riot conditions. Required levels of teamwork can be achieved only through team training. All special riot-control units must receive additional and intensive training in tactics and procedures, as well as in special equipment and weapons.

4. Mobilization plans and emergency procedures must be reviewed in the classroom and practiced in the field. All members of the department must be familiar with riot plans at all times.

5. Mayors and other civil officials must recognize the need and accept the responsibility for initiating regional training and coordination with military and state police personnel, as well as with other agencies of local government.

6. Police agencies must review and become familiar with recent riot experience so that training programs can be realistically adjusted in the light of anticipated problems.

7. In order to help law enforcement agencies improve their knowledge and strengthen their capabilities to prevent and control civil disorders, a national center and clearinghouse should be established to develop, evaluate, and disseminate riot prevention and control data and information.

A serious hazard faced by police officers during disorders is injury from bottles, rocks, and other missiles thrown by rioters. Yet few police departments can furnish every man assigned to civil disturbance duty with the proper equipment to protect head, face, and eyes. The Civil Disorders Commission found that protective clothing,

[14] *Ibid.*, pp. 270–271.

boots, and gloves are generally not available for the police, although most police administrators recommend their procurement and use. Police officers must have the proper personal equipment and clothing to safeguard them against the threat of bodily harm.

On the basis of a survey made of 30 major police departments, the Civil Disorders Commission found that many police forces are inadequately equipped or trained for use of even conventional riot control weapons and materiel. For example, although the police baton has proven to be a very effective weapon in situations where a low level of physical force will control a disorder, many police departments fail to instruct their men in the proper use of this control weapon. The value of the police baton should not be overlooked and police administrators should assure that proper training in its correct and most effective use is given to all police officers.

The only equipment found to be in adequate supply in police departments was hand guns. Experience has shown that these are relatively poor and ineffective weapons for dealing with a civil disorder.

The most serious deficiencies, however, are in advanced nonlethal weapons. Riot control authorities regard nonlethal chemical agents, such as tear gas, as the single most valuable and effective type of middle-range weapons in controlling civil disorders. In listing the priority of force to be applied in a disorder, the FBI manual on riot control, as well as Army and National Guard doctrine, prescribes the use of tear gas (CS and CN) before resorting to firearms. According to the FBI riot control manual: "They are the most effective and most humane means of achieving temporary neutralization of a mob with a minimum of personal injury."

While most of the police departments surveyed possessed some chemical weapons with varying degrees of supplies on hand, they lacked sufficient gas masks to equip even 30 percent of their personnel. The lack of gas masks restricts use of gas by many police forces.

Police and other civil officials have also been inhibited by the unfavorable psychological reaction to the use of any gas or chemical weapon. An additional restraint is created by the presence of large numbers of innocent people in the disorder area who would be affected by the traditional massive use of tear gas.

The recent development of new containers and projectile devices by the U.S. Army now makes it possible to use CS discriminatingly against small groups and even individuals. Police departments could use them to deal effectively and appropriately with looters and snipers.

Some police departments have recently been equipping police officers with a liquid tear gas device. Initial reports indicate that, though less effective than CS, it provides a useful method of dealing with unruly and dangerous individuals. Used properly, it renders offenders harmless for 10 to 15 minutes. Projectors now in production promise to give police a means of acting against lawless small groups or individuals up to a distance of 30 feet.

The use of distinctive colors and odors either added to a chemical agent or projected from a separate device may be an additional way to help police not only identify those engaged in vandalism and other illegal acts, but also deter others.

The exaggerated reports of sniping in many cities experiencing disorders created unwarranted apprehension among some police administrators. This concern has led to a belief in some communities that police officers should be armed with highly destructive implements of war.

The Civil Disorders Commission believed that equipping civil police with automatic rifles, machine guns, and other weapons of massive and indiscriminate destructive force is not warranted by the evidence. Chemical agents provide police forces with an effective and more appropriate weapon. If violence by rioters mounts beyond the control capability of the police, trained military forces should be called in. We should not attempt to convert our police into combat troops equipped for urban warfare.

The true source of police strength in maintaining order lies in the respect and good will of the public they serve. Great harm is likely to result from the use of military weapons of mass destruction by police forces which lack the command and control and firearms discipline of military units. Improper action could destroy the concept of civilian police as a public service agency dependent for effective operations on community cooperation and support.

The development of modern, nonlethal control equipment has languished because police departments lack the resources for tests and evaluation. The decentralized nature of law enforcement and the absence of standard criteria have also limited market opportunities. As a result, private industry has been reluctant to invest in research and development of new police equipment.

Accordingly, the Civil Disorders Commission recommended: [15]

1. The Federal Government should undertake an immediate program to test and evaluate available nonlethal weapons and related control equipment for use by police and control forces.

[15] *Ibid.*, p. 272.

2.   Federal support should be provided to establish criteria and standard specifications which would stimulate and facilitate the production of such items at a reasonably low cost.

3.   Federal funds should be used to develop appropriate tools and materiel for local and state law enforcement agencies.

If these recommendations are adopted, the result will be better maintenance of law and order and better control of disorders with fewer risks to police and the public.[16]

Police Community Relations

Community relations has been previously considered in Chapter 4. It is relevant to re-examine this key zone of police operations within the context of violence prevention and control.

Police officers across the country are analyzing their roles and relationships within the communities they serve. Recent Supreme Court decisions on police practices, problems of control in civil disturbances, accusations of brutality from minority groups, and public demands for improved professional services have highlighted the complexity of police work in a democratic society.

The police officer's role in a democracy is not an easy one, and it seems to become more difficult each day. The police are caught in the middle of myriad and conflicting demands. On the one hand, they are told to "get tough"; on the other, they are accused of brutality. They are pressured to crack down on crime and admonished by the Supreme Court to preserve the rights of individuals. The public insists on crime prevention and an end to riots, while at the same time demanding limited use of force. More positively, police are encouraged to play a more active role in the promotion of law and order and in the solution of urban problems.

The challenge to police work in a democracy is twofold:

1.   To maintain a balance between the security of the community and the rights of the individuals;

2.   To work with the community in the promotion of law and order.

A police administrator at a recent national conference on police-community relations training expressed the first challenge this way: [17]

16 *Ibid.*, pp. 267–272.

17 Francis A. Cizon and William H. T. Smith, *Police-Community Relations Training*, Law Enforcement Assistance Administration, Washington, 1970, p. 1.

The goals of the Police Department are twofold: 1) community security through the prevention of crime and disorder and the promotion of peace; 2) individual security through the protection of life, property and personal liberties. The problem of delicately balancing one with the other has always been the challenge of effective police work in a democracy.

How to protect and promote the common good while at the same time safeguarding the rights of all individuals—the innocent and the guilty—this is the special concern of professional police officers in a democracy.

Another police administrator at the same conference had this to say about police work: [18]

The primary function of the Police Department is to keep the peace and maintain law and order in conjunction with the people. Police work in a democracy implies helping people police themselves.

Traditionally, police officers in the cities have been recruited from the people who lived in the problem areas. The Irish police officer in the Irish community gave little or no special favor to the Irish offender, but he knew and he could identify with the people and conditions in the neighborhoods in which the crimes occurred. The same was usually true in the Polish and Italian communities. Distinctions could be made, in terms of the action of the people of one's own culture, between those who obeyed the law and those who broke the law.

Today, in most urban centers with heavy concentrations of minority groups (particularly Negroes, Puerto Ricans, Mexicans, and Southern Whites), the police do not come from the people living in the areas which have the highest rates of social disorganization. The police officer working in high crime areas is usually operating in what is to him a "totally alien culture." There is little or no real contact or knowledge, let alone identity, with most of the people in inner-city communities. Whatever contact or knowledge he does have of the people in the community is limited to the deviant or criminal elements. Thus, police attitude toward the community is usually a reflection of deviant and criminal elements. Nor do the minority groups see the police as their representatives in the community. They see them as members of an outside group attempting to enforce the codes of an "alien culture." The isolation of the police from the community coupled with an historical mutual antagonism of minority groups and police has prevented effective communication between them. This is the central focus of the special efforts to train police for effective understanding, interaction, and communication with the people of our complex urban communities.

[18] *Ibid.*, p. 2.

Police officers have become extremely sensitive to this problem and to the many demands placed upon them to do something about it. Many resist strenuously any efforts to modernize and professionalize police work with regard to community relations. The police are uncertain as to how they can positively promote law and order among people whom they do not understand and who do not understand them. The police are concerned with what they call the excessive limitations placed upon them in their efforts to arrest suspected criminals and to gather evidence for prosecution. They are not adverse to condemning the concept of community service as one more closely related to social work than to police work. Yet, not too long ago a report on police-community relations in California stated that: [19]

Some California Police Departments realize their particularly important role in helping to solve community race relations problems. Most California Departments realize that good community race relations aid the police in their law enforcement function. These realizations have led to efforts to construct visible community relations programs (with communication the most important point) and officer training programs in race relations.

To foster the growing awareness of the need for police training to improve community relations (and of helping the police resolve some of the difficulties brought on by inconsistent expectations of the public), the Office of Law Enforcement Assistance funded a number of community-relations programs in various cities. OLEA encouraged experimentation with programs and techniques of training for police in the hope of discovering the most effective means of increasing understanding and of strengthening the channels of communication between the police and the people of the community, particularly the poor and the minority groups. Experience with these programs has shown that the task of improving police-community relations through training programs for police is more complex than originally conceived. It has become clear that such special training programs are but a part of the overall police improvements needed.

The sensitivity of police to community relations training programs and the negative reactions with which such programs have been met in the past demands that careful consideration be given to the design, format and educative process of new programs. In previous programs, the officers have been more negative about the orientations and the mechanics of the programs than about their content. Police officers have not objected to training in human relations as much as they have objected to: (1) training programs which seem to be oriented to an accusative, derogatory and condemning approach to police actions;

[19] *Ibid.*, p. 3.

(2) programs which have been developed without full appreciation of the difficult conflict issues with which the police in a democracy are faced; and (3) programs which seem to have "outsiders" telling the police how bad they are and what and how much they "must be taught." Most police officers are aware of the need for police-community relations training, but they want desperately to tell the community their side of the story.

Whether the sensitivity and negative reaction of police officers to such training programs is justified or not, it must be carefully considered in the development of such programs. Changes in police behavior and attitudes through the influence of training programs will occur only if the police are meaningfully involved in the programs. Police-community training programs must be concerned not only with content and speakers but also with providing police officers with an atmosphere conducive to training and with motivations to learn new skills and develop new attitudes which will make their work in the community more effective.

Experiences with police-community relations training programs high-light several factors which seem to be essential to their success. Above all, the tendency of police to be highly resistive to human relations training demands careful planning and preparation for effective motivation and programming. Adult education and on-the-job training are effective only if they motivate toward learning and if they are meaningful in actual job function. The following points seem to be positively related to the most acceptable, meaningful, and, consequently, the most effective programs in the training of police in community relations: [20]

1. Police-Community relations training must be a part of a comprehensive training program for police officers which is designed to improve their knowledge, attitudes and skills consistently and systematically and to foster greater professionalism among police.

2. Departmental policy must not only give verbal support to such training efforts but must be action-oriented in implementing the principles of human relations and community involvement in all of its efforts whether these be relative to internal administration or to community contacts.

3. Program objectives must be positively stated in terms of police improvement, and not negatively in terms of police or community criticism. The content, procedures, and personnel in the program must reflect a sympathetic understanding of police problems and a positive approach to the improvement of police-community relations.

[20] *Ibid.*, p. 43.

4. The achievement of program objectives is directly related to the competency and dedication of the administrative staff. The administrative staff must have an empathic relationship to the men involved in the training and must be keenly aware of law enforcement complexities.

5. The training program should be designed specifically for police officers. It is unrealistic to expect such a program to train the total community. Careful consideration must be given to providing adequate incentives for attendance and meaningful participation in such programs.

6. The content of the program must be well organized and integrated so that each session is clearly related to the one preceding it as well as to the one following it. The logic of the program sequence must be clear at all points in the program. Speakers must be familiar with police problems and should be persons with whom the police can identify.

7. The program content is more important to the success of the program than the speakers; the relevance, continuity and effectiveness of the discussion sessions is more important than either the content or the speakers.

8. Every program should be systematically evaluated as to its effectiveness, but the evaluation research component should not be given priority over the actual training sessions.

The concept of police-community relations is not limited to a professional public relations effort to improve the image of the police in the community. It includes the involvement of the police in the total life of the community in which they serve as well as the enlistment of total community support of law enforcement. It means developing new channels of communication between the police and the community by increasing police contacts with all of the people of the community rather than only with those who come in conflict with the law. It assumes the need for changes in the police understanding of the community and the community understanding of the police. It takes as its goal the re-establishment of police involvement and respectability in the community served. It places a heavy responsibility on police departments to improve themselves and to carry a major responsibility for promoting better police-community relations.[21]

Report of the National Advisory Commission on Civil Disorders, 1968

This Commission cited deep hostility between police and ghetto communities as a primary cause of the disorders surveyed. In Newark, Detroit, Watts, and Harlem—in practically every city that has experi-

---

[21] *Ibid.*, pp. 1–45.

enced racial disruption since the summer of 1964, abrasive relationships between police and Negroes and other minority groups have been a major source of grievance, tension and, ultimately, disorder.

In a fundamental sense, however, it is wrong to define the problem solely as hostility to police. In many ways, the policeman only symbolizes much deeper problems. The policeman in the ghetto is a symbol not only of law, but of the entire system of law enforcement and criminal justice. As such, he becomes the tangible target for grievances against shortcomings throughout that system: Against assembly-line justice in teeming lower courts; against wide disparities in sentences; against antiquated correctional facilities; against the basic inequities imposed by the system on the poor—to whom, for example, the option of bail means only jail.

The policeman in the ghetto is a symbol of increasingly bitter social debate over law enforcement. One side, disturbed and perplexed by sharp rises in crime and urban violence, exerts extreme pressure on police for tougher law enforcement. Another group, inflamed against police as agents of repression, tends toward defiance of what it regards as order maintained at the expense of justice. The policeman in the ghetto is the most visible symbol, finally, of a society from which many ghetto Negroes are increasingly alienated.

At the same time, police responsibilities in the ghetto are even greater than elsewhere in the community since the other institutions of social control have so little authority: The schools, because so many are segregated, old and inferior; religion, which has become irrelevant to those who have lost faith as they lost hope; career aspirations, which for many young Negroes are totally lacking; the family, because its bonds are so often snapped. It is the policeman who must deal with the consequences of this institutional vacuum and is then resented for the presence and the measures this effort demands.

Alone, the policeman in the ghetto cannot solve these problems. His role is already one of the most difficult in our society. He must deal daily with a range of problems and people that test his patience, ingenuity, character, and courage in ways that few of us are ever tested. Without positive leadership, goals, operational guidance, and public support, the individual policeman can only feel victimized. Nor are these problems the responsibility only of police administrators; they are deep enough to tax the courage, intelligence and leadership of mayors, city officials, and community leaders. As Dr. Kenneth B. Clark told the Commission: [22]

This society knows   *   *   *   that if human beings are confined in ghetto compounds of our cities and are subjected to criminally inferior

22 *Ibid.*, pp. 157–158.

education, pervasive economic and job discrimination, committed to houses unfit for human habitation, subjected to unspeakable conditions of municipal services, such as sanitation, that such human beings are not likely to be responsive to appeals to be lawful, to be respectful, to be concerned with property of others.

And yet, precisely because the policeman in the ghetto is a symbol —precisely because he symbolizes so much—it is of critical importance that the police and society take every possible step to allay grievances that flow from a sense of injustice and increased tension and turmoil.

In the work, the police bear a major responsibility for making needed changes. In the first instance, they have the prime responsibility for safeguarding the minimum goal of any civilized society: Security of life and property. To do so, they are given society's maximum power: Discretion in the use of force. Second, it is axiomatic that effective law enforcement requires the support of the community. Such support will not be present when a substantial segment of the community feels threatened by the police and regards the police as an occupying force.

At the same time, public officials also have a clear duty to help the police make any necessary changes to minimize so far as possible the risk of further disorders. Five basic problem areas were identified: [23]

1. The need for change in police operations in the ghetto, to insure proper conduct by individual officers and to eliminate abrasive practices.

2. The need for more adequate police protection of ghetto residents, to eliminate the present high sense of insecurity to person and property.

3. The need for effective mechanisms for resolving citizen grievances against the police.

4. The need for policy guidelines to assist police in areas where police conduct can create tension.

5. The need to develop community support for law enforcement.

The Commission discusses each of these problem areas and follows with specific recommendations which relate directly to achieving more effective law enforcement and to the prevention and control of civil disorders.[24]

[23] The National Advisory Commission on Civil Disorders, Report of the National Advisory Commission on Civil Disorders, 1968, p. 158. For additional studies of riots see: Robert H. Connery, Editor, *Urban Riots*, Vintage Books, New York, 1969, William A. Heaps, *Riots U.S.A.*, The Seabury Press, New York, 1966, and Louis H. Masotti and Don R. Bowen, *Riots and Rebellion*, Sage Publications, Inc., Beverly Hills, 1968.

[24] *Ibid.*, pp. 157–158.

Chapter 15

CHALLENGE AND ASSESSMENT

THIS nation has been the subject of two comprehensive crime surveys, each having extensively analyzed the complexities of the crime phenomenon. In 1929, President Herbert Hoover established the National Commission of Law Observance and Enforcement, popularly identified as the Wickersham Commission, who completed a landmark study of criminality and the American police system. An hiatus of thirty six years occurred until President Lyndon Johnson established the Commission on Law Enforcement and Administration of Justice in 1965.

The Katzenbach Commission was created in response to the urgent recognition of the Nation's crime problem and the depth of ignorance about it. The report of the Commission described the many facets of crime in America emphasizing such phases as those who commit it, those who are its victims, and what can be done to reduce it. The report was the work of 19 commissioners, 63 staff members, 175 consultants, and hundreds of advisors. In the process of developing the findings and recommendations the Commission held three national conferences, conducted five national surveys, held hundreds of meetings, and interviewed tens of thousands of persons.

The Challenge of Crime in a Free Society

This comprehensive report made more than two hundred specific recommendations that the President's Commission on Law Enforcement and Administration of Justice believed would lead to a safer and more just society.

The recommendations called for a greatly increased effort on the part of the Federal Government, the States, the counties, the cities, civic organizations, religious institutions, business groups, and individual citizens. They called for basic changes in the operations of police, schools, prosecutors, employment agencies, defenders, social workers, prisons, housing authorities, and probation and parole officers.

The recommendations were more than just a list of new procedures, new tactics, and new techniques. They were a call for a revolution in the way America thinks about crime.

Many Americans have taken comfort in the view that crime was the vice of a handful of people. This view is inaccurate. In the United States today, one boy in six is referred to the juvenile court.

447

A Commission survey showed that in 1965 more than two million Americans were received in prisons or juvenile training schools, or placed on probation.   Another Commission study suggests that about 40 percent of all male children now living in the United States will be arrested for a nontraffic offense during their lives.   An independent survey of 1,700 persons found that 91 percent of the sample admitted they had committed acts for which they might have received jail or prison sentences.

Many Americans also think of crime as a very narrow range of behavior.   It is not.   An enormous variety of acts make up the "crime problem."   Crime is not just a tough teenager snatching a lady's purse. It is a professional thief stealing cars "on order."   It is a well-heeled loan shark taking over a previously legitimate business for organized crime.   It is a polite young man who suddenly and inexplicably murders his family.   It is a corporation executive conspiring with competitors to keep prices high.   No single formula, no single theory, no single generalization can explain the vast range of behavior called crime.

Many Americans think controlling crime is solely the task of the police, the courts, and correction agencies.   In fact, as the Commission's report makes clear, crime cannot be controlled without the interest and participation of schools, businesses, social agencies, private groups, and individual citizens.

What, then, is America's experience with crime and how has this experience shaped the Nation's way of living?   A new insight into these two questions is furnished by the Commission's National Survey of Criminal Victims.   In this survey, the first of its kind conducted on such a scope 10,000 representative American households were asked about their experiences with crime, whether they reported those experiences to the police, and how those experiences affected their lives.

An important finding of the survey is that for the Nation as a whole there is far more crime than ever is reported.   Burglaries occur about three times more often than they are reported to police.   Aggravated assaults and larcenies over $50 occur twice as often as they are reported.   There are 50 percent more robberies than are reported.   In some areas, only one-tenth of the total number of certain kinds of crimes are reported to the police.   Seventy-four percent of the neighborhood commercial establishments surveyed do not report to police the thefts committed by their employees.

The existence of crime, the talk about crime, the reports of crime, and the fear of crime have eroded the basic quality of life of many

Americans.   A Commission study conducted in high crime areas of two large cities found that: [1]

1. 43 percent of the respondents say they stay off the streets at night because of their fear of crime.

2. 35 percent say they do not speak to strangers any more because of their fear of crime.

3. 21 percent say they use cars and cabs at night because of their fear of crime.

4. 20 percent say they would like to move to another neighborhood because of their fear of crime.

The findings of the Commission's national survey generally support those of the local surveys.   One-third of a representative sample of all Americans say it is unsafe to walk alone at night in their neighborhoods. Slightly more than one-third say they keep firearms in the house for protection against criminals.   Twenty-eight percent say they keep watchdogs for the same reason.

Under any circumstance, developing an effective response to the problem of crime in America is exceedingly difficult.   And because of the changes expected in the population in the next decade, in years to come it will be more difficult.   Young people commit a disproportionate share of crime and the number of young people in our society is growing at a much faster rate than the total population.   Although the 15- to 17-year-old age group represents only 5.4 percent of the population, it accounts for 12.8 percent of all arrests.   Fifteen and sixteen year-olds have the highest arrest rate in the United States.   The problem in the years ahead is dramatically foretold by the fact that 23 percent of the population is 10 or under.

Despite the seriousness of the problem today and the increasing challenge in the years ahead, the central conclusion of the Commission is that a significant reduction in crime is possible if the following objectives are vigorously pursued:

First, society must seek to prevent crime before it happens by assuring all Americans a stake in the benefits and responsibilities of American life, by strengthening law enforcement, and by reducing criminal opportunities.

Second, society's aim of reducing crime would be better served if the system of criminal justice developed a far broader range of techniques with which to deal with individual offenders.

[1] The President's Commission on Law Enforcement and Administration of Justice, *The Challenge of Crime in a Free Society*, U. S. Government Printing Office, Washington, 1967, p. v.

Third, the system of criminal justice must eliminate existing injustices if it is to achieve its ideals and win the respect and cooperation of all citizens.

Fourth, the system of criminal justice must attract more people and better people—police, prosecutors, judges, defense attorneys, probation and parole officers, and corrections officials with more knowledge, expertise, initiative, and integrity.

Fifth, there must be much more operational and basic research into the problems of crime and criminal administration, by those both within and without the system of criminal justice.

Sixth, the police, courts, and correctional agencies must be given substantially greater amounts of money if they are to improve their ability to control crime.

Seventh, individual citizens, civic and business organizations, religious institutions, and all levels of government must take responsibility for planning and implementing the changes that must be made in the criminal justice system if crime is to be reduced.

In terms of specific recommendations, what do these seven objectives mean?

The prevention of crime covers a wide range of activities: Eliminating social conditions closely associated with crime; improving the ability of the criminal justice system to detect, apprehend, judge, and reintegrate into their communities those who commit crimes; and reducing the situations in which crimes are most likely to be committed.

Every effort must be made to strengthen the family, now often shattered by the grinding pressures of urban slums.

Slum schools must be given enough resources to make them as good as schools elsewhere and to enable them to compensate for the various handicaps suffered by the slum child—to rescue him from his environment.

Present efforts to combat school segregation, and the housing segregation that underlies it, must be continued and expanded.

Employment opportunities must be enlarged and young people provided with more effective vocational training and individual job counseling. Programs to create new kinds of jobs—such as probation aides, medical assistants, and teacher helpers—seem particularly promising and should be expanded.

The problem of increasing the ability of the police to detect and apprehend criminals is complicated. In one effort to find out how this objective could be achieved, the Commission conducted an analysis of 1,905 crimes reported to the Los Angeles Police Department during a recent month.   The study showed the importance of identifying the perpetrator at the scene of the crime.   Eighty-six percent of the crimes with named suspects were solved, but only 12 percent of the unnamed suspect crimes were solved.   Another finding of the study was that there is a relationship between the speed of response and certainty of apprehension.   On the average, response to emergency calls resulting in arrests was 50 percent faster than response to emergency calls not resulting in arrest.   On the basis of this finding, and a cost effectiveness study to discover the best means to reduce response time, the Commission recommends an experimental program to develop computer-aided command-and-control systems for large police departments.

To insure the maximum use of such a system, headquarters must have a direct link with every on-duty police officer.   Because large scale production would result in a substantial reduction of the cost of miniature two-way radios, the Commission recommends that the Federal Government assume leadership in initiating a development program for such equipment and that it consider guaranteeing the sale of the first production lot of perhaps 20,000 units.

Two other steps to reduce police response time were recommended: [2]

1.   Police callboxes, which are locked and inconspicuous in most cities, should be left open, brightly marked, and designated "public emergency callboxes."

2.   The telephone company should develop a single police number for each metropolitan area, and eventually for the entire United States.

Improving the effectiveness of law enforcement, however, is much more than improving police response time.   For example a study in Washington, D.C., found that courtroom time for a felony defendant who pleads guilty probably totals less than 1 hour, while the median time from his initial appearance to his disposition is four months.

In an effort to discover how courts can best speed the process of criminal justice, the known facts about felony cases in Washington were placed in a computer and the operation of the system was simulated.   After a number of possible solutions to the problem of delay were tested, it appeared that the addition of a second grand jury—which, with supporting personnel, would cost less than $50,000 a year—would result in a 25-percent reduction in the time required for the typical felony case to move from initial appearance to trial.

[2] *Ibid.*, p. vi.

The application of such analysis—when combined with the Commission's recommended timetable laying out timespans for each step in the criminal process—should help court systems to ascertain their procedural bottlenecks and develop ways to eliminate them.

Another way to prevent crime is to reduce the opportunity to commit it. Many crimes would not be committed, indeed many criminal carreers would not begin, if there were fewer opportunities for crime.

Auto theft is a good example. According to FBI statistics, the key had been left in the ignition or the ignition had been left unlocked in 42 percent of all stolen cars. Even in those cars taken when the ignition was locked, at least 20 percent were stolen simply by shorting the ignition with such simple devices as paper clips or tinfoil. In one city, the elimination of the unlocked "off" position on the 1955 Chevrolet resulted in 50 percent fewer of those models being stolen in 1965 than were stolen in 1964.

On the basis of these findings, it appears that an important reduction in auto theft could be achieved simply by installing an ignition system that automatically ejects the key when the engine is turned off.

A major reason that it is important to reduce auto theft is that stealing a car is very often the criminal act that starts a boy on a course of lawbreaking.

Stricter gun controls also would reduce some kinds of crime. Here, the Commission recommended a strengthening of the Federal law governing the interstate shipment of firearms and enactment of State laws requiring the registration of all handguns, rifles, and shotguns, and prohibiting the sale or ownership of firearms by certain categories of persons—dangerous criminals, habitual drunkards, and drug addicts. After 5 years, the Commission recommended that Congress pass a Federal registration law applying to those States that have not passed their own registration laws.

The Commission's second objective—the development of a far broader range of alternatives for dealing with offenders was based on the belief that, while there are some who must be completely segregated from society, there are many instances in which segregation does more harm than good. Furthermore, by concentrating the resources of the police, the courts, and correctional agencies on the smaller number of offenders who really need them, it should be possible to give all offenders more effective treatment.

A specific and important example of this principle was the Commission's recommendation that every community consider establishing a Youth Services Bureau, a community-based center to which juveniles could be referred by the police, the courts, parents, schools, and social agencies for counseling, education, work, or recreation programs and job placement.

The Youth Services Bureau—an agency to handle many troubled and troublesome young people outside the criminal system—is needed in part because society has failed to give the juvenile court the resources that would allow it to function as its founders hoped it would. In a recent survey of juvenile court judges, for example, 83 percent said no psychologist or psychiatrist was available to their courts on a regular basis and one-third said they did not have probation officers or social workers. Even where there are probation officers, the Commission found, the average officer supervises 76 probationers, more than double the recommended caseload.

The California Youth Authority for the last 5 years has been conducting a controlled experiment to determine the effectiveness of another kind of alternative treatment program for juveniles. There, after initial screening, convicted juvenile delinquents are assigned on a random basis to either an experimental group or a control group. Those in the experimental group are returned to the community and receive intensive individual counseling, group counseling, group therapy, and family counseling. Those in the control group are assigned to California's regular institutional treatment program. The findings so far: 28 percent of the experimental group have had their paroles revoked, compared with 52 percent in the control group. Furthermore, the community treatment program is less expensive than institutional treatment.

To make community-based treatment possible for both adults and juveniles, the Commission recommends the development of an entirely new kind of correctional institution: located close to population centers; maintaining close relations with schools, employers, and universities; housing as few as 50 inmates; serving as a classification center, as the center for various kinds of community programs and as a port of reentry to the community for those difficult and dangerous offenders who have required treatment in facilities with tighter custody.

Such institutions would be useful in the operation of programs— strongly recommended by the Commission—that permit selected inmates to work or study in the community during the day and return to control at night, and programs that permit long-term inmates to become adjusted to society gradually rather than being discharged directly from maximum security institutions to the streets.

Another aspect of the Commission's conviction that different offenders with different problems should be treated in different ways, is its recommendation about the handling of public drunkenness, which, in 1965, accounted for one out of every three arrests in America. The great number of these arrests—some 2 million—burdens the police, clogs the lower courts and crowds the penal institutions. The Commission therefore recommended that communities develop civil detoxification units and comprehensive aftercare programs, and that with the development of such programs, drunkenness, not accompanied by other unlawful conduct, should not be a criminal offense. Similarly, the Commission recommended the expanded use of civil commitment for drug addicts.

The third objective was to eliminate injustices so that the system of criminal justice can win the respect and cooperation of all citizens. Our society must give the police, the courts, and correctional agencies the resources and the mandate to provide fair and dignified treatment for all.

The Commission found overwhelming evidence of institutional shortcomings in almost every part of the United States. A survey of the lower court operations in a number of large American cities found cramped and noisy courtrooms, undignified and perfunctory procedures, badly trained personnel overwhelmed by enormous caseloads. In short, the Commission found assembly-line justice. The Commission found that in at least three States, justices of the peace are paid only if they convict and collect a fee from the defendant, a practice held unconstitutional by the Supreme Court forty years ago.

The Commission found that approximately one-fourth of the 400,000 children detained in 1965—for a variety of causes but including truancy, smoking, and running away from home—were held in adult jails and lockups, often with hardened criminals.

In addition to the creation of new kinds of institutions—such as the Youth Services Bureau and the small, community-based correctional centers—the Commission recommended several important procedural changes. It recommended counsel at various points in the criminal process. For juveniles, the Commission recommended providing counsel whenever coercive action is a possibility. For adults, the Commission recommended providing counsel to any criminal defendant who faces a significant penalty—excluding traffic and similar petty charges—if he cannot afford to provide counsel for himself. In connection with this recommendation, the Commission asks each State to finance regular, statewide assigned counsel and defender systems for the indigent. Counsel also should be provided in parole and probation revocation hearings.

Another kind of broad procedural change that the Commission recommended was that every State, county, and local jurisdiction provide judicial officers with sufficient information about individual defendants to permit the release without money bail of those who can be safely released.

In addition to eliminating the injustice of holding persons charged with a crime merely because they cannot afford bail, this recommendation also would save a good deal of money. New York City alone, for example, spends approximately $10 million a year holding persons who have not yet been found guilty of any crime.

Besides institutional injustices, the Commission found that while the great majority of criminal justice and law enforcement personnel perform their duties with fairness and understanding even under the most trying circumstances, some take advantage of their official positions and act in a callous, corrupt, or brutal manner.

Injustice will not yield to simple solutions. Overcoming it requires a wide variety of remedies including improved methods of selecting personnel, the massive infusion of additional funds, the revamping of existing procedures and the adoption of more effective internal and external controls.

The relations between the police and urban poor deserve special mention. Here the Commission recommended that every large department—especially in communities with substantial minority populations—should have community-relations machinery consisting of a headquarters planning and supervising unit and precinct units to carry out recommended programs. Effective citizen advisory committees should be established in minority group neighborhoods. All departments with substantial minority populations should make special efforts to recruit minority group officers and to deploy and promote them fairly. They should have rigorous internal investigation units to examine complaints of misconduct. The Commission believed that it was of the utmost importance to insure that complaints of unfair treatment are fairly dealt with.

Fair treatment of every individual—fair in fact and also perceived to be fair by those affected—is an essential element of justice and a principal objective of the American criminal justice system.

The fourth objective was that higher levels of knowledge, expertise, initiative, and integrity be achieved by police, judges, prosecutors, defense attorneys, and correctional authorities so that the system of criminal justice can improve its ability to control crime.

The Commission found one obstacle to recruiting better police officers was the standard requirement that all candidates—regardless of qualifications—begin their careers at the lowest level and normally remain at this level from 2 to 5 years before being eligible for promotion. Thus, a college graduate must enter a department at the same rank and pay and perform the same tasks as a person who enters with only a high school diploma or less.

The Commission recommended that police departments give up single entry and establish three levels at which candidates may begin their police careers. The Commission calls these three levels the "community service officer," the "police officer," and the "police agent."

This division, in addition to providing an entry place for the better educated, also would permit police departments to tap the special knowledge, skills, and understanding of those brought up in the slums.

The community service officer would be a uniformed but unarmed member of the police department. Two of his major responsibilities would be to maintain close relations with juveniles in the area where he works and to be especially alert to crime-breeding conditions that other city agencies had not dealt with. Typically, the CSO might be under 21, might not be required to meet conventional education requirements, and might work out of a store-front office. Serving as an apprentice policeman—a substitute for the police cadet—the CSO would work as a member of a team with the police officer and police agent.

The police officer would respond to calls for service, perform routine patrol, render emergency services, make preliminary investigations, and enforce traffic regulations. In order to qualify as a police officer at the present time, a candidate should possess a high school diploma and should demonstrate a capacity for college work.

The police agent would do whatever police jobs were most complicated, most sensitive, and most demanding. He might be a specialist in police community-relations or juvenile delinquency. He might be in uniform patrolling a high-crime neighborhood. He might have staff duties. To become a police agent would require at least 2 years of college work and preferably a baccalaureate degree in the liberal arts or social sciences.

As an ultimate goal, the Commission recommended that all police personnel with general enforcement powers have baccalaureate degrees.

While candidates could enter the police service at any one of the three levels, they also could work their way up through the different categories as they meet the basic education and other requirements.

In many jurisdictions there is a critical need for additional police personnel. Studies by the Commission indicate a recruiting need of

50,000 policemen in 1967 just to fill positions already authorized. In order to increase police effectiveness, additional staff specialists will be required, and when the community service officers are added manpower needs will be even greater.

The Commission also recommended that every State establish a commission on police standards to set minimum recruiting and training standards and to provide financial and technical assistance for local police departments.

In order to improve the quality of judges, prosecutors, and defense attorneys, the Commission recommends a variety of steps: Taking the selection of judges out of partisan politics; the more regular use of seminars, conferences, and institutes to train sitting judges; the establishment of judicial commissions to excuse physically or mentally incapacitated judges from their duties without public humiliation; the general abolition of part-time district attorneys and assistant district attorneys; and a broad range of measures to develop a greatly enlarged and better trained pool of defense attorneys.

In the correctional system there is a critical shortage of probation and parole officers, teachers, caseworkers, vocational instructors, and group workers. The need for major manpower increases in this area was made clear by the findings from the Commissions national corrections survey:[3]

1. Less than 3 percent of all personnel working in local jails and institutions devote their time to treatment and training.

2. Eleven States do not offer any kind of probation services for adult misdemeanants, six offer only the barest fragments of such services, and most States offer them on a spotty basis.

3. Two-thirds of all State adult felony probationers are in caseloads of over 100 persons.

To meet the requirements of both the correctional agencies and the courts, the Commission has found an immediate need to double the Nation's pool of juvenile probation officers, triple the number of probation officers working with adult felons, and increase sevenfold the number of officers working with misdemeanants.

Another area with a critical need for large numbers of expert criminal justice officers is the complex one of controlling organized crime. Here, the Commission recommended that prosecutors and police in every State and city where organized crime is known to, or may exist, develop special organized crime units.

3 *Ibid.*, p. ix.

The fifth objective was that every segment of the system of criminal justice devote a significant part of its resources for research to insure the development of new and effective methods of controlling crime.

The Commission found that little research was being conducted into such matters as the economic impact of crime; the effects on crime of increasing or decreasing criminal sanctions; possible methods for improving the effectiveness of various procedures of the police, courts, and correctional agencies.

Organized crime was another area in which almost no research had been conducted. The Commission found that the only group with any significant knowledge about this problem was law enforcement officials. Those in other disciplines—social scientists, economists and lawyers, for example—have not until recently considered the possibility of research projects on organized crime.

A small fraction of 1 percent of the criminal justice system's total budget is spent on research. This figure could be multiplied many times without approaching the 3 percent industry spends on research, much less the 15 percent the Defense Department spends. The Commission believed it should be multiplied many times.

That research is a powerful force for change in the field of criminal justice perhaps can best be documented by the history of the Vera Institute in New York City. Here the research of a small, non-government agency has in a very short time led to major changes in the bail procedures of approximately 100 cities, several States, and the Federal Government.

Because of the importance of research, the Commission recommended that major criminal justice agencies—such as State court and correctional systems and big-city police departments—organize operational research units as integral parts of their structures.

In addition, the criminal justice agencies should welcome the efforts of scholars and other independent experts to understand their problems and operations. These agencies cannot undertake needed research on their own; they urgently need the help of outsiders.

The Commission also recommended the establishment of several regional research institutes designed to concentrate a number of different disciplines on the problem of crime. It further recommended the establishment of an independent National Criminal Research Foundation to stimulate and coordinate research and disseminate its results.

One essential requirement for research is more complete information about the operation of the criminal process. To meet this requirement, the Commission recommended the creation of a National Criminal Justice Statistics Center. The Center's first responsibility would be to work with the FBI, the Children's Bureau, the Federal Bureau of Prisons, and other agencies to develop an integrated picture of the number of crimes reported to police, the number of persons arrested, the number of accused persons prosecuted, the number of offenders placed on probation, in prison, and subsequently on parole.

Another major responsibility of the Center would be to continue the Commission's initial effort to develop a new yardstick to measure the extent of crime in our society as a supplement to the FBI's Uniform Crime Reports. The Commission believes that the Government should be able to plot the levels of different kinds of crime in a city or a State as precisely as the Labor Department and the Census Bureau now plot the rate of unemployment. Just as unemployment information is essential to sound economic planning, so some day may criminal information help official planning in the system of criminal justice.

Sixth, the police, the courts, and correctional agencies will require substantially more money if they are to control crime better.

Almost all of the specific recommendations made by the Commission will involve increased budgets. Substantially higher salaries must be offered to attract top-flight candidates to the system of criminal justice. For example, the median annual salary for a patrolman in a large city today is $5,300. Typically, the maximum salary is something less than $1,000 above the starting salary. The Commission believed the most important change that can be made in police salary scales is to increase maximums sharply. An FBI agent, for example starts at $8,421 a year and if he serves long and well enough can reach $16,905 a year without being promoted to a supervisory position. The Commission was aware that reaching such figures immediately was not possible in many cities, but it believed that there should be a large range from minimum to maximum everywhere.

The Commission also recommended new kinds of programs that will require additional funds: Youth Services Bureaus, greatly enlarged misdemeanant probation services and increased levels of research, for example.

The Commission believed some of the additional resources—especially those devoted to innovative programs and to training, education, and research—should be contributed by the Federal Government.

The Federal Government already is conducting a broad range of programs—aid to elementary and secondary schools, the Neighborhood Youth Corps, Project Head Start, and others—designed to attack directly the social problems often associated with crime.

Through such agencies as the Federal Bureau of Investigation, the Office of Law Enforcement Assistance, the Bureau of Prisons, and the Office of Manpower Development and Training, the Federal Government also offers comparatively limited financial and technical assistance to the police, the courts, and corrections authorities.

While the Commission was convinced State and local governments must continue to carry the major burden of criminal administration, it recommended a vastly enlarged program of Federal assistance to strengthen law enforcement, crime prevention, and the administration of justice. The program of Federal support recommended by the Commission was directed to eight major needs: [4]

1. State and local planning.
2. Education and training of criminal justice personnel.
3. Surveys and advisory services concerning the organization and operation of police departments, courts, prosecuting offices, and corrections agencies.
4. Development of a coordinated national information system for operational and research purposes.
5. Funding of limited numbers of demonstration programs in agencies of justice.
6. Scientific and technological research and development.
7. Development of national and regional research centers.
8. Grants-in-aid for operational innovations.

The Commission was not in a position to recommend the exact amount of money that would be needed to carry out its proposed program. It believed, however, that a Federal program totaling hundreds of millions of dollars a year during the next decade could be effectively utilized. The Commission also believed the major responsibility for administering this program should lie within the Department of Justice.

The States, the cities, and the counties also will have to make substantial increases in their contributions to the system of criminal justice.

Seventh, individual citizens, social-service agencies, universities, religious institutions, civic and business groups, and all kinds of governmental agencies at all levels must become involved in planning and executing changes in the criminal justice system.

The Commission was convinced that the financial and technical assistance program it proposes can and should be only a small part of the national effort to develop a more effective and fair response to crime.

[4] *Ibid.*, p. xi.

In March of 1966, President Johnson asked the Attorney General to invite each Governor to form a State committee on criminal administration. The response to this request was encouraging; more than two-thirds of the States already have such committees or have indicated they intend to form them.

The Commission recommended that in every State and city there should be an agency, or one or more officials, with specific responsibility for planning improvements in criminal administration and encouraging their implementation.

Planning agencies, among other functions, play a key role in helping State legislatures and city councils decide where additional funds and manpower are most needed, what new programs should be adopted, and where and how existing agencies might pool their resources on either a metropolitan or regional basis.

The planning agencies should include both officials from the system of criminal justice and citizens from other professions. Plans to improve criminal administration will be impossible to put into effect unless those responsible for criminal administration help make them. On the other hand, crime prevention must be the task of the community as a whole.

While this report concentrated on recommendations for action by governments, the Commission was convinced that governmental actions will not be enough. Crime is a social problem that is interwoven with almost every aspect of American life. Controlling it involves improving the quality of family life, the way schools are run, the cities are planned, the way workers are hired. Controlling crime is the business of every American Institution. Controlling crime is the business of every American.

Universities should increase their research on the problems of crime; private social welfare organizations and religious institutions should continue to experiment with advanced techniques of helping slum children overcome their environment; labor unions and businesses can enlarge their programs to provide prisoners with vocational training; professional and community organizations can help probation and parole workers with their work.

The responsibility of the individual citizen runs far deeper than cooperating with the police or accepting jury duty or insuring the safety of his family by installing adequate locks—important as they are. He must respect the law, refuse to cut corners, reject the cynical argument that "anything goes as long as you don't get caught."

Most important of all, he must, on his own and through the organizations he belongs to, interest himself in the problems of crime and criminal justice, seek information, express his views, use his vote wisely, get involved.

In sum, the Commission was sure that the Nation could control crime if it would.[5]

Task Force Report: The Police

The entire report directs its attention to how the police can either overcome or more effectively work within the limitations that are placed on law enforcement agencies of this Nation.   Many of these limitations are functional in nature and can be resolved by improvements or changes in the organizational and operational aspects of police dedepartments.

One area in which the report directed its attention was the need for developing law enforcement policies as guidelines to assist police officers in handling the wide variety of situations with which they are confronted.   Clear-cut and concise administrative policies circumscribing the discretion of the individual police officer are certainly of primary importance if there is to be a basic improvement in law enforcement.

It was pointed out that scientific and technological equipment is sorely needed along with instructions for its practical application.   In addition, personnel who are better educated and well trained to perform their difficult tasks must be attracted to police work.

Emphasis is placed on the problems of public hostility and indifference as the most perplexing facing the police.   Police-community relations, citizen assistance, and police integrity are additional vital topics considered by the task force report.   Lastly, consideration is given to the coordination or pooling of police resources, and the need for state agencies to establish standards for police personnel.

The recommendations of the task force report on the police can serve as guidelines for progressive police administrators.   Each of the 34 recommendations are listed below as they might be utilized as a check list to measure the police fields progress toward full-fledged professionalization:[6]

1.   State legislatures should enact statutory provisions with respect to the authority of law enforcement officers to stop persons for brief questioning, including specifications of the circumstances and limitations under which stops are permissible.

---

5 *Ibid.*, pp. v–xi.

6 The President's Commission on Law Enforcement and Administration of Justice, *Task Force Report: The Police,* U. S. Government Printing Office, Washington, 1967, pp. 1–228.

2. The police should formally participate in community planning in all cities.

3. Police departments in all large communities should have community-relations machinery consisting of a headquarters unit that plans and supervises the department's community-relations programs. It should also have precinct units, responsible to the precinct commander, that carry out the programs. Community relations must be both a staff and a line function. Such machinery is a matter of the greatest importance in any community that has a substantial minority population.

4. In each police precinct in a minority-group neighborhood there should be a citizens' advisory committee that meets regularly with police officials to work out solutions to problems of conflict between the police and the community. It is crucial that the committees be broadly representative of the community as a whole, including those elements who are critical or aggrieved.

5. It should be a high-priority objective of all departments in communities with a substantial minority population to recruit minority-group officers, and to deploy and promote them fairly. Every officer in such departments should receive thorough grounding in community-relations subjects. His performance in the field of community relations should be periodically reviewed and evaluated.

6. Every jurisdiction should provide adequate procedures for full and fair processing of all citizen grievances and complaints about the conduct of any public officer or employee.

7. Police departments should develop and enunciate policies that give police personnel specific guidance for the common situations requiring exercise of police discretion. Policies should cover such matters, among others, as the issuance of orders to citizens regarding their movements or activities, the handling of minor disputes, the safeguarding of the rights of free speech and free assembly, the selection and use of investigative methods, and the decision whether or not to arrest in specific situations involving specific crimes.

8. Each municipality, and other jurisdiction responsible for law enforcement, should carefully assess the manpower needs of its police agency on the basis of efficient use of all its personnel and should provide the resources required to meet the need for increased personnel if such a need is found to exist.

9. Basic police functions, especially in large and medium sized urban departments, should be divided among three kinds of officers, here termed the "community service officer," the "police officer," and the "police agent."

10. Police departments should recruit far more actively than they now do, with special attention to college campuses and innercity neighborhoods.

11. The ultimate aim of all police departments should be that all personnel with general enforcement powers have baccalaureate degrees.

12. Police departments should take immediate steps to establish a minimum requirement of a baccalaureate degree for all supervisory and executive positions.

13. Until reliable tests are devised for identifying and measuring the personal characteristics that contribute to good police work, intelligence tests, thorough background investigations and personal interviews should be used by all departments as absolute minimum techniques to determine the moral character and the intellectual and emotional fitness of police candidates.

14. Police departments and civil service commissions should reexamine and, if necessary, modify present recruitment standards on age, height, weight, visual acuity, and prior residence. The appointing authority should place primary emphasis on the education, background, character and personality of a candidate for police service.

15. Police salaries must be raised, particularly by increasing maximums. In order to attract college graduates to police service, starting and maximum salaries must be competitive with other professions and occupations that seek the same graduates.

16. Salary proposals for each department within local government should be considered on their own merits and should not be joined with the demands of other departments within a city.

17. Promotion eligibility requirements should stress ability above seniority. Promotion "lists" should be compiled on the basis not only of scores on technical examinations but on prior performance, character, educational achievement and leadership potential.

18. To encourage lateral movement of police personnel, a nationwide retirement system should be devised that permits the transferring of retirement credits.

19. All training programs should provide instruction on subjects that prepare recruits to exercise discretion properly, and to understand the community, the role of the police, and what the criminal justice system can and cannot do. Professional educators and civilian experts should be used to teach specialized courses—law and psychology, for example. Recognized teaching techniques such as problem-solving seminars should be incorporated into training programs.

20. Formal police training programs for recruits in all departments, large and small, should consist of an absolute minimum of 400 hours of classroom work spread over a 4-to-6-month period so that it can be combined with carefully selected and supervised field training.

21. Entering officers should serve probation periods of, preferably, 18 months and certainly no less than 1 year. During this period the recruit should be systematically observed and rated. Chief administrators should have the sole authority of dismissal during the probation period and should willingly exercise it against unsatisfactory officers.

22. Every general enforcement officer should have at least 1 week of intensive inservice training a year. Every officer should be given incentives to continue his general education or acquire special skills outside his department.

23. Each State, through its commission on police standards, should provide financial and technical assistance to departments to conduct surveys and make recommendations for improvement and modernization of their organization, management, and operations.

24. Every medium- and large-sized department should employ a skilled lawyer full time as its legal adviser. Smaller departments should arrange for legal advice on a part-time basis.

25. Police departments must take every possible step to implement the guiding organizational principle of central control. Specialist staff units for such matters as planning, research, legal advice, and police personnel should include persons trained in a variety of disciplines and should be utilized to develop and improve the policies, operations, and administration of each police function.

26. Every department in a big or medium-sized city should organize key ranking staff and line personnel into an administrative board similar in function to a corporation's board of directors, whose duty would be to assist the chief and his staff units in developing, enunciating and enforcing departmental policies and guidelines for the day-to-day activities of line personnel.

27. Every department, regardless of size, should have a comprehensive program for maintaining police integrity and every medium- and large-sized department should have a well-manned internal investigation unit responsible only to the chief administrator. The unit should have both an investigative and preventive role in controlling dishonest, unethical, and offensive actions by police officers.

28. Police departments should commence experimentation with a team policing concept that envisions those with patrol and investigative duties combining under unified command with flexible assignments to deal with the crime problems in a defined sector.

29. A comprehensive regulation should be formulated by every chief administrator to reflect the basic policy that firearms may be used *only* when the officer believes his life or the life of another is in imminent danger, or when other reasonable means of apprehension have failed to prevent the escape of a *felony* suspect whom the officer believes presents a serious danger to others.

30. States should assume responsibility for assuring that area-wide records and communications needs are provided.

31. In every metropolitan area the central city or the State should provide laboratory facilities for the routine needs of all the communities in the area. State of multistate laboratories and the FBI laboratory should continue to provide the necessary research to make available to all laboratories more sophisticated means of analysis.

32. Specialized personnel from State or metropolitan departments should assist smaller departments in each metropolitan area on major investigations and in specialized law enforcement functions.

33. Each metropolitan area and each county should take action directed toward the pooling, or consolidation, of police services through the particular technique that will provide the most satisfactory law enforcement service and protection at lowest possible cost.

34. Police standards commissions should be established in every State, and empowered to set mandatory requirements and to give financial aid to governmental units for the implementation of standards.

Task Force Report: Science and Technology

The scientific and technological revolution that has so radically changed most of American society during the past few decades has had surprisingly little impact upon the criminal justice system. In an age when many executives in government and industry, faced with decision-making problems, ask the scientific and technical community for independent suggestions on possible alternatives for objective analyses of possible consequences of their actions, the public officials responsible for establishing and administering the criminal law—the legislators, police, prosecutors, lawyers, judges, and corrections officials—have almost no communication with the scientific and technical community.

More than two hundred thousand scientists and engineers are helping to solve military problems, but only a handful are helping to control the crimes that injure or frighten millions of Americans each year. Even small businesses employ modern technological devices and systems, but the Nation's courts are almost as close to the quill pen era as they are to the age of electronic data processing. The police, with crime laboratories and radio networks, made early use of technology, but most police departments could have been equipped 30 or 40 years ago as well as they are today. Hospitals and clinics draw heavily upon the most recent developments in engineering and medical science, but the overwhelming majority of reformatories, jails and prisons are, technologically speaking, a century or more in the past.

This lack of contact between criminal justice and science and technology is true even in the Federal Government, where, as recently as 1965, the Justice Department was the only Cabinet department with no share of the roughly $15 billion Federal research and development budget.

In order to help bring scientific knowledge and techniques to bear on the problems of criminal justice, the Commission, in collaboration with the Office of Law Enforcement Assistance, established a task force on science and technology in April 1966. The task force was given the job of showing how the resources of science and technology might be used to solve the problems of crime. In the subsequent months, the task force sought:[7]

1. To identify the problems, immediate and long term, that technology is most likely to help solve, and to suggest the kinds of research and development needed.

2. To identify and describe crime control problems in a form susceptible to quantitative analysis.

3. To point out the kinds of important data on crime control and the criminal justice system that are lacking, unreliable or otherwise unusuable, and to propose means of correcting such deficiencies.

4. To analyze problems in crime assessment, police, courts, and corrections as an aid to the Commission and its other task forces.

5. To suggest organizational formats within which technological devices and systems can be developed, field tested, and rendered useful.

With a scope so broad, and limited time and manpower, only a few problems could be studied in detail. The task force gave major attention to computer technology, information systems, communications engineering, and systems analysis, since these appeared to offer the greatest unrealized potentials for system-wide improvement. Within the criminal justice system, the greatest potential for immediate improvement by technological innovation appeared to be in police operations, and so the task force looked particularly hard at the police and

---

[7] Challenge of Crime in a Free Society, *op. cit.*, p. 245.

somewhat less hard at courts and corrections. Some of the results detailed in the task force report included:[8]

1. A compilation of field data examining certain relationships between police patrol operations and the apprehension of criminals.

2. A proposal for improving police responsiveness to calls at minimum cost.

3. A program that could dramatically reduce police radio frequency congestion.

4. A research and development program for developing a semiautomatic fingerprint recognition capability, to replace the present system which cannot regularly trace a criminal with less than a full set of prints.

5. Studies examining possible alternative alarm systems, nonlethal weapons, and other technological innovations for police operations.

6. A review of the application of statistical techniques to decisions about treatment of convicted criminals.

7. Methods for making auto theft more difficult, which automobile manufacturers have agreed to incorporate into the design of future models.

8. An exploratory attempt to apply systems analysis to the overall criminal justice system, which produced several highly suggestive but still tentative results.

9. An outline, but not a detailed design, of a national information system for criminal justice agencies.

10. A proposal for a national research and development program.

These results are only illustrations of the potential contributions of science and technology to crime control. They must be developed in detail for each local situation, and they suggest many other opportunities. As illustrations, however, they appear to offer sufficient promise of the potential benefits from science and technology to warrant major further work immediately.

Modern technology can provide many new devices to improve the operations of criminal justice agencies, and particularly to help the police deter crime and apprehend criminals. It is far easier, however, to imagine and develop devices than to choose the ones in which to invest necessarily limited equipment budgets. Technology can indeed fill most reasonable requests and can thereby provide considerable help to law enforcement. We must still decide what devices we want relative to the price we are willing to pay in dollars, invasion of privacy,

[8] *Ibid.*, p. 245.

and other social costs. It is technically feasible, for example, to cut auto theft drastically by putting a radio transmitter in every car in America and tracking all cars continuously. But this might cost a billion dollars and, even more important, create an intolerable environment of unending surveillance. Science can provide the capability, but the public as a whole must participate in the value discussion of whether or not the capability is worth its financial and social costs.

Furthermore, no one can say what most devices or systems will do about crime; little is known of what anything will do about crime. The effect of this or that device upon crime will be speculative until careful field evaluations are conducted. However, not all technological innovations can be postponed until these evaluations are completed. Judgment must identify where technology appears to offer the greatest promise. This may involve some wasted effort, but the urgency of crime control warrants the risk of some waste.

Introduction of appropriate technology is often hindered by budgets, which not very helpfully distinguish between "equipment" and "personnel" rather than between functions such as "general-purpose police patrol" and "investigation of homicide." For example, since a two-man car on continuous patrol costs about $100,000 per year, it would be surprising if patrol operations could not be significantly improved by a capital investment exceeding the current $3,000 per car. But such an investment might severely strain the equipment budget, and might be passed up, even if it could result in a much larger saving in personnel costs. Dollars could be allocated more rationally by making use of the program budgeting techniques now being used by the Federal Government.

Because of the enormous range of technological possibilities, it is essential to begin not with technology but with problems. Technological efforts can then be concentrated where they are most likely to be productive. Systems analysis has been used most successfully in fields like national defense and mass transportation to determine where technological resources can most usefully be directed over a broad field of concern. These techniques and approaches can be usefully applied to the problems of crime control, relating alternative means to desired ends. Because of the importance of this approach, the task force has illustrated how systems analysis might be applied in a small number of cases: To reduce courtroom delay, to speed police response to a call, and to examine the overall criminal justice system in an integrated way.

Because the task force on science and technology brought a new viewpoint and analytical and quantitative techniques to the subject matter, the Commission encouraged it to examine some of the basic problems of crime and crime control not within the traditional boundaries of science and technology. As a result, a number of ideas and conceptions were uncovered that provided significant new insights into the problems with which the Commission dealt. One of several possible examples can serve to illustrate this point. Although it is common knowledge that the number of arrests made each year in the United States for nontraffic, offenses is very large (the FBI estimates exceed 6 million), it has never been known what percentage of the population is arrested. This percentage depends strongly on the proportion of arrests that are of persons never before arrested. This proportion is difficult to estimate because of the incompleteness of arrest records. A mathematical analysis performed by the task force used a conservative estimate—one new offender in eight arrests—and indicated tentatively that about 40 percent of the male children living in the United States today will be arrested for a nontraffic offense sometime in their lives. The proportion is even higher for boys living in a city.

If sustained by additional data, these startling results refute the common notion that most people never encounter the criminal justice system, and only a small class of "criminals" do. Although this statistic and many like it are vital to understanding how the system operates, there are no estimates, however tentative, of many such numbers. Reasonable estimates of the numbers connected with crime and the criminal justice system are necessary for a systematic analysis of crime control.

Virtually all the efforts of the Commission have been hampered by the pervasive lack of adequate objective information about crime and the possible effects of various techniques for crime control. Each year, judges in this country pass roughly 2 million sentences. Almost all sentencing decisions are made with little or no information on the likely effect of the sentence on future criminal behavior. About 200,000 policemen spend half of their time on "preventive" patrol. Yet, no police chief can obtain even a rough estimate of how much crime is thereby "prevented." The factfinding, analytical, and experimental methods of science offer one approach to identifying some of the important questions and developing the required information.[9]

Task Force Report: Juvenile Delinquency and Youth Crime

Society's efforts to control and combat delinquency may be seen as operating at three levels.

---

[9] The President's Commission on Law Enforcement and Administration of Justice, *Task Force Report: Science and Technology*, U. S. Government Printing Office, Washington, 1967, pp. 1–228.

The first and most basic—indeed, so basic that delinquency prevention is only one of the reasons for it—involves provision of a real opportunity for everyone to participate in the legitimate activities that in our society lead to or constitute a good life: education, recreation, employment, family life. It is to insure such opportunity that schools in the slums must be made as good as schools elsewhere; that discrimination and arbitrary or unnecessary restrictions must be eliminated from employment practices; that job training must be made available to everyone; that physical surroundings must be reclaimed from deterioration and barrenness; that the rights of a citizen must be exercisable without regard to creed or race.

The pursuit of these goals is not inconsistent with the need to strengthen the system of juvenile justice. Some young offenders are dangerous repeaters, responsible for holdups, muggings, aggravated assaults—the crimes that frighten people off the streets. Others, while less threatening, have already shown themselves resistant to noncoercive rehabilitating efforts. Dealing with these youths so as to protect society requires—at least at this point in our understanding of human behavior—custody, adjudication of fact, imposition of sanction. Those measures depend upon an effective, efficient system of juvenile justice. Swift apprehension, thorough investigation, prompt disposition—carried out by persons carefully selected and trained for their functions—should maximize the system's deterrent impact and the respect accorded the law it upholds. Insofar as the juvenile justice system does deal with delinquency, its dealings should be characterized by these attributes.

Further, the system should operate with all the procedural formality necessary to safeguard adequately the rights that any person has when he is subject to the application of coercive power. Juveniles should be represented by counsel; they should be able to confront those complaining of their conduct; their fate should not be determined by hearsay or gossip. They should not be unnecessarily detained.

Between these two aspects of delinquency control—the first relevant to all young people, the second reserved for those who appear to need the coercive authority of the court—there is a third: response to the special needs of youths with special problems. They may already have delinquency records. They may be law-abiding but alienated and uncooperative in making use of education or employment or other opportunities. They may be behavior or academic problems in school, or misfits among their peers, or disruptive in recreation groups. Whatever the nature or degree of the difficulty, today they are all too likely to be excluded by most agencies and institutions, which find these youngsters, whom ostensibly they exist to help, in fact more than their limited resources can manage. They may restrict the participation of such youths in extra-curricular school activities, keep them segregated from their fellows in special classes, eliminate them from recreation groups, rate them ineligible for certain sorts of therapy.

For such youths, it is imperative to furnish help that is particularized enough to deal with their individual needs but does not separate them from their peers and label them for life. Providing sufficiently specialized services while yet avoiding destructive labeling and stigma poses one of the central dilemmas in the delinquency prevention area. The Commission suggested some methods of meeting it—by minimizing the separation in special classes of children who need additional help in school and by returning them to regular routine as soon as possible; by involving whole groups of young people, rather than just the troublemakers, in community activities; by requiring that the Youth Services Bureau accept and deal with all youth and encouraging it, by means of specially earmarked funds, to develop intensive programs for delinquents. Whatever the specific methods chosen, the problem must be attacked, for it is with these young people that most youth-serving agencies today are having the least success.[10]

Task Force Report: Organized Crime

Organized crime is a society that seeks to operate outside the control of the American people and their governments. It involves thousands of criminals, working within structures as complex as those of any large corporation, subject to laws more rigidly enforced than those of legitimate governments. Its actions are not impulsive but rather the result of intricate conspiracies, carried on over many years and aimed at gaining control over whole fields of activity in order to amass huge profits.

The core of organized crime activity is the supplying of illegal goods and services—gambling, loan sharking, narcotics, and other forms of vice—to countless numbers of citizen customers. But organized crime is also extensively and deeply involved in legitimate business and in labor unions. Here it employs illegitimate methods —monopolization, terrorism, extortion, tax evasion—to drive out or control lawful ownership and leadership and to exact illegal profits from the public. And to carry on its many activities secure from governmental interference, organized crime corrupts public officials.

---

[10] The President's Commission on Law Enforcement and Administration of Justice, *Task Force Report: Juvenile Delinquency and Youth Crime*, U. S. Government Printing Office, Washington, 1967, pp. 1–428.

Robert F. Kennedy, when he was Attorney General illustrated its power simply and vividly. He testified before a Senate subcommittee in 1963 that the physical protection of witnesses who had cooperated with the Federal Government in organized crime cases often required that those witnesses change their appearances, change their names, or even leave the country. When the government of a powerful country is unable to protect its friends from its enemies by means less extreme than obliterating their identities, surely it is being seriously challenged, if not threatened.

What organized crime wants is money and power. What makes it different from law-abiding organizations and individuals with those same objectives is that the ethical and moral standards the criminals adhere to, the laws and regulations they obey, the procedures they use, are private and secret ones that they devise themselves, change when they see fit, and administer summarily and invisibly. Organized crime affects the lives of millions of Americans, but because it desperately preserves its invisibility many, perhaps most, Americans are not aware how they are affected, at all. The price of a loaf of bread may go up one cent as the result of organized crime conspiracy, but a housewife has no way of knowing why she is paying more. If organized criminals paid income tax on every cent of their vast earnings everybody's tax bill would go down, but no one knows how much.

But to discuss the impact of organized crime in terms of whatever direct, personal, everyday effect it has on individuals is to miss most of the point. Most individuals are not affected, in this sense, very much. Much of the money organized crime accumulates comes from innumerable petty transactions: 50-cent bets, $3-a-month private garbage collection services, quarters dropped into racketeer-owned jukeboxes, or small price rises resulting from protection rackets. A one-cent-a-loaf rise in bread may annoy housewives, but it certainly does not impoverish them.

Sometimes organized crime's activities do not directly affect individuals at all. Smuggled cigarettes in a vending machine cost consumers no more than tax-paid cigarettes, but they enrich the leaders of organized crime. Sometimes these activities actually reduce prices for a short period of time, as can happen when organized crime, in an attempt to take over an industry, starts a price war against legitimate businessmen. Even when organized crime engages in a large transaction, individuals may not be directly affected. A large sum of money can be diverted from a union pension fund to finance a business venture without immediate and direct effect upon the individual members of the union.

It is organized crime's accumulation of money, not the individual transactions by which the money is accumulated, that has a great and threatening impact on America. A quarter in a jukebox means nothing and results in nothing. But millions of quarters in thousands of juke-boxes can provide both a strong motive for murder and the means to commit murder with impunity. Organized crime exists by virtue of the power it purchases with its money. The millions of dollars it can invest in narcotics or use for layoff money give it power over the lives of thousands of people and over the quality of life in whole neighbor-hoods. The millions of dollars it can throw into the legitimate economic system give it power to manipulate the price of shares on the stock market, to raise or lower the price of retail merchandise, to determine whether entire industries are union or nonunion, to make it easier or harder for businessmen to continue in business.

The millions of dollars it can spend on corrupting public officials may give it power to maim or murder people inside or outside the or-ganization with impunity, to extort money from businessmen, to con-duct businesses in such fields as liquor, meat, or drugs without regard to administrative regulations, to avoid payment of income taxes, or to secure public works contracts without competitive bidding.

The purpose of organized crime is not competition with visible, legal government but nullification of it. When organized crime places an official in public office, it nullifies the political process. When it bribes a police official, it nullifies law enforcement.

There is another, more subtle, way in which organized crime has an impact on American life. Consider the former way of life of Frank Costello, a man who has repeatedly been called a leader of organized crime. He lived in an expensive apartment on the corner of 72nd Street and Central Park West in New York. He was often seen dining in well-known restaurants in the company of judges, public officials, and prominent businessmen. Every morning he was shaved in the barber-shop of the Waldorf Astoria Hotel. On many weekends he played golf at a country club on the fashionable North Shore of Long Island. In short, though his reputation was common knowledge, he moved around New York conspicuously and unashamedly, perhaps ostracized by some people but more often accepted, greeted by journalists, recog-nized by children, accorded all the freedoms of a prosperous and suc-cessful man. On a society that treats such a man in such a manner, or-ganized crime has had an impact.

And yet the public remains indifferent. Few Americans seem to comprehend how the phenomenon of organized crime affects their lives. They do not see how gambling with bookmakers, or borrowing money from loan sharks, forwards the interests of great criminal cartels.

Businessmen looking for labor harmony or non-union status through irregular channels rationalize away any suspicions that organized crime is thereby spreading its influence. When an ambitious political candidate accepts substantial cash contributions from unknown sources, he suspects but dismisses the fact that organized crime will dictate some of his actions when he assumes office.

President Johnson asked the Commission to determine why organized crime has been expanding despite the Nation's best efforts to prevent it. The Commission drew upon the small group of enforcement personnel and other knowledgeable persons who deal with organized crime. Federal agencies provided extensive material. But because so little study and research have been done in this field, we also secured the assistance of sociologists, systems analysts, political scientists, economists, and lawyers. America's limited response to organized crime is illustrated by the fact that, for several of these disciplines, the call for assistance resulted in their first concentrated examination of organized crime.[11]

The task force made twenty specific recommendations that can readily be identified as strategy to combat organized crime based on a close examination of its distinctive characteristics and methods of operation.

Task Force Report: Crime and its Impact—An Assessment

The most natural and frequent question people ask about crime is "Why?" They ask it about individual crimes and about crime as a whole. In either case it is an almost impossible question to answer. Each single crime is a response to a specific situation by a person with an infinitely complicated psychological and emotional makeup who is subject to infinitely complicated external pressures. Crime as a whole is millions of such responses. To seek the "causes" of crime in human motivations alone is to risk losing one's way in the impenetrable thickets of the human psyche. Compulsive gambling was the cause of an embezzlement, one may say, or drug addiction the cause of a burglary or madness the cause of a homicide; but what caused the compulsion, the addiction, the madness? Why did they manifest themselves in those ways at those times? There are some crimes so irrational, so unpredictable, so explosive, so resistant to analysis or explanation that they can no more be prevented or guarded against than earthquakes or tidal waves.

[11] The President's Commission on Law Enforcement and Administration of Justice, *Task Force Report: Organized Crime*, U. S. Government Printing Office, Washington, 1967, pp. 1–126.

At the opposite end of the spectrum of crime are the carefully planned acts of professional criminals. The elaborately organized robbery of an armored car, the skillfully executed jewel theft, the murder of an informant by a Cosa Nostra "enforcer" are so deliberate, so calculated, so rational, that understanding the motivations of those who commit such crimes does not show us how to prevent them. How to keep competent and intelligent men from taking up crime as a life work is as baffling a problem as how to predict and discourage sudden criminal outbursts.

To say this is not, of course, to belittle the efforts of psychiatrists and other behavioral scientists to identify and to treat the personality traits that are associated with crime. Such efforts are an indispensable part of understanding and controlling crime. Many criminals can be rehabilitated. The point is that looking at the personal characteristics of offenders is only one of many ways, and not always the most helpful way, of looking at crime.

It is possible to say, for example, that many crimes are "caused" by their victims. Often the victim of an assault is the person who started the fight, or the victim of an automobile theft is a person who left his keys in his car, or the victim of a loan shark is a person who lost his rent money at the race track, or the victim of a confidence man is a person who thought he could get rich quick. The relationship of victims to crimes is a subject that so far has received little attention. Many crimes, no matter what kind of people their perpetrators were, would not have been committed if their victims had understood the risks they were running.

From another viewpoint, crime is "caused" by public tolerance of it, or reluctance or inability to take action against it. Corporate and business—"white-collar"—crime is closely associated with a widespread notion that, when making money is involved, anything goes. Shoplifting and employee theft may be made more safe by their victims' reluctance to report to the police—often due to a recognition that the likelihood of detection and successful prosecution are negligible. Very often slum residents feel they live in territory that is useless for them even to try to defend. Many slum residents feel overwhelmed and helpless in the face of the flourishing vice and crime around them; many have received indifferent treatment from the criminal justice system when they have attempted to do their duty as complainants and witnesses; many fear reprisals, especially victims of rackets. When citizens do not get involved, criminals can act with relative impunity.

In a sense, social and economic conditions "cause" crime. Crime flourishes, and always has flourished, in city slums, those neighborhoods where overcrowding, economic deprivation, social disruption and racial discrimination are endemic. Crime flourishes in conditions of affluence, where there is much desire for material goods and many opportunities to acquire them illegally. Crime flourishes when there are many restless, relatively footloose young people in the population. Crime flourishes when standards of morality are changing rapidly.

Finally, to the extent that the agencies of law enforcement and justice, and such community institutions as schools, churches and social service agencies, do not do their jobs effectively, they fail to prevent crime. If the police are inefficient or starved for manpower, otherwise preventable crimes will occur; if they are overzealous, people better left alone will be drawn into criminal careers. If the courts fail to separate the innocent from the guilty, the guilty may be turned loose to continue their depredations and the innocent may be criminalized. If the system fails to convict the guilty with reasonable certainty and promptness, deterrence of crime may be blunted. If correctional programs do not correct, a core of hardened and habitual criminals will continue to plague the community. If the community institutions that can shape the characters of young people do not take advantage of their opportunities, youth rebelliousness will turn into crime.

The causes of crime, then, are numerous and mysterious and intertwined. The description of crime in a city precinct tries to convey a sense for the great variety of human acts and relationships involved in the crimes that police typically encounter in their daily patrols. It shows that crimes are sometimes simple and sometimes complex, sometimes easy and sometimes hard to understand. Even to begin to understand them, one must gather statistics about the amounts and trends of crime. The task force took a close look at the data regularly reported and the results of special studies that might shed light on the amount, rate, and trend for different types of crime. It explores what is known and what can be surmised about changes in the social and economic conditions of the country and the characteristics and distribution of the population which might account for the volume and trends of crime. It considers as well some of the ways in which the reporting practices of criminal justice agencies and the willingness of citizens to report their victimization may affect our knowledge of crime in America.

A different picture of the crime problem emerges when we examine the costs of different types of crime. Even though this subject has been much neglected and it is difficult to secure accurate estimates of what crimes cost victims or what we pay to prevent or control crime and to process apprehended offenders, nevertheless the available data presents a disconcerting picture of the economic burden of crime for individuals, households, businesses, and organizations throughout the country.

The fact that crime rates are higher in some regions of the country than in others and that the rates for different types of offenses vary considerably among large and small cities suggests the importance of trying to relate these variations to differences in the characteristics of the population and the cultural and economic conditions of life. Such comparisons between regions and cities are explored to the extent that the available data and published research studies permit. However, more intensive work has been done on the distribution of the place of occurrence of different offenses and the residences of offenders among the various community areas *within* cities, and the results of such studies are considered in the report. The purpose is not just to show that the rates of offenses and offenders vary considerably between urban areas, but to assess the conditions of life which are most closely associated with these variations.

If we knew more about the characteristics of both offenders and victims, the nature of their relationships and the circumstances that create a high probability of criminal conduct, it seems likely that crime prevention and control programs could be made much more effective. Though the Task Force could not undertake new research studies of offenders, an effort was made to add further information about the characteristics of victims and their relationships with offenders, particularly in regard to aggressive crimes against persons. The results of these victim studies are considered together with the findings of previous studies on the characteristics of victims and offenders.

One of the major undertakings of the Task Force was the initiation of a national survey, and a more intensive survey of selected police districts in three cities, concerning the experience of citizens and households as victims of crime. Estimations derived from these surveys of the amount of reported and unreported crime and the reasons for nonreporting are discussed as well as the characteristics of victims. However, the surveys also provided an excellent opportunity to explore in greater detail than ever before public attitudes toward crime and law enforcement, the crime problems that particularly concern people, and the measures they take to protect themselves from being victimized. These results are presented along with data on the public's views on the causes and cures of crime.

There is a review of certain special crime problems that pose particularly difficult challenges for crime prevention and control and raise different types of issues for the system of law enforcement and criminal justice. The problem of the professional criminal, whose principal employment and source of income is derived from criminal activity, is considered and some of the difficulties and dilemmas in developing effective law enforcement against the broad range of offenses characterized as "white collar crime" is considered. Though not a great deal is actually known about many of the characteristics and operations of the various types of professional criminals, it seems likely that they contribute substantially to the burden of crime, if for no other reason than that they become skilled at committing crime and evading detection and also work full time at it. It also seems likely that the crimes of embezzlement, tax fraud, food and drug violations, securities fraud, anti-trust violation, price-fixing, and other forms of white collar crime impose a far heavier burden on the operation of our social and economic institutions than the small number of cases successfully prosecuted would imply. The increasing difficulty of preventing or regulating such activities, as the organizational complexity of our society increases, raises questions concerning the utility of criminal as compared to other regulatory procedures which bear closer study.

The destructive riots which have broken out in recent years in the slum neighborhoods of many large cities pose a totally different problem of crime prevention and control. The discussion of this problem is not intended as a definitive examination of the causes of riots or a means of their prevention. Instead riots are considered from the perspective of the types of criminal activity which find release in the riot situation and the problems of prevention and control that they represent.

The final section is devoted to an appraisal of the current national system of statistical accounting on crime and criminal justice matters. It tries to identify needs for information and analysis that we are not yet meeting well enough or at all. It offers a series of proposals which the Task Force believes will greatly enhance the capacity of local, State and Federal governments to keep informed about the many different types of crime problems in our society and to organize a more effective response to them.[12]

---

[12] The President's Commission on Law Enforcement and Administration of Justice, *Task Force Report: Crime and Its Impact—An Assessment*, U. S. Government Printing Office, Washington, 1967, pp. 1–215.

*

APPENDICES

APPENDIX A

(PLEASE POST)

Announcement of Competitive Examination
for Position of

CHIEF OF POLICE, SEATTLE, WASHINGTON

The City of Seattle announces a nation-wide, open competitive examination for the position listed above, which will be filled through appointment by the Mayor from a list of three eligible candidates recommended by the examining board. Selection will be based upon the results of the competitive examination.

FINAL DATE FOR FILING APPLICATIONS

Applications must be filed in the office of Mr. Kenneth Colman, Chairman of the Police Advisory Committee, Colman Building, Seattle, Washington, on or before 5:00 p. m., or post-marked not later than midnight, May 15, 1946. To secure application form, wire Mayor's Office, Seattle 4, Washington.

EXAMINATION DATE

Written examination—Friday, May 31, 1946.

Oral examination—June 24 to 29 inclusive.

PLACE OF EXAMINATION

For the convenience of applicants in the several geographical areas of the nation, written examinations will be held at the following locations:

Institute of Government University of Washington Seattle, Washington	Department of Political Science University of California Berkeley, California
Traffic Institute Northwestern University Evanston, Illinois	Department of Legal Medicine Harvard University Cambridge, Massachusetts

Bureau of Municipal Research
University of Texas
Austin, Texas

And such other places throughout the United States as the number of applicants and conditions require. The oral examination will be held in Seattle, Washington only.

Only those candidates whose experience and written examinations satisfy the examining board will be called to Seattle for the oral examination. The oral interview will be supplemented by a confidential investigation of the character and professional record of candidates who qualify. Competitors who attain an eligible rating may be investigated with the object of securing additional evidence as to their qualifications and fitness for this position, and to secure evidence as to their honesty, integrity, habits, loyalty and general character.

Applicants called to Seattle for oral examination will defray their own expenses.

The decisions of the examining board in the selection of three eligible candidates will be final.

SALARY

Minimum, $7,500.00 per year.

TENURE OF OFFICE

Indefinite tenure.

QUALIFICATIONS

Not less than ten years full time employment in public safety or law enforcement work within the last 15 years, of which a part must have been in an administrative capacity. The nature and extent of the applicant's administrative experience are considered of the highest importance. In considering the length of time served in public safety and law enforcement organizations, time spent on leave of absence in the Armed Forces will be considered as continuous service.

Military experience, especially at command levels, is conceded to be an asset to a police executive and careful consideration will therefore be given to the applicant's military service record.

EDUCATION

Equivalent to that represented by completion of the twelfth grade or graduation from high school. College level training in public administration, police science and administration, criminal law, psychology, sociology, economics or business administration, or a combination of these fields of study, may be substituted for not more than two years of the required experience. In evaluating experience, major consideration will be given to the quality, importance and breadth of experience rather than to years of experience.

AGE LIMIT

Applicants for this position must have reached their 32nd birthday on the closing date for receipt of applications specified at the head of this announcement.

DUTIES OF POSITION

The duties of this position include the following:

1. Organization of the Seattle Police Department over a period of five years in accordance with professional standards.

2. Planning and execution of a professional police program for the protection of life and property, preservation of peace and order, control and prevention of crime and vice, and the regulation and control of traffic.

3. Planning and direction of the total organization and operations of a metropolitan Police Department.

4. Selection and appointment, subject to Civil Service provisions, of officers and employees best qualified to carry on the police program, and supervision of their training, assignment and performance.

5. Interpretation of police policies and objectives to personnel of the Department, the public and the press.

6. Such other duties as may be necessary in the projection of police service in Seattle, on a professional career basis.

Applications are invited from qualified applicants throughout the United States.

EXAMINING BOARD

CHARLES W. DULLEA
Western Vice President, International Ass'n Chiefs of Police
Chief of Police
San Francisco, Calif.

COL. HOMER GARRISON, Jr.
Director,
State Department of Public Safety
Fourth Vice President, International Ass'n Chiefs of Police
Austin, Texas.

V. A. LEONARD,
Chairman
Department of Police Science and Administration
State College of Washington
Pullman, Washington

ADDRESS ALL APPLICATIONS TO:

KENNETH B. COLMAN, Chairman
Police Advisory Committee
Colman Building
Seattle 4, Washington

CITY OF SEATTLE, WASHINGTON

Application for the Position of Police Chief

Application No. ....

Date received ....

GENERAL INSTRUCTIONS

Applications must be typewritten or in ink, sworn to before a notary or other officer authorized to administer oaths and filed in the office of Kenneth B. Colman, Chairman of the Police Advisory Committee, Colman Building, Seattle, on or before 5:00 p. m., or postmarked not later than midnight, May 15, 1946.

Applicants should read carefully the announcement in the bulletin submitted with this form.

It is important that each statement or answer in this application be complete, truthful and accurate. Incomplete, false or misleading statements or answers may be cause for rejection. Where spaces on this blank are insufficient, supply additional information on bond paper $8\frac{1}{2}$ x 11 size.

1. Name .... Address ....
2. Age ...... Place and date of birth ....
   U. S. citizen? ....
3. Marital status .... Number of children ....
4. Height .... Weight (in street clothes) ....
5. Is your health such as to enable you to perform regularly and efficiently the duties of this position?
6. Have you any defect of hearing, sight, speech or limb? (Eligible candidates will be given a medical examination in Seattle at time of oral interview)
7. Are you addicted to the moderate or immoderate use of alcohol, or to the use of drugs in any form?
8. Have you ever been arrested, indicted or convicted for any law violation other than a minor traffic offense?
9. Have you ever been discharged or forced to resign from a position?
10. Education. (Give details)
    Grammar and High School
    College or University
    Post-graduate work

11. Courses completed in the fields of public administration and police administration. (Give details of university or college program)

12. Special honors received

13. Military experience and record

14. Publications authored (books, articles, reports—give exact titles and references)

15. Professional associations to which you belong

16. List any income other than your present salary

17. List all business interests or connections outside of police service

18. List all organizations to which you belong as a member

19. Positions of professional or civic leadership which you have held

20. Employment record. Present and former employments. (Beginning with present or latest employment, list in reverse order all positions held for the last fifteen years, stating in each case reason for leaving previous position. Use separate sheet of paper)

21. For each of the above positions in police work give a brief description of the principal tasks you performed, the number of employees supervised by you, the assistance and supervision required from your supervisors, and any other information indicating the nature and responsibilities of the position.

22. Write a brief personal statement commenting upon significant aspects of your professional experience and educational training which in your judgment qualify you to discharge with distinction the duties and responsibilities of this position.

23. Do you object to the Committee making inquiry of your present employer regarding your character and qualifications?

24. Names, addresses and occupations of five persons, not relatives, nor employers, nor supervisors, who have knowledge of your character and ability

25. Attach to this application a 5 x 7 photograph of yourself and one set of fingerprints. These are a part of your application.

. . . .
Signature of Applicant

AFFIDAVIT

State of ....
County of ....
On this ...... day of ...., 1946, before me
personally appeared ....
who stated on oath that he is the author of this application and that the
information contained therein is true and correct to the best of his
knowledge and belief.

Witness my hand and seal.

....
Notary Public.

  * * *

List all jobs you have held in the last ten years. Put your present
or most recent job first. By being complete you may improve your
chances for employment. If you need more space, you may attach
additional sheets. Include military service in proper time sequence
and temporary part-time jobs.

....
FROM _____ TO _____ EXACT TITLE OF POSITION _____
  Month and Year Month and Year
NAME AND ADDRESS OF EMPLOYER YOUR DUTIES ARE:
NAME & TITLE OF YOUR SUPERVISOR
REASON FOR LEAVING   NUMBER SUPERVISED SALARY PER
             MONTH:

....
FROM _____ TO _____ EXACT TITLE OF POSITION _____
  Month and Year Month and Year
NAME AND ADDRESS OF EMPLOYER YOUR DUTIES WERE:
NAME & TITLE OF YOUR SUPERVISOR
REASON FOR LEAVING   NUMBER SUPERVISED SALARY PER
             MONTH:

....
FROM _____ TO _____ EXACT TITLE OF POSITION _____
  Month and Year Month and Year

APPENDIX B

Model Police Standards Council Act Drafted by * The International Association of Chiefs of Police

Model Police Standards Council Act of

(Title should conform to State requirements. The following is a suggestion: "An act establishing a Police Standards Council; providing certain educational and training requirements for members of police forces; and for related purposes.")

(Be it enacted, etc.)

Section 1.—Findings and Policy

The legislature finds that the administration of criminal justice is of statewide concern, and that police work is important to the health, safety, and welfare of the people of this State and is of such a nature as to require education and training of a professional character. It is in the public interest that such education and training be made available to persons who seek to become police officers, persons who are serving as such officers in a temporary or probationary capacity, and persons already in regular service.

Section 2.—Police Officer Defined

As used in this Act:

"Police officer" means any full-time employee of a police department which is a part of or administered by the State or any political subdivision thereof and who is responsible for the prevention and detection of crime and the enforcement of the penal, traffic, or highway laws of this State.

Section 3.—Police Standards Council

(a) There is hereby established a Police Standards Council, hereinafter called "the Council," in the Executive Office of the Governor. The Council shall be composed of 15 members, as follows: Five chief administrative officers of local government police forces, at least 3 of whom shall be from forces maintained by incorporated municipalities; 5 officials or employees of local government who have general executive or legislative responsibilities with respect thereto so chosen as to represent county government and municipal government; (the head of the

---

* See V. A. Leonard, *Police Communications Systems*, Springfield, Illinois, Charles C. Thomas, Publisher, 1970.

State police), 1 representative of higher education, 2 public members and the Attorney General.

(b) Except for the Attorney General and the (head of the State police) who shall serve during their continuance in those offices, members of the Council shall be appointed by the Governor for terms of 4 years: provided that no member shall serve beyond the time when he holds the office or employment by reason of which he was initially eligible for appointment. Notwithstanding anything in this section to the contrary, the terms of members initially appointed to the Council by the Governor upon its establishment shall be: three for 1 year, three for 2 years, three for 3 years, and four for 4 years. The Governor, at the time of appointment, shall designate which of the terms are respectively for 1, 2, 3 and 4 years. Any vacancy on the Council shall be filled in the same manner as the original appointment, but for the unexpired term.

(c) The Governor annually shall designate the chairman of the Council, and the Council annually shall select its vice chairman. The chairman and vice chairman shall be designated and selected from among the members of the Council.

(d) Notwithstanding any provision of any statute, ordinance, local law, or charter provision to the contrary, membership on the Council shall not disqualify any member from holding any other public office or employment, or cause the forfeiture thereof.

(e) Members of the Council shall serve without compensation, but shall be entitled to receive reimbursement for any actual expenses incurred as a necessary incident to such service.

(f) The Council shall hold no less than four regular meetings a year. Subject to the requirements of this subsection, the chairman shall fix the times and places of meetings, either on his own motion or upon written request of any (five) members of the Council.

(g) The Council shall report annually to the Governor and legislature on its activities, and may make such other reports as it deems desirable.

Section 4.   Powers

In addition to powers conferred upon the Council elsewhere in this act, the Council shall have power to:

1. Promulgate rules and regulations for the administration of this act including the authority to require the submission of reports and information by police departments within this State.

2. Establish minimum educational and training standards for admission to employment as a police officer: (a) in permanent positions, and (b) in temporary or probationary status.

3. Certify persons as being qualified under the provisions of this act to be police officers.

4. Establish minimum curriculum requirements for preparatory, inservice and advanced courses and programs for schools operated by or for the State or any political subdivisions thereof for the specific purpose of training police recruits or police officers.

5. Consult and cooperate with counties, municipalities, agencies of this State, other governmental agencies, and with universities, colleges, junior colleges, and other institutions concerning the deveolpment of police training schools and programs or courses of instruction.

6. Approve institutions and facilities for school operation by or for the State or any political subdivision thereof for the specific purpose of training police officers and police recruits.

7. Make or encourage studies of any aspect of police administration.

8. Conduct and stimulate research by public and private agencies which shall be designed to improve police administration and law enforcement.

9. Make recommendations concerning any matter within its purview pursuant to this act.

10. Employ a Director and such other personnel as may be necessary in the performance of its functions.

11. Make such evaluations as may be necessary to determine if governmental units are complying with the provisions of this act.

12. Adopt and amend bylaws, consistent with law, for its internal management and control.

13. Enter into contracts or do such things as may be necessary and incidental to the administration of its authority pursuant to this act.

Section 5. Education and Training Required

(a) Police officers already serving under permanent appointment on the effective date of this act shall not be required to meet any requirement of subsections (b) and (c) of this section as a condition of tenure or continued employment; nor shall failure of any such police officer to fulfill such requirements make him ineligible for any promotional examination for which he is otherwise eligible. The legislature finds, and it is hereby declared to be the policy of this act, that such police officers have satisfied such requirements by their experience.

(b) At the earliest practicable time, the Council shall provide, by regulation, that no person shall be appointed as a police officer, except on a temporary or probationary basis, unless such person has satisfactorily completed a preparatory program of police training at a school approved by the Council, and is the holder of a bachelor's degree from an accredited institution. No police officer who lacks the education and training qualifications required by the Council may have his temporary or probationary employment extended beyond 1 year by renewal of appointment or otherwise.

(c) In addition to the requirements of subsections (b), (e), and (f) of this section, the Council, by rules and regulations, shall fix other qualifications for the employment and promotion of police officers, including minimum age, education, physical and mental standards, citizenship, good moral character, experience, and such other matters as relate to the competence and reliability of persons to assume and discharge the responsibilities of police officers, and the Council shall prescribe the means for presenting evidence of fulfillment of these requirements.

(d) The Council shall issue a certificate evidencing satisfaction of the requirements of subsections (b) and (c) of this Section to any applicant who presents such evidence as may be required by its rules and regulations of satisfactory completion of a program or course of instruction in another jurisdiction equivalent in content and quality to that required by the Council for approved police education and training programs in this State.

(e) After the effective date of this act, each candidate for employment as a police officer who receives passing scores on his employment entrance examinations shall have credits, as established by the Council, added to his total examination scores for studies which he has satisfactorily completed at an accredited institution of higher learning in a program leading to a degree.

(f) Each police officer who is a candidate for promotion also shall receive educational credits as determined in section 5 on promotional examinations.

Section 6.   Police Training Schools and Programs: Grants Under the Supervision of Council and the State

(a) The Council shall establish and maintain police training programs through such agencies and institutions as the Council may deem appropriate.

(b) The Council shall authorize the reimbursement to each political subdivision and to the State 50 percent of the salary and of the allowable tuition, living, and travel expenses incurred by the officers in attendance at approved training programs, providing said political subdivisions or State agencies do in fact adhere to the selection and training standards established by the Council.

Section 7.   Appropriations

(a) Except as otherwise specifically provided in this Section, the Council shall be supported only by appropriations made by the legislature.

(b) The Council may accept for any of its purposes and functions under this act any and all donations, both real and personal, and grants of money from any governmental unit or public agency, or from any institution, person, firm, or corporation, and may receive, utilize, and dispose of the same.   Any arrangements pursuant to this subsection shall be detailed in the annual report of the Council.   Such report shall include the identity of the donor, the nature of the transaction, and the conditions, if any.   Any monies received by the Council pursuant to this subsection shall be deposited in the (State treasury) to the account of the Council.

(c) The Council, by rules and regulations, shall provide for the administration of the grant program authorized by this Section.   In promulgating such rules, the Council shall promote the most efficient and economical program for police training, including the maximum utilization of existing facilities and programs for the purpose of avoiding duplication.

(d) The Council may provide grants as a reimbursement for actual expenses incurred by the State or political subdivisions thereof for the provisions of training programs to officers from other jurisdictions within the State.

Section 8.   Severability.

The provisions of this act shall be severable and if any phrase, clause, sentence, or provision of this act is declared to be contrary to the Constitution or laws of this State or of the United States or the applicability thereof to any government, agency, person, or circumstance is held invalid, the validity of the remainder of this act and the applicability to any government, agency, person, or circumstance shall not be affected thereby.

Section 9.   Repealing Clause

All acts or parts of acts not consistent with this act are hereby repealed.

APPENDIX C

THE PROFESSIONAL CODE OF ETHICS PROMULGAT-
ED BY THE INTERNATIONAL ASSOCIATION
OF CHIEFS OF POLICE

The Law Enforcement Code of Ethics which follows, was adopted by the International Association of Chiefs of Police at the 1957 Conference in Honolulu by unanimous approval of the delegates present.

The Code, together with a proposed Canons of Police Ethics, was the subject of a six-month study by a special committee of the Association's Executive Committee, comprised of Past President Andrew J. Kavanaugh, Wilmington, Del.; Assistant Director Quinn Tamm, of the Federal Bureau of Investigation, and Franklin M. Kreml, Director, Northwestern University Transportation Center. The Conference action was taken following favorable recommendation of the Executive Committee.

The Code was first developed jointly and adopted by the California Peace Officers Association and the Peace Officers Research Association of California. It was released in December, 1956 and given wide distribution throughout the state. It has been adopted also by the National Conference of Police Associations. The special IACP committee, in considering the Code of Ethics, also drafted Canons of Police Ethics. The resolution of the Honolulu Conference approving the Code also provided that it be implemented by the Canons of Ethics authored by this committee.

LAW ENFORCEMENT CODE OF ETHICS

As a Law Enforcement Officer, my fundamental duty is to serve mankind; to safeguard lives and property; to protect the innocent against deception, the weak against oppression or intimidation, and the peaceful against violence or disorder; and to respect the Constitutional rights of all men to liberty, equality and justice.

I will keep my private life unsullied as an example to all; maintain courageous calm in the face of danger, scorn, or ridicule; develop self-restraint; and be constantly mindful of the welfare of others. Honest in thought and deed in both my personal and official life, I will be exemplary in obeying the laws of the land and the regulations of my department. Whatever I see or hear of a confidential nature or that is confided to me in my official capacity will be kept ever secret unless revelation is necessary in the performance of my duty.

I will never act officiously or permit personal feelings, prejudices, animosities or friendships to influence my decisions. With no compromise for crime and with relentless prosecution of criminals, I will enforce the law courteously and appropriately without fear or favor, malice or ill will, never employing unnecessary force or violence and never accepting gratuities.

I recognize the badge of my office as a symbol of public faith, and I accept it as a public trust to be held so long as I am true to the ethics of the police service. I will constantly strive to achieve these objectives and ideals, dedicating myself before God to my chosen profession . . . law enforcement.

APPENDIX D
CLASSIFICATION OF POLICE HAZARDS *

Persons

Criminals
Migrants
Perverts
Inverts
Alcoholics
Dope Addicts
Prostitutes
Gamblers
Pimps
Drug Peddlers
Saloon Keepers
Pawnbrokers
Second Hand Dealers
Feebleminded
Insane
Agitators
Fanatics
Subversive Agents
Juvenile Delinquents
Problem Children
Solicitors
Peddlers
Taxi Dancers
Car Hops

Places

Main Arteries
  Railroad
  Automobile
  Pedestrian
Shipping Docks
Ferry Landings
Rendezvous or Residence of
  Individuals Listed under Persons
Railroad Stations
Radical Headquarters
Saloons
Gambling Places
Pool Halls
Amusement Parks
Pawn Shops
Second Hand Stores
Transitional Areas
Foreign Born Areas
Negro Areas
Streets in Vicinity of Theaters

Property

Unoccupied Dwellings
Warehouses
Fraternity, Sorority Houses and Dormitories

Safes
Autos
Buildings under Construction.
Gas Stations
Banks
Business places where
1. Insurance companies prohibit open stock risks.
2. Open stock risks which are prohibited without alarm systems.
3. Open stock risks which must be referred to the home office.

Situational

Athletic Events
Political Meetings
Parades
Conventions
Radical Meetings
Racial Conflicts
Celebrations
Disaster
Mobs
Labor Conflicts
Strikes
Note:
  Police Hazards must be further classified as to whether or not they are:
High Frequency
Low Frequency
High Value
Low Value

Places

Houses of Prostitution
Taverns
Bars
Night Clubs
Dance halls
Low rent rooming houses

Situational

Seasonal
Time Limited
Density
Opportunity
Temporary
Removable
Fixed
  Police records, where these are properly kept, will always give a true picture of the police hazards in any community.

* Based upon a compilation made by Chief August Vollmer.

495

APPENDIX E

MODIFIED MERCALLI INTENSITY FOR EARTHQUAKES [1]

By WOOD and NEUMAN (abridged)

I. Not felt except by a very few under especially favorable circumstances.

II. Felt only by a few persons at rest, especially on upper floors of buildings. Delicately suspended objects may swing.

III. Felt quite noticeably, especially on upper floors of buildings, but many people do not recognize it as an earthquake. Standing motor cars may rock slightly. Vibration like passing of truck. Duration estimated.

IV. During the day felt indoors by many, outdoors by few. At night some awakened. Dishes, windows, doors disturbed; walls made cracking sound. Sensation like heavy truck striking building. Standing motor cars rocked noticeably.

V. Felt by nearly everyone; many awakened. Some dishes, windows, and so forth broken; a few instances of cracked plaster; unstable objects overturned. Disturbances of trees, poles, and other tall objects sometimes noticed.

VI. Felt by all; many frightened and ran outdoors. Some heavy furniture moved; a few instances of fallen plaster or damaged chimneys. Damage slight.

VII. Everybody runs outdoors. Damage negligible in buildings of good design and construction; slight to moderate in well-built ordinary structures; considerable in poorly built or badly designed structures; some chimneys broken; noted by persons driving motor cars.

VIII. Damage slight in specially designed structures, considerable in ordinary substantial buildings with partial collapse; great in poorly built structures. Panel walls thrown out of frame structures. Fall of chimneys, factory stacks, columns, monuments, walls. Heavy furniture overturned. Sand and mud ejected in small amounts. Changes in well water. Persons driving motor cars disturbed.

IX. Damage considerable in specially designed structures; well designed frame structures thrown out of plumb; great in sub-

[1] Perry Byerly, *Seismology*, Prentice-Hall Inc., New York, 1942, pp. 56–64.

stantial buildings, with partial collapse. Buildings shifted off foundations. Ground cracked conspicuously. Underground pipes broken.

X. Some well-built wooden structures destroyed; most masonry and frame structures destroyed with foundations; ground badly cracked. Rails bent. Landslides considerable from river banks and steep slopes. Shifted sand and mud. Water splashed (slopped) over banks.

XI. Few, if any (masonry), structures remain standing. Bridges destroyed. Broad fissures in ground. Underground pipe lines completely out of service. Earth slumps and land slips in soft ground. Rails bent greatly.

XII. Damage total. Waves seen on ground surfaces. Lines of sight and level distorted. Objects thrown upward into the air.

Leonard Police Org. & Man. 3rd Ed.F.P.—32

APPENDIX F

SCOPE AND CONTENT OF AN INSTRUCTIONAL PROGRAM IN SAFETY AND DRIVER EDUCATION *

I. Teaching the Beginning Driver the Social Responsibilities of Driving.
1. Developing the student's ideas of "traffic citizenship" as a part of all good citizenship.
2. Developing knowledge and habits of observance of traffic laws and safe driving roles.
3. Developing friendly and cooperative attitudes toward traffic enforcement officers and traffic courts.
4. Developing safe drivers in situations where the student's family and friends are not exemplary drivers.

II. Testing and Identifying Abilities, Limitations and Progress of the Student Driver.
1. Anticipating by tests and observations a student's probable driving record.
2. Explaining to the student his limitations, as shown by physical fitness, reaction time, visual and other psychophysical tests, and helping him to compensate for his limitations.
3. Testing and grading a learner's performance.

III. Selecting Materials, Equipment, and Arrangements for Driver Education Classes and Driving Groups.
1. Turning to the community.
2. Selecting and evaluating classroom teaching aids.
3. Devising and evaluating ways to supplement a student's at-the-wheel experience.
4. Selecting the route over which students should operate cars, or the effective use of practice areas.
5. Making the "observation time" in the practice driving car a profitable learning experience.
6. Making use of the demonstration technique both in the class-room and in the practice car.
7. Teaching the basic mechanical operations of the car, including evaluations of the teaching aids used.

* Reproduced through the courtesy of the National Education Association, 1201 Sixteenth Street, N. W., Washington, D. C. See their publication, *How Experienced Teachers Develop Good Traffic Citizens*, 1958.

IV. Teaching the Operations of Driving and Developing the Judgments Required.
1. Developing good habits of routine things to do and check.
2. Teaching the efficient habits and skills necessary in the use of clutch, accelerator, gear-shift and brakes.
3. Teaching the beginning driver to steer the car smoothly and slowly forward and backward.
5. Preparing students to drive under hazardous conditions, such as on icy or slippery roads, through rain, snow, fog, high winds etc.
6. Preparing students to make proper maneuvers in cases of blowout, brake failure, or other mechanical failure.

VI. Teaching Driver Education to Special Groups.
1. Making the instruction profitable to a class which includes both experienced and inexperienced drivers.
2. Helping the tense student.
3. Teaching driver education to meet the special problems of students who are physically handicapped.
4. Teaching driver education to the slow learner or student of low ability.
5. Teaching driver education to adults.

BIBLIOGRAPHY

BOOKS

ALEXANDER, Myrl E., *Jail Administration*, Charles C. Thomas, Publisher, 1957.

ALLEN, Edward J., *Merchants of Menace*, Charles C. Thomas, Publisher, 1962.

AMERICAN MUNICIPAL ASSOCIATION, *Motorized Police Patrol—One-man or Two-man Crews?* Report No. 140, Chicago, 1940.

APPLEWHITE, Philip B., *Organizational Behavior*, Englewood Cliffs, Prentice-Hall, Inc., 1965.

ARGYRIS, Chris, *Understanding Organization Behavior*, Homewood, Illinois, The Forsey Press, Inc., 1960.

ASHENHUST, Paul H., *Police and the People*, Charles C. Thomas, Publisher, 1947.

ASSOCIATED POLICE COMMUNICATIONS OFFICERS, INC., *The Public Safety Standard Operating Procedure Manual*, New Smyrna, Beach, Florida, 1969.

AUBRY, Arthur S., *The Officer in the Small Department*, Charles C. Thomas, Publisher, 1960.

AUMANN, Francis R., *The Changing Legal System*, Ohio State University, 1940.

BAKKE, E. W., *The Fusion Process*, New Haven, Yale University Press, 1953.

BARNARD, Chester L., *Organization and Management*, New York, Harvard University Press, 1948.

BARNARD, Chester L., *The Functions of the Executive*, Cambridge, Harvard University Press, 1938.

BISCAILUZ, Eugene W., *Los Angeles County Major Disaster Emergency Council*, Los Angeles County Sheriff's Department, 1941.

BLAU, Peter M., *The Dynamics of Bureaucracy*, Chicago, University of Chicago Press, 1955.

BONNER, Hubert, *Group Dynamics: Principles and Applications*, New York, The Ronald Press Company, 1959.

BOUDIN, Louis B., *Government by Judiciary*, New York, William Godwin, 1932.

BRISTOW, Allen P., *Field Interrogation,* Charles C. Thomas, Publisher, 1958.

BRISTOW, Allen P., *Decision-Making in Police Administration,* Charles C. Thomas, Publisher, 1961.

BRISTOW, Allen P., *Effective Police Manpower Utilization,* Springfield, Illinois, Charles C. Thomas, Publisher, 1969.

BROWN, Thorvald T., *The Enigma of Drug Addiction,* Charles C. Thomas, Publisher, 1961.

BURT, Cyril, *The Young Delinquent,* D. Appleton & Co., 1914.

BURTT, Harold E., *Principles of Employment Psychology,* Harper and Bros., 1942.

BYERLY, Perry, *Seismology,* Prentice-Hall, Inc., 1942.

CARR, L. J., *Delinquency Control,* Harper and Bros., 1941.

CARTWRIGHT, Darwin and ZANDER, Alvin, *Group Dynamics —Research and Theory,* New York, Harper and Company, 1953.

CHAPMAN, Samuel G., *Dogs in Police Service,* Public Administration Service, 1960.

CHAPMAN, Samuel B., *Police Patrol Readings,* Springfield, Illinois, Charles C. Thomas, Publisher, 1964.

CIZON, Francis A., and SMITH, William H. T., *Police Community Relations Training,* Washington, Law Enforcement Assistance Administration, 1970.

CLAUSEWITZ, Carl Von, *On the Principles of War,* Kegan, Paul, Trench, Trubner & Co., Ltd., 1911.

CLEVELAND BUREAU OF GOVERNMENTAL RESEARCH, INC., *A Survey of Police-Fire Integration in the United States and Canada,* October, 1961.

CLIFT, Raymond E., *A Guide to Modern Police Thinking,* Cincinnati, W. H. Anderson Company, 2nd ed., 1965.

CLOWERS, Norman L., *Patrolman Patterns, Problems and Procedures,* Charles C. Thomas, Publisher, 1962.

COLLITON, Patrick, *The Evaluation of the Research-Planning Function in the American Police Services,* a Master's Thesis, Washington State University, 1962.

CONNERY, Robert H., *Urban Riots,* New York, Vintage Books, 1969.

CONWAY, James V. P., *Evidential Documents,* Charles C. Thomas, Publisher, 1959.

COOPER, R. Weldon, *Municipal Police Administration in Texas,* Bureau of Municipal Research, University of Texas, 1938.

CRESSEY, Donald R., *Theft of the Nation,* New York, Harper and Row, 1969.

CROCKETT, Thompson S., and STINCHCOMB, James D., *Guide Lines for Law Enforcement Education in Community and Junior Colleges,* Washington, American Association of Junior Colleges, 1968.

CROUCH, Winston W., *Metropolitan Services: Studies of Allocation in a Federated Organization, Part II, The Police Function,* Bureau of Governmental Research, University of California at Los Angeles, 1962.

CURRY, J. E., and KING, Glen D., *Race Tensions and the Police,* Charles C. Thomas, Publisher, 1962.

CURTIS, S. J., *Modern Retail Security,* Charles C. Thomas, Publisher, 1960.

DAHL, Raymond A., and BOYLE, Howard H., *Arrest, Search and Seizure,* Supplement, Milwaukee, Hammersmith-Courtney, 1967.

DAVID, Ralph Currier, *Industrial Organization and Management,* Harper and Bros., 1940.

DAVIS, John E., *An Introduction to Tool Marks, Firearms and the Striagraph,* Charles C. Thomas, Publisher, 1958.

DAVIS, John R., *Industrial Plant Protection,* Charles C. Thomas, Publisher, 1957.

DEPARTMENT OF JUSTICE, State of California, *A Guide to Race Relations for Police Officers,* Sacramento, 1946.

DEPARTMENT OF THE ARMY, *Civil Disturbances and Disasters,* FM 19–15, Washington, U. S. Government Printing Office, 1968.

DEWHURST, H. S., *The Railroad Police,* Charles C. Thomas, Publisher, 1955.

DIENSTEIN, William, *Are You Guilty?,* Charles C. Thomas, Publisher, 1953.

DIENSTEIN, William, *Technics for the Crime Investigator,* Charles C. Thomas, Publisher, 1959.

DEINSTEIN, William, *How to Write a Narrative Investigation Report,* Springfield, Illinois, Charles C. Thomas, Publisher.

DOUGHERTY, Edward, *Safety in Police Pursuit Driving,* Charles C. Thomas, Publisher, 1961.

DUDYCHA, George J., *Psychology for Law Enforcement Officers,* Charles C. Thomas, Publisher, 1960.

EARLE, Howard H., *Student Instructor Guide on Police-Community Relations,* Springfield, Illinois, Charles C. Thomas, Publisher, 1970.

EARLE, Howard H., *Contract Law Enforcement by the Los Angeles County Sheriff's Department,* a Master's Thesis, University of Southern California, June 1960.

EDWARDS, Loren E., *Shoplifting and Shrinkage Protection for Stores,* Charles C. Thomas, Publisher, 1958.

EVANS, Henry K., and KREML, Franklin M., *Traffic Engineering and The Police,* National Conservation Bureau and International Association of Chiefs of Police, 1946.

FEDERAL BUREAU OF INVESTIGATION, *Prevention and Control of Mobs and Riots,* Washington, U. S. Government Printing Office, 1967.

FERRY, Enrico, *Criminal Sociology,* Appleton-Century Co., Inc., 1896.

FIELD, Annita T., *Fingerprint Handbook,* Charles C. Thomas, Publisher, 1959.

FLYNN, Edward J., *You're the Boss,* The Viking Press, 1947.

FORTAS, Abe, *Concerning Dissent and Civil Disobedience,* New York, Signet Books, 1968.

FOSDICK, Raymond B., *American Police Systems,* The Century Company, New York, 1916.

FOSDICK, Raymond B., *European Police System,* The Century Company, New York, 1915.

FOSDICK, Raymond B., *Police Administration,* Part III of the Cleveland Foundation Survey of Criminal Justice in Cleveland, 1921.

Frost, *A Forward Look in Police Education,* Charles C. Thomas, Publisher, 1959.

GABARD, E. Caroline and KENNEY, John P., *Police Writing,* Charles C. Thomas, Publisher, 1957.

GAMMAGE, Allen Z., *Basic Police Report Writing,* Charles C. Thomas, Publisher, 1960.

GERBER, Samuel R., and SCHROEDER, Oliver, *Criminal Investigation,* Cincinnati, W. H. Anderson Company, 1962.

GERMANN, A. C., *Police Personnel Management,* Charles C. Thomas, Publisher, 1958.

GILSTON, David H., and PODELL, Lawrence, *The Practical Patrolman,* Charles C. Thomas, Publisher, 1959.

GOCKE, B. W., *Police Sergeants Manual,* O. W. Smith Book Co., 1943.

GOCKE, B. W., *Practical Plant Protection,* Charles C. Thomas, Publisher, 1957.

GOOTNICK, Louis, *A Survey of Police Use of the Lie Detector,* a Master's Thesis, New York University, October 1959.

GOURLEY, C. Douglas and BRISTOW, Allen P., *Patrol Administration,* Charles C. Thomas, Publisher, 1961.

GOURLEY, C. Douglas, *Public Relations and the Police,* Charles C. Thomas, Publisher, 1953.

GRAHAM, George A., and REINING, Henry, Jr., *Regulatory Administration,* John Wiley & Sons, Inc., 1943.

GREENING, J. A., *Report of the Committee on Professionalization of Police Service,* Yearbook of the International Association of Chiefs of Police, 1938–39.

GRIFFIN, John I., *Statistics Essential for Police Efficiency,* Charles C. Thomas, Publisher, 1958.

GUEST, Robert H., *Organization Change: The Effect of Successful Leadership,* Homewood, Illinois, The Dorsey Press, 1962.

GULICK and URWICK, *Papers on the Science of Administration,* Institute of Public Administration, Columbia University, 1937.

HAMMOND, Harold F., *Traffic Engineering Handbook,* Institute of Traffic Engineers, 1950.

HARNEY, Malachi L., *The Narcotic Officer's Notebook,* Charles C. Thomas, 1961.

HARNEY, Malachi L., and CROSS, John C., *The Informer in Law Enforcement,* Springfield, Illinois, Charles C. Thomas, Publisher, 1965.

HAZELET, John C., *Police Report Writing,* Charles C. Thomas, Publisher, 1960.

HARNEY, Malachi and CROSS, John C., *The Informer in Law Enforcement,* Charles C. Thomas, Publisher, 1959.

HEALY, William, *The Individual Delinquent,* Little, Brown & Co., Boston, 1915.

HEAPS, William., *Riots USA,* New York, The Seabury Press, 1966.

HECK, H. N., *Earthquake History of the United States,* U. S. Coast Geodetic Survey, Special Publication, No. 49.

HEFFRON, Floyd N., *The Officer in the Courtroom,* Charles C. Thomas, Publisher, 1955.

HIGGINS, Lois L., *Policewoman's Manual,* Charles C. Thomas, Publisher, 1961.

HOLMAN, Mary, *The Police Officer and the Child,* Charles C. Thomas, Publisher, 1962.

HOOTON, Arnest, *The American Criminal, An Anthropological Study,* Harvard University Press, 1939.

HOOVER, J. Edgar, Federal Bureau of Investigation, *Crime in the United States,* Washington, U. S. Government Printing Office.

HOUTS, Marshall, *The Rules of Evidence,* Charles C. Thomas, Publisher, 1956.

HOUTS, Marshall, *From Arrest to Release,* Charles C. Thomas, Publisher, 1958.

HOUTS, Marshall, *From Evidence to Proof,* Charles C. Thomas, Publisher, 1956.

INBAU, Fred E., *Lie Detection and Criminal Interrogation,* The Williams and Wilkins Co., 2nd edition, 1948.

INTERNATIONAL ASSOCIATION OF CHIEFS OF POLICE, *Police Unions,* revised edition, August 1958.

INTERNATIONAL CITY MANAGERS ASSOCIATION, *The Municipal Yearbook,* 1959 and 1963.

INTERNATIONAL CITY MANAGERS ASSOCIATION, *Questions and Answers—About the Council—Manager Plan and the City Manager Profession,* Washington, 1968.

JAMES, James B., *Limitations on Evidence in Criminal Cases,* Ann Arbor, Dean Hicks, 1966.

JONES, Leland V., *Scientific Investigation and Physical Evidence,* Charles C. Thomas, Publisher, 1959.

JURIS, Harvey A., and HUTCHINSON, Kay B., *The Legal Status of Municipal Police Employee Organizations,* Working Paper No. 3, Madison, Center for Law and Behavioral Science, University of Wisconsin, 1969.

KENNEY, John P. and PURSUIT, Dan G., *Police Work With Juveniles,* Charles C. Thomas, Publisher, 1954.

KENNEY, John P., *Police Management Planning,* Charles C. Thomas, Publisher, 1959.

KENNEY, John P. and WILLIAMS, John B., *Police Operations,* Charles C. Thomas, Publisher, 1960.

KEY, V. O., *Politics, Parties and Pressure Groups*, Thomas Y. Crowell Co., 1947.

KILLIAN, Lewis M., *The Impossible Revolution*, New Work, Random House, 1968.

KING, Everett M., *The Officer Speaks in Public*, Charles C. Thomas, Publisher, 1958.

KING, Everett M., *The Auxiliary Police Unit*, Charles C. Thomas, 1960.

KING, Glen D., *First-Line Supervisor's Manual*, Charles C. Thomas, Publisher, 1961.

KNEIER, Charles M., *City Government in the United States*, Harper and Brothers, New York, 1934.

KNEIER, Charles M., *City Government in the United States*, Harper and Brothers, revised edition, 1947.

KRESS, A. L., *Foremanship Fundamentals*, McGraw Hill Book Company, 1942.

KOOKEN, Don L., *Ethics in Police Service*, Charles C. Thomas, Publisher, 1957.

LADD, Walter D., *Organizing for Traffic Safety in Your Community*, Charles C. Thomas, Publisher, 1959.

LANGFORD, Beryl; SHEEHAN, Robert; LOBKOVISH, Thomas F., and WATSON, Paul J., *Stopping Vehicles and Occupant Control*, Charles C. Thomas, Publisher, 1960.

LEE, Alfred McClung, *Race Riot*, The Dryden Press, Inc., 1943.

LEE, Clarence D., *The Instrumental Detection of Deception*, Charles C. Thomas, Publisher, 1952.

LEONARD, V. A., *The Police Communication System*, Berkeley, University of California Press, 1938.

Survey and Reorganization of the Seattle Police Department, City of Seattle, 1945.

Police Organization and Management, Mineola, New York, The Foundation Press, Inc., 2nd ed., 1964, 3rd ed., 1971.

The Police of the 20th Century, Mineola, New York, The Foundation Press, Inc., 1964.

A Guide to the Study of Police Organization and Management, Pullman, Washington, Washington State University Press, 1965.

Police Science for the Young American, Springfield, Illinois, Charles C. Thomas, Publisher, 1968.

The Police, the Judiciary and the Criminal, Springfield, Illinois, Charles C. Thomas, Publisher, 1967.

The Police Enterprise, Its Organization and Management, Springfield, Illinois, Charles C. Thomas, Publisher, 1968.

Police Personnel Management, same publisher, 1968.

The Police Records System, same publisher, 1968.

The Police Communications System, same publisher, 1969.

Police Patrol Organization, same publisher, 1969.

The Police Detective Function, same publisher, 1969.

Criminal Investigation and Identification, same publisher, 1969.

Police Traffic Regulation and Control, same publisher, 1971.

Police Crime Prevention, same publisher, 1971.

Police Pre-Disaster Preparation, same publisher, 1971.

LEONARD, V. A., and MORE, Harry, W., *The General Administration of Criminal Justice,* Mineola, New York, 1966.

LIKERT, Rensis, *The Human Organization: Its Management and Value,* New York, McGraw-Hill, 1967.

LONG, Honorable William G., Judge of the Seattle Juvenile Court, *The Relation of Juvenile Courts to Other Agencies,* Proceedings of the Fifth Pacific Northwest Law Enforcement Conference, State College of Washington, Pullman, 1944.

MASOTTI, Louis H., and BOWEN, Don R., *Riots and Rebellion,* Beverly Hills, Sage Publications, Inc., 1968.

MATSON, Theodore M., SMITH, Wilbur S., and HURD, Frederick V., *Traffic Engineering,* New York, McGraw-Hill, 1955.

McCORMICK, Charles C., *Cases and Materials on the Law of Evidence,* St. Paul, West Publishing Company, 1948.

McCRACKEN, Dwight, *Traffic Regulation in Small Cities,* Chicago, Municipal Administration Service, 1932.

McGREGOR, Douglas, *The Professional Manager,* New York, McGraw-Hill.

MERKELEY, Donald K., *The Investigation of Death,* Charles C. Thomas, Publisher, 1957.

MICHIGAN STATE UNIVERSITY, *Survey of Police Community Relations,* Field Survey V, Washington, D. C., U. S. Government Printing Office, 1967.

MILINOSKI, Bronislaw, *The Dynamics of Culte Change,* New Haven, Yale University Press, 1945.

MORE, Harry W., Jr., *The New Era of Public Safety,* Springfield, Illinois, Charles C. Thomas, Publisher, 1970.

MOSHER AND KINGSLEY, *Public Personnel Administration,* Harper and Bros., 1941.

MOYNAHAN, James M., Jr., *Police Ju Jitsu,* Charles C. Thomas, Publisher, 1962.

NATIONAL ADVISORY COMMISSION ON CIVIL DISOR-DERS, *Report to the President,* Washington, U. S. Government Printing Office, 1968.

NATIONAL ADVISORY COMMISSION ON CIVIL DISOR-DERS, *Supplemental Studies,* Washington, U. S. Government Printing Office, 1968.

NATIONAL COMMISSION ON THE CAUSES AND PRE-VENTION OF VIOLENCE, *Violence in America,* Washington, U. S. Government Printing Office.

NATIONAL COMMISSION ON THE CAUSES AND PRE-VENTION OF VIOLENCE, *To Establish Justice, To Insure Domestic Tranquility,* Washington, U. S. Government Printing Office, 1966.

NATIONAL COMMISSION ON LAW OBSERVANCE AND ENFORCEMENT, *Report on the Police,* Washington, U. S. Government Printing Office, 1931.

NATIONAL MUNICIPAL LEAGUE, *Forms of Municipal Government and How They Have Worked,* New York, 1966.

NATIONAL MUNICIPAL LEAGUE, *The Story of the Council-Manager Plan,* New York, 1964.

NATIONAL MUNICIPAL LEAGUE, *Facts About the Council-Manager Plan,* New York, 1965.

NATIONAL MUNICIPAL LEAGUE, *Best Practice Under the Manager Plan,* New York, 1965.

NATIONAL MUNICIPAL LEAGUE, *City Employes and the Manager Plan,* New York, 1966.

NELSON, A. T., and SMITH, Howard E., *Car Clouting, The Crime, the Criminal and the Police,* Charles C. Thomas, Publisher, 1958.

NEW YORK CITY POLICE DEPARTMENT, *Operational Manual for Disasters,* 1962.

NELSON, Truman, *The Right of Revolution,* Boston, Beacon Press, 1968.

NICOLAIDIS, Nicholas G., *Policy Decision and Organization Theory,* Los Angeles, John W. Donner Fund Publication No. 11, University of Southern California Book Store, 1960.

O'HARA, Charles C., *Fundamentals of Criminal Investigation,* Springfield, Illinois, Charles C. Thomas, Publisher, 2nd ed., 1970.

OTTOLENGHI, S., *The Italian Police Upper School and Its Technical Services,* Polygraphic Institute of the Italian State Library, Rome, 1933.

PARKER, W. H., *Los Angeles Police Daily Training Bulletin,* Charles C. Thomas, Publisher, 1958, Vols. I and II.

PENOFSKY, Daniel J., *Guidelines for Interrogation,* Rochester, Jurisprudence, 1967.

PEPER, John P., *A Recruit Asks Some Questions,* Charles C. Thomas, Publisher, 1954.

PERKINS, Rollin M., *Elements of Police Science,* Foundation Press, Inc., Brooklyn, N. Y., 1942.

PERKINS, Rollin M., *Police Examinations,* The Foundation Press Inc., Chicago, 1947.

PERKINS, Rollin M., *Criminal Law and Procedure, 2nd,* Mineola, New York, The Foundation Press, Inc., 1959.

PFIFFNER, John M., *The Supervision of Personnel,* Englewood Cliffs, New Jersey, Prentice-Hall, Inc., 1958.

PFIFFNER, John M., and PRESTHUS, Robert, *Public Administration,* 5th ed., New York, The Ronald Press Company, 1967.

PFIFFNER, John M., *Municipal Administration,* The Ronald Press Company, New York, 1940.

PFIFFNER, John M., *Public Administration in the United States,* Ronald Press Co., New York, 1936.

PORTERFIELD, Austin L., *Crime, Suicide and Social Well-Being in Your State and City,* (Porterfield and Robert H. Talbert), with the assistance of Herbert R. Mundhenke, The Leo Potishman Foundation, Texas Christian University, Fort Worth, 1948.

PORTERFIELD, Austin L., *Youth in Trouble,* The Leo Potishman Foundation, Texas Christian University, Fort Worth, 1946.

POUND, Roscoe, *"Criminal Justice in Cleveland,"* The Cleveland Foundation, 1922.

PRESIDENT'S COMMISSION ON LAW ENFORCEMENT AND ADMINISTRATION OF JUSTICE, *The Challenge of Crime in a Free Society,* Washington, U. S. Government Printing Office, 1967.
Task Force Report: The Police, same source, 1967.
Task Force Report: Juvenile Delinquency, same source, 1967.

Task Force Report: Science and Technology, same source, 1967.

Task Force Report: Organized Crime, same source, 1967.

Task Force Report, Crime and Its Impact: An Assessment, same source, 1967.

RECKLESS, Walter C., *The Crime Problem,* Appleton-Century-Crofts, New York, 1950.

RECKLESS, Walter C., *The Etiology of Delinquent and Criminal Behavior,* Social Science Research Council, New York, 1943.

RECKLESS, Walter C., *Juvenile Delinquency* (Reckless and Smith), McGraw-Hill, New York, 1932.

RECKLESS, Walter C., *Criminal Behavior,* McGraw-Hill, New York, 1940.

RECKLESS, Walter C., *Social Psychology* (Krueger and Reckless), Longsman, Green & Co., 1931.

REINHARDT, James M., *Sex Perversions and Sex Crimes,* Charles C. Thomas, Publisher, 1957.

REITH, Charles, *The Police Idea,* Oxford University Press, 1939.

RIDLEY, Clarence E., and SIMON, Herbert A., *Measuring Municipal Activities,* International City Managers' Association, 1938.

RIZER, Conrad, *Police Mathematics,* Charles C. Thomas, Publisher, 1955.

ROBINSON, Carlton C., *Traffic Engineering,* New York, Universal Publishing and Distributing Company, 1966.

ROBINSON, Oliver Prescott, The Fundamentals of Military Strategy, U. S. Infantry Association, Washington, D. C., 1928.

ROETHISBERGER, F. S., and DICKSON, J., *Management and the Worker,* Cambridge, Harvard University Press, 1939.

SALERNO, Ralph and THOPKINS, John S., *The Crime Confederation,* Garden City, New Jersey, Doubleday and Company, 1969.

SCHELL, Erwin Haskell, *The Technique of Executive Control,* McGraw-Hill Book Company, Inc., New York, 1942.

SCHWARZ, John I., *Police Roadblock Operations,* Charles C. Thomas, Publisher, 1962.

SCOTT, Clifford L., and GARRETT, Bill, *Leadership for the Police Supervisor,* Charles C. Thomas, Publisher, 1960.

SCOTT, Charles C., *Photographic Evidence,* Vernon Law Book Company, 1955.

SCOTT, James C., *An Analysis of Lateral Entry as a Means of Obtaining Municipal Police Supervisors and Administrators in the United*

States, Master's Thesis, Pullman, Washington, Washington State University, 1965.

SCOTT, Walter R., *Fingerprint Mechanics,* Charles C. Thomas, Publisher, 1951.

SECKLER-Hudson, Catherine, *Organization and Management: Theory and Practice,* Washington, The American University, 1955.

SELZNICK, Philip, *Leadership and Administration,* Evanston, Row, Peterson, 1957.

SIMON, Herbert A., *Administrative Behavior,* New York, McMillan Company, 1958.

SMITH, Bruce, *Police Systems in the United States,* Harper and Brothers, New York, 1940.

SMITH, Bruce, *The State Police,* The MacMillan Company, New York, 1925.

SMITH, R. Dean, *Computer Applications in Police Manpower Distribution,* Field Service Division, International Association of Chiefs of Police, 1961.

SNYDER, LeMoyne, *Homicide Investigation,* Charles C. Thomas, Publisher, 1959.

SUNNYVALE (CALIFORNIA) DEPARTMENT OF PUBLIC SAFETY, *A Decade of Public Safety* (Police-Fire Integration).

TAYLOR, Frederick W., *Scientific Management,* New York, Harper and Bros., 1947.

TAYLOR, Frederick W., *Shop Management,* Harper & Brothers, New York, 1911.

THOMPSON, Craig and RAYMOND, Allen, *Gang Rule in New York,* Camden, 1940.

THORNDYKE, E. L., *Your City,* Harcourt, Brace and Company, 1939.

TRAFFIC INSTITUTE, Northwestern University, *Traffic Accident Investigator's Manual,* 1957.

TURNER, Ralph F., *Forensic Science and Laboratory Technics,* Charles C. Thomas Publisher, Springfield, Illinois, 1949.

VANDERBOSCH, Charles C., *Criminal Investigation,* Washington, Professional Standards Division, International Association of Chiefs of Police, 1968.

VOLLMER, August, *The Police and Modern Society,* University of California Press, Berkeley, 1936.

VOLLMER, August, *The Police Beat,* Proceedings of the Fortieth Annual Conference of the International Association of Chiefs of Police, 1933.

VOLLMER, August, *The Criminal,* Foundation Press, Inc., Brooklyn, N. Y., 1948.

VOLLMER, August, *Community Coordination,* Coordinating Councils, Inc., March-April, 1939.

VOLLMER, August, *Pre-delinquency,* Journal of Criminal Law and Criminology, XIV, 2, Aug. 1923.

VOLLMER and PARKER, *Crime and the State Police,* University of California Press, Berkeley, 1936.

WALDO, Dwight, *The Administrative State,* The Ronald Press Company, New York, 1948.

WALKER, Harvey, *The Legislative Process,* Ronald Press, Co., New York, 1948.

WALKER, Harvey, *Training Public Employes in Britain,* New York and London, McGraw-Hill Book Co., 1935.

WALKER, Harvey, *Federal Limitations Upon Municipal Ordinance Making Power,* Ohio State University Press, 1929.

WALKER, Harvey, *Law Making in the U. S.,* Ronald Press Co., New York, 1934.

WALKER, Harvey, *Public Administration in the United States,* Farrar and Rinehart, Inc., 1937.

WESTON, Paul B., *Combat Shooting for the Police,* Charles C. Thomas, Publisher, 1960.

WESTON, Paul B., *The Police Traffic Control Function,* Charles C. Thomas, Publisher, 1960.

WESTON, Paul B., *The Police Traffic Control Function,* Springfield, Illinois, Charles C. Thomas, Publisher, 2nd. ed., 1968.

WHITE, Leonard D., *Introduction to the Study of Public Administration,* New York, McMillan Company, 1955.

WOOD, Mayor Sterling A., *Riot Control by the National Guard,* Military Publishing Co., 1940.

WYNNE, G. Ray, *Transportation Management,* Studio City, California, Coda Publications, 1965.

YORK, Orrell A., *Municipal Police Training in New York State,* Municipal Police Training Council, Albany, New York, 1961.

ZINK, Harold, *Government of Cities in the United States,* The MacMillan Co., 1939.

ZINN, Howard, *Disobedience and Democracy,* New York, Vintage Books, 1968.

POLICE SURVEYS AND REORGANIZATIONS

BEALL,William P. Jr., *Survey and Reorganization of the Police Department of Medford, Oregon,* 1951.

EASTMAN, George D., *Survey and Reorganization of the St. Paul Bureau of Police,* 1963.

GREENING, J. A., *Police Beat Survey,* Police Department, Berkeley, California, 1944. (mimeographed.)

GREENING, J. A., *Survey and Reorganization of the Honolulu Police Department,* 1934.

GREENING, J. A., *Survey and Reorganization of the Mason City, Police Department,* 1930.

HOLSTROM, J. D., *Police Beat Survey,* Police Department, Berkeley, California, 1945. (mimeographed.)

Illinois Association for Criminal Justice, *Illinois Crime Survey,* 1929.

LEONARD, V. A., *A Proposed Survey and Reorganization of the Ft. Worth Police Department,* Master's Thesis, Texas Christian University, 1940.

LEONARD, V. A., *Survey and Reorganization of the Seattle Police Department,* 1945.

Public Administration Service, Chicago, *Survey of the Police Department, Greenwich, Conn.,* 1938.

Reorganization Scheme—Redistribution of Manpower in Accordance with Formula Based on Weighted Mileage, Metropolitan Police, London, R.U.F./1, M.P. 30–17282/200.

SMITH, Bruce, *The Baltimore Police Survey,* Institute of Public Administration, New York, 1941.

SMITH, Bruce, *The New Orleans Police Survey,* Bureau of Governmental Research, Inc., New Orleans, 1946.

VOLLMER, August, *Survey and Reorganization of the Dallas Police Department,* 1944.

VOLLMER, August, *Survey and Reorganization of the Havana Police Department,* 1929.

VOLLMER, August, *Survey and Reorganization of the Kansas City Police Department,* 1928.

VOLLMER, August, *Survey and Reorganization of the Los Angeles Police Department,* 1925.

VOLLMER, August, *Survey and Reorganization of the Minneapolis Police Department,* 1930.

VOLLMER, August, *Survey and Reorganization of the Syracuse Police Department,* 1944.

VOLLMER, August, *Survey and Reorganization of the Police Department of Portland, Oregon,* 1947.

WILSON, O. W., *Survey and Reorganization of the Police Department of Hartford, Connecticut,* 1942.

WILSON, O. W., *Survey and Reorganization of the Greensboro Police Department,* 1941.

WILSON, O. W., *Survey and Reorganization of the Pasadena Police Department,* 1940.

WILSON, O. W., *Survey and Reorganization of the San Antonio Police Department,* 1933.

WILSON, O. W., *Survey and Reorganization of the Wichita Police Department,* 1930.

WILSON, O. W., *Distribution of the Police Patrol Force,* Public Administration Service, Chicago, 1941.

WILSON, O. W., *Standards of Effective Criminal Investigation,* Proceedings of 44th Annual Conference of International Association of Chiefs of Police, 1937.

WILSON, O. W., *Police Administration,* McGraw-Hill Book Co., first edition 1950; second edition 1963.

WILSON, O. W., *Police Records and Their Installation,* Public Administration Service, 1951.

WILSON, O. W., *Police Planning,* Charles C. Thomas, Publisher, 1958.

WILSON, O. W., *Parker on Police,* Charles C. Thomas, Publisher, 1956.

PERIODICALS

BELLMAN, Arthur, *A Police Service Rating Scale,* 26 Journal of Criminal Law and Criminology, 1935.

BODIN, Nathan, *Do Problem Children Become Delinquents and Criminals?* Condensed from a Master of Arts Thesis, University of California, Journal of Criminal Law and Criminology, November-December, 1936.

COOK, Walter W., *"Scientific Method and the Law,"* American Bar Association Journal, 1927, Vol. 13.

DIXON, A. L., *The English Police System,* The Annals of the American Academy of Political and Social Science, Vol. CXLVI, p. 177, Nov. 1929.

DUNBAR, Walter, *California Youth Authority,* Vol. 16, No. 1, spring 1963.

EASTMAN, George D., *The Flexible Unit—A Unique Striking Force,* Police, July-August 1960.

ELLIS, James H., *The Connecticut Resident State Police System,* Police, September-October 1960.

Federal Security Agency, Division of Social Protection, *The Program of Division of Social Protection,* Bulletin issued by Region XII, San Francisco, California, November, 14, 1941.

HEARLE, Edward F. R., *Can Electronic Data Processing Be Applied to All Police Agencies?,* Logistics Department, The Rand Corporation, The Police Chief, February 1962.

HOLMES, Benjamin, *Selection of Patrolmen,* The Journal of Criminal Law and Criminology, No. XXXII, No. 5, January-February, 1942.

JESSUP, Jacob A., *A Study of the Use of Police Reserves or Auxiliaries,* Police, January-February 1960.

MATSCHECK, Walter, *Kansas City, Where the Manager Plan Has Failed,* The Annals of the American Academy of Political and Social Science, September, 1938.

National Commission on Law Observance and Enforcement *Report on the Police,* Vol. 14, Washington, D. C., 1931.

OLIPHANT, Herman, *"A Return to the Stare Decisis,"* American Bar Association Journal, Vol. 13, 1928.

PARRATT, Spencer D., *A Critique of the Bellman Police Service Rating Scale,* 27 Journal of Criminal Law and Criminology, 1937.

PARRATT, Spencer D., *How Effective is a Police Department,* The Annals of the American Academy of Political and Social Science, Philadelphia, Vol. 199, Sept. 1928.

RANKIN, James H., M. D., *Preventive Psychiatry in the Los Angeles Police Department,* Police, July-August 1957.

SMITH, Bruce, *"Politics and Law Enforcement,"* The Annals of American Academy of Political and Social Science, Vol. 169, September, 1933.

SUPPLEMENT

NUMBER OF LAW ENFORCEMENT DEGREE PROGRAMS AVAILABLE IN THE UNITED STATES AND OUTLYING AREAS

State	Associate Degree Programs (2-Year)	Baccalaureate Degree Programs (4-Year)	Master's Degree Programs	Doctorate Degree Program	Number of Separate Institutions
Alabama	2	0	0		2
Alaska	2	0	0		2
Arizona	3	2	1		5
Arkansas	0	0	0		0
California	60	7	7	2	67
Colorado	4	1	0		4
Connecticut	5	2	1		5
Delaware	1	0	0		1
District of Columbia	2	1	0		2
Nebraska	1	1	0		1
Nevada	2	1	0		2
New Hampshire	1	0	0		1
New Jersey	4	0	0		4
New Mexico	1	1	0		1
New York	18	1	2	2	20
North Carolina	8	0	0		8
North Dakota	0	0	0		0
Ohio	8	3	0	2	10

State					
Florida	14	1	1	0	14
Georgia	5	1	1	1	5
Hawaii	1	0	0	0	1
Idaho	2	1	0	0	2
Illinois	13	3	0	0	15
Indiana	1	2	2	0	3
Iowa	6	0	2	0	7
Kansas	4	0	0	0	4
Kentucky	1	2	0	0	2
Louisiana	1	1	0	0	1
Maine	0	0	0	0	0
Maryland	7	1	0	0	8
Massachusetts	4	1	0	0	4
Michigan	10	2	1	1	12
Minnesota	0	0	0	0	0
Mississippi	0	1	0	0	1
Missouri	5	2	0	0	7
Montana	1	0	0	0	1
Oklahoma	1	2	0	0	3
Oregon	6	2	0	0	8
Pennsylvania	9	2	0	0	10
Rhode Island	1	1	0	0	1
South Carolina	2	0	0	0	2
South Dakota	0	0	0	0	0
Tennessee	1	1	1	0	1
Texas	12	1	1	1	13
Utah	2	2	0	0	3
Vermont	0	0	0	0	0
Virginia	6	2	0	0	6
Washington	12	2	1	1	14
West Virginia	1	1	0	0	1
Wisconsin	4	1	0	0	5
Wyoming	1	0	0	0	1
Guam	1	0	0	0	1
Virgin Islands	1	0	0	0	1
	257	55	21	7	292

PROGRAM LISTINGS BY STATE

Institution	Address (Zip Code in Parentheses)	Degree	For Information Contact Department of
ALABAMA			
Jefferson State Junior College	2601 Carson Rd. Birmingham (35215)	A.S. (Transfer) A.A.S.	Police Science and Criminology
The Marion Institute	Marion (36756)	A.A., A.S. (Law Enf.)	Law Enforcement
ALASKA			
Anchorage Community College	2533 Providence Ave. Anchorage (99504)	A.A. (Police Admin.)	Police Administration
University of Alaska	College (99701)	A.A. (Police Admin.)	Political Science
ARIZONA			
Cochise College	Douglas (85607)	A.A. (Law Enf.)	Law Enforcement
Glendale Community College	6000 West Olive Ave. Glendale (85301)	A.A. (Law Enf.)	Cont. Education
Northern Arizona University	Box 5752 Flagstaff (86001)	B.S. (Police Sc., Criminalistics)	Police Science and Administration
Phoenix College	1202 W. Thomas Rd. Phoenix (85013)	A.A. (Police Sc.)	Law Enforcement
University of Arizona	Tucson (86001)	B.S.P.A., M.P.A. (Law Enf., Correcs.)	Public Administration
CALIFORNIA			
Allan Hancock College	800 S. College Drive Santa Maria (93454)	A.S. (Law Enf., Correcs.)	Law Enforcement

Institution	Address	Degree	Program
Antelope Valley College	3041 West Avenue K Lancaster (93534)	A.A. (Police Sc.)	Guidance and Counseling
Bakersfield College	1801 Panorama Drive Bakersfield (93305)	A.A. (Police Sc.)	Vocational-Technical Education
Barstow College	2700 Barstow Rd. Barstow (92311)	A.A. (Law Enf.)	Law Enforcement
Cabrillo College	6500 Soquel Drive Aptos (95003)	A.A. (Police Sc.)	Police Science
California State College at Long Beach	6101 E. Seventh St. Long Beach (90804)	B.S. (Police Sc.) M.S. (Police Admin., Criminalistics)	Criminology
California State College at Los Angeles	5151 State College Drive Los Angeles (90032)	B.S., M.S. (Police Sc., Criminalistics)	Police Science and Administration
California, University of	Berkeley (94720)	A.B., B.S., M., D. (Criminology)	Criminology
Cerritos College	11110 E. Alondra Blvd. Norwalk (90651)	A.A. (Police Sc.)	Social Science
Chabot College	25555 Hesperian Blvd. Hayward (94545)	A.A. (Police Sc.)	Police Science
Chaffey College	5885 Haven Ave. Alta Loma (91701)	A.A. (Police Sc.)	Police Science and Corrections
Citrus College	11824 E. Foothill Blvd. Azusa (91702)	A.A. (Police Sc.)	Police Science
College of the Desert	43-500 Monterey Ave. Palm Desert (92270)	A.A. (Police Sc.)	Vocational-Technical Education
College of the Redwoods	1040 Del Norte Eureka (95501)	A.A. (Police Sc.)	Public Safety
Compton College	1111 E. Artesia Blvd. Compton (90221)	A.A., A.S. (Police Sc.)	Police Science

Institution	Address (Zip Code in Parentheses)	Degree	For Information Contact Department of
Contra Costa College	2600 Mission Bell Drive San Pablo (94806)	A.A. (Law Enf., Correcs.)	Police Science
De Anza College	21250 Stevens Creek Blvd. Cupertino (95014)	A.A. (Law Enf.)	Law Enforcement
Diablo Valley College	Golf Club Rd. Pleasant Hill (94523)	A.A. (Police Sc.)	Police Science
East Los Angeles College	5357 E. Brooklyn Ave. Los Angeles (90022)	A.A. (Police Sc.)	Police Science
El Camino College	16007 S. Crenshaw Blvd. Torrance (90506)	A.A. (Police Sc.)	Police Science
Fresno City College	1101 E. University Ave. Fresno (93726)	A.A., A.S. (Police Sc.)	Police Science
Fresno State College	Fresno (93726)	B.S., M.S. (Law Enf., Correcs.)	Criminology
Fullerton Junior College	321 E. Chapman Ave. Fullerton (92634)	A.A. (Police Sc.)	Police Science
Gavilan College	5055 Santa Teresa Blvd. Gilroy (95020)	A.A. (Police Sc.)	Police Science
Glendale College	1500 N. Verdugo Rd. Glendale (91208)	A.A. (Police Sc.)	Police Science
Golden West College	15744 Golden West St. Huntington Beach (92647)	A.A. (Law Enf.)	Law Enforcement
Grossmont College	8800 Grossmont College Dr. El Cajon (92020)	A.A., A.S. (Criminology)	Criminology
Hartnell College	156 Homestead Ave. Salinas (93901)	A.A. (Police Sc., Correcs.)	Police Science

College	Address	Degree	Program
Imperial Valley College	P. O. Box 158, Hwy 111 at Ira Alten Rd. Imperial (92251)	A.A. (Police Sc.)	Police Science
Long Beach City College	4901 E. Carson St. Long Beach (90808)	A.A. (Police Sc.)	Police Science
Los Angeles City College	855 N. Vermont Ave. Los Angeles (90029)	A.A. (Police Sc.)	.Police Science
Los Angeles Harbor College	1111 Figueroa Place Wilmington (90744)	A.A. (Police Sc.)	Police Science
Los Angeles Valley College	5800 Fulton Ave. Van Nuys (91401)	A.A. (Police Sc.)	Police Science
Marin, College of	Kentfield (94904)	A.A., A.S. (Police Sc.)	Vocational and Technical Education
Merrit College	5714 Grove St. Oakland (94609)	A.A.	Police Science
Mira Costa College	Barnard Drive Oceanside (92054)	A.S., A.A. (Police Sc.)	Vocational and Technical Education
Modesto Junior College	College Ave. Modesto (95350)	A.A. (Police Sc.)	Police Science
Monterey Peninsula College	Monterey (93940)	A.A., A.S. (Police Sc.)	Police Science
Mount San Antonio College	1100 N. Grand Ave. Walnut (91789)	A.A. (Police Sc.)	Public Safety and Service
Napa College	2277 Napa Vallejo Hwy. Napa (94558)	A.A. (Police Sc.)	Police Science
Palo Verde College	811 W. Chanslorway Blythe (92225)	A.A. (Police Sc.)	Vocational Education

Institution	Address (Zip Code in Parentheses)	Degree	For Information Contact Department of
Pasadena City College	1570 E. Colorado Blvd. Pasadena (91106)	A.A. (Police Sc.)	Engineering and Technology
Peralta Colleges	5714 Grove St. Oakland (94609)	A.A. (Police Sc.)	Police Science
Rio Hondo Junior College	3600 Workman Mill Rd. Whittier (90608)	A.A. (Police Sc.)	Police Science
Riverside City College	3650 Fairfax Ave. Riverside (92506)	A.A. (Police Sc.)	Police Science
Sacramento City College	3835 Freeport Blvd. Sacramento (95822)	A.A. (Police Sc.)	Service Occupations
Sacramento State College	6000 "J" Street Sacramento (95819)	B.A., M.A. (Police Sc.)	Police Science and Administration
San Bernardino Valley College	701 S. Mount Vernon Ave. San Bernardino (91786)	A.A. (Police Sc., Correcs.)	Public Protection
San Diego Junior Colleges	835 12th Ave. San Diego (92101)	A.S. (Police Sc.)	Police Science
San Francisco, City College of	Ocean Ave. at Phelan San Francisco (94112)	A.A. (Police Sc.)	Criminology
San Joaquin Delta College	3301 Kensington Way Stockton (95204)	A.A. (Police Sc.)	Police Science
San Jose City College	2100 Moorpark Ave. San Jose (95114)	A.A. (Law Enf.)	Law Enforcement
San Jose State College	125 South Seventh St. San Jose (95114)	A.B. (Law Enf., Penology), M.S. (Law Enf.)	Law Enforcement and Administration

College	Address	Degree	Program
San Mateo, College of	1700 W. Hillsdale Blvd. San Mateo (94402)	A.A. (Police Sc.)	Social Science
Santa Ana College	1530 W. 17th St. Santa Ana (92706)	A.A. (Police Sc.)	Police Science
Santa Barbara City College	721 Cliff Drive Santa Barbara (93105)	A.A., A.S. (Police Sc.)	Vocational-Technical Education
Santa Monica City College	1815 Pearl St. Santa Monica (90406)	A.A. (Police Sc.)	Police Science
Santa Rosa Junior College	7501 Mendocino Ave. Santa Rosa (95401)	A.A. (Police Sc.)	Police Science
Sequoias, College of the	915 S. Mooney Blvd. Visalia (93277)	A.A. (Police Sc.)	Police Science
Shasta College	Old Oregon Trail Redding (96001)	A.A. (Police Sc.)	Law Enforcement
Sierra College	Rocklin Rd. Rocklin (95677)	A.A. (Police Sc.)	Police Science
Solano College	100 Whitney Ave. Vallejo (94590)	A.A. (Police Sc.)	Police Science
Southern California, University of	University Park Los Angeles (90024)	B.S., M.S., D.P.A. (Police; Correcs., Admin.)	Public Administration
Southwestern College	5800 Otay Lakes Rd. Chula Vista (92010)	A.A. (Police Sc.)	Police Science and Administration
Ventura College	4667 Telegraph Rd. Ventura (93003)	A.A. (Police Sc.)	Police Science and Public Administration
West Valley College	44 E. Latimer Ave. Campbell (95008)	A.A. (Law Enf.)	Law Enforcement
Yuba College	North Beale Road Marysville (95901)	A.A., A.S. (Police Sc.)	Police Science

Institution	Address (Zip Code in Parentheses)	Degree	For Information Contact Department of
COLORADO			
Arapahoe Junior College	5987 So. Rapp Littleton (80120)	A.A.S.	Police Science
El Paso Community College	5 West Las Vegas Ave. Colorado Springs (80906)	A.S.	Occupational Studies
Metropolitan State College	250 W. 14th Ave. at Civic Center Denver (80204)	A.A.S., B.S. (Law Enf., Police Sc.)	Law Enforcement and Criminology
Trinidad State Junior College	600 Prospect St. Trinidad (81082)	A.A.S. (Law Enf.)	Law Enforcement
CONNECTICUT			
Eastern Connecticut State College	Willimantic (06226)	A.S. (Law Enf.) 4 Year - Part Time	Law Enforcement
Manchester Community College	P. O. Box 1046 Manchester (06040)	A.S. (Police Sc., Correcs.)	Law Enforcement
New Haven College	300 Orange Ave. West Haven (06516)	A.S., B.S. (Law Enf.)	Law Enforcement
Norwalk Community College	300 Highland Ave. Norwalk (06854)	A.A.	Law Enforcement
University of Hartford	West Hartford (06117)	A.S., B.S. (Police Admin.) M.P.A.	Public Administration
DELAWARE			
Brandywine College	P.O. Box 7139, Concord Pike Wilmington (19803)	A.S. (Police Sc.)	Police Science and Administration

DISTRICT OF COLUMBIA

Institution	Address	Degree	Program
American University	Mass. & Neb. Ave., N.W. Washington (20016)	A.A., A.B. (Police Admin.)	Continuing Education
Washington Technical Institute	4100 Connecticut Ave. Washington (20008)	A.A. (Police Sc.)	Police Science

FLORIDA

Institution	Address	Degree	Program
Brevard Junior College	Clearlake Rd. Cocoa (32922)	A.S.	Police Administration
Broward Junior College	3501 Davie Rd. Fort Lauderdale (33314)	A.S., A.S. (Police Sc.)	Police Science
Central Florida Junior College	P. O. Box 1388 Ocala (32670)	A.A. (Law Enf.)	Law Enforcement
Daytona Beach Junior College	P. O. Box 1111 Daytona (32015)	A.A., A.S. (Police Admin.)	Law Enforcement
Florida Junior College at Jacksonville	Cumberland Campus Jacksonville (32205)	A.A., A.S. (Police Sc.)	Police Science and Administration
Florida Keys Junior College	Stock Island Key West (33040)	A.S. (Police Sc.)	Police Administration
Florida State University	Tallahassee (32306)	A.S., A.B., B.S., M.A., M.S., Ph.D. (Law Enf., Criminalistics)	Criminology and Corrections
Lake-Sumter Junior College	Leesburg (32748)	A.A. (Correcs.)	Law Enforcement
Miami-Dade Junior College	11380 N.W. 27th Ave. Miami (33167)	A.A., A.S. (Police Sc.)	Police Science and Criminology

Institution	Address (Zip Code in Parentheses)	Degree	For Information Contact Department of
Palm Beach Junior College	4200 Congress Ave., Lake Worth (33460)	A.S. (Law Enf.)	Social Science
Pensacola Junior College	1000 College Blvd. Pensacola (32504)	A.S.	Law Enforcement
St. Petersburg Junior College	6605 - 5th Ave., N. St. Petersburg (35733	A.A. (Police Admin.)	Police Administration
Tallahassee Junior College	444 Appleyard Drive Tallahassee (32303)	A.A., A.S.	Law Enforcement
Valencia Junior College	P. O. Box 3028 Orlando (32802)	A.S. (Law Enf.)	Law Enforcement
GEORGIA			
Albany Junior College	2400 Gillionville Albany (31705)	A.A. (Police Admin.)	Social Science
Armstrong State College	Savannah (31406)	A.A. (Police Admin.)	Police Science
DeKalb College	555 N. Indiana Creek Dr. Clarkston (30021)	A.A. (Police Sc.)	Police Science
Georgia State College	33 Gilmer Road Atlanta (30303)	A.A., B.S, M.S.	Criminal Justice
Kennesaw Junior College	Marietta (30060)	A.A. (Police Admin.)	Admissions
HAWAII			
Honolulu Community College	874 Dillingham Blvd. Honolulu (96817)	A.S. (Police Sc.).	Public Administration

IDAHO

Institution	Address	Degree	Program
Boise College	1907 Campus Drive Boise (83707)	A.A., B.A., B.S. (Criminology)	Governmental Services
College of Southern Idaho	1300 Kimberly Rd. Twin Falls (83301)	A.S. (Law Enf.)	Vocational-Technical Education

ILLINOIS

Institution	Address	Degree	Program
Black Hawk College	1001 16th Street Moline (61265)	A.A.	Governmental Services
Carl Sandburg College	139 S. Cherry St. Galesburg (61401)	A.A.S. (Law Enf.)	Police Science Technology
College of Dupage	20 North 235 Ferry Rd. Naperville (60540)	A.A., A.A.S. (Police Sc.)	Police Science Technology
Danville Junior College	2000 E. Main St. Danville (61832)	A.A.S.	Police Science
Illinois Central College	P. O. Box 2400 East Peoria (61611)	A.A.S. (Police Tech.)	Police Science Technology
Joliet Junior College	201 E. Jefferson St. Joliet (60432)	A.S.	Vocational-Technical Education
Loop College	64 East Lake St. Chicago (60601)	A.A. (Law Enf.)	Law Enforcement
Prairie State College	P. O. Box 487 Chicago Heights (60411)	A.A.S., B.S. (Law Enf.)	Occupational Services
Rock Valley College	Rockford (61111)	A.S.	Technology
Southern Illinois University	Carbondale (62901)	A.A. (Law Enf.)	Center for Study of Crime
Triton College	2000 Fifth Ave. River Grove (60171)	A.S.	Police Science Administration

Institution	Address (Zip Code in Parentheses)	Degree	For Information Contact Department of
University of Illinois at Chicago Circle	P. O. Box 4348 Chicago (60680)	B.A. (Criminal Justice)	Criminal Justice
Waubonsee Community College	Route 47 & Harter Rd. Sugar Grove (60554)	A.A.S.	Vocational-Technical Education
Western Illinois University	Morrill Hall Macomb (61455)	B.S. (Law Enf.)	Law Enforcement
William Rainey Harper College	Algonquin & Roselle Rds. Palatine (60067)	A.S. (Law Enf.)	Police Science
INDIANA			
Indiana State University	Terre Haute (47803)	B.S., M.S.	Criminology
Indiana University	Bloomington (47401)	A.B., M.P.A. (Law Enf.)	Police Administration
University of Evansville	P. O. Box 329 Evansville (47704)	A.A. (Law Enf.)	Law Enforcement
IOWA			
Iowa Central Community College	330 Ave. M Fort Dodge (50501)	A.A.	Arts & Science
Iowa Western Community College	923 E. Washington Clarinda (51632)	A.A.S.	Social Science
Kirkwood Community College	Box 2068 Cedar Rapids (52406)	A.A.	Law Enforcement
North Iowa Area Community College	220 E. State St. Mason City (50401)	A.A. (Law Enf.)	Law Enforcement
Southeastern Iowa Area Community College	Hwy 34 West Burlington (52601)	A.A. (Law Enf.)	Law Enforcement

Institution	Location	Degree	Program
State University of Iowa	Iowa City (52240)	M.A. (Law Enf., Correcs.)	Sociology
University of Iowa	Iowa City (52240)	A.A. (Law Enf.), M.A. (Law Enf., Correcs.)	Sociology
KANSAS			
Allen County Community Junior College	Iola (66744)	A.A. (Police Sc.)	Police Science
Cowley County Community College	2nd & 5th Ave. Arkansas City (67005)	A.A.S. (Police Sc.)	Occupational Education
Hutchinson Community Junior College	1300 N. Plum St. Hutchinson (64111)	A.A.S. (Police Sc.)	Vocational-Technical Education
Wichita State University	1845 Fairmount Wichita (67208)	A.A.S. (Police Sc.)	Police Science
KENTUCKY			
Eastern Kentucky University	Richmond (40475)	A.A., B.S. (Law Enf.)	Law Enforcement
University of Louisville	Belknap Campus Louisville (40208)	B.S. (Police Admin.)	Police Administration
LOUISIANA			
Loyola University	6363 St. Charles Ave. New Orleans (70118)	A.A., B.A. (Criminology)	Evening Division
MARYLAND			
Anne Arundel Community College	Arnold (21012)	A.A.	Law Enforcement

Institution	Address (Zip Code in Parentheses)	Degree	For Information Contact Department of
Catonsville Community College	800 S. Rolling Rd., Catonsville (21228)	A.A. (Police Admin., Correcs.)	Police Administration and Corrections
Cecil Community College	Booth Street Corner Elkton (21921)	A.A.	Law Enforcement
Community College of Baltimore	2901 Liberty Heights Ave. Baltimore (21215)	A.A. (Police Sc.)	Urban Affairs
Essex Community College	Essex (21221)	A.A. (Police Sc.)	Social Science
Hagerstown Junior College	751 Robinwood Drive Hagerstown (21740)	A.A.	Law Enforcement
Montgomery College	Rockville (20850)	A.A. (Police Sc.)	Police Science
University of Baltimore	1420 North Charles St. Baltimore (21201)	B.S. (Law Enf.)	Law Enforcement
MASSACHUSETTS			
Cape Cod Community College	Hyannis (02601)	A.A.	Social Science
Mount Wachusett Community College	Gardner (01440)	A.S. (Law Enf.)	Evening Studies
Northeastern University	360 Huntington Ave. Boston (02115)	A.A., B.S. (Law Enf. & Security)	Criminal Justice
Worcester Junior College	Worcester (01608)	A.A. (Police Sc.)	Police Administration
MICHIGAN			
Delta College	University Center (48710)	A.A. (Law Enf.)	Social Science

Institution	Address	Degree	Field/Title
Flint Community Junior College	1301 E. Court St. Flint (48503)	A.A. (Police Sc.)	Law Enforcement
Glen Oaks Community College	Centreville (49032)	A.A.	Dean of Instruction
Grand Rapids Junior College	143 Bostwick Ave., N.E. Grand Rapids (49502)	A.A. (Public Safety)	Public Safety
Kellog Community College	450 North Ave. Battle Creek (49016)	A.A.	Admissions
Lansing Community College	419 N. Capitol Ave. Lansing (48914)	A.A. (Law Enf.)	Law Enforcement
Macomb County Community College	16500 Hall Rd. Mt. Clemens (48043)	A.A. (Law Enf.)	Public Services
Michigan State University	East Lansing (48823)	B.S., M.S., Ph.D. (Criminal Justice, Criminology)	Police Administration and Public Safety
Oakland Community College	Auburn Hills Campus 2900 Featherstone Rd. Auburn Heights (48057)	A.A. (Police Sc.)	Business
St. Clair County Community College	323 Erie Street. Port Huron (48060)	A.A. (Law Enf.)	Law Enforcement Education
Schoolcraft College	18600 Haggerty Rd. Livonia (48151)	A.A. (Technology)	
Wayne State University	5257 Cass Ave. Detroit (48202)	B.S. (Police Admin.)	Police Administration

MISSISSIPPI

Institution	Address	Degree	Field/Title
University of Mississippi School of Business & Government	University (38677)	B.A. (Police Admin.)	Political Science

Institution	Address (Zip Code in Parentheses)	Degree	For Information Contact Department of
MISSOURI			
Central Missouri State College	Warrensburg (64093)	A.B., B.S. (Law Enf.)	Law Enforcement
Florissant Valley Community College	3400 Pershall Rd. St. Louis (63135)	A.A.	Law Enforcement
Forest Park Community College	5600 Oakland Ave. St. Louis (63110)	A.A.S.	Law Enforcement
Meramec Community College	959 S. Geyer Rd. Kirkwood (63122)	A.A.S.	Law Enforcement
Missouri Southern College	Newman & Duquesne Roads Joplin (64801)	A.S. (Law Enf.)	Law Enforcement
Penn Valley Community College	560 Westport Rd. Kansas City (64111)	A.A. (Police Sc.)	Police Science
University of Missouri	8001 Natural Bridge Rd. St. Louis (63121)	B.S. (Admin. of Justice)	Administration of Justice
MONTANA			
Dawson College	Box 631 Glendive (59330)	A.A. (Police Sc.)	Police Science
NEBRASKA			
University of Nebraska at Omaha	Box 688, Downtown Station Omaha (68101)	A.A., B.S. (Law Enf., Correcs.)	Law Enforcement and Corrections
NEVADA			
Nevada Technical Institute	Stead Campus Reno (89507)	A.S. (Law Enf.)	Law Enforcement

Institution	Address	Degree	Program
University of Nevada	4505 Maryland Pkwy. Las Vegas (89109)	A.S. (Law Enf.) B.A.	General and Technical Studies
NEW HAMPSHIRE			
St. Anselms College	College Rd. Manchester (03102)	A.A.	Police Science
NEW JERSEY			
Atlantic Community College	Mays Landing (08330)	A.A., A.S.	Dean of Instruction
Ocean County College	Hooper Ave. Toms River (08753)	A.A. (Law Enf.)	Law Enforcement Option
Rider College	P. O. Box 298 Trenton (08602)	A.A. (Law Enf.)	Special Programs
Rutgers, The State University	77 Hamilton St. New Brunswick (08903)	A.S. (Police Sc.)	Law Enforcement
NEW MEXICO			
New Mexico State University	P.O. Box 487, University Park Las Cruces (88001)	B.S. (Police Sc.), A.A. (Police Sc.)	Police Science
NEW YORK			
Auburn Community College	Auburn (13021)	A.A.S. (Police Sc.)	Continuing Education
Dutchess Community College	Pendell Road Poughkeepsie (12160)	A.A. (Police Sc., Correcs.)	Social and Service Technologies

Institution	Address (Zip Code in Parentheses)	Degree	For Information Contact Department of
Elmira College	Elmira (14901)	A.A.S.	Evening and Summer Sessions
Erie Community College	Main St. & Youngs Rd. Buffalo (14221)	A.A.S.	Police Science
Hudson Valley Community College	80 Vandenburgh Ave. Troy (12180)	A.A.S. (Police Sc.)	Police Science
Jamestown Community College	525 Falconer St. Jamestown (14701)	A.A., A.A.S., A.S.	Continuing Education
John Jay College of Criminal Justice	315 Park Ave. South New York (10003)	A.S., B.S. (Police Sc.), A.A., B.A.	Police Science
Mohawk Valley Community College	1101 Sherman Dr. Utica (13501)	A.A.S. (Police Sc.)	Continuing Education
Monroe Community College	1000 E. Henrietta Rd. Rochester (14623)	A.A.S. (Police Sc.)	Police Science
Nassau Community College	Nassau (12123)	A.A. (Police Sc.)	Police Science
New York State University	Farmingdale, L.I. (11735)	A.A. (Police Sc.)	Police Science
New York University	4 Washington Square N. New York (10003)	M.P.A., Ph.D. (Public Admin.)	Law Enforcement
Onondaga Community College	700 E. Water St. Syracuse (13210)	A.S., A.A.S.	Police Science
Orange County Community College	Middletown (19040)	A.A. (Police Sc.)	Police Science
Rockland Community College	145 College Rd. Suffern (10901)	A.A.S.	Law Enforcement
State University of New York	221 Ontario St. Albany (12203)	M.A., Ph.D. (Crim. Justice)	Criminal Justice

Institution	Address	Degree	Program
State University of New York	Farmingdale, L.I. (11735)	A.A.S.	Police Science
Suffolk County Community College	533 College Rd. Seldon, L.I. (11784)	A.A.S.	Police Science
Ulster County Community College	Stone Ridge (12484)	A.A.S. (Police Sc., Correcs.)	Public Service
Westchester Community College	75 Grasslands Road Valhalla (10595)	A.A.S.	Police Science
NORTH CAROLINA			
Central Piedmont Community College	Elizabeth Ave. at Kings Drive Charlotte (23204)	A.A.S.	Police Science and Criminology
Davidson Community College	P. O. Box 1083 Lexington (27292)	A.A.S.	Police Science and Criminology
Durham Technical Institute	P. O. Box 11307 Durham (27703)	A.A.S.	Vocational-Technical Education
Forsyth Technical Institute	2100 Silas Creek Parkway Winston-Salem (27102)	A.A.S.	Vocational-Technical Education
Gaston College	P. O. Box 1397 Dallas (28034)	A.A. (Police Sc.)	Police Science
Pitt Technical Institute	P. O. Box 97 Sylva (28779)	A.A.S.	Police Science
Southwestern Technical Institute	P. O. Box 95 Sylva (28779)	A.A.S.	Social Science
Wilson County Technical Institute	902 Herring Ave. Wilson (27893)	A.A. (Police Sc.)	Police Science

Institution	Address (Zip Code in Parentheses)	Degree	For Information Contact Department of
OHIO			
Clark County Technical Institute	Springfield (45505)	A.A.S.	Police Science
Cuyahoga Community College	2900 Community College Ave. Cleveland (44115)	A.A., A.S. (Police Sc.)	Law Enforcement
Kent State University	Kent (44240)	B.A. (Law Enf. Admin.)	Political Science
Lakeland Community College	Mentor (44060)	A.A.S.	Technical Education
Lorain County Community College	1005 N. Abbe Rd. Elyria (44035)	A.A.S. (Police Sc.)	Police Science
University of Akron	Community & Technical College Akron (44278)	A.S.	Law Enforcement
University of Cincinnati	Cincinnati (45221)	A.S. (Police Sc.)	Police Science
University of Dayton	Dayton (45409)	B.S.S.	Law Enforcement
University of Toledo, The	2801 W. Bancroft St. Toledo (43606)	A.A.	Law Enforcement Technology
Youngstown State University	410 Wick Ave. Youngstown (44503)	A.A., B.A. (Law Enf., Correcs.)	Criminal Justice
OKLAHOMA			
Northern Oklahoma College	1220 E. Grand Tonkawa (74653)	A.A. (Law Enf.)	Social Sciences
University of Oklahoma	455 W. Lindsey Norman (73069)	A.B. (Political Sc.)	Political Science
University of Tulsa, The	6th at College Tulsa (74104)	B.S. (Police Sc.)	Sociology

OREGON

College	Address	Degree	Program
Blue Mountain Community College	P. O. Box 100 Pendleton (97801)	A.S. (Law Enf.)	Vocational-Technical Division
Clatsop Community College	16th & Jerome Sts. Astoria (97103)	A.A. (Police Sc.)	Police Science
Lane Community College	Eugene (97405)	A.S. (Law Enf.)	Social Science
Portland Community College	12000 S.W. 49th Portland (97219)	A.A. (Police Sc., Correcs.)	Public Safety
Portland State University	P. O. Box 751 Portland (97207)	B.S. (Behavioral Sc.)	Law Enforcement
Southern Oregon College	1250 Siskiyou Blvd. Ashland (97520)	B.A., B.S. (Law Enf.)	Law Enforcement
Treasure Valley Community College	650 College Blvd. Ontario (97914)	A.A. (Police Sc.)	Law Enforcement
Umpqua Community College	P. O. Box 967 Roseburg (97470)	A.A. (Police Sc.)	Vocational-Technical & Adult Education

PENNSYLVANIA

College	Address	Degree	Program
Bucks County Community College	Newton (18940)	A.S. (Police Admin., Police Sc., Correcs.)	Law Enforcement
Community College of Allegheny County	East Campus Monroeville (15146)	A.A., A.S. (Police Sc., Admin.)	Police Science & Administration
Community College of Beaver County	609 3rd Ave. Freedom (15042)	A.S.	Law Enforcement
Harrisburg Area Community College	3300 Cameron Street Rd. Harrisburg (17110)	A.S. (Police Sc., Public Admin.)	Police & Public Administration

Institution	Address (Zip Code in Parentheses)	Degree	For Information Contact Department of
Indiana University of Pennsylvania	Indiana (15701)	A.A., B.A. (Crim., Law Enf.)	Criminology
Lehigh County Community College	2370 Main St. Schnecksville (18078)	A.A., A.A.S.	Police Science Administration
Montgomery County Community College	612 Fayette St. Conshohocken (19428)	A.A.S.	Science & Technology
Pennsylvania State University	University Park (16802)	B.S. (Law Enf. and Correcs.)	Law Enforcement and Corrections
Temple University	Broad and Berks Philadelphia (19111)	A.A. (Law Enf.)	Law Enforcement
York College	Country Club Rd. York (17405)	A.S.	Law Enforcement

RHODE ISLAND

Institution	Address (Zip Code in Parentheses)	Degree	For Information Contact Department of
Bryant College	129 Hope St. Providence (02906)	A.S., B.S. (Law Enf.)	Law Enforcement

SOUTH CAROLINA

Institution	Address (Zip Code in Parentheses)	Degree	For Information Contact Department of
Palmer College	125 Bull St. Charleston (29404) & 1700 Laurel St. Columbia (29201)	A.A.	Education
Spartanburg Junior College	Spartanburg (29301)	A.A. (Police Sc.)	Police Science

TENNESSEE

Institution	Address	Degree	Program
Memphis State University	Memphis (38111)	A.A., B.S., M.A. (Law Enf.)	Sociology, Division of Law Enforcement

TEXAS

Institution	Address	Degree	Program
Amarillo College	Box 447 Amarillo (79105)	A.A.S. (Police Sc.)	School of Technology
Central Texas College	Hwy. 190 West Killeen (74651)	A.A.S. (Law Enf.)	Law Enforcement
El Centro College –of the Dallas City Jr. College District	Main & Lamar Dallas (75202)	A.A.S.	Police Science
Grayson County Junior College	P. O. Box 979 Denison (75020)	A.A.	Law Enforcement
Lee College	Baytown (77520)	A.A.	Social Science
McLennan Community College	Waco (76703)	A.A.S.	
Odessa College	P. O. Box 3752 Odessa (79760)	A.A. (Police Sc.)	Police Science
Sam Houston State University	Huntsville (77340)	A.B., B.S., M.A. (Police Sc., Law Enf.), Ph.D. (Criminal Justice)	Law Enforcement
San Antonio College	1300 San Pedro San Antonio (78212)	A.A.S. (Law Enf.)	Law Enforcement
San Jacinto College	8060 Spencer Hwy. Pasadena (77571)	A.A., A.S.	Technical Education
South Texas Junior College	1 Main Street Houston (77002)	A.A.	Police Administration
Tarrant County Junior College	1400 Fort Worth Nat'l Bank Bldg. Fort Worth (76102)	A.A.	Police Administration

Institution	Address (Zip Code in Parentheses)	Degree	For Information Contact Department of
Texarkana College.	1024 Tucker St. Texarkana (75501)	A.A. (Police Tech.)	Police Technology)
UTAH			
Brigham Young University	Provo (84601)	A.A., B.S. (Law Enf.)	Law Enforcement Education
University of Utah	Salt Lake City (84112)	B.A., B.S. (Sociology)	Sociology
Weber State College	Ogden (84403)	A.A., A.S. (Police Sc.)	Police Science
VIRGINIA			
Central Virginia Community College	P. O. Box 4098 Ft. Hill Street Lynchburg (24502)	A.A.S. (Police Sc.)	Police Science
Northern Virginia Community College	8333 Little River Turnpike Annandale (22003)	A.A.S.	Police Science
Old Dominion University	P. O. Box 6173 Norfolk (23508)	A.A. (Law Enf.)	Law Enforcement
Richmond Professional Institute	901 W. Franklin St. Richmond (23220)	A.A., B.S. (Law Enf.)	
Virginia Commonwealth University	901 W. Franklin St. Richmond (23220)	A.A., B.S. (Law Enf.)	Sociology
Virginia Western Community College	3095 Colonial Ave., S.W. Roanoke (24015)	A.A.S.	Police Science
WASHINGTON			
Bellevue Community College	3000 - 145th Place, S.E. Bellevue (98004)	Assoc. in Technology	Law Enforcement

College	Address	Degree	Program
Clark College	1800 McLaughlin Blvd. Vancouver (98661)	A.A. (Police Sc.)	Police Science
Everett Community College	801 Wetmore Ave. Everett (98201)	A.A. (Law Enf.)	Law Enforcement
Fort Steilacoom Community College	6010 Mount Tacoma Drive S.W. Tacoma (98499)	A.A. (Law Enf.)	Occupational Education
Green River Community College	12401 S.E. 320th St. Auburn (98002)	A.A. (Law Enf.)	Law Enforcement
Highline Community College	Midway (98031)	A.A.S. (Police Sc.)	Law Enforcement
Madison Area Technical College	211 N. Carroll St. Madison (52703)	A.A. (Police Sc.)	Police Science
Olympic College	16th & Chester Bremerton (98310)	A.T.A. (Police Sc.)	Police Science
Pacific Western College of Liberal Arts	20005 Jones Rd. Renton (98055)	B.S. (Police Sc.)	Police Science
Seattle Community College	1625 Broadway Seattle (98109)	A.S.	Curriculum & Instruction Laboratory
Shoreline Community College	16101 Greenwood Ave., N Seattle (98177)	A.A.A. (Police Sc.)	Vocational-Technical Education
Tacoma Community College	5900 South 12th St. Tacoma (98465)	A.A.	Community Services
Washington State University	Pullman (99163)	B.S., M.A. (Police Sc.)	Police Science
Yakima Valley College	16th & Nob Hill Blvd. Yakima (98902)	A.A. (Police Sc.)	Occupational Education

WEST VIRGINIA

Institution	Address (Zip Code in Parentheses)	Degree	For Information Contact Department of
West Virginia State College	Institute (25112)	A.A., B.S. (Law Enf.)	Law Enforcement

WISCONSIN

Institution	Address (Zip Code in Parentheses)	Degree	For Information Contact Department of
Kenosha Technical Institute	3520 - 30th Ave. Kenosha (53140)	A.A.S. (Police Sc.)	Police Science
Madison Area Technical College	Madison (53703)	A.A.S.	Law Enforcement
Marquette University	1217 W. Wisconsin Ave. Milwaukee (53233)	A.A. (Law Enf.)	Continuing Education
Milwaukee Area Technical College	1015 North 6th St. Milwaukee (53227)	A.S. (Police Sc.)	Police Science
Wisconsin State University	Platteville (53818)	B.S. (Police Sc.)	Police Science and Administration

WYOMING

Institution	Address (Zip Code in Parentheses)	Degree	For Information Contact Department of
Casper College	125 College Dr. Casper (82601)	A.A. (Law Enf.)	Law Enforcement

U. S. OUTLYING POSSESSIONS

GUAM

Institution	Address (Zip Code in Parentheses)	Degree	For Information Contact Department of
University of Guam	P. O. Box EK Agana (96910)	A.A. (Police Sc.)	Police Science & Law Enforcement

VIRGIN ISLANDS

Institution	Address (Zip Code in Parentheses)	Degree	For Information Contact Department of
College of the Virgin Islands	P. O. Box 1826 St. Thomas (00801)	A.A. (Police Sc.)	Social Science

[80—Z1]

INDEX

References are to Pages

A

B

C

INDEX
References are to pages

F

G

H

I

J

References are to pages

S

T

Training function—Continued
    Limitations of in-service training, 157
    Pre-service police training, 158
    Recruit training, 148
    Regional in-service training, 155
    Roll-Call training, 162
    State Commissions on Minimum Recruiting and Training Standards, 159
    University police training, 165
Tucson Police Department, 239

U

Underworld, 25
United States Civil Service Commission, 133
Unity of command, 65
University police training, 165
Urwick, L., fn, 95, fn, 154

V

Vanderbosch, Charles C., fn, 222, fn, 280
Veterans' preference, fn, 134
Vice control, 285
    Audit of, 412
Violence, tide of, 421–446
Vollmer, August, fn, 47, fn, 128, fn, 175, fn, 192, fn, 231, fn, 232, fn, 236, fn, 267, fn, 287, fn, 311, fn, 314, fn, 317, fn, 384

W

Walker, Harvey, fn, 187
Walkie-talkie, 345
Warren, Chief Justice Earl, 255
Weber, Max, fn, 95, 96
Weisz, William J., fn, 351
Weston, Paul B., fn, 292, 293, 302, 308
White, Leonard D., fn, 94
Wickman, E. K., fn, 314
Wigmore, John Henry, 256, fn, 257, 280, fn, 281
Wilson, Chief Jerry V., 172
Wilson, O. W., fn, 192, 194, fn, 305, fn, 308, fn, 317, fn, 338
Wilson, W. F., fn, 388
Wood, Major Sterling A., fn, 374

Y

Yoder, Norman M., fn, 119
York, Orrell, fn, 159

Z

Zander, Alvin, fn, 95, 96
Zink, Harold, fn, 18, fn, 188
Zinn, Howard, fn, 426

END OF VOLUME

DATE DUE

AP 27'87	MAY 5 '87		

DEMCO 38-297